DIVAS AND SCHOLARS

Divas

AND

Scholars

PERFORMING

ITALIAN

OPERA

PHILIP GOSSETT

THE UNIVERSITY OF CHICAGO PRESS

CHICAGO AND LONDON

Philip Gossett is the Robert W. Reneker Distinguished Service Professor
in Music and the College at the University of Chicago.

The University of Chicago Press, Chicago 60637
The University of Chicago Press, Ltd., London
© 2006 by The University of Chicago
All rights reserved. Published 2006
Printed in the United States of America

15 14 13 12 11 10 09 08 07 06 1 2 3 4 5
ISBN-13: 978-0-226-30482-3 (cloth)
ISBN-10: 0-226-30482-5 (cloth)

Library of Congress Cataloging-in-Publication Data
Gossett, Philip.
Divas and scholars : performing Italian opera / Philip Gossett.
p.   cm.
Includes bibliographical references (p.) and indexes.
ISBN 0-226-30482-5 (cloth : alk. paper)
1. Opera.   2. Opera—Production and direction.
3. Opera—Performance.   I. Title.
ML1700.G7397 2006
782.10945—dc22
2005032151

TO HAROLD GOSSETT,

My father and most enthusiastic supporter

CONTENTS

PREFACE

This book, written by a fan, a musician, and a scholar, is about performing nineteenth-century Italian opera. It is addressed to all those who share my passion for the music of Rossini, Bellini, Donizetti, and Verdi. I trust that fans will be intrigued by an occasional technical explanation, musicians will find something of value in the social and textual history of their art, and scholars will indulge me the backstage gossip indigenous to the opera house.

While these three elements of my operatic being are now hopelessly merged, they developed consecutively. My earliest exposure to opera was the Metropolitan Opera's weekly broadcasts, and my father assures me that as a child I sang along with gusto. Unfortunately, my vocal skills have not improved with age. The first opera I actually saw was *Carmen* with Rise Stevens at the old Met, during the mid-1950s, but memories of this event have long been inseparable from family anecdote. An opera-loving uncle, Jules Schwartz, collected early LPs, which we devoured together. Having studied piano since the age of five, I frequented Juilliard Preparatory Division in uptown Manhattan during my high school years (from 1955 to 1958) for piano lessons and theory classes. By noon on most Saturdays I caught the subway downtown to join the standing-room queue at the Met. I must have heard all the great singers of the period, and there were many, but at that age I was not very discriminating about voices: it was the extraordinary music and drama that captured my imagination.

Heading off to Amherst College in the fall of 1958, I brought along my trusty reel-to-reel tape recorder. Tapes of Uncle Julie's LPs and others borrowed from the New York Public Library were my constant companions, and they ranged from Mozart through Verdi and Wagner to Berg and even Britten: indeed, it was a recording of *Peter Grimes* that convinced me that opera remained a living art. On our first New York date, I brought my Smith College girlfriend to stand at the Met through a Birgit Nilsson *Tristan und Isolde.* Despite three-inch spike heels (I hadn't warned her about the opera's length), she survived.

Every opera fan has a favorite story, and here is mine. During a summer of French study at the Cannes campus of the University of Aix-en-Provence in 1960 (I say that with a straight face), my Wagnerian fascination drove me, ticketless, to Bayreuth. After expressing astonishment at my presumption, a sympathetic box-office agent directed me to an annual youth music festival, the Rencontres Internationales de Jeunesse Musicale, meeting that summer in Bayreuth, for whose participants some tickets had been reserved. That very morning their rehearsal pianist for a production of *Così fan tutte* had jumped ship, and suddenly my skill at keyboard sight-reading was rewarded. Along with my assignment came tickets for *Das Rheingold, Siegfried,* and *Götterdämmerung* in the legendary Wieland Wagner productions, with Nilsson as Brünnhilde. After *Rheingold* I knew I *had* to see *Die Walküre.* In my desperate search for a ticket, I made my way to the office of the English widow of Richard Wagner's son Siegfried, Winifred Wagner, who had run Bayreuth during the Nazi years and was known for her close association with Hitler. Although control of the festival had passed to her sons, Wieland and Wolfgang, she remained a presence at postwar Bayreuth. While she must have been amused by my cock-and-bull stories, she was surprisingly kind. Still, there simply were no tickets. Instead of admitting defeat, I followed several violinists into the orchestra green room, where, fortunately, there were *two* bathroom stalls, into one of which I promptly locked myself. When I heard the storm music and knew that Siegmund was dragging himself to Hunding's hearth, I emerged and opened the first door marked "Verboten" (that much German I knew). There I was, atop a lighting tower high over the stage, and it was from there—not quite twenty—that I saw my first, unforgettable *Walküre.*

Making a career in opera was the furthest thing from my mind. While I took an occasional music course, continued to study piano, and accompanied the Smith-Amherst Glee Club, I was a declared physics and math major, and even won a prestigious fellowship from the Woods Hole Oceanographic Institute after my junior year. However, an intense summer of applying the Navier-Stokes equations to rotating bodies convinced me that scientific research was not for me. My teacher and mentor, the physicist Arnold Arons, who understood me better than I understood myself, suggested I explore music history. After a year of courses at Columbia University and a final year

of undergraduate study at Amherst (under the tutelage of the kind and brilliant Henry Mishkin), I knew that this direction was right.

I undertook graduate work in music at Princeton University. And what did
we study? Certainly not Italian opera and even more certainly not Italian *bel
canto* opera. The very idea seemed risible. No, we did *serious* musicology: medieval notation, Byzantine chant, tempo and meter in the music of the Renaissance, the history of music theory, analysis of twelve-tone music, the operas of Wagner, Bach cantatas, Beethoven piano sonatas. Yet when it became
time to choose a topic for my doctoral dissertation, I announced my intention to write about Italian opera. My professors believed (or so I imagined)
that this bright young scholar was about to ruin his career.

As I embarked on the SS *France* to undertake dissertation research in Paris
in the fall of 1965, preparing new scholarly and performing editions of this
repertory was far from my mind. Not that graduate school had left me untouched by the rigors of textual scholarship. From my wife, Suzanne (my
Tristan und Isolde date), who was pursuing her own studies of the Jacobean
dramatists Beaumont and Fletcher, I first heard the dread name of the dean
of American bibliographers and textual scholars, Fredson Bowers, and
learned of early seventeenth-century compositors and their unfortunate pen-
chant for turning little pieces of type upside down. But it was one of my own
teachers, Arthur Mendel, who demonstrated the significance of pinholes,
stitchholes, and stabholes. Painstakingly he analyzed the history of the pages
that made up the tormented autograph manuscript of Bach's *St. John Passion*,
revised and rebound again and again and again as the composer performed
it with his Leipzig choir over a period of twenty-five years. After sitting
through ten weeks of seminars that would ultimately result in the longest
scholarly report ever included in the *Neue Bach-Ausgabe*, I vowed that textual
scholarship was not going to dominate *my* scholarly career. No, for me the
pleasures of criticism and musical analysis.

I had chosen my project with the help of another Princeton professor,
Oliver Strunk, whose elegant prose style reflected his upbringing as the son
of William Strunk Jr., one-half the team of Strunk and E. B. White, authors
of *The Elements of Style.* Though a scholar of Byzantine chant, the younger
Strunk loved Italian opera with the passion of a patrician slumming at a blues
joint. He pointed out to me that Rossini, Bellini, Donizetti, and Verdi, at crucial moments during their careers, all composed works for Parisian theaters.
But what happened to the style of an Italian composer when he sought to
adapt his art to the needs of a foreign society in a city that considered itself "la

capital del mondo," as the Parisian Contessa di Folleville asserts in Rossini's *Il viaggio a Reims?* That was a subject worth pursuing.

There were abundant grounds for investigating the question. Three of the composers (Rossini, Donizetti, and Verdi) had written operas for Italian theaters, which they subsequently adapted to French texts for performance at the Paris Opéra; three (Rossini, Bellini, and Donizetti) had prepared operas expressly for the Théâtre Italien, a theater frequented by cultural luminaries such as Balzac, Stendhal, and Delacroix; three (Rossini, Donizetti, and Verdi) had composed new operas in French for the Opéra. Strunk used to describe scholarship not as searching for needles in haystacks, but rather as getting inside a haystack and kicking the straw around. Well, here was plenty of straw waiting to be kicked.

I set to work examining the French career of the earliest of these composers, Gioachino Rossini. Rossini presented his first opera in 1810, when he was eighteen, at the Teatro di San Moisè in Venice.[1] Between 1810 and 1823, he wrote thirty-four operas for Italian theaters, ranging from early one-act *farse,* through the comic operas of the mid-1810s, to the great serious operas, largely associated with the Teatro San Carlo of Naples. His success was overwhelming: by the 1820s as much as half the repertory in the operatic season of any Italian theater consisted of works by Rossini.[2] Furthermore, the new approaches he developed to musical dramaturgy and form were models that dominated the thinking of Italian composers for the next half century. As Rossini's slightly younger contemporary, Giovanni Pacini, wrote in his memoirs: "Let me be permitted to observe that at the time all my contemporaries followed the same school, the same mannerisms, and thus were imitators, like me, of the *Great Star.* But good heavens! what was one to do if there was no other means to make your way? If I was a follower of the great man of Pesaro, then, so were all the others."[3] Then, in 1823, Rossini moved to Paris, where he lived until 1829. He served as director of the Théâtre Italien, mounting several earlier Italian operas and writing *Il viaggio a Reims* for the coronation of Charles X in 1825. For the Opéra, Rossini first adapted two Neapolitan serious operas, *Maometto II* and *Mosè in Egitto,* into works performed in French, as *Le Siège de Corinthe* (1826) and *Moïse* (1827); he subsequently used part of the music of *Il viaggio a Reims* for a French comic opera, *Le Comte Ory* (1828); finally, in 1829, he mounted an entirely new work, one of the most successful and complex compositions ever given at the Opéra, *Guillaume Tell.* After *Tell,* Rossini abandoned the operatic stage and lived another thirty-eight years in semiretirement, first in Paris, then in Italy, and eventually (after 1855) back in Paris.

When I arrived in Paris, then, the steps I needed to pursue seemed clear: chart the changes Rossini made when he transformed his Italian operas for the French stage; investigate the performances he directed of his own operas at the Théâtre Italien; and analyze *Guillaume Tell.* By adding similar studies for other Italian composers, one could be assured of ample material to construct a thesis. There was no collected edition of Rossini's music, of course, nor had most of the operas been printed in full orchestral score, but the Bibliothèque nationale, the Bibliothèque du Conservatoire, and the Bibliothèque de l'Opéra were rich in musical sources. And so, in my first weeks, I began to study printed reductions for piano and voice, orchestral manuscripts of the operas, and even Rossini's own autograph scores, several of which are in Parisian collections. It did not take me long to realize the morass into which I had fallen.

In my dazed state it seemed as if every source of an opera I examined was different from every other one. I compared printed editions, librettos (which in the early nineteenth century were published for individual performances and were intended to reproduce the words the audience would actually hear in the theater), manuscripts of the operas (copied all over Europe), and complete autograph scores, as well as fragments. How could I talk rationally about changes the composer made in his operas for Paris if I had no way of defining the "original" to which the "changes" were made? I needed to understand which versions stemmed from performances with which he was associated, and which reflected other contemporary practices. I needed to comprehend the theatrical system in which textual decisions were made, not to mention the performers for whom they were made. Furthermore, if sources in Paris were so problematic, how could I avoid examining other collections? Little by little, I was sucked into the quicksand of textual scholarship. The result has been my thirty-year involvement with the *Edizione critica delle opere di Gioachino Rossini,* and then *The Works of Giuseppe Verdi.* There will be more to say about these projects and their history during the course of this book.

While I had studied music from childhood, I never sought a career as a pianist, even though I frequently performed chamber music in public or accompanied singers and choruses in concert. My involvement in critical editions of Italian opera, however, led directly to close collaboration with singers, conductors, and stage directors, and since the mid-1970s I have been actively involved in performances, many of which will find a place in the following pages. Having worked hard to get accurate scores into the hands of performers, I was hardly ready to abandon the works I had come to love at the moment they emerged from the printed page into the public domain of performance in the opera house. At first I simply observed and tried to learn; later, as I grew more confident, I worked directly with productions on matters involving style, vocal ornamentation, and decisions about cuts and versions.

You cannot publish critical editions of nineteenth-century Italian operas without studying the performing traditions of that period and their subsequent transformations. And in studying the traditions you begin to understand the relationship between history and practice. Without knowing something about the instruments for which Rossini and Verdi were writing, you cannot understand why their scores look the way they do. Without instruction in the art of vocal ornamentation from Rossini and his own singers (Giuditta Pasta, Manuel García, and Laure Cinti-Damoreau), you are forced to trust the practices of late nineteenth-century divas like Estelle Liebling, who tended to confuse the music of Rossini with the Bell Song from Délibe's *Lakmé*. Without grasping nineteenth-century stagecraft, you will inevitably be puzzled by the structure of a nineteenth-century libretto. And without comprehending the social milieu for which these operas were written, you cannot draw lessons from the history of their transmission.

History and practice, in short, go hand in hand: they did so in the nineteenth century and they do so today. I have had the privilege of working directly with some of today's finest artists (the equal of artists of any generation): singers such as Marilyn Horne (who for me will always take pride of place), Cecilia Bartoli, Rockwell Blake, Renée Fleming, Juan Diego Flórez, Cecilia Gasdia, Bruno Praticò, and Samuel Ramey; conductors such as Claudio Abbado, Bruno Bartoletti, Riccardo Chailly, Valéry Gergiev, James Levine, Riccardo Muti, Roger Norrington, and Evelino Pidò; and stage directors such as Jonathan Miller, Pier Luigi Pizzi, Jean-Pierre Ponnelle, Luca Ronconi, and Francesca Zambello. I have learned an enormous amount from them, and I hope that I have made some small contribution in return. Opera production at its best, after all, depends not on the presence of superstars, but on the assembling of a team that operates well together (a concept many superstars fully understand, but others do not).

As fan, musician, and scholar, then, I aim in this book to address the many problems that theaters and performers face when they produce a nineteenth-century Italian opera, concentrating on the period from the advent of Rossini in 1810 through Verdi's revision of *Macbeth* for Paris in 1865.[4] Even in today's intellectual climate, where all artistic production is ever more understood to result from collaborative processes, nineteenth-century Italian operas seem particularly embedded in the social history of their composition and performance, in the hurly-burly of impresarios' demands, singers' egos, and audiences' expectations. Manuel García, the first Almaviva in *Il barbiere di Siviglia,* was paid three times as much for singing the work as Rossini got for composing it, and the latter's contract obliged him "to make where needed all those alterations necessary either to ensure the good reception of the music or to meet the circumstances and convenience of those same singers, at the simple request of the Impresario, because so it must be and no other way."[5] The artistic world has changed less than one might imagine.

The public is both intrigued and confused by what it gleans about these problems through journalistic discussion of multiple versions, cuts, vocal ornamentation, changes in instruments and instrumental technique, and the reconstruction of historical staging practices. But journalism generally reflects immediate controversy about individual performances and performers. Few efforts have been made to proceed more systematically: to understand how modern concerns are rooted in the history of Italian opera; to elaborate principles that assist scholars and the public in thinking about these questions; to assist performers who need to make practical decisions.

Although I love the beautiful sounds that are part (but only part) of what characterizes fine *bel canto* singing, I am not a professional voice teacher and claim no particular expertise on how to produce or evaluate those sounds. While no opera fan can resist an occasional parenthetical comment, the magic of great singing is not the central subject of this book. Nor is this a book that indulges in diva worship, although I love a Maria Callas recording as much as the next fan. I offer no speculation as to how Giuditta Pasta sounded when she first intoned "Casta Diva," nor can I explain how Giambattista Rubini executed that legendary high *f* in Bellini's *I puritani,* before which many a modern tenor has quivered. I care primarily about great and not-so-great works of operatic art and about the real musicians working in the opera house who face eminently practical problems in bringing these operas to the stage. It continues to be the extraordinary music and drama of Italian opera that most captures my imagination, although I am fully aware that the works I love come to life thanks to the singers who interpret them.[6]

Divas and Scholars opens with a report on two opera festivals with which I worked closely during the summer of 2000, the Santa Fe Opera and the Rossini Opera Festival of Pesaro. Through discussions of five productions mounted during these festivals (and comparisons with earlier productions of these operas with which I was associated), I have tried to suggest the purpose of this book and the kinds of questions it will address. Part I, "Knowing the

Score," traces the social history of nineteenth-century Italian theaters in order to explain the nature of the musical scores from which performers have long worked. There are wonderful books about this social history (particularly those of the late historian John Rosselli, who made such important contributions to this field),[7] but none draws the necessary conclusions about the history, transmission, and editing of the music. The concept of the critical edition as it applies to Italian opera is deliciously colorful, and I have tried to tell that story through case studies that illustrate the "romance" of the critical edition (not such an oxymoron as it might appear), with reference to Rossini's *Tancredi* and *Il viaggio a Reims* and Verdi's *Stiffelio.*

In an "intermezzo" devoted to the production of Rossini's *Semiramide* at the Metropolitan Opera in 1991, I seek to clarify what it means to talk about "performing" from a critical edition (notice, *not* "performing a critical edition") and to set to rest some of the absurdities that still surface about the relationship between scholarship and performance. Part II, "Performing the Opera," consists of a series of chapters devoted to different aspects of modern performance. "Choosing a Version" focuses on the problem of determining what music to adopt when multiple versions of an opera exist, a problem that needs to be analyzed in terms of the social environment in which these operas were conceived and in that of today's theaters. "Serafin's Scissors" discusses the omitting of passages from an opera in performance, examining the history of the practice and its advantages and disadvantages. A series of chapters then addresses issues pertaining to vocal style (ornamentation and transposition), the matter of texts, translations, and adaptations (of particular importance for operas written in French by Italian composers, which often continue to be performed in Italian translation), instrumentation, and certain aspects of stage direction and set design.

Divas and Scholars concludes with a "coda" describing two unusual sets of performances with which I was involved during the 2002–3 season in Scandinavia, Verdi's *Gustavo III* (the first version of *Un ballo in maschera*) in Gothenburg and Rossini's *Il viaggio a Reims* (with a partially new text added by Dario Fo) in Helsinki. In both cases my colleagues and I tested the limits of history and practice.

There are other topics I would have liked to cover in this book, but they will have to await another occasion. For those interested in the question of Verdi's metronome markings and their use in performances of his operas, I recommend the work of Roberta Montemorra Marvin and John Mauceri.[8] Although it covers many different repertories, Clive Brown's *Classical and Romantic Performing Practice 1750–1900* is a mine of information on such matters as accentuation, dynamics, articulation and phrasing, bowing, tempo indications, vibrato, and so on.[9] On the subject of dance in Italian opera, the best general treatment remains that of Kathleen Kuzmick Hansell; for a consideration of Verdi's ballet music for Paris, see the important study of Knud Arne Jürgensen.[10]

The subject of this book has been with me for some twenty years, and parts of it were presented as a series of Gauss Seminars at Princeton University in 1992; other parts were delivered as the Hambro Lectures in Opera at Oxford University in 2000. I am grateful to both institutions (and, in particular, to Victor Brombert at Princeton and to Reinhold Strohm and Margaret Bent at Oxford) for their kindness. All the opinions expressed in this book are my own, and I normally use the first-person singular in the text. On occasion, though, when I am identifying myself with other scholars or with a group of performers, I adopt the first-person plural. Even in those cases, however, no other individuals or institutions should be held responsible for my personal views. Musical examples are cited from the critical editions where these have been prepared; otherwise, a source is specified. Earlier versions of several chapters have been previously published: chapter 4 in *The New Republic;*[11] chapter 6 in the newsletter of the American Academy of Arts and Sciences in 1992; an Italian version of chapter 10 in the proceedings of a conference from the bicentenary of Bellini's birth;[12] the second part of chapter 14 in a festschrift for Agostino Ziino.[13] Passages from other chapters have appeared in various conference papers I have delivered over the past decade, which will be cited in the appropriate places.

ACKNOWLEDGMENTS

To acknowledge all those whose help, example, encouragement, and thinking have gone into this book would mean listing all the institutions that have fostered my scholarly and practical efforts over the years (universities, opera houses, publishers, libraries), as well as all those individuals with whom I have lived, worked, gone to the theater, and discussed Italian opera. I have of necessity been somewhat more selective here, but I am no less grateful to everyone who has provided assistance, sustenance, and friendship.

Among institutions the University of Chicago must take pride of place. I joined the faculty in 1968 and have long felt that no other institution could have offered me such an intellectually stimulating environment in which to grow, nor such tangible and intangible support of my efforts. A series of presidents (especially Hanna H. Gray and Hugo Sonnenschein), provosts

(Gerhard Casper, Geoffrey Stone, and Richard Saller), deans (Karl J. Weintraub, Stuart Tave, and Janel Mueller), and department chairs and colleagues (among them Leonard B. Meyer, Edward E. Lowinsky, Howard Mayer Brown, Ellen Harris, and Anne Walters Robertson) have always been there for me; without them, none of this would have been possible. Nor will I ever forget that the stimulus to publish *The Works of Giuseppe Verdi* and continued support for the project came directly from the University of Chicago Press, its directors (Morris Philipson and Paula Duffy), its editors (John Ryden, Wendy Strothman, Penelope Kaiserlian, and Alan Thomas), and its music editors (Gabriele Dotto and Kathleen Kuzmick Hansell). "What do you mean there's no complete edition of the works of Verdi!" said John Ryden, having read a footnote in which I lamented that such an edition did not exist: "We'll do it." And so they have.

A few years earlier, a similar commitment was made by the Fondazione Rossini of Pesaro. Bruno Cagli, artistic director of the Fondazione for thirty-five years and now also president of the Accademia di Santa Cecilia in Rome, has been my colleague since the early 1970s, when the Fondazione embraced our vision of publishing the *Edizione critica delle opere di Gioachino Rossini*. With the active support of a series of presidents (Wolframo Pierangeli, Giorgio de Sabata, Vincenzo Emiliani, and Alfredo Siepi), the Fondazione helped us through the political intricacies of a small Italian seaside town, and gave us the confidence and determination to move ahead.

Neither the University of Chicago Press nor the Fondazione Rossini could have undertaken these projects alone. Our partnership with Italy's greatest music publisher, Casa Ricordi of Milan, has been fundamental. I want to thank the administrators of the company, who—while not always sure where we were going—retained confidence in us: Guido Rignano and, in particular, Mimma Guastoni, whose inspiring leadership ensured that the critical editions of Rossini and Verdi would not remain on the library shelves. The institutional relationship continues to flourish under the new administrative structure of BMG Ricordi. What I have learned from the professional staff of Casa Ricordi (Luciana Pestalozza, Fausto Broussard, Gabriele Dotto, and Ilaria Narici, among others) is incalculable. Without their constant encouragement and institutional memory, as well as their willingness to offer me full access to the treasures in the Ricordi Archives, much of my work would have been impossible.

The Istituto Nazionale di Studi Verdiani of Parma, founded in 1959, is a younger institution than the others, but it has been a beacon for Verdi studies through its conferences, its publications, its library. The present director of the Institute, Pierluigi Petrobelli, befriended my wife and me when I first came to Italy to study Italian opera in 1966, and since then we have worked together continuously. Without the example of Petrobelli's own scholarship and his patient efforts on behalf of others, Verdi studies could not have flourished as they have over the past decades.

I have mentioned above some of the performers from whom I have learned the most, and the list could be extended many times over, but let me here thank several opera houses and festivals that have been particularly supportive of my efforts. Not all references in this book to their productions are positive, but I would not want my criticisms to hide my profound gratitude for all they have done and continue to do for Italian opera. After all, if the scholar in the opera house cannot function as a gadfly, what is he doing there? Lyric Opera of Chicago has been my home company since 1968, and I want to express my appreciation to the late Ardis Krainik, one of the finest impresarios of our time; to the company's remarkable conductor and artistic director for so many years, Bruno Bartoletti, who always kept me honest; to its former artistic adviser, Matthew Epstein, an eternal font of operatic wisdom; and to the king of press agents, Danny Newman, because no one has been so kind to me as he. I cut my operatic teeth as a standee at the Metropolitan Opera of New York, and I have kept learning over the years from its entire musical staff, beginning with the music director, James Levine, but continuing through coaches, conductors, and orchestral musicians, as well as its librarian, John Grande, who helped me understand what I was doing. Eve Queler, with her Opera Orchestra of New York, takes the challenge of presenting lesser-known works in concert, and I have had the pleasure of working and talking opera with her since 1978, when we presented the new edition of *Tancredi*, with Marilyn Horne and Katia Ricciarelli.

In Italy I treasure particularly many of my experiences at the Rossini Opera Festival of Pesaro, which will—necessarily—play an important role in this book. While I have not always agreed with their artistic decisions, I know that the head of the festival for twenty-five years, Franco Mariotti, has done more than anyone to make sure that the works of Rossini live on the modern stage. The opportunity to work at the festival with Claudio Abbado, Gianluigi Gelmetti, Roger Norrington, and many other fine conductors, at the Teatro alla Scala of Milan with Riccardo Muti, at the Teatro Comunale of Bologna with Riccardo Chailly, and in various other Italian theaters with fine conductors and singers has allowed me to understand the world of Italian opera from within and to avoid easy generalizations. Many thoughts and formulations in this book reflect long conversations during weeks of rehearsals with

Richard Buckley in Chicago and Santa Fe, and with Evelino Pidò in Belgium, France, Italy, and the United States. To both of them go my sincerest admiration and affection.

The world of operatic scholarship is equally broad, and I have enjoyed working closely with students and colleagues in several countries, including all those who have prepared critical editions of the works of Rossini and Verdi under my direction. Each has found his or her way into this book, but I want particularly to acknowledge several of them. The late M. Elizabeth C. Bartlet, professor of music at Duke University, was the editor of *Guillaume Tell* and our foremost scholar of French eighteenth- and nineteenth-century opera. I began as her teacher and ended as her student. Margaret Bent, medievalist extraordinaire and fellow of All Souls' College, Oxford, is also an opera fanatic on the side (with, alas, *oltremontane* tendencies). Her edition of *Il Turco in Italia* finally brought that score back into the public view, and her ability to join philology and musicality is unrivaled. Patricia Brauner has been at my side in the Rossini edition since the 1980s, and I could not have done this work without her. Smart and sensible in equal parts, she has kept the project on an even keel when it threatened to teeter out of control. She and her husband, Charles (editor most recently of the critical edition of *Mosè in Egitto*), have helped give a human face to all the years of effort. Azio Corghi, one of Italy's greatest living composers, was also the editor of *L'Italiana in Algeri* and remains a friend of long standing, with whom I have had the pleasure of conversing frequently about art and life.

My gratitude to Will Crutchfield can hardly be described. We have been talking about Italian opera for twenty years, and I never fail to be challenged and inspired by his thoughtful and genuinely helpful criticism. He knows more about this repertory than anyone else, and his own forthcoming book on elements of performance practice will fill out much of what I have to say here. If there is a model to which I have aspired in writing about music for a nonscholarly audience, it is that of my friend and colleague Andrew Porter, whose many years at the *New Yorker* produced the most sustained and brilliant example of music criticism for our time. As if that were not sufficient, his singing translations, scholarly activity on the Verdi operas (in particular *Don Carlos*), and efforts at resurrecting nineteenth-century staging practices have all played a key role in helping me to develop my ideas. Working with Fabrizio Della Seta on the critical edition of both *La traviata* and (for the Rossini edition) *Adina* was as positive an experience as any general editor could hope to have. That the new Bellini edition is in his capable hands (with his fine colleagues Alessandro Roccatagliati and Luca Zoppelli) gives me great confidence in the project. Even more, he has been a soft-spoken but incisive colleague and a friend of the greatest integrity, and I continue to learn from him. I met the Italo-American musician, composer, and scholar Gabriele Dotto when he had just begun to work for Casa Ricordi during the 1980s, and promptly carried him off to Chicago. He prepared the critical edition of Rossini's *Bianca e Falliero* and served for many years as managing editor of *The Works of Giuseppe Verdi*, before Casa Ricordi stole him back. Now general editor (with Roger Parker) of the new Donizetti edition, Gabe knows what it is like from inside as no one else, and I will always be grateful to him for his insight and warmth. Ellen Harris is no specialist in nineteenth-century Italian opera, just a great Handel scholar, a fine singer (our lecture/concert on ornamentation in Rossini was the first version of what has become chapter 9 of this book), and a trusted friend. Colwyn Philipps (Lord St. Davids), has been a font of endless knowledge about printed music for twenty years, and his superb Rossini collection is now part of the library of the Fondazione Rossini.

During the course of my work on this book, several students—many of them now respected scholars and teachers in their own right—have assisted me in one task or another. Let me mention Stefano Castelvecchi of King's College, Cambridge, editor of Verdi's *Alzira;* Jeffrey Kallberg, our finest Chopin scholar, professor at the University of Pennsylvania and editor of Verdi's *Luisa Miller;* Doug Ipson, who is preparing the edition of Verdi's *La battaglia di Legnano;* Daniela Macchione, whose superb work with the Fondazione Rossini over the past five years has been a breath of fresh air; Hilary Porris, assistant professor at the College Conservatory of Music at the University of Cincinnati, whose own studies of substitute arias has changed much of our way of thinking about the phenomenon; and Alberto Rizzuti, who teaches at the University of Turin and is preparing the critical edition of Verdi's *Giovanna d'Arco.*

A number of friends and colleagues have read some or all the chapters of this book and have provided me with extremely useful feedback. They obviously bear no responsibility for what I may have done with their advice, but I do want to thank them most warmly for their efforts to set me straight. They include, among those I have already cited, Charles and Patricia Brauner, Will Crutchfield, Andrew Porter, and Alan Thomas. Let me add Denise Gallo of the Library of Congress, who is preparing the edition of Rossini's *Musica per banda;* Helen Greenwald of the New England Conservatory, coeditor of *Zelmira* for the Rossini edition and a truly supportive friend; Kathleen Kuzmick Hansell, managing editor of *The Works of Giuseppe Verdi* and editor of Verdi's

Stiffelio; Linda and Dick Kerber of the University of Iowa, a historian and a cardiologist, who love opera and—in the case of Linda—go back to my high school years; Ron Mellor, professor of classics and history at the University of California, Los Angeles, who seems to get to every opera performance I attend, in any country and at any time of year; Roger Parker, professor at Cambridge University and distinguished scholar of Italian opera from Donizetti to Puccini; Federica Riva, librarian of the Parma Conservatory, thoughtful commentator on the Italian operatic scene, and dear friend; and Leon Wieseltier, author, political commentator, literary editor of the *New Republic,* and Rossini fan (who would have known?). I am particularly grateful to Margaret Mahan, whose skilled editorial labors made a real difference, and Alan Thomas, who shepherded the book through the Press with the proper mix of kindness and rigor.

My family has put up with me all these years, pushed, prodded, rolled their eyes, and given me loving support. Suzanne, who has been with me from the start and has always kept her faith in this project, even when I seemed to be losing it, subjected the entire manuscript to her rigorous editorial control and tried to make sure that most of the time I was writing in a way that nonmusicians could follow. As children, David and Jeffrey were kind enough to pretend they were interested, and it has been one of the great pleasures of my life to see that, as adults, they really are. It is to my biggest supporter, though, my father, that I dedicate this book. Since accepting the fact that I was going to be a musicologist, whether he liked it or not, he and his wonderful wife, Jean, have always been at my side. May this book express in some way my love and appreciation.

Philip Gossett
Chicago, 2005

PROLOGUE

1

MARE O MONTI:
TWO SUMMER FESTIVALS

Every summer Italians find themselves engaged in delicate negotiations on which the happiness of a family depends: Should they spend their vacation at the seaside or in the mountains, *mare o monti?* Some believe in the virtues of clean air and brisk walks on carefully marked paths far above the heat and humidity of an Italian August. Some prefer sea breezes, swimming in the Mediterranean (less polluted than a decade ago), and quiet rest under an umbrella in one of the symmetrically arranged beach chairs that line Italy's shores. If *papà* loves the mountain scenery, *mammà* looks forward to joining her friends at the sea; if thirteen-year old Emma expects to hit the trail before daybreak, eighteen-year old Massimo wants only to ogle the procession of teenage beauties in ever briefer bathing attire on their endless walks for his benefit, up and down the hot Adriatic sands. There is no hope of resolving this dispute, only various degrees of compromise. A mountain refuge with an all-night discothèque will help control Massimo's hormones, while a beach resort with tennis courts will allow Emma to keep in shape. And a range of cultural activities can provide sufficient distraction for all concerned.

Tourism supports the economy of large parts of Italy, not to mention the United States. Since cultural tourism broadens the appeal of a vacation destination, many summer festivals are located in places that compete for tourist dollars. The resulting transformations in local institutions do not win universal approval. Ask long-time residents of Santa Fe, New Mexico, at the foot of the Sangre de Cristo mountains, what they think about the hordes of visitors pouring into their town for the summer Opera Festival, about brand-name chains replacing local stores, about restaurants with international cuisine transforming a dining community once known for regional specialties. The increased cost of real estate in Santa Fe has forced many locals to seek homes in Albuquerque, some sixty miles south. The situation isn't much different in

Pesaro, an Italian beach resort where a three-to-four-month summer season provides resources that sustain the region and its workers for an entire year. But the international clientele of the Rossini Opera Festival in Pesaro each August has also brought shops devoted to designer clothes by Versace and Max Mara, expensive leather goods, and restaurants earning Michelin stars. Local businesses can no longer sustain themselves on the main street, where rents keep rising, and trattorias that used to serve the local population find it harder and harder to survive.

Each festival has a particular repertory niche.[1] Since 1957, Santa Fe, while offering a broad range of opera, has emphasized the works of Richard Strauss and contemporary music. Since 1980, the younger festival in Pesaro has celebrated the works of a native son, Gioachino Rossini, born in the Adriatic city in 1792. Young artist programs in both festivals help ensure the liveliness of the community, and stars of future seasons often begin their careers as apprentices. The early success of each festival was due to the presence of significant artistic figures. Igor Stravinsky became a central participant in the making of the Santa Fe Opera, where *The Rake's Progress* was featured in the first festival in 1957. Maurizio Pollini and Claudio Abbado played defining roles in Pesaro. Pollini conducted *La donna del lago* in 1981, a landmark production in the revival of interest in the Rossini serious operas. Abbado, in what is widely viewed as one of the great musical events in Italy of the past half century, unveiled in 1984 the modern premiere of the reconstructed *Il viaggio a Reims,* written for the coronation of Charles X in 1825 and long believed to be lost. Both festivals, dogged by their past successes and frequently accused of having lost their way, are urged to reinvent themselves year after year.

The renovated Santa Fe opera house sits on a hill, high above the surrounding landscape, open to the skies on both sides and—when the set permits—through the back of the stage. As with all outdoor theaters, acoustics require careful attention, but the sound is usually glorious and stage designers have access to the latest technology. There is ample room for operas to be performed in repertory. In contrast, although for several years Pesaro tried to alternate two or three operas at the thousand-seat Teatro Rossini—a traditional Italian theater built in the mid-1810s and inaugurated by Rossini himself with a revival of *La gazza ladra* in 1818—the experience was nervewracking. Parts of the set often slept under the stars; fortunately there is little rain in Pesaro during August. The Rossini Opera Festival soon added the Sala Pedrotti, a concert hall in the Conservatory with excellent acoustics and a stage that can accommodate a simple set. In the absence of an orchestra pit, players sit at the level of the audience, exactly the way Italian orchestras performed during the first half of the nineteenth century. Finally, the festival commandeered an indoor sports arena, cleverly transformed. While particularly appropriate for monumental operas, it served equally well for comedies in the hands of imaginative directors and designers, until what is widely regarded as real-estate speculation forced its closing after the season of 2005.

During the summer of 2000 I worked in both Santa Fe and Pesaro. Five nineteenth-century Italian operas were on the boards: in Santa Fe Rossini's *Ermione* and Verdi's *Rigoletto;* in Pesaro three operas by Rossini: *Le Siège de Corinthe, La scala di seta,* and *La Cenerentola.* I participated directly in some productions, advised informally for others, and watched from the sidelines for the rest. This introductory chapter suggests some of the problems we faced in bringing these works before the public. The issues and questions that arose in these particular productions are representative of those that recur in opera houses throughout the world when facing this repertory. No one should take my remarks as being particularly critical of a specific institution: in every opera house or festival highly successful productions rub shoulders with questionable ones, but even within productions that succeed, many issues require further reflection. My examples, in short, are intended to make clear why all of us—scholars, performers, and audiences—need to think harder about what it means to perform Italian opera.

ERMIONE FINALLY SEES THE LIGHT OF DAY

An expectant and knowledgeable public gathered at the Teatro Rossini of Pesaro during the summer of 1987 to witness the first staged performance of *Ermione* since the spring of 1819. This was one of nine serious operas written by Rossini for Naples between 1815 and 1822, but unlike other Neapolitan works (*Otello, Armida,* or *Zelmira*), *Ermione* was almost entirely unknown. After its unsuccessful premiere on 27 March 1819, and six additional performances that season, the opera disappeared.[2] Except for a fleeting reference to its failure to please, no written records document this inaugural season. Withdrawing the score from the Neapolitan impresario Domenico Barbaja, Rossini is alleged to have said, "You'll see it again sooner or later, and perhaps then the Neapolitan public will recognize its mistake."[3] Although he tried to resurrect individual numbers in other operatic contexts, he basically put *Ermione* away. Asked whether he would allow a French translation, he responded, "No, it is my little Italian *Guillaume Tell,* and it will not see the light of day until after my death."[4] We can't be sure, of course, that he actually said any of these things, but none of them is implausible.

Scholars who had performed *Ermione* over and over in their imaginations were convinced that it was one of Rossini's most important serious operas. The long-standing claim that it was "all recitative and declamation," words Ferdinand Hiller attributed to Rossini in 1855, seemed absurd.[5] There are important scenes of dramatic recitative, accompanied by the orchestra, and intense moments of impassioned declamation, to be sure, but the score abounds in beautiful melody and artfully devised florid passages. Furthermore, the librettist, Andrea Leone Tottola, treats the opera's literary source, Racine's *Andromaque,* with both respect and appropriate freedom. The principal characters are the unhappy children of the Greek heroes of the Trojan War: Pirro, son of Achilles; Oreste, son of Agamemnon; and Ermione, daughter of Menelaus and Helen of Troy; as well as Andromaca, the widow of the Trojan leader, Hector. All four protagonists are locked into an impossible chain of love and hate that leads inevitably to the death of Pirro, the destruction of both Ermione and Andromaca, and the despair of Oreste. In Ermione herself, furthermore, Rossini created one of the most complex characters in the *bel canto* repertory.

Nonetheless, the 1987 performances of *Ermione* in Pesaro received a chorus of boos, the worst reception of any opera ever performed at the festival. I had to restrain myself from joining the chorus. There were many fine things about this *Ermione.* Marilyn Horne was a superb Andromaca, a relatively small but significant part. As always she turned up for the first rehearsal with the entire role memorized, ornamentation in place, and a fine sense of her character and its relationship to the dramaturgy of the whole. The tenors performing Oreste and Pirro were stalwarts of the Rossini renaissance of the 1980s, Rockwell Blake (known affectionately throughout the operatic world as "Rocky") and Chris Merritt, both of whom were well received.

But even those three stars could not prevail within a production that worked against the opera and the singers, a conductor who seemed utterly lost, and a prima donna who didn't belong there. Roberto De Simone, famous for his reinterpretations of the popular dramatic traditions of Naples, was well regarded as an operatic stage director, and his 1985 Pesaro production of Rossini's *farsa, Il signor Bruschino,* had been a delight, even if the Gallic wit of the original was transformed into Neapolitan slapstick. For *Ermione,* however, he invented a stage that severely restricted the space available to singers for entrances, exits, and movement. It hardly mattered, since the prima donna was basically motionless all evening, with two principal gestures: lifting her left arm and pointing a menacing finger to the left, and lifting her right arm and pointing a menacing finger to the right. One can sympathize with the reluctance of stage directors to impose Greek togas on a modern audience, but De Simone's setting in the Naples of 1819, the post-Napoleonic Bourbon reign in the Kingdom of the Two Sicilies, had little resonance with the story of *Ermione*.

Still, De Simone's inoffensive staging would not itself have aroused public ire. That was reserved for the conductor and the prima donna. I knew the production was in trouble from the first orchestral reading, which I attended with the provisional critical edition in hand, in case errors had slipped into our score that required immediate attention.[6] Errors, after all, translate into wasted rehearsal time, a serious matter, given the expense involved. But it soon became apparent that Gustav Kuhn had arrived at this reading without knowing the music.[7] A man of considerable talent and instinct, Kuhn must have assumed he would learn the opera during rehearsals. He began the reading with *Ermione*'s unusual sinfonia, beating time mechanically, while its series of atypical tempo and meter changes, its use of an off-stage chorus, its complex orchestration, and its structural abnormalities began to unfold. Perhaps realizing how badly he had miscalculated, he appeared uncomfortable, even terrified. And so the rehearsal period went. Rather than providing musical leadership, Kuhn strove to catch up with the rehearsal accompanists and singers, most of whom had been hard at work for months. He never succeeded.

Even this, however painful, could have been forgiven were it not for Montserrat Caballé's difficulties with the title role. Blame must be shared. How could the management of the festival not have known that Caballé no longer had the vocal skills or the histrionic ability to perform this challenging part? How could Caballé have accepted the role at that point in her career? In her prime she was a singer of great gifts, breathtaking *pianissimi*, elegant coloratura, fine musicianship. By the late 1980s she had become a caricature of herself. Often she caricatured the operas in which she appeared: during Rossini's *Il viaggio a Reims* in London in 1992, she compensated for her inability to sing the role of Madama Cortese by playing the buffoon, mugging and throwing apples at the conductor, Carlo Rizzi. But what could she do with *Ermione*? Physical ills had restricted her range of movement. Most of all, she could not sing the music and did not seem to understand that it mattered.

It is normal for singers to make small adjustments to help them negotiate passages they find particularly difficult (nineteenth-century musicians called these adjustments *puntature*).[8] It is quite another thing for a singer to omit or rewrite to the point of unintelligibility large portions of a score. At the climax of Ermione's "gran scena," she dispatches the love-sick Oreste to kill Pirro at the altar, where he is exchanging marriage vows with Andromaca. Caballé mortally weakened Rossini's melodies by radically simplifying them, then by altering the notes at the climactic moment of the melodic line. Why? Simply, as she told me directly, because she found it harder to sing the phrase Rossini had written. In Ermione's final duet with Oreste, where she berates the confused son of Agamemnon for not understanding that she continues to love the man he has murdered, Ermione is supposed to repeat obsessively, six times, a pattern of four sixteenth notes (with the text "hide yourself from the eyes of living beings, murderer, traitor"); then she must leap *fortissimo* to a high *b♭*, one of the highest notes she is asked to sing anywhere in the opera, precisely on the powerful syllable "[tradi]-tor" [traitor]. Caballé reduced the passage to one fleeting four-note pattern, then let loose with a resounding high *b♭*, as if that were all her fans had come to hear. Having decimated the musical content of the part, she presented herself before the booing public with a copy of the score, pointing to it as if to assert, "I have sung what Rossini wrote."

ERMIONE MEETS ROBERT E. LEE

Subsequent productions of *Ermione* have been more successful, including notable revivals in Rome in 1991 and Glyndebourne in 1995 (a fine staging by Graham Vick, with Sir Andrew Davis conducting). The decision by Santa Fe Opera to produce *Ermione* during the summer of 2000 was a new direction for the theater, which had never been particularly interested in this repertory. As rehearsals proceeded, however, buzz developed around the project, and more and more people (even the founding director of Santa Fe Opera and Strauss champion, John Crosby, no admirer of *bel canto* opera) made their way into the Tusuque public school, where a mock-up of the stage had been constructed. As in Glyndebourne, *Ermione* was well received by public and critics (excluding a *New York Times* observer, whose vocabulary to describe Rossini's style was limited to "chirpy").[9]

Yet even in a production where all the pieces fall into place, many controversial decisions need to be taken, affecting music, drama, stage setting, and costumes. The public sees a finished product, but every staging of an Italian opera embodies a series of responses to difficult questions. The opera was performed from the critical edition prepared by Patricia Brauner and myself. But the conductor, Evelino Pidò, who had led an earlier set of performances in Rome, was perplexed by one change between the provisional critical edition he had used in 1991 (before the edition was actually published) and the published critical edition he now had before him. In the chorus that introduces Ermione in the second scene of the opera, an orchestral figure recurs

EXAMPLE 1.1. GIOACHINO ROSSINI, *ERMIONE*, CORO (N. 2), MM. 1–11.

several times. It had been played in the provisional edition by a flute, two oboes, and two clarinets, in octaves, *fortissimo*, then echoed by a single clarinet, *piano;* in the printed score the same figure was assigned to four horns in unison, echoed by one solo horn (example 1.1). Not only did Pidò want to know why this had been changed, he was quite reasonably concerned about the ability of four horns to play this figure in unison.

The question was fully justified. In Rossini's own manuscript for this chorus, which we will refer to as his "autograph manuscript" or simply as his "autograph," the version for four horns was physically altered by the composer himself to that for flute, oboes, and clarinets. If Rossini himself modified the passage, why did we want to return to the version he seems to have canceled? The truth is that Brauner and I had at first misunderstood the history of this passage. Seeing the composer's correction, we imagined that he made the change because the passage was too challenging for four horns. But we were wrong. The autograph of this chorus is not with the remainder of *Ermione* in the Bibliothèque de l'Opéra in Paris, but in Pesaro in the collection of the Fondazione Rossini, with autograph materials for *Le Siège de Corinthe* and the Italian opera on which it is based, *Maometto II.* Convinced that *Ermione* would never be revived, Rossini inserted this chorus into *Le Siège de Corinthe* in 1826, providing a text in French, writing a new orchestral introduction, and modifying the orchestration of this figure. He made this modification not because the original passage was too difficult to play but because the dramatic situation had changed. In *Le Siège de Corinthe,* "L'hymen lui donne" is sung by Ismène and the chorus of Turkish women at the beginning of a *divertissement* (with choruses and ballet), inviting the Greek Pamyra to enjoy the fruits of love by entering into marriage with the Turkish sultan Mahomet. "Dall'Oriente l'astro del giorno," the same chorus in *Ermione,* is sung by Cleone and a chorus of Spartan women, armed with bows and arrows, who invite the sorrowing Ermione to join the hunt. That Rossini would use four horns for a hunting chorus, and replace them when the Greek huntresses became Turkish maidens in a *divertissement,* is perfectly comprehensible. When completing our research into *Ermione* in order to publish the critical edition, furthermore, we examined all surviving manuscript copies of the opera: every one of them had the version with four horns.

Pidò was right: playing this unison passage at a rapid pace is no easy feat for four horns (not even for nineteenth-century natural horns, without valves), but as rehearsals continued, the performers gained confidence and the sound was splendid. Did they ever make mistakes? Sure, but who has ever heard a performance of an opera (even *Siegfried* under James Levine) in which a horn has not emitted a few croaks? You write for horn, you take your lumps.

Ermione is a relatively short opera and does not require cutting to reduce its length. Pirro's aria (which includes sections for the chorus and all major soloists) is long, but so much action and character development takes place that it is difficult to shorten. A lovely "duettino" for Pilade (friend of Oreste) and Fenicio (adviser to Pirro) may not be essential to the drama, but this scene allows some respite for the prima donna between her gran scena and the explosive scena and duet that brings the opera to a close. Just imagine the reaction of the fine Santa Fe Ermione, Alexandrina Pendatchanska, who again sang the role with distinction at New York City Opera in the spring of 2004, had we proposed to cut the duettino! Composers were sensitive to such matters, and many seemingly superfluous passages in Italian opera serve intensely practical needs.

We did make some cuts in the recitative. In his libretto, Tottola frequently provided short lines for handmaidens, lieutenants, and friends, briefly commenting on the action. He may have thought he was imitating an element of French classical tragedy, but when set to music these asides acquire more importance than they can sustain. After Oreste challenges Pirro to turn over Astianatte, the son of Hector and Andromaca, so that the Greeks can put the boy to death, Andromaca and Ermione comment, "How unhappy I am!" and "How will the ingrate respond?" But before Pirro is allowed to erupt into his aria, Tottola provided further text for two aides, Attalo and Fenicio: "How boldly he expresses himself!" and "Heavens! I anticipate Pirro's anger, I turn cold and am confused!" We eliminated or abbreviated similar passages, carefully adjusting the sequence of chords so that harmonic continuity was preserved.

Working with the stage director Jonathan Miller on *Ermione* was stimulating and challenging. But why, many asked, did he and his designer, Isabella

Bywater, not only dress the characters in mid-nineteenth century costumes but specifically clothe the Trojans as defeated Confederate soldiers and the Greeks as victorious Yankees? What was the point of turning a story of the aftermath of the Trojan War into one visually invoking the American Civil War, while not changing a word of the libretto? For dramas set in classical Greece, Miller believed that modern audiences are too easily distanced from events on stage. The mythic qualities and formal austerity of the *Oresteia* or *Oedipus Rex,* however, are different from the dramatic intensity of *Ermione.* For Miller, the setting allowed an American audience to get closer to these tormented characters. *Gone with the Wind, The Little Foxes, Ermione:* it is not an unlikely combination. Oreste's troubled entrance as an ambassador from one Northern general to another, for example, with his aide-de-camp Pilade trying to keep him focused on his task, gives these characters immediacy. Is the transposition *necessary?* Hardly. Would the setting have been equally relevant to a Czech audience in Prague? Surely not, although the same could be said about most theatrical productions. Did it create moments that were historically implausible? Only if a viewer insisted on interpreting every detail in terms of the Civil War.

Rather than insisting upon the historical moment, Miller successfully offered suggestion and understatement. Every personal interchange among characters and most details of the dramaturgy followed precisely Rossini's indications (although the Southern belles, not traditionally known for their prowess as hunters, appeared without bows and arrows). This was in no sense a "radical staging," alienating us from the work to comment critically on it.[10] It was a conventional staging, attentive to the dramatic values of Rossini and aware of the underlying traditions of French classical tragedy. Indeed, Miller boasted that he was surely the only person in the world who had staged not only *Ermione* but also *Andromaque* (with the Old Vic). Still, approaches to staging remain among the thorniest issues in performing Italian opera, and another summer 2000 production, *Le Siège de Corinthe,* as we shall see, posed this problem in a far more outrageous manner.

RIGOLETTO AND THE PHOTOCOPIER

Butter or ice? It was over twenty years ago, in March 1983, that Riccardo Muti conducted the first performances of the critical edition of *Rigoletto*—the first volume to appear in *The Works of Giuseppe Verdi*—at the Vienna Staatsoper.[11] Much of that week is impressed in my memory, although I remain unable to recall whether the sculpture of the hunchback that served as a centerpiece for the after-theater reception was carved from butter or ice.

It is not the only imponderable about those performances. More perplexing is why this event took place in Vienna at all, a city that treats Italian opera
with the studied scorn due a former colonial culture. Verdi was all right, as
long as his tunes were passed from one hurdy-gurdy to another, but in the
temple of great art only *Otello* and *Falstaff* were admissible. The common
public, with its debased taste, might need to be humored by allowing childish
melodramas to be produced, but the less energy put into the process, the better. A critical edition of *Rigoletto?* Only an intellectual half-wit would devote
himself to such a project, unless he were the dupe of voracious music publishers eager to make money on works long out of copyright. In fact, I was accused publicly of being both a half-wit and a dupe at a conference in which the
new edition of *Rigoletto* was presented. Over a coffee *mit Schlag* in a Viennese
café, Rudolf Stephan, who was to become director of the Arnold Schönberg
edition, chided me for wasting my time on Italian opera.

Muti prepared the performance with care, and the Rigoletto (Renato
Bruson) and the Gilda (Edita Gruberova) were excellent. The orchestra played
with elegance, and many details corrected in the new edition emerged with
convincing clarity. The production, while not particularly interesting, was free
from scandal. Many individuals inside and outside the theater, however,
wanted the project to fail, for it was widely considered to be the brainchild of
Lorin Maazel, then director of the Staatsoper, who had political problems in
Vienna's complex society. Maazel's own reaction to the political turmoil was
philosophical: during intermission on opening night he compared himself to
Mahler, whose shabby treatment by the Viennese is legendary.

Unfortunately the performance was severely marred by the tenor, or rather
by a succession of tenors. The originally scheduled Duke of Mantua withdrew
several weeks into the rehearsal period. His replacement fell ill and had to bow
out altogether after the dress rehearsal, leaving this new production without
a Duke. Rather than postponing the opening, Muti chose a tenor then in
Vienna who he thought would respond to intensive coaching and whom he
might teach the most important elements of the new edition overnight.

He was wrong. The late Franco Bonisolli was one of those Italian tenors
with good lungs, a strong sound, but little musical intelligence. He knew just
fine how to sing the role of the Duke, thank you, and he was perfectly willing
to perform it — on his own terms. I cannot imagine the nature of those coach-
ings between Muti and Bonisolli, to which no one had access, but in the performance Bonisolli was appalling. His Duke was vocally coarse, dramatically
vulgar, and indifferent to this production's efforts to rediscover and interpret
Verdi's original text and music. Add to that his outrage that Muti wanted him

to sing the music *as written,* which meant in particular that he was not permitted to sing and sustain a high *b* at the conclusion of "La donna è mobile" in the third act. Muti wanted the aria treated as a popular tune, a feather in the breeze, not an excuse for tenor high jinks. That particular battle Muti won, but to no avail, for Bonisolli found many ways to express his distaste for the proceedings. His outrageous behavior with Maddalena conveyed nothing of the eroticism of Verdi's quartet, but invoked the spirit of the burlesque hall. When the Duke is finally allowed a *pianissimo* high *b* as he makes his exit from the opera intoning "La donna è mobile" offstage, Bonisolli bellowed the note at full volume and sat on it. And sat. And sat. He couldn't see either Bruson's anxiety as he stared impatiently at the sack that is supposed to contain the Duke's body or Muti's furious glares. Many in the audience understood this gesture of defiance and there were pockets of nervous laughter. During the curtain calls, Bonisolli received a solid round of boos, at which point he ostentatiously thrust his rear end at the public. The Viennese press scoffed at what they took to be Maazel's discomfiture.

In all the turmoil, who could remember that serious artistic aims were at stake, that scholars and performers alike, convinced that *Rigoletto* was a work of art deserving a better fate than it had been accorded, were attempting to revisit this staple of the repertory? As the first series of performances based on the first critical edition published in *The Works of Giuseppe Verdi,* it was anything but an auspicious occasion. But it woke an entire generation of Verdi scholars—all of whom in one way or another were to collaborate over the next decades with this major editorial project of the University of Chicago Press and Casa Ricordi—to the realities of the operatic world. And as the hunchback in butter was consumed (or the hunchback in ice melted), we vowed to continue our efforts.

Music publishers are in business to make money by selling printed music and renting performance materials to theaters and concert organizations. If they don't make money, as any good economist could predict, they go out of business. If a publishing house reprints and sells nineteenth- or early twentieth-century scores and parts, its costs are few. The less work it does, the higher its profits. If Kalmus sells a vocal score purporting to be Rossini's *Il Turco in Italia* in which some 50 percent of the music is not from that opera, *caveat emptor.*[12] A publishing house will invest in preparing a new edition, on the other hand, only if it both believes the edition to be necessary and hopes to earn a reasonable return on its investment. Casa Ricordi, now BMG Ricordi, Italy's premier music publisher since 1808, has traditionally sold vocal scores and some orchestral scores, while renting performance materials. But producing a full orchestral score of Bellini's *La straniera* or Donizetti's *Adelia* will never be commercially viable. That is why Ricordi has entered into agreements with private and public institutions—the University of Chicago Press, the Fondazione Rossini, the cities of Bergamo and Catania—to produce critical editions of the works of this repertory. Ricordi opens its archives to these institutions and their scholars, then works closely with them in the preparation of new scores, of which it distributes performing materials. Rental fees and royalties from licensing performance rights (in countries offering limited protection for critical editions) are shared with the editors and with co-publishers, which reinvest them in future projects. While hardly a perfect system, it has proved viable for some twenty-five years.

Economic judgments are made all the time in performing Italian opera. Does a theater hire an expensive tenor or does it use local talent? If it hires an expensive tenor, does it skimp on the soprano and baritone? Does it create a new production or dust off sets warehoused two decades ago? And how does one decide between several desiderata? If 95 percent of the public can't tell what musical edition is being used, but everyone is pleased when just a little more gold paint is applied to the set, how do you spend your limited resources?

Many opera houses therefore decide to forgo the new editions, particularly of repertory operas for which there is a serviceable score in circulation. Having invested in *Ermione* during the summer of 2000, Santa Fe determined that *Rigoletto* would be performed with materials already in hand. And so, one might think, the fruits of the research and editorial work that resulted in the critical edition of *Rigoletto* did not reach audiences in the Sangre de Cristo mountains. But that is not quite accurate. In *Rigoletto* there are significant corrections in the notes, rhythms, text, and dynamics in the parts of Gilda, Rigoletto, and the Duke. New vocal scores have been in print for more than a decade, and many singers have studied them. Peculiar contradictions can result. In a fascinating *Rigoletto* in Los Angeles during the winter of 2000, which did not officially use the new edition, the Duke of Mantua became "Duke," a Hollywood mogul, and the opening festivities took place around his swimming pool in Beverly Hills, following the preview of Duke's new movie (*Vendetta*). Whatever one may have thought of the staging (I liked it), Gilda and the Duke incorporated the many corrections of the new score, while Rigoletto sang the old notes, many of them wrong.

In Santa Fe all principal singers adopted the corrected readings. More important, the conscientious conductor, Richard Buckley, was determined to incorporate as many corrections as possible. Between my rehearsals for *Ermione* and his for *Rigoletto,* we went over the score page by page, and I shared with him the corrections I could remember. I had neither the time nor the energy to check every symbol in the old Ricordi score against the critical edition. So, we fixed dynamic levels in the Prelude; we made sure the flute and clarinet played their last note before "Questa, o quella," where the old Ricordi edition carelessly omitted the resolutions; we got the rhythm right after the "Perigordino," ignoring a wrongly interpolated measure of rest; we differentiated between accents and diminuendo hairpins in the accompaniment for "Veglia, o donna, questo fiore" and the orchestral introduction to "La donna è mobile."

Among the most striking corrections in the critical edition is the restoration to their original form of several elements in the storm and trio of the last act, during which Gilda enters the inn and is murdered by Sparafucile. These include Verdi's markings for thunder, lightning, and storm noises, as well as his original choral parts. The old Ricordi scores eliminated most of the former, which used a notation Verdi invented for the purpose, and simplified the latter (a men's chorus backstage, "a bocca chiusa," that is, humming). To get the choral entries right in Santa Fe, the photocopier went into operation, so that the chorus actually learned this section of *Rigoletto* from the new edition.

For Verdi's storm effects there was to be no metal sheet to strike for thunder and no traditional wind machine. Instead, the finest new electronics were at Santa Fe's disposal. Thunder, lightning bolts, rain, wind: all were carefully synthesized and timed to coincide precisely with Verdi's markings. Yet when the sound effects were unveiled at the piano dress rehearsal, they were a disaster: too loud, too soft, now on, now off, and badly coordinated with the score. The men's chorus was inaudible from behind a sound-deadening wall. By the final dress rehearsal most of this had been worked out. Volume and timing of the electronics were better regulated, and the chorus was placed in the orchestra pit, from where they could be heard.

When opening night came, we were confident that the storm effects would function correctly. What we failed to take into account was the weather. Although Santa Fe's theater is now covered, so that well-dressed patrons are no longer drenched during a sudden downpour (a regular feature of earlier operagoing in Santa Fe), the theater remains open along its sides to stunning mountain views. It is also open to the sounds of nature, which on opening night of *Rigoletto* included a spectacular storm. Murmurs of thunder began with the Prelude and returned, on cue, for the beginning of the storm and trio in the third act. The counterpoint between actual thunder and electronic thunder was a bonus Verdi had not envisioned.

Other additions to Verdi's score raised more complicated issues. Richard Buckley is a second-generation conductor. His father, the late Emerson Buckley, was the guiding light of the Greater Miami Opera for many years and a long-time favorite conductor for Luciano Pavarotti. The younger Buckley, while friendly to the new Verdi editions, also knows his performing traditions. He is bothered neither by inserted high notes nor by an occasional ornamental flourish, and so the Duke sang an unwritten high *b* at the end of "La donna è mobile" and Rigoletto leaped to the stratosphere for "All'onda, all'onda." As will be seen in chapter 9, I do not reject interpolated high notes in principle, but there is one traditional singer's modification in *Rigoletto* that I find offensive, for it ruins a musical effect that Verdi calculated with care. The fine Rigoletto, Kim Josephson, sang this very interpolation during the dress rehearsal of the opera.

The moment comes just before the jester attacks the cabaletta of his second-act duet with Gilda, "Sì, vendetta, tremenda vendetta." Monterone has crossed the stage between guards. Observing the portrait of the Duke, he muses bitterly: "Since you have escaped my calls for revenge, you will apparently live happily, o Duke!" Rigoletto, his sobbing daughter beside him, calls after Monterone: "Old man, you are wrong, you will have an avenger." Verdi wrote the roles of Monterone and Rigoletto as mirror images. The strains of Monterone's curse and of Rigoletto's fearful "That old man cursed me" ring through the opera, beginning with the first measures of the prelude. Time and again they involve simple declamation on middle *c,* a comfortable note in the upper middle of a baritone's tessitura. In the second act, then, Monterone emphasizes this middle *c* and the key of *C minor* in the phrase he addresses to the Duke's portrait, imitating precisely Rigoletto's angry dismissal of the courtiers. Rigoletto returns to this *c* to proclaim himself Monterone's avenger, after which the music shifts abruptly, in a harmonically unexpected manner, to the key of *A♭ major* for "Sì, vendetta, tremenda vendetta" (example 1.2). Generations of Rigolettos have shown off their upper register by altering the final *c* of "un vindice avrai" to *e♭,* a minor third higher. But that gesture completely changes the sense of the music, for this *e♭* functions as a dominant degree to the new tonic (*A♭ major*). Verdi's stark declamation and sudden attack are made to seem harmonically consequential, with a link across the rests between the sections, in a way he never intended.[13]

EXAMPLE 1.2. GIUSEPPE VERDI, *RIGOLETTO*, SCENA E DUETTO (N. 10), MM. 192–196.

The day before the *Rigoletto* premiere, at lunch in the Tesuque Market Café (a hangout for Hollywood stars who buy multimillion-dollar villas in the hills), I expressed my reservations about this interpolation to Buckley, who listened carefully. I did not expect anything to change as the result of that conversation: singers need to be left alone in the days between dress rehearsal and opening night, and told how wonderful they are. So I was surprised on opening night to hear this spot corrected: Josephson held firm on the *c* before attacking "Sì, vendetta, tremenda vendetta." I wish I could say that I was satisfied, but I wasn't. He sang the note hesitantly, uncertain, as if he didn't quite understand the point. In performing Italian opera, it is not enough to sing the right notes: they must be sung with authority, even in the mountains of New Mexico.

LE SIÈGE DE CORINTHE AND *THE PIRATES OF PENZANCE*

Although the Rossini Opera Festival on the shores of the Adriatic employs the new critical editions of the works of Rossini prepared by the Fondazione Rossini, life in the theater is more complex than the principles scholars invoke.

And choosing an edition is only one of the decisions to be made when performing Italian opera. Even the so-called home of "practical musicology," as Pesaro in its golden years used to be called, can become a battleground for differing visions of theater, incompatible musical opinions, and the conflicts that inevitably emerge when strong personalities (singers, conductors, directors, even scholars) clash. Two of the three productions at Pesaro in August 2000 were deeply contested; the third was a blessed example of what happens when all the gears mesh.

The festival opened with the first Pesaro performance of *Le Siège de Corinthe*, Rossini's earliest French opera, which had its premiere at the Paris Opéra in 1826. It was based, in turn, on one of Rossini's finest Neapolitan operas, *Maometto II*, prepared in 1820. There had been legendary performances of the latter in Pesaro in 1986 and 1993, an elegant production by Pier Luigi Pizzi, with Cecilia Gasdia as the heroine, Anna (Venetian in *Maometto II*), and Sam Ramey, then Michele Pertusi, as her beloved who turns out to be the Turkish sultan Maometto II. While the Neapolitan premiere of *Maometto II* shared the doubtful reception there of *Ermione*, Rossini was determined not to leave this work's reputation to posterity. He revised it for Venice in 1823, then recast it as a battle between Greeks and Turks for Paris. With *Le Siège de Corinthe*, Italian vocal style and operatic forms entered forcibly into the temple of French culture; the resulting clash and reconciliation laid the groundwork for French grand opera.[14]

There is no acceptable, let alone critical, edition of *Le Siège de Corinthe*. Indeed, until *Maometto II* is published, it will be impossible to approach Rossini's first French opera responsibly. The directors of the Rossini Festival were indifferent: having produced *Guillaume Tell* in 1995 (using the edition of the Fondazione Rossini), then *Moïse* in 1997 (using a nineteenth-century score that was functional but of questionable authority), they were determined also to undertake *Le Siège de Corinthe*. As in the case of *Moïse*, the festival adopted an orchestral score issued by Rossini's French publisher, Troupenas. Scholars at the Fondazione tried to explain, to no avail, that the Troupenas score of *Siège* was a mess, with errors and inconsistencies, major confusions about the order and content of pieces, and dramaturgical absurdities. At the end, for example, the male Greek defenders of Corinth are all dead, yet they manage to sing from offstage "O patrie," in a conclusion that merges incoherently several versions of the final measures. Only by sorting out the performance history will it be possible to produce a coherent text, as was accomplished with *Guillaume Tell*, an edition on which Elizabeth Bartlet labored for many years.[15]

The conductor, Maurizio Benini, found himself facing error-filled materials with nothing but instinct to guide him. To make matters worse, the Troupenas orchestral score often differed from the Troupenas vocal score. The cavatina, or opening aria, for Maometto in *Maometto II,* for example, is a showstopper. Rossini organized his opera so that there would be few opportunities for audience applause until this entrance of the hero/villain. The opera's introductory ensemble is followed by Anna's cavatina, which is short and in a single section: while it is beautiful, it is definitely not showy. After that cavatina the opera continues with one of the longest and most splendid ensembles in all Italian opera, the *terzettone* (Rossini's unusual name employs the Italian suffix *-one,* meaning "great big"), but its orchestral conclusion modulates to a new key, robbing the audience of whatever opportunity they might have had to applaud.[16] Now the chorus of Turks and their Sultan enter, and Maometto sings his fabulous solo with a blockbuster conclusion. In Pizzi's production the effect was startling, with the young and dashing Sam Ramey, his chest bared to the delight of a host of swooning admirers, perilously perched high on the outstretched hands of his warriors.

In *Maometto II* the piece consists of a chorus, a cantabile ("Sorgete"), in which Maometto exhorts his followers to battle, a *tempo di mezzo* (a transitional section, featuring the chorus), and the cabaletta (a quicker final section, whose main period is repeated, giving the singer a chance to introduce ornamentation), in which Maometto promises with their help to conquer the universe. In *Le Siège de Corinthe* the same piece is presented in the Troupenas orchestral score with the chorus, a new recitative, the *tempo di mezzo,* and the cabaletta (the cantabile is omitted). The vocal score agrees with the orchestral score, but it *also* has the cantabile. Benini and his Mahomet, Michele Pertusi, decided to include the cantabile. While the music is appealing, the result is a historically incorrect conflation of two versions. But their incompatibility goes further. Not only do the new recitative and the old cantabile cover exactly the same dramatic ground, but the recitative ends on a chord (a dominant seventh) that resolves naturally to the key of the *tempo di mezzo* (*D minor*). As one intelligent nineteenth-century edition specified, "if you want to sing the cantabile, you have to omit the preceding recitative."[17] Instead, Pesaro heard them both.

Such issues, though, rapidly faded away in comparison with the directorial hijinks that surrounded this production. They tell me that Massimo Castri is one of Italy's most significant directors of prose theater, which only suggests how badly people of talent can go wrong. It was Castri's first attempt at operatic staging. Other Italian theatrical wizards (Luchino Visconti, Giorgio

Strehler, Luca Ronconi, and Dario Fo) have made the transition brilliantly. Instead of trying to learn how opera and theater differ, however, Castri expressed his scorn for the lyric theater. What do you mean he couldn't cut music here, shift scenes there, add material wherever it suited his whim, just as he did in prose theater? What is this music stuff that interfered with his notion of theatrical time? Furthermore, why couldn't these singers behave like actors? And how dare Ruth Ann Swenson, the beautiful Pamyra, complain that she couldn't sing while Castri chain-smoked his way through rehearsals?

Worse, he made up his mind (and told the newspapers) that *Le Siège de Corinthe* could not be taken seriously, and that Rossini's music was an ironic response to the plot. So much for the European commitment to the plight of Greeks fighting for their freedom against Turks during the 1820s, the background against which Rossini's opera was written and received. Castri instead decided to provide what he termed an ironic staging. It began by employing a steeply raked (that is, sloping) stage, covered with thick artificial grass, over which in act 1 were strewn bright white Corinthian capitals (only capitals) that seemed made from styrofoam. In act 2 these capitals were replaced by nineteenth-century divans in red brocade with gold fringe for the Turkish maidens (who began the act by giggling as they smoked their hookahs). In act 3 the divans gave way to grave markers, which at Pamyra's suicide sank into the earth while comic-book lightning was projected on the bare cyclorama around the back of the stage: *shazam!* The wounded Greeks were dressed as Byronic heroes, wearing top hats into battle; the Turks as Victorian orientalist caricatures, the men wearing red fezzes and handlebar mustachios.

With the set at such a perilous rake, no singer could do anything but seek out a stable position and remain stationary, so stage movement between protagonists was almost nonexistent. Only perversity or hostility could have imposed this stage on an opera in which a formal *divertissement,* with several elaborate dances, takes up about a third of the second act. The potentially witty action invented by the choreographer, in which six Pamyras and six Maomettos pantomimed a scene of courtship on six red divans, became tiresome, for the dancers had nowhere to go. No wonder that Mauro Bigonzetti choreographed only two of the three dance movements, then left town. Pamyra and Mahomet were supposed to watch these events on a divan upstage, while drinking Turkish coffee, and so they did on opening night, looking for all the world like an *opera buffa* couple, Fiorilla and Selim in *Il Turco in Italia.* But after Castri departed (stage directors are not obliged to remain at a theater after the show has opened), Ruth Ann Swenson informed Michele

Pertusi, five minutes before the beginning of act 2 at the second performance, that she planned to exit as soon the "ballet" began. He could follow or remain in solitary splendor. Off they went.

So little happened on stage that the foolishness of what *did* happen became even more apparent. The chorus of Greek women implored God's help wearing frilly dresses and twirling parasols. And the Turkish women demonstrated their victory by waving around those same parasols, presumably the spoils of war. In the chorus that opened the second act, Ismène begged the heavens to assist Pamyra and "dry her tears." This handmaiden then ostentatiously minced around during Pamyra's aria and her duet with Mahomet drying *her own* tears with a big handkerchief (shades of *Otello*). The end of the second act pits the Greeks against the Turks, but Castri kept the Greeks off-stage, so no one in the audience could have any idea what was happening. And after Pamyra exhorts the Greek women to die by their own hands rather than surrender, Castri had the ladies carried away by the soldiers, as if reenacting the rape of the Sabine women.

The problem with staging an Italian/French opera of the *primo Ottocento* as a mockery of itself is that for an Italian audience it produces nothing but confusion, while for an Anglo-American audience it suggests the accomplishment of two geniuses of the English theater, Gilbert and Sullivan. Their Savoy operas are conceived as send-ups of Italian opera. They are more than parodies, of course, because Gilbert was a brilliant writer and Sullivan knew how to clothe his verses with music that brought forth their wit or gave them deeper expression. But who could parody act 2 of Verdi's *Ernani*, in which old Silva hides Ernani behind one of the portraits of his ancestors, better than Gilbert and Sullivan in *Ruddigore?* Who has ever laughed more deliciously at Donizetti's *L'elisir d'amore* than the authors of *The Sorcerer*, whose Doctor Dulcamara figure, J. Wellington Wells, "a dealer in magic and spells," sells his wares surrounded by a demonic troupe imported from *Der Freischütz*, via English Christmas pantomimes. Who has ever parodied an Italian opera chorus better than the Savoyards, witness the response of *H.M.S. Pinafore*'s Ralph Rackstraw to his supportive followers: "I know the value of a kindly chorus ... but choruses yield little consolation." And there are the maidens, parasols twirling and fresh as the morning dew, making their way to the inaccessible pirates' lair in *The Pirates of Penzance* to the strains of "Climbing over rocky mountain, tripping rivulet and fountain." To treat *Le Siège de Corinthe* ironically in the wake of Gilbert and Sullivan runs the risk of confusing the parodied with the parody. Instead of Castri's parasols serving as a commentary on Rossini's opera, they seemed an importation from *Pirates*. In the best of circumstances, English and American audiences need to suppress their memories of the Savoy operas in order to give Italian opera its due. Castri's *Siège de Corinthe* was pablum by comparison.

RUMMAGING IN A TRUNK FOR *LA SCALA DI SETA*

The five one-act operas Rossini wrote before he was twenty-one years old (known as *farse*, as we have seen) were all prepared for the Venetian Teatro San Moisè, a small opera house that specialized in this kind of spectacle. It was a wonderful place for young composers to develop their skills in a venue less demanding than the major opera houses in northern Italy—La Scala or the Teatro La Fenice of Venice. For many years Rossini's autograph manuscript of *La scala di seta*, one of the best of his *farse*, was presumed lost. In fact, it had been acquired by a Swedish musician and naval officer, Rudolf Nydahl, who assembled an extraordinary collection of musical manuscripts. After his death in 1973, this collection became accessible to scholars, and the Fondazione Rossini eventually learned that among its treasures was the autograph of *La scala di seta*. It is a lovely document, with every note in the hand of the composer. Using this manuscript as his principal source, Anders Wiklund—a Swedish scholar—prepared the critical edition of *La scala di seta* for the Fondazione. A provisional version of his score was first performed at the Rossini Opera Festival during the summer of 1988; the opera was actually published by the Fondazione three years later.[18]

La scala di seta had practically no performing history in the nineteenth century, for one-act operas did not circulate widely. After the spring season of 1812 at the San Moisè, where it was performed twelve times, the *farsa* was revived in even smaller theaters: Senigaglia in 1813, Siena in 1818, Lisbon in 1825.[19] For none of these revivals do printed librettos survive, so we have no further information about them. While Ricordi published a vocal score in 1852, only in the twentieth century did the *farsa* begin to be seen with regularity. There was never any question about its structure, although that structure was not always respected in modern performances. For several years an inauthentic overture (a potpourri of Rossini themes from other operas) circulated side by side with the original. At least one conductor, Herbert Handt, stretched Rossini's one act into two by bringing down the curtain after the quartet, taking an intermission, and opening the "second act" with this pseudo-overture.[20] Once the autograph of the opera was rediscovered, any lingering doubts about the overture disappeared, and it became possible to marvel at all the delicious details Rossini strewed with youthful abandon throughout this superb score.

In its earlier production of *La scala di seta,* first performed in 1988, the Rossini Festival performed this *farsa* very well. The set by Emanuele Luzzati and Santuzza Calì was beautiful to see, a backdrop that gave the impression of stained glass. The staging of Maurizio Scaparro was elegant, emphasizing more the Romantic elements of Rossini's score than the comic ones, but perfectly willing to revel in the latter. (None of us will forget a very young Cecilia Bartoli in the part of Lucilla, singing her "aria di sorbetto" from behind a translucent screen while tearing the clothes off the young man she had determined to conquer.) It was wonderful to find in *La scala di seta* a perfectly constructed theatrical mechanism, not too long, not too short, each element falling precisely into place.

After a production, however successful, has been seen several times, it is time to move on, and in the summer of 2000 the festival called upon director Luca de Filippo and designer Bruno Garofalo to devise a new staging of *La scala di seta.* Although de Filippo, like Castri, was new to the lyric stage, he felt no need to undermine the work he was directing. He brought to it, however, a sensibility influenced by his own theatrical lineage as the son of one of the giants of twentieth-century Italian theater, Eduardo de Filippo, playwright and director of Neapolitan comic theater. It comes as no surprise, then, that Luca de Filippo chose to emphasize the farcical elements of the work.

A few details may immediately determine the character of an operatic staging. In *La scala di seta,* for example, the curtain opens on the apartment of the heroine (Giulia) in the home of her tutor (Dormont). She has remained closed in her apartment all day with her secret husband (Dorvil), but she is plagued by her servant (Germano) and her cousin (Lucilla). Both have been sent by her tutor, who wants to discuss the marriage he is arranging between Giulia and a wealthy suitor (Blansac). According to the printed libretto, after Giulia chases Germano and Lucilla away, she opens the door to a small side room, where Dorvil has been hiding. The de Filippo staging, instead, had Dorvil emerge from a large but narrow clothes closet, where he presumably had been stifling during the first scene. At his entrance, then, our tenor hero was already made to seem ridiculous. Also according to the libretto, Dorvil gains access to Giulia's apartment by means of the silken ladder of the title, which Giulia keeps folded in a dresser drawer, then attaches to a balcony on the other side of a glass door (which gave rise to the stained glass of the earlier Pesaro production). De Filippo turned each element into an opportunity for broad comedy. Instead of using a balcony, Dorvil entered and exited through a high window, access to which required Giulia to shove a heavy table across stage, on top of which she precariously balanced a chair. The gossamer silken ladder became a contraption of slats and thick cord, which she extracted from a trapdoor in the center of the stage like a magician producing strings of colored cloth from his hat, and then tossed through the high window; it landed with a resounding thud.

There is nothing outrageous here: the audience enjoyed de Filippo's devices, which were often effective, and Rossini's musical magic survived. That I personally would have preferred a staging more sensitive to the elegant and sentimental elements characteristic of this work is not an opinion that need be held by others. Were there not room for considerable interpretive latitude, performing Italian opera would be a dreary business. No, what outraged me about this production was a musical decision, taken with what the Italians would call *leggerezza* (insouciance), that contradicted much of what the Rossini Opera Festival had stood for over its twenty-year history. I had been engaged to prepare suggestions for variations and cadenzas for this production. When I arrived for the piano dress rehearsal, a week before the scheduled premiere, I discovered on the piano a concert aria Rossini had prepared for a Venetian patron, Filippo Grimani, probably in 1813, "Alle voci della gloria." I knew the piece well, having prepared this very edition for Samuel Ramey to include in a CD of Rossini arias issued by Teldec in 1992.[21] But what was "Alle voci della gloria" doing in a rehearsal for *La scala di seta?*

Apparently it had been decided to add it for Blansac, who doesn't otherwise have a solo aria. While in the nineteenth century operatic scores were sometimes manipulated in performance, the work of the Fondazione Rossini and the Rossini Festival had been dedicated, in principle, to presenting Rossini's operas as he conceived them, complete and intact. When he himself created multiple versions or introduced alternative arias, these were fair game, but other interpolations had been avoided. That rigor helped define the festival for two decades. I would not cry scandal if a theater in Reggio Emilia or Paris introduced an interpolation. An argument could even be made that the Rossini Festival should experiment with the whole problem of the arias early nineteenth-century singers carried around with them (figuratively— and sometimes literally—in their "trunks," hence *arie di baule*) to insert in an opera when they felt their parts were too small or the original music wasn't flashy enough. But that was a decision to take only after a careful assessment of its implications.[22]

In addition to the principle, there is the piece. "Alle voci della gloria" is an elaborate scena and aria written to a text from an *opera seria*, with a large

EXAMPLE 1.3. GIOACHINO ROSSINI, "ALLE VOCI DELLA GLORIA," MM. 104–107.

orchestra, employing trumpets, trombones, and percussion, none of which appear in *La scala di seta*. It had been accommodated to its imposed home for Pesaro by omitting the scena and the first section of the aria. This left a truncated piece in two sections, a fragment of an aria that begins in one key and ends in another, very much contrary to Rossinian practice. The tune of the florid cabaletta, furthermore, is generic (example 1.3). It resembles many other Rossinian cabalettas, such as Rosina's "Io sono docile" from her cavatina "Una voce poco fa" in *Il barbiere di Siviglia*. The addition also meant that there were now four consecutive arias, decidedly unbalancing the opera's structure. And what was gained? An able but hardly stellar Blansac struggled through half a virtuoso piece he had no business singing, and de Filippo invented a superfluous situation in which Blansac filed through and tossed away what seemed to be snapshots of his earlier conquests. While we're at it, why don't we give an aria to Antonio in *Le nozze di Figaro* (it isn't bad enough that Mozart gave arias to Marcellina and Basilio) or Jacquino in *Fidelio* or Fiorello in *Il barbiere di Siviglia?* Poor dears, the composers neglected them: we need to compensate for their oversight.

A performance is a public statement. Since scholars working with the Fondazione Rossini could not put on a counterperformance, I made a public statement of my own, calling attention to what I hoped would be a "momentary aberration" in the cultural mission of the festival. That phrase led to articles in local newspapers, comments by reviewers, interviews on local and national radio, with tempers running high. Differences of opinion are fair game, but fabrications are not. Yet representatives of the festival fraudulently claimed that Rossini himself had added this aria to *La scala di seta*. War was averted only by the intervention of the mayor of Pesaro, who sat us down in his office overlooking the town's main square and told us to behave ourselves. Egos and politics are never far removed when Italian opera is performed.

THEATRICAL MAGIC IN *LA CENERENTOLA*

Yet sometimes it all comes together. Rossini's 1817 retelling of the Cinderella story never disappeared from the stage. In the title role he created a perfect part for coloratura mezzos, who have never relinquished it to their soprano stepsisters. But the score in use during the first seventy years of the twentieth century was appalling (the old edition of *Rigoletto* was perfection by comparison), clumsily reorchestrated at the end of the nineteenth century, long after Rossini's death, and rendered intolerably noisy with added brass and banging percussion. To its shame, Ricordi had only this horrid pastiche available; to the continuing shame of the world of Italian opera, there are still opera companies who purchase reprints of this old Ricordi score (from Kalmus) and continue to use it. What renders the situation so piquant is that these companies must therefore hire additional orchestral musicians to play inauthentic material, paying much more in labor costs than it would cost them to rent an accurate edition.

In 1969, in honor of the 1968 centenary of Rossini's death, I published a facsimile of the autograph manuscript of *La Cenerentola*, together with a description of its authentic sources.[23] Soon after, Alberto Zedda prepared a provisional edition of the score on the basis of those sources, and Claudio Abbado's performances in 1973 at the Teatro alla Scala in the production of Jean-Pierre Ponnelle, which still circulates thirty years later, restored the opera to its rightful position in the repertory. Finally, in 1998, the Fondazione Rossini developed this preliminary edition into an accurate critical edition.[24] While there are still singers who learned their roles from older scores, the corrected readings are so obviously superior that the only objection ever raised to them is that it is difficult to unlearn old habits. When the Metropolitan Opera performed *La Cenerentola* for the first time ever in 1997, a performance for which I served as stylistic adviser, the opera was under the baton of James Levine (a first-rate Rossini conductor), and Cecilia Bartoli was enchanting in the title role. But the friendly and accommodating Simone Alaimo, our Don Magnifico (Cenerentola's stepfather), couldn't get his throat around one of the corrections. In the old score of his cavatina, Magnifico interprets the "magnificent dream" from which Cenerentola's stepsisters have awoken him, then imitates their babbling: "col ci ci, col ci ci, col ci ci, col ci ci." But Rossini, aware that repeating the same sounds at a rapid tempo produces a tongue twister, alternated syllables: "col ci ci, col ciù, ciù, col ci ci, col ciù, ciù." Although the latter is *much* more gracious to sing and the former a mistake, Alaimo never got it quite right. His difficulties became such a joke that Levine would enter rehearsals, patented towel draped over his shoulder, to the strains of "col ci ci, col ciù ciù."

The Metropolitan's *Cenerentola* was musically excellent. We shortened the opera a bit by making cuts in the recitative by Luca Agolini and omitting two pieces by the same composer performed at the opera's premiere: a chorus for the courtiers at the beginning of the second act and an aria for one of the stepsisters, Clorinda.[25] A third Agolini composition, an aria for the Prince's tutor, Alidoro, was replaced by Rossini's own substitute aria, "Là del ciel." Otherwise no cuts were made, nor were they necessary, for all the singers were experts at the style and at the art of embellishing repeated passages.

The production, though, was rather mixed. There were some fine things. The chorus, apparitions from a Magritte painting, hilariously appeared and disappeared from trapdoors and holes all over the stage. Ramon Vargas was a convincing Prince (at first disguised as his own servant), and Alessandro Corbelli showed New York his widely acclaimed interpretation of Dandini (the servant disguised as the Prince). Cecilia Bartoli was musically glorious, naive, spunky, and funny as the scullery maid, but less successful as the consort of the Prince. It is not clear whether the fault lay in her or in the vision of her communicated by the director, Cesare Lievi, focusing too much on her serving-girl persona. In the first-act finale, building on a line from Dandini ("Today, since I am playing the part of the Prince, I want to eat for four"), the concluding ensemble—in which food is not mentioned—became the excuse for a prolonged and vulgar food-fight. The end of the second act wasn't much better: Don Ramiro and Cenerentola were dressed in formal garb, like dolls on a wedding cake. Sure enough, an enormous cake soon filled the stage, atop which the lovers scrambled awkwardly. This Cenerentola had much to learn about being a Princess.

A festival and a regular opera house can make different decisions. The Luca Ronconi production of *La Cenerentola* at Pesaro, first performed during the summer of 1998, and repeated in 2000, included every note of the score, those by Rossini and those by Agolini (though, as at the Met, replacing Agolini's Alidoro aria with Rossini's). Is this a good thing? These Pesaro performances were the first in modern times to incorporate the chorus by Agolini opening act 2, in which the supercilious courtiers deride Don Magnifico and his two daughters. While the music is undistinguished, the piece provides a more distinctive opening for the act then the *secco* recitative usually heard. More important, Ronconi staged it well (although Ruth Ann Swenson would have objected to the cigarette smoke swirling around stage from the mimes who played courtiers). But I find myself bored by Agolini's aria for Clorinda, which seems pretentious and long. There is a reason, however, for inserting an aria at that point in the opera: it occupies the time needed to transport us back from Don Magnifico's house to the palace. Here the Pesaro production miscalculated. The scene change was made only *after* Clorinda had finished, negating the practical purpose for the aria.

Yet one could forgive this flaw, for the stage design of this *Cenerentola* was remarkable. The opera was produced at the sports arena transformed into an opera house (the "Palafestival"). With monumental operas, filling its large stage is no trouble, as Hugo De Ana's imposing *Semiramide* demonstrated in 1992; when operas are more intimate, directors and designers must not only use the large space well but also carve out smaller playing areas for their singers. For the scene in Don Magnifico's house, Ronconi and his designer, Margherita Palli, created an intimate space, in front of a large chimney-place. There Cenerentola sat alone by the fire, Alidoro disguised as a beggar asked for alms, and the disguised Prince met his future bride. The remainder of the set was a vast concatenation of furniture, pieces piled high, with a dizzying array of surfaces, beds, chairs, dressers, sofas. This surreal mound reflected the text of the opera: since half the impoverished Magnifico's house has fallen down, the implicit conceit was that he ended up throwing one piece of furniture on top of another. Time and space were indeterminate, but art deco skyscrapers in the back were consonant with the arrival of the disguised Dandini and the courtiers in a black limousine from the 1930s. Gags and pratfalls were made possible by the furniture, but there were ample flat surfaces so that sentimental scenes could be played straight.

When it came time for Cenerentola to be transported to the Prince's palace, she disappeared for a moment in the direction of the chimney, still in her rags, as Alidoro began his aria. Toward its end a resplendent Cenerentola in a flame-red gown emerged from the top of the chimney in the beak of a large stork, who transported her across the top of the stage. Vesselina Kasarova—five months pregnant—sang the title role in 1998, and some were horrified to see her carried across the stage, but it was all theatrical wizardry. Neither Kasarova nor Sonia Ganassi in 2000 personally flew across the stage: doubles made that traversal. Now stagehands appeared, in work clothes and rubber boots. Down came a row of "sky-hooks," which they attached to pieces of the furniture, and the entire set was hoisted upward. Below it the Prince's palace (like a piece in a three-dimensional jigsaw puzzle) was revealed. The backdrop flats began to twirl in a gaudy ballet of surfaces, warm lights bathed the playing area, and suddenly we were in the luxurious palace of the Prince. Several stunning chimney-places appeared, down one of which the flame-red

Cenerentola (the real one) appeared. Opera lovers often scorn productions in which the biggest applause of an evening is earned by the scenery, but this brilliant set and set change were integrated into a production in which almost every element functioned. Unfortunately, the set change happened twice more in act 2—a return to Don Magnifico's house, then back to the palace for the final scene—and it began to seem long. Ronconi needed to adopt a twentieth-century equivalent of an old nineteenth-century practice, using recitatives and the Clorinda aria to cover these scene changes, but the movements of the massive set might have been distracting. A polite audience therefore sat quietly as the luminous scene change in act 1 lost its luster in act 2.

How much recitative should be cut in an opera? Again, there is no simple answer. Jacopo Ferretti's libretto for *La Cenerentola* is brilliant (especially now that its many jokes and puns have been restored to their original form). Hearing the text declaimed well is a joy, whether the singers are native Italians or simply well schooled in Italian traditions. The Pesaro audience needed no overhead projections to guffaw throughout the evening, nor could the immediacy of their reaction ever be achieved through supertitles. Overall, I believe that supertitles have had a positive role in opera, but it cannot be denied that something has been lost in their now universal adoption in the United States: James Levine's long resistance had a core of truth.

In Pesaro, Carlo Rizzi conducted with verve the fine orchestra of the Teatro Comunale of Bologna. While none of the singers tossed him an apple, one of Don Magnifico's pillows did fall into the orchestra pit during a performance, and Rizzi was soon on its receiving end. But the cast was superb—professionals who understood Rossini's music and its style, knew about appoggiaturas and ornamentation, phrased well, and did not push their sound. Kasarova was the most elegant Cinderella I have ever seen and introduced remarkable details (I will never forget her tentative and self-conscious dance steps when she begs to be taken to the ball). Juan Diego Flórez showed us why he is now unmatched among Rossini tenors (throwing off the many high *c*s with abandon), while Bruno Praticò was a funny, yet menacing Don Magnifico.

It is rare that opera houses (whether in the mountains or by the sea) provide us with performances in which underlying musical choices, the singers, set design, and staging all serve a composer and his art to the delight of the public. But even in a disappointing production some individual interpretation or detail can make the experience memorable. All the controversies introduced in this prologue, the triumphs, the absurdities, the battles, reflect basic and recurring themes in performing Italian opera, and they will be considered at greater length in the following chapters. To treat these issues as if history (social history, music history, textual history) were irrelevant to performance is irresponsible. It is equally irresponsible to assume that performers should simply turn to history for solutions, without recognizing that every decision made in the theater today is rooted in the world in which we live and work. The purpose of this book is to suggest how scholars and performers, working toward common goals, can bring history and practice together.

PART I

Knowing the Score

2

SETTING THE STAGE

OPERA IN ITALIAN SOCIETY

Opera was at the center of Italian culture throughout the first half of the nineteenth century.[1] Every major city had more than one theater, sometimes open in different seasons or specializing in different repertories. Opera lovers in Naples could attend performances not only at the great San Carlo, home of *opera seria,*[2] but also at the Teatro del Fondo, the Teatro Nuovo, and the Teatro dei Fiorentini. The Fiorentini and later the Nuovo featured *opera buffa,* frequently with comic characters like Don Bartolo in Rossini's *Il barbiere di Siviglia* or Don Magnifico in *La Cenerentola* singing and speaking in Neapolitan dialect. In Milan, seasons at La Scala were rivaled by those at the Teatro Carcano and the Teatro della Canobbiana, and for a few years during the 1810s the Teatro Re. Rome boasted the Teatro Valle, the Teatro Argentina, and the Teatro Apollo,[3] while Venice featured a host of smaller theaters, as well as the elegant La Fenice.[4] Most smaller cities or villages provided a stage for operatic performances. Some had full seasons, others a few performances during annual trade fairs held in the summer or early fall.

New operas were constantly in demand. A major operatic season would consist of three or four different operas, at least one of which would be new, introduced singly, then—if all were successful—performed in repertory. When they could find the means and appropriate younger talent, provincial theaters also tried to obtain new works. *Le nozze in villa,* Donizetti's first full-length *opera buffa,* was written for the Teatro Vecchio of Mantua, Rossini's *L'equivoco stravagante,* his second opera to be staged, for the Teatro Comunale of Bologna. As a result, there were ample opportunities for composers to ply their trade.

Complaints about the terrible conditions under which Italian composers were expected to function, the dreadful pressure and impossible deadlines, must be put into context. It is perfectly true that *Il barbiere di Siviglia* was composed, rehearsed, and performed in less than a month, as were *L'Italiana in Algeri* and *La sonnambula*. While Donizetti continued making corrections during rehearsals, *Don Pasquale* was completed within the same time frame.[5] But it is also true that these are all masterpieces of the operatic stage. Verdi in 1858 complained about the years he spent in frenetic activity "in the galleys," but he used the term "galley years" to refer not only to the 1840s, during which he composed his early operas, but also to the widely admired scores of the early 1850s, *Rigoletto, Il trovatore,* and *La traviata.*[6] And not all operas were prepared and performed under such intense pressure. Rossini spent at least four months (from October 1822 through the beginning of February 1823) principally concerned with *Semiramide.* As late as Verdi's *Aida* in the early 1870s, three months was considered ample to prepare a major work. When Bellini boasted that he wrote only one opera yearly, thereby differentiating himself from those he portrayed as his workaday contemporaries (chiefly Donizetti), he did not mean it took an entire year for him to write that opera. Bellini's actual compositional habits were largely indistinguishable from those of Donizetti, who in a career twice as long wrote seven times as many operas. Bellini's pronouncement, of course, had an economic subtext: since he wrote fewer operas, he expected each to command a higher fee from commissioning theaters.[7]

A composer was normally hired by a specific theater to write an opera for a specific season to be performed by a specific company of singers. The theater might turn to one of the acknowledged masters—Rossini, then Donizetti or Bellini, finally Verdi, but also significant were Mayr, Mercadante, Pacini, or Petrella. Most theaters depended on an impresario who controlled artistic and administrative decisions, though he in turn was beholden to regulations enforced by local royalty, political leaders, and censors. Impresarios bore significant financial responsibility for their companies: many suffered tremendous losses, a few grew rich. When capital was accumulated, it did not derive from operatic receipts alone. For a number of years the lobby of the San Carlo in Naples provided theater patrons with opportunities for gambling. The fortune of the great impresario Domenico Barbaja was largely made in that lobby. To keep Rossini in Naples between 1815 and 1822, effectively as musical director of the Neapolitan theaters, Barbaja ultimately offered the composer a stake in the gambling business. In Paris, Rossini talked his way into funding directly from the governmental purse; indeed, he made completion of *Guillaume Tell* dependent on his receiving a guaranteed pension from the state.

In the typical Italian theater of the time, the more socially prominent patrons sat in several rows of private boxes built around a horseshoe-shaped auditorium. When not under direct governmental control, theaters were built or maintained by local families, each of which owned one or more boxes. These families constituted a society that hired an impresario to administer the theater, while attempting to keep some control over their investment, both financial and artistic. Such a society differed only marginally from the board of trustees of a modern American opera house. Still other theaters were run for limited periods by individuals who produced operatic seasons in cities without a regular opera company or in competition with more established theaters. An extraordinary venture of this kind occurred in 1830–31, when dilettantes took over the Teatro Carcano of Milan, commissioning Donizetti to write *Anna Bolena,* and Bellini *La sonnambula.*

Fundamental to most Italian opera houses during the first half of the nineteenth century was the operatic "season." Companies did not provide continuous entertainment throughout the year, but functioned instead during periods often tied to the church calendar. The most important was carnival, which began on the night of St. Stephens (26 December) and continued through the beginning of Lent or even until the start of Passion week, depending on local custom. Where operatic performances continued into Lent, works with a religious orientation were sought. A tradition of Lenten operas in Naples provided the context for Rossini's *Mosè in Egitto,* first performed on 5 March 1818, or Donizetti's opera about the biblical Noah, *Il diluvio universale,* on 28 February 1830, both prepared for the San Carlo.[8] Seasons in different cities were more variable. At La Scala, opera was presented in the autumn, but the theater usually closed its doors for Advent. In Rome, both the Argentina and the Valle would produce opera during carnival, but in the spring or autumn one house would offer operatic entertainment, while the other might feature a company presenting prose drama.

Singers were normally hired for an entire season, not for a single opera. If three different works were to be performed, the same singers would participate in them all. The artistic ramifications of this commercial organization are palpable. It is no surprise, of course, that composers prepared new works with the particular characteristics of individual singers in mind. Before contracting to write an opera, a mature Donizetti or Verdi would demand to know which singers were in the theater's company for the season; if the company had not yet been determined, the composer's contract was often contingent on his subsequent approval of the singers engaged.[9] Popular operas written for certain singers, however, would be revived in a later season or a different city with new artists, whose talents might be more appropriate to another of the operas to be performed. Impresarios tried to program a group of works suitable to the available personnel, of course, but they were not always successful. Many of the revisions and adaptations common to Italian operas during this period result from this structural organization of the theaters. The situation was particularly devastating for operas written for an unusual combination of voices. That San Carlo regularly engaged two principal tenors in its company during Rossini's tenure (Andrea Nozzari and Giovanni David) imposed characteristics on the composer's Neapolitan *opere serie* that other opera houses could rarely meet.[10] The tormented contemporary history of these works directly reflects the circumstances in which they were composed.

Into this world stepped the composer, whose contract with a theater required that he would prepare an opera to be performed during a given season, sometimes with a specific date (if it was to open the season), sometimes simply as the second or third opera of the season. The contract might have been signed as long as a year in advance, or it might have been concocted at the last moment. Rossini was commissioned to write *L'Italiana in Algeri* less than a month before its premiere, when a desperate impresario at the San Benedetto of Venice found himself without the opera that had previously been commissioned from Carlo Coccia. We do not know why Coccia relinquished his commission, but—for obvious reasons—composers who did not fulfill their contractual obligations were rare. On the other hand, Rossini's contract with La Fenice for *Semiramide,* which had its premiere on 3 February 1823, was signed six months earlier, in mid-August of 1822.[11] But hiring a composer was not enough: his art depended on the words he would set to music. A librettist was needed.

THE LIBRETTIST AND *LE CONVENIENZE TEATRALI*

During the eighteenth century, composers typically set the same basic libretto again and again, often texts by Pietro Metastasio, the Caesarian court poet in Vienna from 1729 until his death in 1782, whose mellifluous texts continued to be used into the nineteenth century. By early in that century, however, new librettos were generally written for most Italian operas. They were often adaptations of spoken drama from the French or German theater. But librettists also found inspiration in Spanish drama or in English Romantic literature, particularly the poems and stories of Scott and the epics and verse dramas of Byron. Fashions changed considerably during the first half of the nineteenth century. Early in the century source plays might predate the derived opera by some forty or even fifty years. Rossini's *Tancredi* (1813) is based on a play by Voltaire from 1760, while his *Ermione* (1818) goes back even further, to Racine's seventeenth-century drama *Andromaque*. By the 1830s, Italian composers and librettists were turning to the latest creations of the emerging Romantic theater, and Donizetti's *Lucrezia Borgia* (1833) was written the same year as the verse drama by Victor Hugo on which it was based.[12]

While it had become less typical for composers to set anew texts previously used by other composers, this common eighteenth-century practice did continue into the nineteenth. Looking for a libretto that would force him to try his compositional skills on the more grisly elements of Romantic melodrama, Donizetti came across the *Gabriella di Vergy* of Andrea Leone Tottola (written in 1816 for the composer Michele Carafa) and composed his own setting of the text ("for my own pleasure") in 1826.[13] The haste required to get *L'Italiana in Algeri* on stage made it essential to choose a preexisting libretto, and Rossini employed one written by Angelo Anelli for Luigi Mosca five years earlier. (It is possible that Anelli himself made important changes in the text that brought the libretto within the orbit of Rossinian *opera buffa*.) Verdi's *Un giorno di regno* of 1840 was based on a libretto that Felice Romani had written in 1818 for the Bohemian composer Adalbert Gyrowetz (*Il finto Stanislao*). For many Italian librettists of the time, French operatic texts were a rich vein to be mined: Antonio Somma's *Un ballo in maschera* (1859) for Verdi, derived from Scribe's 1833 libretto for Auber (*Gustave III*), is only the most famous example.

The choice of a librettist generally fell to the management of the theater, and librettists often developed close ties with local theaters: Romani with La Scala, Ferretti with Roman theaters, Gaetano Rossi and Francesco Maria Piave with La Fenice, and Salvadore Cammarano with San Carlo. They were responsible not only for preparing the text of an opera, but also for providing the modest staging required by contemporary theatrical practice. Most composers accepted the librettist suggested by the theater commissioning the work, but more prominent composers could impose their own choices. Bellini preferred Romani, and the two collaborated on operas first performed in Venice and Parma, but these collaborations (*Zaira* of 1829, *I Capuleti e i Montecchi* of 1830, and *Beatrice di Tenda* of 1833) were as a whole less satisfactory than the work they did together in Milan, where Romani knew better the ambience of the theater and the taste of the public. From *Lucia di Lammermoor* (1835) until his 1838 departure from Italy for Paris, Donizetti preferred Cammarano for his serious operas, even when first performed away from Naples: *Belisario* (Venice, 1836), *Pia de' Tolomei* (Venice, 1837), *Maria di Rudenz* (Venice, 1837). In insisting on Cammarano, in fact, Donizetti specifically contradicted the wishes of the Venetian theaters.

In theory, the choice of subject lay in the hands of the theater and its librettist, and composers were expected to set to music whatever text was put into their hands: there is no evidence, for example, that Rossini intervened in the librettos of his early operas or that Verdi modified the libretto of Antonio Solera's *Nabucco* (1842). Increasingly, however, composers participated in these decisions. There is good reason to believe that Rossini played a significant role in choosing the subjects for many of his Neapolitan operas, while Romani certainly consulted Rossini about the subject of their 1819 collaboration for La Scala, *Bianca e Falliero*.[14] Rossi wrote much of the libretto to *Semiramide* in the villa outside Bologna belonging to Rossini's wife, the soprano Isabella Colbran, as Rossini then and there began composing the score. Donizetti's correspondence from the 1830s demonstrates his active participation in choosing the subjects of his operas, and in a number of cases (particularly with comic operas) the composer was his own librettist. During his early career, on the other hand, Donizetti had significantly less choice about his texts. Verdi's struggles with theaters, censors, and librettists are well known, yet almost from the beginning the composer was actively involved in the search for subjects and usually suggested them himself. In Verdi's *Copialettere*—copybooks in which he drafted his correspondence and included other business dealings— there is a page (probably written in 1849) with a list of possible subjects for operatic treatment.[15]

Verdi went even further: he frequently provided his librettists with a prose outline of a subject, often called a *selva*, indicating precisely how he wanted subjects to be organized in operatic terms, with the succession of musical numbers laid out and a great deal of the text specified.[16] One of the most fascinating documents of this kind to survive is his *selva* for the second act of *La forza del destino*.[17] In it he laid out the structure of the entire act, specifying the kind of music he envisaged for each section (whether recitative or a lyrical number—aria, *ballata*, duet) and often making specific recommendations to the poet as to the verse forms he should use. At the end of the duet for Leonora and the Padre Guardiano, for example, he indicated "lirici di metro piuttosto breve" (lyric verses in a relatively brief poetic meter—i.e., a small number of syllables in each line).[18] At the end of the act, where the monks take their farewell from Leonora, who intends henceforth to live as a hermit, Verdi wrote the following words in his *selva*:

La Vergine degli Angeli [May the Virgin of the Angels cover you
vi copra del suo manto, e with her cloak, and may the Angel of the
l'angelo del Signore vegli Lord keep watch in your defense.]
alla vostra difesa.

While the words seem to be written as four lines of poetry, they are not metrically consistent and are not rhymed, but the organization of the words on
the page suggested that Verdi wanted a quatrain of seven-syllable verse (*settenario*) here. That is precisely what Piave gave him:

La Vergine degli Angeli	[May the Virgin of the Angels cover you
Vi copra del suo manto,	with her cloak, and may the blessed Angel
E voi protegga vigile	of God vigilantly protect you.]
Di Dio l'Angelo santo.	

A document of this kind makes it clear why Verdi is said to have played such
a significant role in the drafting of the librettos for some of his operas.[19]

While it was primarily the responsibility of the librettist to derive from
the subject a drama *per musica,* organized into a series of musical numbers, with the poetry written in standard verse forms, during the first half of
the nineteenth century many conventions—some fixed, some changing—
governed the way the librettist was expected to proceed. Similar eighteenth-
century conventions were satirized in Benedetto Marcello's famous treatise *Il
teatro alla moda.* Donizetti's wicked *Le convenienze ed inconvenienze teatrali*
(in either its 1827 or its 1831 version) is only one of a string of operatic satires
on the subject.[20] Some of these conventions reflected the fact that opera companies were assembled for a specific theatrical season. They consisted of
a certain number of soloists of varied artistic stature (with a *prima* donna
clearly differentiated from a *seconda* donna) and vocal register (soprano, contralto, tenor, bass). Each principal singer was expected to participate appropriately in the work, with an adequate number of solo pieces, duets,
and ensembles. And these pieces needed to be spread out over the course
of the opera, so that there would be ample time for a singer to rest. During the first two decades of the century a secondary singer might also demand his or her moment in the sun, a so-called *aria di sorbetto* (sherbet aria),
whose name suggests the level of audience attention to the piece. But this
particular convention, left over from the aria-dominated style of eighteenth-
century opera, gradually disappeared as librettos derived from Romantic
melodrama became more streamlined and individual musical numbers grew
more expansive.

Some conventions had to do with matters of "priority." For a certain time,
at least, a prima donna presumed she would conclude the opera with a major
solo number (often referred to as a *rondò,* even though its structure by this
time had little to do with the classical rondo).[21] Librettists, supported willingly
or unwillingly by the composer, arranged the action accordingly, knowing

that the success of an opera could depend on a contented prima donna. On some occasions the convention functions well: Rossini's *La donna del lago,* with its happy ending, and Donizetti's *Anna Bolena,* with its tragic one, are excellent examples. At other times the convention may seem to border on the absurd: the original version (1833) of Donizetti's *Lucrezia Borgia,* in which Lucrezia sings a spectacular *rondò* about how much she loved the son she has just poisoned, "Era desso il figlio mio." For a revival of the opera several years later (Milan, 1840), Donizetti replaced his original ending with a more dramatically pertinent conclusion. Sometimes a composer would take a principled stand. The soprano Sofia Löwe expected that *Ernani* would conclude with a stand-up-and-sock-it-to-them *rondò* for her alone, but Verdi, who early in his work on the opera had written to Piave, "For the love of God do not end with a rondò but write a trio: and this trio must be the best piece in the opera," would not be budged.[22] More than one prima donna has protested vigorously the structure of *Lucia di Lammermoor,* which produces the worst indignity imaginable for a soprano: she must die *before* the tenor. Unfortunately, the story would permit no other dénouement, and our heroines have had either to settle for a penultimate mad scene or to reverse the scenes and destroy all semblance of dramaturgical structure.

But more was involved in organizing a libretto than assuaging the sensibilities of singers concerned primarily with the size and scope of their own part, rather than with the quality of the opera as a whole. *Ernani,* first performed at the Teatro La Fenice of Venice at the end of the carnival season of 1844, serves as a particularly good example for the problems librettists and composers faced in achieving a workable libretto, in this case one based on a revolutionary work of French Romantic drama, Victor Hugo's 1829 *Hernani.* Not only was *Ernani* Verdi's first collaboration with Piave, who was later at his side for operas such as *Rigoletto* and *La traviata,* but it was one of the librettist's first efforts. By 1843, Verdi had had considerable experience in the theater, both as an assiduous operagoer during his formative years in Milan and as a composer (he had written four operas for La Scala, the last two of which, *Nabucco* and *I lombardi alla prima crociata,* had been very well received). Thus, he felt obliged to point out serious problems in the libretto Piave proposed, while showering praise on Piave's poetry (which the composer actually considered secondary to matters such as dramatic action, timing, and structure).

When Piave began to bristle under Verdi's criticism, the composer wrote directly to Guglielmo Brenna, one of the administratiors of La Fenice, explaining his motivations. His letter includes a clear, explicit description of what needed to be taken into account when planning a libretto:

> For my part, I would prefer never to trouble a poet to change a verse for me; and I wrote music to three librettos of Solera [the poet for *Oberto* (1839), *Nabucco* (1842), and *I lombardi* (1843)], and comparing the originals, which I have kept, with the printed librettos, only a very few lines will be found to have been altered, and these because Solera himself wanted it.[23]
>
> But Solera had already written five or six librettos and knows the theater, dramatic effect, and musical forms. Sig. Piave has never written, and therefore it is natural that in these things he is deficient.
>
> In fact, what woman would be able to sing one after another a big cavatina, a duet that finishes as a trio, and an entire finale, as in this first act of *Ernani?* Sig. Piave will have good reasons to advance, but I have others, and I answer that the lungs will not hold up under this effort. What maestro would be able to set to music without boring the audience a hundred lines of recitative, as in this third act? In all four acts of *Nabucco* or of *I lombardi,* you will surely not find more than a hundred lines of recitative.
>
> And the same could be said of so many other small things. You who have been so kind to me, I pray you to make Piave understand these things and persuade him. However little experience I may have, I nevertheless go to the theater all year long, and I pay the most careful attention: I have seen myself that so many compositions would not have failed had there been a better distribution of the pieces, a more careful calculation of the dramatic effects, clearer musical forms... in short, if the poet and composer had had more experience. So many times a recitative that is too long, a phrase, a sentence that would be most beautiful in a book and even in a spoken drama, just make the audience laugh in a sung drama.[24]

The order of pieces, proper and physically reasonable demands on the capacities of singers, a concern for brevity, an awareness of the difference between the requirements of spoken drama and opera, the clarity of structure of individual numbers—all were basic to the proper layout of a musical drama.

THE POETRY OF A *DRAMMA PER MUSICA*

In the beginning was the word. At least most of the time. Occasionally, to be sure, a composer decided to reuse music written for an older opera in a new one, and obedient librettists were called upon to write appropriate poetry.

The practice extends beyond Rossini, who certainly made ample use of it at certain moments in his career. Even Romani was called upon to play this game when Bellini sought to salvage in *I Capuleti e i Montecchi* some music from the ruins of their unsuccessful *Zaira*. But then again, Bellini liked to compose textless, abstract melodies in the morning (he called them his "daily exercises"), which he later sought to place in his operas. Many pages of these exercises exist; the tunes for which he had found a home are neatly crossed out.[25] Other composers, for one reason or another, might prepare melodies for specific scenes in an opera before they had any text in hand or when faced with a text they did not like. Letters from both Donizetti and Verdi to their librettists sometimes request poetry of a certain meter with a precise number of lines, a sign that the music was already written. But these counterexamples are relatively few in number. Generally, the libretto came first.

To understand the nature of Italian opera in the first half of the nineteenth century, it is essential to understand how the poetry of a libretto was organized. This was such an obvious matter to composers and librettists that they rarely needed to comment upon it in their letters. Printed librettos, issued for each production and reflecting the contents of those performances, preserved the shape and organization of the poetry, so that contemporary audiences followed the dramatic and poetic structure (either during performances or away from the theater) with ease. It would be clearer to modern audiences had not many editors of librettos and recording companies, who include librettos in their "packages," developed the atrocious practice of obscuring the structure of the text. They have conceived the "typical listener" as someone curled up at home with a compact disc, a libretto, and precious little intelligence. They presume that this listener, with limited knowledge of Italian, will be unable to recognize repetitions of words unless those repetitions are written out, so they repeat words or phrases over and over, instead of leaving the poetry as written. They further presume that the listener is incapable of following dialogue among characters unless the interventions of each character are drastically set off from those of other characters by typographically intrusive methods (beginning the first words of each character flush left, for example, so that the structure of the poetry is obscured). The organization of the poetry is therefore sacrificed to what is deemed to be easy comprehensibility. Given this "disorganization" and the introduction of superfluous text repetitions, it becomes almost impossible to read the text for pleasure or to understand its poetic structure, and generations of opera lovers have suffered the consequences. Yet to understand how a composer wrote an opera, with all its implications for how we should edit and perform that opera, we need to have a clear sense of the structure of the libretto.

Italian librettos, well into the latter part of the nineteenth century, were almost always written exclusively in poetry, not prose, and the poetry was governed by quite specific rules.[26] The libretto (and therefore the opera) was divided into individual musical "numbers," compositions called arias (or a variety of other names specifying a piece featuring a solo singer), duets, trios, introductions (the first number in an opera or, occasionally, the first number of a later act), and finales to one or more acts. For each genre there developed certain rules about internal structure, rules that could be observed, bent, or broken, but which composers and librettists recognized. Between these formal numbers were scenes of dialogue or monologue intended to be set as recitative, usually accompanied primarily by a keyboard instrument early in the century, almost always with orchestral accompaniment by the third decade. The nature of the poetry differed depending on the dramatic situation and its potential musical significance, but the most basic division was between poetry intended for recitative and that intended for formal numbers.[27]

Rendering terms describing Italian verse into what might appear to be simple English equivalents is profoundly misleading. An Italian *settenario* is not really a "seven-syllable" line of verse, since it can have six, seven, or eight syllables, depending on whether the line is: (a) *tronco* (concluding with an accented syllable, a so-called masculine ending, hence six syllables); (b) *piano* (the form according to which the poetic meter is measured, concluding with an accented syllable and an unaccented one, a so-called feminine ending, hence seven syllables); or (c) *sdrucciolo* (concluding with an accented syllable and two unaccented syllables, hence eight syllables). Here are some representative examples of the three kinds of *settenari* verses, all with a final accent on the sixth syllable, from a duet in *Rigoletto*:

1 2 3 4 5 6 7
Tut-te le fe-ste al tem-pio (*settenario piano*)
[Each feast day at the church]

1 2 3 4 5 6 7 8
Se i lab-bri no-stri ta-cque-ro, (*settenario sdrucciolo*)
[Although our lips were silent,]

1 2 3 4 5 6
Da- gl'oc-chi il cor par-lò. (*settenario tronco*)
[Our hearts spoke through our eyes.]

Notice that, in Italian verse, the final vowel of one word and the first of the next elide and are considered a single syllable: hence "[fe]-ste al," "Se i," and "[gl'oc]-chi il" are counted as single syllables. Similar considerations affect *senari, ottonari, decasillabi,* and *endecasillabi* verses ("six," "eight," "ten," or "eleven" syllables, respectively, but which can normally exist in *tronco, piano,* or *sdrucciolo* forms). To avoid this confusion, I use Italian metrical terms wherever appropriate throughout this book.

Verses for recitative were written in what is known as *versi sciolti,* poetry consisting of *endecasillabi* and *settenari* freely mixed, with only an occasional rhyme. A single line of poetry could be assigned to a single character, or divided among several characters, and grammatical units might well run on from one verse to the next. If the poetry is printed correctly, the way librettists intended them to be printed and the way they were printed during the nineteenth century, the poetic structure is almost always quite rigorous.

Here are the first three lines of the opening recitative in the last act of *Rigoletto,* a dialogue for Rigoletto and Gilda, in which she insists that she still loves the Duke. As written by Piave, it consists of a *settenario* followed by two *endecasillabi.* The beginning of each verse is written flush left; when the lines are split among more than one character, the continuation of the line is indented:

Rig. *E l'ami?*	And you love him?
Gil. *Sempre.*	Always.
Rig. *Pure*	And yet
Tempo a guarirne t'ho lasciato.	I gave you time to heal.
Gil. *Io l'amo!!*	I love him!!
Rig. *Povero cor di donna! Ah il vile infame!..*	Poor woman's heart! The vile scoundrel!..

The division of a single line of verse among characters, the irregular (though not unplanned) changes in the length of lines, the occasional but not prevalent use of rhyme, all imply a musical setting in a freer, declamatory style, that is, recitative. Faced with such a text, composers usually set them accordingly.

That does not mean, however, that recitative verse, *versi sciolti,* can never be set lyrically. Indeed, one of the ways in which the operas of the generation of Bellini and Donizetti differ from those of Rossini and composers of his time is in the extent to which later composers pepper their recitative scenes with lyrical periods, even when the verse forms do not easily lend themselves to this practice. In Romani's libretto for Donizetti's *Anna Bolena,* the second act begins with recitative, a scene between Queen Anna and King Henry's new favorite, Giovanna Seymour. Anna, alone, is musing to herself on the shame she feels. Giovanna enters, pities Anna's state, and finally addresses her. Here are the first eight lines of recitative, of which the first and seventh are *settenari*, all the rest *endecasillabi*:

Anna	*Dio, che mi vedi in core,*	God, who sees in my heart,
	Mi volgo a te... Se meritai quest'onta	I turn to you... You decide whether I merit
	Giudica tu.	This shame.
Gio.	*Piange l'afflitta... Ahi! come*	The afflicted one weeps... Oh! how
	Ne sosterrò lo sguardo?	Can I bear her glance?
Anna	*Ah! sì, gli affanni*	Ah! yes, the sorrows
	Dell'infelice Aragonese inulti	Of the poor Aragonese will not be
	Esser non denno, e a me terribil pena	Unavenged, and your rigor
	Il tuo rigor destina...	Intends a terrible fate for me...
	Ma terribile è troppo...	But it is too terrible...
Gio.	*O mia regina!*	O my queen!

These eight lines of recitative, with a rhyme between the last two lines ("destina" and "regina") to mark the moment in which Giovanna reveals her presence to Anna, are perfectly standard in their construction. Concluding rhymes of this kind have much the same function as does the rhymed couplet at the end of a scene in Shakespeare: to provide momentary closure.

At the start of this scene, however, Donizetti chose to provide a lyrical moment for Anna, using her first words as the basis for a short lyrical prayer. To render these irregular recitative verses into verses appropriate for a regular musical period, with balanced phrases, the composer was forced to push and prod recalcitrant material, arriving finally at something like the following poetic "stanza" in mock *settenari*:

> *Dio, che mi vedi in core,*
> *Mi volgi a te, o Dio...*
> *Se meritai quest'onta*
> *Giudica tu, o Dio.*

Despite the awkward arrangement of the poetic text, Donizetti created a touching lyrical moment, filling out the emotional world of his protagonist. Which is to say that composers, while heavily dependent on the text presented to them by their librettists, were not slaves to it.

Verses intended for formal numbers are quite different. In the simplest case, solo arias, they consist of stanzas of rhymed poetry in a single meter, or first in one meter, then in another. Here is the text of Lindoro's entrance aria (his cavatina) from Rossini's *L'Italiana in Algeri*. First he laments at being far from his beloved; then he reflects that even the thought of her brings calm to his soul:

Languir per una bella	To yearn for a beauty
E star lontan da quella,	And be far from her,
È il più crudel tormento,	Is the worst torment
Che provar possa un cor.	That a heart can experience.
Forse verrà il momento:	Perhaps the moment will come,
Ma non lo spero ancor.	But I do not yet hope for it.
Contenta quest'alma	This soul seeks happiness
In mezzo alle pene	Amidst sorrow
Sol trova la calma	And finds calm only
Pensando al suo bene,	Thinking of its beloved,
Che sempre costante	Whom, ever constant,
Si serba in amor.	It continues to love.

There are two six-line stanzas here, the first using *settenari,* the second *senari.* The metric change between the stanzas is a specific invitation to the composer to prepare an aria in two separate sections, with different vocal rhythms, different tempos, and different meters. Even before the composer began his work, the poet had defined Lindoro's cavatina as being a piece in two musical sections. Rossini, who was as comfortable with the convention as the librettist, set the piece accordingly, with an initial Andantino in 6/8 followed by an Allegro in common time.[28]

Poetry in fixed meters was used not only for lyrical sections but also for dialogue falling within musical numbers (as opposed to the *versi sciolti* employed for dialogue falling *between* musical numbers). The difference is significant, and using the term "recitative" to refer indiscriminately to both kinds of music hides distinctions that are important for how we must hear and perform the passages in question. Within a musical number dialogue (or *parlante* as it was often called in the nineteenth century) was frequently organized into more regular rhythmic units, with the orchestra providing continuity and structure, while the vocal line fits itself into the texture more freely, following the implications of the dramatic situation.

Between the lyrical sections of his scena and aria at the end of act 3 of *Il trovatore,* for example, Manrico is informed that the gypsy he believes to be his mother, Azucena, has been taken captive by the Conte di Luna and is about to be burned at the stake. Although Cammarano's text for this passage has some of the qualities of recitative verse (in particular the use of single lines of poetry divided among several characters, with grammatical units running on from one verse to the next), its use of meter and rhyme gives it an urgency that *versi sciolti* do not normally have.[29] I have introduced spaces between certain lines to clarify visually the stanzaic structure.

Ruiz	*Manrico?...*	Manrico?...
Man.	*Che?...*	What?...
Ruiz	*La zingara,*	The gypsy,
	Vieni, tra ceppi mira....	Come, see her in chains....
Man.	*Oh Dio!*	Oh God!
Ruiz	*Per man de' barbari*	The barbarians
	Accesa è già la pira....	Have already lit the pyre....
Man.	*Oh ciel!.. mie membra oscillano....*	Oh heaven!... my limbs are unsteady....
	Nube mi cuopre il ciglio!	Clouds cover my eyes!
Leo.	*Tu fremi!..*	You tremble!..
Man.	*E il deggio!... Sappilo,*	As I must!.. Know, then,
	Io son....	I am....
Leo.	*Chi mai?*	What then?
Man.	*Suo figlio!...*	Her son!..
	Ah vili!.. Il rio spettacolo	Vile ones!..The awful vision
	Quasi il respir m'invola....	Almost takes my breath away....
	Raduna i nostri... affretati,	Gather our men together... hurry,
	Ruiz.... va..... torna... vola!	Ruiz... go.... return... fly!

In fact the poetic structure (three four-line stanzas of *settenari*, rhyming second and fourth lines) is identical to the structure Cammarano employed for the *primo tempo* (first section) of Manrico's aria, which begins:

Ah! sì, ben mio, coll'essere	Ah! yes, my beloved, when I am
Io tuo, tu mia consorte,	Your husband and you my wife,
Avrò più l'alma intrepida,	I will have a more intrepid soul,
Il braccio avrò più forte.	My arm will be stronger still.

Not until after the dialogue between Manrico, Ruiz, and Leonora does Cammarano finally change the poetic structure, employing a compound meter that the Italians call *quinari doppi* for the famous conclusion of Manrico's aria. In *quinari doppi*, each line of poetry is made up of two separate *quinari* (often printed with additional space between them), and each half-line can conclude with a word that is *tronco* ("spe-gne-rò," with the accent on "-rò"), *piano* ("pi-ra," with the accent on "pi-"), or a *sdrucciolo* ("spe-gne-te-la," with the accent on "-gne-"):

Di quella pira l'orrendo fuoco	The horrid fire of that pyre
Tutte le fibre m'arse, avvampò!...	Burns all my fibers, sets me ablaze!...
Empi spegnetela, o ch'io, tra poco,	Villains, put it out, or I will soon
Col sangue vostro la spegnerò!....	Extinguish it with your blood!....

A more pressing invitation to a rousing cabaletta could not have been offered to a composer.[30]

Verdi sought to stimulate the conservative Cammarano to provide him with unusual verse patterns and continuous structures by writing to his poet, "If in opera there were neither cavatinas, duets, trios, choruses, finales, etc. etc., and the whole work consisted, let's say, of a single number, I should find that all the more right and proper."[31] Similar pleas would be repeated over and over again in the composer's correspondence, until—many years later and in very different historical circumstances—he found in the person of Arrigo Boito a librettist able to understand and embrace his half-understood desires. Their resulting collaborations, on the revision of *Simon Boccanegra* (1881) and on *Otello* (1887) and *Falstaff* (1893), belong to a different esthetic plane, even though they are rooted in Verdi's previous achievements. Earlier, however, Cammarano (just like Piave and Antonio Ghislanzoni—the librettist for a relatively late Verdi opera, *Aida,* of 1871) provided Verdi with a libretto in which most numbers were carefully laid out in an essentially traditional fashion, the fashion that dominated Italian opera from the early nineteenth century through the 1860s—the period with which this book is primarily concerned. Had they done anything else, the composer might not have been prepared to cope with the artistic challenge.

By purely poetic means, then (the use of different meters, the use of stanzas of verse for a single character, the use of dialogue, etc.), librettists—often in consultation with the composer—materially influenced the structure and character of both the entire opera and each individual piece. They provided composers with recitative verse and with formal numbers, so that the poetry shaped important musical decisions. For the most part, composers took the structural parameters implicit in the poetry, fashioning each composition accordingly and from those parameters developing the shape of the entire opera.[32]

A COMPOSER'S PRIVATE DOCUMENTS: SKETCHES

Though a completed libretto might be delivered on time to a composer, often it arrived piecemeal, leaving him in a state of anguish and uncertainty, even about the number of acts into which the drama was to be divided. Contemporary documents suggest that when the subject of the opera on which Cesare Sterbini and Rossini were to collaborate was altered at the last minute, Sterbini fed the composer the libretto of *Il barbiere di Siviglia* in installments, and Rossini prepared each piece as the text was handed to him. Bellini suffered immeasurably from Romani's failure to provide poetry for *Beatrice di Tenda* in adequate time, leading to an ugly dispute in the Venetian press and a formal break in their relations. Donizetti waited impatiently in Florence for almost a month while the libretto Romani was supposed to be preparing for *Parisina* failed to arrive. Both knew that Romani was terribly overworked and notoriously dilatory, but he was also considered to be the finest contemporary librettist.[33] Verdi worked closely with his poets in determining the shape and contents of his operas. Once he began to receive poetry, he tormented them, demanding extensive changes in the texts they had sent. Because Verdi frequently worked in a different city from his librettists, and rarely traveled to the city in which an opera was to be performed until rehearsals began, there is extensive correspondence between the composer and his poets.[34] Such documentation is less ample for earlier composers and librettists, but there are many indications that they consulted with one another in working out the dramaturgy of an opera and the structure of its poetry.

With a libretto (or at least part of one) in hand, the composer set to work. Time was short even under the best of circumstances. Under the worst, the need for disciplined creativity must have been overwhelming. While extant documents in the composer's hand, sketches or autograph manuscripts, are an inadequate guide to the complex mental processes (conscious or intuitive) through which a composer produced a new work, they are all we have. Understanding these documents is crucial, for the dissemination—or what I will refer to as the transmission—of nineteenth-century Italian operas in handwritten or printed form begins with them. Many of the difficulties in producing an edition of an opera or performing that opera derive directly from problems inherent in these earliest autograph sources.

Sketches were strictly private, not intended for any eye other than that of the composer. The very few known sketches in Rossini's hand pertain to some of his most complex music: the *terzettone* in *Maometto II*, two extensive numbers from *Semiramide* (the first-act finale and the great scena and aria for

Arsace in the second act), the trio "A la faveur de cette nuit obscure" from *Le Comte Ory,* and the second-act finale added to the French *Moïse.* What the composer chose to write down, however, often involves details: only the sketches for *Semiramide* and *Le Comte Ory* establish the musical content for long stretches of a composition. Still, nothing suggests that Rossini habitually had recourse to extensive sketches during the preparation of most of his operas.[35] He probably adopted them largely for the final works of his Italian career (after 1820) and then again in preparing music for the Opéra (1826–1829). A similar pattern seems to be true for Donizetti. Bellini, on the other hand, often worked quite differently, as we have seen, writing down page after page of melodies before he had a libretto in hand. Later, he would return to those pages as a bank of ideas from which to draw the lyrical capital he would transform into the vocal lines of an opera.

Of the four major Italian opera composers working during the first half of the nineteenth century, Verdi alone employed independent sketches extensively. Since 1941, when the Verdi family permitted Carlo Gatti to publish the sketches for *Rigoletto* in facsimile, scholars have been intrigued by this material.[36] While the *Rigoletto* sketches contain a few miscellaneous jottings pertaining to individual melodic ideas, they mostly consist of a draft of the entire work, beginning in the festive atmosphere at the court of the Duke of Mantua and concluding with the tragic death of Gilda and desperation of Rigoletto. Verdi worked out the opera in order, number by number, in a form that included the principal vocal lines with a bass part, as well as significant orchestral melodies. This type of sketch is commonly referred to as a "continuity draft" of the opera. According to Gatti, similar sketches exist at Verdi's home in Sant'Agata for every opera from the 1849 *Luisa Miller* through the 1893 *Falstaff,* as well as for the major nonoperatic works such as the *Messa da Requiem* of 1874. In his *Verdi nelle immagini* Gatti provided a few barely legible samples from other operas, whetting the appetites of all those who study Verdi's music.[37]

Study of the *Rigoletto* sketches makes it clear that Verdi's repeated requests for changes in the libretto were almost all formulated during the process of sketching, which is what he called the "creative work" for an opera. Employing the text supplied by his librettist, Verdi used the continuity draft to set out the basic musical structure of each piece in the opera. When problems arose with the words, he would improvise a solution or even draft a passage without text, immediately shooting off a letter to the librettist requesting modifications or even entirely new poetry in a specific meter or with specific accentual patterns.[38]

Our knowledge of the Verdi sketches has increased significantly since Gatti's publications. Recently the family, through the good offices of the Istituto Nazionale di Studi Verdiani, has made available to editors of *The Works of Giuseppe Verdi* the sketches for *Stiffelio, La traviata, Un ballo in maschera,* and *La forza del destino.* These manuscripts usually have continuity drafts of individual numbers or even entire acts, similar to those we know from the sketches for *Rigoletto.* To a greater extent than in the case of *Rigoletto,* however, they also provide preliminary notations for an opera or significantly different earlier versions. The sketches for *Stiffelio* offer many early ideas for solo compositions, ideas independent of any continuity draft.[39] The *Ballo* continuity draft has an entirely different orchestral introduction for the Amelia aria that opens the second act. For *La traviata* Verdi laid out in an abbreviated form the basic structure of the entire first act before receiving any poetry from Piave, even before knowing what the characters' names would be in Italian. He set down in words and with a few selected themes his sense of how the drama would be shaped.[40] Among the wordless themes staring at us from this intriguing page are the *brindisi* or toast ("Libiamo ne' lieti calici"), "Ah forse è lui," and "Sempre libera." We do not yet know enough about Verdi's working habits, however, to gauge whether this page is an anomaly or whether he regularly wrote down ideas for his operas before having the libretto in hand.

By using extensive independent sketches (usually continuity drafts) for all his mature operas, Verdi interposed a level of advance planning in the compositional process that earlier nineteenth-century Italian opera composers rarely employed. Only after preparing these continuity drafts did he begin to lay out the autograph manuscript of an opera, the public document that would subsequently be used by copyists and editors. First he would prepare what we call a "skeleton score," basically entering the same material he had included in his continuity draft (vocal lines, bass, important instrumental ideas), now in a more complete form and with each element in its proper position in what would become the full score; subsequently he would fill out the skeleton, so to speak, by completing the orchestration.

Sometimes there are quite significant differences between the continuity drafts and the final product. This is particularly true for operas such as *Un ballo in maschera,* where fifteen months of battles (from November 1857 through January 1859) with the censors of two cities (Naples, then Rome) gave the composer a longer time than usual to ponder the music he had earlier sketched.[41] It is also true for *La forza del destino,* where the illness of a prima donna caused the postponement of the first performance in St. Petersburg from the beginning of 1862 to November of the same year.[42] On most occasions, however,

Verdi's continuity draft for a musical number is quite similar to the final version, and the task of copying the vocal lines, bass, and important orchestral melodies from that draft into his autograph manuscript was largely mechanical. No composer of the period, of course, would ever have "copied" his own music without touching up details of articulation, rhythm, even pitches, and confusions resulting from this process remain visible throughout the autograph manuscripts. Access to the sketches, then, turns out to be of great assistance to scholars and performers who wish as complete a view as possible of the written sources for a Verdi opera.

What Verdi prepared as an independent continuity draft and then copied over as a "skeleton score," Rossini, Bellini, and Donizetti usually entered straightaway into their autograph manuscripts. They certainly worked ideas out at the keyboard, and they sometimes jotted thoughts down on paper, but for these composers the "skeleton score" *was* their continuity draft. They wrote their music in its skeletal form (vocal lines, bass, and significant orchestral ideas) directly into their autograph manuscripts. This difference in the way they composed explains many of the physical differences between the autograph manuscripts of Verdi, on the one hand, and those of Rossini, Bellini, and Donizetti, on the other. It also explains many of the contradictions and problems that emerge when one studies or performs their completed operas.

A COMPOSER'S PUBLIC DOCUMENTS:
AUTOGRAPH MANUSCRIPTS

Paper. A composer of Italian opera could not begin to prepare the autograph manuscript of a work until he had procured music paper. This was not a trivial matter. Four issues, some interrelated, needed to be considered: the quality of the paper, its physical dimensions and format (whether oblong—wider than it is high—or vertical), the number of staves ruled on each page (already present when the paper was purchased), and its structure (single pages, bifolios, or gatherings). The choices a composer made at this stage were important for the state in which his opera would be transmitted to the musical world.

Most composers during the first half of the nineteenth century employed paper of excellent quality, and their autograph manuscripts have survived in exemplary condition. It was not until the second half of the century that the quality of the materials regularly used in papermaking deteriorated to the point that many documents from that period are today disintegrating, to the dismay of librarians, collectors, and scholars. But even earlier in the century there could be severe and unfortunate discrepancies in the paper. In composing *Elisabetta, regina d'Inghilterra* (1815), *Mosè in Egitto* (1818), and *La donna del lago* (1819), Rossini used paper of excellent quality for the musical numbers, but of poorer quality for the intervening recitatives, even though these are all accompanied by the orchestra. The ink has bled through the paper, often making his notation difficult to read. This bleeding must have begun early in the history of the documents, for pages within passages of recitative surely composed by Rossini or entire recitatives perhaps composed by him were recopied by another hand and inserted into the autograph manuscripts.[43]

In *La donna del lago* these recitatives in the hand of a collaborator are particularly unfortunate, since Rossini *also* employed an anonymous assistant to compose the aria for Duglas ("Taci, lo voglio") in the first act. As a result, we cannot always be certain which recitatives were composed by Rossini and which by his assistant. That knowledge is of more than theoretical significance. When Houston Grand Opera staged *La donna del lago* in 1981, the general manager, David Gockley, realized during the dress rehearsal that he was facing the costly specter of double overtime for the orchestra. Five minutes needed to be cut from the score, he told me, and five minutes were indeed cut. But in making those eminently practical decisions, it would have been nice to know which recitatives were actually by Rossini himself.[44]

As operatic scores during the first half of the nineteenth century became more complex orchestrally and more often employed large ensemble scenes, the size of manuscript paper used for those scores gradually increased. The change was by no means uniform. Rossini's paper for his Neapolitan works during the 1810s is in oblong format and measured around 28 cm in width by 23 cm in height, but his *Guillaume Tell* of 1829 required much larger paper, measuring 33 cm by 25 cm, hardly different from that used by Verdi for most of his operas in the 1840s. The Verdian scores, however, were mostly written on paper in vertical format, approximately 24 cm in width by 33 cm in height. There could occasionally be extreme variations in these proportions. The composer Saverio Mercadante, a figure to be reckoned with in the world of Italian opera from the 1820s through the 1840s, began to lose his sight toward 1840, and he tended to require ever larger manuscript paper, sometimes involving two sheets pasted together.

More significant than changes in the size of the paper was the transformation in its format. Early in the century composers wrote their operas on music paper in oblong format; by the 1840s vertical format had become standard. Vertical paper allowed a composer to write fewer measures per page, but provided enough staves for complex ensembles, using an expanded orchestra, stage band, soloists, and chorus. In *Rigoletto,* for example, Verdi employed up-right paper with thirty staves per page for his massive "Introduzione," the Duke of Mantua's *festa* that comprises the entire first scene. Oblong paper allowed composers to write more measures per page, but limited the number of staves available. For the operas of Cimarosa and Paisiello, oblong paper had been adequate, as it was for Rossini's earlier operas. At a certain point, however, the number of staves that could comfortably be drawn on standard oblong paper was insufficient for many composers' needs, and it led them into various compromises.

In the ensemble sections of the first-act finale of *Il pirata,* for example, the sheer size of the forces led Bellini, who was still using oblong paper, to write out the vocal parts in one section of the manuscript and the instrumental parts elsewhere. If this did not promise enough confusion, the vocal parts of the final ensemble ("Ah! partiamo, i miei tormenti") are notated in one key (*C minor/major*) and the instrumental parts in another (*B♭ minor/major*). At some point between preparing the vocal parts and completing the orchestration, the composer changed his mind, but this history remains to be unraveled.[45]

Even without going to such extraordinary lengths, most large ensembles by Rossini cannot be accommodated on the oblong music paper he chose for his autograph manuscripts, so that he was obliged to employ what composers referred to as *spartitini,* "little scores," in which were gathered instrumental parts that could not fit into the main score because of space limitations. They are almost always mentioned in the main score, where Rossini wrote phrases such as: "Tromboni, Timpani e Gran Cassa in fine" (Trombones, Timpani, and Bass Drum at the end). But often these original *spartitini* have disappeared, and secondary sources preserve multiple versions. The autograph manuscript of Rossini's *Semiramide,* for example, refers to a number of *spartitini,* but none are present in the manuscript. The confused and contradictory readings of secondary sources suggest that these *spartitini* were misplaced almost at once. Only in 1990, during preparation of the critical edition of the opera for its first performance at the Metropolitan Opera, when the original orchestral parts were closely examined by my associates at the Fondazione Rossini, Patricia Brauner and Mauro Bucarelli, did the autograph *spartitini* of *Semiramide* emerge, hidden among thousands and thousands of pages in the hands of various copyists. For the first time since 1823 it was possible to restore Rossini's original orchestration.[46]

That the paper used throughout an opera was generally of the same size and format is hardly surprising; it is not difficult to imagine the problems that could (and did) arise in binding and preserving an autograph manuscript whose papers were of varying sizes. But there was no reason for every composition in an opera to use paper pre-lined with the same number of staves. Indeed, to ensure maximum legibility, it was advantageous for a composer to choose manuscript paper for each composition with the fewest possible staves, consonant with vocal and orchestral requirements. The larger the staves and the more room between them, the easier it was for a composer to write clearly his signs of articulation, notes, and text. Thus, in Verdi's *Alzira*, the vertical paper ranges from sixteen to twenty-four staves, with *spartitini* added for the finales to the second and third acts.[47] In Rossini's *Otello*, the oblong paper ranges from ten to sixteen staves, with a *spartitino* added for the finale to the first act; in *Guillaume Tell*, on the other hand, the larger oblong paper used by Rossini ranges from twelve to twenty-two staves, with *spartitini* for the finales to the first, third, and fourth acts.[48]

This physical description of the paper has exquisitely musical implications. In Rossini's *Tancredi*, the composer chose ten-stave paper for Amenaide's prayerful aria in the second act, "Giusto Dio, che umile adoro."[49] These staves are assigned to the following instruments:

First Violins	2 Clarinets
Second Violins	2 Horns
Violas	2 Trumpets
1 Flute	Amenaide
2 Oboes	Violoncellos and Double basses

(Notice the typical nineteenth-century layout of the score, with upper strings at the top, followed by winds and brass, vocal parts, and then lower strings.) But Rossini also wanted two bassoons to play, for in the margin he wrote "I Fagotti nella riga del basso" (the bassoons with the bass line), suggesting that the bassoons should join with the violoncellos and double basses. Yet, the situation is more complex: in six measures within the aria, explicit bassoon parts are notated on the staff normally assigned to trumpets (silent at this point). Did Rossini *really* want the bassoons to play everywhere else with the bass of the strings? Even in passages scored for pizzicato strings alone, where the presence of the bassoons would create a dubious effect? Had Rossini chosen twelve-stave paper, we would not have to guess. As it is, his choice of ten-stave paper created uncertainties with which every generation of copyists, performers, and editors has had to cope. Perhaps when he began drafting the number he did not know there was going to be a problem; realizing too late that there was one, he improvised an unsatisfactory solution rather than rewrite the entire score or provide a *spartitino* for the bassoons.

Nor are the Verdi autographs immune to such problems. Elvira's cavatina in *Ernani* ("Ernani, Ernani, involami") is written on sixteen-stave vertical paper, organized as follows: [50]

First Violins	2 Horns in B♭
Second Violins	2 Trumpets in E♭
Violas	2 Bassoons
1 Flute	3 Trombones and Cimbasso
1 Piccolo	Elvira
2 Oboes	Chorus of Women
2 Clarinets	Violoncellos
2 Horns in F	Double basses

Whenever a composer places the parts for two instruments on the same staff (even identical instruments, such as two oboes), problems arise, unless he is explicit—and few of the composers under discussion were—about how many instruments should be playing at any moment in those measures where only a single melodic line is present. But the problems become truly daunting in this *Ernani* example, where Verdi notated three trombones and a cimbasso on a single staff. When Verdi wrote four notes, the matter is clear; when he wrote three, it becomes ambiguous; when he wrote two or one, it is incomprehensible. In Elvira's cavatina at one point he indicated "cimbasso solo." A later passage is marked simply "solo." But which instrument should play that solo, a trombone or the cimbasso? Verdi's notation provides no further information. The old Ricordi performing parts assigned the part to the first trombone, but the logic of the musical situation suggests it should be played by the cimbasso. Had the composer chosen eighteen-stave paper, we would not have to guess. [51]

The structure of the paper used by a composer also had serious implications for the transmission of his work. Music paper was not supplied to composers in individual leaves, but rather in the form of gatherings of bifolios (each bifolio having two attached leaves or four pages: see example 2.1). Composers such as Rossini, Bellini, or Donizetti, who did not make extensive sketches in advance, tended to employ either a string of single bifolios or, at most, small gatherings of two bifolios. Verdi, whose previous sketching allowed him to anticipate quite precisely the length of each musical number in an opera, used much larger gatherings, of five, six, or as many as ten or twelve nested bifolios (i.e., one inside the other). That he used these large gatherings even for operas preceding *Luisa Miller,* the first opera for which we have reason to believe that complete sketches exist in the family home at

EXAMPLE 2.1. A BIFOLIO OF OBLONG PAPER.

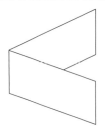

Sant'Agata, suggests that he employed sketches throughout the 1840s.[52] Taking the process a step further, copyists, who knew in advance the precise length of every piece in an opera, tried to use single gatherings for each of them wherever possible.

It is not difficult to intuit the reasons behind these choices. Composers or copyists who could anticipate the length of a piece used a structure in large gatherings that simplified the task of organizing and binding the manuscript: it is manifestly more difficult to keep track of ten consecutive bifolios than of a single gathering of ten nested bifolios. Yet composers working out the exact dimensions of a composition directly in their autograph manuscripts, rather than in independent continuity drafts, had every reason to employ single bifolios or gatherings of two bifolios. Not only were they uncertain about the length of each piece, they were much more likely to change their mind about a passage as they drafted it. Removing a single bifolio containing music that was not going well was much easier than dismantling a larger gathering. In the autograph of Donizetti's *Don Pasquale,* for example, the composer used the convenience of the structure in single bifolios to introduce various modifications during the course of composition. He drafted a theme to serve as the conclusion to the first act ("Vado, corro al gran cimento"), then decided to change it altogether, by adding new bifolios as needed. Under normal circumstances, he would have removed the bifolios that no longer contained music pertaining to the revised version. In this case, however, he was to change his mind again, and ultimately developed the definitive version of the passage by combining and adapting elements from both of the earlier versions. All his manipulations can be followed in detail, since nothing was removed from the manuscript during his process of revision.[53] His alternative would have been to write the entire cabaletta out from scratch, but it was not the solution he chose.

For purposes of binding and preservation, of course, single bifolios or small gatherings also presented significantly greater risks than larger gatherings. In the Bellini autographs individual bifolios from the composer's original score are frequently missing; some have been replaced by a copy, some have just disappeared. It is not always certain whether the absences are the workings of accident or actual cuts desired by the composer. When the operas are those of Bellini, who was ever ready to introduce revisions for a new set of singers or a new theater, the resulting problems can be maddening, and the issues can be far from trivial. The concluding *A major* section in the "Guerra, guerra" chorus in *Norma,* for example, is missing in Bellini's autograph, but its absence may or may not be related to a composer-sanctioned cut.[54] On other occasions a series of single bifolios can become hopelessly muddled. Cataloguing of the incomplete autograph manuscript of Rossini's *Il viaggio a Reims* at the Library of the Santa Cecilia Conservatory in Rome was made more difficult because of the baffling order in which its bifolios had been transmitted.

WRITING DOWN THE OPERA:
"SKELETON SCORES" AND *PARTICELLE*

With the paper on which he was going to write his autograph manuscript before him, where did the composer begin? He could normally expect a rehearsal period of three weeks, barring unforeseen events that might expand the time available (the illness of a singer) or shrink it (the failure of a preceding opera in the season). During that time, singers had to learn the parts of a new work, staging—however elementary—had to be worked out, orchestral materials prepared and rehearsed, sets painted and assembled, and the entire opera realized as a music drama. Working toward such a close and specific deadline, the composer kept firmly in mind the priorities of composition and of production, at least on those occasions when he was not being fed the libretto piecemeal, at the last moment.

Composers were sensitive to the particular needs of preparing the chorus. Even if choral interventions were relatively simple and the requirements for stage movement minimal, choristers tended to be poorly trained and even musically illiterate. Thus, preparing numbers in which the chorus appeared demanded a certain priority.[55] But getting music into the hands of the principal soloists was equally important. Working within a relatively stable group of conventions, most singers were able to commit music quickly to their voices and memories. While composers did what they could to assist the process, soloists were not necessarily given their major numbers first. After all, if a composer was unfamiliar with the abilities of a certain prima donna or feared that time may have ravaged a once glorious instrument, he might prefer to prepare first the ensembles in which she would appear, finalizing her solo music only after the rehearsal period had begun.

We may marvel at the prodigious feats of memory of nineteenth-century singers, but experience in the modern opera house helps redimension our wonderment. During the summer of 1996 the Rossini Opera Festival was scheduled to perform for the first time the new critical edition of the composer's *Matilde di Shabran,* an *opera semiseria* of monumental size and complexity. When the tenor scheduled to sing the principal tenor role of Corradino fell ill less than three weeks before opening night, no other singer in the world knew the role or had even seen the complete score. Yet the young Juan Diego Flórez, who had been hired for a smaller part in another opera, learned the principal aria by memory overnight, auditioned with it, and was engaged to assume the role of Corradino. He sang the part without a hitch, and with these performances launched what is proving to be an impressive career. Eight years later, a fully mature artist, he triumphantly returned to his debut role during the summer of 2004 in one of the most impressive productions of the festival in recent years, directed by Mario Martone and conducted by Riccardo Frizza.

Least urgent was the overture, of course, for which no stage rehearsals were needed (contemporary stage directors to the contrary). It is no wonder that throughout operatic history, overtures were invariably the last compositions prepared, and stories of composers arriving the night of the premiere with the ink still wet on the orchestral parts of their unrehearsed overture are legion. It is also no wonder that on occasion Donizetti or Rossini would borrow an overture from an earlier, unsuccessful work. Indeed, as the century progressed, many composers were happy to leave their operas without overtures altogether. Most of the famous Rossini overtures introduce his earlier operas: for his seven last Neapolitan *opere serie,* written between 1817 and 1822, he prepared only one full-fledged overture, for *Ermione* (with its unusual chorus of Trojan prisoners singing from behind the lowered curtain, as we have seen).[56] Verdi added an overture to *Alzira* in 1845 only at the insistence of the Neapolitan management, and he demanded extra payment for it.[57]

Although for every musical number or recitative the composer would plan the layout of the entire score, indicating which instruments would be playing and normally allotting a staff for each of them, he would begin by writing only a skeleton score, as described above. From a compositional point of view, this procedure makes perfect sense. The vocal parts, bass, and principal melodic lines, representing the main musical ideas and determining their melodic and harmonic development, had to be devised before the music was orchestrated, and that remained true whether they had first been written down elsewhere (in a continuity draft) and copied into the autograph manuscript (Verdi) or were written down for the first time directly into the autograph manuscript (Rossini, Bellini, Donizetti). The procedure also made practical sense. Vocal lines, whether for soloists or chorus, were required immediately for rehearsals: they had to be learned and memorized. Orchestral rehearsals tended to begin only a few days before the premiere of an opera. Filling in the staves left blank in the skeleton score and preparing parts for the orchestral musicians, then, was less urgent.

Several important manuscripts from this period, operas projected and pursued extensively before being abandoned, provide eloquent testimony to the way composers worked. Bellini began an opera based on Hugo's *Hernani,* to a libretto by Romani, during the autumn of 1830, just a few months after the first performance of the play caused a political and artistic uproar in Paris. Intended to serve as the second new opera in the carnival season at Milan's Teatro Carcano of 1830–31, which opened with Donizetti's *Anna Bolena,* this *Ernani* soon ran into significant difficulties with the Austrian censors. Rather than disfigure their text, Romani and Bellini substituted a new opera in a different genre, *La sonnambula.* Many pages from *Ernani* exist, including melodic sketches and some completed pages but mostly sections in skeleton score.[58] (Significantly, the part of Ernani was to be written for a female singer *en travesti,* Giuditta Pasta, precisely the vocal casting Verdi was to refuse in 1844.)

In a similar state is most of the third and fourth acts of the almost completed *Le Duc d'Albe* by Donizetti. Intended by the composer for performance in 1840 as his second work for the Opéra in Paris (after *Les Martyrs,* itself an adaptation of his Neapolitan *Poliuto*), this was a major effort for Donizetti—his first entirely new work in French. It was written to a libretto by the most important French librettist, Eugène Scribe, and a colleague, Charles Duveyrier; Scribe later developed from it a libretto for Verdi, *Les Vêpres siciliennes.*[59] Unfortunately, the director of the Opéra, Léon Pillet, was not prepared to mount any work without a central role for his mistress, the mezzo-soprano Rosine Stolz. And so Donizetti left *Le Duc d'Albe* with its first two acts basically complete and its third and fourth acts in skeleton score. Instead, he turned to another work that had gone unperformed, his *L'Ange de Nisida,* written for a theater that had gone bankrupt, the Théâtre de la

Renaissance, and from it he constructed one of his very finest operas, *La Favorite*, with the superb role of Léonor perfectly adapted to the talents of Pillet's own "Favorite," la Stolz.[60]

Rossini left an entire work in this form, his setting of choruses from Sophocles' tragedy *Oedipus at Colonus* in the Italian translation (*Edipo Coloneo*) prepared by the Bolognese poet Giambattista Giusti. It was probably in 1815 that Giusti asked the composer to write music for these choruses. Although no specific performance appears to have been planned, Rossini acquiesced and prepared a complete skeleton score. He wrote the vocal lines (a part for the chorus leader and the male chorus—without always including the lower choral parts), some of the bass line (particularly where there were significant modulations), and important instrumental solos. In a few cases, such as the brief sinfonia, he entered a fuller complement of instruments. In this state Rossini offered the manuscript to Giusti.

Giusti, who cared a great deal about these choruses, was deeply offended. In notes to the printed edition of his translation (Parma, 1817), he explained that he had employed a special poetic style for them, so that (as in the Greek theater) they could be sung:[61]

> To us it therefore seemed praiseworthy to try this experiment, and we wanted our choruses to be set to music. Meanwhile, while we await a favorable occasion to have the work performed on stage, we have wanted to make this translation public, from the style of which, and in particular from that of the choruses, the impartial reader will judge the effect that sung choruses might produce. That effect will be further clarified by experience, when that becomes possible.

In an explanatory note, Giusti added:

> A famous Maestro di Cappella set my choruses to music and was generously paid by me. Shortly after I realized that on many pages the accompaniments were lacking. I went back to him, and returned the pages. For a year since that time, and despite the numerous requests I have made, I have been unable to get them back. His friends say that this is his way of playing a joke on me; but jokes of that kind resemble those of a certain famous jester who, during the celebration of a feast and in the presence of a King (who enjoyed the action), plucked with admirable dexterity the gold boxes from the pockets of the astonished courtiers.

It is unlikely that Rossini intended to play a joke on Giusti. Rather, he behaved as did all composers of Italian opera during the first half of the nineteenth century. For Rossini the main creative work was done, and he would have been prepared to complete the orchestration when a performance was to take place. In this case, however, Rossini never did return to the score, nor do we know whether Giusti got his fee back.

The manuscript surfaced again in the early 1840s, when it was offered for sale in Paris by the Bolognese composer Vincenzo Gabussi, a good friend of Rossini's. It is at least possible that Rossini presented the manuscript to Gabussi as a gift. *Edipo Coloneo* was ultimately acquired by the French publisher Troupenas, who derived from it an "aria" for Oedipus (actually an introductory section of one of the choruses, set by Rossini as a solo for the *choregus*) and two female choruses (which he entitled "Faith" and "Hope"). To these two choruses Troupenas persuaded the composer to add a third, leading to the publication in 1844 of what became *Three Religious Choruses: Faith, Hope, and Charity.* But the manuscript that turned up in Paris and now, after various international journeys, resides in the Pierpont Morgan Library in New York is fully orchestrated. Another composer (probably the same person who composed the aria for Duglas in *La donna del lago*) "filled in the blanks," i.e., completed the orchestration. Because the layers are in different hands, we can identify precisely what was in Rossini's skeleton score. Although we cannot usually separate the layers so precisely, it is perfectly clear that this is how *all* Rossini's autograph manuscripts were prepared. To exemplify in this unusual case just what a skeleton score looked like, the critical edition of *Edipo Coloneo* printed the added orchestration over a grey background, so that the compositional stages are immediately evident.

Verdi worked the same way, and sometimes we can follow his steps. From his home at Sant'Agata he sent to Venice on 5 February 1851 the skeleton score of act 1 of *Rigoletto,* not including the prelude, and of act 2 except for the final duet. From these manuscripts, which included vocal lines and only some of the orchestral accompaniment, Verdi instructed the Venetian copyist to extract vocal parts and consign them to the appropriate singers. He added, "I will bring the rest of the opera with me and I will orchestrate the score during the rehearsals."[62] Verdi actually arrived in Venice on 19 February: there is no reason to think that the singers had yet seen any of act 2 or the final duet. The first performance of *Rigoletto* took place on 11 March. In those three weeks, then, Verdi orchestrated most of the opera, while the singers were learning their parts and the entire work was staged. When Verdi completed his orchestration, orchestral parts were prepared and the orchestra was rehearsed and integrated into the performance.

Working to such a tight schedule, it is hardly surprising that composers proceeded in this manner; they needed to get vocal parts in the hands of singers as soon as possible. For most operas written in Italy we lack these original singers' parts, *particelle* as they were often called. They have fallen victim to the ravages of time, the social system that put opera seasons under the control of a series of changing impresarios, or the destructive powers of fire or housecleaning. But some original parts do exist, such as those for *Semiramide* at the La Fenice. (These parts had been transferred to the Fondazione Levi of Venice before the theater was again destroyed by fire in 1996.) We are more fortunate with works written for the Parisian theaters. At the Opéra, a vast number of individual parts prepared for singers exists, sometimes with annotations in the hands of the composers. Even from the archives of the Théâtre Italien, the Parisian theater that played such an important role in the spread of this repertory in northern Europe, the theater through which French writers and artists (Delacroix, Balzac, Stendhal) came to know Italian opera, many *particelle* are extant. Those pertaining to *Il viaggio a Reims* are crucial sources. All surviving parts for individual singers present the same picture: the solo vocal line for a number or an act, together with vocal lines pertaining to one or more other characters in ensembles, with occasional vocal cues from other parts. Of the orchestral music, only the bass line is present (and rarely complete), together with a few significant instrumental cues to assist the vocalist. Such *particelle* could easily have been prepared from a skeleton score, and for the first performances of an opera they surely were. In the case of Verdi's *Macbeth,* the publisher Ricordi certainly had choral parts for the opera engraved in 1847 directly from the composer's skeleton score.[63]

ORCHESTRATING THE OPERA

With the singers in possession of their music, copyists returned the autograph manuscripts, still in skeleton score, to the composers. In their letters, Donizetti and Verdi state repeatedly that orchestration took place while they were rehearsing an opera with the singers. We do not have analogous Rossini letters, but the manuscripts themselves, with their different shades of ink, suggest a similar procedure. During breaks from rehearsals, composers would complete the orchestral lines; for those large ensembles where all instruments could not fit on the regular manuscript paper, they added the requisite *spartitini.*

In the nineteenth century, composers normally orchestrated their own operas from beginning to end. Although Rossini would occasionally use a collaborator to write recitative or to compose an *aria di sorbetto,* there are only two or three instances in which he permitted another composer to orchestrate an operatic number for which he wrote the skeleton score.[64] Italian opera composers may have worked in conditions that resemble those of the American musical theater, but the idea that there was another person waiting in the wings to orchestrate their scores, such as Broadway's famous Robert Russell Bennett, would have been anathema. That haste was required for the task did not mean it was done without care. Indeed, the most striking orchestral effects were probably conceived, even if not fully written down, together with the vocal lines. The remainder of the orchestration followed well-understood principles, more a matter of craft than of invention or inspiration. Autograph manuscripts of Rossini, Donizetti, and Verdi show an easy mastery of orchestral writing; those of Bellini a more hesitant grasp, although his direct experience with the orchestra during rehearsals usually led him to effective solutions.

Still, composers simplified the task of completing the orchestration whenever possible, allowing themselves a wide range of shortcuts. Where the structure of the music demanded repetition of a section (the reprise of the principal theme of a cabaletta, for example), Bellini and Donizetti did not even bother to lay out the measures, preferring to write "Dall'A al B" ("From A to B") across the score, meaning that the next measures repeated identically the measures between the ones marked "A" and "B." They would begin notating the music again with the measure after the repeat. Somewhat less cavalier, Rossini and Verdi usually marked off the necessary measures, but entered only the vocal lines and bass. (In larger ensembles they might even leave a series of blank measures.) At the beginning of the repeated passage they too would write either "Come Sopra" ("As above"—typical of Rossini) or "Dall'A al B" (Verdi), specifying that all material not written in full should be derived from the first appearance of the passage. In some autograph manuscripts, copyists filled in the blank measures.

Only in one respect did composers turn to other musicians to complete their orchestration: they did not prepare full scores for the wind bands, frequently supplied by the local military garrison, which appeared onstage (*sul palco*) during certain operas. After Rossini first employed such a *banda sul palco* in his *Ricciardo e Zoraide* of 1818, these bands played an ever more important role in Italian serious opera. Normally a composer would prepare a short score of the music to be played by the *banda,* written on two staves, as if for piano. A local bandmaster would arrange this music for whatever contingent of band instruments could be made available by municipal or military authorities. That procedure is as true for Rossini in *Semiramide* as for

Verdi in *Nabucco* and *Un ballo in maschera*.[65] Only once did Rossini himself make a *banda* realization, in a very special circumstance. Revising his *Mosè in Egitto* in 1819, he added the famous Prayer in the third act, just before the Hebrews cross the Red Sea. The accompaniment of that Prayer employs both orchestra and *banda*, and Rossini himself wrote the *banda* parts.[66] Even when Rossini did not directly write *banda* parts, he consulted closely with the bandmaster. No one but the composer could have taken responsibility for the extraordinary use of stage band in the first-act finale of *La donna del lago*, where nine trumpets and four trombones accompany the entrance of Malcom, to which a more normally constituted *banda* is later added, for a total of some thirty-five band instruments *sul palco*. The French found the effect intolerable, and after the work was first given in Paris in 1824, Rossini was compelled to have a new band reduction prepared, for a more modest group of instruments.[67]

Many peculiarities persisting in modern editions of Italian operas from the first half of the nineteenth century, to the confusion of instrumentalists, singers, and conductors, can be understood only by examining the layers in which the autograph manuscripts were generated and by interpreting the abbreviations composers employed. Some discrepancies deriving from the compositional layers are trivial. Frequently, for example, the value of the note in the violoncellos and double basses is not the same as the value of the notes in all other instrumental parts. In the lovely duet for Pippo and Ninetta (N. 12) in the second act of Rossini's *La gazza ladra*, the section preparing for the repetition of the cabaletta theme closes with a *G-major* chord for the entire orchestra and voices. The note in the violoncellos and double basses is a half note, but in every other orchestral part there are quarter notes. There is a discrepancy only because Rossini wrote the note in the violoncellos and double-basses into his score before he wrote the other orchestral parts; nothing in the music suggests that the composer wanted to prolong the sound of the violoncellos and double basses alone.[68]

But not every case is trivial. This is Verdi's continuity draft for the end of Rigoletto's soliloquy, "Pari siamo," in which he compares himself to the assassin, Sparafucile (example 2.2). The chord in the second measure appears on the second beat, immediately after Rigoletto sings his high *e*. Compare Verdi's autograph manuscript of *Rigoletto*, where the passage is scored for voice and strings. In the example the upper string parts are condensed on a single staff (example 2.3). Verdi could not have wanted lower strings to enter on the second beat and upper strings on the third, as shown here. Rather, this is a quintessential error reflecting successive layers in the autograph. Copying

EXAMPLE 2.2. GIUSEPPE VERDI, *RIGOLETTO*, SCENA E DUETTO (N. 4),
MM. 67–68 IN THE CONTINUITY DRAFT.

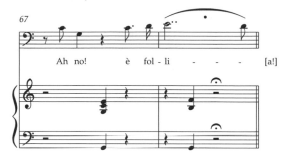

the version of the continuity draft into his skeleton score, Verdi wrote the note in the lower strings as it appears in that draft. Completing the orchestration (and influenced by the chord he had correctly written in the preceding measure), he placed the chord in the upper strings on the third beat, without having noticed the discrepancy with what he had previously written down. Verdi's incoherent notation was encouraged by the layout of the manuscript, with upper strings filling the top three staves and lower strings the bottom two, separated by winds, brass, percussion, and vocal parts. Writing Rigoletto and lower strings, then, Verdi was using adjacent staves; adding upper strings he was writing at the top of the page.

What did Verdi intend here? Editors and performers must make a judgment, one dependent both on aesthetic considerations and on our understanding of the process by which *Rigoletto* was notated. Most contemporary manuscripts blindly follow the original. Those few secondary sources keen enough to be aware of the problem, including the orchestral parts and vocal

EXAMPLE 2.3. GIUSEPPE VERDI, *RIGOLETTO*, SCENA E DUETTO (N. 4),
MM. 67–68 IN THE AUTOGRAPH MANUSCRIPT.

score issued by Verdi's publisher Ricordi, adopted the principle that "majority rules," opting for the version of the upper strings. Yet there is good reason to favor the rhythmically striking placement of the chord on the second beat, as in the lower strings (written both in the continuity draft and in the skeleton score, while Verdi was thinking more closely about the relationship between the chord and the vocal line), rather than the the more pedestrian placement on the third beat (written while the composer was furiously completing the orchestration).[69] Whatever one's choice, however, there is no way to be certain of what Verdi intended. What is certain is that he did not intend what he wrote and that the problem must be fixed in both the printed score and in performance.

Many puzzles and inconsistencies reflect abbreviations used by composers during the orchestration of their scores. Once we understand that copyists may have filled in orchestral lines marked "Come Sopra" by a composer, we can avoid giving these additions the same weight as the composer's own notation, a mistake that occurs in so many nineteenth-century secondary sources. From a secondary source, of course, it is impossible to know that the autograph manuscript was not all in the composer's hand, so that variants introduced by copyists appear to have the same weight as a composer's own notation.[70] When we understand that a composer used shorthand for passages in which the orchestration is derived "Come Sopra," furthermore, we better appreciate that even autograph differences in the bass line in such passages may have been introduced inadvertently by the composer, who was probably writing from memory. Finally, if we keep in mind the physical appearance of these autograph manuscripts, we can be sensitive to situations where a composer began to write anew after a "Come Sopra" passage. Writing without actually seeing the preceding measures, a composer frequently introduced banal errors in the instrumentation or infelicities in the way an instrumental part resolves.

Verbal instructions for one instrumental part to be derived from another are equally perilous. Following eighteenth-century practice, where violas tended to join the lower strings, Rossini and Donizetti (but also Bellini and Verdi on occasion) sometimes mark the viola staff "col basso." The meaning is clear: violas double the part of the lower strings. But realizing this instruction in practice is not always so simple. Cellos and double basses usually read from the same line and play the same music (with double basses sounding an octave below the cellos—even that not unequivocal, since the notes available on nineteenth-century instruments were not everywhere the same). But when violas, whose lowest note is the *c* below middle *c,* are asked to play together with cellos, whose lowest note is the c an octave below the lowest viola note, should they play the same notes as the cellos or an octave above? Should they switch from one register to the other, and if so where? How do we know precisely where the composer wanted the violas to play? Did he even consider the problem? The context often provides a clear picture, but there are many occasions when editors and instrumentalists are thrust back on their own resources. That, too, is a consequence of the way these autograph manuscripts were prepared.

All these matters had both immediate and long-range implications for the transmission of Italian operas from the first half of the nineteenth century. They continue to have ramifications for musicians and scholars trying to decide what a composer may have meant. The process here described, however, hardly encouraged composers to think about posterity. There is ample documentary evidence that they were conscious of their artistic stature and faced their tasks with seriousness and confidence. Yet they were compelled by the nature of the system within which they worked to concentrate their attention, all their attention, on a performance whose fast-approaching reality imposed severe constraints. With opening night three days hence, the soprano was battling with her lover (the tenor), the bass was incapable of learning his music, the first oboe turned out to be a clarinettist in disguise, and the entire viola section (both players) was sick.[71] If anyone had told Rossini in 1816 that *Il barbiere di Siviglia* would still be entertaining the public in the twenty-first century, he would have been incredulous. After all, there was practically no "active repertory" in 1816. Apart from a handful of operas by Gluck, Mozart, Paisiello, and Cimarosa (all composers either still alive or dead less than thirty years), most of the operas being performed at all, and *all* the operas being performed regularly, were newly or recently composed.

With an opera fully orchestrated, the composer's autograph manuscript now went back to the copyists, who drew out parts for the individual members of the orchestra. Finally, it was possible to rehearse the orchestra. For *Rigoletto*, the first orchestral rehearsal took place on 4 March 1851, precisely one week before the premiere of the opera.

3

TRANSMISSION VERSUS TRADITION

Your copyists work too quickly: if they are paid by the page, pay them by the
hour, augment their salary, do what you want, but try to remedy this disorder.

Giuseppe Verdi to Tito Ricordi, 17 January 1863

REHEARSALS AND FIRST PERFORMANCES

However hectic the period of preparation may have been, rehearsals were
even more intense. At best a completed opera would be rehearsed for a
month; in dire circumstances rehearsals would begin before the last act had
been drafted. Composers and stage directors (usually their librettists) worked
first with the singers, some of whom might have received part of their music in advance. Rehearsals with full orchestra began only a few days before
the premiere, when composers finally completed the orchestration. Opening
night approached with frightening rapidity. That first performances were
underrehearsed, tentative, and frequently disappointing is no surprise, and
the fabled opening-night disasters of *Il barbiere di Siviglia* and *Norma* owed
much to the circumstances of their production. Composers hoped for immediate popular triumphs, to be sure, and sometimes even got them, but
they knew that the production would improve over the course of the season.

From reviews, letters, diaries, and contemporary reports, as well as from
hints in musical sources, we learn much about rehearsals and premieres, and
capturing the flavor of this activity helps orient us to problems we continue
to face. For example, composers often tailored their scores to the abilities of
their singers. When Verdi sent vocal parts to Felice Varesi and Marianna
Barbieri-Nini, his original Macbeth and Lady Macbeth, in 1847, before the rehearsal period, he urged them, "Let me know if there are any passages that lie
badly for you," so that he might make modifications before orchestrating the
score. For Macbeth, Verdi prepared alternative versions of a passage and
asked the baritone to select the one that suited him better.[1]

While assisting with preparations in London for the premiere of *I mas-nadieri* during the summer of 1847, Verdi's student and colleague Emanuele Muzio, who accompanied the composer on this trip, wrote frequently to Verdi's father-in-law in Busseto, Antonio Barezzi. Muzio described with admiration some of the artistic qualities of their leading lady, the "Swedish nightingale" Jenny Lind, but disparaged her style of singing: "Her agility is incomparable, and often to show off her skill in singing she errs on the side of *fioriture,* turns, and trills, things that pleased last century, but not in 1847. We Italians are not accustomed to this manner; and, should Lind come to Italy, she would abandon this mania she has for ornamentation and would sing more simply."[2] While Muzio's opinions probably reflected those of Verdi, the composer was not about to ignore the particular talents of Lind. Both the autograph manuscript of *I masnadieri* and the singer's part derived from it show many changes in Amalia's vocal lines, which were originally much simpler, perhaps because Verdi did not directly know her voice; the changes were introduced during rehearsals to accommodate Lind's style. Amalia's cavatina, "Lo sguardo avea degli angeli," is thus well represented with just the kind of *fioriture,* turns, and trills that Muzio deplored.[3] What we do not know, of course, is the additional ornamentation Lind may have introduced during rehearsals and performances of the opera.

Composers made many modifications for artistic reasons, independent of the predilections of individual singers. Revision and polishing continued throughout the rehearsal period, often creating confusion in the subsequent transmission of an opera. A single note might be involved, as in "Caro nome" in *Rigoletto.* At the end of this beautiful evocation of "Gualtier Maldè" (the false name the Duke invents during his duet with Rigoletto's daughter), Gilda repeats the name twice. All printed scores of the opera have her ascend both times from b ("Gualtier Mal-[dè]") to the tonic e for the final syllable ("[Gualtier Mal]-dè"). But in Verdi's autograph manuscript he unequivocally altered those final e, opting to hold the voice on the lower b (example 3.1). It is not difficult to understand the appeal of this change. The ascent provides a strong cadential gesture, an effect diametrically opposed to the dreamy repetition of the name that results from holding the pitch unchanged. Furthermore, the ensuing return of the main theme, "Caro nome," begins on that same e: if the voice has already ascended there, the freshness of this reprise is compromised. Why, then, did printed scores not incorporate Verdi's change? We know the answer. Verdi's publisher, Ricordi, anxious to print a vocal score as soon as possible, sent a copyist from Milan to Venice, where *Rigoletto* was in rehearsal. Ricordi's copy—with the earlier version of "Caro nome"—was

EXAMPLE 3.1. GIUSEPPE VERDI, *RIGOLETTO*, ARIA GILDA (N. 6), MM. 63–71.

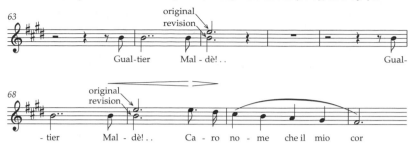

finished and forwarded to Milan before opening night. Every vocal score published by Ricordi (and those derived from them by other publishers) and every subsequent manuscript copied in Milan followed that earlier version of the melody. Indeed, the only source—apart from the autograph manuscript—that has Verdi's revision is a copy of *Rigoletto* prepared by La Fenice *after* the premiere. Thus, we know for certain that Verdi changed Gilda's melodic line between the time the Ricordi copy was made (toward the end of February 1851) and the time the Fenice copy was prepared (early in March).[4]

While composers frequently introduced important revisions into their scores just before or after the premiere, only some of these emendations made their way into materials from which the operas were later performed. Rossini modified the *Pas de trois* and Tyrolean chorus ("Toi que l'oiseau ne suivrait pas!") from *Guillaume Tell,* bringing the chorus back for a rousing conclusion, but Rossini's French publisher, Troupenas, never registered the change.[5] When the duet for Percy and Anna in the first-act finale of *Anna Bolena,* "S'ei t'abborre, io t'amo ancora," fell flat, Donizetti replaced it with a new duet, "Sì, son io che a te ritorno," but printed scores included only the former.[6] And Donizetti was dissatisfied with the ending of the second-act duet for Don Pasquale and the Dottore in *Don Pasquale,* making numerous changes both during rehearsals and afterwards: the laughing conclusion, for example, was added for a revival in Vienna several months after the Parisian premiere of 3 January 1843. While the Ricordi score ultimately got this right, other editions published during the 1840s are chaotic.[7]

When the curtain finally rose on a new opera, the composer was normally required to be physically present, alongside the orchestra and in full view of the public, for the first three performances. Contracts often referred to his leading the performance "from the cembalo," suggesting that he gave cues, set tempi, and personally accompanied *secco* recitative, but the phrase continued to be used even after cembalos and the *secco* recitative with which they were associated had disappeared. According to an oft-repeated anecdote, told first by the original Rosina, Geltrude Righetti-Giorgi, during the notorious premiere of *Il barbiere di Siviglia* in 1816 Rossini ostentatiously applauded the singers (and, implicitly, his own music) at the end of the first act, bringing further howls of abuse from an angry public.[8]

As the century progressed, contracts no longer specified the composer's presence at the "cembalo," but he was still expected to be in the theater for the first three evenings. Verdi's contract with La Fenice for *La traviata*, for example, has the following clause, which appears to have been standard: "Maestro Verdi must remain in Venice at least until after the third performance of his new opera, and he must be present at all rehearsals for it, large or small, as well as at the first performances."[9] Verdi's bitterness at the dreadful failure of his second opera for La Scala, *Un giorno di regno,* whose first performance took place on 5 September 1840, just a short time after the death of his first wife, Margherita Barezzi (both their infant children had died within the past three years), was unquestionably exacerbated by his having to appear in the theater—perhaps even at the cembalo, for this *opera buffa* still has *secco* recitative. As he wrote in a famous letter to his publisher, Tito Ricordi, almost twenty years later:

> Since that time I never again saw *Un giorno di regno,* and it is probably a bad opera, although who knows how many operas no better have been tolerated or even perhaps applauded. Oh, if then the public had only—not applauded—but had borne that opera in silence, I would not have had sufficient words to thank them![10]

In success or failure, the composer was there to receive directly the audience's reaction.

Whatever problems may have arisen in coordinating the performance (setting tempos, fixing dynamic levels, correcting mistakes in the parts) would have been handled by a word here, a gesture there. Communication between the singers and the orchestra was more direct, for there was no Wagnerian orchestra pit, no "mystic gulf" in which the instrumentalists were hidden: the orchestra sat on the same level as the audience.[11] Likewise, there was no conductor with a baton beating time—just the composer, for his three obligatory performances, and the leader of the first violin section, who was responsible for keeping things together. This violinist worked not from a complete orchestral score of the opera, but rather from a "violino principale" part, a special first violin part that included the main vocal lines and instrumental solos, so that necessary cues could be provided. Independent conductors in Italy were not common until the 1850s, although they were regularly employed at the Paris Opéra already during Rossini's years there, from 1826 through 1829.[12]

We must try to understand how these first performances in Italian theaters were prepared and executed, since these were the conditions in which scores for Italian operas from the first half of the nineteenth century were prepared. They allowed no time to verify individual instrumental parts, to eliminate notational errors or infelicities, to fix details in ensembles. Only the most obvious errors, those which immediately sprang to a composer's attention aurally, could possibly have been corrected. Indeed, nineteenth-century performance materials actually used in the theater are so filled with mistakes that one wonders how the performers ever got through an evening. If they were good musicians, though, instrumentalists presumably knew where they were harmonically, had some sense of where they were likely to be going, and negotiated the difficulties intelligently.

While there was considerably more rehearsal time in Paris, the never-ending changes and the presence of many individuals seeking to control the process left such confusion about what should be played that the theater was soon awash in incomprehensible and contradictory indications. When oral tradition faded, the Opéra had to return to the printed score of Rossini's *Guillaume Tell* to find a comprehensible text. In the process, they lost many of the modifications Rossini made during the rehearsal period.[13] Verdi's pronouncements about "la grande boutique," as he not so affectionately called the commercial enterprise that was the Paris Opéra, reflected a common feeling among Italian composers: despite the high performance royalties, the enticing possibilities for elaborate staging, the superior quality of the orchestra, and the attention paid to the literary quality of librettos, operas written for France lacked a unified artistic vision. Verdi was no fan of opera by committee.[14]

After the first three performances, the composer was free to depart. Now his opera began to make its way without his presence. If we are to understand materials used for performance in the nineteenth century, from which are derived many of those still employed today, we must know not only how they came into existence but, even more, how they were transmitted from the time of the first performance until the present. The process of transmission changed radically between 1810 and 1865, and the changes were related to a transformation in the economics of composition. Rossini was a prime example of the earlier system, centered on a theater and its impresario (who commissioned an opera and paid the composer a fee for his work) and on copyists of that theater (who often had a contract granting them the right to distribute manuscript copies of operas performed there, with no further payment to the composer). Verdi was rooted in the later system, dependent on both a theater commissioning a work (for which the composer was paid a fee) and a publisher who acquired directly from the composer subsequent distribution rights (against payment of a further fee and/or royalties). Composers of the generation of Bellini and Donizetti belonged to a time of transition between these two economic systems.

It is crucial to differentiate between the way that operas were transmitted through written sources (whether manuscript copies, printed editions, or performing parts)—the subject of this chapter—and performing traditions associated with those same operas (changes introduced into the vocal line by singers, added cadenzas and high notes, cuts or interpolations, modifications in instrumentation made by contemporaries, etc.). The texts transmitted through written sources—however problematic they may be—do not embody what I am describing as performance traditions. Only rarely does a particular reworking of an opera by later performers become part of a continuous written record, although some transmitted reworkings have had a pernicious influence on the history of a work (as when Ricordi for half a century distributed a late nineteenth-century reorchestration of *Il barbiere di Siviglia* or other Rossini comedies). Modifications made by individual singers or cuts, on the other hand, tend to be exemplified in single copies, and are not transmitted from one written or printed source of a work to another. The occasional publication of an aria with the ornamentation of a favorite singer, for example, almost never influenced the text of the work from which the aria was taken. So we need to differentiate between operas as transmitted by manuscript and printed sources, and performance practices that develop over time and are passed down from one generation to another. The persistent failure to separate transmission from performance traditions continues to plague efforts to think clearly about Italian opera.

ROSSINI AND HIS AUTOGRAPH MANUSCRIPTS

Let us begin with the transmission of Rossini's operas and those of his contemporaries. After the obligatory three performances for a new work, Rossini would usually depart for the city of his next commission or return to visit his family in Bologna. Even during his residency in Naples (1815–22), he often left that city after a major premiere. The future of the opera just composed would depend on the contract Rossini had with the theater that had commissioned it. That there could be significant disagreement as to the meaning of such a contract emerges from the dispute that developed between Rossini and the Neapolitan impresario, Barbaja, after the premiere on 16 February 1822 of the composer's last opera for Naples, *Zelmira*. This opera was written just before the company transferred for the spring season to Vienna, where its residency at the Kärntnertortheater won the favor of the Viennese public and many intellectuals (including a delighted Hegel), raising the hackles of local musicians, Beethoven among them. The dispute between Rossini and Barbaja also reflected their animosity in 1822, motivated by Rossini's decision not only to leave Naples but also to rob Barbaja of his prima donna (and perhaps former mistress) by marrying Isabella Colbran. However titillating the context, the dispute reveals much about the transmission of Italian operas during the early 1820s.

On 17 April 1823, after the premiere of *Semiramide* and before Rossini began the trip that would take him to Paris and London, he wrote the following letter to a Neapolitan friend, Carlo de Chiaro, living at that moment in Vienna or St. Petersburg:

Dear friend: I can do nothing less than thank you for the interest you take in me, but unfortunately you have undertaken a mission that, despite your good heart and sense of justice, will go badly for you. I have not responded to that last letter from Barbaja because I do not possess a style dignified enough to respond categorically. I will say only that if I had sums belonging to Barbaja deposited with me and if I could not or would not give them back to him, I would at least have the scruples to pay him interest. He has six thousand ducats in hand, a year has passed since the society came to an end, and he has neither paid nor proposed paying any interest and only sets forth stupid reasons against paying, simply to get revenge.

I own all my original manuscripts, it being custom and law that a year after an opera is given, authors have the right to have their autographs back. Did I perhaps steal my originals from Barbaja's archive? I asked him for them, and he granted them to me; then why now does he reclaim them?

He pretends that I made provisions for the full score of *Zelmira* [Rossini seems to be referring to the distribution of the full orchestral score], while I made no other contracts but that with Vienna [for the publication of a reduction for piano and voices, with the Viennese music publisher Artaria], as he knows well; and if he finds a contract in which I made provisions for the full score of *Zelmira*, I will pay any penalty at all. He has words, not documents. None of the operas written in Naples brought a single penny of gain to Barbaja in terms of distribution rights, since the copyist has the right to give the score to whomever he pleases. Should *Zelmira* alone be the opera that serves as an exception? [15]

Rossini's departure from Naples was not happy. Barbaja apparently kept a sum of money Rossini had invested in a business enterprise in which they were partners, presumably the one that controlled the gambling concessions at San Carlo, and had neither repaid the sum nor given him interest on his investment. Faced with the composer's demands, Barbaja claimed instead that Rossini had defrauded him by stealing the autograph manuscript of *Zelmira* from Barbaja's archive, thereby robbing the impresario of income that would have come to him from controlling the distribution of the opera, marketing the product he had acquired when he commissioned the work, and making copies for other theaters.

Rossini denies the accuracy of this economic contention. According to him, the impresario had no rights at all to further commercial exploitation of operas first produced in his theater. Rather, the composer had the right to have his autograph manuscript returned to him a year after the first performance of a work, and Rossini claimed to own all his own autograph manuscripts: there was no justification for Barbaja to differentiate *Zelmira* from the others. A copy of that autograph manuscript would have been made by the copyist associated with the theater, and the right to produce further copies belonged to that copyist, not to the impresario. Of the nine *opere serie* Rossini composed for Naples between 1815 and 1822, the composer did indeed keep at least eight autograph manuscripts his entire life. Upon the death of his second wife, Olympe Pélissier, five of these (*Elisabetta, regina d'Inghilterra, Otello, Armida, La donna del lago,* and *Maometto II*) passed to the city of his birth, Pesaro, where the Fondazione Rossini was formed to administer his legacy and establish a conservatory. Another three (*Mosè in Egitto, Ermione,* and *Zelmira*), now in various Parisian libraries, were given by Olympe as personal gifts, perhaps in lieu of cash payments, to her doctor, her lawyer, and others. Fortunately these manuscripts eventually made their way into public collections. Only the autograph of *Ricciardo e Zoraide* is in Naples (now at the conservatory library), where it has probably remained since its composition in 1818.

Thus, copies of these scores made in Naples, from which other copies were made, and then copies of the copies, as the operas spread from one theater to another in Italy and then elsewhere in Europe, were the sources used for performances of Rossini's Neapolitan operas as they circulated in the nineteenth century. The autograph manuscripts remained with the composer.

The accuracy of that first copy was therefore a crucial matter, as was the ability of successive copyists to produce accurate renderings in turn. But that, as we shall see, was precisely the problem.

Rossini, however, was being less than truthful with Carlo de Chiaro, and hence with Barbaja. He may well have had a contract with Naples that specified this disposition of his autograph manuscripts, but there was no "standard" procedure either within a single opera house or throughout the Italian peninsula. Individual contracts, rather than any generalizable custom or law, determined individual practice. Between 1810 and 1813 Rossini wrote five one-act *farse* for the Venetian Teatro San Moisè. Not a single autograph manuscript for these *farse* remained in Rossini's possession. Two have disappeared (*La cambiale di matrimonio* and *L'inganno felice*), one recently resurfaced in a Swedish collection (*La scala di seta*)—as we saw in chapter 1—and two others turned up in the hands of Rossini's friends, presumably purchased from previous owners. During the 1850s these friends hastened to Paris to find the aging Rossini and have him authenticate their treasures. On the autograph manuscript of *L'occasione fa il ladro,* Rossini wrote in 1855 or 1858 (the last number is difficult to read), "I recognize this score as my autograph." On that of *Il signor Bruschino,* owned by Prince Giuseppe Poniatowski, himself an amateur musician and composer of operas, Rossini wrote in a more spirited tone on 10 February 1858, "I, the undersigned, declare that this is the autograph of my *Bruschino,* composed in Venice in 1813. It pleases me moreover to declare that I am Blessed that this Sin of my youth is in the hands of my worthy friend and patron, Prince G. Poniatowski." [16]

After the first performances, these Venetian manuscripts became the property of the copyist of the San Moisè, Giacomo Zamboni. Indeed, after applying his stamp twice to the first page of the autograph of *L'occasione fa il ladro,* Zamboni wrote, "Original of Maestro Rossini. When making cuts or other changes, please do not ruin it by using ink, etc." He signed his name: "G. F. Zamboni owner [*proprietario*]." The copyist of the San Moisè, then, apparently had not only the right to distribute the opera but also the right to keep the autograph manuscript itself, a right very similar to that gradually wrested from Milanese theaters by Giovanni Ricordi, patriarch of the firm whose name is intimately related to the history of Italian music for the past two centuries. We will take up that story later in this chapter.

The situation in Rome was less clear. Of the five operas Rossini wrote for three different Roman theaters, he apparently kept the autograph manuscript only of the last, the *opera semiseria* he composed for the Teatro Apollo in 1821, *Matilde di Shabran,* at whose first performances Niccolò Paganini himself, the great Italian violinist and composer, served as "violino principale." It presumably passed from Rossini to his young Belgian friend Edmond Michotte, in whose collection at the Brussels Conservatory it currently resides.[17] The autograph manuscript of Rossini's first Roman opera, *Torvaldo e Dorliska*, written to open the carnival season of 1815–16 at the Teatro Valle, is found in the Bibliothèque du Conservatoire, one of the treasures inherited from the French collector Charles Malherbe. Its previous history is unknown. The autograph manuscript of the only *opera seria* Rossini wrote for Rome, *Adelaide di Borgogna*, first performed at the Teatro Argentina on 27 December 1817, appears to be lost.

Of particular interest, of course, are the autograph manuscripts of the two *opere buffe* written by Rossini for Rome, *Il barbiere di Siviglia* (Teatro Argentina, 20 February 1816) and *La Cenerentola* (Teatro Valle, 25 January 1817). Both manuscripts ultimately became part of the collection of a Bolognese friend of Rossini's, the lawyer Rinaldo Bajetti, at whose death in 1862 they were donated, respectively, to the libraries of the Bologna Liceo Musicale (where Rossini had been a student) and the Accademia Filarmonica (to which Rossini had been admitted in 1806, at the age of fourteen).[18] We cannot trace the history of the autograph manuscript of *Il barbiere di Siviglia* between the opera's premiere and the time of Bajetti's gift to the Liceo Musicale. For *La Cenerentola*, a clause in the original contract specified that the manuscript would remain with the impresario of the Teatro Valle, Pietro Cartoni (the score will "remain the full and absolute property of Sig. Cartoni, without the said Maestro's being able to reclaim his original after a year").[19]

As we saw in the discussion of recent New York and Pesaro performances in chapter 1, *La Cenerentola* is an opera for which Rossini made extensive use of a collaborator, the Roman musician Luca Agolini, known as Luca "lo zoppo" because of a characteristic limp. Agolini wrote the *secco* recitative and three musical numbers: arias for the Prince's tutor (Alidoro) and one of the stepsisters (Clorinda), and a short chorus at the beginning of the second act. In Rossini's autograph manuscript, all the recitative and Clorinda's aria are present, in Agolini's hand, while the chorus is missing.[20] Where the Alidoro aria should occur, however, just before the first-act finale, the manuscript includes neither Agolini's "Vasto teatro è il mondo" nor the aria with which Rossini replaced it in 1821 for a later performance at the Teatro Apollo in Rome, "Là del ciel nell'arcano profondo," a piece whose size and difficulty give the role of Alidoro an altogether different weight. Instead, the manuscript has another aria, written in yet another hand, "Fa silenzio, odi un rumore." This aria was performed during a revival of *La Cenerentola* in 1818 at the Teatro

Apollo of Rome to celebrate a state visit of the King of Naples and his family. Rossini's autograph manuscript, then, was still in the hands of the Roman impresario at that time, and the substitution was made without the composer's knowledge or approval. When Rossini prepared "Là del ciel" for Alidoro in 1821, he kept its autograph manuscript, which is part of the collection he willed to the Fondazione Rossini. Reconstructing the history of Rossini's involvement with the music of *La Cenerentola*, in short, requires control over a set of autograph sources (and manuscript copies) in many different libraries.

MANUSCRIPT COPIES OF ITALIAN OPERAS

After the first run of performances, then, the autograph manuscript of an opera composed in Italy had largely served its function. The situation was quite different in France, where the production of new operas was centered in one major city, Paris. Music publishers there regularly used the autograph manuscripts and other materials supplied by composers of new works to print orchestral scores, and reductions for piano and voice, of operas first performed in the capital.[21] These, in turn, could be employed in theaters scattered in smaller provincial centers around the country, theaters that would buy or rent orchestral parts from the publishers. Normally these publishers were commercial entrepreneurs, although early in the century a group of composers joined forces to form a cooperative society for the publication of their operas.[22]

But in Italy during the first few decades of the nineteenth century there was no obvious center of musical and cultural life, and no music publisher powerful enough to dominate the market throughout the peninsula.[23] Major theaters existed in several different cities, and one must always remember that "Italy" was a geographical area, not a political entity. After the defeat of Napoleon and the return of the Restoration monarchs in 1815, Naples was in the Kingdom of the Two Sicilies, ruled by the Spanish Bourbons; Milan was part of the Hapsburg, Viennese empire, to which the independent Venice had been annexed in the wake of Napoleon's peace treaty with the Viennese at Campoformia in 1797; Rome and the Papal States were ruled by the Pope, whose claims were sustained by various political forces; Parma was an independent duchy; and so on. Lines of communication were scanty, laws differed from one state to the next, and theaters did the best they could.

Each major theater in Italy had a close association with one or more *copisterie*, which copied entire scores, orchestral parts, and *particelle* for individual singers. In Rome, for example, local *copisterie* were run by Leopoldo

Ratti and Gian-Battista Cencetti, who later formed a publishing company together.[24] When an opera was successful, the copyists, who usually had the right to distribute the work (as Rossini pointed out), might prepare several copies of these materials, hoping to earn additional income by renting or selling them to other theaters. If they still had access to the composer's autograph, they might use it as a source; if not, they worked from whatever copy was available. When the Teatro alla Pergola of Florence decided to perform immediately a work that had been an outstanding success in Rome, perhaps even with the same cast, the theater needed to contact Ratti and Cencetti, who would rent or sell them a manuscript and performing materials. Unless, of course, another musician had surreptitiously prepared a copy of the score from the composer's autograph manuscript or from whatever copy was in the theater archive. Strictly speaking, of course, he had no right to do this, but control was lax. And, like a good capitalist, he probably could undersell Ratti and Cencetti, with their *copisterie* costs. Thus, the illegal copy may have found its way to Florence, at a cheaper price. From it, other copies might be drawn, in a constantly expanding network.[25]

Copisterie also frequently prepared extracts from operas, or (by the 1820s) entire operas, in reductions for piano and voice or for piano alone. Although these also served the needs of singers, their most important audience was the growing middle-class public, which could enjoy at home the most popular numbers from works they had applauded in the opera houses. In the first decades of the century there was a large market for manuscript copies of excerpts, but as new techniques of engraving, lithographing, and printing brought the price of each copy down, and as Italian nineteenth-century opera grew ever more popular, it became possible to publish more economically than to copy. Still, it was remarkable how quickly printed editions of excerpts could be published. One popular number from Rossini's *Ermione*, a duet from the first-act finale, hit the streets less than a week after the opera's Neapolitan premiere in 1819, and a second (the famous cavatina for Oreste, "Che sorda al mesto pianto," followed a few days later.[26] Even complete vocal scores, in the second quarter of the century, were made available within a few months.[27]

But these printed editions, especially those of a complete opera, opened new possibilities for clever entrepreneurs, which may have been why Italian publishers resisted printing complete operas—even in vocal score—for such a long time. Indeed, the first editions of most of Rossini's Italian operas were printed north of the Alps, reflecting the European popularity of Italian opera. Italian publishers finally succumbed to the practice only after reductions printed in France, Germany, and Austria began to be imported into Italy.

After all, if you took your vocal score to the theater and made a few observations about instrumental effects, you would have a pretty good idea about the original orchestration. What was to prevent a competent musician from reorchestrating the entire score and selling it to another theater as the original or even as an inexpensive imitation? We can often reconstruct extraordinary cases of fraud or of attempts to make the best of an uncertain situation.

Rossini himself, for example, revised *Tancredi* several times. For a Milanese revival at the end of 1813 he wrote two new arias for the tenor, Argirio. His first-act aria in Milan, "Se ostinata ancor non cedi," replaces the original Venetian "Pensa che sei mia figlia" of February 1813. The pieces, while musically unrelated, are dramaturgically similar (Argirio attempting to convince his daughter, Amenaide, to accept a political marriage to the haughty Orbazzano).[28] Contemporary sources are divided: some have one piece, some the other. The most amusing source, though, is a Florentine manuscript, probably associated with a local performance. It has "Se ostinata ancor non cedi," but the orchestration differs entirely from that known in all other sources; the vocal line is basically the same, but there are many small variants.[29]

How can we explain this peculiar Florentine source for "Se ostinata ancor non cedi"? Here is a possible scenario. Florence, having decided to perform *Tancredi,* obtains a score, whether legitimately or not, and assembles a cast. Rehearsals begin. When it comes time for his first-act aria, Argirio steps forward, but as the pianist begins to play "Pensa che sei mia figlia," the singer's mouth drops open in astonishment. "Excuse me, maestro, what is that?" "Argirio's aria," comes the reply. "But no," says our Argirio, who had just sung the role for the first time in Genoa, "that's not the aria. The aria goes like this." At which point he sings some snatches from "Se ostinata ancor non cedi," explaining that the score used in Genoa came from Milan, where Rossini had directed performances last year. "In any event," he concludes, "that's the aria I know, and that's the aria I intend to sing." And out he storms. Panic in the Florentine theater. After a quick discussion (remember that the production is scheduled to open in a week), Argirio is called back. "Sing the melody," he is told by the *maestro al cembalo,* who does his best to copy it down. "And what do you remember about the orchestration?" After receiving indications about instrumental solos, the *maestro* goes off. In a few hours he returns with an orchestration of "Se ostinata ancor non cedi." "Is that more or less how it goes?" he asks our tenor. "That's it," responds the contented Argirio, and so a new orchestration of "Se ostinata ancor non cedi" appears, which may very well circulate to other theaters (although in this case the version seems never to have left Florence).

But outright thievery was rampant, even in the 1830s, when composers such as Donizetti and Bellini began to make commercial agreements with publishers like Ricordi in Milan for the distribution of their operas. Donizetti's letters are filled with complaints about operas which are supposed to be Ricordi's property, yet have been pirated, and often reorchestrated. To his friend Andrea Monteleone, a musician associated with the Teatro Carolino of Palermo, where Donizetti spent a year as music director in 1826, Donizetti wrote on 12 October 1834:

> I might have truly believed from your long silence that I mattered very little to you, but I was wrong, and it is better for me, because losing friends is very sad, just as it is very sad for me to learn that *L'elisir d'amore* will fall on its face. It is even sadder because I fear that it is the *false* one, for now in Milan, Bellini's music and my own circulates in bastardized form. Indeed, I warn you that if one day *Parisina* should fall into the hands of the Palermo impresario, unless it has been sold to them by Ricordi, try if you can—in my name—by every means to impede the performance, for it is certainly the *false* one. The sellers of this manhandled music are Artaria and Lucca, and their correspondents. Let this serve as a rule for you, because there exists a *false Elisir,* a *false Norma,* a *false Bolena,* and a *false Parisina.* Be a champion of justice and defend the honor of your friends, for as you will understand right away the instrumentation [of these false adaptations] is *arciarabo* [absolutely incomprehensible].[30]

Bellini could become rabid on the same subject. Indeed, when his *La sonnambula,* first performed at the Teatro Carcano of Milan on 6 March 1831, began to circulate in a falsified version, he published an "Avviso musicale" in the Milanese press on 1 December 1831:

> It is appropriate to warn all theater Directors, Impresarios, and music sellers that a Theatrical Correspondent has permitted himself to orchestrate my opera *La sonnambula* from the reduction of it for piano, and to palm it off as that written by me for the Teatro Carcano of Milan at the last carnival. If such falsifications damaged only the financial interests of artists, I would perhaps not be tempted to protest, but they damage their reputation, for they spread imperfect works, monstrous and damaging even for those who acquire them in good faith, especially with the aim of using them in the theater. For this reason I appeal to theater Directors, Impresarios, and music sellers, begging them to consider spurious any score of *Sonnambula* offered them, except for copies signed by me or Signor

Giovanni Ricordi, who has the only original. With this will be safeguarded my honor and their own interests, and the falsifiers will be taught that it is time to respect even here the rights of creators and not to compromise their reputation and dignity.[31]

The warning had little effect. More than a year later, on 17 February 1833, Bellini wrote to his friend Francesco Florimo, librarian of the Naples Conservatory, lamenting another thievery, this time of *Norma* in Naples, which the composer refers to as his own country:

> You tell me that they are working on my *Norma;* and from whom have they gotten the score? I own it myself, and anyone else could only have given it orchestrated by some hack. [...] And should the presidency of our theaters, deaf to your complaints (complaints you may make in my name, allowing him to see, if necessary, even this letter), insist on producing my opera in this way, I believe you have the right to ask the competent authorities to put on the poster: *Norma,* vocal lines by Bellini, orchestrated by somebody else. I would like to be able to boast that in my country this justice will not be denied me.[32]

The negative ramifications of these spurious orchestrations continue to our own day. When Fabio Biondi conducted *Norma* for the Verdi Festival of Parma in March 2001, he chose to perform the original version of the first-act finale of the opera, in which the composer highlighted equally the three protagonists, Norma, Adalgisa, and Pollione—a version printed in the earliest Ricordi vocal score of the opera.[33] But Bellini later modified the passage in his autograph manuscript by crossing out a number of measures and by removing several pages, thus significantly reducing the presence of Adalgisa in the ensemble. Both musicians and scholars have found fault with this modification, which surely reflected the composer's nervousness after the opera was poorly received at its Milanese premiere (Teatro alla Scala, 26 December 1831).[34] Seeking to restore the passage to its original form, Fabio's brother, Fabrizio Biondi, located the relevant measures in manuscript copies of the full score of *Norma* at the Conservatories of Naples and Milan. Despite their present location, however, both manuscripts were prepared in Naples, and it soon became apparent that they are examples of just the kinds of manuscripts Bellini had protested, in which the orchestration of the entire opera (not just the first-act finale) was falsified. Fortunately, Fabrizio and I realized the problem in time to develop a more plausible orchestration of the missing measures for the Parma performances. And, of course, this editorial orchestration was identified as such so that performers could judge for themselves whether it was successful or not, without assuming it was Bellini's own work.

Nor was reorchestration the only fraud perpetrated by unscrupulous copyists. As his first introduction to Parisian musical life, Donizetti was commissioned early in 1834 to write a new opera for the Théâtre Italien the following year. Resident composer in Naples at the time, Donizetti had the libretto of *Marino Faliero* prepared by a local poet, Emanuele Bidera. Before departing for Milan, where his *Gemma di Vergy* was to open the carnival season at La Scala on 26 December 1834, Donizetti had composed most of the Parisian opera. He left Milan for Paris on the last day of 1834. Once there, complications arose. Not only did various problems become evident in Bidera's libretto, but Donizetti also received musical advice from Rossini, éminence grise of the Théâtre Italien during the first half of the 1830s and the person responsible for his commission. Furthermore, Donizetti had his first opportunity to hear music in Paris, not only at the Théâtre Italien, but at native Parisian theaters, the Opéra and the Opéra-Comique. As a result, he made extensive alterations in the new opera. In this revised state *Marino Faliero* was performed with reasonable but not overwhelming success, on 12 March 1835. For Donizetti, that score, and that score alone, was *Marino Faliero*.[35]

Imagine his consternation when he discovered that copies of the opera were circulating with the earlier version, which he considered to have been superseded. The culprit was Gennaro Fabbricatore, a Neapolitan copyist. Another copyist, with free access to Donizetti's scores, had sworn to make only a single copy of *Marino Faliero* as it existed when the composer left Naples. Instead he made two, selling one of those copies to Fabbricatore for one *carlino* per page. From this copy, Fabbricatore soon made the score available to others, and thus illegal copies of the score circulated without even the need for reorchestration. Donizetti knew instantly that fraud was involved, as he told Ricordi in a letter of 20 October 1835: "As fortune would have it, in Paris I composed many new pieces, and added a great many things, and so the altered libretto and the new music testified to their being scoundrels."[36] But the problem would not go away. On 2 November 1836 he wrote to his friend Luigi Spadaro Del Bosch in Messina:

> I hear that in Messina they are doing *Belisario* and *Marino Faliero*. I am almost certain in my belief that both these scores are false, and therefore I beg you to ask the Impresarios if they would have the kindness to send me a piece of each opera, and I, by immediate courier, will respond with a yes or

a no. In any case, try to find out if *Marino* begins with a sung Introduzione in B♭. If the stretta of the finale is in E♭. If the aria of the tenor or the first scene is in *C minor,* if the text of the duet for two basses in the stretta is "Trema o Steno, tremate o superbi," etc.

If all of this is true, it may be the real score, but if not would you please go to the Superintendent to have them suspend the performance, as happened in Palermo.[37]

Ill will, fraud, and thievery: all complicated the problem of transmission.

Even in the absence of dishonesty, even when manuscript copies were made without the intent to deceive, the more popular a work and the longer it remained in the repertory, the more complex and confused its transmission became. Rossini's *L'Italiana in Algeri* had its enormously successful premiere at the Teatro San Benedetto of Venice on 22 May 1813, after which Rossini himself directed revivals in Milan in 1814 and Naples in 1815.[38] He kept his autograph manuscript until the Milanese revival, at the Teatro Re in early April 1814, at which time it became the property of the copyist of that theater, Giovanni Ricordi, whose activities we will be investigating shortly. By the time the score arrived in Ricordi's hands, Rossini had made important changes in the opera. To cite a particularly interesting one, for Milan he modified extensively the original version of the second-act cavatina for Isabella, "Per lui che adoro," the alternatively funny and tender piece in which Isabella prepares her *toilette* in front of a mirror, fully aware that her three suitors, Lindoro, Taddeo, and Mustafà, are looking on from their respective hiding places.

In the Venetian original of "Per lui che adoro," the orchestral introduction features a lovely solo for cello; in the revision, prepared for the Teatro Re and the only version present in Rossini's autograph manuscript, the solo is assigned to a flute. Rossini surely made this change because the small Teatro Re, whose orchestral forces were described as inadequate in a contemporary review, had no appropriate cellist.[39] But of some twenty-five manuscript copies I have personally examined of the opera, only one (in the library of the Parma Conservatory) has the version with flute; every other score contains the version with cello, which existed *before* Ricordi had acquired Rossini's autograph manuscript. In other words, even before April 1814, eleven months after the Venetian premiere, enough scores were already in circulation to guarantee that the opera's early transmission would be independent of the Milanese copyist and publisher. Only at the end of the nineteenth century and in the twentieth did Ricordi effectively control the transmission of

L'Italiana, and during that time the version with cello largely disappeared. I have been told, however, that a recording of the aria by Zara Dolukhanova made in Russia, where Ricordi's scores were less prevalent, still used the original cello.[40] The critical edition of the score, edited by Azio Corghi, makes both versions available, of course, and the first American performance in this century of the version with cello took place in a Metropolitan Opera production of 1984, conducted by James Levine, with Marilyn Horne the unforgettable Isabella. In this case, the manuscript copies provide evidence that the autograph manuscript no longer preserves.

Tracing the transmission of an early-nineteenth-century Italian opera, in short, is not always simple, yet the issues involved are fundamental to the music we have before us as we attempt to perform an opera. *L'Italiana in Algeri,* in fact, provides a useful case study.

THE TRANSMISSION OF *L'ITALIANA IN ALGERI*

Opera houses during the first decades of the nineteenth century based their productions on manuscript copies, from which orchestral parts were drawn. But the copies in circulation were of many different types, and this diversity reveals how fraught with uncertainty was the transmission of an opera, especially one as popular as *L'Italiana in Algeri.* The problem is well exemplified by four different manuscripts of the opera preserved in the library of the Naples Conservatory. They demonstrate how scores still in use during the first three-quarters of the twentieth century acquired their particular characteristics.

Copying the Warts and All

The manuscript copy identified as "Rossini 22–1–59, 60" of the Naples Conservatory was made directly from Rossini's autograph of *L'Italiana in Algeri* (or from another copy equally strict in reproducing its contents). It preserves every mistake of the original, every peculiarity of layout, every wart. Here is an example. Since the opera was produced under enormous time pressure, its libretto was derived from a preexisting one by Angelo Anelli, prepared for the Teatro alla Scala in 1808 (where it was set to music by Luigi Mosca) and revised in 1813 to suit Rossini's requirements.[41] To assist him in meeting his deadline, Rossini employed an anonymous collaborator, who composed Haly's aria "Le femmine d'Italia," perhaps Lindoro's second-act "Ah come il cor di giubilo," and all the *secco* recitative. This collaborator worked mostly from the printed libretto of 1808, using a separate bifolio (or bifolios) of music paper for each individual passage of recitative. These separate bifolios could then be placed in the right order within the complete score, between the musical numbers Rossini was preparing.

Here is the text of the final section of the first lyrical number of Rossini's opera (its "introduction") and the beginning of the ensuing recitative. The text is identical to the libretto prepared by Anelli in 1808. The introduction concludes with a quatrain in *ottonari*, whereas the recitative, as always, is a mixture of *settenari* and *endecasillabi*.

SCENA 1 (conclusion)	SCENE 1 (conclusion)
Tutti: *Più volubil d'una foglia*	More changeable than a leaf
Va il mio/suo cor di voglia in voglia	My/His heart goes from desire to desire
Delle donne calpestando	Trampling over women's
Le lusinghe, e la beltà.	Hopes and beauty.
Mus.: *Ritiratevi tutti. Haly, t'arresta.*	Leave, all of you. Haly, remain.
Zul.: *(Che fiero cor!)*	(What a proud heart!)
Elv.: *(Che dura legge è questa!)*	(What a hard law this is!)

SCENA 2: Mustafà, e Haly (beginning)	SCENE 2: Mustafà and Haly (beginning)
Mus.: *Il mio schiavo Italian farai, che tosto*	Have my Italian slave come right away,
Venga, e m'aspetti qui... Tu sai, che sazio	And let him await me here... You know
Io son di questa moglie,	That I'm tired of this wife,
Che non ne posso più. Scacciarla... è male.	And have had enough. To send her packing... is bad.
Tenerla... è peggio. Ho quindi stabilito	To keep her... is worse. I've therefore decided
Ch'ella pigli costui per suo Marito.	That she should take him as her husband.

Rossini's collaborator failed to notice that scene 1 concludes with two lines of recitative, "Ritiratevi tutti. Haly, t'arresta. / (Che fiero cor!) (Che dura legge è questa!)," before continuing—still in recitative—with scene 2 for Mustafà and Haly. Thus, he set this recitative only from the beginning of scene 2. After the manuscript of the opera was assembled, with Rossini's introduction followed by the copyist's incomplete recitative, someone became aware that the two lines of recitative at the close of scene 1 had inadvertently been omitted. Since Rossini had completed his introduction on the front side of the paper (its recto), the maestro responsible for the recitative entered a setting of the missing lines on the back side of that page (its verso), which had previously been blank. This peculiarity in the structure of Rossini's autograph is altogether without musical importance, but it offers a revealing glimpse of how the (not entirely) autograph manuscript of the opera was put together.

The faithful copyist of "Rossini 22–1–59, 60" repeated precisely this physical organization, an absurdity: every other manuscript source keeps all the measures of recitative together. But throughout the score, "Rossini 22–1–59, 60" similarly preserved every quirk and error of the original. Identifying such copies can be of great importance when Rossini's own manuscript no longer survives. They give us access to a missing autograph through the eyes of a contemporary musician who tried not to exercise personal intelligence but aimed simply to reproduce what was in front of him. In the case of *L'Italiana in Algeri,* however, for which the autograph has survived, a copy of this kind is wholly without interest.

Hackwork

Manuscripts that reveal such a strict attitude toward copying are rare. More typical is the manuscript "Rossini 22–1–57, 58," preserved at the Naples Conservatory library but prepared "in Florence in the music *copisteria* of Francesco Minati da Badja." While this score incorporates essential features of *L'Italiana in Algeri* and makes no fundamental alterations to the sequence of musical numbers or their internal structure, it fails to respect the details of Rossini's notation. Concerned primarily with getting down on paper the pitches, text, and rhythms, most copyists worked quickly. When rhythms proved complex or contradictory, especially in ensembles, copyists would simplify the notation, replacing a double-dotted rhythm by a single-dotted one: it is extremely rare to find a copyist who transforms a simple rhythm into a more complex one. Once a copyist had falsified Rossini's notation, of course, others followed along or introduced further simplifications. Articulation signs (staccatos, accents, slurs) or dynamic signs (dynamic levels, crescendos, diminuendos) suffered a similar fate. Autograph manuscripts are hardly meticulous in their presentation of such signs, but examples entered by the composer are sufficiently extensive to provide necessary information for editors and performers. Manuscript copies, on the other hand, rarely preserve more than 50 percent of the signs of articulation or dynamics present in an autograph. Even those they do preserve are too often misread or misinterpreted.

Early in the nineteenth century, for example, "closed" crescendos, diminuendos, or accents were used extensively in northern Italy. I have seen them in autographs of Simone Mayr and Rossini, but there is every reason to believe they were fairly widespread (example 3.2).[42] That a "closed" diminuendo

EXAMPLE 3.2. "CLOSED" ACCENTS, DIMINUENDOS, AND CRESCENDOS, ALL SIGNS
CHARACTERISTIC OF ROSSINI'S AUTOGRAPH MANUSCRIPTS.

or crescendo is sometimes present in one part while a *sf* (sforzato, or sudden
and intense accent) followed by a diminuendo, or a crescendo leading to a *sf,*
is present in another helps us interpret the signs: a "closed" crescendo indicates an increase in volume, leading to a *sf;* a "closed" diminuendo indicates
a *sf* attack, followed by a diminuendo; a "closed" accent suggests a more intense accent than normal. Copyists, particularly in Rome or Naples, unfamiliar with this notation, inevitably substituted regular crescendos, diminuendos, and accents, abandoning a group of signs highly characteristic of
Rossini's style.

The presence of closed signs in manuscript copies, on the other hand, suggests that these copies are particularly close to the autograph. In a work from
Rossini's youth such as *L'equivoco stravagante,* for which no autograph survives, the one manuscript containing these signs immediately acquires authority. Although this manuscript is preserved in Paris, it comes from Bologna, where the opera was first performed in 1811, and could easily have been
copied from Rossini's original. Since no other surviving manuscript contains
closed signs, the Paris copy could *not* derive from them: no copyist would
have *added* such signs. This is only one of the reasons why the Paris manuscript of *L'equivoco stravagante* turns out to be the best surviving source. In
it, for example, we find many distinctly off-color expressions, forbidden by
the Bolognese authorities and absent in most other sources. Then again, one
could well ask what Rossini was thinking when he set to music a libretto in
which the heroine pretends to be a eunuch in disguise to avoid an unacceptable suitor![43]

Copies of *L'Italiana in Algeri* such as "Rossini 22–1–57, 58," in short, represent an opera's bare outlines. This is the kind of hackwork found in the vast
majority of manuscript copies through which Rossini's operas normally circulated during the nineteenth century.

L'Italiana Transformed *"in Farsa"*

A worse fate faced Rossini's score in Naples. In the manuscript "Rossini
22–1–62" of the Naples Conservatory library, *L'Italiana in Algeri* was "transformed *in farsa,"* i.e., arranged according to Neapolitan practice in a single act
with spoken dialogue replacing the *secco* recitative. This combination of musical numbers and spoken dialogue was well known in the Naples comic the-

ater: Donizetti's one-act *farsa, La romanziera e l'uomo nero,* first performed
at the Teatro del Fondo on 18 June 1831, was a work of just this type. From
printed librettos, we also know that Rossini's *Il barbiere di Siviglia* and *La
Cenerentola* were often performed in Naples with spoken dialogue. Preparing
the *farsa* version of *L'Italiana,* the reviser used a hackwork manuscript, eliminating many musical numbers and all the recitative. What remained was a
series of musical numbers to be linked by spoken dialogue. In one case the
copyist actually specified "Segue Prosa" at the end of a musical number. The
Neapolitan provenance is further confirmed by the substitution for the original "Taddeo" of the typical Neapolitan name "Pompeo," a practice followed
in Naples even when the opera was performed complete—with recitatives—
under Rossini's direction in 1815.[44]

What is most amusing about the manuscript, though, is that bound at its
beginning, in an entirely different hand, is a complete set of *secco* recitatives,
not to the original libretto but clearly to the text that had been spoken in this
one-act *farsa.* Since the dialogue had been heavily cut and manipulated, a
later musician provided a new setting of this modified text, using quite a different musical style from Rossini's original collaborator. In two stages within
"Rossini 22–1–62," then, *L'Italiana in Algeri* was first transformed *in farsa*
with spoken dialogue, in the Neapolitan manner, then transformed into a
one-act *opera buffa* with new *secco* recitative.

While one might complain that this sort of manipulation is disastrous for
Rossini's opera, it reflects well-defined objectives, inherently practical and
specific. Those musical numbers preserved, furthermore, are indeed Rossini's,
and they constitute many of the finest moments in the opera. "Highlights from
L'Italiana in Algeri," "ROSSINI'S GREATEST HITS": a similar urge still motivates
those who produce CDs and those who purchase them.

Transforming *L'Italiana:* The Censor

The most insidious aspects of transmission are those that transform a work
from within, responding to pressures exerted by censors, altering the original
structure or changing the sound to suit the perceived needs of a later generation. They are insidious because they are invisible, assuming an aura of authority to which they have no right. The fourth manuscript of *L'Italiana in
Algeri* in the Neapolitan collection "Rossini 22–1–61" exemplifies all these
problems. Originally prepared in the Roman *copisteria* of Giulio Cesare Martorelli, the score is entitled *Il naufragio felice* [The Fortunate Shipwreck] *ovvero
L'Italiana in Algeri,* as the opera was known in its first Roman performances
during the 1814–15 season.[45] In this form the manuscript represented the

hackwork standard among contemporary copies. But it goes a step further, incorporating alterations and accretions that reflect censorship, the pretensions of singers, and shifts in musical taste.

We are still today performing operas with their librettos modified by nineteenth-century censors, even though in many cases we could easily recapture the original text. Since censored versions of *L'Italiana in Algeri* did not circulate widely, the opera avoided that fate, but more than one manuscript was affected. The Martorelli copy reflects practices in Rome, the city in which theatrical censors brought the most exasperating criteria to bear. Anything related to "la patria" had to be suppressed, and so Isabella's famous *rondò*, encouraging the Italian slaves to flight, became "Pensa allo scampo" (Think of escape) instead of the original "Pensa alla patria" (Think of your country). Another Roman substitution, attested to in a libretto from 1819, was "Pensa alla sposa" (Think of your wife).[46] But in Rome the word "patria," in whatever context, was regularly replaced by "dover" (duty) or "affetto" (feelings).[47]

The effect on Italian opera of political and religious censorship throughout the first half of the nineteenth century was often devastating. The refusal of Neapolitan censors to permit the staging of Donizetti's *Poliuto*, in which the life of a saint became material for a melodrama, led to the composer's departure from Naples (and contributed to the depression that led the tenor scheduled to create the title role, Adolphe Nourrit, to commit suicide by throwing himself from the window of his Neapolitan apartment).[48] In order to have *I puritani* produced in Naples, Bellini felt obliged to omit its most successful single number, the patriotic duet "Suoni la tromba."[49] Verdi's experiences with *Stiffelio*, *Rigoletto*, and *Un ballo in maschera* (written, respectively, for Trieste, Venice, and—originally—Naples) are only the better-known cases of a long-smoldering problem.

Despite its buoyant exterior, *L'Italiana in Algeri* was more problematic to the censors than many other Rossini operas. One manuscript of the period shows a fascinating alteration for political motives. Announcing themselves ready to fight for freedom, the chorus of Italian slaves sings:[50]

Pronti abbiamo e ferri, e mani	Our weapons and hands are ready
Per fuggir con voi di qua,	To fly with you from here,
Quanto vaglian gl'Italiani	What Italians are worth
Al cimento si vedrà.	You'll see in the moment of trial.

These lines, which were already present in the 1808 libretto for Luigi Mosca, might have been considered dangerous in the best of circumstances. Rossini made them much worse by accompanying the last two verses with a melody

EXAMPLE 3.3. GIOACHINO ROSSINI, *L'ITALIANA IN ALGERI*, CORO,
RECITATIVO E RONDÒ ISABELLA (N. 15), MM. 26–27, ORCHESTRAL MELODY,
AND A PHRASE FROM *LA MARSEILLAISE*.

"Quanto vaglian gl'Italiani"

La Marseillaise

prominently featured in the orchestra that is an unmistakable reference to the French Revolutionary anthem, *La Marseillaise* (example 3.3). The irony was pungent: by 1813 the French had overstayed their welcome in Italy and hardly constituted a model of patriotic virtues. Nonetheless, two early manuscripts of *L'Italiana,* prepared in Venice and its surrounding region, recast the music of this chorus to avoid this potentially subversive quotation.[51]

If politics was taboo, so was sex, especially in Papal Rome. Describing how she can have her way with any man ("So a domar gli uomini come si fa"), Isabella in the original version of *L'Italiana in Algeri* concludes with these *quinari* verses:

Tutti la chiedono,	All men ask for it,
Tutti la bramano	All men yearn for it
Da vaga femmina	From a beautiful woman
Felicità.	Happiness.

But not even this suggestive snicker (which in Marilyn Horne's interpretation could become pretty raunchy) was acceptable to Roman censors in 1819, who transformed the verses into:

Per noi sospirano,	They sigh for us,
Per noi delirano,	They are mad for us,
Sol da noi sperano	From us alone they hope for
Felicità.	Happiness.

Much more moral.

The *locus classicus* of censorial morality, of course, is *Rigoletto,* where censors had much to preoccupy them, as Verdi knew.[52] At one time he and Piave planned to incorporate the scene in Hugo's play (itself banned from the Parisian stage after a single performance on 22 November 1832) in which the abducted Blanche (Gilda) seeks protection from the courtiers by locking herself in a room, which turns out to be the King's bedchamber. The third act concludes with the King's producing the key, opening the door, and disappearing within. That was hardly going to pass muster in Italy any more than in France, and Verdi himself found it in questionable taste. As he wrote in a ribald letter of 25 November 1850:

> I carefully examined the second act, and I think that for us too it would be better to find a [different] place for an aria for Francesco [King François I / the Duke of Mantua]: think about it, and I'll do the same, and write to me about it. We ought to find something more chaste and get rid of that much too obvious *fotisterio* [brothel]. And remove the *chiave* [key] which suggests the idea *chiavare* [to fuck] etc. etc. Oh Heavens! they are simple things, natural, but the *patriarca* [patriarch or religious official] can't take delight in this idea any more!![53]

This is a problem that Piave and Verdi never did fully resolve, and if *Rigoletto* has a weakness, it lies in the ambivalent feelings of the Duke for Gilda, which the Duke's second-act aria only succeeds in sentimentalizing.

When the husband of the singer Teresa De Giuli Borsi wrote to Verdi in 1852 requesting an additional aria for Gilda, the composer responded by insisting that his "miserable talent" had done its best. Where, in any case, could the piece be added? "One place there would be, but Heaven help us! We would be whipped. We would have to show Gilda with the Duke in his bedchamber!! You understand? In any case it would be a duet. Magnificent duet!! But the priests, the monks, and the hypocrites would cry scandal."[54] But Verdi did not believe other elements of his opera required modification. He could not imagine why censors would care if the body of Gilda was deposited in a sack. It might not work on stage, of course, but he alone should be the judge of that, not the censors.

To one little change, however, Verdi appears to have assented. When the Duke enters the inn of Sparafucile in the last act, he says (in all secondary sources of the opera, manuscripts and printed editions alike):

Duca: *Due cose e tosto...* (a Sparafucile)		Two things and right away...
		(*To Sparafucile*)
Spa.:	*Quali?*	What?
Duca: *Una stanza e del vino...*		A room and some wine...

These verses are different from what Verdi had written both in his sketch and in his autograph:

Duca:	*Due cose e tosto...* (a Sparafucile)		Two things and right away...
			(*To Sparafucile*)
Spa.:		*Quali?*	What?
Duca:	*Tua sorella e del vino...*		Your sister and some wine...

We know, of course, that the Duke has been enticed to the inn by Maddalena, so that these lines offer no new information. Yet the bald statement, taken directly from Hugo, was too much for the Venetian censors. In Verdi's autograph "tua sorella" is dutifully crossed out and "una stanza" added, not in Verdi's hand. So it had been performed ever since, even when the Duke all but raped the girl on stage, until the critical edition made the original text available in the early 1980s.[55]

Transforming *L'Italiana:* Structural Changes

During the first half of the nineteenth century composers were often asked to direct one of their older operas for a new city, at a new theater, in a new production, and with new singers. In the process a composer sometimes modified his score. To make sense of nineteenth-century sources and to make intelligent decisions for modern performances, one must understand these alterations and the motives behind them. Sometimes composers felt that sections of their original were weak, musically or dramaturgically; occasionally there were sections that had been prepared by other musicians. Given the opportunity to intervene, composers did so.[56] Thus, for a revival of *L'Italiana in Algeri* at the Teatro Re of Milan in the spring of 1814, Rossini replaced a solo for Lindoro in the second act ("Ah come il cor di giubilo"), probably prepared by an associate, with an aria of his own.

Other revisions favored particular singers, who, because of their vocal range or other characteristics of their voices, could not negotiate the original versions. More insidious vanities were not infrequent: singers felt their parts were too small or that their solos did not adequately display their gifts. In a world where the prima donna was paid considerably more than the composer (a world that has changed little today), operas were at the mercy of such caprice. To suit the talents of Maria Marcolini, an Isabella who may have been uncomfortable with the sexual innuendos of "Cruda sorte" discussed above, Rossini prepared the more heroic "Cimentando i venti e l'onde" for a performance in Vicenza later in 1813.

Important revisions were frequently tied to performances in a different cultural environment. In Restoration Naples, Isabella's "Pensa alla patria" was impossible, and Rossini replaced it with an aria that avoids all mention of patriotism, "Sullo stil de' viaggiatori." Adaptations often took place when an Italian opera was performed in France or Vienna; similar changes were made when a French opera was performed in Italy. Audiences, even in major European capitals, were notoriously provincial, and a composer was expected to bend his talents to local custom. Coming to grips with multiple versions of an opera, all prepared by its original composer, is one of the most difficult aspects of performing Italian opera.[57]

None of these problems disappeared when the composer himself was absent: weaknesses in the score were equally palpable; singers did not become more timid in their demands or more flexible in their throats; and if a theater felt that alterations in a score were necessary for its local audience, it had no compunction about intervening. Unauthorized rearrangements of opera were commonplace in the nineteenth century, although some theaters began to develop a sense of responsibility, identifying in printed librettos those compositions added to a score. There are many documents, letters, and reviews that testify to a growing appreciation of the integrity of a composer's work, but this idea made its way slowly during the first half of the century.

The Martorelli manuscript of *L'Italiana in Algeri*, "Rossini 22–1–61," has only a small problem of this kind. In its main body one piece from the Venice 1813 score is missing, Haly's aria, "Le femmine d'Italia." While a lovely piece, it is not by Rossini: this is one of the compositions he assigned to an associate. Was it originally missing from the Martorelli manuscript and did Haly object to a part that had no solo? Or was it originally present and did Haly find "Le femmine d'Italia" not right for his voice? In any case, a new aria was prepared, "Ad amare un vago oggetto," and it was included as an appendix to the manuscript. While there is no reason to assume the music is by Rossini, in at least one series of performances it became part of his score. Its significance in the textual history of *L'Italiana in Algeri*, however, was marginal.

Transforming *L'Italiana:* The Orchestration

The worst transformations visited upon *L'Italiana in Algeri*, however, infected the very texture of the score, and the Martorelli manuscript, "Rossini 22–1–61," gives eloquent witness to the process by which the disease took root. Rossini's use of the orchestra was both highly personal and characteristic of his time, a period of significant changes in orchestral technique.[58] In his first operas, even those for major opera houses, Rossini made no use of trombones. In earlier Italian opera these instruments were generally reserved for special effects: oracles, scenes of hell and damnation, stone guests. Only gradually during the 1810s did their use become widespread in Italian opera, particularly in *opera seria*. Rossini employed a single trombone in *Il Turco in Italia* (Milan, La Scala, 14 August 1814), but only in Naples did he introduce three trombones, which soon became the norm. Occasionally he added a fourth low brass instrument, the "serpentone," more akin to the Verdian "cimbasso" than to the modern tuba, which is *not* the sound Rossini (or Verdi) envisioned.[59] For no work did he ever employ more than two bassoons. And he had a particular inclination for using the piccolo in soloistic contexts and in special orchestral combinations. The overture to *L'Italiana in Algeri,* where a theme is played by bassoon and piccolo at a distance of three octaves, is a lovely example (see mm. 184–192).

By midcentury, feelings about orchestration were quite different. Every opera employed three trombones and cimbasso (the standard scoring in Verdi). No one would have dreamed of writing a serious opera with only two horns, as in the orchestration of Rossini's *Otello* (except for its sinfonia). Four bassoons were sometimes available (Meyerbeer had employed two bassoons and a contrabassoon in his Italian opera of 1824, *Il crociato in Egitto*.)[60] Piccolos were no longer used soloistically. As a result, the few Rossini operas regularly performed during the second half of the century were heavily revised by musicians of the time anxious to bring them into line with orchestral values of that period. These late revisions were among the very few elements of performing practice transmitted through printed scores.

In the Martorelli manuscript, Rossini's original orchestration is heavily edited by later hands: three trombones are supplied for most ensembles; to compositions without trumpets, two trumpet parts are added; passages written for piccolo are assigned to flute; additional flute and bassoon lines are invented. These modifications were at first made directly on the original score or provided as separate fascicles, so that one could see where Rossini's notation ended and where the reviser's work began. When the modifications became too numerous, however, entire numbers or sections were copied anew with the revised orchestration. For anyone picking up the newly prepared score, then, these passages *were* Rossini's opera, and there was no way to differentiate between what he had written and what was imposed on his score more than fifty years later.

A score of *L'Italiana in Algeri* manipulated in a similar way was to be the basis of the rental score and parts prepared by Ricordi late in the nineteenth century and provided to opera houses until about 1973, when Azio Corghi's critical edition of the opera, later published by the Fondazione Rossini, finally restored the opera to its correct orchestral format. The delicacy, lightness, and precision of Rossini's orchestration was sacrificed to a late nineteenth-century vision of orchestral sonority and was then sanctified by ignorant twentieth-century musicians as belonging to the "tradition," a "tradition" invented by musicians with no sense of Rossini's orchestration and totally extraneous to the opera that delighted all Europe during Rossini's lifetime. A similar fate greeted *La Cenerentola,* where the trombones, instrumental doublings, and thumping bass drum and cymbals that pepper the score in many twentieth-century performances are totally inauthentic. But some modern opera houses, concerned about being charged rental fees to use performing materials for the new editions, continue to opt for these deficient scores, as we saw in chapter 1, thereby compelling themselves to hire extra orchestral musicians to play instrumental parts that Rossini never wrote and that denature his orchestration.

ENTER GIOVANNI RICORDI

Rossini's operas suffered much worse from this system of transmission, leading—as it invariably did—to freewheeling and unprincipled interventions, than did those of Bellini and Donizetti; their operas in turn suffered worse than those of Verdi. The key figure in this cultural transformation was a music copyist turned publisher, Giovanni Ricordi, a genius and positive force in the history of Italian opera, despite occasional misdeeds. The company he founded, still Italy's largest music publisher and one of the most significant in the world, although now linked to the multinational BMG, supported and fostered much of the development of Italian opera in the nineteenth century and into our own time. Giovanni Ricordi and his sons and their sons were friends and associates of Rossini, Bellini, Donizetti, Verdi, and Puccini, creating a vast publishing empire. Their approach blended commercial acuity with a recognition of the rights—artistic and pecuniary—that should accompany a composer's creative work.[61]

The history of copyright legislation, particularly international copyright, is complex. The early nineteenth century was a period of confused and contradictory laws. Some countries, such as England and France, had strict legislation, but it applied only to works first published within their borders. In the geographical reality and political fiction that was Italy, it was more difficult to rationalize the system.[62] Nor should we imagine that effective copyright legislation solves all problems. It is easy to favor laws that guarantee artists the right to appropriate financial recompense for their labor and a way to maintain the integrity of their work. Yet copyright has its insidious side. When Stravinsky decided to reorchestrate *Petrushka* in the 1940s, he was seeking in part "to safeguard his copyright position."[63] Whether there were always artistic gains in this reorchestration is a matter for debate: the original work has a coherence perhaps compromised in the stylistically more eclectic revision.

But we have already considered the alternative. The failures of the system of distribution and the inadequacy of protection given to composers in early nineteenth-century Italy were evident, and Giovanni Ricordi shrewdly turned these problems to his advantage. In a series of contracts Ricordi signed with Milanese theaters one can follow the birth of an idea, an inspiration. He parlayed a *copisteria* into an archive, an archive into a publishing house, a publishing house into a quasi monopoly on the theatrical production of Italian composers.[64]

There are strokes of fortune that come only to those prepared to recognize them. The Teatro alla Scala had an archive in which were deposited scores prepared for the theater (autograph manuscripts or manuscript copies) and derivative materials. As the copyist attached to the theater, Ricordi was responsible for preparing parts for performances and providing complete manuscripts where needed. Although his position allowed him the right to profit from scores commissioned by the theater, precise limits to his activities were defined. Gradually he expanded those limits. At first he could make manuscript copies of extracts alone (arias, duets, but not concerted numbers— ensembles, introductions, and finales), which he could sell to dilettantes who sought to play and sing the most successful numbers from the latest opera in the privacy of their homes. The orchestral parts and manuscripts he was asked to produce, on the other hand, were jealously guarded by the theater. Then Ricordi found a quicker, more satisfactory means of providing copies of *morceaux favoris:* to engrave the music on copper plates and print multiple copies. Here too his rights were limited: he could print single numbers but not complete scores, for the prohibition against concerted numbers remained in force. By withholding these pieces, after all, the theater sought to maintain control over subsequent performances of the work, and to make it more difficult for an unscrupulous musician to reorchestrate an opera from a vocal score and sell it to theaters elsewhere on the peninsula.

No such restrictions prevented French or German publishers from making complete vocal scores of favorite operas, however, and Ricordi was painfully aware that beautiful editions began crossing the Alps in the late 1810s and early 1820s. No copyright problems existed, since the works had been first performed in Italy and hence were unprotected under French and German law. Publishers unmercifully pirated each other's work. Shortly after the premiere of Rossini's *La donna del lago,* for example, Ricordi published a few extracts. These made their way to Leipzig, where the German publisher Breitkopf & Härtel found them so attractive that the firm decided to bring out a complete score of the opera. For this purpose they used all available Ricordi extracts *and* a complete manuscript copy. They simply followed the Ricordi piano reductions for numbers the Milanese publisher had issued as extracts; for the other numbers and recitatives not previously published by Ricordi they had new reductions made. In this way Breitkopf & Härtel cobbled together one of the earliest editions of *La donna del lago.* Ricordi gained a modest revenge several years later. Finally relieved of contractual impediments to publishing complete operas, the company not only made use of the new Breitkopf reductions for its own complete edition but even borrowed ornamental designs that had first appeared on the title page of the Breitkopf score.[65]

We do not know just how Giovanni Ricordi succeeded in wringing evergreater concessions from the Milanese theaters. His *copisteria* was undoubtedly efficient, of course, and theaters turned to him increasingly to receive the best possible materials. At a certain point, however, he stopped being an employee of the theaters and became a private entrepreneur, from whom theaters rented materials. Most extraordinarily, the Teatro alla Scala appears to have been so pleased with this arrangement that they ceded to Ricordi the entire archive of operatic manuscripts, autographs, copies, and performing materials, related to works that had been presented at or commissioned by the theater. For a while Ricordi needed to make a new contract for each new opera performed at La Scala, but soon the passage of rights to Ricordi became automatic. By the mid 1820s, he controlled a vast archive and wielded immense power.

The key to Ricordi's fortune was its insistence on renting full orchestral scores and instrumental and vocal materials to theaters for performance, rather than publishing these full scores. In Italy, after all, with no central authority and only regional laws, nothing could stop local theaters from making their own parts and proceeding without a thought for the composer or his publisher. Indeed, among Italian publishers only Leopoldo Ratti and Giovanni Battista Cencetti in Rome behaved differently: during the 1820s and 1830s they issued full scores of eight Rossini operas. Though typographically attractive (and therefore much in demand by collectors today), the Ratti and Cencetti publications resemble hackwork manuscripts, with articulation poorly marked, notes and rhythms inaccurate. In no case do they derive from a Rossini autograph: the publishers worked from faulty secondary sources.

Ricordi, on the other hand, knew that this route would not offer him financial or artistic success. To a growing number of composers he stressed the advantages of his not only publishing vocal scores of their operas but also representing their interests in dealing with theaters. He would assure them proper compensation for their artistic labors both when they wrote an opera (through fees from the opera house and the sale of proprietary rights to Ricordi) and for a certain period of time *after* the first performances (through royalties on sales of vocal scores and a percentage of fees paid by opera houses to perform the work). The interests of the composer and the publisher, in short, appeared to be the same. They were, indeed, the same in principle, but different elements of the relationship had a different relative importance for the two parties: that was the zone in which serious problems were eventually to emerge.

In the meanwhile, the system was gradually put into place, and Ricordi brought into his orbit Bellini, Donizetti, Pacini, Mercadante, Verdi, and a host of lesser-known composers. These composers still sometimes made agreements with opera houses that gave the commissioning theaters complete possession and all rights to their new scores, including the right to control and profit from all future performances. More and more Italian composers, however, accepted smaller payments from the commissioning theaters in order to reserve for themselves all subsequent rights to the commercial exploitation of their own music. These, in turn, they ceded to Ricordi along with the original autograph manuscripts of the works; Ricordi, then, would represent them in all further commercial dealings. This was a crucial element of Ricordi's success, since these autograph manuscripts guaranteed that the editor had access to a reliable source for each opera he acquired. Ricordi thus accumulated an enormous collection of autograph manuscripts, including almost every opera by Verdi and Puccini, and an impressive array of scores by earlier composers. Even when composers sold their rights to a theater, the impresarios in turn frequently sold them to Ricordi, either directly or through the mediation of a local *copisteria*. La Fenice, for example, wanted to purchase all rights to *Rigoletto*, but Verdi—always a shrewd negotiator—asked an exorbitant price. A compromise was achieved: Verdi retained the rights (which he immediately ceded to Ricordi), but in recognition of La Fenice's special status as commissioning theater, they were permitted to have their *copisteria* prepare a manuscript copy to keep in the theater archives. The copy could not be made available to any other theater, but could be used as the basis for future performances at La Fenice, without additional payment. As a result of this arrangement, which proved satisfactory to Verdi, La Fenice, and Ricordi, *Rigoletto* joined the Ricordi stable.[66]

CASA RICORDI, TRANSMISSION,
AND PERFORMING TRADITIONS

Ricordi's rental service originally consisted only of manuscript full scores and parts, prepared in his *copisteria*. By midcentury he realized the financial advantages of printing string and choral parts, for which multiple copies were needed, thereby guaranteeing uniformity. Thus, when an opera was likely to be successful, Ricordi quickly printed string and choral parts; for the winds, brass, and percussion, where only a single part was required, he continued at first to provide manuscripts. That was the fate of *Ernani, Macbeth,* and *Luisa Miller.* Only when Verdi's operas began to gain rapid and widespread distribution in the 1850s did Ricordi begin to print all the orchestral parts for *Rigoletto, Il trovatore,* and *La traviata.*[67] During the 1880s and 1890s the company finally printed wind, brass, and percussion parts for some earlier operas that still held the stage. Clearly we need to think differently about parts prepared during a period in which the composer was actively involved in productions (even though he had little role in the editorial process), and wind parts prepared later when the composer took no interest in the process and was not involved in productions in which the parts were used.

Once he acquired rights to a work, Ricordi made it his business to create a market for that work. From the 1830s, he published vocal scores of operas that had some hope of success, using them to generate public interest and to serve singers. How seriously did composers take these publications? It is difficult to say. Preparing a vocal score, with a reduction of the orchestral fabric for piano, was considered a mechanical job, often assigned to students or young composers. It is one of music history's most delicious ironies that the vocal score of Donizetti's *La Favorite* was prepared by a young German musician of apparently limited promise, who was trying desperately to gain entrée into Parisian musical circles during the 1840s, one Richard Wagner.

Vocal scores of some early Verdi operas were made by his student Emanuele Muzio, but Verdi did not supervise the work closely. To Antonio Barezzi, the father of Verdi's first wife and the man most responsible for providing Verdi the opportunity to pursue musical studies in Milan during the 1830s, Muzio reported that Ricordi was angry with him because there were errors in the vocal score of *Macbeth,* and "it was my responsibility, having done the reduction, to assist with the printing." No one said that Verdi bore any responsibility. When Muzio prepared a reduction for four hands, he managed to get Verdi to play through the first act with him, and he told Barezzi that "it seemed to have the effect of an orchestra."[68] Exceptionally Verdi might become involved, as with the sinfonia to *Alzira*. Prevailed upon by the Neapolitan impresario to add a sinfonia to an opera that originally lacked one, Verdi himself prepared the piano reduction. Engravers' marks on his autograph, preserved in the Accademia Filarmonica of Bologna, demonstrate that this manuscript was used by Ricordi to produce the edition of the sinfonia in the vocal score of *Alzira*.[69] But such occasions were rare.

After an opera was published, however, Verdi was quick to complain if the score came out badly or if he noticed errors. In 1855, in a fit of anger (and as a bargaining point in negotiations about fees), Verdi wrote angrily to the company in words that have long echoed to its embarassment, "I complain bitterly of the editions of my last operas, made with such little care, and filled with an infinite number of errors."[70] Of course, Verdi's anger might have been better directed at himself: for a composer to pay such scant attention to the publication of his music encouraged the proliferation of errors. The autograph manuscripts, while relatively clear, are not always unequivocal. In later years, freed from the pressures of the "galleys," as he called the life of an iterant composer,[71] he paid closer attention to publications. For the *Messa da Requiem* there exist in New York's Pierpont Morgan Library a few proof sheets from the first edition of the vocal score, with corrections by Verdi. They demonstrate that the composer cared about the score; they also demonstrate that he was a lousy proofreader, as Verdi himself was fully aware.[72]

It would be as inaccurate to suggest that composers had no involvement in these publications as to pretend that they examined them closely. Donizetti's correspondence is filled with fascinating details. In 1833, for example, he sent Ricordi the vocal score of *Il furioso all'isola di Santo Domingo*, "ready to be copied and printed."[73] A copyist had laid out the vocal lines, and Donizetti himself probably supplied the piano accompaniment (the terms of the letter are ambiguous, but this interpretation seems most likely). This transaction turned out badly, since the impresario of the theater and other publishers became embroiled in complex negotiations. Other cases were clearer. On 1 August 1833, Donizetti sent Ricordi corrections for *Parisina*, one passage of which "seemed like a church cadence" and needed to be replaced.[74] In 1839, from Paris, he reassured Ricordi concerning the latter's rights to *Roberto Devereux*:

> I sold my opera *Roberto Devereux* to Barbaja [the Neapolitan impresario], ceding to him all proprietary rights imaginable, and I also know for certain that Barbaja ceded and sold those same rights to Gennaro Fabbricatore, director of the *copisteria*. If you purchased my score of *Roberto*

Devereux from him, you are the legitimate owner, through the legitimate transmission of rights from me to Barbaja, from the latter to Fabbricatore, and from Fabbricatore to you. I can't see where any doubt might enter.[75]

But Donizetti's relations with Ricordi were not always happy. In 1839 and 1840 there were bitter disagreements as to whether Donizetti had ceded Ricordi complete rights to certain operas or only the right to publish a vocal score; and for a few years Donizetti, like Verdi in the late 1840s, transferred his allegiance to a rival Milanese publisher, Francesco Lucca. To Lucca, Donizetti sold at least some rights to his opera *Adelia,* for which he himself prepared the piano reduction. On 7 March 1841 he wrote to Lucca, "I hope that you have already received *Adelia,* reduced by myself. Please ask our friend Mandanici to verify if there are errors, either by the copyists in the vocal lines or by me in the piano reduction."[76] He listed corrections that needed to be made in the score, but said nothing about further controls. Instead: "Keep a close watch so that the edition is really correct." Donizetti could not have been very pleased with Lucca's work, because by 1842 he was again doing business in Italy primarily with Ricordi.

By midcentury, then, Ricordi's business consisted principally of renting orchestral materials (some printed, some manuscript) and full scores (normally in manuscript), and selling vocal scores, whose piano part was sometimes arranged by the composer, more often by others. Once these materials entered Ricordi's control, composers never reviewed them systematically. When an opera house wanted to perform a work, they made arrangements through Ricordi, who would demand a fee, a percentage of which was shared with the composer. Here are the figures for Verdi's *Rigoletto.* He sold the opera and all proprietary rights to Ricordi for 14,000 francs (700 napoleons), to be paid in precise installments. Ricordi also contracted to pay the composer 30 percent of income from rental agreements and 40 percent from sales (of the vocal scores, extracts, etc.) for ten years, after which all further income reverted to the publisher. In the *Copialettere* Verdi wrote out the terms of the contract and listed the dates on which he received payments. After the 700 napoleons were received, he crossed out the page and wrote "Paid." On a separate page he marked down the sums received on sales and rentals, listing each performance over the first ten years of the opera's life, together with the income received.[77] Verdi was reasonably content with the system, as was Ricordi. Indeed, Verdi was quick to remind Ricordi, whenever their negotiations for a new work grew heated, that his operas were largely responsible for Ricordi's financial success.

With Ricordi in control of most of the process, distribution became centralized; with the formation of the Italian nation, uniform copyright laws could be better enforced, although some thievery continued. But other problems were unchanged. Copies of the full score and printed or orchestral parts were prepared quickly. They had to be, since prompt fulfillment of business contracts depended on it. When gross errors existed in the model from which this material was prepared, Ricordi's copyists made marks in the margin. Sometimes corrections were introduced by the composer, but most of the time copyists did their best to interpret the notation, glossing over lacunae or ambiguous signs. In theory, a manuscript score and parts would go off to a theater and come back to Ricordi unchanged; in practice, changes were regularly introduced, often by well-intentioned musicians of a later generation unable to understand or interpret properly what they had in front of them. Some changes were incorporated into later scores and parts, though not into the autograph manuscripts (which could be used for archival reference).

It soon became impossible to tell where a composer's notation ended and a copyist's or an orchestral musician's began. Time pressures rarely allowed consultation of the autograph manuscript, for there were always new operas to process. Since full scores were sent around in manuscript, differences from one to another easily went unnoticed or uncorrected. Verdi's fury at the state of the manuscript of *La forza del destino* he received in Madrid in 1863 is clear from the epigraph to this chapter, and in that case there was no intention whatsoever to falsify the original.[78] While it was rare for large-scale alterations to be introduced into Verdi operas, those of Rossini, Bellini, and Donizetti, victims of an earlier system of distribution, suffered innumerable distortions. If a conductor in 1860 wanted an extra trombone, it was added, and its origin was soon masked. Donizetti and Bellini were dead, and Rossini had been out of the fray for thirty years. By the end of the century, materials rented by Ricordi were frequently far removed from the composer's original. Indeed, for *L'Italiana in Algeri* and *La Cenerentola*, as we have seen, Ricordi rented exclusively materials that had largely been reorchestrated.

There was no malicious intent to falsify, but the entire system encouraged a laissez-faire attitude. Contrast the situation in Germany or France, where composers controlled printed editions of their music, taking a direct interest and correcting proofs. Since most Ricordi materials were transitory manuscripts, copied, sent around, then destroyed, the composer could hardly control them. With few exceptions, Ricordi published no full orchestral scores of the operas of Rossini, Bellini, Donizetti, or Verdi until the 1880s, when the orchestral score of Verdi's *Otello*, composed in 1886–87, was engraved. That publication marked the beginning of the modern era in the transmission of Italian opera.

Before the end of the century, Ricordi prepared printed orchestral scores of all the operas by these four composers that still held the stage. Never intended for sale, these rental scores replaced the manuscript copies Ricordi had previously made available to theaters. Not only did the firm prepare the printed scores in a very short time, but it often had no autograph manuscripts available, especially for works by Rossini, Bellini, and Donizetti. Instead, it adopted whatever score was at hand. Even when the company possessed an autograph, such as Rossini's *L'Italiana in Algeri,* it might prefer a version modified for late nineteenth-century taste. Most of the composers were long dead; Verdi had no role in this work (with the exception of the orchestral scores of *Otello* and *Falstaff,* where the nature of his participation remains to be fully understood). Only at the beginning of the twentieth century did Ricordi begin to sell printed orchestral scores of the most famous Verdi operas, of *Il barbiere di Siviglia,* of *Lucia di Lammermoor.* By that time, *all* the composers were dead, some for over fifty years, and contemporary taste had shifted fundamentally.

To speak of these printed editions—these scores prepared to satisfy proximate commercial needs at the end of the nineteenth century or during the first decades of the twentieth—as if they represented a continuous "performing tradition" is absurd. Yet these are the scores that were used in opera houses throughout the world until critical editions began to be prepared during the late 1960s. Apologists for the status quo, who claim that Italian opera should be performed according to "performing traditions" embodied in these scores, fail to understand that they were prepared at Casa Ricordi by functionaries who gave no thought to performing traditions. It is equally misguided to praise the obsession for accuracy in a Toscanini or a Muti who is using these scores. Accuracy to what? Certainly both conductors could and did ask Ricordi to verify ambiguous points in the editions they employed, since it was widely believed that the Ricordi scores accurately preserved in print the music of Rossini, Bellini, Donizetti, and Verdi. But when Vittorio Gui instigated a comparison of the score Ricordi had published as *Il barbiere di Siviglia* with Rossini's autograph manuscript, he decided to prepare his own performing materials, which he used in performances in 1942 at the Maggio Musicale Fiorentino and throughout the remainder of his career as a conductor.[79]

This discussion of the transmission of Italian opera has dealt with the actual musical materials used in theaters and printed by editors, especially Ricordi, not with performing traditions, which I described above as "changes introduced into the vocal line by singers, added cadenzas and high notes, cuts and interpolations, modifications in instrumentation made by contemporaries, etc." About performing traditions and their validity there are legitimately differing viewpoints, to be considered in the second half of this book.[80] About musical materials used in theaters around the world since the early twentieth century, long believed (and still believed by some) to reflect accurately the written form of a composer's intentions and to embody a continuous performance tradition, there can be no equivocation: although prepared by relatively competent musicians of the late nineteenth and early twentieth centuries, these scores do not reflect and never were the product of careful editorial work, nor do they embody performing traditions in any serious manner. The aim of present-day critical editions is to replace them at the earliest possible moment. Yet, like many worthwhile goals, it is simpler to formulate than to achieve. A consideration of events of the past forty years can help us understand why this should be the case.

4

SCANDAL AND SCHOLARSHIP

27,000 ERRORS

In July 1958, *La Scala*, an Italian periodical devoted to news of Italian opera and musical life, published a polemical article by a young Australian musician, Denis Vaughan.[1] Having become an assistant conductor to Sir Thomas Beecham four years earlier, Vaughan had grown fascinated by the asymmetries of phrasing, the subtle gradations of color and dynamics, the nonuniform use of staccato articulation that he felt characterized Beecham's interpretations and gave the music that passed under his baton an inner life of great power and variety. Largely ignorant of the social history of Italian opera and its implications for the editorial processes through which nineteenth-century works were distributed in print, Vaughan was astonished to discover that the autograph manuscripts of certain works by Verdi and Puccini were significantly different from printed editions in circulation during the 1950s. Whereas printed editions offered relatively homogenous dynamics, articulation, and phrasing, the autograph manuscripts—read literally—showed marked asymmetries in phrasing, diverse gradations of dynamics, a selective use of accents, and so on.

For an admirer of Beecham's art, it seemed nothing short of a revelation. Convinced that his discoveries would prompt a reinterpretation of the art of these composers, Vaughan devoted his article to the *Messa da Requiem* and *Falstaff,* both of whose autograph manuscripts were available in excellent facsimiles. In his introduction Vaughan declared war on the Verdi interpretive tradition and also on Verdi's editors at Casa Ricordi:

> The purpose of this study, rigorously critical, conducted on some original autograph manuscripts of Verdi and on recent printed editions of these scores, is to underline the great importance of the musical signs written by Verdi himself, and therefore clearly felt and wanted by him, for all

that concerns melody, harmony, tempos, dynamics, phrasing, accents, and articulation. Signs that, although perfectly evident in the original scores, strangely have not been reproduced in the printed editions of the operas in question.

I give below some examples which will serve to demonstrate the enormous value that a critical edition of the works of Verdi might have, by following and reproducing with scrupulous observance the indications, quite precise, left by him. I need only point out that in the *Messa da Requiem* alone one can recognize as many as some 8,000 discrepancies between the original and the print, while in *Falstaff* these discrepancies mount up to 27,000.

Twenty-seven thousand discrepancies! Vaughan's statements no sooner hit the press than an international furor erupted in the musical world.

Verdi, after all, was no ordinary mortal. For many years his picture graced the equivalent of the one-dollar bill in Italy, where he has served for a century and a half as a national icon. His most famous melodies are still in the air, hummed and whistled by members of every social sphere. Even if mass access to Verdi's music today is largely through television commercials, the symbolic meaning of that music remains strong, and the hold over the popular imagination of a composition such as "Va pensiero sull'ale dorate," the chorus of Hebrew slaves in *Nabucco,* extends well beyond its musical beauties.

Verdi's carefully self-constructed public image cast him forward as a leading figure in the movement for national independence, and his operas from the 1840s are filled with moments whose potential relevance to contemporary political situations was not lost on his compatriots. During the revolutionary uprisings of 1848, the composer set a libretto of explicitly patriotic sentiments, *La battaglia di Legnano,* whose final act is titled "Morire per la patria." And the chorus in *Nabucco* continued to resonate in the minds and spirits of the Italian people. When the Teatro alla Scala was reconstructed after the bombings of World War II, the first music that resounded through its halls, under the baton of Toscanini, was "Va, pensiero." [2]

It is thus not difficult to imagine the public reaction to the idea that Verdi's scores had been so severely misrepresented that there were twenty-seven thousand discrepancies between the composer's autograph of *Falstaff* and the opera's printed edition. In journalistic circles "discrepancies" quickly became "errors," and heated letters and denunciations circulated throughout the European press. Vaughan produced letters of support from many musicians and conductors, while others—led by Gianandrea Gavazzeni—ridiculed his examples. At a special concert/debate in Milan, the public was asked to compare passages performed according to the "traditional" versions of the printed scores with the same passages as sanctioned by Vaughan.[3] Parliamentary debates were held in Rome, leading to the foundation of the Istituto Nazionale di Studi Verdiani of Parma, one of the primary tasks of which was supposed to be the preparation of a critical edition of the composer's works.[4]

And yet, despite the transmission problems discussed in chapter 3, with their profound implications for the worth of current printed scores, Vaughan's campaign for new editions fizzled out. There were several reasons, some tactical, some substantive. By mounting a publicity barrage about his "discoveries" and claiming to identify astronomical numbers of "discrepancies," Vaughan offended Italian national honor. Worse, he emphasized time and again the brilliance of Sir Thomas Beecham and the parallels between Beecham's approach and what Vaughan thought he saw in the Verdi autographs, while explicitly criticizing the scores in use in Italy and implicitly claiming that the interpretations of Italian conductors lacked the inner life that only the great English conductor had been able to achieve. In response, Gavazzeni wrote:

> After the cataloguing of all that has allegedly been neglected in Verdi and altered in Puccini to the detriment of the composers' original inspiration and its expression in manuscript, what is Vaughan and with him the school for textual criticism and orchestral conducting of Sir Thomas Beecham trying to prove? Obviously that Toscanini, and the other Italians after him who devoted their interpretive powers to the study of Verdi and Puccini, mutilated the scores and betrayed the composers in their performances.[5]

This chauvinistic defense inevitably damaged Vaughan's credibility.

But three substantive problems were more significant: the terrain on which Vaughan joined battle, the logic of his argument, and his reading of the sources. We know for certain that Puccini, another subject of Vaughan's polemic, played a significant role in the printing of his own operas, and his autograph manuscripts do not always reflect the changes he made over time. Often he introduced or permitted significant changes in his music, and these were reflected in the printed editions made available to the public, even when they were not definitively notated in his autograph manuscripts. Was Puccini wrong to have abandoned the original, two-act version of *Madama Butterfly*? Should he not have depended on Toscanini to edit the dynamics and articulation in the printed full score of *Manon Lescaut* or to improve the orchestration of many passages in *La fanciulla del West*?[6] And was he misguided when he omitted the "canzone dei fiori" in *Suor Angelica*?[7] However one may answer these and a host of similar questions, there is no evidence that this composer, who followed every stage in the dissemination of his works, really wanted musicians to return to the readings of his original autograph manuscripts and mistakenly allowed flawed printed editions to circulate. Thus Puccini's manuscripts, important as they are for an understanding of his operas, cannot be considered a court of last resort when editing his music. For Verdi the situation is more equivocal. Early in his career he played largely a supervisory role in the publishing of his works, but by the 1880s he was much more intimately involved. Vaughn, by examining works for which Verdi is known to have participated in the editorial process, chose distinctly inhospitable terrain. In the 1950s nobody could accurately assess the extent of Verdi's participation in the editorial process for *Otello* or *Falstaff*, and the matter remains unresolved even today.[8]

The logic of Vaughan's argument was equally problematic. From the generally true proposition that we should give great weight to signs actually written by Verdi in his manuscripts, Vaughan assumed that the absence of signs meant that the composer did not want them. This doesn't follow logically; nor does it reflect what we know about the preparation of autograph manuscripts by nineteenth-century Italian composers. Vaughan paid lip service to an alternative possibility, but quickly dismissed it:

> Objectively one must, however, recognize that even in the original Verdian scores one encounters some lacunae. But these lacunae are easily identifiable only with study and with the direct experience acquired by faithfully and assiduously copying out these same complete autographs. For in this way one enters directly into Verdi's "forma mentis."[9]

It's one thing to assert that it can be useful to write out sections of a score to get a feeling for the rhythm of its writing; quite another to believe that lacunae can be identified only by copying out an entire manuscript.

And Vaughan proved to be an inaccurate literalist in his reading of Verdi's autographs. He wrote, for example, "On this first page [of *Falstaff*] there are 125 discrepancies. On the first chord the *ff* is only for the oboes, bassoons, trumpets, and timpani, the first and second violins and the violas. The others are *f*."[10] To which Gavazzeni responded, in the essay cited above, "Nothing and nobody will ever convince me that Verdi intended in the first bar to differentiate, *f* from *ff*, instrumental sections and instruments belonging to the same section." Quite apart from whether Gavazzeni could ever be convinced (and it is difficult not to agree with his musical instincts), Vaughan's list does not faithfully reproduce the readings of Verdi's autograph, which has an unmistakable *ff* for cellos.[11] Many instruments have no signs, and since when does the absence of a sign signify *f?*

EXAMPLE 4.1. GIUSEPPE VERDI, *MESSA DA REQUIEM*, "DIES IRÆ" (N. 2),
AT THE "LACRYMOSA DIES ILLA," MM. 625–629.

The argument between Vaughan and Gavazzeni on the subject of slurs for one of the most beautiful phrases in the *Messa da Requiem*, the "Lacrymosa dies illa," is of breathtaking silliness. The melody, as sung originally by the mezzo-soprano at mm. 625–629 of the "Dies iræ" movement, with the articulation as specified in the critical edition, is shown in example 4.1.[12] Here is Vaughan's description of a later reappearance of the melody:

> Double phrasing; the melody is slurred in one part while the notes are separately articulated in the other. While the first bassoon, the solo tenor, the tenors of the chorus and the cellos, together with the third horn, have a singing legato, the third bassoon, the solo bass, and the basses of the chorus articulate the phrase. Verdi frequently uses this procedure, which was then copied also by Puccini. Thus, it is not an oversight of Verdi's.[13]

To which Gavazzeni retorted, "Just try humming the 'Lacrimosa' staccato without slurring and then sing praises to the fetish of 'double phrasing.'"

Years later, Vaughan returned to the fray and tried to provide a "musical" explanation for Verdi's notation, arguing that Verdi provided longer slurs for upper instruments or voices, shorter slurs for lower ones. In this way, he "was trying to ensure that the phrase was sung cantabile, but without turgidity: by avoiding the uniform slur over the entire phrase, he has created an inner articulation which gives the whole statement an extra rhythmic vitality."[14] The ghost of Sir Thomas Beecham is still hovering in the wings.

In fact, neither Vaughan nor Gavazzeni looked carefully at either the musical situation or the musical sources. Vaughan's description of Verdi's crowded autograph is an idealization: apart from his frequent misreadings, "slurs" are often groups of slur fragments, and a change of manuscript page in the middle of the melody confuses the issue further.[15] His explanation, too, lacks common sense: although Vaughan treats the first bassoon as an "upper" instrument and the third bassoon as a "lower" one, these identical instruments are playing in unison. The presence or absence of slurs in Verdi's autograph is actually a function of available physical space: there was ample space for a full slur for the choral tenors, and so Verdi wrote it; there was no room for a slur for the choral basses, and so he omitted it. Above the staff for the first bassoon Verdi easily wrote a slur (actually two slur fragments, meeting in the middle of a held note); above the staff for the third bassoon there was simply no room, although Verdi did manage to include a partial slur under the first four notes of the melody, between the parts of the third and fourth bassoon (which are written on a single staff).

Gavazzeni's sneer was no more justified. What neither realized was that the slurring of the "Lacrymosa dies illa" melody in all Ricordi editions of the *Messa da Requiem* through the mid-1980s had been dead wrong. It is slurred in multiple ways in its various appearances, but the diversities are determined by page turns in the autograph manuscript and the division of the music into pages and systems in printed editions. No conductor with any musical sense ever paid attention to those printed signs, and performers instinctively treated the melody as a legato phrase. Blinded by his theories, Vaughan failed to understand the nature of the problem; and Gavazzeni, accustomed to hearing the melody as a legato phrase, failed to realize that the printed edition was faulty.

Twenty-seven thousand errors like this? Not only did Italian musicians turn their collective back on Vaughan's claims; they conveniently identified musical scholarship or "philology" and calls for "critical editions" with his ideas: if this is what scholars mean when they demand "critical editions," they implied, let us return to our vaunted "tradition," as printed in the old editions. A chorus of relieved conductors could thus sing in unison, "If it was good enough for Toscanini, it's good enough for me." Vaughan's challenge had been met and dismissed, and one could believe again that commercially available scores of nineteenth-century Italian operas were trustworthy. As Giuseppe Patané put it in a note to his recording of *Il barbiere di Siviglia* as late as 1989, "Truth, in my opinion, is only reflected in a certain tradition which we cannot forget. Should this tradition disappear, operas as an art form would suffer as a whole and we would gradually see the disappearance of the works themselves." [16]

There matters rested during the first part of the 1960s. Casa Ricordi, honestly believing that Vaughan's claims were without merit, found no pressing commercial reason to replace its editions, although the publisher did employ a local musician, Mario Parenti, to correct obvious errors in the more popular operas. But meetings to establish a national edition of the works of Verdi led nowhere, because nobody knew where to begin. There were valuable biographical and critical studies pertaining to the composer, but no one had looked carefully at the manuscript sources or the printed editions, no one had analyzed Verdi's compositional process or his involvement in the performance history of his works, no one had fully investigated his collaborations with his librettists.[17] With the exception of the autograph manuscripts owned by Casa Ricordi, no one even knew which sources had survived or where they were located. Under such circumstances, discussions of "critical editions" seemed decidedly premature.

Many people in the music world believe that during this period Casa Ricordi, anxious to avoid further scandals, grew selective about whom it permitted to examine its archives. The belief is so widespread that it is unlikely to be totally baseless, but it is unsupported by my own experience. When I arrived in Milan in the fall of 1966, a fresh-faced graduate student working on a doctoral dissertation, I was given access to the collection, and the personnel of Casa Ricordi never ceased to be helpful and interested far beyond what courtesy would require. And I was not alone. Intrigued by the Vaughan affair and nourished by a love for Italian opera, several young musicologists were patiently examining the sources of nineteenth-century Italian opera. They came from Italy, the United States, Britain, Germany, and New Zealand. They knew the impressive textual work being done on the new complete editions of the works of Bach and Mozart; they observed the Berlioz research in England, under the direction of Hugh Macdonald. Without crying scandal, these scholars began to turn their musicological training to Italian opera.

In the light of the transformation in our knowledge over the past forty years, it is difficult to imagine the spirit with which we began our work. I remember sitting in the reading room of the Music Department at the Bibliothèque Nationale in Paris in the autumn of 1965, studying for the first time a complete score of Rossini's *Maometto II*. What an extraordinary work, I thought—and what a shame that I will never hear it, let alone see it on stage. I can imagine a Donizetti scholar, such as William Ashbrook, having a similar experience.[18] And there were young Verdians, such as David Lawton and David Rosen, who became aware that Verdi left far more music for his operas (suppressed scenes, revisions, alternative arias) than printed editions contained.[19] This scholarly work was beginning to constitute a foundation over which the question of critical editions of Italian opera could again be raised when the time grew ripe.

IL BARBIERE DI SIVIGLIA

We honor artists of the past by celebrating the centennials and other anniversaries of their births and deaths. The major celebration relating to Italian opera during the 1960s was the hundreth anniversary of the death of Rossini. In 1968, Rossini was a one-opera composer. To be sure, everyone knew he had written some forty operas, and there had been occasional twentieth-century revivals under Vittorio Gui. The Maggio Musicale Fiorentino in the early 1950s gave hearings to *Armida* (for Maria Callas), *Tancredi,* and *La donna del lago;* Gavazzeni directed a *Turco in Italia* (with Callas). But in the minds of the public, Rossini was *Il barbiere di Siviglia.*

When plans were laid for celebrating the centennial of the composer's death, it was to that opera that almost everyone turned. A young Italian conductor named Alberto Zedda was called upon to lead one of those revivals. During an earlier stay in America (as a conductor at the New York City Opera and a faculty member at the Cincinnati Conservatory of Music), he had directed a number of performances of *Il barbiere.* Several American wind players complained about peculiar readings in their parts, awkward melodic lines, unlikely rhythms. Since the Ricordi archives had no manuscript of the opera, Zedda—unaware of the earlier activities of Vittorio Gui[20]—decided to check these readings directly with Rossini's autograph manuscript, which is preserved at the Bologna Conservatory.

Seeking neither scandal nor publicity (the Vaughan fiasco was still smoldering), Zedda carried his score of the opera from Milan to Bologna, together with instrumental parts rented from Ricordi, on both of which he planned to enter his emendations. Having never before examined an autograph by Rossini (or any other composer), he had no points of comparison. Unable to identify securely Rossini's hand, he believed the *secco* recitative in *Il barbiere* to be by Rossini, whereas those pages are actually composing scores in other hands. He did not know that Rossini had later prepared additional music for his work; nor was he aware of several Rossini manuscripts containing cadenzas and variations.[21] Faced with serious textual problems, he was thrown back upon his own resources, those of an intelligent musician with limited knowledge of Rossini's other works.

But there was so much to see that quibbles over details faded away. The Ricordi edition was fundamentally different from Rossini's manuscript. Melodic lines were changed, rhythms modified, harmonies altered, orchestration transformed. Extra brass and percussion had been added. Where Rossini called for a piccolo, the edition substituted a flute. Signs of articulation (slurs, staccatos, accents) were unrecognizable. It is not that Rossini's manuscript was structurally different from the printed edition. Often as the opera may have been performed with disfiguring cuts, the printed edition was essentially complete. The differences, rather, were in the tissues and sinews of the opera.

Perplexed, disbelieving, Zedda entered into his score and parts as many modifications as possible, performed his corrected version of the opera, and returned the rented materials to the publisher.

Since a publisher rents the same set of orchestral parts to various conductors and opera houses, contracts specify that materials must be returned in good condition. Zedda's parts were so heavily marked up that no other conductor could have used them, and so Ricordi did what any self-respecting publishing house would have done—it billed Zedda for the cost of the materials he had rendered useless. Zedda protested: the Ricordi materials were not *Il barbiere di Siviglia,* but a deformation of it. From an Australian conductor concerned with contradictory slurs, such charges might be rejected; but here was an Italian conductor demonstrating the problems on page after page of the score in the privacy of Ricordi's Milan offices.

Unbeknownst to Zedda and Ricordi, not to mention Gui, many scholars were fully aware of these problems. In 1864 a Florentine publisher, Giovanni Guidi, had issued a full score of the opera based strictly (even too strictly) on the autograph manuscript, which—as we have seen in chapter 3—had been given to the library of the Bologna Conservatory in 1862. Guidi's score, in turn, was reissued several times, including a version by a New York publisher, Broude Brothers, which further corrected the score on the basis of a good manuscript of the first act of the opera in the New York Public Library (believed, erroneously, to have annotations in Rossini's hand).[22] Side by side with these scores, however, there circulated the Ricordi edition—the version considered "traditional," the one adopted by most theaters, the one Zedda had corrected. Whence did this score derive? How could these two versions of *Il barbiere* be reconciled? Since no one had a response, it was simpler for Ricordi to continue shipping its materials around the world.

Finally convinced that a problem did exist, and confident that Zedda could produce a score both faithful to Rossini's autograph and acceptable to performers, Ricordi entrusted him with preparing a critical edition of *Il barbiere.* Published at the end of 1969, Ricordi's belated contribution to the Rossini centennial, it was the first critical edition of a nineteenth-century Italian opera.[23] Whatever its deficiencies, Zedda's *Barbiere* had the merit of having tackled a difficult, even intractable task. In particular, Zedda was able to show that contemporary manuscripts and printed editions of the opera followed almost without exception the basic outlines of Rossini's original score. There were lacunae, pieces often cut in performance (such as the Count's second-act aria, "Cessa di più resistere"). There were rare substitutions: Bartolo's hilarious aria "Ad un dottor della mia sorte" was sometimes replaced by the simpler (and musically inferior) "Manca un foglio," written in 1816 by Pietro Romani for a revival of the opera in Florence. Also there were small changes in the orchestration: pizzicato cellos accompanied the Count's "Ecco ridente in cielo" in a few manuscripts, reflecting the practice of theaters with no access to a guitar. And Rossini's articulation was copied incompletely and inaccurately, while his rhythms were invariably simplified, eloquent testimony that contemporary copyists made fewer strokes of the pen wherever possible. Still, contemporary manuscripts and printed editions otherwise reflect the text of the opera as the composer notated it in his autograph manuscript.

About the so-called "traditional" version of the opera, Zedda was less incisive. He stated that its readings, "even if they may have been produced and taken hold while Rossini was alive, find no confirmation in a written source."[24] In fact, there is no evidence that anything resembling the Ricordi material was in use during Rossini's lifetime. The "traditional" *Barbiere* was a deformed version prepared long after Rossini's death, for reasons that may have seemed pressing at the time but have no validity today, such as filling out Rossini's chamberlike orchestration with heavier sounds; avoiding Rossini's characteristic use of the piccolo; facilitating the process whereby Rosina became a high soprano, rather than a Rossinian contralto/mezzo-soprano. Instead of deriving from a long-standing performance tradition, the old Ricordi edition simply reflected editorial decisions in the late nineteenth century to print an easily available score of *Il barbiere di Siviglia* (perhaps one then in use at the Teatro alla Scala), rather than searching out Rossini's manuscript. Even Zedda's critical edition has not completely erased the unfortunate effect of that decision on the performance history of Rossini's opera.

CLAUDIO ABBADO AND A TENOR ROMEO

Critical editions of musical works are different from those of literary works. While the critical edition of a poem or a novel can be read with pleasure, its details dissected by the devoted scholar, its obscurities and its curiosities enjoyed by the informed amateur, a critical edition of a musical work is not intended for the library or the study alone. It is intended to be used as the basis for performances.[25] When the work is as much a part of the popular imagination as *Il barbiere di Siviglia*, the first performance based on a new edition can become a cultural event. On 9 December 1969 La Scala was the site, an extraordinary cast was assembled (featuring Teresa Berganza as Rosina), and Jean-Pierre Ponnelle was the stage director. The man entrusted with bringing the new *Barbiere* to light was not Zedda but rather the rising star of Italian conductors, Claudio Abbado.

Abbado at that moment was the object of controversy. Having become interested in Bellini's setting of the Romeo and Juliet story, *I Capuleti e i Montecchi*, he had prepared a new performing edition of that opera, which he conducted at La Scala on 26 March 1966. He altered the arrangement of the voices by substituting a tenor as Romeo for the mezzo-soprano required by Bellini, who had followed a tradition to which many Rossinian *opere serie* (*Tancredi, La donna del lago, Semiramide*) belong. Abbado's aim was comprehensible: he wanted to revive Bellini's opera in a way the public might more easily accept, since few works being performed during the 1960s featured female heroes *en travesti*. Neither Francesca Zambello (the stage director) nor I will ever forget the conversation of two elderly women during a rehearsal of Rossini's *Bianca e Falliero* almost twenty years later, at Greater Miami Opera in 1988, before supertitles had transformed audience understanding: "Do you see what I see?" one whispered to the other, "two women—making love?"

But Bellini's score was not so easily manipulated. He had planned the music with certain effects of sonority, and a tenor Romeo was decidedly not what he had had in mind. Perhaps the most impressive moment in the opera occurs at the end of the first-act finale, when, from opposite sides of the stage, the forcibly separated Giulietta and Romeo sing in unison an archetypical Bellinian melody, "Se ogni speme è a noi rapita," over a *sottovoce* staccato accompaniment from male soloists and the all-male chorus. The significance and the beauty of the passage lies in those two female voices, lost in one another, soaring over the male ensemble, intoning a melodic idea that goes on and on in ever-inventive and rhythmically subtle detail, thirty-one measures of continuous melody ("melodie lunghe, lunghe, lunghe," as Verdi described Bellini's melodies).[26] Substitute a tenor for the second woman's voice, and the magic is gone.

The implications of the revised vocal scoring were broader still. In an opera as dependent upon ensembles as *I Capuleti e i Montecchi*, Bellini's delicate web of vocal parts unravels when Romeo is recast as a tenor. In their duet, Romeo and Tebaldo (the latter played by the young Luciano Pavarotti in Abbado's production) frequently sing in parallel sixths, with Romeo above Tebaldo. One cannot transpose Romeo down an octave and hope for acceptable results: the music is not conceived for two male voices in thirds.

Nor did Abbado's interventions stop with the vocal parts. Despite Bellini's considerable talents, he was far less expert in handling orchestral sonority than

Rossini or Donizetti. The autograph manuscripts are replete with alterations that suggest insecurity, not an idealized search for perfection.[27] The resulting sound is often heavy, for Bellini began with a larger orchestra than Rossini's and kept most instruments playing too much of the time. Similar problems are not unknown to the German symphonic tradition. Should orchestras today play Schumann's symphonies or a revision of them by another composer (say, the composer-conductor Gustav Mahler) or conductor (a Georg Szell or a Leopold Stokowski)? Schumann, after all, was an active participant in the first performances of these symphonies, working directly with his conductor (Felix Mendelssohn) and making alterations where he felt artistic results obtained during rehearsals and performances were unsatisfactory.[28]

Bellini had similar responsibilities: he was contractually required to rehearse his new operas and to participate in their first three performances. The sound was verified directly in the theater by the composer. If we think that Bellini's operas are worth performing, then they are arguably worth performing as they were conceived, with problems of balance resolved through careful control of orchestral size and seating, the use of dynamic gradations, and so forth.[29] But Abbado chose instead to "revise" Bellini's orchestration, and his interventions were present on every page of the score.

Abbado's *Capuleti* might have circulated in this form had not the dean of Italian music critics, Fedele d'Amico, blown the whistle. In a sharply worded article he deplored the operation, lamenting that Bellini's beautiful opera lay fallow while this pointless "revision" was allowed to circulate.[30] Abbado appears to have taken this criticism to heart. His edition of *I Capuleti e i Montecchi* was withdrawn from circulation shortly thereafter; and when the first performance of a nineteenth-century Italian opera based on a critical edition, Zedda's *Barbiere di Siviglia,* was planned for La Scala, it was Abbado who took command.

Abbado's *Barbiere* was a revolutionary reading of the opera. Not only did he employ the critical edition, but he adhered to the text with almost fanatical strictness. No significant cuts were sanctioned and few ornaments were permitted. This was a performance with a message: Rossini was to be presented at a level of precision usually reserved for the German masters.[31] The slapstick antics that the work had endured for decades were replaced by a clean and eminently funny staging by Jean-Pierre Ponnelle, where physical action emerged from the music. The singing was elegant, while the orchestral execution brought out every detail of the Rossinian palette.

Yet not everyone approved. Isolated voices, paying no heed to the evidence of the sources and insisting on a "tradition" invented at the end of the nine-

teenth century, preferred the old Ricordi version. (As late as 1989 Giuseppe
Patané made it a point of honor that his recording of the opera did not use the
critical edition.) [32] And there was the more complicated objection of those
who wondered whether this was how a Rossini opera should be performed.
Did purging the opera of the vocal fireworks that coloratura sopranos had ap-
pended to melodic lines never written for them in the first place also mean that
a mezzo-soprano Rosina or a contralto Rosina was compelled to sing only the
notes printed in the score? Did eliminating traditional licenses (speeding up,
slowing down, introducing pauses for stage business) also mean that the music had to be performed with quasi-metronomic regularity?

Abbado's performance had been technically perfect, but still there were
complaints that it lacked the wit and the vivacity that characterized Rossini's
art. And in a transference that has become standard, uncertainties about the
performance grew into doubts about the edition. Is that what it meant to use
a "critical edition"? Did the new edition encourage, or even require, this kind
of performance? Was spirit the price of scholarship?

THE SIEGE OF LA SCALA

One year later a different Rossinian production graced the same theater. The
work was *L'assedio di Corinto,* and it was given on 11 April 1969 under the
direction of Thomas Schippers. It also marked the debut at La Scala of two of
the greatest American singers of our time, Beverly Sills and Marilyn Horne.
With several changes in the score and cast (and, sadly, without the presence
of Horne), this production was imported to New York six years later (7 April
1975) for the arrival of Sills in the promised land of the Metropolitan Opera,
after her two decades' wandering in the desert of the New York City Opera.
Schippers and his colleagues subjected Rossini's score to alterations far more
drastic than those imposed by Abbado on *I Capuleti e i Montecchi.* Although
they did not reorchestrate the music, they cut and rearranged so much of it
that large parts of the opera were unrecognizable.[33] From a serious work of
music drama they concocted a showpiece for two prima donnas.

L'assedio di Corinto has a complicated history, as we saw in chapter 1. The
opera was originally written as *Maometto II* for the Teatro San Carlo of
Naples in 1820. Rossini revised it first for Venice to open the carnival season
of 1823 (on 26 December 1822), and in 1826 he used it as the source for *Le Siège
de Corinthe,* his earliest opera in French. This version was then translated
back into Italian (badly) as *L'assedio di Corinto.* But the versions performed
by Schippers at La Scala and the Met were not merely this retranslation into

Italian of Rossini's French opera, but a conflation of the various versions, to which—on the recording and in New York—was added an extraneous piece (from a revision of the opera by another composer) to favor even more the part of the soprano.[34]

The original *Maometto II* and *Le Siège de Corinthe* are both coherent works of art, but they are very different. The unusual dramaturgical and musical design of *Maometto II*, Rossini's most innovative Italian serious opera, must have bewildered his contemporaries, even among the relatively sophisticated public of Naples. What Rossini calls a *terzettone* in his autograph manuscript—a big fat trio—is a continuous musical composition that occupies almost a third of the first act. Anna's heroic scene at the end of the second act opens with some of the most difficult and expressive florid music that Rossini ever wrote, but instead of concluding with an elaborate *rondò*, the opera's final moments witness the arrival of the Turkish forces, Anna's abrupt suicide, and the shocked reaction of Maometto and the rest of the cast.[35]

In the best neoclassical tradition, *Maometto II* is a tragedy of love and honor, focused on four principal characters: Paolo Erisso, a tenor, the leader of the Venetian colony at Negroponte; Anna, a soprano, his daughter; Calbo, a contralto *en travesti*, a Venetian warrior in love with Anna; and Maometto II, a bass, the leader of the besieging Turkish forces. Anna and Maometto had fallen in love at an earlier time and in a different place, with Maometto in disguise; but now they must play out their personal story in hopeless circumstances. She betrays her beloved in order to save her father and her people, weds Calbo (whom she respects but does not love), and ultimately kills herself before her mother's tomb.

In *Le Siège de Corinthe*, Rossini transformed his Neapolitan masterpiece into a nascent French grand opera, in a style that would strongly influence Meyerbeer.[36] The protagonists become Greeks and Turks instead of Venetians and Turks, to reflect the political events of the 1820s;[37] but this was the least significant alteration. The vocal lines of the Italian original were greatly simplified, following the more declamatory style in use at the Opéra in Paris.[38] In further homage to French traditions, Rossini expanded the spectacular elements of the score. Choruses, dances, and pantomimes often overwhelm those elements of the tragedy that remain from *Maometto II*. A scene of prophecy for a new character (Hiéros) and a group of Greek soldiers invoking Marathon, exalting martyrdom, and promising a glorious future for Greece foretells the conclusion of *Le Siège*, a mass suicide, rather than the individual suicide of Anna.[39] Almost every detail of this scene (except the mass suicide) was imitated by Verdi in the well-known scene that concludes the third act of *Nabucco.*

These alterations in dramaturgy were accompanied by changes in the solo roles. Heroic parts *en travesti* were not acceptable in French opera; hence the contralto role of Calbo was transformed into the tenor Néocles. Since Calbo's original aria ("Non temer: d'un basso affetto," with its cabaletta "E d'un trono alla speranza") is a quintessential solo for coloratura contralto, and absolutely inappropriate for a tenor, Rossini replaced it with a new aria for Néocles ("Grand Dieu! faut-il qu'un peuple qui t'adore"). Rather than lose the Calbo aria altogether, Rossini modified its cabaletta for the soprano (now called Pamyra) and allowed it to conclude her major aria (derived from the incomplete aria that Anna had sung at the end of *Maometto II,* before her suicide), which in *Le Siège* opens the second of the opera's three acts. Then, in order to provide solo music for Pamyra near the end, before the mass suicide, Rossini inserted the prayer for Anna that had been included within the *terzettone* from *Maometto II.* The manipulations, although they sound complicated when described, produce a perfectly coherent work.

While most scholars and performers are convinced that *Maometto II* is musically and dramatically more powerful than *Le Siège de Corinthe,* there are legitimate reasons to favor one opera or the other. But Schippers tried to merge the two. His fundamental error was to imagine that *Le Siège* could be performed with a contralto (Horne) as Néocles and a high soprano (Sills) as Pamyra. Each decision had unhappy ramifications. By reintroducing the hero *en travesti* into a French opera written for tenor, Schippers found himself forced to turn to *Maometto II* to find appropriate music for Horne's aria. The resulting piece was of a monstrously large size, and it was constructed on the assumption that more is better (the kitchen sink principle, we might call it), drawing freely on music written for both Calbo and Néocles.

The presence of a coloratura contralto in *Le Siège* compromised the work's general shift to a simpler vocal style, even when singers' interpolations are taken into account. With Néocles now reassigned Calbo's original cabaletta, the Pamyra aria at the beginning of the second act suddenly found itself without a concluding movement. What should one do? Choose a cabaletta, of course, any cabaletta, and stick it in. Sills sang one from *Ciro in Babilonia,* an opera written by Rossini early in 1812, with a ludicrous result. From the elaborate orchestral web of Rossini at his most mature, the sound suddenly dissolved into the Cimarosan ideal of his youth.[40] (One could argue that if this music was to be added, it should at least have been reorchestrated in the style

EXAMPLE 4.2. GIOACHINO ROSSINI, *CIRO IN BABILONIA*, ARIA AMIRA ("VORREI VEDER LO SPOSO"), ORCHESTRAL THEME BETWEEN STATEMENTS OF THE CABALETTA THEME, TO WHICH BEVERLY SILLS VOCALIZED IN *LE SIÈGE DE CORINTHE*.

etc.

of *Maometto II.*) And as if that were not sufficient, Sills vocalized along with the rambunctious orchestral theme between the two statements of the caba-letta theme, strewing high notes hither and yon (example 4.2). She needed to have *something* to sing, after all, since her effective tessitura was so much higher than what Rossini wrote for either Anna or Pamyra. With the soprano's line regularly transposed up an octave, ensembles sounded unbalanced.

Despite this travesty of the music of Rossini, the ladies sang their hearts out, and *L'assedio di Corinto* was a triumph for the prima donnas. In the case of Marilyn Horne, it continued her demonstration of what Rossini's vocal lines could be when sung by an artist with the requisite technical skills. Still, just as voices were raised against Abbado's *Barbiere,* many protested this operation. Few knew the opera well, of course, and almost no one had even a passing ac-quaintance with *Maometto II,* but a vocal score of *L'assedio* was available from Ricordi, and some had even heard the reprise of the opera at the Maggio Musicale on 4 June 1949, with a young Renata Tebaldi as Pamyra. I threw in my two bits at a well-attended public lecture at the New York Public Library at Lincoln Center, to which music critics flocked, the night before the opening.[41] For my pains I earned this barb from Sills: "I think some so-called musicolo-gists are like men who talk constantly of sex and never do anything about it."[42]

The contrast between Abbado's *Barbiere* and Schipper's *Assedio* embodies two extreme approaches to the performance of Italian opera. For the one, the text of an edition, especially a "critical edition," is—in principle—sacrosanct and must be respected in every detail; for the other, an opera is an entertain-ment and can be freely manipulated as long as the result is a good show. Since the music of Rossini was largely unknown and unknowable during the late 1960s, the second approach seemed feasible. But the controversy that greeted the La Scala revival of *L'assedio di Corinto* had one important result: it gave impetus to the formation of the *Edizione critica delle opere di Gioachino Rossini.*

RICCARDO MUTI AND THE PEOPLE'S GIFT TO VERDI

It was a stroke of good fortune that, after the Vaughan skirmishes, the real battle for critical editions of nineteenth-century Italian opera and a revitalized performance practice to go with them was engaged first on Rossinian soil. After all, neither audiences nor musicians had much knowledge of *Tancredi, La donna del lago, Il Turco in Italia,* or *Il viaggio a Reims.* The appearance of new editions became a cause for rejoicing: singers and conductors accepted them readily, and audiences were delighted to hear what amounted to new works. An occasional crotchety critic (particularly one who disliked the *bel canto* repertory anyway) might snort something about "scholarship," but knownothingism has never seemed a worthy platform.

When the terrain shifted to the operas of Giuseppe Verdi, however, howls of anguish and even anger arose from some quarters, and studied indifference from others. The more familiar the work, the stronger the reaction. A belief in the rectitude, the sanctity, of what is perceived to be a modern performance tradition spilled over into a belief that the current printed text could lay equal claim to validity. This confusion is at the heart of contemporary controversies about editing and performing the music of Verdi. And the name around which these controversies have swarmed for almost three decades is that of Riccardo Muti.

With a rigorous approach to the scores that overshadows even that of the legendary Toscanini, Muti's Verdi is inextricably tied to the search for a reconceptualized performance practice of Italian opera. More than any other Italian conductor, Muti has been associated with a strict reading of the printed score. Yet this "cause of fidelity," as Muti has defined it, "must not be understood as the cold reproduction of a text, but as an intuitive interpretation through the written signs of a whole spiritual world that exists beyond the written signs." [43] That spiritual position is achieved by insisting on integral performances and refusing to allow singers "traditional" liberties and interpolations.

When the works involved were tangential to the repertory, Muti's approach won a chorus of approval. His *Guglielmo Tell* at the Maggio Musicale in 1972, although sung in Italian and based on a problematic edition, was a revelation. Yes, the work lasted more than five hours, and one had to be in optimal physical and mental condition simply to attend. (I was fortunate enough to hear the dress rehearsal.) Yes, it was performed in an execrable nineteenth-century translation, when it should have been done in the original French.[44] Yes, the tenor Nicolai Gedda, a fine Arnold, bowed out before the end of the run. (At the repeat of Arnold's phrase "Ah! Mathilde, idole de mon âme!" in $A\flat$ *major,* a full tone higher than its original statement in $G\flat$ *major,* Gedda was so obviously struggling that I worried about his health.) All this is true, but perfection is something we seek, not something we attain. Muti's rendering of Rossini's *William Tell* for the first time clarified for this modern listener the fascination that Rossini's last opera had for nineteenth-century musicians.

With the works of Verdi, matters were very different. Whatever else anyone may or may not have heard in Florence when Muti directed *Il trovatore* in December 1977 at the Teatro Comunale, all that anyone talked about was the end of "Di quella pira," the cabaletta for Manrico that concludes the third act. The reason was that Muti's Manrico did not sing the high *c* traditionally interpolated to bring down the curtain amid a storm of applause. Indeed, the production has gone down in public consciousness and critical lore as Muti's defiant challenge—the "*Trovatore* without a high *c*"—to the contemporary performing tradition. A similar reaction emerged when he conducted the same opera on 7 December 2000 to open the season at La Scala, marking the hundredth anniversary of Verdi's death. As Loretta Bentivoglio wrote the next day in *La Repubblica:*

> Fury and battles in the *loggione* of La Scala for a high *c.* "Shame," some one screamed from above, when the tenor Salvatore Licitra failed to introduce the high note at the end of the cabaletta "Di quella pira," which Riccardo Muti, as even children know, removed from the *Trovatore* that opened the season at La Scala last night.[45]

But Muti's 1977 *Trovatore* was, in fact, much more. The American Verdi scholar David Lawton had taken the initial steps toward preparing the critical edition of the opera (which was ultimately published in 1993), carefully comparing the printed text of the Ricordi edition then commercially available with Verdi's manuscript.[46] Through this process he was able to identify errors and misreadings and begin to clarify the meaning of the composer's notation. But the efforts of Lawton, Muti, the singers, the orchestra, and the production team were overshadowed: everything dissolved into the hullabaloo over the high *c.*

What makes the controversy particularly absurd is that the note in question never existed in *any* printed edition of the opera. The "great moment" is in fact an interpolation. In this respect, Lawton's edition of the opera was unchanged with respect to the older printed edition. Muti's insistence that the interpolated note not be sung, however, marked not only his performance but also Lawton's edition, which became "the *edition* of *Il trovatore* without a high *c.*" But why should anyone care so much? Does it make such a difference if the tenor ascends to that note rather than remaining on the *g,* as in the printed text?[47]

Looking exclusively at the end of the aria, the interpolated note is nothing but harmless pyrotechnics. As assertive a cabaletta as Verdi ever wrote, the piece closes the third act, brings down the curtain, and moves the opera pre-cipitously to the final catastrophe. Verdi's conclusion demonstrates his wish to preserve an unusual level of tension. Manrico would ordinarily have ended the aria by descending from the *g* of "All'armi" to the lower *c.* Instead Verdi holds the voice on the *g* so that Manrico concludes on the fifth of the *C major* chord, while the first tenors take the *e* below it and the second tenors and basses sing middle *c.* The result is a full tonic triad, with Manrico alone on the highest note.[48]

Why did Verdi not intensify this effect further, by giving *c, e,* and *g* to the male chorus, with Manrico free to ascend to high *c?* Musical analysis, which can be invoked to support all sides of an argument, is painfully unsuited to this kind of question. But here is a relatively simple explanation—a histori-cal explanation, not a musical one. Verdi wrote the role of Manrico for Carlo Baucardé, a tenor whose effective range it presumably reflects. The part has a high tessitura, sitting for long stretches in the sixth between middle *c* and high *a,* but *a* (which recurs frequently) is the highest note that Verdi expected Manrico to sing easily. Only at a single point in the opera does the composer notate a high *bb* for Manrico, in the context of the stretta that concludes the first-act trio. In this section, the Conte di Luna has a part of his own ("Di geloso amor sprezzato"), while Leonora and Manrico sing two different texts to essentially the same music. They begin together, at the octave, until Leo-nora ascends to high *bb,* at which point Manrico is assigned a lower note, *g* (example 4.3). When the theme is repeated, now with an accompanimental

EXAMPLE 4.3. GIUSEPPE VERDI, *IL TROVATORE*, SCENA, ROMANZA E TERZETTO (N. 3), MM. 229–236.

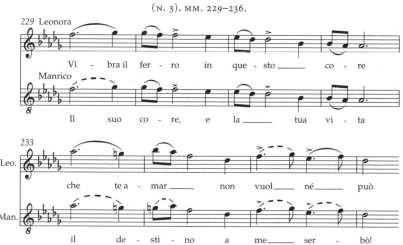

EXAMPLE 4.4. GIUSEPPE VERDI, *IL TROVATORE*, SCENA, ROMANZA E TERZETTO (N. 3), MM. 259–262.

line for the Conte, Leonora must ascend by leap to the *b*♭. To avoid interrupting the octaves being sung by Manrico and the prima donna, Verdi gave the tenor a choice: either *b*♭ (the only time in the opera) or the lower *d*♭, should the singer be unable to handle the higher pitch (example 4.4). Verdi, in short, did not feel that Baucardé had a usable high *c,* nor a high *b,* and only a most uncertain high *b*♭.[49]

It would be possible, of course, to broaden this discussion to include the issue of Verdi's writing for tenor in the 1840s and the first part of the 1850s, at a time when an earlier vocal style, characterized by a lighter upper register (think of Tonio's *cavatine* "Pour mon âme quel destin," with its eight high *c*s in Donizetti's *La Fille du Régiment*), was giving way to a more robust sound, extending into the highest register. In that context, the role of Manrico is perfectly characteristic of how Verdi wanted to write for tenor at that moment in his life. Later, to be sure, he tended to push his tenors higher, as techniques of vocal production changed and, with them, Verdi's entire approach to a tenor's tessitura.

But it is quite irrelevant whether or not, as a famous anecdote would have it, Verdi actually told the singer Enrico Tamberlick, who had boasted of the success of his high *c* with the public, "Far be it from me to deny the public what it wants. Put in the high *c* if you like, provided it is a good one."[50] The real disaster of the interpolated high *c* is its effect on the choice of an appropriate tenor to sing the role of Manrico. The sine qua non for an opera house today, as it casts the part, has become the ability of a tenor to let loose a stentorian high *c* at the end of "Di quella pira." The interpolated note has come to dominate the conception of the part, and everything else is planned around an effect that Verdi never intended. To produce the high *c,* furthermore, singers generally cut the cabaletta by half and omit the notes that they should be singing with the chorus, so as to preserve breath and energy for the final pitch.

At the time of Muti's *Trovatore* in Florence, one Italian critic commented that the high *c*, even if not written by Verdi, was a gift that the people had given to Verdi. This bit of sentimentality hides the basic issue: whether Manrico does or does not produce a high *c* is of little artistic importance. What is artistically devastating is that the perceived need to hit the stratospheric note has transformed our conception of the role. Give me a tenor who can sing Manrico as Verdi conceived the part and chooses to add a ringing high *c*, and I will join the *loggione* in applauding him. Failing that, let Manrico, in Rossini's famous words to the same Tamberlick, leave his high *c* on the hat rack, to be picked up on his way out of the theater.[51]

"LA CABALETTA, FILOLOGO"

The opening of the operatic season at La Scala on the evening of 7 December, the day honoring Milan's patron saint, Sant'Ambrogio, is present-day Italy's most keenly awaited musical event each year. "Scala" supplements are published in the major newspapers; what the Italians call the *cronaca* pages report gleefully on those members of the government and society likely to be in attendance and what they will be wearing; protest movements (involving party politics or animal rights) know that their activities will be publicized. Through all the social trappings, some attention is even paid to the music. The performances of Verdi's *Ernani* at La Scala for Sant'Ambrogio in 1982 were particularly in the public eye: it was the first time that this prestigious event was to be entrusted to Riccardo Muti.

For weeks before the premiere, the word *filologia* ("philology") was tossed around by critics and the public. For this, Muti was more than a little responsible. Just before the performance he told the *Corriere della Sera*: "This will be the *Ernani* of Giuseppe Verdi, that is, an edition extremely faithful to the manuscript, without cuts; the opera will be performed exactly as it was conceived."[52] It was a peculiar statement. First of all, Muti used the manuscript of *Ernani* largely to investigate a single issue, as we shall see. The score that he employed was the standard edition, prepared by Ricordi at the end of the nineteenth century, with more than its share of mistakes and misreadings. Muti could justifiably have talked about a performance "extremely faithful to the Ricordi edition," but hardly about fidelity to Verdi's autograph.

But there was another, graver problem. What does it mean to perform an opera "exactly as it was conceived"? How do we know how a work was conceived? We cannot ask Verdi how he conceived *Ernani*. Perhaps we must settle for something far more banal: choose an edition derived as closely as possible from authentic sources, and then use that edition as the basis for a performance, bringing to bear what the composer wrote down, other historical information, our knowledge about performances Verdi himself directed, our awareness of modern performing traditions, and—most of all—our own musical and dramaturgical intuitions. In any event, the claim to an *Ernani at La Scala the way Verdi wanted it*" (the invention of a *Corriere della Sera* headline writer) was imprudent under the best of circumstances.

Just as a polemic about a single note characterized Muti's *Trovatore* in Florence, a single piece served as the lightning rod for his *Ernani* in Milan: the cabaletta for Silva, "Infin che un brando vindice," within the first-act finale. The piece was not in the original version of the work, performed at the Teatro La Fenice of Venice on 9 March 1844.[53] Although this movement is included in most editions of the opera, Muti decided to omit it. He set forth his reasons in the same *Corriere della Sera* interview:

> Just recently I happened upon a vocal score from the second half of the nineteenth century, in which the cabaletta for the bass, "Infin che un brando vindice," is missing. My curiosity aroused, to keep faith with my rigor and my philological scruples I decided to examine Verdi's manuscript: from Casa Ricordi I obtained a copy of the original, and I had confirmation that the cabaletta is not there. Driven, as always, by a need to return to the sources and to arrive at the truth of the written sign, I sought documentation by calling on the musicologist Francesco Degrada and consulting the book of Julian Budden. These explain clearly that almost certainly the cabaletta is not by Verdi and was inserted for the first time by the bass Ignazio Marini, who sang it in the fall of 1844 in Milan.
>
> At the time, the critic of a Milanese paper reacted negatively, going so far as to protest strongly this abusively inserted cabaletta and to hold Marini (then a well-known bass) responsible for having introduced it into the opera. Having verified this, I also found the answer to a problem that had been disturbing me: Why was it that the [arias for the] soprano, tenor, and bass had both cantabiles and cabalettas, while [that for] the baritone alone had no cabaletta, leaving the relationship among the four unbalanced? The answer appeared in Verdi's original manuscript: the soprano and tenor had both a cantabile and cabaletta, but neither the bass nor the baritone had a cabaletta. I thus decided to follow the precise indications of the composer and to omit a passage almost certainly not by Verdi or, at least, of which there is no trace in the original manuscript.

Notice the uneasy slippage here between analytical explanation and philology. As for analysis, do we really know how many characters in a "typical" Italian opera of 1845 have multipartite arias and how many have arias in a single tempo? And as for philology, Degrada and Budden are much more cautious than Muti: they describe factors that might suggest the piece is by Verdi and others that suggest it is not, leaving the matter open.[54]

But a performance does not have the luxury of being indecisive. Silva cannot proceed to the footlights and explain the situation to the audience: "Ladies and gentlemen, we are not sure whether the cabaletta that follows in some sources is really by Verdi, so I'm going to (*a*) sing it or (*b*) leave it out." And the glamor of opening night at La Scala blends poorly with uncertainty. Muti took a legitimate doubt and made an entirely plausible artistic decision. After all, composers and performers of Italian opera in the nineteenth century were frequently called upon to make just such decisions for particular occasions on practical grounds, to meet the needs of theaters and singers. Then Muti buttressed his decision with claims that it was philologically motivated and analytically just. Rumors circulated widely in Milan that the real motivation for omitting the cabaletta was the inability of an aging Nicolai Ghiaurov to sing it well.

By the time of the old Spanish grandee's entrance toward the end of the first act, the opening-night audience at La Scala was already hostile to the staging by Luca Ronconi and the sets of Ezio Frigerio, whose price was the subject of vociferous debate and whose awkward multiple levels subjected the singers to unaccustomed gymnastics. I particularly recall Mirella Freni as Elvira teetering perilously on a platform as she was carried up and down flights of stairs. The singers in turn reacted with a tentative performance that did not sit well with *mélomanes* in the audience. Finally Silva appeared and sang his cantabile, "Infelice! e tu credevi." As he continued with the finale, omitting "Infin che un brando vindice," a cry was heard from the recesses of the theater: "La cabaletta, filologo!" The last word was spat out with palpable scorn. Muti dug in his heels and carried on.

The incident was worthy of the theater of the absurd. Ostensibly, Muti acted with philological responsibility by omitting the cabaletta, while the gallery patrons demonstrated their attachment to the "traditional" way of singing *Ernani*. But in truth all of them got it wrong. What the *loggionisti* did not understand was that in the performing tradition of *Ernani*, the Silva cabaletta was usually omitted. Although it is present in Ricordi materials (which, as so often, take their cue from a Milanese production), in most extant copies of these materials the music is firmly crossed out. And Muti erred in not understanding that the music he actually performed was a philologist's nightmare, an erroneous conflation of two separate versions.

Whoever introduced the cabaletta into the score *also* felt it necessary to modify the preceding two bars of music. When Ricordi first printed string parts of the opera soon after its premiere, the publisher followed Verdi's autograph, without the Silva cabaletta. When the string parts were reprinted to include the cabaletta, Ricordi modified the two previous bars. Parts for winds, brass, and percussion for *Ernani* were first printed in the 1880s, and they contain only the modified bars introducing the cabaletta. Each version has its own musical and harmonic integrity. As Verdi originally conceived the piece, Silva's "L'antico Silva vuol vendetta, e tosto..." concluding in *F minor*, easily lead to his "Uscite..." (addressed to his followers) in *Db major* (example 4.5). In the revision, the music emphasizes the dominant of *F minor*, then continues directly with Silva's cabaletta by leaping to that key's relative major, *Ab*, a common harmonic progression in Italian opera of the period (example 4.6). It is similar to the progression we find leading into the final cabaletta of act 2

EXAMPLE 4.5. GIUSEPPE VERDI, *ERNANI*, FINALE PRIMO (N. 5), ORIGINAL VERSION, MM. 55–58.

EXAMPLE 4.6. GIUSEPPE VERDI, *ERNANI*, FINALE PRIMO (N. 5), WITH THE ADDED
CABALETTA FOR SILVA, MM. 55A–59A.

in *Rigoletto,* as discussed in chapter 1 (see example 1.2). What Verdi never intended, however, was the version played at La Scala. Muti performed the bars
that had been rewritten in order to introduce the cabaletta, and then he cut
the cabaletta. Philology indeed! But he was hardly alone in having made that
mistake. Ever since Ricordi in the 1880s printed wind, brass, and percussion
parts containing only the revised version, there was no way to perform Verdi's
own music. Everyone who omitted the Silva cabaletta fell into the same trap.
Only when the critical edition of *Ernani* became available was it possible to
perform the music either as Verdi had originally written it or with the added
cabaletta. Performances, by their very nature, cannot pretend to be philological: that is the purpose of editions.

Subsequent research has clarified much of the history of "Infin che un
brando vindice." The cabaletta is indeed by Verdi, but he did not write it for
Ernani. It was composed at the request of Marini for insertion into a revival in
Barcelona in 1842 of Verdi's first opera, *Oberto, Conte di San Bonifacio.* Roger
Parker first identified the Spanish libretto, which includes the relevant text;

and Claudio Gallico, in the preface to the critical edition of *Ernani,* first transcribed the letter from Verdi to Marini that accompanied the manuscript on its voyage to Barcelona.[55] We should not be surprised, then, that it was the same Marini who introduced "Infin che un brando vindice" into *Ernani.* What we still do not know is whether Verdi gave his blessing to the operation, or merely tolerated it.

By the time of the *Ernani* follies at La Scala, there was good reason to hope that similar problems might be easier to avoid in the future. The University of Chicago Press and Casa Ricordi had announced their intention to publish *The Works of Giuseppe Verdi* in new critical editions, and the inaugural volume in the series, *Rigoletto,* was about to appear. The conductor who first used the new *Rigoletto* in the theater was the conductor who had demonstrated how deeply he cared about the issues it sought to address: Riccardo Muti.

5
THE ROMANCE OF THE CRITICAL EDITION

The words "critical edition" strike a mixture of scorn and terror in the hearts of many conductors, singers, and music administrators. That reaction is comprehensible: musicians have enough to do preparing a performance of a work without being told that the printed scores they are using are inaccurate or incomplete. The less they need to think about such problems, the happier they are. Moreover, most of them can recite an endless number of anecdotes about new editions that are worse than the old, musicologists who cannot interpret properly the notation of transposing instruments, guitar chords with seven notes for an instrument having only six strings, pages strewn with extraneous symbols, and so on. I have seen critical editions embraced by conductors with a rigor contrary to their true meaning, ignored by nervous singers unwilling to change a note or a word of an interpretation they believe to be authorized by some mystical tradition, denounced by pecunious administrators as the brainchild of rapacious music publishers, and debated in the popular press (particularly in Italy) with a passion that defies understanding.

Critical editions of literary works have a long history in Western culture, with roots in biblical scholarship, in Shakespearean scholarship, and in the editing of Greek and Latin texts—the triumph of Renaissance humanism.[1] By debating the relative merits of Shakespearean quartos and folios, literary scholars sought answers about what might have been Shakespeare's lost original: they developed sophisticated techniques for comparing multiple copies of a printed edition, investigating the mechanisms by which authorial manuscripts (essentially none survive) might have passed through the hands of compositors to assume printed form. By comparing and filiating medieval sources of ancient texts, classical scholars attempted to plunge back into antiquity, to comprehend the transmission of a work, and to move closer to that single source from which all later sources were thought ultimately to derive.

Everything we know about Plato and Aristotle, about Aeschylus, Sophocles, and Euripides, about Virgil and Homer is owing to the patient work of generations of early scholars, comparing manuscripts in libraries all over Europe and the Middle East, at a time when the most far-flung sources, separated from one another geographically and from the original texts—whatever they may have been like—by millennia, needed to be examined and collated individually. Implicit in most traditional textual criticism, of course, was the profound faith that there is a work and that it can be recovered.[2] In the case of the Bible, of course, there was the added implication that in its original form the text was God-given.

More recent studies foster a less absolutist view toward the history of a literary text. Instead of focusing on a single "definitive" version, the final form a work assumed in the hands of its author (what the Germans call the *Fassung letzter Hand*), genetic textual criticism conceives a poem, a novel, a drama, or an essay as the sum of all creative work expended on it. Drafts, canceled layers, published versions, later revisions: all are given weight. The "work" is not embodied in a single "authorized" version but is expressed through the various stages of a complex intellectual and artistic process, which is presented to the reader.[3] Other textual critics, influenced particularly by the work of Jerome J. McGann, envision the text within a broader social context, of which the author is only one part: the context could comprise autograph manuscripts, to be sure, but also manuscript (or typed) copies, editorial interventions by publishing houses, publication in multiple editions in differing formats, public or private readings, theatrical productions, and so forth. For these critics, a literary work is social at its very core, and the quest for an authorial "original," independent of that social context, is spurious and quixotic.[4]

Critical editions of nineteenth-century Italian operas make available the best texts that modern scholarship, musicianship, and editorial technique can produce. Fully cognizant of modern theory, they do not return blindly to one "original" source, although the composer's autograph manuscript is often our best single guide. Instead, they reconstruct the circumstances under which a work was written, the interaction of composer and librettist, the effect of imposed censorship, the elements that entered into the performance, the steps that led to publication, and the role the composer played in the subsequent history of the work. They interpret the notation, often incomplete or contradictory, so that musicians have available not only a text prepared with an ear toward eventual performance, but also one that permits them to distinguish signs that stem directly from the composer from signs that derive from secondary sources or are provided by the editor. For works that exist in multiple versions, they either incorporate the versions within a single text (with "ossia"—alternative readings—indicated) or choose a basic perform-ing text (with appendixes that make possible the practical realization of any version prepared under the direction of the composer).[5]

WHAT IS "VERDI'S *RIGOLETTO*"?

Most literary texts continue to be read by individuals in the quiet of their homes or in libraries. Even most editions of plays are intended for reading, and adaptations prepared for performance are rarely consigned to print. Many contemporary writers, including Nabokov, Calvino, and Eco have played with that relationship in fiction such as *Pale Fire* or *If on a winter's night a traveler...*, creating literary works together with their textual and ana-lytical commentary. Calvino's *The Baron in the Trees* was born with a com-mentary for junior-high-school students as part of the text. Approaches to scholarship and creative work reflect common cultural roots.

Editions of musical scores (together with derivative parts and vocal scores) serve quite different purposes. The number of "readers" who can consult or consume the critical edition of an opera in the privacy of their home or in a library is minuscule in proportion to the number who may ul-timately see and hear a performance of that opera in the theater or on televi-sion or will come to know it through recordings. Because of the size and com-plexity of the vocal, choral, and orchestral forces that need to be marshaled, furthermore, a musical performance cannot adopt quite so casual a relation-ship to a printed text as a play can. Stage directors who lack experience in op-era rapidly learn that even a cut in the *secco* recitative cannot be made simply by striking out the unwanted lines of text: music must be rewritten, har-monies modified, an army of support personnel informed.

By comparison to the exertions of textual scholars reconstructing from later sources literary texts for which we lack authorial manuscripts, the task of editors preparing critical editions of the operas of Rossini, Bellini, Donizetti, and Verdi should be straightforward. In most cases we actually possess the au-thor's original manuscript and a wide range of sources documenting his fur-ther involvement with the work, not to mention the involvement of all those who formed part of the social and editorial process through which the opera came to be known by musicians and the public. To our distress, however, these documents—whether autograph manuscripts or derivative sources—are far from unequivocal. They are the source of all truth, so to speak, but they are also the root of all uncertainty.

Verdi's direct involvement with *Rigoletto* was limited to its first series of performances, at the Teatro La Fenice of Venice during the carnival season of 1850–51. For a long time, as we have seen, it was also the only opera by Verdi for which the composer's sketch was available to scholars. Thus, the simplicity of its history and the easy accessibility of relevant sources led the editors and publishers of *The Works of Giuseppe Verdi* to choose *Rigoletto* as the first Verdi opera to be prepared in a critical edition, which was edited by Martin Chusid.[6] Those same qualities allow it to serve our needs as we consider the practical meaning of the phrase "Verdi's *Rigoletto*."

We can reconstruct with precision the genesis of *Rigoletto* from its first conception to its premiere on 11 March 1851. Already by the spring of 1850, Verdi and his librettist, Francesco Maria Piave, had decided that the drama *Le Roi s'amuse* by Victor Hugo would be an ideal subject for their Venetian commission. During the summer Piave, who had already collaborated with Verdi on *Ernani, I due Foscari, Macbeth,* and *Il corsaro,* drafted a scenario, on the basis of which the librettist was assured that local censors would not object to the projected work. By the end of September he had almost completed the libretto, entitled at that point *La maledizione* (The Curse). By mid-October Verdi had received the text, and Piave was paid for it. As far as we know, the composer had written no music yet. He was fully occupied with *Stiffelio,* also to a libretto by Piave, whose premiere took place in Trieste on 16 November 1850.[7] After that premiere Verdi threw himself wholeheartedly into *La maledizione.* He quickly sketched the first act, using names modeled on Victor Hugo's play, which focused on the court of King François I of France: "Il Re" rather than "Il Duca," "Triboletto" rather than "Rigoletto," and "Bianca" rather than "Gilda."

But Verdi knew the difficulties Hugo's drama had encountered in Paris and remained concerned about censorship. By early December he was informed that the libretto had indeed been refused. Outraged, he offered to direct *Stiffelio* for Venice, since it was impossible for him to compose yet another opera. Piave, meanwhile, tried desperately to mollify both Verdi and the censors, proposing a revised libretto, *Il Duca di Vendome.* When Verdi received a copy, he rejected it out of hand, explaining precisely why the new libretto was impossible and concluding: "My notes, whether beautiful or ugly, are never written at random, and I always try to give them a specific character. In short, an original and powerful drama has been transformed into one that is quite common and cold."[8] After further consultations at Verdi's home in Busseto, and subsequently between the librettist, theater, and censors in Venice, an agreement was reached: *La maledizione,* soon to be known as *Rigoletto,* was approved, with only a few alterations of details.

From the moment he heard about the censor's original objections, Verdi halted all work on *Rigoletto*. Only after Piave had traveled back to Venice from Busseto on 5 January 1851 did the composer return to his task. Since composer and librettist were in different cities, a helpful series of letters chronicles their activities. Verdi sketched his way through acts 2 and 3, generally following the order of the libretto. By 14 January he had finished the Duke's aria (he may have written Rigoletto's aria earlier), by 20 January the remainder of the second act, by 5 February the third act.

At the same time he began to draft in skeleton score what would become his complete autograph manuscript, inserting vocal lines, the bass, and occasional instrumental indications. In this form he sent to Venice on 5 February all of the first act and most of the third (with the exception of the final duet), so that copyists could prepare *particelle,* parts from which each of the singers could study his or her role. Verdi did not himself arrive in Venice until 19 February, carrying with him the second act and the final duet of the third. We know that he had done no orchestration as of 11 February, for on that date he wrote to Ricordi that he had sent several pieces to Venice so that vocal lines could be extracted: "only the vocal lines," he said, "because I have not yet been able to do a note of the instrumentation."[9] Perhaps some of the material he carried with him on 19 February was already orchestrated, but the first act and most of the third were certainly orchestrated while he rehearsed with the singers. Orchestral rehearsals began about 4 March, by which time the orchestration must have been largely completed and the parts copied; the first performance followed one week later.

Whenever we think about the sources for "Verdi's *Rigoletto,*" we must bear in mind the speed with which the opera was written. Furthermore, as soon as Verdi arrived in Venice on 19 February, his activities were extremely diverse. He had to orchestrate his music, coach the singers, oversee the physical production and staging, and prepare the orchestra. There was no aspect of the production to which he did not turn his attention. It is hardly surprising, then, that many details in the autograph manuscript were overlooked in his drive to meet the imminent deadline of performance. Immersed as all the participants were in a single stylistic ambience, the composer could take a great deal for granted from his singers and orchestral musicians. A gesture or a few words of explanation during rehearsals would provide whatever correctives seemed crucial. Nor did Verdi ever reconsider those details, as he might have done had he anticipated that the full score would actually be published. Instead, he trusted Ricordi to provide reasonable copies of the score and to prepare adequate materials. Once the initial set of performances was over, the autograph manuscript of *Rigoletto* became the property of Casa Ricordi, and

Verdi never touched it again. His emotions at consigning his autograph to his publisher were probably not as strong in 1851 as in 1886, when he wrote to Arrigo Boito, librettist of *Otello,* that the last two acts had been consigned to the Ricordi *copisteria:* "Poor *Otello!* He will never return here again!!!"[10]

Strictly speaking, what is "Verdi's *Rigoletto*"? Philosophers have debated "the identity of the musical work" extensively.[11] Many believe that the identity of *Rigoletto* must be sought in some "ideal" conception of the work as Verdi imagined it, of which the written notation is but an approximation. One can understand and even sympathize with this viewpoint, but it addresses primarily nonmusicians, those uncomfortable with the ambiguities of actual musical notation. Few would use such arguments for literature. When literary scholars try to push back our knowledge of a Shakespearean play beyond surviving printed sources to a hypothetical manuscript in the author's hand, they believe that they are seeking to recover the lost ideal state of "Shakespeare's *The Tempest.*" In the presence of such an authorial text, they would hardly describe the penned words of Shakespeare as a mere approximation of characters and actions imagined by the writer, even while acknowledging that once an "ideal text" enters the theater, it becomes part of a complex social framework and lies open to modification and intervention from one or more hands. The problem about identifying a musical work with some "ideal performance" of that work as imagined by the composer is that there is no such thing. The very notion negates the nature of musical art, in which there is a composition and there is a set of performances of that composition. Nor does it help to evoke performances directed by a composer: Stravinsky's interpretations of his own music differ profoundly from recording to recording.

We know nothing more about "Verdi's *Rigoletto*" than what we find in the autograph manuscript of that opera (together with its antecedent sketch). No other source whatsoever, not a single variant, can be demonstrably linked to the composer.[12] As performers and editors, we can (and should) broaden our concerns to include the editorial history and performing traditions of *Rigoletto.* We can acquire useful information by studying letters in which Verdi comments on the opera, by reading contemporary reviews and periodicals, by examining instruments and instrumental practice in the 1850s, by understanding the structure of theaters and the nature of contemporary stagecraft, by following the careers of the singers for whom Verdi was writing. But the only trace we have of "Verdi's *Rigoletto*" is that autograph manuscript.

Would it not be enough, then, simply to study this document, either directly or in a beautiful facsimile reproduction, or—to assist those who find Verdi's handwriting too confusing for easy consultation—in a diplomatic transcription? In some cases it might indeed be enough. Since transforming into print the written notation of many compositions of our own time can pose intractable problems, publishers frequently resort to reproducing autograph manuscripts. Composers have met this challenge by developing a clarity of notation and a level of accuracy that would have astonished a Beethoven, the illegibility of whose hand was legendary in his own time. For Verdi, however, consultation of his autograph manuscript is rarely adequate. The extreme pressure under which he worked led him into errors, lacunae, and inconsistencies of every kind.

Here is one example from the opening scene of *Rigoletto*. In Verdi's autograph the Count of Ceprano, after feeling the sting of Rigoletto's tongue, vows revenge. He tells the other courtiers, "In armi chi ha core / Doman sia da me" (Let him who has courage come to my house, armed, tomorrow). But a moment later the same Ceprano turns to the same courtiers and exhorts them, "Stanotte chi ha core / Sia in armi da me" (Let him who has courage come to my house, armed, tonight). Did Ceprano intentionally change the appointment from one day to the other?

From Verdi's letter to Piave of 14 January 1851, we know that the composer was troubled about the time sequence of the opera.[13] All events of the first two acts were originally intended to take place in a single night. But Verdi complained that "after the party Triboletto [sic] changes, sings a duet with the assassin, an endless scene with Gilda, [who has] a duet with the Duke, and an aria, and finally this abduction. This cannot all happen in a single night, since if the party finishes toward dawn, Triboletto [sic] cannot meet the assassin toward evening, and it isn't very likely that Bianca [sic] would remain awake all night." Thus, Verdi asked Piave to alter the verses of the chorus in the middle section of the Duke's aria:

Poiché la festa cessò di corte	Once the party at Court was finished
Moviamo uniti prima del dì.	We set out together before dawn.

Piave agreed and gave the courtiers these verses instead:

Scorrendo uniti remota via	Passing together on a remote street
Brev'ora dopo caduto il dì,	Just after nightfall,

Verdi was perfectly happy with these new verses, which he entered directly into his autograph manuscript.

At the same time, the composer pointed out to his librettist that the time sequence also had to be changed in the first act, where Ceprano (at that time still called "Cavriano") originally had the following interchange with the courtiers:

Cav.:	*Stanotte chi ha core*	Let him who has courage
	Sia in armi da me.	Come to my house, armed, tonight.
Tutti:	*Sì.*	Yes.
Cav.:	*È detto.*	It's agreed.
Tutti:	*Sarà.*	We'll be there.

In place of this text, Piave provided Verdi with new words:

Cav.:	*In armi chi ha core*	Let him who has courage
	Doman sia da me.	Come to my house, armed, tomorrow.
Tutti:	*Sì.*	Yes.
Cav.:	*A notte.*	At nightfall.
Tutti:	*Sarà.*	We'll be there.

Verdi dutifully scratched out of his autograph manuscript the offending words (which he had used in the skeleton score) and replaced them with the new text.

But the composer forgot that the text is repeated a few measures later, and hence failed to correct the second appearance of the text.[14] Thus, Ceprano first invites the courtiers to meet him "tomorrow," then two minutes later asks them instead to come "tonight." As incredible as it may seem, no printed edition of the opera ever corrected this blatant error, and countless performances made before preparation of the critical edition blithely employed the faulty text. Does the time sequence of *Rigoletto* really matter? Well, it mattered enough to the composer and his librettist for them, after a careful correspondence, to correct it. Does that mean that every production of *Rigoletto* must endeavor to render this time sequence palpable? Not necessarily: the relationship between a written score and a performance is a complex one, which forms the subject of the second part of this book. But no matter how performers may wish to manipulate stage time for the purposes of a particular production, it is clear that "Verdi's *Rigoletto*," as preserved in his autograph manuscript, is incoherent at this point.

Of a different order are the many places in the autograph manuscript of *Rigoletto* in which the composer omitted signs, the kinds of problems on which Denis Vaughan's polemic foundered. The initial orchestral presentation of the melody of "La donna è mobile," for example, is played simultaneously (in varying registers) by flute, piccolo, oboe, clarinet, bassoon, first violins, and cellos. The first five notes are normally articulated with three

EXAMPLE 5.1. GIUSEPPE VERDI, *RIGOLETTO*, SCENA E CANZONE [DUCA]
(N. 11), MM. 38–41.

accents and a diminuendo. All printed editions before the critical edition, it is worth pointing out, print these signs as accents over the first *four* notes, a very different effect and not reflecting at all the notation of the autograph manuscript, which is unusually precise (example 5.1). But in notating the various instrumental parts playing the melody, Verdi wrote a diminuendo at m. 39 only for flute, first violins, and cellos, omitting it in piccolo, oboe, clarinet, and bassoon, whereas at m. 41 he wrote it explicitly in each part.[15] Are we supposed to believe that "Verdi's *Rigoletto*" was meant to be performed with some instruments playing a diminuendo and the others remaining unchanged? At the courtier's entrance in the middle section of the Duke's aria ("Duca, Duca! L'amante fu rapita a Rigoletto!"), Verdi wrote *ff* in the first violins to signal a loud chord. In the next measure, however, where the instrumentation is vastly reduced (to oboes, bassoons, and strings), there is a *pp* for bassoons, cellos, and double basses, but no additional marking for the first violins. Are we expected to believe that in "Verdi's *Rigoletto*" these violins must continue to play *ff* while the bassoons, cellos, and double basses assume the lower volume?[16]

And so on through a range of many trivial and a significant number of nontrivial matters, affecting almost every measure of the autograph of *Rigoletto*. Some tangible intervention is required to transform "Verdi's *Rigoletto*," as incorporated in his autograph, into a musical score that can be used to perform the opera. Such intervention is necessarily the work of some later musician or musicians. The musical score commonly known as *Rigoletto* in whatever edition, whether "critical" or not, as opposed to "Verdi's *Rigoletto*," results from a series of editorial interventions. The *Rigoletto* most commonly available before publication of the critical edition in 1983 was the product of interventions that began with the first preparation by the Ricordi firm of a printed full orchestral score for rental during the 1890s, continued with the first publication of a full orchestral score for purchase early in the twentieth century, and was followed by further interventions each time it was reprinted during the twentieth century. If we believe that performers should play the work "as Verdi conceived it," to which *Rigoletto* should they turn?

Editorial interventions deemed essential by one generation of musicians are quite different from those deemed essential by another. Nowhere is this more keenly felt than in music written before 1830, where the pendulum of editorial technique has swung from editions adding a full panoply of expressive markings and slurs (in music whose sources had few), to those supplying so little information as to be practically diplomatic transcriptions of an old source, to those accepting again modest editorial interventions. Although the finest scholars of the nineteenth century provided *Gesamtausgaben* (editions of the complete works) of Bach, Handel, Mozart, Beethoven, and Schubert, over the past fifty years the music of these composers has been (or is being) reedited in new complete editions. Certainly we know more today about their life and works than did nineteenth-century editors, and access to better musical sources can lead to new editions strikingly different from the old. Often, though, the same sources are simply being employed in different ways by a new generation of scholars, committed to a new set of editorial principles.[17]

Yet it is extremely unlikely that two musicians asked to prepare a printed edition of *Rigoletto* today would agree in every case about where the score requires editorial intervention and what this intervention should be. Editors make those adjustments they consider necessary on the basis of the historical moment at which they are working, the musical culture by which they are surrounded, their specific knowledge of the music of Verdi and its sources, their inherent musicality, and their insight and intelligence. A critical edition of *Rigoletto*, then, is necessarily an interpretation of "Verdi's *Rigoletto*"—as is any edition whatsoever. The difference is that a critical edition makes its substantive interventions graphically explicit, and explains them in ample critical notes. Users of the score can ascertain where "Verdi's *Rigoletto*" ends and editorial intervention begins. A critical edition also differs from other editions in its insistence that criteria for editorial interventions be clear and that such interventions be restricted to those which derive from Verdi's explicit indications or meet levels of consistency and logic that reflect Verdi's notational practice. But it would be naive to assume that universal agreement could ever be reached as to what those levels should be.

FINDING THE SOURCES

Although a scholar's work is often accomplished in the library or in his or her study, the preparation of critical editions depends fundamentally on locating and using sources, particularly autograph sources, hidden in nooks and crannies of public or private libraries, in venerated collections of noble families, in bank vaults in Switzerland. Some library collections are well catalogued and preserved, although particular items may go unmentioned or be unknown for decades. Sometimes identifications are faulty, even in responsible libraries. The Library of the Conservatory of Milan long thought it possessed the autograph manuscript of Rossini's *La gazzetta,* while the real autograph was (and still is) in the library of the Naples Conservatory. The copy that ended up in Milan, part of the "Noseda" collection, was "authenticated" by the nineteenth-century librarian of the Naples Conservatory, Francesco Florimo, who was thoroughly knowledgeable about Rossini's handwriting and surely knew that his identification was fraudulent.[18] Then again, the library of the Bologna Conservatory believed for years—against all appearances—that it owned the autograph manuscript of Rossini's *Stabat Mater,* when the composer's original was sitting in the British Library in London, where it remains.[19]

Entire library collections can be in sad disarray. Among Rossini sources at the Naples Conservatory in the mid-1960s were autograph manuscripts that had gone unidentified, including several works presumed lost. Only by asking to see every item related to Rossini in the library (and extending a projected two-week stay to six weeks) was I able to sort them out. Among the unknown works was Rossini's 1820 *Messa di Gloria,* of which the original performing parts (with autograph annotations by Rossini) turned out to be in the collection.[20] The problem is not restricted to Italy. Edmond Michotte was a close friend of Rossini's in his youth and later director of the Brussels Conservatory, to which he left his important collection of manuscripts.[21] Visiting the conservatory for the first time in 1965, I found a pile of uncatalogued manuscript pages, few of which had ever been examined. As I worked through that pile, a treasure trove appeared: alongside the autograph of an entire Rossini opera, *Matilde di Shabran,* were autograph manuscripts of arias from operas, songs, and sketches; copyist's manuscripts belonging to Isabella Colbran and Giuditta Pasta (sometimes with ornamentation in Rossini's hand); and other sources. There was also the one surviving page of the autograph manuscript of the *Messa di Gloria,* which Rossini had given to Gustave Vaëz in 1846.[22] Not until the 1970s did the Music Department of the Bibliothèque Nationale in Paris admit grudgingly, to Elizabeth Bartlet (a Canadian scholar working on the operas of Méhul) that they owned a considerable collection of manuscript parts from the archive of the Théâtre Italien. That collection ultimately yielded the first musical sources to surface in the twentieth century pertaining to Rossini's *Il viaggio a Reims.* I will have more to say about that work and its discovery later in this chapter.

The quest for manuscripts in private collections can be especially satisfying or especially frustrating. A fleeting glimpse of an important source in an auction or a dealer's catalogue or a casual reference in a book can lead to an extended search, sometimes crowned with success, sometimes not. Since the publication of the first volume of Julian Budden's magisterial *The Operas of Verdi,* for example, it has been known that Verdi prepared a new romanza, "Sventurato! Alla mia vita," for his opera *Attila* when the Russian tenor Nicola Ivanoff sang the role of Foresto in Trieste during the autumn of 1846 (shortly after the opera's Venetian premiere on 17 March of the same year).[23] Ivanoff was a great friend of Rossini's, and it was Rossini himself, in a letter of 21 July, who commissioned Verdi to write the piece for his protégé. Verdi was not fond of "substitute" arias, but he could hardly refuse Rossini. And so Verdi, in turn, penned this wonderful note to Piave on 10 August:

> I need a favor: a romanza with recitative and two quatrains; the subject will be a lover who is moaning about the infidelity of his beloved (old hat!). Write me 5 or 6 lines of recitative, then two quatrains of *ottonari;* there should be a masculine ending every other line, because it's easier to set that way...
>
> Make sure they're pathetic and tearful: have that imbecile of a lover say that he would have given up his share of paradise and that she rewarded him with... Horns... Long live those horns: bless them!... If I could, I'd like to give them out myself all the time![24]

By early September, Ivanoff had his romanza.

Ivanoff sang the romanza for the final time in Turin in 1849, after which all traces of it disappeared. Then, more than thirty years ago, Verdi's autograph manuscript was acquired by a distinguished London antiquarian music dealer, Albi Rosenthal, who nevertheless refused to show it to anyone. After he sold the manuscript, its new owner would not even allow his identity to be revealed. Finally, in the spring of 1992, I was asked to write an article for a memorial book in honor of the collector Hans Moldenhauer, who had recently died, leaving an extensive group of manuscripts to the Library of Congress. The library wanted me to describe a Verdi aria in the collection, which they believed to have been written for *Ernani.* It turned out to be "Sventurato! Alla mia vita." This beautiful romanza, acquired by Moldenhauer from Rosenthal and then willed to the Library of Congress, will be published in an appendix to the critical edition of *Attila.* Its first modern performance in the context of *Attila* took place at Lyric Opera of Chicago during its 2000–2001 season, where it was well received.

Many quests are less successful. The autograph manuscript of the principal soprano aria ("Quelle horrible destinée") that Rossini added to his Italian opera *Mosè in Egitto* when he transformed it as *Moïse* for the Opéra of Paris in 1827, sits inaccessible in a private collection. It appeared fleetingly in an exhibit of musical manuscripts owned by collectors in Basel, but all subsequent efforts to see it have failed.[25] In an 1864 biography of Rossini, the French critic Aléxis Azevedo mentions that he owns the autograph manuscript of a chorus from the same opera, but no one has ever found it.[26] In 1916 a manuscript of Verdi's sketches for a major scene in *Jérusalem* was sold in New York: its subsequent whereabouts are unknown.[27] Donizetti's manuscript for *La Favorite* was owned by a wealthy Milanese family, the Treccani degli Alfieri, in the 1940s, but has since disappeared. Although a microfilm copy is deposited in the New York Public Library, the manuscript is so complex (much of it began life as a different, unperformed work, *L'Ange de Nisida*) that access to the original would be an enormous boon.[28] Verdi letters fundamental to our understanding of his middle-period operas are regularly bought anonymously at auction and disappear for decades. Most auction houses will send requests for information to new owners, to be sure, but when the owners disregard those requests, there is no recourse.

Even if we grant collectors their right to privacy, musical manuscripts are sometimes bought and sold with noticeable avidity and even duplicity. In 1979, Christie's in London attempted, unsuccessfully, to auction what they claimed to be the autograph manuscript of a wedding *Cantatina* by Rossini. From a reproduction in the auction catalogue, it was perfectly clear to Rossini scholars that the manuscript was not in the composer's hand.[29] Nor could it have been a copy of a piece by Rossini, since the score was obviously a composing manuscript, not a copyist's rendering. I immediately wrote to Christie's, alerting them to their error; they ignored my letter. But when the manuscript remained unsold, it was duly returned to the owner, who later brought it to be seen by scholars at the Fondazione Rossini. We informed him in no uncertain terms that the manuscript was not in Rossini's hand. But, the owner insisted, the musical style is similar to Rossini's (and whose style in Italy in 1832 wasn't?); further, the manuscript was certainly written early in the nineteenth century (and what does that have to do with Rossini's handwriting?). Many years later he was still trying to convince us. Finally, in 2003, he persuaded the artistic director of the "Hampstead & Highgate Festival" to give the *Cantatina* its "world premiere," listing it as "Rossini (attrib.)." The printed program included two pictures: part of Rossini's autograph manuscript for the *Stabat mater* and a snippet from the *Cantatina*. Look at the capital "E," the program notes suggested, ignoring the fact that the clefs and time signature, absolutely characteristic of Rossini's handwriting, were entirely different from those in the *Cantatina*. And so disinformation continues to spread.

On another occasion a manuscript dealer from Los Angeles, Scriptorium, claimed that an authentic Rossini manuscript was a fraud. The story pertains to one of the first volumes published in the Rossini critical edition, a volume of piano music from his *Péchés de vieillesse* (Sins of Old Age), as Rossini called his late Parisian music, 1855–68. This volume was entitled *Quelques Riens pour album* (Several Nothings for Album), in that ironically self-deprecating manner typical of late Rossini.[30] These twenty-four piano pieces, complex and often fascinating, are anything but traditional album leaves. Not surprisingly, Respighi used several of their themes in the ballet score he arranged in 1919 from Rossini's late piano music, *La Boutique fantasque*, for the Ballets russes. All but one of the twenty-four autograph manuscripts are in the collection of the Fondazione Rossini; the remaining autograph is in the private collection of a generous American music lover, Mario Valente, who kindly shared it with us.

After completing the autograph manuscript of a piece from those late years, the composer habitually instructed a copyist in his employ to prepare a manuscript copy of it. The copy was used when the composer himself or other musicians performed the piece, sometimes at the musical salons (the *samedi soirs*) that Rossini and his wife Olympe held at their Chausée d'Antin apartment. The composer would personally correct the copy, usually sign it, and sometimes even add performance indications not present in his original autograph. For the purposes of a critical edition, therefore, such copies are significant, for they can provide information unavailable elsewhere.[31]

Unlike the autograph manuscripts of the *Péchés de vieillesse*, however, which the composer generally kept, willing them first to his wife and then, after her death, to the city of Pesaro, the *copies* were purchased from Rossini's widow in 1873 by the Englishman "Baron" Grant (the title was granted him by the Italian king in appreciation for his having developed the property that became the Galleria in central Milan).[32] When his business affairs turned sour, Baron Grant tried to realize some gain by auctioning off these copies. The auction, held by the London firm of Puttick & Simpson on 30 May 1878, was a fiasco.[33] Rossini was hardly a leading figure in musical Europe during the late Romantic period: even if his operas still had a certain prestige, no one understood these late piano pieces and songs with their incomprehensible titles ("A Caress for My Wife," "Little Caprice in the Style of Offenbach,"

"My Hygienic Morning Prelude," etc.). Hence, few of the manuscripts were purchased.

The manuscripts not acquired at the 1878 sale arrived a hundred years later in the hands of an outstanding English music dealer, Richard Macnutt, who sold them to the Houghton Library at Harvard University. The lots that *were* purchased were acquired by collectors, music dealers, and speculators from all over Europe. Some have since surfaced; others have not. Copies of the twenty-four *Quelques Riens pour album,* as well as several other piano pieces and songs, were acquired for the French music publisher Heugel by Armand Gouzien. And, indeed, between 1880 and 1885 Heugel published all the music that Gouzien had acquired. Since inquiries in Paris concerning the where-abouts of these manuscripts proved fruitless, we presumed that the editor preparing *Quelques Riens pour album* would have access to them only through the Heugel editions, from which he would have to deduce what Rossini may actually have added to the manuscripts.

What was our surprise when in November 1975, shortly before work began on the critical edition of *Quelques Riens pour album,* a German auction com-pany, Hauswedell & Nolte, announced that a member of the Heugel family had made available for sale these very manuscript copies, signed by Rossini and with his autograph emendations. We sought information about them from the auction house, which put us in touch with the Los Angeles buyer. Scriptorium, in turn, informed us that it did indeed have the manuscripts, that it would not allow us to examine them unless we wished to purchase them (and could Scriptorium make us a deal?), but that, in any case, it was returning them to the auction company. As Charles Sachs, of Scriptorium, informed me in a letter dated 5 April 1976, a well-known New York manu-script dealer, the late Charles Hamilton, had "denounced their genuineness in the sense that he does not believe that either the corrections or the signa-tures at the end of each manuscript are in the hand of Rossini." Hamilton's claims to expertise in fields ranging from Elizabethan theater to the Hitler diaries are well known, not only to scholars but to readers of the *New York Times.* Having reconstructed the complete history of these Rossini manu-scripts, we were astonished. Were we merely cynical to wonder whether this claim for inauthenticity was related to Scriptorium's inability to find a buyer?

Back to Germany went the Heugel manuscripts. Before accepting the claim that the manuscripts were inauthentic, however, Hauswedell & Nolte decided to seek expert advice, and they, in turn, sent them off to none other than the Fondazione Rossini of Pesaro. There, it was possible for me and my colleagues to examine them thoroughly, to catalogue their autograph markings (many of them fascinating), and to return them to the auction company with every assurance that the manuscripts were authentic. And back they went to Los Angeles, where Scriptorium ultimately succeeded in selling them. A later auction and a later buyer finally placed these Heugel manuscripts in the hands of a friendly collector, and they are now available for study by scholars preparing critical editions.

THREE TRIUMPHAL TALES

A Happy Ending for the Tragic Finale of *Tancredi*

Many stories about my own quests for musical sources of the operas of Rossini and Verdi are piquant enough for fiction. Indeed, in Fréderic Vitoux's 1983 novel, *Fin de saison au Palazzo Pedrotti*, there is a character who rediscovers in the collection of a noble Italian family the lost tragic finale of *Tancredi*, Rossini's first great *opera seria*. I would like to believe, however, that the only personal similarity between myself and the highly disagreeable American musicologist in the novel, Edmund Green, might be found in the following description: "Green sang, and he sang as loudly as possible, in a hoarse voice, terribly out of tune, without the least scruple."[34] Perhaps I should add that I have never actually *met* Vitoux; nor (as far as I know) has he ever heard me sing.

This is what really happened. Although I had loved opera from my early teens, I did not encounter my first real prima donna until the late 1960s, and it was my particular good fortune that she was Marilyn Horne. Horne's 1966 performance as the young hero Arsace (one of the great roles for a contralto/mezzo-soprano *en travesti*) in the recording of *Semiramide*, with Joan Sutherland in the title role, had been a revelation: so this was what Rossini's serious operas, with all those cascades of notes, could sound like when interpreted by a superb artist.[35] And if a contralto/mezzo-soprano could develop the technique to sing this music, why not a tenor or a bass? My meeting with Horne during the autumn of 1972 was arranged by one of her fans, Conrad Claborne (later a respected artist's agent in New York), who knew that I had recently returned from a year of research in Europe on Rossinian sources. She received us graciously in her home in New Jersey, and we sat together for hours, trading information and operatic gossip. As we were about to leave, she asked me about Rossini's *Tancredi*: "Have you found the tragic finale?" No, I admitted, but I hoped it might yet surface. "If you ever do find it," she said, "let me know: I've always wanted to perform the part [another heroic role *en travesti*], but I don't find the happy ending convincing." At the time, neither of us anticipated that in the fall of 1977 Jackie (as she is affectionately known to friends) would sing in the first performance of *Tancredi* based on the critical edition of the opera, with its newly rediscovered tragic finale. The Houston Grand Opera performances launched Rossini's opera on a series of revivals that has brought it into theaters throughout the world.

In adapting Voltaire's play *Tancrède* for Rossini, the librettist Gaetano Rossi introduced a happy ending in place of the original death of the Sicilian hero in battle against the Saracens. Soon after the highly successful original performances of *Tancredi* in Venice at the Teatro La Fenice (the premiere took place on 6 February 1813), Rossini and much of the original cast proceeded to Ferrara, where they produced *Tancredi* again. In Ferrara, however, several changes were made, as attested by the libretto printed on that occasion. A new aria for Tancredi was added near the end of the opera, "Perché turbar la calma," replacing the weaker original, and it immediately gained pride of place in future performances. Most important, the conclusion of the opera was rewritten to follow Voltaire more closely, with the death of the hero bringing down the curtain. The new lines are practically a translation into Italian verse of Voltaire's text, clearly by a poet who understood and treasured the original. Recitative (in the standard *settenari* and *endecasillabi*) leads to a concluding quatrain in *settenari*:

Amenaide... serbami	Amenaide... remain
Tua fé... quel... cor ch'è mio,	Faithful to me... that... heart that is mine,
Ti lascio... ah! tu di vivere	I leave you... ah! you must swear
Giurami,... sposa... addio.	To live,... my wife... farewell.

Unlike the new aria added for Ferrara, the tragic finale was poorly received. A contemporary review noted: "The death of Tancredi, introduced there [in Ferrara] and to which that public did not want to adapt itself [...], did not please."[36] Until the mid 1970s, no musical source was known to exist.

There the story would have ended were it not for the kindness of the late Count Giacomo Lechi of Brescia and his family.[37] Count Lechi, reviewing the family's papers in 1976, came upon several musical manuscripts. One was a manuscript that bore the following delightful attestation, written in the hand characteristic of Rossini's old age:

Dichiaro (e non senza Rossore)	[I declare (and not without Shame)
essere questo un mio autografo	that this is an autograph of mine
del 1813!! A Venezia fu vergato,	from *1813!!* It was penned in Venice,
che tempi!!!!! Aujourd'hui c'est	what times!!!!! Today is quite another
autre chose. G. Rossini.	matter. G. Rossini.
(Paris 22 Nov.ʳᵉ 1867.)[38]	(Paris, 22 November 1867.)]

Curious about the manuscript, Count Lechi sent copies of a few pages to the Fondazione Rossini, asking for assistance in identifying it. On a fall day a few months later, Bruno Cagli (artistic director of the Foundation), Alberto Zedda, and I drove to Brescia at the invitation of Count Lechi to examine what we knew was going to be the autograph manuscript of the tragic finale of *Tancredi,* the unique surviving source of a composition whose where-abouts had been unknown for over 160 years. We were shown into a splendid villa, whose library contained many treasures documenting the family's cul-tural, political, and scientific activities over several centuries. And with the assistance of Count Lechi, I was able to reconstruct the history that had brought Rossini and the Lechis together.

The Lechis are a distinguished northern Italian family. Two Lechi broth-ers (Giuseppe and Teodoro), hoping that their support of the French em-peror would ultimately lead to the formation of an independent Italian state, were active in the Napoleonic wars. Indeed, Giuseppe was a commander in the Legione Lombarda, which invaded Pesaro twice in 1797, freeing it tempo-rarily from the Papal States. Rossini's father, also named Giuseppe, one of Pesaro's most outspoken patriots, was instrumental in the local revolt and personally received a message from Lechi informing him of the time planned for the arrival of the French. As a result, Giuseppe Rossini was imprisoned for almost a year after the French forces were routed and the Papal government returned.

A younger Lechi brother, Luigi (1786–1867) played another, quite different role in the life of Gioachino Rossini. Luigi Lechi studied medicine and sciences in Pavia in 1809 and in Paris from 1810 to 1811, but his main interests were lit-erary. He was part of the circle of students at the University of Pavia sur-rounding the great Italian poet Ugo Foscolo, who had been appointed profes-sor of Italian rhetoric there in 1808. During this period Lechi first met the singer Adelaide Malanotte, who was to create the title role in Rossini's *Tan-credi.* We do not know how or when they were introduced, but we do know that Foscolo was well acquainted with "a beautiful woman from Verona, dear to the Graces and the Muses," as he referred to Malanotte in a letter of 2 March 1809 to Giuseppe Mangili.[39] Born in Verona in 1785, she is said to have come from a bourgeois family. She married a Frenchman, Montrésor, and bore him two children. Matrimonial strife led to her undertaking a career as a singer, which she pursued in earnest beginning in 1809.

Foscolo's feelings about Malanotte are expressed in a letter to Giuseppe Grassi, a scholar from Turin famous for studies of the Italian language and translator of Goethe's *Werther.* This letter of 4 December 1809 provided an introduction for Grassi to Malanotte, who was to perform in Turin during the approaching carnival season:

> My dear Grassi — If we did not occasionally encounter the Graces and the Muses in our earthly pilgrimage, and if the Graces and the Muses did not open for us the door of Courtesy and Love, I would no longer find either motive or interest in continuing the journey of life through so many difficulties and dangers. And because I believe that you and all gentle souls feel the same way, I send you this letter, which will permit you to encounter the Graces and the Muses. With it you will visit the Signora Malanotte, and you will greet with my love and with your love her large and ever so dark eyes. I do not recommend you to her, nor her to you: you will be dear to one another because she is beautiful and a great singer, and because you are courteous and a fine writer. Be careful only not to fall in love. And live happily.[40]

Grassi may have followed Foscolo's advice "not to fall in love," but Luigi Lechi did not. By late 1812, Luigi Lechi and Adelaide Malanotte had begun the liaison that bound them together until the singer's death in 1832.

Not only did Luigi Lechi accompany Adelaide Malanotte to Venice and Ferrara for her performances in *Tancredi* in 1813, but he himself also prepared the text of the tragic finale added in Ferrara. The failure of the tragic finale to please the Ferrarese public suggested to the composer that it would never again be performed in the Italian operatic world he knew. Thus, he presented the autograph to either Malanotte or Lechi. Just before the death of Luigi Lechi on 13 December 1867, the manuscript of the tragic finale was taken to Paris by Count Faustino Lechi, son of Luigi's brother Teodoro, and Luigi's sole heir. It was on that occasion that Rossini wrote on the manuscript the attestation concerning its authenticity.

In 1976 the Fondazione Rossini decided to proceed with the critical edition of *Tancredi,* and my phone call to Marilyn Horne followed immediately. That, in turn, led to the Houston premiere of the opera in the critical edition I prepared, in which the tragic finale was performed for the first time. Audiences who have experienced the stunning performances of *Tancredi* with Horne (or Lucia Valentini-Terrani or Daniela Barcellona) know that this conclusion is one of the most unusual compositions in Rossini's operas, indeed in Italian opera from the early nineteenth century. It begins with a brief choral number, "Muore il prode." What must have been a *secco* recitative follows, during which the dying hero is carried in. No music for that recitative is preserved in the Lechi manuscript, although it was almost surely set by

Rossini himself. Since the dramaturgical shape of the opera requires that these words be heard, I provided an original setting for the critical edition (clearly marked as having been composed by the editor).[41]

Writing such a recitative *ex novo* required bringing together analytic control of Rossini's musical language in the recitatives of *Tancredi* on the one hand, and a free response to the exigencies of the text and dramatic moment on the other. I prepared a table of harmonic progressions used in recitative by Rossini throughout the opera, to keep myself stylistically honest. Yet the poignancy and urgency of the moment, in which the dying Tancredi learns that Amenaide was indeed faithful, required an intense musical setting. How does one measure one's success in preparing such a passage? One's ego wants the passage to be appreciated; one's superego wants it to pass unobserved, perfectly integrated into the whole. And so I reacted with a mixture of emotions when one conductor (Gianluigi Gelmetti), unaware that I had written this recitative, praised it for its expressiveness and called it "Monteverdian": that suggested I may have gone too far!

But, of course, what really matters in the tragic finale of *Tancredi* is Rossini's concluding music. In their starkness, the accompanied recitative and "Cavatina Finale," as Rossini called the concluding moments of the opera, depart so completely from typical finale designs of the period that we can easily comprehend their failure to gain popular approval. Gone are the coloratura flourishes; gone is a more elaborate orchestration; gone are requirements of phrase construction and cadential repetition; gone, in short, are the conventions that usually rule Italian opera. Instead, the concluding moments of the opera mirror each word of the dying hero, supported essentially by strings alone. One feels in the presence of the Gluckian ideal, adapted even in this quasi-declamatory music to the beauty of Italian melody and the simplicity of Italian harmony. The ideal may have been transmitted from Luigi Lechi and his neoclassical vision of art, but in this piece Rossini made that vision his own.

The Voyage (through Paris, Rome, Vienna, and New York) *to Rheims*

In a world where the authority of kings had so nearly been overthrown as Europe in the 1820s, celebrations for the coronation of a new king were meant to reinforce the legitimacy of the Restoration and its monarchs. Every Parisian institution and every artist supported directly or indirectly by the government was expected to participate in the celebrations that accompanied and followed the coronation of Charles X at Rheims on 29 May 1825.[42] The major contribution of the Théâtre Italien was *Il viaggio a Reims,* designated a "cantata scenica" in its printed libretto (but in every other respect a full-length opera), its music composed by Rossini, the theater's musical director since 1824. First performed on 19 June 1825 in the presence of the king, repeated twice more in the following days and a final time (as a "représentation extraordinaire") in September, the work had an enormous success with critics and public alike. But because *Il viaggio a Reims* was so closely associated with a historical event, the celebration of which forms an integral part of the libretto, Rossini decided quite early to withdraw his score from circulation and to reuse parts of it on another occasion, introducing them into an opera more likely to have a longer stage life.[43]

That occasion presented itself a few years later, when about half of the score, with important modifications, was integrated into Rossini's third opera in French, *Le Comte Ory*, which had its premiere at the Opéra on 20 August 1828. Using the text by Luigi Balocchi printed in the original libretto for *Il viaggio a Reims*, as well as contemporary testimony, I was able in 1970 to suggest which pieces from the earlier Italian work had been inserted into the later French opera, though no musical sources directly related to *Il viaggio a Reims* were at that time known to exist.[44] Indeed, only a handful of autograph fragments associated with *Le Comte Ory* survived, and none contain music borrowed from *Il viaggio a Reims*. When the tentative structure of the *Edizione critica delle opere di Gioachino Rossini* was proposed in 1974, space was left for *Il viaggio a Reims* among the operas, but the title was marked "subject to the recovery of the musical sources."

Miracles happen. During the course of her doctoral research at the University of Chicago, Elizabeth Bartlet was permitted in 1974 to examine a group of manuscripts at the Music Department of the Bibliothèque Nationale in Paris—performance materials for operas given during the first half of the nineteenth century at the Théâtre Italien—that had not yet been catalogued. The library had long before accounted for all the manuscript copies of full operas or extracts in its possession, but it had set aside these orchestral and vocal parts for later consideration. While Bartlet was seeking materials from the years immediately following the French Revolution, she spotted a group of parts identified as *Il viaggio a Reims* or *Andremo a Parigi?* She knew that no musical sources for Rossini's opera had previously been identified; she also knew that *Andremo a Parigi?* was an adaptation of *Viaggio* performed at the Théâtre Italien in 1848, without Rossini's participation. In it, the travelers originally seeking to arrive in Rheims for the coronation of Charles X became travelers on their way to Paris to see the barricades. She wrote to me immediately about her discovery and, at my urgent request, arranged for a microfilm to be made of all the parts.

The manuscripts were indeed performance materials (orchestral parts, a few vocal and choral parts, and a short section of the prompter's part) for many sections of *Il viaggio a Reims* and its adaptation as *Andremo a Parigi?* Wherever possible the 1848 adaptation used original 1825 parts, emended as appropriate; where the changes introduced in 1848 were too numerous, new parts were made. These Parisian parts were incomplete, however, and some passages were missing altogether (including the legendary 1825 finale, which brings together travelers from all over Europe to celebrate the new king, a scene irrelevant in 1848). The parts confirmed most of my hypothetical derivations in *Le Comte Ory* from *Il viaggio a Reims*.[45] They also provided a first glimpse of some music Rossini wrote for *Viaggio* that had previously been unknown, especially the lengthy sextet, but the many lacunae in the vocal parts made it impossible to prepare a complete reconstruction. The Paris material was tantalizing, but did not alone offer sufficient information to bring *Il viaggio a Reims* back to life.

In 1976–77 I had a sabbatical leave in Rome from the University of Chicago, during which I prepared the critical edition of *Tancredi*. At various points during the year, I visited the library of the Rome Conservatory, "Santa Cecilia," a collection I thought I knew well. During earlier stays in Rome, in fact, I had studied every Rossini item listed in the catalogue, most of the operatic sources there for the operas of Bellini, Donizetti, and Verdi, and operas by a host of related composers. The staff knew me well and were aware of my interests. They even dreaded my appearances, which were sure to give them more work. One day toward the end of the spring of 1977, the librarian, Emilia Zanetti, appeared with a glint in her eye. "There's something here," she said, "that I think you might find interesting." And a few moments later she reappeared with a pile of manuscript pages, on the cover of which was written in Rossini's unmistakable script: "Alcuni Brani della *Cantata* Il Viaggio a Reims. Mio Autografo. G. Rossini" (Several pieces from the *Cantata* Il Viaggio a Reims. My autograph manuscript. G. Rossini). Below, Rossini's widow had added: "Given to my friend the dear Doctor Vio Bonato, 1 March 1878, Olympe V.ve [Widow] Rossini."[46]

The bifolios of the manuscript were largely out of order, and my first task was to reassemble them consecutively with the assistance of the printed libretto and a knowledge of the way Rossini prepared manuscripts. When I had finished, there before me lay Rossini's autograph manuscript for practically all the music from *Il viaggio a Reims* that he had *not* reused in *Le Comte Ory*: almost all the *secco* recitative (which he wrote personally), the sextet, part of an aria for bass, a full-fledged duet for tenor and mezzo-soprano, and the finale. Yes, the finale about which I had read in Parisian reviews of 1825, with its series of national anthems and characteristic songs in praise of Charles X. Some were traditional, some newly invented, but all combined delicious musical detail with the faintly ironic touch that Balocchi and Rossini had sprinkled liberally over their entire concoction. The finale concluded with a superb set of variations on the French song "Vive Henri IV" (each statement masterfully reharmonized).

How do you describe the experience of reading through a score that no one had seen for more than 150 years, reproducing its melodies and its rich orchestral textures in your mind? No one knew at that time how the manuscript had come to the Biblioteca di Santa Cecilia, but it had been there for years.[47] While Emilia Zanetti had included *Il viaggio a Reims* in the early 1950s in the very smallest of small print in a German musical encyclopedia (as part of a long list of sources in the library), the music had never figured in the library's catalogues.[48] Still, it was enough finally to know that we were ever so much closer to reconstructing Rossini's lost opera. For the music not reused in *Le Comte Ory,* we had almost all of Rossini's autograph manuscript; for the music reused in *Ory,* we had the full score of that opera printed by Rossini's French publisher, Troupenas, surely derived from sections of the autograph manuscript of *Viaggio,* as modified for *Le Comte Ory.* Using the performance materials surviving in Paris, then, we could work our way back from *Andremo a Parigi?* and *Le Comte Ory* to the music as it probably existed in *Il viaggio a Reims.* Responsibility for the edition was placed in the hands of Janet Johnson, now professor of music at the University of Southern California.[49]

As Johnson began to assemble the score, we became ever more aware of its brilliance and wit. Many numbers reused in *Le Comte Ory* were actually more effective in their original home in *Il viaggio a Reims:* the strophic musical structure of Don Profondo's catalogue aria, for example, in which he lists the possessions of each traveler, produced a more compelling marriage of words and music than when essentially the same music was used to underpin Raimbaud's consecutive narrative in *Le Comte Ory.* But we also grew aware that there were significant lacunae. Even as we permitted the Rossini Opera Festival to program the first performances since 1825 for the summer of 1984, we were not sanguine. Then, in the spring of 1983, I visited Vienna on the occasion of those first performances of the critical edition of Verdi's *Rigoletto.* During breaks from rehearsals, I spent time in the Österreichische Nationalbibliothek, which preserves an important collection of manuscripts associated with Viennese theaters. Many Rossini operas are included, mostly in German adaptations. As I reached the end of the card catalogue, my heart jumped: here was a composition entitled *Il viaggio a Vienna*. Now Rossini had never written an opera by that name, but I knew of another city...

What I had found in Vienna, as Janet Johnson later established, were performing parts for an adaptation of Rossini's opera, made in 1854 by unknown hands for the wedding of Emperor Franz Joseph I to his "Sissy," Elizabeth of Bavaria. The revisers must have had available to them earlier performing materials from both *Il viaggio a Reims* and *Andremo a Parigi?* In several cases, in fact, the Viennese materials help establish readings for *Il viaggio a Reims* that cannot be found in other sources.

With these materials in hand, it was possible for Johnson to complete a provisional critical edition of the score, which had its glorious first performance in Pesaro in 1984, under the direction of Claudio Abbado and with one of the most extraordinary *bel canto* casts ever assembled (including Katia Ricciarelli, Lucia Valentini-Terrani, Lella Cuberli, Cecilia Gasdia, Samuel Ramey, Ruggero Raimondi, Francisco Araiza, Leo Nucci, Bernadette Manca di Nissa, Enzo Dara, and William Matteuzzi). The inventive staging of Luca Ronconi, adored by Italian critics, loathed by Anglo-American ones, played with the idea of "rediscovery" by filling the stage with television monitors and turning the voyage of Rossini's opera into a staged event in which the inside of the theater was linked to the city where the opera was being performed.[50] As the king and his retinue processed through the real streets of the city, images of what was happening inside the theater were projected onto screens set up throughout the city, while images of what was happening in the streets were projected inside the theater. It was one thing to do this in Pesaro, of course, a small city on the Adriatic, and quite another to bring it off in Milan and Vienna, but I can testify that the Milanese effort was a banner event in the life of that city. Normally the "king" was a handsome young extra, who appeared in the theater at the very end of the performance to take his place on stage as the ensemble sang "Viva la Francia e il prode regnator" (Long live France and its valiant ruler). But during the performances at Ferrara in 1992, marking the Rossini bicentennial, Abbado and the cast almost didn't make it to the final curtain, when they discovered that the "extra" portraying the "king" had been replaced at the last moment by a singer who happened to be in Ferrara recording Rossini's *Il barbiere di Siviglia* with Abbado, one Placido Domingo.

At the time of the Pesaro performances in 1984, we were aware that there was still a missing composition. A chorus, "L'allegria è un sommo bene,"originally followed the dances that open the finale of *Il viaggio a Reims;* although its text was in the 1825 printed libretto, however, no source preserved any music. While the chorus may be dramaturgically expendable, the *divertissement* suffers from its absence. As I subsequently reexamined the one surviving Parisian performing part pertaining to the finale, I realized that there *was* something where the chorus should have been: a treble clef, a key signature (three sharps), a meter (3/8), and an indication of 381 (the correct number should actually be 379) blank measures. All textual scholars experience occasional moments of illumination, and in this case the lightbulb flashed on: I knew that piece. The only composition among the Rossini operas that came even close to sharing these characteristics was a women's chorus from *Maometto II* that Rossini omitted from the 1826 *Siège de Corinthe.* Sure enough, the text of "L'allegria è un sommo bene" fit perfectly under the music of "È follia sul fior degli anni" from *Maometto II:* Rossini had reused the chorus, to a new text, in *Il viaggio a Reims.*

That explained, finally, why the autograph manuscript of this chorus was no longer together with the autograph materials for *Maometto II,* preserved in the collection of the Fondazione Rossini. The autograph of the chorus is now in the Music Division of the New York Public Library, purchased for the Library from the Swiss autograph dealer M. Slatkine & Fils in 1972 in memory of Rossini's American biographer Herbert Weinstock.[51] The chorus, with the words from *Il viaggio a Reims,* was included in concert performances of that opera at the Newport Festival during the summer of 1988, and finally was included within staged performances of the work in London, Pesaro, and Ferrara during the Rossini bicentennial. We are not certain that Rossini reworked the women's chorus of *Maometto II* into a mixed chorus for *Il viaggio a Reims,* but the dramatic situation makes it more than likely. On the occasion of the first staged performance of the opera in New York during the autumn of 1999, at the New York City Opera, I prepared a version for mixed chorus.[52] Whatever its relation to what Rossini may actually have prepared in 1825, my reconstruction seeks to capture the spirit of *Il viaggio a Reims.*

One never knows, of course, where another manuscript might appear: just around the corner, in another angle of yet another library, in another private collection or bank vault, or in the next auction catalogue from Sotheby's. Somewhere the autograph manuscript of *Le Comte Ory* might appear, within which we would surely find the missing autograph material for *Il viaggio a Reims.* Given our present knowledge of the sources, which remains incomplete, Janet Johnson invented some inner parts in the unaccompanied passage for thirteen solo voices that opens the "Gran Pezzo Concertato" (transformed into an ensemble for seven soloists and chorus in *Le Comte Ory*); the vocal line in the section preparing the cabaletta of Don Profondo's aria remains uncertain; and for one recitative (in which the company learns that

KNOWING THE SCORE / 158

no horses are available to take them to Reims), we prepared several dramatically crucial measures from scratch.[53] But one cannot wait forever: *Il viaggio
a Reims* is finally available in print, even as the search for additional sources
continues.

Religion and Sex in *Stiffelio*

Censorship was a sore problem for Italian opera throughout the first half of
the nineteenth century. The instability caused by constantly shifting political
winds created a climate in which periods of relative liberality were followed
by periods of harsh governmental and ecclesiastical suppression. Although
the operas of Donizetti were seriously affected by censorship, particularly
during the 1830s in Naples, it was Verdi who had the most numerous and
difficult confrontations with the censors. These became increasingly intense
during the years immediately following the revolutionary uprisings that
swept Europe in 1848, when expectations for a new social and political order
were brusquely checked, and reigning governments became morbidly sensitive to signs of political or cultural liberalism.

Nineteenth-century censors had a significant role in the creation and
transmission of many works still being performed today. In some cases their
intervention took place late enough in the compositional process that it is
possible to undo their nefarious work; in other cases it is more difficult.
Donizetti's *Maria Stuarda* and *Poliuto,* for example, were banned in Naples
only after the composer had completed the operas. The sight of one queen
calling another "vile bastard" on the stage of the Teatro San Carlo in *Maria
Stuarda* was too much for the Neapolitan sensibility; and while Racine's
Polyeucte might have been an acceptable play in France, the court society surrounding the strongly religious Queen of Naples would not permit a theatrical spectacle dealing with the life of a saint. *Maria Stuarda* finally reached the
stage in Naples as a heavily revised *Buondelmonte; Poliuto* was transformed by
its composer into a French opera, *Les Martyrs,* and was first performed at the
Paris Opéra. The survival of the autograph for *Poliuto* at the Ricordi Archives
in Milan made it possible to edit and perform that work as Donizetti conceived
it. The reappearance in the Nydahl collection in Stockholm of the autograph
of *Maria Stuarda* (long believed to be lost) led to the publication of the opera
as the first volume of the new critical edition of the works of Donizetti.[54]

Most censorial interventions in Verdi's *Rigoletto* took effect before the
composer completed his sketching. Returning *Rigoletto* from the court of the
Duke of Mantua to Victor Hugo's court of King François I of France, in
short, would require rewriting passages without having any Verdian model.

Editorial interventions of this magnitude could not be seriously proposed in a printed edition of the opera, critical or otherwise, although that does not mean that a modern director should not experiment with such a transformation for a particular production. Among surviving sources for Verdi's *Un ballo in maschera,* on the other hand, there is enough autograph material to permit the reconstruction of an earlier layer in the opera's history, recapturing the Swedish ambiance of *Gustavo III,* rather than using the Boston setting Verdi ultimately accepted in order to have the work performed at all.[55]

For Verdi, however, the most difficult case has always been *Stiffelio,* the opera first performed at the Teatro Grande of Trieste on 16 November 1850. The total disappearance of this work beween the late 1850s and 1968 had never ceased to puzzle those intimately familiar with the Verdi canon. Was it possible that the opera immediately preceding *Rigoletto,* with a text by the same librettist, Francesco Maria Piave, could have so little interest? Although Ricordi did publish a vocal score before the end of 1852, this edition already incorporated changes demanded by the censors in Trieste, presumed necessary to permit the opera's performance on the Italian peninsula. For a long time, however, it was widely believed that no orchestral manuscript of *Stiffelio* had survived. Not only was Verdi's autograph per se not present in the Ricordi archives, but before 1968 no manuscript copy of the opera had been located. Only after copies were identified in Naples could the first modern revival be attempted, at the Teatro Regio of Parma in that same year. (Another, somewhat superior copy was found later, in Vienna.) But these surviving copies were all problematic. They presented either censored versions of the work or, in some cases, complete, unauthorized rewritings to an entirely different libretto (*Guglielmo Wellingrode*).[56]

It is not difficult to understand why censors could object to a plot that mixes sex and religion in a potent theatrical concoction. The protagonist of *Stiffelio* is a Protestant minister whose wife, Lina, has committed adultery before the curtain rises. During the course of the opera, Lina's father, Stankar, kills the seducer of his daughter, Stiffelio forces his wife to agree to a divorce, and then—before his assembled congregation—he reads aloud the passage from the Gospel in which Christ speaks about the woman taken in adultery. The words of pardon ("He that is without sin among you, let him cast the first stone... And she arose pardoned") are echoed by the congregation, and Lina's pardon—at least before God—is assured. The power of the story resides precisely in the emotional travail of a religious leader, whose high moral precepts as a public figure do not sustain him when he is faced with an intense private drama. Still smarting from the treatment his beloved

Giuseppina Strepponi received from provincial society—including his former father-in-law—when he brought her to Busseto, Verdi must have found
Stiffelio irresistible.[57]

But the censors required a vast number of changes in the text (omission
of all biblical references, removal of all religious imagery, changes even in the
way Stiffelio is addressed—no longer a *pastor* [minister], but simply an *ora-
tor* [speaker]).[58] Disgusted by these changes and convinced that there was
little likelihood of the opera circulating as he had intended, Verdi soon withdrew the work from circulation. In 1857, he transformed many parts of *Stiffelio* into a new opera, *Aroldo.* Close study of the autograph manuscript of
Aroldo in the Ricordi Archives, however, reveals that for music absorbed
from *Stiffelio* Verdi simply used sections extracted from his previous manuscript of that opera, on which he made the necessary corrections. As in the
case of *Il viaggio a Reims,* then, a complete autograph of *Stiffelio* no longer existed. But what happened to the passages from *Stiffelio* that Verdi did not
reuse in *Aroldo?* Were they destroyed or lost?

The problem of Verdian sources has perturbed scholars since serious textual work began on the Verdi canon during the 1960s. When John Ryden,
then editor-in-chief at the University of Chicago Press, first suggested to me
that Chicago might be interested in collaborating with Ricordi on the publication of *The Works of Giuseppe Verdi,* one of my main concerns was that the
Verdi heirs, some of whom still inhabit the Villa Verdi at Sant'Agata, near
Parma, had always resisted sharing with scholars the composer's musical
manuscripts thought to be in the heirs' possession. The principal autograph
manuscripts for Verdi's music, those on which a critical edition would primarily be based, are located in the Ricordi Archives, but there was good reason to suspect that other autograph manuscripts (sketches for the major
works from *Luisa Miller* on, passages later replaced from works such as *Simon
Boccanegra* and *La forza del destino,* alternative arias or instrumental pieces,
and juvenilia) were preserved at Sant'Agata where the composer made his
home for more than fifty years. Verdi was not a man who would wantonly destroy important papers, particularly those of musical significance, although
he may have requested shortly before his death that the manuscripts preserving his earliest compositions be destroyed.[59]

Gaining access to those sources has occupied our attention since we began
work on the Verdi edition. Indeed, the order in which we have published volumes in the edition has not been chronological but has been determined,
in part, by the availability of sources. We began with *Rigoletto* because Verdi
never prepared alternative music for it, and the sketches for the opera, as we

have seen, were reproduced in a facsimile edition in 1941. The political context of this facsimile is clear from its preface: it was published as part of the
celebrations on the fortieth anniversary of Verdi's death, "decreed by il Duce,
longtime and enlightened admirer of Verdi." [60] Despite this publication, the
family still did not want to show us the original manuscript. As volumes of
the critical edition have appeared and as the new scores have been adopted
by important conductors, however, the family has begun to understand our
work better and has become more cooperative. With their help, our knowledge of the art of Verdi has greatly increased. Here is one example.

Following the death of Rossini in 1868, Verdi conceived a project in which
all the most important composers of Italy would collaborate on a composite
Mass to honor the first anniversary of the older composer's death. In 1869,
then, Verdi prepared his own contribution, the final movement, "Libera me."
For a complicated set of political and practical reasons, this Mass, although
fully prepared, was never performed. A manuscript of the entire composite
Mass languished in the Ricordi Archives, some sections in the hands of
its various composers, some sections—including Verdi's "Libera me"—in
manuscript copies.[61] It was clear, however, that the "Libera me" Verdi prepared for the composite Mass later became the basis for the "Libera me"
he included in his own, complete *Messa da Requiem* of 1874, composed after
the death of the great Italian literary figure whom Verdi so deeply admired,
Alessandro Manzoni.

When plans were made to prepare the critical edition of the *Messa da Requiem,* edited by Professor David Rosen of Cornell University, it seemed essential that the 1869 "Libera me" figure as an appendix. We had access to the
copyist's manuscript at the Ricordi Archives, but it was filled with mistakes:
an edition based on that source would have required massive editorial interventions, whose relationship to Verdi's original could not be confirmed. At
that point the Istituto di Studi Verdiani had the wonderful idea of preparing
an edition of the entire composite Mass for Rossini, David Rosen to be joined
by a group of young Italian scholars, each of whom would be responsible for
one piece. The editing was accomplished, and the very first performances
ever of the Mass were planned for Stuttgart (11 September 1988) and Parma
(15 September 1988), under the direction of Helmut Rilling, who himself conducted a later revival at the New York Philharmonic. With this splendid occasion before them, the Verdi family offered Rosen access to the autograph
manuscript of the original "Libera me." Indeed, the event was so memorable
that they allowed its publication in facsimile, with an opening statement by
the then president of Italy, Francesco Cossiga.[62] Thus, the critical edition of

Verdi's *Messa da Requiem* could provide documentation for this stage in the history of Verdi's work on the music. It turned out that the original version of the "Libera me" was musically compelling in itself, and there have been several later performances with great success, including a particularly moving one by Riccardo Muti and the orchestra and chorus of La Scala in November 2000 to inaugurate the Verdi celebrations of 2001.

Soon after, the editors of *The Works of Giuseppe Verdi* began to discuss with the Metropolitan Opera of New York a production of Verdi's *Stiffelio* to take place in October of 1993—with James Levine conducting and Placido Domingo in the title role—as part of celebrations for Domingo's twenty-fifth anniversary on the stage of the Met. We were eager to proceed, but the problems of the censored text and the absence of much of the autograph weighed heavily on us. How could we do justice to Verdi's music and drama without knowing exactly what he had written? Finally, both Ricordi and the Istituto di Studi Verdiani explained to the Verdi heirs the significance of the occasion and the importance original materials might have for future performances of a major but unknown Verdi opera. The family agreed to see what it might have, and it wasn't long before Professor Petrobelli of the Istituto informed me that manuscripts had been delivered to Parma, where I would be welcome to join him in examining them.

I will not soon forget the day in February 1992 when I traveled to Parma to see the *Stiffelio* manuscripts. At the time I was in Italy for celebrations of the Rossini bicentennial. On the previous night, Claudio Abbado had conducted a revival of *Il viaggio a Reims* in Ferrara (the very revival at which Placido Domingo appeared as the "king"); on the following night I was scheduled to be in Bologna, where Abbado, Ruggero Raimondi, and I were to be inducted as honorary members of the Accademia Filarmonica di Bologna, the oldest musical society in Italy, which counted among its membership Rossini and Mozart. I traveled to Bologna via Parma, where, at the Istituto di Studi Verdiani, Petrobelli and I studied the treasures the family had put at our disposal. To our immense joy, they had shared with us the autograph manuscript of the music Verdi had written for *Stiffelio* and not reused in *Aroldo* (only a few pages were missing), as well as the complete sketches for both operas, almost sixty pages of them.[63] It was the first time since the publication of the sketches for *Rigoletto* in 1941 that anyone had seen a major Verdian sketch.

The *Stiffelio* manuscripts proved to be of the utmost importance. With this material available, Kathleen Hansell, music editor at the University of Chicago Press, was able to prepare an excellent critical edition of the score, and several scholars could examine Verdi's sketches.[64] The most astonishing changes were in the libretto of the work. Instead of the pallid censored text that Verdi was forced to accept in Trieste, the autograph manuscripts revealed the original words of the opera. Where previously available sources refer to "l'empio" (the villain) or to "il Giusto" (the just one), Verdi originally invoked the names of "Judas" and "Christ"; where in other sources Stiffelio returns to his senses during the second-act finale by saying "Stiffelio io sono" (I am Stiffelio), the autograph has the words "Sacerdote io sono" (I am a minister).[65]

The emotional center of the work is a duet, where Stiffelio demands that his wife, Lina, agree to a divorce. After trying unsuccessfully to reason with her husband, she signs the papers. Then, no longer his wife, she confronts him anew: "I am not speaking to my husband, but to a minister of the Gospel" ("l'uomo del Vangelo"—a phrase the censors had changed to "l'uom di santo zelo," the man of sacred zeal).[66] She then continues: "Even on the cross He opened the paths of heaven to sinners. It is no longer a woman who begs you, but a sinner." Stiffelio (whose given name is Rodolfo) tries to stop her, but she will not be silenced. "Rodolfo, ascoltatemi" (Rodolofo, listen to me), she says; at least, that is what the secondary sources show. But those are not the words Verdi set to music. Instead, in Verdi's autograph manuscript, Lina, freed from her marital bonds, turns on her former husband and demands: "Ministro, confessatemi" (Minister, confess me). Verdi set those "parole sceniche," a phrase he often invoked for words that sum up and embody a drama, so that they can be clearly understood.[67] His understanding of Protestant theology may not be quite right, but the increased dramaturgical power of the scene in its original form is striking.

The sketches for *Stiffelio* have provided many new insights into the opera, but one of the most fascinating things we learned from them bears on Verdi's next opera, *Rigoletto*. Verdi had a great deal of difficulty finding the theme for the cabaletta of Lina's principal aria, at the beginning of the second act. In this section, she addresses the man who seduced her:

Perder dunque voi volete[68]	So you wish to destroy
Questa misera tradita!..	This poor betrayed woman!..
Se restate, la mia vita	If you remain, my life
Tutta in pianto scorrerà!..	Will know only tears!..

The melody Verdi ultimately chose is not one of the opera's finest moments. But among the versions of this cabaletta that he tried out is a very well-known tune (example 5.2). That the innocent Gilda's "Caro nome" was originally sketched for the betrayed Lina's "Dunque perdere volete" has implications for our understanding of Verdi's treatment of text and music and, more generally, his compositional process.[69]

EXAMPLE 5.2. GIUSEPPE VERDI, *STIFELLIO*, A SKETCH FOR THE CABALETTA
OF THE SCENA ED ARIA LINA (N. 6).

Before these implications can be fully investigated, however, scholars will need to have wider access to Verdi's sketches and other manuscripts. The Verdi family has since allowed the editors of the critical editions of *La traviata, Un ballo in maschera,* and *La forza del destino,* Fabrizio Della Seta, Ilaria Narici, and myself (with the late William C. Holmes) to examine the fascinating sketches for those operas, and there is every reason to hope that they will continue to be helpful in the future.[70] Certainly our ability to solve the many problems surrounding *Simon Boccanegra, Falstaff,* and even *Aida* will depend heavily on that continuing cooperation. What there is to be gained is an even stronger presence of Verdi's own voice on today's operatic stages.

Although *Tancredi, Il viaggio a Reims,* and *Stiffelio* represent spectacular stories in the work on critical editions of the music of Italy's major nineteenth-century composers, they are hardly unique. Rossini's *Petite Messe solennelle* led me to the Chateau d'Offémont in Saint-Crépin-aux-Bois, just outside Compiègne, where Count Jacques Pillet-Will, a descendant of the family that originally comissioned the work, shared with me a manuscript of the Mass that Rossini had given to the count's illustrious ancestors. It revealed an even earlier version of the work—from 1864—than had previously been known. First performed at the Rossini Opera Festival during the summer of 1997 in the presence of Countess Elizabeth Pillet-Will (sadly, Count Jacques had died earlier that year), this version proved to be musically compelling, and it has since circulated widely in Italy and elsewhere.[71] Preparation of the critical edition of *I masnadieri* led its editor, Roberta Marvin, into the whirlwind surrounding the musical archives of the Covent Garden opera house as that venerable institution was in the process of self-destructing during the mid-1990s. As a result, she managed to find fascinating evidence for the artistic interactions between a well-known prima donna, Jenny Lind, and a still relatively young composer, one Giuseppe Verdi, in his first musical experience outside his native soil.[72]

Musical editions exist on the page, not in the theater; but all theatrical presentations begin with a printed score and parts. These documents have their own stories, and the history of the scores generally available during most of the twentieth century, especially for operas written between 1800 and 1870, is not a happy one. Critical editions of this repertory engage with the history of each work, seeking to recognize the social systems that underlay its composition, first performances, and revivals; tracing its transmission; remaining sensitive to the participation of composers, librettists, singers, publishers, and instrumentalists. Editors—and other scholars on whose labors they build— must find and evaluate sources, struggle with their contradictions and uncertainties, seek feedback from performers, proofread over and over in order to eliminate inadvertent error (not even the best edition is error-free). There is romance, to be sure, but also much *Sitzfleisch*. Through all of this, however, the critical editions continue to recognize the composer as the central figure in the Italian operatic landscape and to seek where possible to reproduce his voice as fully and accurately as possible.

INTERMEZZO

6

SCHOLARS AND PERFORMERS: THE CASE OF *SEMIRAMIDE*

THE CHIMERA OF AUTHENTIC PERFORMANCE

Musical scholarship and musical performance are often represented as occupying hostile worlds. The mutual dependence that actually governs these spheres engenders, perhaps inevitably, a certain degree of mutual distrust. Similar divisions are deeply embedded throughout Western culture, where theory and practice are treated as binary opposites: economists versus business executives, computer scientists versus software hackers, critics versus artists. "Thinkers" and denizens of "ivory towers," on the one hand, jut up against "doers" and inhabitants of the "real world" on the other. The word "academic" is regularly used by those in and out of institutions of higher learning to set theoretical discourse apart from the practical world. In the arts, where the creation of new works or the representation of old ones is linked to the idea of "inspiration," even "divine inspiration," the imagined gulf sometimes seems unbridgeable.

Over the past quarter century, much of this controversy in music has centered on the efforts of musicologists and some performers to look beyond the present and the immediate past when thinking about the performance of older musical compositions or repertories. Such concerns, of course, are hardly new. From the moment in which musicians sought to perform music on which the ink had already dried, the problem of coming to grips with the music of an earlier time arose in one form or another. In the medieval cathedral of Notre-Dame, the compositions of Léonin (written in the latter part of the twelfth century) were reinterpreted by Pérotin and his followers in the next generation. Renaissance musicians debated the appropriate way to interpret musical notation that indicated only incompletely the presence of sharps or flats. The growing number of instructional manuals during the seventeenth century for interpreting the notation of ornaments in Baroque music or for

accompanying concerted music from a keyboard instrument through the realization of a so-called "figured bass" testify to a common practice that was
neither so common that it did not have to be explained nor so certain that controversies did not arise with regularity.[1]

But the problems intensified when two historical forces intersected: musical antiquarianism led to the recovery of repertories for which there were few
guides in contemporary artistic life, while musical modernism was alienating
many twentieth-century audiences from the music of their own time. Thus,
diverse repertories—often bearing with them only the most modest indications of how their notations might be interpreted by performers—were
introduced into the living musical museum. As long as the repertories under
discussion were primarily the concern of those involved in the study and performance of music before the time of Bach, squabbles about the way to perform a Machaut *ballade,* a Josquin motet, a Frescobaldi organ prelude, or a
Monteverdi madrigal were generally confined within a relatively small community of scholars and performers. During the past decades, however, as the
questions began impinging on music closer to our own time—music still
dear to performers and audiences—these issues became increasingly real to
an ever-wider public.

The case of late Baroque music is instructive. There is simply no continuous editorial or performing tradition for all but a few of the works of Bach,
Handel, and the composers of their time. When Bach's major vocal music began to be resurrected (partly under the leadership of Felix Mendelssohn) in
the 1820s and 1830s, it was necessary to invent a style of performance. It is
hardly to the discredit of the Romantic sensibility that musicians of the era
depended heavily on their own sound ideal.[2] Yet it was not long before the developing field of musicology, particularly in Germany, began to investigate
Bach's art. A critical edition of the complete works was prepared,[3] documents
and archival records from Bach's life were consulted, theoretical treatises and
critical writings of the epoch were analyzed. From this intensive study arose
a new understanding of the music of Bach, the circumstances for which it was
written, the forces by which it was performed, and the sound ideal of the late
Baroque era in music. Gradually these ideas found a sympathetic reception
among performers, many of whom were themselves active researchers. The
harpsichord was reborn.[4] Recorders and baroque trumpets were developed,
and techniques for playing them relearned and then mastered. String players
and singers recognized that the techniques appropriate for a Brahms symphony or a Wagner opera might not be the same as those required for a Bach
concerto or a Handel oratorio. It is only later that they would be asked to con-

sider whether the techniques they used in Brahms and Wagner might need reexamination in their turn. But first, through this revolution in public sensibility, performances of late Baroque music took on new life.

This does not mean to suggest that all musicians and scholars agree about details, even today, after the flurry of new scholarship into the music of Bach that accompanied the publication of the *Neue Bach Ausgabe* (*New Bach Edition*).[5] The invective that characterized debate over Joshua Rifkin's performances of Bach's *Mass in B minor,* for example, with a single singer on each part (a scoring that Rifkin traced to his interpretation of documents associated directly with Bach's performances in Leipzig), almost obscured the valuable lessons to be learned from his effort.[6] Controversies about how to interpret ornaments, realize the accompanying *continuo,* or understand "unequal notes" or "double-dotting" continue to rage. Through all the turmoil, many of us, in the privacy of our homes, persist in gaining enormous pleasure by playing the *Well-Tempered Clavier* on modern pianos. We also enjoy participating in sing-along *Messiahs* with a chorus of thousands. Some may even cast a nostalgic glance at Leopold Stokowski's orchestration of the *Prelude and Fugue in D minor.* No matter. There is simply no doubt that the search for information about performing late Baroque music has transformed our understanding of the repertory. It has allowed us to confront the historical gap in the performance history of these works, often with splendid aesthetic results.

Nor must we be deterred by the perfectly obvious fact that our "reconstructions" are a product of our modern sensibilities. We neither can nor should deny those sensibilities when approaching works of art from the past. At the same time, we should not imagine that the attempt to learn more about the past will guarantee success. Poor performers, poor scholars, and poor critics have always existed, whether they carry shields emblazoned with the devices "authentic early music performance," "Romantic sensibility," "tradition," or "modernist revisionism." No amount of philosophical investigation about the impossibility of objective history, and no amount of economic reductionism about the relationship of historically informed performance to the record industry, can obscure the fact that we approach Bach today with a far broader understanding of the composer's music and his world than did mid-nineteenth-century or most twentieth-century performers. The best musicians filter what they know through their own modern sensibilities to achieve compelling performances. Those who insist on increasing their knowledge do so out of a profound conviction that the effort to understand Bach's music in its historical setting is a crucial part of this process. We want to perform Bach because we care primarily about *his* music, not about nineteenth-century or early-twentieth-century visions of that music, however interesting the latter may be for certain historical studies. That our own sensibilities will inevitably influence the questions we ask and the ways we actually bring the music to aural life is a fact so obvious that it hardly needs constant reiteration. In no way does it diminish the importance of the quest for understanding.

As soon as we pass beyond the Baroque era, however, to the historical periods commonly labeled Classical and Romantic, the century from approximately 1770 through 1870, the situation becomes more difficult. At stake is a significant part of the standard repertory, those compositions that have long formed the bulk of the music performed by our symphonic and choral organizations and in our opera houses. These works seem to have a continuous history of performance from the time of their composition to the present day, although not necessarily a coherent one. Suddenly proposals for performance that challenge an established norm seemed more threatening. Those who play Mozart's keyboard concertos on the fortepianos for which they were written are regularly excoriated for their lack of passion and individuality;[7] those who perform these same pieces on Steinway grands with all the trappings of late nineteenth-century phrasing and pedaling are pilloried for their insensitivity to historical practice. And when a performer such as Malcolm Bilson renders early Beethoven on the fortepiano, including more passionate works (the *Pathétique Sonata* or the *Trio in C minor,* Op. 1, No. 3), unquestionably written with that instrument in mind, he arouses some musicians and members of the public to intense anger.

The anger extends from the merely petulant to the insidiously demagogic. I recall hearing a radio interview with the late flautist Jean-Pierre Rampal in which he denounced all work on historical performance as a travesty of musical and instrumental sense: how could anyone imagine listening to those tootling recorders when the magnificent flute was at their disposition. Daniel Barenboim not only conducts Bach with musicians of the Chicago Symphony Orchestra, but urges them on to apply more and more vibrato.[8] Modern Italian conductors express incredulity and astonishment at the aesthetic attitudes embodied in the recordings of Beethoven symphonies under the direction of Roger Norrington and at their commercial success. And during the autumn of 1994, while I was pursuing studies in Rome, a performance of Beethoven's *Ninth Symphony* directed by John Eliot Gardiner at the Teatro alla Scala, using early instruments and attempting to recapture early nineteenth-century performing styles, was the object of sustained journalistic attacks, which at least had the honesty to admit that the Milanese public had been enthusiastic. Fabio

Biondi's brilliant performance of Bellini's *Norma* with early nineteenth-century instruments at the Parma Verdi Festival in March 2001, and the uncomprehending, infuriated reaction of some *loggionisti*, will be discussed in chapter 12.

The battles about authentic performance also encompass matters pertaining to the texts being employed and the use being made of them. Alfred Brendel and his critics clash in the pages of the *New York Review of Books* as to whether Schubert's last piano sonata, in B♭ *major*, should be played with or without the repeat of the exposition indicated by the composer.[9] Errors in editions of piano music and their unthinking acceptance by many performers is a theme Charles Rosen often touches upon.[10] No conductor can program a Schumann symphony without facing those who think the composer knew how to write for the orchestra and those who do not. It sometimes seems that half of every review of a Bruckner symphony is devoted to explaining what has or has not been performed and why the choice is correct or incorrect.

Since the publication of *Text and Act,* a collection of Richard Taruskin's earlier essays and reviews—edited and refurnished with a new set of zingers against his critics—Taruskin has emerged as the leading naysayer concerning the study and use in modern performance of historical practices, and his views seem to have become text to the *New York Times,* where he occasionally acts out.[11] Taruskin's principal point, repeated endlessly by himself and by some reviewers for that newspaper, is that much of what we have thought of as "authentic" performance practice (Taruskin's scare quotes) over the past twenty-five years is essentially modernist performance style imposed on the past. This is, in its way, a brilliant perception, although perhaps not so brilliant as Taruskin might like us to believe. After all, if Stravinsky found something in Baroque music that appealed to his modernist sensibility, something he could use for his own purposes, it is not necessarily because the performance of eighteenth-century music needed to be remade in Stravinsky's image. What he found, though, was in part what scholars and performers attempting to reconstruct Baroque practice had already discovered there. These scholars and performers may have been wrong about details, and they were certainly part of the culture in which both they and Stravinsky lived, but it was not their commitment to some version of "modernism" that drove them to undertake the studies that transformed knowledge of the Baroque repertory in the first decades of the twentieth century.[12]

Still, words such as *authentic,* once proudly descriptive of musical performances informed by historical study, have lost whatever meaning they may once have possessed: whether emblazoned on banners or (more often) on the covers of CDs as symbols of truth and beauty or treated as objects of opprobrium and scorn, they have become at best slogans, at worst commercial ploys. Indeed, their continued use is merely confusing. Are we willing to say, after all, that a performance faithful to a musicological reconstruction is authentic, while one ignorant of such reconstructions but embodying the interpretation of a committed artist within different parameters is not?[13] The term *authenticity* begs too many questions. It also reinforces categorical divisions that deny the interdependence of theory and practice, embodying in banalities complex issues that every performer and every scholar must confront. Traditionalist performers and critics reject a vast amount of serious thought on performance by rejecting caricatures of that thought. But scholars can be no less intransigent in sustaining dearly held theories while ignoring modern realities and the complexity of historical data.

In nineteenth-century Italian opera, where tempers are hotter and prima donnas more imperious, disputes descend to a level of rhetoric astonishing to those not already captivated by the customs of the lyric stage. Some critics, annoyed with what they take to be disastrous performances masquerading under the guise of authenticity, respond with a thick sarcasm aimed at issues that have little bearing on the reasons for their displeasure. I still recall a review by Kenneth Furie of Riccardo Muti's recording of *Cavalleria rusticana* and *I pagliacci,* in which Furie complained, "And what is Muti doing all this while, with disaster overtaking from all directions? *He's by God giving us pure, authentic performances!* Yessirree, it's back to the autograph scores, boys and girls! For the first time we hear *Pagliacci* as Leoncavallo really meant it."[14] But who, in fact, believes that going back to the autograph scores will result in successful performances, let alone authentic ones? And who believes that refusing to play the notes written by a composer guarantees musical success? Is there no way to decrease the volume engendered by these meaningless controversies, whose only result is to confound the public?

Few musicologists are so naive as to imagine that all our queries about historical and modern performance would be solved were a time machine to transport us to a nineteenth-century theater. No one holds as a model the first performance of *Il barbiere di Siviglia,* where it seems likely that the singers barely knew their parts, the orchestra was underrehearsed, the performing materials were atrociously (mis)copied at the last moment, and the audience (according to the first Rosina, Geltrude Righetti-Giorgi) hooted and jeered.[15] Nor does anyone seek to recreate theaters in which we draw the curtains of our boxes while awaiting major arias, chatting with friends, eating ices, and *amoreggiando,* as so vividly described by contemporary writers such as Stendhal and Balzac.[16] When public social activity centered around the opera house and the same work was performed night after night, that was a reasonable way of listening to music. How we listen today is inextricably related to how we live today.

What would it mean, after all, to ask an artist to "sing only what's written." Is there any evidence that performers in the nineteenth century strived to erase their personality and individuality of tone? Should orchestral musicians invariably ignore the technical advances made in the construction of their instruments or the techniques for playing them? Does anyone seriously suggest that stage designers, as a matter of course, should reproduce period productions or that directors should limit themselves to following nineteenth-century staging manuals?[17] Practical musicians, designers, directors, and impresarios shrink from what they consider to be attitudes bearing little relation to the theater as they understand it. Some operatic personalities relish these extreme formulations: by ridiculing them, they can avoid facing the serious issues involved.

That we can learn much by reconstructing mentally (or even physically) a nineteenth-century performance, analyzing historical vocal technique, scenic design, stage direction, and instrumental practice seems self-evident, and this knowledge has implications for modern performance.[18] That scholars expect performers to abandon themselves blindly to historical reconstruction is a gross misrepresentation. I do not mean to suggest that extreme formulations cannot be found somewhere in the writings of the thousands of performers and scholars that have interested themselves in the question over several generations, but I must agree with Charles Rosen when he writes: "[Taruskin's] most crushing arguments are often reserved for opinions that no one really holds."[19] The straw man of authenticity simply gets in the way of a reasoned approach to the complex interactions of theory and practice, history and contemporaneity, tradition and innovation.

SEMIRAMIDE AT THE METROPOLITAN OPERA

On 30 November 1990, the Metropolitan Opera unveiled a new production of Gioachino Rossini's *Semiramide,* conducted by James Conlon, in a production directed by John Copley and designed by John Conklin. (The most difficult aspect of rehearsals was remembering which J.C. one happened to be talking to at any given moment.) Prepared for the Teatro La Fenice of Venice, *Semiramide* was the last of some thirty-four operas Rossini wrote for Italian theaters between 1810 and 1823. The best of these operas dominated stages in

Italy and abroad for thirty years, and their influence continued to be felt long after Rossini's serious operas disappeared from the repertory for a variety of historical and cultural reasons. The Met's decision to revive *Semiramide* was both a tribute to one of the great singers of modern times, Marilyn Horne, and a belated recognition by America's oldest opera house of the growing, worldwide interest, by musicians and the public alike, in Rossini's noncomic operas.

Although I admire *Semiramide* greatly, I frankly would not have chosen it as the first Rossini *opera seria* to be presented to the Metropolitan Opera audience. However brilliant its music may be, *Semiramide* is a neoclassical drama and a work whose structural formality makes it Rossini's single longest Italian opera. When major opera houses wish to perform a Rossini serious opera, I normally suggest one of two Neapolitan works, *Ermione* and *Maometto II:* both have the advantages of being considerably shorter and of having a more fluid structural design. But the former has a relatively small mezzo-soprano role (and hence would have been inappropriate as a work chosen in part to celebrate Marilyn Horne), and the latter was compromised by the Met's controversial presentation of *Le Siège de Corinthe,* an opera largely derived from *Maometto II,* already discussed in chapter 4. Furthermore the popularity of several individual compositions in *Semiramide* provided a point of contact with the public: the queen's "Bel raggio lusinghier" or Arsace's "Eccomi alfine in Babilonia" continued to be *morceaux favoris* for sopranos and contraltos long after the public had any idea what the opera was about. And so, *Semiramide* it was.

The dramatic precepts of eighteenth-century neoclassical drama are unfamiliar to modern America. *Semiramide* was probably the first contact with a play by Voltaire in any form for 99 percent of the audience who attended the Metropolitan or watched the public-television program that brought *Semiramide* before the largest audience it had ever known.[20] The remaining 1 percent of the audience consisted mostly of opera lovers who had seen Rossini's *Tancredi,* also based on a Voltaire play, at Chicago, Houston, Los Angeles, San Francisco, or in Europe. Thus, a certain puzzlement at the formal (even static) dramaturgy was to be expected. Not everyone would feel comfortable with a work whose aesthetic bases are in such sharp contrast with the precepts of the Romantic theater underlying most nineteenth-century Italian opera. Nonetheless, the theater audience was enthusiastic, and standing ovations greeted Lella Cuberli and June Anderson (alternating in the title role), Marilyn Horne, Chris Merritt, and Sam Ramey, even though the evening began at 7:30 and did not conclude until almost midnight.

Among those left relatively unmoved by *Semiramide* was Donal Henahan, at that time chief music critic of the *New York Times*. What interested me was not his opinion of the opera but the way it was expressed. Reviewing the entire Metropolitan Opera season, he wrote, "'Semiramide,' revived after nearly a century, was played in a new edition that put exhaustive scholarship before operatic effectiveness." [21] There it is, laid out for all to see: "exhaustive scholarship" versus "operatic effectiveness." Journalistic *bon mot* or not, it embraces a common misconception. In fact, this production of *Semiramide,* for which I served as "stylistic adviser" and which employed the new critical edition of the opera that I had prepared for the Fondazione Rossini drawing on earlier efforts by Alberto Zedda, provides a paradigmatic introduction to the interaction of scholarship and performance in the opera house, an interaction a good deal more complex than might appear from Henahan's banal dichotomies. The issues, like this book, can be divided into two categories: knowing the score and performing the opera.

PREPARING A NEW EDITION OF *SEMIRAMIDE*

Whatever theoretical value philosophers—in their search for the "ideal" musical work—may assign to or withhold from a written musical score, few performers of nineteenth-century repertory learn their music by ear, and even those who do must rely on someone who is reading a score. In order to perform *Semiramide,* then, the Met needed a full score for the conductor (one containing all orchestral and vocal parts), vocal scores for singers and rehearsal pianists, and individual orchestral parts from which everyone from violinists to timpanists could play. In the nineteenth century, the full score of *Semiramide* circulated almost exclusively in manuscript; orchestral parts were also prepared by hand.[22] With one exception, only vocal scores were printed. (The exceptional publication, an orchestral score printed by the Roman firm of Ratti and Cencetti, with the same criteria they used for manuscript copies prepared in their *copisteria,* had a limited circulation.) Rossini's own autograph manuscript of the opera remains in the archives of the theater for which *Semiramide* was written, the Teatro La Fenice of Venice (whose archives are deposited at the Fondazione Levi). From this autograph the theater's copyists prepared parts (which still exist) and a complete manuscript of the full score. From that manuscript copy, other copies and other sets of parts were prepared. These derivative scores and parts were used for performances in the nineteenth century and occasionally in the first half of the twentieth, all over the world.

By the end of the nineteenth century, despite its presence in three early seasons at the Metropolitan Opera (in 1892 with Adelina Patti and in 1894 and 1895 with Nellie Melba), *Semiramide* had largely disappeared from the stage. Most nineteenth-century performing materials were allowed to rot in theater basements or were trotted out for an occasional revival (such as the one led by Tullio Serafin at Florence's Maggio musicale in 1940), and whatever once existed in the Ricordi archive in Milan, Italy's most extensive collection of parts and scores, was destroyed by Allied bombardments in 1944.[23] Thus, when *Semiramide* was given its first modern performances on 17 December 1962 at La Scala, which was looking for a vehicle especially suited to the talents of Joan Sutherland and Giulietta Simionato, it was necessary to prepare a new full score and parts. Photographic reproductions of nineteenth-century vocal scores were available and could be corrected to take account of decisions made in the new score.[24] The 1962 full score, although unsigned, was prepared in a serious manner and appears to have been based on Rossini's autograph at the Teatro La Fenice. Nonetheless, many problems remained. The edition reflected the needs of those particular performances at La Scala. It was based exclusively on musical sources known and available in 1962, before serious research on nineteenth-century Italian opera texts had begun. And it could not draw on the wealth of experience the new critical edition of Rossini's works has provided, experience gained in preparing, among other things, editions of most of Rossini's thirty-nine operas, twenty-eight of which are currently in print or in proof.

As best as I can tell, until the Metropolitan Opera's 1990 production, the 1962 La Scala score, copies of it, and materials derived from it, served as the basis for modern revivals of *Semiramide*. (Since 1962, some seventy opera houses have included the work in one or more seasons.) During those years, however, theaters employing this material complained bitterly about its condition, for reasons we will examine below. Zedda made an effort to improve the situation by correcting the score and materials, but there were too many difficulties associated with the original product. I therefore agreed to prepare the critical edition so that it could be used for the first time as the basis for the performances at the Metropolitan Opera. There are four principal ways in which the new critical edition differs from the older score: (1) it is complete; (2) it uses autograph material unknown to previous editors; (3) it reconstructs the stage band Rossini employed in 1823; (4) it renders Rossini's opera more accurately and provides a more idiomatic treatment of articulation, dynamics, and so forth. Each element deserves further consideration.

1. THE NEW CRITICAL EDITION IS COMPLETE. *Semiramide* is a very long opera, even by early nineteenth-century standards. It is not surprising, therefore, that the first significant twentieth-century effort to stage the work used a heavily abridged score. The decision to omit certain passages from Rossini's *Semiramide* in the performances at La Scala in 1962, however, was made *before* the edition was prepared, and only the material that was to be included in the performance was actually edited. Thus, a great deal of music Rossini composed for the opera was lacking in the score. But not every subsequent opera house presenting *Semiramide* agreed with the La Scala cuts. For example, although the tenor, Idreno, has only limited dramatic importance, Rossini did write two arias for him. In 1962, when few tenors could sing Rossini's florid *opera seria* arias, it was prudent to omit one aria altogether and to reduce the length of the other. When better prepared tenors assumed the role in later productions, they wanted to restore some of that music.[25]

In 1962, the art of vocal ornamentation in Rossini was poorly understood. Musical forms constructed to give singers an opportunity to decorate the repetition of a melodic line seemed superfluous, and many repetitions were omitted from the edition. Almost twenty years later, Samuel Ramey, a bass capable of electrifying an audience in this repertory, assumed the role of Assur for the first time. When he wished to follow Rossini by repeating (with added ornaments) the theme of the cabaletta in Assur's aria, the missing bars had to be restored. In the 1962 La Scala production, particular attention was placed on *Semiramide* as a vehicle for soloists, and the quality of Rossini's choruses went unrecognized. Until she performed the role of Arsace in 1990, in the production based on the critical edition, Marilyn Horne—as she told me during rehearsals—had never even *heard* the extraordinary chorus that opens Arsace's scene in the second act, a particularly splendid passage.

As each new performance made different demands or produced different requirements, pages were added to (or omitted from) the La Scala score, and orchestral parts were cut up and pasted together in new configurations. Finding your way through the material seemed like negotiating a maze. Indeed, the situation was so bad that the Ricordi firm, which distributed the materials, was threatened with lawsuits demanding compensation for time lost in rehearsal, as I was told by more than one employee. The critical edition of *Semiramide,* for the first time, contains the complete opera Rossini wrote in 1823. While making no presumption that a theater should perform everything, it ensures that eventual cuts can be decided after performers know the entire opera and on the basis of the particular needs of a production.

"Complete," nonetheless, remains a relative term: the new edition is as complete as it can be, given our current knowledge. There is strong evidence that Rossini revised the conclusion of the opera for the Théâtre Italien of Paris in 1825, adding additional recitative after Arsace (Ninius) strikes down Semiramide. The dialogue is an affecting moment of forgiveness and reconciliation between mother and son, before the curtain falls with what must have been a solemn chorus of grief. The words of this new finale are preserved in a libretto printed at the time, and the music of the recitative alone is found in a vocal score printed in Paris in 1825. But no orchestral score of this recitative is known, and no musical source heretofore identified gives the final chorus in any form whatsoever. The search for this alternative finale to *Semiramide* continues. Meanwhile, the critical edition has published the new recitative exactly as it is found in the Parisian vocal score. Perhaps one day soon we will suggest an orchestration so that a theater can more easily use it, should it so choose.

There are some things, however, that the critical edition does not contain. When *Semiramide* was revived for Joan Sutherland, her husband, the conductor and coach Richard Bonynge, manipulated the opera to favor the title role. The recording they made together in 1964 shows how the score was altered, with arias omitted, important choruses deleted, measures snipped away throughout. Most important, Bonynge invented—out of whole cloth—a conclusion in which the hero Arsace kills the villain Assur rather than his own mother, the queen Semiramide, as in Voltaire's tragedy and Rossini's opera. Thus, as the final curtain descended, Sutherland was on her feet, alive and well. Since this manipulation of Rossini's opera had been incorporated into performing materials of the work, a number of revivals subsequently used it. The *New York Times* critic, reviewing the Metropolitan Opera production of *Semiramide,* talked about the Bonynge invention as if it were traceable to Rossini. I am emphatically not questioning Bonynge's right to make such an adaptation for particular circumstances with which he was directly involved as a performer in the early 1960s. My objection is to seeing his version attain a textual status that it never claimed for itself nor deserves to have.

2. THE NEW CRITICAL EDITION USES MATERIAL UNKNOWN TO PREVIOUS EDITORS. Although the editors of the 1962 *Semiramide* had access to the Venetian autograph, other autograph materials were lacking. As we saw in chapter 2, Rossini composed his operas using paper in an oblong format rather than the vertical format that became typical later in the nineteenth century. Oblong paper allows a composer to write more measures per page, while sacrificing the number of staves available. When, in a large ensemble, everyone sings and plays at once, the opera composer using oblong paper is forced to re-

sort to *spartitini* (little scores) to accommodate the overflow of instruments. These autograph *spartitini,* usually bound at the end of a manuscript, can easily be misplaced. For *Semiramide,* they were all missing. Using secondary sources, the La Scala score filled in some missing instruments, but its compilers were often compelled to invent new horn, trumpet, and percussion parts.

Although the musical archives of the Teatro La Fenice contain the original performing materials for *Semiramide,* these materials had never been consulted in conjunction with the preparation of a modern edition of the opera. After much travail, a microfiche copy of the entire set of materials was obtained, and during the summer of 1989, two scholars working with the Rossini Foundation, Mauro Bucarelli and Patricia Brauner, indexed the more than four thousand manuscript pages. I remember the day when they came into my office looking particularly self-satisfied. "There's something we think you should see," they said. There, photographed between a part for trombone and a part for bass drum, they had found the complete autograph *spartitini* for *Semiramide.* The parts were a revelation in many ways, often quite different from *spartitini* preserved in other nineteenth-century sources of the opera. It seems likely that Rossini's *spartitini* were mistakenly placed with performing materials during that very first season, limiting their role in the further transmission of the opera. Thus, the critical edition, for the first time since 1823, was able to include throughout the composer's own wind, brass, and percussion parts for major ensembles.

One small lacuna remained. In the opera's introduction, Rossini wrote a note in his main score signaling that parts for the third and fourth horns were to be found in a separate *spartitino,* but no such *spartitino* came to light. The La Scala score, based in part on the Ratti and Cencetti edition, seemed suspect: for long stretches the third and fourth horns doubled the bassoons, an orchestral technique foreign to Rossini's style. Indeed, a close look at Rossini's orchestration demonstrates that he had used here two bassoons and the first and second horns to produce an accompaniment in four-part harmony. This instrumental technique, which Rossini often adopted, requires bassoons and horns to play in a way that creates a unified, balanced sound, producing a more modulated sound in softer passages (such as the chorus "Di plausi qual clamor" within the *Semiramide* introduction) than chords played by four horns. Here, performing parts from La Fenice came to the rescue: from them we could reconstruct the missing third and fourth horn parts. They provide useful punctuations in the orchestral sound, but do not double work already being accomplished by the bassoons. Thus, the new critical edition could present the full orchestration of *Semiramide* as Rossini conceived it.

In another way the parts were of great importance. In the *particella* for the tenor Idreno, there were no marks at all in his first-act aria (and signs in the orchestral parts suggest that this aria was probably cut during the first season), but in the second-act aria a series of ornaments for the cabaletta were added to the *particella*. Although not in Rossini's hand, they may reflect modifications introduced by the composer. Unusually, these ornaments, instead of decorating the theme when it is repeated, *simplify* the melody of the theme on its first appearance by substituting fewer notes with less difficult intervals between them, after which the transition and repetition of the theme were cut. Rossini's Venetian Idreno, John Sinclair (whose name appears on the part), may have been incapable of singing the vocal lines Rossini had prepared. But given the highly florid and rhythmically complex theme, the markings in Sinclair's part turn out to be aesthetically quite suggestive. Indeed, the tenor Rockwell Blake, the first to study this *particella* closely, often begins by singing the simplified version of the vocal line, so that the more florid setting composed by Rossini is heard as a "variation." Whatever an individual singer may decide to do, the critical edition documents more fully Rossini's thoughts about this aria.

3. THE NEW CRITICAL EDITION RECONSTRUCTS THE STAGE BAND ROSSINI EMPLOYED IN 1823. In three pieces, *Semiramide* requires a band of winds, brass, and percussion to play either in costume onstage (*sul palco*) or in the wings. Rossini was the first nineteenth-century Italian composer regularly to introduce a *banda sul palco* into his operas, but he did not normally prepare a complete score for that band: instead, he sketched the band music on one or two staves, expecting the local bandmaster to complete the orchestration using appropriate forces. (Verdi behaved in much the same way.) For operas that have a continuous tradition, such as Verdi's *Rigoletto*, theaters tend to use a modified version based on nineteenth-century models, but with fewer instruments. For operas lacking such a tradition, modern theaters will either commission a new orchestration for the *banda* or else forego the use of a stage band altogether and rewrite the music so that it can be played by instruments in the orchestra.

After studying this problem thoroughly, the editors of the critical edition of Rossini's works decided to include, in each opera for which Rossini requires the presence of a stage band, a separately bound volume containing the original, early nineteenth-century setting of the band music for that opera, edited on the basis of surviving materials. These original orchestrations of the band music often circulated together with manuscript copies of the opera. While theaters might modify the *banda* setting to accommodate local circumstances, they tended to use the original orchestration as a point of reference. In some cases the results are remarkable. In *La donna del lago,* as we have seen in chapter 2, the original band consisted of two separate ensembles: one is a normally constituted band of some twenty-five players using a variety of band instruments; the other is a special ensemble of nine trumpets, four trombones, and percussion, associated with Malcom and the military forces he leads within the first-act finale, where the special ensemble is used both as a separate entity and in counterpoint with the fuller band. All these players were placed directly onstage, as we know from descriptions of the first staging of *La donna del lago* under Rossini's direction in Paris in 1824. However a modern theater may decide to proceed, anyone seeking to understand the effect of Rossini's opera in the early nineteenth century must take into account the sound that emerged from the stage at the end of the first act.

Among the La Fenice performing materials for *Semiramide,* we found what must have been the original scoring for the *banda sul palco,* a scoring present in a number of other manuscripts of the opera. Twenty-two instruments were employed by the anonymous arranger—winds, brass, and percussion—and rehearsals for the 1990 production at the Metropolitan Opera with the stage band alone demonstrated the scoring to be fluent and effective.[26] In theory, then, there should have been no reason for a modern theater not to use this music, and at a production of *Semiramide* at the Rossini Opera Festival of Pesaro during the summer of 2003 the original ensemble was used to splendid effect. What actually transpired in New York we will see shortly.

4. THE NEW CRITICAL EDITION RENDERS ROSSINI'S OPERA MORE ACCURATELY AND PROVIDES A MORE IDIOMATIC TREATMENT OF ARTICULATION, DYNAMICS, AND SO FORTH. Every composer has different habits, some determined by personal considerations, some by external ones. When an opera composer is accustomed to the idea that his autograph will be used to prepare a printed edition of the complete orchestral score, he is motivated to be more precise about details, ensuring that there are dynamic markings in each part, that articulation is clear and reasonably coherent, that errors are corrected. He is precise because the medium in which his score will circulate is a precise one. When an opera composer expects his score to circulate in manuscript, as Rossini usually did, he tends to be less precise, since copyists' manuscripts are prepared in haste and rarely reflect with accuracy a composer's text. If a modern edition of an opera does not resolve contradictions and imprecisions in the autograph, chaos plagues the rehearsals. Rossini could count on musicians thoroughly familiar with his style, but the stylistic orientation of orchestral players today mutates with each work they perform. In its social

framework, then, an edition of an opera differs markedly from an edition of a novel or even of a piano sonata. Experience dealing with Rossini autographs provides a framework within which to resolve these problems.

Sometimes errors and confusions in the autograph are amusing. At the beginning of *Semiramide*, for example, the Babylonians are celebrating the day in which their queen will announce her choice for their new king. Peoples from around the Middle East offer gifts and pay homage. Many nineteenth-century sources carefully copy the following choral text from Rossini's autograph: "Dal Gange aurato, dal Nilo altero, dall'Orso indomito, dall'orbe intero" (From the golden Ganges, from the proud Nile, from the indomitable Bear, from the entire world). Indomitable Bear? What is this "Bear" doing among the major rivers of the ancient world? It is, of course, a Rossinian mistake. While entering the text of the libretto, Rossini wrote "Dal Gange aurato, dal Nilo altero, dall'orbe," before realizing that he had skipped a line, "da Tigri indomito" (from the indomitable Tigris). Thus, the Tigris is properly invoked together with the Ganges and the Nile. But, as my associate editor, Patricia Brauner, commented when she first noted this problem, Rossini's error is perfectly comprehensible: he simply substituted a bear (*orso*) for a tiger (*tigre*).

In our editorial efforts, of course, we assumed that we could reasonably control both the editorial process and the end product. *Semiramide*, however, was the first title in the Rossini edition to be prepared and typeset through computer processing. The advantages are manifold: changes and corrections are much simpler than they used to be, when every sign was punched into copper plates, and corrections entailed punching out signs already introduced and flattening the plate so that it could be punched again. Furthermore, computer processing allows performance parts to be generated directly from the full score, without the need to prepare those materials anew. However much we may lament the disappearance of the craft of music engraving, previously passed down from generation to generation, most music is now being processed through computer technology. But *Semiramide* was a first for us, and it soon became clear how many bugs were swarming around the computer program. As we corrected wave after wave of proof, we realized to our horror that new errors kept emerging. The process was controlling us, rather than the other way around. A correction made on page 225 in the cellos caused changes on page 227 in the bassoons because of linkages that had been made while the music was being entered into the computer. The lines seemed to be identical, and it was so easy for the computer operator to copy one from the other. What no one understood was that the linkage continued to be operative even when it was no longer appropriate. I personally read the proofs of *Semiramide* five times from beginning to end, swearing each time that I would never allow a score to be done on the computer again (an oath I promptly forgot). I don't want to think how many readings were done by my staff or by Casa Ricordi.[27]

We ultimately produced that more accurate score we promised, and it required not only exhaustive but also exhausting scholarship. Nonetheless, the critical edition of *Semiramide* uses that scholarship (and more than a little imagination) to make Rossini's opera available to performers in as complete and correct a form as modern textual criticism allows, recognizing fully that this edition (as with every edition of a musical or literary text) is a product of our era and its complex relationship to the past.

PERFORMING FROM THE CRITICAL EDITION OF *SEMIRAMIDE*

What did the *New York Times* critic mean when he said that *Semiramide* "was played in a new edition that put exhaustive scholarship before operatic effectiveness"? If by "edition" he was referring to the new critical edition of *Semiramide,* the meaning of the sentence is obscure: by whatever criteria Rossini's opera may be judged effective or ineffective, an *edition* of *Semiramide* (as opposed to an adaptation) cannot transform it into something else. *Semiramide* is not *Les Contes d'Hoffman* or *Carmen* or even *Don Carlos,* operas in which there are significant doubts about what music should be present in the score, either because the composers (or others) revised the works so many times that the situation is unclear or because they never lived to see their operas performed at all. Rossini wrote an opera called *Semiramide* with a certain musical-dramatic structure: the critical edition presents that opera as the composer conceived it, to the best of our knowledge. *Punto e basta,* as the Italians say.

If "edition" here means only production, on the other hand, the phrase is even harder to understand, since there was nothing "scholarly" about the Metropolitan Opera's production in any commonly understood sense of that term. Although there are many surviving drawings of sets and costumes for this once highly popular opera, no effort was made to employ them. At most, the production followed nineteenth-century practice by changing sets without dropping the curtain, thereby sparing the audience those interminable pauses in a dimly lit theater typical of opera productions of thirty years ago.[28] Although a great deal of ornamentation used in *Semiramide* by early nineteenth-century singers survives, none was adopted by the cast, all of whom developed, either by themselves or with the help of coaches, ornamentation they considered suitable for their own voices.[29] Neither the audience nor the critics judged ineffective the ornamentation used by Lella Cuberli, June Anderson, Marilyn Horne, or Samuel Ramey (each of whom ornamented his or her music in different ways). Although scholars know a great deal about the instruments Rossini would have had at his disposal in 1823, no member of the Metropolitan orchestra was asked to leave his or her modern instrument at home. At most, dynamic levels in their parts were changed to reflect, for example, the different weight of a modern brass instrument or the different ways instrumentalists were arranged physically during nineteenth-century performances. And although Rossini had only a single pair of tuned drums available to him, the fine Metropolitan timpanist (who employed four individually tuned drums) followed modern practice in substituting chordal notes when the composer, to keep the timpani playing in an ensemble passage, resorted to a nonharmonic tone.

Once the critical edition of *Semiramide* was in the hands of the performers, in short, no participant in the production had any thought other than creating an operatically effective performance for a modern New York City audience. Yet the question remains: What happens at the point of intersection between scholarship, with its effort to develop accurate texts and to provide precise historical knowledge, and performance? What kinds of questions are asked? What kinds of answers are deemed acceptable? What are the limits beyond which the performer feels constrained or the scholar feels compromised? And what happens when those limits are crossed?

Of the four categories of differences between the new critical edition and the earlier score, two are relatively unproblematic: no one has suggested it would have been better as a matter of principle not to use Rossini's orchestration; no one has suggested any changes in the basic editorial procedures employed. That does not mean that every editorial decision is unimpeachable, either in theory or as it affected tangibly this particular production. But the critical editions currently in progress of the operas of Rossini, Donizetti, and Verdi take as a point of pride that, wherever possible, first performances of a new edition use proofs and not a published score. Critiques of editorial decisions by fine musicians help scholars reassess their solutions and, if necessary, produce a more accurate and nuanced text. In addition, nothing reveals a simple mistake faster than when a clarinettist plays a $b\natural$ in a $B\flat$-*major* chord.

The other two categories of differences between the new critical edition of *Semiramide* and the earlier score, the use and orchestration of the stage band and the problem of cuts, are more controversial and therefore more interesting. They raise problems that arise at the point of intersection between scholarship and performance, problems to be explored in the second part of this book. We will also look briefly at some specific issues faced by the performers of *Semiramide* when employing vocal variations and ornamentation neither specified by the composer nor deriving, whether directly or indirectly, from his intervention.

Orchestration and Editorial Procedures

The computer wars did not end with the production of the full score. Performance materials derived from the score sported errors we could not have anticipated, which emerged only during rehearsals for the orchestra alone, without the singers. On several occasions the second violin part was printed a second or a third too low, even though the line was correct in the orchestral score. There is almost nothing as infuriating as watching costly rehearsal time tick away in order to correct nonsense beyond one's control. It was even worse for me to realize that we had occasionally failed to correct notes in the clarinet and horn parts—transposing instruments (that is, what you see is *not* what you get, and a written *c* actually sounds *d*, *e♭*, *f*, *g*, *a♭*, *a*, or *b♭*, depending on the transposition). These were places where Rossini's accidentals (sharps and flats) were wrong, yet we had neglected to intervene. There were only a handful of errors in the whole 1400-page orchestral score of *Semiramide*, but each one sent a dagger through me. Nonetheless, we somehow got through orchestral readings, errors in the parts were corrected, and we were able to begin rehearsals with the singers.[30]

The Metropolitan Opera orchestra consists of players who are serious professionals and fine musicians, but rehearsal conditions were not ideal. For repertory operas the players are so good that lengthy rehearsal is counterproductive, but for a work new to them the rehearsal time available was inadequate. On many days after the readings for orchestra alone, the players went right into the pit for run-throughs of entire acts or the whole opera. There was not even a *Sitzprobe* scheduled, a musical rehearsal in which the conductor works on musical details with orchestra, soloists, and chorus. Some of the fault for this scheduling lies in the common misperception that Rossini operas are relatively simple for the orchestra to play. If that means that the orchestral score is less dense or contrapuntally complex than a score by Wagner or Berg's *Lulu*, fair enough. But if it means that the style can be grasped and the orchestral lines brought to life by musicians not accustomed to playing similar music, it is totally false. Indeed, American orchestras need considerably *more* rehearsal time to play Rossini well than to play Wagner. They need to understand how the accompaniments, ostensibly simple, must be shaped, phrased, and articulated in order to sustain, envelop, and give radiance to the vocal lines. More than in most repertories, players also have to deal with fermatas, freedom in tempo, and modifications in the literal values of notes, all elements that cannot simply be inferred from the notes in the parts on their music stands.

Furthermore, the personnel making up the orchestra were highly variable. Because the orchestra has so many calls for rehearsals and performances each week, there is no "single" Metropolitan Opera orchestra but rather a group of musicians who belong to the orchestral family, as well as a group of "stringers" who come in when called. Some musicians were assigned permanently to *Semiramide* rehearsals and performances; others came and went without warning. As long as a body with the right instrument filled the requisite seat, Maestro Conlon was expected to be satisfied. That system might work for a composer whose style was well known to the players, but it was a nightmare for Rossini.

Never have I seen a set of parts marked up with such a surfeit of additional signs as were these *Semiramide* materials.[31] Rossini normally writes his famous orchestral crescendos beginning at a dynamic level of **pp.** After eight measures there might be a "cresc.," after another eight a *f,* and finally a *ff.* Editions of Rossini's music, whether critical or not, follow his notation, as they should, intervening or regularizing only where there are inconsistencies or unusual problems. Given the nature of modern instruments, the size of the modern opera orchestra, and today's theater acoustics, however, it is standard for a conductor to tell the orchestra to start a Rossini crescendo as softly as it can play, to keep it at that same level even after the word "cresc." appears, letting the increase in the number of instruments take care of the crescendo effect at first, and to save increases in dynamic level for the very end of the passage. Stated clearly once, such an explanation covers many similar situations throughout an opera.[32] But not at the Met. Since Maestro Conlon could never know who would be sitting at each desk during a rehearsal or even at a performance, it was decided to mark each and every crescendo in the performance materials in a way that would have been considered ludicrous in most other opera houses. At the start of each crescendo all of Rossini's **pp** were turned into **ppp;** all indications of "cresc." were crossed out and postponed for four or eight measures, and so on. In a few cases, it was so difficult to get the message across to players who were showing up for one rehearsal or another that we actually removed some of Rossini's doublings in order to be certain that the vocal lines would be heard. Once we did the opposite, reinforcing a line that Rossini assigned to first violins alone by having all the second violins play along in order to give it sufficient weight.

Throughout these manipulations of details, I could not help wondering what the orchestral balances would have been like had we been using early nineteenth-century trombones, horns, and trumpets, instead of our "new and improved" modern variety. How absurd to change every *ff* in the trombones and tuba to *f* or even *mf*, so that they would not overpower the remainder of the orchestra. With a stable orchestral contingent, the players could have been told once and for all that their instruments are more powerful than those Rossini had in mind; hence they should never play louder than *mf* or *f*, even in a *tutti* passage. But in the real world of the Metropolitan Opera, with modern instruments, we were compelled physically to alter every single dynamic marking in Rossini's score so that a musician reading his or her part for the first time would know what was expected.

The *Banda sul Palco*

Rossini projected the use of a band during three numbers of *Semiramide,* sometimes onstage (with its members in costume), sometimes in the wings. As we have seen, the original scoring of this band, for twenty-two instruments, functioned well in rehearsals for band alone (with only minor modifications). Both scholarship and good sense would suggest, then, that the original band parts be used.[33]

In the nineteenth century, the local militia provided players for the band. In today's world, unionized theaters do not have the option of calling on the fire department, and few theaters are prepared to engage twenty-two additional union musicians for a few minutes of music. None has been willing to put a brass band onstage, where Rossini often expected it to be, whether because of the cost of costumes, the necessity to pay supplements to the members of the band, or a feeling of discomfort at the convention, which has long since disappeared from opera houses around the world. For most performances of *Semiramide* and similar operas, the music written for the *banda sul palco* is assigned to instruments in the pit, a most unwelcome compromise since the stage band is usually meant to represent music "actually heard" by the protagonists, whereas music emerging from the pit normally (but not always) exists in a different realm. Eliminating the stage band altogether, then, disturbs the dramaturgical and musical structure of the work. Important theaters, such as the Metropolitan, compromise: they hire a band (often with reduced numbers) and put it in the wings, where, of course, problems of coordination between the band and the conductor become serious, even in the presence of television monitors.

Given the physical production of *Semiramide* at the Met, there were two places in the wings where the band could be placed: upstage right or downstage left. We began upstage right, a site from which the sounds arriving in the theater, which had seemed perfectly balanced during rehearsals of the band alone, were so distorted that the treble instruments, piccolos and high clarinets, completely overpowered the bass, giving the impression of a handful of pennywhistles. We then moved the band to downstage left: better, but the acoustics still distorted the sound. And so, working together, the scholar and the bandmaster modified the orchestration to suit the acoustic conditions, removing some of the higher-pitched instruments and strengthening the bass. Those modifications resolved the orchestration problem for the intervention of the stage band in the second act, where the band is intended to play alone offstage: by quoting music heard earlier in the opera the band announces impending festivities that directly bear on the dramatic confrontation taking place onstage.

More difficult to resolve were the two interventions of the stage band in the first act, where the band must play *together* or in close coordination with the pit orchestra. Rossini begins his first-act finale with an important choral movement. The orchestra plays a lengthy passage alone, allowing the chorus and the band time to enter and take their positions onstage. The music is then repeated with the chorus and the band joining the orchestra. It is not difficult to imagine a splendid effect achieved by this combination of musical forces. When the band is in the wings, however, two problems arise: first, it is difficult for it to produce a sound weighty enough to balance the fortissimo of the orchestra and the singing of the chorus; second, the problem of coordination becomes difficult, and in a passage where band and orchestra must often play the same music, the effect can be ragged. We rehearsed the passage numerous times, but ultimately all participants in the production agreed that the benefits to be gained by employing the offstage band did not offset the dangers of failed coordination between musical forces. Thus, the band was omitted from the first-act finale.

To the chagrin of everyone involved in the production, scholars and performers alike, the band parts for the Allegretto chorus of the introduction, "Di plausi qual clamor," were also omitted, with the notes assigned to instruments in the pit. The band here has a specific dramaturgical function: it announces the imminent arrival of Semiramide and her court, representing in sound the offstage "clamor" described in the text. The effect Rossini was

EXAMPLE 6.1. GIOACHINO ROSSINI, *SEMIRAMIDE*, INTRODUZIONE (N. 1),
THE CHORUS "DI PLAUSI QUEL CLAMOR," MM. 365–374.

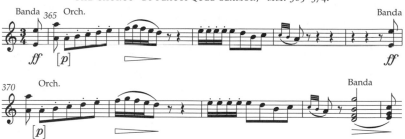

seeking depended upon integrating the band within the entire musical context. The band plays only a few notes, but those notes either introduce and
give rhythmic impulse to each musical phrase or effect tonal modulations between phrases (example 6.1). The nineteenth-century scoring was unproblematic, and given the dynamic context in the orchestra, *piano* and *pianissimo,* there was no problem hearing the band. Because the coordination of
band and orchestra requires absolute rhythmic precision, however, placing
the band offstage turned out to be a severe handicap. With sufficient rehearsal
time, this handicap might have been overcome, but in 1990 at the Met, that
time was unavailable. Once rehearsals moved from the rehearsal rooms to the
theater, the band entries were never rhythmically correct.

The band interventions were therefore written into the orchestral parts,
using those few instruments not already playing. The result was a pallid imitation of the original, with no musical force, no dramatic logic, and no sense.
Exhaustive scholarship and operatic effectiveness were both sacrificed on the
altar of practical expedience.

Cuts

While only those thoroughly familiar with *Semiramide* or professionals directly involved in the production were aware of problems with the *banda sul
palco,* everyone who attended the performances could talk knowingly about
the length of Rossini's opera. That cuts would have to be made in Rossini's
score was a principle accepted from the beginning by all. Although prepared
to do whatever the performers felt necessary to present the work responsibly,
the company's judgment was that *Semiramide* would have greater public success if it could be brought in at just over four hours in length, including intermission and applause but not final curtain calls. In the modern world, all theaters try to hold overtime to a minimum, but the crucial element for the

Metropolitan's budget was to get the theater emptied before midnight. They were prepared to have a seven o'clock curtain if necessary, but their experience suggested that beginning an opera before 7:30 created undue difficulties for a New York audience, difficulties that could be overcome only for works that had already developed a place in a particular repertory, such as *Götterdämmerung* or *Parsifal*. (Do not think such constraints affect only modern theaters: practical considerations caused Rossini to make major cuts for the first performances of *Guillaume Tell* and Verdi to do likewise for *Don Carlos*.)[34]

Without cuts, the music of *Semiramide* runs approximately three hours and forty-five minutes. Adding a half-hour intermission and anticipating audience enthusiasm for a work that highlights virtuoso singing (on opening night as much as four minutes of applause greeted certain scenes), we knew that between fifteen and thirty minutes of music needed to be eliminated. Our challenge was to make those cuts in an effective and responsible manner. We can identify four categories of cuts: (1) recitative; (2) choral movements; (3) complete numbers; (4) internal cuts, usually of repeated passages.

1. RECITATIVE. Performing a little-known opera in an enormous theater that in 1990 still refused to employ supertitles (a situation reversed a decade later) guarantees that details of the dramatic action and subtleties of character motivation will remain mysterious to an overwhelming majority of the audience. Although all the recitative in *Semiramide* is accompanied by the orchestra, is written with care, and is by Rossini (unlike *Il barbiere di Siviglia*, where nary a note of the recitative is his),[35] significant cuts can be made. There are always gains and losses. After the massive introduction, a short recitative helps clarify (to those who understand the words) some of the action already witnessed. Omitting it saves three minutes. What are the negative results? Some useful dramaturgical development of individual characters is sacrificed, including elements important for later relations between those characters. There is an awkward tonal shift from the key of the introduction, *F major,* to the key at the beginning of the next musical number, *G major.* Although Rossini's recitative mediates between those keys, audience applause after the introduction tends to alleviate the tonal problem. More unfortunate, cutting the recitative means the loss of a dramaturgically effective conclusion to the entire opening of the work. The High Priest, Oroe, is left alone. He addresses another prayer to the gods, and reenters the temple to a reprise of the solemn music that had opened the entire introduction. Still, loss of this recitative and a number of similar passages throughout the opera cannot be said to have damaged the work significantly. Indeed, many of the recitative cuts taken at the Metropolitan Opera were already being made during the 1820s.

2. CHORAL MOVEMENTS. The massive choral interventions that introduce five of the thirteen numbers of *Semiramide,* and play an important role in two others, lend an air of solemnity and monumentality to the opera. The indiscriminate removal of choruses changes the character of the work. In some cases, such as the chorus opening Arsace's scene in the second act, the cuts are not only disfiguring but remove genuinely distinguished music. In other cases, discreet excisions are possible.

Often Rossini constructs a choral movement by providing an orchestral introduction (A), repeating that introduction with choral parts added (A'), providing a contrasting section (B), and then repeating the opening music with chorus once again (A'); additional cadences bring the chorus to a conclusion. Stage directors such as the late Jean-Pierre Ponnelle, who keep their forces in constant movement, know how to make choruses scenically interesting; those who are more visually oriented, sculpting beautiful stage pictures, such as John Copley, the stage director for *Semiramide* at the Metropolitan, find them excessively long.

In deciding what to cut at the Met, dramatic needs, scenic needs, and judgments about musical value were invoked. As a result, three identically constructed choruses (with the form AA'BA', followed by cadences) were handled in three different ways. In the introduction to the first act, the structure was reduced to AA' cadences, a form Rossini regularly uses in other operas. In this case the excision of the B section removed one of the two extended passages in the opera in which the *banda sul palco* plays independently of the orchestra. (The other such passage, within the duet at the start of the second act, was left untouched.) The musically splendid chorus that opens the first-act finale, on the other hand, was left intact.

The most intrusive cut occurred in the chorus at the beginning of the finale of the second (and final) act, which takes place in the subterranean tomb of the murdered King Nino. Although the entire chorus was rehearsed, the choral movement itself was judged musically weak and dramatically problematic by both the conductor and the stage director. Yet cutting this passage entirely was impossible for two reasons: first, it quotes material from the overture, transforming it from duple to triple meter, an effect that no one wished to lose (example 6.2). Second, fragments from the music appear in the recitative for Arsace that follows the chorus in the finale, and their appearance there would make no sense if none of this music had appeared earlier. As a result, it was decided to reduce this choral movement to the introductory orchestral statement of the theme (the very first A), with all participation by the chorus eliminated. This completely transformed the significance of the music. Instead of

EXAMPLE 6.2. GIOACHINO ROSSINI, *SEMIRAMIDE*, SINFONIA, MM. 112–115,
AND FINALE SECONDO (N. 13), OPENING CHORUS, MM. 17–20.

being heard as part of a chorus, it essentially became an orchestral introduction to the accompanied recitative—a structural device not dissimilar to musical techniques Rossini employs elsewhere (Calbo's great aria in the second
act of *Maometto II* is one of many possible examples). A listener familiar with
Rossini's style, but not with this particular composition, would have had no
compelling reason to think the score was anything but intact.

    3. COMPLETE NUMBERS. The least painful way to make cuts in an opera is
to remove entire numbers. It is also the way Rossini most often countenanced
in productions with which he was involved. As we have seen, the tenor, Idreno,
is given two arias in *Semiramide,* one in each act. The pieces are musically attractive, but they function more as concert arias than as integral elements in
the drama. In fact, the first-act aria was almost never performed in the nineteenth century, and it was probably omitted already within the 1823 Venetian season. The second-act aria, on the other hand, could not be so lightly
removed, since it provides a necessary moment of repose for the mezzo-
soprano: without it, she would be forced to sing a twenty-minute solo scene,
followed immediately by one of the most difficult duets in Italian opera
("Ebben, a te, ferisci").

    Conductor, scholar, administrators: all of us looked longingly at Idreno's
first-act aria, a full eight minutes toward our temporal goal. The role of
Idreno, however, marked the debut at the Metropolitan Opera of Chris Merritt, who in the early part of his career was known principally as a fine Rossini
tenor. But Merritt was hired on the explicit understanding that he would sing
both arias, and he was *going* to sing both arias. Ultimately, we were forced to
settle for a series of internal cuts in each piece, cuts that displeased me musically and that were stylistically awkward. But opera is about people as well as
about art: the singer's will could not be ignored.

4. INTERNAL CUTS. Performers of Italian opera often make internal cuts in musical numbers. Singers who understand the technique of vocal ornamentation, on the other hand, are loath to countenance cuts in their solo arias. They understand that repeated passages offer them the opportunity to demonstrate their art. Except for Idreno's arias all solo arias in *Semiramide* were performed intact. Some cuts of repeated passages were made in duets, largely in recognition of the sheer endurance required for the soprano, mezzo-soprano, and bass to perform this score. For the most part, these cuts followed practices for which Rossini himself offers ample precedent. In the duet for Arsace and Assur, for example, the concluding cabaletta, "Va, superbo," consists of a theme sung by the bass, its identical repetition by the mezzo-soprano, a short transition, a repeat of the theme for bass alone, then a repeat for mezzo-soprano, now with the bass providing a contrapuntal line (AA trans. AA'). At the Met, the music after the transition was reduced to just the final A, with Arsace singing the melody and Assur providing a counterpoint.

But at least one cut made in some performances of *Semiramide* at the Metropolitan Opera belongs to the well-known category of "vanity cuts." Modern basses tend to conclude Assur's "mad scene" by leaping up to a high *f*, rather than descending to the tonic as Rossini wrote. Leaving aside the advisability of this practice (a matter that will be discussed in chapter 9), when basses produce a solid *f* they want it to ring out for several measures. In the orchestral conclusion to Assur's aria, however, Rossini quotes in abbreviated form an orchestral pattern that had served him earlier in the piece, with an alternation of tonic and dominant harmonies in two-measure groupings. After two measures on *F major,* the harmony shifts to the dominant chord, and the bass's sustained high *f* cannot be continued without creating a harmonic clash (example 6.3). Basses yearn to cut those measures on the dominant, leaving the piece to conclude with seven consecutive measures on the tonic. Indeed, during rehearsals Samuel Ramey was so discontent about performing the music Rossini had written that at one point he showed his displeasure by alternating *f* and *e* (example 6.4). Nonetheless, the decision to respect Rossini's score prevailed, and on opening night Ramey held his high *f* for two bars, then exited to a resounding and deserved ovation. But singers' egos need constant stroking. When I returned for a later performance, the orchestral measures on the dominant had disappeared, and the audience had to listen to all those bars of tonic harmony, an effect Rossini would certainly not have countenanced, not even for a bass with a voice as beautiful and powerful as Ramey's. I like to think, though, that Gioachino was watching these shenanigans: after two bars

EXAMPLE 6.3. GIOACHINO ROSSINI, *SEMIRAMIDE*, SCENA, CORO,
E ARIA ASSUR (N. 12), MM. 475–479.

EXAMPLE 6.4. SAMUEL RAMEY'S MODIFICATION OF THE VOCAL CONCLUSION
IN THE SCENA, CORO, E ARIA ASSUR (N. 12), MM. 475–479.

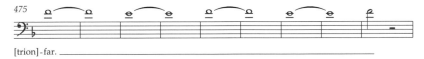

of high *f*, Ramey's voice cracked, leaving the orchestra to repeat the tonic chord in solitary splendor.

Vocal Variations and Ornamentation

The introduction of a high note at the end of a musical number, although an effect particularly dear to twentieth-century singers and audiences, was practically unknown to singers active during the years when Rossini was composing his works for Italian theaters and supervising performances of them. But there were many other ways in which singers were expected to modify the notes actually written down by the composer, and a study of various forms of contemporary evidence allows us to understand such practices quite precisely. Our knowledge of these performance techniques has increased enormously over the past thirty years. Disagreements among professionals can (and do) arise over details, and many singers have developed their own personal way of ornamenting their music. Certain techniques are recognizably associated with Marilyn Horne, others with Rockwell Blake, still others with Cecilia Bartoli. Yet it is only when a performance diverges profoundly from the accepted standard that the public or the critics tend to comment on the matter, and that certainly did not happen in the Met's *Semiramide.* In most respects the singers participating in these performances provided fine realizations of the score in the appropriate style.

Almost all the singers, for example, introduced appoggiaturas in an appropriate manner. Some understood from long experience exactly how to handle these small modifications in the vocal line, whose function is to provide a musical accent to match the accent that falls on the next-to-last syllable of a verse with a feminine ending (in a word like "[a]-mo-[re]"). Composers of the first part of the nineteenth century often wrote two equal notes for the next-to-last and last syllable ("[a]-mo-re") but expected that the first would be modified by the singer (usually sung as the note a tone above). Although the need to employ such appoggiaturas in early nineteenth-century Italian opera is a principle that has been stated often and authoritatively,[36] many professional singers, older or younger, continue to arrive at rehearsals with the music learned literally, and a surprising number of conductors do not know the difference. I have sat in early rehearsals for operas at Pesaro, New York, St. Louis, Miami, Chicago, and Rome, marking necessary appoggiaturas in the scores of singers.

Only at one point in *Semiramide,* however, did I feel that the performance of appoggiaturas was wrongheaded. It came at the beginning of the cantabile section in the great "mad scene" for Assur. Sam Ramey's performance of the scene was for the most part so extraordinary that a group of New York wags rechristened the opera "Sammy Ramey Day." Yet Ramey got it into his head that at the beginning of this cantabile, Rossini's notation, which clearly implies appoggiaturas in both the first two measures, should be interpreted by singing only the second measure with an appoggiatura (example 6.5). Is this just a matter of taste? No, it is not: Ramey sang the wrong note. An equivalent error would be to perform the beginning of Rigoletto's aria in the second-act of Verdi's opera without the appoggiaturas Verdi specified (example 6.6). But Verdi was composing thirty years after Rossini, when singers were less con-

EXAMPLE 6.5. GIOACHINO ROSSINI, *SEMIRAMIDE*, SCENA, CORO,
E ARIA ASSUR (N. 12), MM. 278–279.

versant with the conventions, and he consequently wrote out every appoggiatura required. He also sought to differentiate passages where he did not
want appoggiaturas, often passages involving declamation over an orchestral
melody, as opposed to recitative-like passages.

Apart from appoggiaturas, the style of nineteenth-century Italian opera
before Verdi (with some important extensions even into Verdi) required singers to add appropriate cadenzas where the composer did not write them in
full, or to modify those the composer did write to suit their individual vocal
abilities. The practice also was based on the assumption that singers would
vary certain repeated passages, even though these were notated identically by
the composer. Such interventions were not considered "optional": the structure and style of the music were conceived in order to favor them. Nineteenth-
century sources, including manuscripts prepared by Rossini for singers of
his time, provide sets of variations used by singers from the first half of the
century, and theoretical treatises on singing offer an enormous amount of
information about these practices. There is no one "correct" way to proceed.
Rather, the art of ornamentation is a creative interaction between historical
style and individual personality. There are as many different ways appropri-

EXAMPLE 6.6. GIUSEPPE VERDI, *RIGOLETTO*, SCENA ED ARIA
RIGOLETTO (N. 9), MM. 78–79.

ately to add cadenzas and to vary repeated lines as there are singers, and most performers today operate within perfectly acceptable boundaries.

Certainly all the singers in the Metropolitan Opera's *Semiramide* were well versed in these techniques, even though they went about their tasks quite differently. Some prepared their own materials anew; others combined variations and cadenzas they had sung before with new ones. Some had everything written out well in advance; others developed material during rehearsals. In one duet for Semiramide and Arsace, Lella Cuberli and Marilyn Horne sang a splendid joint cadenza that Richard Bonynge had developed for performances with Joan Sutherland and Horne during the 1960s. For the Met, I prepared a complete set of suggestions for the entire opera, which were sent to the singers before rehearsals began in New York. They used what they liked, rejected what they didn't, and made substitutions and emendations to suit their needs. During rehearsals we fixed places that didn't work. All eyes, of course, were on the conductor, and when Maestro Conlon grimaced, it was back to the drawing board. The last thing anyone was concerned about was "scholarship."

The world of the theater is not a place where one pays obeisance to a written score, but rather a place where one finds real singers performing with real orchestral musicians; audiences with trains and buses to catch; administrators who must watch both the cash box and the artistic product; successive generations of critics, each of which invokes a past golden age but fails to appreciate its own; costumes that come apart just as the heroine launches into a cabaletta, forcing her to sing complicated runs and variations while worrying that she'll soon be naked; choruses that must be shepherded onto and off the stage because the director wants to make a "pretty picture"; massively inappropriate sets that must be changed in the middle of a musical number; ghosts that emerge in clouds of smoke sending prima donnas to their bed with coughs; tenors that jet from one theater to another and arrive for rehearsals barely knowing the music. That's what the world of the theater is like. And musicologists who truly love opera would have it no other way.

An edition is not a performance, a performance is not an edition, and scholarship and operatic effectiveness are not mutually exclusive. Once we know the score, once a critical edition enters the world of the theater, it is used in much the same way as any other edition is used. It is to the issues that arise when performing Italian opera from any edition, critical or otherwise, that the rest of this book is dedicated.

PART II

Performing the Opera

7

CHOOSING A VERSION

MODERN PERFORMERS AND HISTORY

The relationship between modern performers and the history that should sustain them has rarely been so tormented as in our current musical environment. Increasing numbers of critics, conductors, scholars, and instrumentalists are calling into question many of the basic tenets that guided musical practice through much of the twentieth century. We distrust tradition, we distrust instinct, we distrust scholarship, we distrust our ability to judge among competing aesthetic positions and interpretive strategies. These concerns have become ever more troublesome as they have touched the performance of music written in the late eighteenth and the nineteenth centuries, the music we grew up believing was "ours," a repertory that seems to recede further and further into the past with the new millennium.

Musicians and critics who posit the existence of a continuous musical tradition linking the present to nineteenth-century practices are faced with increasingly persistent evidence that this apparent continuity is a chimera.[1] Instruments and the techniques for playing them, vocal styles and the use of ornamentation, the social role of music and its implications for musical structure and performance—all have undergone vast changes since the time of Beethoven, Chopin, or Rossini, not to mention Grieg, Elgar, and Bartok. Some conductors arrogantly dismiss this evidence as ignorant posturing by nonmusicians or the refuge of poor souls unable to play in tune. But even those most contemptuous of efforts to find for the so-called standard repertory a performance practice more responsive to the historical circumstances under which it was created and first performed cannot dismiss a movement whose popular reception has been enthusiastic.[2]

The principles embraced by musicians and critics committed to the development of more sensitively historicized performance styles, on the other hand, are equally under siege. Battles rage in the scholarly literature and popular press about numerous details: the best way to apply ornamentation in various repertories, the interpretation of tempo markings, and the choice of instruments to be employed (whether in the orchestra, for solo keyboard works, or in the accompaniment of *secco* recitative). But the very possibility of developing such alternative styles with a sensitivity to historical circumstances has been attacked by those who insist that conductors from Toscanini to Roger Norrington are merely demonstrating the triumph of "modernism" in performance, an anti-Romantic sensibility that has nothing whatsoever to do with the historical past and everything to do with a present-day revolt against more proximate performing styles.

We are surrounded by proponents and critics of either a loosely defined tradition, or a questionable search for authenticity, or a pessimistic, even nihilistic insistence that all our efforts lead to our merely embodying the modernist or postmodernist (or whatever tomorrow's "-ist" may be) tendencies of our current society. We also belong to a generation of musicians and music lovers formed by a century of mechanical reproduction of music. Our memories merge evenings in the theater with innumerable recordings. We lose track of what real performances sound like, so confused and enchanted are we by the doctored sounds served up by record companies. Small wonder that a minor industry has arisen in comparative analysis of early recordings: its device, a stopwatch to compare performances of Beethoven symphonies frozen on disc with the composer's own metronome markings, whatever those highly contested numbers might mean.

Let me state at the outset that I do not consider modern performers to be under any obligation (moral or otherwise) to respect either the particular qualities of a work or the general characteristics of its composer's style. To take an example that some musicians found disturbing, I had nothing but profound admiration for Peter Brook and his *La Tragédie de Carmen,* theatrical art at its most memorable. This adaptation and transformation of a novella by Prosper Mérimée, using melodies by Georges Bizet reorchestrated intelligently for a small instrumental ensemble, had no pretense to be Bizet's *Carmen.* It aspired to be a work in its own right, with its own aesthetic integrity.

Once they set aside the Peter Brook model and claim to be presenting a nineteenth-century opera, however, performers find themselves in a different situation. Even here, I have no interest in invoking the language of moral obligation. Yet conductors, singers, and stage directors (even the most iconoclastic) inevitably approach their tasks enriched or encumbered with their knowledge of previous performances of a work or similar works, whether through personal experience in the theater, secondary accounts (the opinion of teachers and coaches, for example), or recordings. Everything has been filtered further through sensibilities reflecting those experiences that make us all international citizens of the early twenty-first century. Performances, in short, are already "historical through and through."

The call to historicize further our knowledge of Italian opera, then, is not a subterfuge for escaping our modern identity or the personal passions of an artist in favor of historical models. It stems rather from the belief that performers can find more satisfactory answers to some of their concerns if they make the effort to supplement their present knowledge with awareness of a work's original historical, dramaturgical, musical, and social context: indeed, much in the shape of a typical nineteenth-century Italian opera is meaningful only in such a context. Neither invocations of the authority of tradition (which too often is a euphemism for the status quo) nor obeisance to the idol of historical reconstruction will offer as promising a path.

This chapter and the ensuing ones will provide access to this context for a variety of issues that performers confront each time they perform an Italian opera written during the first half of the nineteenth century. By combining historical evidence, theoretical models, and actual examples, these discussions may help all those concerned with Italian opera—whether as performers, critics, or listeners—to understand the ways in which the lessons of history and the realities of today's musical culture can interact effectively in the opera house.

"IT IS ALL BELLINI'S WORK"

Before rehearsals for an opera begin, performers must decide what music to incorporate in the particular production being planned. A first set of decisions involves the choice among alternative versions, when these exist, as they almost always do: that is the subject of the present chapter. Once a basic version has been chosen, performers need to address the problem of whether to make any cuts: that is the subject of the next chapter. Too often these questions implicitly or explicitly are couched in terms, whether aesthetic or practical, that limit the history they invoke to the immediate past.

In an opera such as *Lucia di Lammermoor,* traditionalists insist on adhering to a rigidly defined, heavily cut version, whose historical roots they ignore. Whether consciously or not, they are essentially following the version of *Lucia* recorded under the baton of Tullio Serafin in the 1950s. This version, furthermore, was given a semblance of permanence in one of the most wrongheaded books ever written about Italian opera, entitled *Style,*

Traditions, and Conventions of Italian Melodrama of the Eighteenth and Nine-teenth Century, published (in Italian) by Ricordi in 1958, to which we will return in the next chapter.[3] The failure to think through the performance history of individual works, though, extends well beyond operas like *Lucia,* which did, after all, have a fairly continuous performance history from the time of its composition to the present.

In 1977, when directing at New York City Opera the first performances of Rossini's *Il Turco in Italia* in the new critical edition, Tito Capobianco, a well-known stage director, told me that certain decisions about versions and cuts in the opera were traditional, as if those decisions went back to the nineteenth century. But there was no continuous performing tradition for *Il Turco in Italia,* which had disappeared from the repertory for a hundred years before being revived under the direction of Gianandrea Gavazzeni at the Teatro Eliseo of Rome in 1950 (with the participation of Maria Callas). The opera was recorded at La Scala during the summer of 1954, then presented at the theater the following March, always with Callas. I know these performances, of course, only from the recording, but on that basis one observes the intelligence of most of Gavazzeni's musical choices and the stylistic mastery of Callas's interpretation.[4] Writing in the program book, John Steane comments that "she excels in recitative." And referring to the conclusion of the opera, after the great quartet at the masked ball ("Oh! guardate che accidente"), he adds, "Then in the final solo of the opera, *Sì, mi è forza partir* (Yes, I must leave), the sentiment is real; the tragic accent now marks a genuine development and the character gains a new warmth and depth in a way which perhaps only an artist with Callas's skills and experience could bring out." What Steane failed to understand is that this part of the opera has been decimated. In the version they chose to perform, surely unbeknownst to Callas, Gavazzeni omitted her principal aria and one of the most stunning single compositions in the opera, "Squallida vesta" (Squalid clothes). This is the aria in which Fiorilla, having learned that her husband has barred the doors of his house to her, repents her flighty behavior. The trivial *secco* recitative that follows ("Sì, mi è forza partir")—written by one of Rossini's collaborators, not by the composer himself—is utterly void of any dramatic meaning without that previous scene. Who told her that she would have to leave Naples for her parents' home in Sorrento? Of course, one wonders what Callas would have had to say about performing *Il Turco in Italia* in Gavazzeni's version had she been aware of this cut!

On the other hand, in their monolithic insistence that every note of a score such as *La traviata* be played in the theater, reformers show equally little awareness of the textual and performance history of the works they champion and the theatrical conditions that prevailed, even in the best of circumstances, during the first half of the nineteenth century. As Charles Rosen has argued, it is highly suspect to historicize the performance of a musical artifact, concerning ourselves with its notes, rhythms, orchestral forces, and vocal style, while abstracting the work from the historical and social circumstances that gave it birth—to presume, in short, that one can create an authentic performance in an inauthentic environment. And yet, who would feel it obligatory, while improving the musical text of a nineteenth-century opera, also to reproduce the appalling circumstances under which many acknowledged masterpieces of our musical heritage were born?[5]

These rigidly drawn lines succeed only in obscuring the issue: how can we use our knowledge of the history of performance, our grasp of the social realities of nineteenth-century Italian opera, our analytic skills, and our aesthetic perceptions to develop a more responsible approach to choosing what music to include in modern performances? In order to address this question, we need to recall the social realities of Italian opera and their implications for the nature of operatic "texts." Can we talk about an opera that exists in multiple versions as being, in any meaningful sense, a "work"? Or must we consider these operas to be loose agglomerations of music that can be manipulated in any way we find convenient?

However much we may avoid the language of moral obligation when discussing performance, it remains commonplace to speak of the obligation of a critical edition to print a work in a form as close as possible to an author's intentions, even though the philosophical and practical difficulties in understanding "authorial intention" are legion. These difficulties are well known to literary editors: the multiple texts of *King Lear,* Dreiser's *Sister Carrie,* and the poems of W. H. Auden are notorious examples. Different versions of a poem or novel can be contemplated and compared by a solitary reader, even if critics disagree about which text to favor through the physical organization of a book. Should they put alternative versions face to face, in footnotes, or in a principal text and a series of appendixes? Although plays in their theatrical realizations present problems similar to those of opera, there remains a need for reading texts prepared with criteria similar to those employed for other literary works.[6]

For composers of Italian opera, on the other hand, publication was important primarily as a way to facilitate performance. Indeed, through about 1820 even the most popular operas circulated only in manuscript or in incomplete reductions for piano and voice (lacking, for example, the recitative). Ricordi began publishing complete vocal scores in the mid 1820s, as we have seen, but it was not until near the end of Verdi's life that some full orchestral scores of his operas appeared (those for *Otello* and *Falstaff*), and even then the composer was only tangentially involved with the process.[7] It is not surprising, then, that authorial intentions in Italian opera are often bound up with the requirements of particular productions.

Although it was more lucrative for composers to prepare new works than to mount new productions of old ones, various circumstances could lead to their involvement in revivals: they might be preparing a new opera for a theater that was simultaneously mounting a production of an earlier one (as Rossini did when he presented a new version of *Maometto II* to open the Venetian season of carnival 1822–23, for which he wrote *Semiramide*);[8] they might agree to participate in a revival for a special circumstance, such as the opening of a new theater (as Bellini did when he revised *Bianca e Fernando* for the opening of the Teatro Carlo Felice in Genoa);[9] they might seek to accommodate the wishes of an admired singer (as Donizetti did when he transformed a secondary tenor role in *Maria di Rohan,* Armando di Gondì, to a principal role *en travesti* for the contralto Marietta Brambilla at the Théâtre Italien of Paris a year after its Viennese premiere);[10] they might genuinely feel an opera needed revision on aesthetic grounds (as Verdi did when he prepared a major new version of *La forza del destino* for Milan in 1869, seven years after the St. Petersburg premiere).[11] We can usually document, reconstruct, and publish these versions, however they may originally have been motivated (whether to meet changing needs of the performing forces or the diverse tastes of different publics), but we need to be cautious about assigning them relative worth. This is true even in the case of a composer such as Verdi, whose treatment of his own autograph manuscripts suggests he intended to leave his operas in what he considered to be definitive versions.[12] It is not intuitively obvious, however, that the Verdi responsible for the 1865 *Macbeth,* revised for Paris, could look with sympathy or even with equanimity at the original 1847 version of that opera.[13] The availability of multiple versions prepared by the composer, then, creates a first problem that must be addressed by modern performers of Italian opera.

Some commentators, such as Carl Dahlhaus, blinded by the influence of social and theatrical structures on this process of revision, withhold altogether from Italian *bel canto* operas the status of a "work," preferring to see them as amorphous collections of individual compositions given temporary shape by particular productions.[14] By emphasizing abuses of the Italian theatrical system, this position attempts to ignore the evidence of composers' letters (particularly those of Bellini, Donizetti, and Verdi), who railed against theaters and performers tampering arbitrarily with their works. One could argue, to be sure, that some of that railing was itself theatrical, a product less of deep artistic conviction than of an effort to ensure control over theaters (and of the royalties that accrued from such control). Thus, during the late 1840s Verdi regularly asked Ricordi to insert in every rental contract with theaters a clause of this type:

> With the aim of impeding the alterations often made in opera houses, it is prohibited to make any change in this score, any mutilation, to lower or raise the key, in short to make any alteration that requires even the smallest change in the orchestration, under penalty of a fine of 1000 francs, which I will demand from you whenever any theater whatsoever makes such an alteration in the score.[15]

But there is considerable contemporary testimony, even before Verdi's diatribes to Ricordi, that composers, singers, and theaters were sensitive to the status of Italian operas as "works," whose structure should be respected, where possible, for both practical and aesthetic reasons. Let me offer examples from 1828, 1834, and 1836, pertaining to Bellini and Rossini.

A Composer

From the viewpoint of a prima donna, Rossini's *Otello* (first performed at the Teatro del Fondo of Naples on 4 December 1816) had one major flaw: Desdemona appears on stage first in a scena and duettino with her friend Emilia. Later in the opera, to be sure, she has a great deal of solo singing (the second-act finale is essentially an aria for Desdemona, and the first half of the third and final act is devoted to her willow song and prayer), but major singers longed then—and continue to long today—for the opportunity to display themselves in solo song when they first enter. Printed librettos of the epoch demonstrate that Desdemonas of the period often introduced a cavatina before the scena and duettino with Emilia, sometimes omitting the duettino altogether.[16] The revival of the opera in Rome during the carnival of 1820 is infamous for Rossini's having prepared a "happy ending" for the opera, at the request of the theater, inserting a duet from his *Armida* and a final ensemble from *Ricciardo e Zoraide*. In the same production, however, the prima donna, Girolama Dardanelli, appeared on stage in the first act with a chorus ("Esulta, patria omai") and cavatina ("Quanto è grato all'alma mia") borrowed with only a few adjustments in the text from Rossini's first Neapolitan opera, *Elisabetta, regina d'Inghilterra,* of 1815. We don't know whether Dardanelli's insertion was made with or without Rossini's approval (he was not present for the rehearsals or the performance).[17]

It is quite certain, on the other hand, that Rossini had nothing to do with the first production of *Otello* given in Paris at the Théâtre Italien in 1821. On that occasion, Giuditta Pasta made her debut in the role of Desdemona. She wanted a scena and cavatina, and in the absence of one in the original version of *Otello* she had no compunctions whatsoever about adding a piece that Rossini had prepared for Malcom in *La donna del lago:* the recitative "Mura felici" (Happy walls) became "Mura infelici" (Unhappy walls), while the cavatina "Elena! oh tu, che chiamo!" (Ellen! you whom I call) became "Palpita incerta l'alma" (My uncertain soul trembles). Since the original piece was written for a contralto, Pasta transposed the cavatina up a fourth (from *E major* to *A major*), and in that key it was printed in all French editions of the opera.[18] When she brought the opera to London in 1822, she also brought with her the added scena and cavatina. And when Rossini arrived in London and Paris to supervise productions of *Otello* in 1824, he did not tamper with this fait accompli.

Yet Pasta's added cavatina for *Otello* caused a chain reaction. When Rossini introduced *La donna del lago* to Paris on 7 September 1824, he replaced Malcom's scena and cavatina (by now too well known to the Parisians from *Otello*) with the scena and cavatina for Arsace from *Semiramide,* "Ah! quel giorno ognor rammento," creating yet further confusion when *Semiramide* was first sung in Paris in 1825, where the cavatina was simply omitted.[19] By 1827–28, Rossini finally succeeded in setting matters right. Henriette Sontag assumed the role of Desdemona in a revival of *Otello* early in 1828, and Rossini took the opportunity to get his operas back into the form he had written them. Fearful, though, that Sontag might be criticized for not singing the scena and cavatina to which Pasta had accustomed the French, the composer sent a letter to the *Journal de Commerce:*

> Mlle Sontag would have wished to sing the role of Desdemona as it was originally given in Paris by M.^{de} Pasta, but since the cavatina "Oh quante lagrime" has been returned to *La donna del lago,* for which it had originally been written, Mlle Sontag has agreed to sing the role just as I composed it for the Neapolitan Theater. To avoid any other interpretation, I beg you, sir, to have the kindness to insert this letter into your next number.[20]

Although he was perfectly prepared to make or accept a modified version of *Otello* when necessary, Rossini was also prepared to set matters right when he had the chance.

A Singer

In preparing his Romeo and Juliet opera, *I Capuleti e i Montecchi,* which had its premiere at the Teatro La Fenice of Venice on 11 March 1830, Bellini paid particular attention to the work's conclusion. Felice Romani, his librettist, had prepared a libretto in 1825 on the same subject for Nicola Vaccai, *Giulietta e Romeo,* many verses from which he recycled for Bellini.[21] Some verses Romani had to invent anew, since Bellini had decided to import into *Capuleti* several compositions from their previous, unsuccessful collaboration, *Zaira* (whose premiere took place at the Teatro Ducale of Parma on 16 May 1829).[22] But some verses, particularly at the very conclusion of the opera, had to be newly written because the composer did not want to close his opera with elaborate solo music, as in Vaccai, but rather with a touching duet for the lovers, sung in fragments that strain for a moment of lyricism, then die away. We are convinced by this splendid effect, but the contemporary public was not: the audience was no more attuned to such a conclusion than were the audiences that twenty years earlier had refused the tragic finale of Rossini's *Tancredi.*[23]

Furthermore, Bellini was not taking into account the predilections of singers. In particular, his finale to *I Capuleti e i Montecchi* did not much please Maria Malibran, daughter of Manuel García (the original Count Almaviva in Rossini's *Il barbiere di Siviglia*). Malibran, who often performed the role of Romeo during the early 1830s, was one of the finest singers of her time, a legendary musician and a captivating personality, of whom Bellini became immediately enamored when he first saw her in London in 1833. He wanted nothing more than to write an opera for her, but the only tangible result of this desire was the Neapolitan version of *I puritani,* which (for reasons we will examine below) was never performed during their lifetimes. Malibran was also the very model of a capricious prima donna, and she decided that Bellini's conclusion for *I Capuleti* did not show her vocal skills to full advantage. As a result, she introduced into Bellini's opera, in performances in Bologna during October 1832, sections of the finale borrowed from Vaccai's earlier opera.[24] When Giuditta Grisi made the same substitution in Turin during the carnival season of 1836, Romani wrote a scathing article attacking the practice: "The third act of Vaccai was glued to the opera of Bellini, as in the punishment by which Mesenzio attached a dead body to a live one."[25] Then, taking off from a verse from his own libretto, Romani proclaimed:

> Ah! if you sleep, awake now ["Ah! se tu dormi svegliati!"], good Italian sense, and no longer permit yourself to be swindled in this way by the whims

of virtuosos! Awake, if you sleep, public judgment, and do not permit the most beautiful operas of our imagination to be so perverted, mutilated, ruined! Awake, if you sleep, modesty, and cry aloud to singers that the time has come for the musical theater no longer to be disfigured by their peculiarities, by their pastiches, by their ridiculous habits [*convenienze*]! Awake, reason, awake, criteria, awake, taste, love for truth, desire for beauty, awake!

But so many other singers imitated Malibran that Ricordi, in its vocal score of the opera, took to printing the Vaccai conclusion as if it were a valid and "sanctioned" alternative to Bellini's.[26]

When Giuseppina Ronzi De Begnis assumed the role of Romeo in Florence in 1834, it was suggested to her that she too follow the lead of Malibran, but she refused what she called this *pasticcio alla Malibran,* insisting instead that "if I make a fiasco, at least it will be all Bellini." The performance instead was a great success, as she announced in triumph:

> I assure you that I was trembling, as the Florentines have the vice of not listening; and you know that in this third act there are no things that flatter the ear, and that to enjoy the beauties, whether of music or of declamation, there must be religious silence. I obtained that, and once the audience had seen me, they remained as if unable to move. In short, to make the matter brief, it gave great pleasure, and after it we were all called out.
>
> Things seem to me to be going well; I really am content. To tell you the truth, I would have been very unhappy if this opera had failed; and I am the more content because it is all Bellini's work. There were people who said: how does Malibran happen to change the third act? It seems to me that, as a singer who is supposed to be such an actress, she should be content. Does this seem to you a small triumph?[27]

For Bellini it was a great one.

A Theater

Even more surprisingly, theaters themselves recognized that introducing changes into operas for reasons having to do with needs of local productions, however necessary they might seem and however carefully they might be done, could be damaging to the works themselves. In 1836, the Teatro alla Scala mounted Rossini's *Armida,* an opera that had practically disappeared from the stage after its premiere, but whose most famous numbers had occasionally been inserted (even by Rossini) into performances of other operas.[28] In the libretto printed for this occasion, the Scala management informed the public:

In offering this opera, which the famous Maestro wrote for the Royal Teatro San Carlo of Naples in 1817, we have sought to reproduce it in its original form, even though some pieces have been heard in other operas. This has been done because of the difficulty of adding pieces which equal (let alone better) the beauties of the originals and because Rossini's genius must be respected in every way possible.[29]

"Rossini's genius must be respected in every way possible" (il genio di Rossini vuol essere in ogni maniera rispettato): those are words that one hardly expects to find spoken by a commercial Italian theater in the mid-1830s, and yet they represent the contemporary realization that the greatest composers of Italian opera had written works whose integrity was worthy of respect. While it is true, then, that Italian composers were part of a commercial system in which the shape of operas could be modified by themselves or by others to meet performance needs, there was a keen sense that their operas were also works of art whose "constitutive properties" (to adopt Nelson Goodman's term)[30] were to be respected. This sense was shared by composers, librettists, publishers, singers, and sympathetic critics. Every time we decide what version of an Italian opera to perform in the theater, and every time we make decisions about cuts, we are reliving—and provisionally resolving—this historical and aesthetic conflict.

SOCIAL CONTEXT AND OPERATIC TEXTS

The perception that Italian operas may need to be modified in performance today, and sometimes presented with a different sequence of musical numbers or in an abbreviated form, is in part a function of the difference between the social conditions in which these operas were performed in the nineteenth century and those of modern society.[31] Under normal circumstances, modern audiences do not appear to have what the theatrical clock would suggest was the staying power of early-nineteenth-century audiences. After all, performances at the Teatro alla Scala of Milan in the 1810s began with the first act of an opera (lasting approximately two hours), to be followed by a full-length heroic ballet unrelated to the opera (an hour in length), the final act of the opera (an hour and a half), and a shorter comic or semiserious ballet (a half hour). When Rossini's *Bianca e Falliero* was first performed at La Scala on 26 December 1819, according to the original printed libretto, the evening began with the first act of the opera, continued with the "ballo tragico" *Cimene* by Salvatore Viganò (divided into six "acts"), proceeded with the second act of the opera, and concluded with the "secondo ballo" *La campanella d'argento* by Filippo Bertini (divided into three "acts").[32] Stendhal and other contemporary writers refer to evenings in the theater that began around seven o'clock in the winter and nine o'clock in the summer and continued for approximately six hours.[33] Even by midcentury, when ballets on extraneous (or even related) subjects were no longer performed between the acts of an opera, a theatrical evening often included a full-length opera, followed by a full-length ballet.[34]

Yet we must avoid drawing false conclusions about the attention span of nineteenth-century audiences in Italy. Theaters were not temples of art, where lights would be extinguished and a rapt public would concentrate all its attention on the stage. Theaters fulfilled then, as they do now, many social and aesthetic functions. In cities as diverse as Milan, Venice, and Naples, the opera house was the center of public social interaction for the nobility and the professional classes, while some areas in the theater were also economically accessible to students and tradesmen.[35] The public viewed the operas from an open area in front of the stage, known as the *platea* (our modern orchestra): depending on the theater, this included some fixed seats (which could be rented) and benches, as well as a considerable area for spectators to view the opera on foot. The *platea* was surrounded by a horseshoe-shaped set of four to six superposed rows of boxes (*palchi*), either owned by noble and wealthy families or rented by them on a yearly or multiyear basis. These boxes were laterally closed off from one another, and most were supplied with curtains that could isolate the occupants from public view. (In the most tightly controlled society in the peninsula, the Bourbon monarchy in Naples, such curtains were banned.) Despite architectural modifications of various kinds, eighteenth- and nineteenth-century theaters constructed along these lines remain prevalent today throughout Italy, from the Teatro alla Scala of Milan and the Teatro San Carlo of Naples to the Teatro Regio of Parma and the smaller Teatro Rossini of Pesaro.

Illustrations and descriptions of theater life during the first half of the nineteenth century are remarkably consistent in showing free movement in the *platea*, with audiences purchasing food and drink from itinerant vendors, conversations among spectators, individuals moving in and out of the theater. The name *aria di sorbetto* reflects the practice of buying and consuming ices during short arias sung by secondary characters. Even at the Teatro San Carlo, one of the few theaters to fill the entire *platea* with benches and, later, individual seats (another political effort to control the public), there was adequate room between rows to allow easy access during a performance.[36] Furthermore, theaters were illuminated throughout the performance, first by candlelight or oil, later by gas, so that movement was unhindered by darkness.[37] Operatic managements, in short, would not have understood modern concerns about the incompatibility of an act that lasts two hours with an audience's need to use bathroom facilities.

For the nobility in the *palchi,* social intercourse was even freer. Stendhal's *La chartreuse de Parme,* Balzac's *Massimilla Doni* (with its fictional portrait of the countess Cristina Belgiojoso),[38] and countless literary invocations of Italian theatrical life suggest the atmosphere in which opera was received. Across from the *palchi,* there were comfortable rooms, furnished by the box holders, in which social gatherings could be held, meals served, intimate meetings arranged, and servants instructed to wait. As Stendhal wrote, "La Scala [...], situated as it is in a city with a damp winter climate, soon grew to be a general meeting-place for the whole town. A well-heated, well-lit establishment, where one may be quite certain of meeting people on almost any evening in the week, is a most invaluable institution for any city."[39] In the large public areas that led to the *platea* and *palchi,* gaming rooms provided another form of public entertainment, until they were largely banned by approximately 1820. Even fee structures reflected the multiple uses of the opera house. Everyone who entered was charged an *ingresso* (an entrance fee), but those who came only to gamble or to visit with friends in public areas removed from the actual theatrical space were not expected to pay an additional charge for the right to be present at the performance.[40] A similar fee structure persisted in many European opera houses well into the 1960s, although I am sure that few of those who paid or collected these fees understood their historical source.

As we have seen, the theatrical year was usually divided into several seasons, each lasting two to three months, during which a fixed company of singers presented to a largely unchanging audience three or four different operas, at least one of which was newly composed. If a work pleased the public, it would be performed night after night. Thus, for the carnival and Lenten season in 1821 (which began on the preceding St. Stephen's eve, 26 December 1820), La Scala offered three works: the premiere of Simone Mayr's *Fedra,* which opened the season and played thirty-seven times; a revival of Rossini's Neapolitan opera, *La donna del lago,* based on the narrative poem by Sir Walter Scott, which opened 8 February and played thirty-two times; and a new opera by Giuseppe Mosca, *Emira, Regina d'Egitto,* whose short and unsuccessful run began on 6 March and ended after a mere three performances. Each opera was, as usual, accompanied by ballets.[41]

There is ample evidence from newspaper reports and an analysis of musical sources, that theaters made modifications during the course of a season, even for an ostensibly successful work, in response to public opinion, the capabilities of singers, and the wishes of composers. For revivals in later seasons or different cities, printed librettos, usually prepared anew for every season in which an opera was to be given and intended to mirror the words actually performed on stage, provide extensive documentation of the ways in which some operas were modified or cut. From them we observe that the integrity of certain works was regularly maintained, while other works were routinely dismembered.[42]

This partial reprise of our earlier discussion of the social realities of Italian opera performance and composition in the nineteenth century suggests that it is perfectly appropriate for a modern opera house, functioning under extremely different social constraints, to concern itself with the structure and length of an Italian opera, to weigh alternative versions, and to consider making cuts. The call to invoke the early history of these works, in an effort to further our understanding, demands neither the reconstruction of a hypothetical "ideal" nineteenth-century performance nor the re-creation in today's opera house of a documentable version from the past. Rather, it encourages undertaking practical decisions sensitized to the social and cultural history of Italian opera in general and to both the composition and the reception history of individual works. These practical decisions are a function of aesthetic judgments, familiarity with the repertory, local theatrical custom, the abilities of singers, the changing taste of audiences, union wage regulations, train or bus schedules, and restaurant opening and closing hours. Such issues, whether directed by the composer or not, determined the shape of operas in their premiere performances and contemporary revivals. They remain determinant in our present-day operatic culture.

"MANCA UN FOGLIO...": NONAUTHORIAL MULTIPLE VERSIONS

Surprisingly few well-known Italian operas exist in a unique version identifiable with the composer: among them are Rossini's *Il signor Bruschino* and *Il viaggio a Reims*, Bellini's *La sonnambula* (although the opera presents serious textual issues that have yet to be resolved),[43] and Verdi's *Luisa Miller* and *Rigoletto*. By and large these are operas the composers staged only once. Donizetti's name does not appear on this list: he supervised productions of his most successful works not only in Italy but also in Paris and Vienna, constantly introducing variants. Even in the case of Verdi, who wrote (by most counts) twenty-six completely distinct operas and made a habit of insisting on their integrity, only eight exist in unique versions.[44] A vast body of information, mixing in unequal parts serious research and folklore, has developed around multiple authorial versions, but complete explanations and performance materials exist only for works available in critical editions.

Alongside these multiple authorial versions, we find an impressive array of nonauthorial versions, versions prepared in the absence of the composer. The contents of these performances can most easily be reconstructed from printed librettos. Theaters and performers may well have had strong reasons for proceeding as they did, and had the composer been present to supervise the revival, he might well have made similar adjustments. In his absence, however, theaters did what administrators, musical directors, singers, or governmental censors thought best. Few of these nonauthorial versions entered the preserved musical record. Indeed, what is most impressive about surviving musical sources is how uniform they tend to be: only a handful of pieces in the sources for Rossini's operas cannot be traced directly to an authorial version. This is true even for an opera such as *Aureliano in Palmira* (first performed at La Scala on 26 December 1813), probably the most unstable Rossinian text in the contemporary performance tradition, judging from printed librettos.[45]

When nonauthorial versions do become part of the written musical tradition, the misinformation they convey can have serious consequences for the subsequent performance history of a work, extending well beyond the performances for which they were introduced. Don Bartolo's aria "A un Dottor della mia sorte," from Rossini's *Il barbiere di Sivigilia,* must have been considered too difficult, too long, or just not congenial by Paolo Rosich, the singer who participated in the Florentine revival of the opera at the Teatro di Via della Pergola during the autumn of 1816, just a few months after its Roman premiere. The local music master was Pietro Romani, a highly respected craftsman of his time, whose work as musical director for the Florentine theaters was, in the absence of a composer, necessary and significant.[46] "A un Dottor della mia sorte" is one of the more demanding buffo arias in the entire repertory; it is also one of the greatest, when sung well. But with the local Bartolo in grief, Romani came to the rescue by providing a simpler, distinctly inferior aria of his own composition, "Manca un foglio." With gratitude, Rosich performed Romani's piece, leaving that of Rossini aside.[47] Because other singers had a similar problem, "Manca un foglio" began to circulate more widely, both in manuscript and in printed form.[48] During the course of the century, some printed editions, giving no hint of this history, simply substituted Romani for Rossini, while others printed Romani in an appendix, marking "A un dottor della mia sorte" with notes such as: "This aria is never performed, and that of Pietro

Romani, published as an appendix, is preferred."[49] In some German editions both arias were printed, that of Rossini in act 1, that of Romani—with a modified text (sometimes only in German)—to open act 2.[50] Confusion began to spread: Just what piece *did* Rossini write? Even artists perfectly capable of singing the original found that they were expected to sing Romani's piece. Thus, a change made to suit the needs of a particular singer had become writ: a "tradition" had been born. Fortunately it is a tradition that has been reversed. While modern Bartolos may complain that Rossini's aria is very difficult (and while they may insist on abbreviating it when they find themselves incapable of doing justice to the entire piece), there is little chance that Romani will return with any regularity.[51]

For at least one Rossini opera, an unauthorized revision ended up in print, confusing generations of music critics and performers, even today. Rossini's *Il Turco in Italia,* first performed at La Scala on 14 August 1814, started life under unfortunate circumstances. Just a year earlier Rossini had written *L'Italiana in Algeri* for Venice, and the opera had an immediate and widespread success. (As late as 1830, a Venetian critic could think of no better way to emphasize how much the public had liked Bellini's *I Capuleti e i Montecchi* at its premiere than by comparing its reception to that of *L'Italiana,* first performed seventeen years earlier.)[52] The composer himself brought *L'Italiana* with him to Milan, where he directed a well-received revival at the smaller Teatro Re during the spring of 1814.[53] Perhaps to capitalize on that success, Rossini and the librettist assigned to him by the Teatro alla Scala, Felice Romani (near the beginning of his career), decided to compose an opera whose theme is ostensibly the reverse: not an Italian lady who goes to Algeria in search of her beloved, but a Turkish prince who comes to Italy in search of the delights that Italian women legendarily bestow on their favorites. In fact, Romani's libretto is not completely original: the idea behind it, as well as many verses and details (including the presence of a poet who attempts to control the action but instead is controlled by it), are taken from a libretto of the same name by Caterino Mazzolà, written for the theater in Dresden in 1788, where it was set to music by Franz Seydelmann.[54]

The characters in *Il Turco in Italia* are very different indeed from those in *L'Italiana in Algeri.* Fiorilla, the heroine of *Turco* and married to Don Geronio, is an outrageous flirt, who flits from man to man dropping favors and demanding obedience but whose wiles are delicious to watch; Isabella, the heroine of *L'Italiana* and a lady of spirit and strength, is devoted to her beloved Lindoro but knows how to use a woman's weapons to advance her aims. Elvira, the wife of Mustafà in *L'Italiana,* is cardboard, too good, too true—one understands why Mustafà wants to send her away; Zaida, whom Selim (the Turk) unjustly sentenced to death before the curtain rises in *Turco,* has independence and fire, and her reconciliation with Selim provides the impetus for the opera's happy ending. *L'Italiana*'s Mustafà is a buffoon, easily manipulated by Isabella; *Il Turco*'s Selim has stature and character, despite his roving eye, and the role is really that of a *basso nobile.* Taddeo, too, the gallant attached to Isabella in *L'Italiana,* is a thoroughly comic character, while Don Geronio in *Turco* employs much the same vocal style but is a more sympathetic presence. The reconciliation of Don Geronio and Fiorilla takes place only after he pretends to send her back to her parents, and Fiorilla's realization of her folly is set by Rossini to an aria of repentance with great strength and beauty. (Beverly Sills, in the New York City Opera revival of 1977, sang it as if it were a facetious "mad scene," at the end of which she threw herself on the ground, then lifted her head and winked at the audience, bringing down the house but completely falsifying the opera.)[55] Over the whole enterprise is the poet, Prosdocimo, whose genial presence keeps the work moving ahead with witty comments on the *convenienze* of Italian opera.

The Milanese were probably unconcerned with these details, for they took it for granted that Rossini was palming off on them an inversion of his earlier work, with music indistinguishable from it.[56] After this poor reception, *Il Turco in Italia* made its way only slowly on Italian stages. Rossini himself returned to the work for a Roman revival in 1815, removing two and a half of the three numbers prepared by an unknown assistant in Milan (leaving only the *secco* recitative and the end of the second-act finale), and adding several new numbers of his own composition. This revised authorial version, completely unknown until the publication of the critical edition, provides many interesting suggestions for modern performances.[57] It is not to that Roman *Turco* I wish to turn, however, but to another, nonauthorial version.

Ferdinand Paër (1771–1839), an Italian composer living in France and serving as director of the Théâtre Italien during the late 1810s and early 1820s, decided to produce *Il Turco in Italia* for his Parisian audiences.[58] He was under pressure from the authorities to bring more works by Rossini into the repertory of the theater. Reports had been circulating about this new genius in Italy whose works were beginning to dominate Italian theaters, yet few of them had found their way to Paris. There were those, among them Rossini's first biographer, Stendhal, who felt that Paër was making a determined effort to keep the Parisians from knowing Rossini's operas, since knowledge of those works might lead to a rejuvenation of the Théâtre Italien's repertory, sweeping aside operas by composers of Paër's generation.[59] Rather than simply performing Rossini's opera, however, Paër patched together a compendium of pieces from several works: he cut many pieces from *Turco,* while inserting parts of Rossini's *La Cenerentola* and other operas, an aria by Fioravanti, and still other pieces by composers unknown. This was the concoction presented to the Parisian public as Rossini's *Il Turco in Italia* on 18 May 1820. Few in Paris could have known the difference, of course, because the score had never been performed or printed in France. The immediate result was to destroy the effect of the first performances of *La Cenerentola* two years later, when Rossini was accused of having borrowed extensively from *Il Turco in Italia* in writing the later opera. Thus, the manipulation of one score cast doubts on the quality of two.[60]

What made this particular adaptation so disastrous was that the music publishers of Paris soon printed not Rossini's *Turco in Italia* but Paër's adaptation. Through almost two centuries, critics (beginning with Stendhal) have used these scores as the basis for their discussion of Rossini's opera. Books and program notes are still being written that claim that in *La Cenerentola* Rossini borrows extensively from *Il Turco in Italia.* Indeed, an American reprint publisher, Kalmus, continues to keep one of these French scores in print as Rossini's *Il Turco in Italia,* without giving its readers any warning. As recently as the spring of 1997, when I assisted in preparing a production of the opera for the Teatro Ponchielli of Cremona and La Scala of Milan, under the direction of Riccardo Chailly, there were still singers who were confused by those reprinted scores. If, as Stendhal opined, Paër sought to discredit Rossini's operas, in this particular case he succeeded far better and for a far longer time than he could ever have imagined possible.

It is generally agreed today that if you are going to perform Rossini's *Il Turco in Italia* at all, you probably should avoid Paër's adaptation. But similar efforts at "adapting" and "revising" have been made in our time. One Rossinian example is the version of *La gazza ladra* made for a performance at the Teatro Nuovo of Pesaro in 1941 by the composer Riccardo Zandonai (also at the time director of the Conservatory in Pesaro, founded by and named for Rossini), who revised, reorchestrated, and abysmally mistreated the original score, to what end it is difficult to imagine. His version, needless to say, soon disappeared, almost without a trace.[61] So has the version that the brilliant German stage director Günther Rennert prepared during the 1950s of *Il Turco in Italia.* Whatever one may think of this adaptation, and many admired it greatly, it was absurd to grant it permanence by putting it into print. Yet that was precisely what Ricordi did in 1962, making it possible for many years to purchase Rennert's *Turco,* but not Rossini's.

CHOOSING AMONG AUTHORIAL VERSIONS

Authorial variant versions sometimes involve little more than the substitution of one or more musical numbers (usually arias) for others with similar structural functions. But there are also striking examples of large-scale changes in the overall structure and dramaturgy of entire operas, often involving cross-cultural adaptations from France to Italy or vice versa (Rossini's *Maometto II* and *Le Siège de Corinthe,* Bellini's *I puritani,* Donizetti's *Poliuto* and *Les Martyrs,* and Verdi's *Don Carlos* are famous and complex examples). In general, we can conceptualize the process of deciding which version to perform in terms of a grid in three dimensions on which to measure our alternatives. These dimensions involve: (1) aesthetic and analytic matters; (2) historical circumstances; and (3) the practical conditions of modern performance.

Aesthetic and Analytic Matters

Aesthetic and analytic matters involve our individual judgments concerning the relative musical worth of alternative versions, the musico-dramatic character of each piece, and the larger dramaturgical consequences of adopting one version rather than another.

Many issues need to be considered in judging relative musical worth: the quality of invention, the coherence of each variant in the context of the entire work, the tonal implications of different key schemes (both between adjacent numbers and within the opera as a whole), the vocal style, and so forth. We should presume neither that the results of different parts of our inquiry will reinforce one another nor that unanimity of opinion is possible. Few musicians today would argue that the quality of invention in Lady Macbeth's aria "Trionfai!" in the original, 1847 version of Verdi's *Macbeth* is superior to that of the revised aria he prepared for Paris in 1865, "La luce langue." Still, the new piece belongs to a different stylistic world from the rest of Lady's music, especially her first-act aria, "Vieni! t'affretta!" and even her remarkable sleepwalking scene, neither of which Verdi altered for Paris.[62] And proceeding from "La luce langue" to the following, unrevised chorus of murderers is a bit like stepping from the pages of Joyce's *Ulysses* into his *Dubliners.*

The new aria for Lady Macbeth also changes the nature of her character both musically, by replacing a virtuoso showpiece with a more inward, lyrical moment, and dramatically, by introducing an element of self-doubt that is lacking in the earlier composition; hence, the choice between the two is significant for developing a coherent approach to the role. There are similar examples throughout the repertory. An Isabella in *L'Italiana in Algeri* who sings the lengthy, loving, and heroic cavatina, "Cimentando i venti e l'onde," which Rossini added to the opera for a revival in Vicenza immediately after the original 1813 Venetian season,[63] announces herself in terms very different from one who shows off her wares as a sexual commodity in the risqué (and frequently censored) "Cruda sorte" (see chapter 3). The choice between them affects the pacing of the opera, the character of the protagonist, and her further interpretation of the part. A young and frisky singer may prefer "Cruda sorte!"; a more mature one, "Cimentando." The opera can support either interpretation. Likewise, the love between Percy and Anna in Donizetti's *Anna Bolena* is presented in a more lyrical and passionate vein in their duet "Sì, son io che a te ritorno" than in the composition it replaced during the course of the opera's first season at the Teatro Carcano of Milan during the carnival of 1831, "S'ei t'abborre, io t'amo ancora," a much darker piece. The alternatives need to be weighed in that light.[64]

On some occasions, alternative versions have dramaturgical implications that affect fundamentally the way we perceive an opera. The interaction of Ernani and Silva and the significance of Ernani's dreadful oath are transformed when the final section of their duet at the end of the second act of Verdi's *Ernani* is replaced by the aria for Ernani Verdi wrote just a few months after the opera's premiere (9 March 1844) for a performance with Rossini's protégé, the young Russian tenor Nicola Ivanoff, that opened the following carnival season at the Teatro Ducale of Parma (26 December 1844).[65] Such changes are even more striking when they affect the final moments of an opera. As we have seen, Rossini's tragic *Otello* was provided with a happy ending by the composer himself, who had earlier replaced the happy ending of *Tancredi* with a tragic one. The effect is equally startling, although the plot is unchanged, when a superb but exhibitionistic concluding *rondò* for the prima donna and surviving assembled cast in Donizetti's *Lucrezia Borgia* (first performed at the Teatro alla Scala on 26 December 1833) is replaced by a more intimate final scene for Lucrezia and the son she has poisoned: that is the substitution Donizetti made for performances at the Teatro alla Scala beginning on 11 January 1840.[66] At the same time, however, Donizetti seems to have made peace with his Scala Lucrezia, Erminia Frezzolini, by adding a florid, cadenza-laden cabaletta ("Si voli il primo a cogliere") to Lucrezia's *romanza* in the opera's prologue ("Come è bello").[67]

Historical Circumstances

The second dimension of our grid consists of the specific events that lead a composer to create an alternative piece and the implications of those events for the way we evaluate the resulting music. Among such circumstances are cases in which a composer replaces music originally written by an associate, revisions that result from actions of political censors, and changes introduced to suit the needs or desires of specific performers. As we discuss these situations, we will face again and again different compositional attitudes to the problem of "definitive" and "nondefinitive" revisions.

Faced with sharp pressures of time, early nineteenth-century composers occasionally called on younger colleagues to prepare recitative and even complete musical numbers for their operas, or else they borrowed music from one of their own earlier operas. Sometimes the music in question is integral to a work: the second-act finale of Rossini's *Il Turco in Italia,* for example, is by another composer, and the opera cannot be performed without using at least its concluding sections.[68] (It would be comforting to believe, but it is unlikely, that Rossini assigned this piece to a collaborator out of impatience with its relatively conventional resolution to a most unconventional libretto.) Most of the time, though, the principal composer can easily replace those pieces by another composer or those borrowed from an earlier opera, especially in the absence of a looming deadline. Still, subsequent performers may not always choose to follow the principal composer's last word. When Rossini worked against the clock to complete *Matilde di Shabran* for performance in Rome at the Teatro Apollo on 24 February 1821, he entrusted two entire musical numbers, as well as part of a third, to the young Giovanni Pacini, who probably prepared all the *secco* recitative as well. Just a few months later, for a revival in Naples at the Teatro del Fondo on 11 November 1821, under the name *Bellezza e Cuor di ferro* (*Beauty and Heart of Stone,* we might call it), Rossini eliminated all Pacini's contributions except for the *secco* recitative, while adding several new pieces of his own. In this case, the new Rossini compositions had a limited circulation outside of Naples since he had recast the role of the poet Isidoro in the local Neapolitan dialect.[69] Equally interesting, in Rome Rossini had introduced as the penultimate number of the opera an aria for Corradino, "Anima mia, Matilde," derived almost without change from the tenor cavatina ("S'Ella m'è ognor fedele") in an earlier Neapolitan opera, *Ricciardo e Zoraide* (Naples, Teatro San Carlo, 3 December 1818). But it was one thing to borrow a number from *Ricciardo e Zoraide* for an opera having its premiere in Rome, quite another to present the same piece to a Neapolitan public who knew the previous opera well. Thus, for the Teatro del Fondo, Rossini replaced the Corradino aria with a duet for Corradino and Edoardo (a trousers role), "Da cento smanie, e cento." But what do we do with tenors who want to sing an aria at that point in the opera? There are reasons in favor of each solution.

Italian opera houses in the first half of the nineteenth century, furthermore, worked under difficult and constantly evolving political conditions. Censors played an active role in determining what could or could not be presented at a particular moment. In extreme cases, entire operas were revised, while other operas were banned outright. Verdi knew very well that the censors in Naples were likely to object to the subject of *Gustavo III* when, in the autumn of 1857, he began to sketch his opera about the assassination of the Swedish king.[70] Nonetheless, he urged the librettist, Antonio Somma, to complete his work while they awaited further notice. After the governmental objections were received, poet and composer spent Christmas of 1857 together at Sant'Agata, devising the modified libretto, *Una vendetta in dominò*, with the action moved to a middle-European duchy. Convinced that they could now proceed, Verdi finished sketching the opera and laid out his entire skeleton score. In early January he traveled to Naples, prepared to deliver that skeleton score to the copyists so that they could prepare parts for the singers. Staging and musical rehearsals were scheduled to begin at once, during which Verdi was to orchestrate the work. What he could not have expected was Felice Orsini's foolhardy attempt to assassinate Napoleon III in Paris on 14 January 1858. As a result of this incident, in which there were several deaths and many injuries, a newly sensitized censorship in Naples grew even more intractable, and Verdi was informed that not even *Una vendetta in dominò* would be permitted. The censors submitted to him a new text, with the plot moved to medieval Florence, *Adelia degli Adimari,* which Verdi contemptuously refused (calling it *Adelia degli Animali*).[71] More than another year would pass (following further battles with censors in Naples and Rome) before Verdi's opera would emerge from these trials as *Un ballo in maschera*. But work for the critical edition of *Un ballo in maschera* has revealed that—from what Verdi would have considered the *creative* point of view—*Una vendetta in dominò* was in fact completed, and it is possible to reconstruct that opera (with a fair degree of probability) as Verdi conceived it. Some relatively simple orchestration is all that is needed to bring it finally to the stage.[72]

In other cases of censorship, only individual pieces were eliminated. The Neapolitan censors seem to have been particularly nervous in the period following the restoration of the Bourbon monarchy in 1815. Rossini, recently arrived in the city, appears to have mollified them by replacing Isabella's patriotic *rondò* in *L'Italiana in Algeri*, "Pensa alla patria" with the politically neutral and musically bland (though attractive) "Sullo stil de' viaggiatori."[73] In it, Isabella and the chorus no longer invoke "patria" or the "worth of the Italians"; instead she treats the story as an adventure, which they will chat about when they get home, "sullo stil de' viaggiatori" (as all travelers do). Far from having

Isabella incite the Italians with thoughts of patriotic fervor, Rossini presents her actions as merely "l'inganno della beltà" (the strategem of beauty). Written for a specific situation, a specific historical moment, "Sullo stil de' viaggiatori" is hard to take seriously as an alternative in the modern opera house. But one could imagine with dread a political climate in which once again it might be impossible to sing "Pensa alla patria." As far as we know, the replacement aria was never performed again in the nineteenth century, and its survival is quite fortuitous: it occurs in a single source, a copyist's manuscript now preserved in Milan but of Neapolitan provenance.[74]

Most variant versions, however, reflect the different technical capabilities or dramatic propensities of singers engaged for a revival of an opera. Nineteenth-century Italian composers wrote their music with specific singers in mind. When they were unfamiliar with the characteristics of particular voices, they would refrain from preparing solo music for those singers until they had an opportunity to work with them or at least to learn more about their voices. When Verdi was sketching the first version of *Macbeth* in 1847, as mentioned in the beginning of chapter 3, he kept in contact with his singers by letter, sending them vocal parts and asking for comments. To his first Lady Macbeth, Marianna Barbieri-Nini, he wrote, "In the 3/8 Adagio of this duet, there is a chromatic scale at the end [example 7.1]. It must be sung *rallentando* and end in a *pianissimo;* if this proves difficult for you, let me know."[75] Although the passage was ultimately replaced, this ending chromatic scale and its surrounding measures are still present, as an earlier layer, in Verdi's autograph manuscript; under the right circumstances and for the right singer, the original version might even be performed.[76] To his first Macbeth, Felice Varesi, Verdi sent two proposals for an important phrase that occurs during the scene of the apparitions of the eight kings in the third act, adding: "do the one that suits you best, and write to tell me which one I should orchestrate."[77] Because he had never heard Barbieri-Nini sing, he refrained from composing her "Trionfai" solo at the beginning of the second act, informing her instead (in the same letter quoted above), "All that is needed to complete your part is a cabaletta, which I shall write for you in Florence so that it will suit your voice perfectly and be sure to make an effect."

EXAMPLE 7.1. GIUSEPPE VERDI, *MACBETH,* SCENA E DUETTO (N. 5), AN EARLY CADENTIAL FIGURE FOR LADY MACBETH FROM THE CANTABILE.

In revivals, composers and singers themselves routinely made *puntature,* small adjustments in the melodic lines to suit new voices. There is a lovely letter from Verdi to Donizetti on the occasion of one of the very first revivals of *Ernani,* in Vienna just a few months after the Venetian premiere of March 1844. Since the composer could not attend the Viennese rehearsals, he asked Donizetti, who was music director of the Viennese theater, to follow preparations in the theater carefully, adding: "I beg you to occupy yourself both with the general direction and with the *puntature* that may be necessary, especially in Ferretti's part [Luigi Ferretti played the role of Ernani]."[78] When appropriate singers were unavailable, and *puntature* were insufficient, composers intervened more heavily. Only in a few early performances, following its Venetian premiere of 1824, could Meyerbeer's *Il crociato in Egitto* feature a castrato, Giambattista Velluti, in the leading role of Armando. But Velluti, the last important operatic castrato, was at the end of his career, and Meyerbeer subsequently rewrote the part for mezzo-soprano: in that version, particularly with the exceptional Giuditta Pasta as its interpreter, the opera could circulate.[79]

Some revisions made by Italian composers to suit the needs of available singers seem appalling by modern standards. For an 1824 Parisian revival of *La donna del lago,* for example, Rossini lacked two tenors capable of doing justice to the second-act trio "Alla ragion deh rieda." Instead, he inserted two fine but irrelevant pieces from another opera, *Bianca e Falliero,* neither of which required a virtuoso tenor.[80] The intervention did not go unnoticed. Stendhal, reviewing the performance in the *Journal de Paris* of 9 September 1824, referred specifically to the omission of the trio: "To tell the truth, thanks to Bordogni and Mari it was necessary to omit a [...] piece from the original score of *La donna del lago* that would have pleased the public."[81] We cannot properly evaluate this alternative version of *La donna del lago* apart from the historical circumstances that gave it birth. Rossini frequently lacked appropriate singers—particularly two virtuoso tenors—to perform his Neapolitan operas in other Italian or European theaters. When contemplating a revival of *La donna del lago* in Rome during the carnival season of 1822, a performance that did not ultimately take place, the composer had already suggested the introduction of the two pieces from *Bianca e Falliero* in place of the trio from *La donna del lago.*[82]

One should not imagine that composers always undertook such revisions reluctantly: many variant versions for specific singers were prepared with alacrity. After the highly successful premiere of *I Capuleti e i Montecchi* in Venice during the carnival season of 1830, the Venetian impresario Giuseppe

Crivelli determined to mount the opera again to open the following carnival season at the Teatro alla Scala of Milan, where he also served as impresario. For the role of Giulietta, however, Crivelli had engaged Amalia Schütz-Oldosi, a mezzo-soprano with a considerably lower tessitura than the original Giulietta, Rosalbina Caradori Allan. Thus, Bellini was obliged to modify the part considerably.[83] He did this by intervening massively on a complete manuscript copy of the entire opera. In some cases he simply provided an alternative vocal line for Giulietta, leaving the rest of the score unchanged; in some cases he completely rewrote significant passages, transposing both of Giulietta's solo compositions down by a full tone or by a minor third, and even transposing her duet with Romeo down (but only by a half tone).[84] In Giulietta's aria at the beginning of the second act he inserted a stunning new lyrical section, "Morir dovessi ancora" (Even if I must die).[85] Although the editor of the critical edition does not suggest it, I cannot imagine that soprano Giuliettas will need much encouragement to transpose the passage up by a minor third and to include it in their performances. Despite all this work, however, Bellini was not altogether pleased with the results, as he informed his friend Giovanni Battista Perucchini on 3 January 1831:

> For me the opera made only half the effect of the one I heard in Venice: whether because the theatre is larger, because Rolla's tempi are too broad,[86] because in all the ensembles the voices of the two women cannot blend well since both are mezzo-sopranos, because such a large theater is harmful to Grisi, but when all is said and done I no longer hear the *Capuleti* of Venice, and yet the theater is always full of abundant applause.[87]

The public does indeed seem to have been pleased, and the opera was performed twenty-five times during the course of the season. The particular characteristics of its cast, however, leave modern performers with a choice of versions for performing *I Capuleti e i Montecchi*.

In concluding this discussion of historical circumstances, we find ourselves inevitably, if unwillingly, faced with the problem of authorial intention. It has been dogging us throughout. Although it is only one factor in our considerations, a composer's attitude toward the text of an opera matters. That Donizetti transformed *Maria Stuarda* into *Buondelmonte* with a heavy heart, because the censors refused permission to perform the original opera, cannot help but influence our choice of which work to perform.[88] Although Verdi was willing to compose an alternative cabaletta for *I due Foscari* as a gesture of friendship to the influential tenor Mario, he specifically requested that Mario return the manuscript after he had used the piece and not allow copies to be made.[89] This is consistent with Verdi's tendency to leave his autograph manuscripts in what he considered to be a "definitive state." Even if we are not obliged to be guided by this evidence, we can hardly be indifferent to it.

Practical Conditions of Modern Performance

The third and final dimension of our grid consists of the technical capabilities and the explicit desires of singers; the theatrical practices of a particular opera house, located in a particular city, with a particular audience; the artistic vision of conductors or stage directors.

The questions faced by modern performers are not different in kind from those of their nineteenth-century predecessors. The technical problems posed by Rossini's music for tenor remain formidable. The incompatibility of a robust prima donna and the consumptive Violetta in *La traviata* was as apparent when Montserrat Caballé sang the role as when Fanny Salvini-Donatelli created it. Prima donnas remain divided between those, like Ronzi De Begnis, who are proud to perform *I Capuleti e i Montecchi* as Bellini conceived it and those prepared to choose a *pasticcio alla Malibran* because it seems vocally more satisfying, between those unwilling to change so much as a single word in a rendition once learned and those constantly reexploring the dramaturgical and musical meaning of a part.

It is difficult for the public to comprehend the extent to which some singers are prisoners of what they believe to be "tradition," generally identical to the music they have already memorized. Logic, meaning, and evidence are to no avail. In the second act of Verdi's *Ernani*, for example, the king of Spain, Don Carlo, in pursuit of the bandit Ernani, arrives unexpectedly at the château of Don Silva. Silva, who has promised Ernani the rights of hospitality, helps the bandit escape the fury of the king by hiding him behind a painting in the family portrait gallery. (Gilbert and Sullivan fans recognize in this setting the origin of the wonderful scene in the second act of *Ruddigore* where the bad baronet's relatives emerge from the frames of their portraits to insist that he continue his life of crime.) Don Carlo has followed Ernani, and knows he is in the house. In Victor Hugo's play, from which the libretto is derived, the king poses a series of alternatives to Silva: "Réponds, duc, ou je fais raser tes onze tours!" (Respond, Duke, or I'll have your eleven towers razed); "Je veux sa tête, ou bien la tienne" (I want his head, or else your own).

Verdi rendered this confrontation as an aria for the king, with a secondary part for Silva. In the standard edition of *Ernani*, the king addresses Silva in a ringing phrase, beloved of baritones: "Il tuo capo, o traditore, altro scampo, no, non v'è" (Your head, traitor, there is no other escape). That doesn't offer

Silva much of a choice! One can understand why a singer might enjoy declaiming "o traditore" in the face of the old man, but not only is the text meaningless, it is not what Francesco Maria Piave printed in his libretto or what Verdi wrote in his autograph score. The correct text is "Il tuo capo, o *il traditore, altro scampo, no, non v'è*" (Your head or the traitor, there is no other escape). Yet when Piero Cappuccilli portrayed Don Carlo in the first performance of the new critical edition of *Ernani*, at the Lyric Opera of Chicago during the 1984–85 season, he flatly refused to change anything (including this word) in the way he had always sung the part.

It is not that Cappuccilli was unwilling to historicize his performance: he merely refused to think past the history he already knew. Indeed, one of the most interesting developments over the past decades has been the enthusiasm with which some singers have participated not only in historical reconstructions of so-called authentic versions of operas, but even in reconstructions of versions associated not with a composer but with an earlier singer. Although it was fascinating to hear the Vaccai finale when Marilyn Horne performed Romeo in Bellini's *I Capuleti e i Montecchi* in Dallas in 1977, no one (least of all Horne) believed that this choice of a performing version improved the work.[90] Horne was also featured in the mid-nineteenth-century Pauline Viardot version of Gluck's eighteenth-century *Orfeo ed Euridice*, in part arranged by Berlioz. She never did convince an opera house to stage Rossini's *Otello* with the title role (originally written for tenor) assigned to a mezzo-soprano, as Malibran performed it as a "novelty" in a benefit evening on her behalf in Paris toward the end of 1831,[91] but it was not for lack of trying. The festival in Martina Franca finally did produce the opera with a mezzo-soprano during the summer of 2000, confirming the wisdom of those who had previously refused to undertake this operation. Nor is the interest in such historical stagings limited to Marilyn Horne: in 1989 the Teatro dell'Opera in Rome successfully performed Cimarosa's *Gli Orazi ed i Curiazi* of 1796 with inserted florid arias by Marco Portogallo, a version that had circulated widely in Italy at the beginning of the nineteenth century.

However problematic these reconstructions may be for those who believe in the aesthetic superiority of the works in versions conceived by their composers, they testify to a refreshing vitality in modern performance. Opera houses, in fact, remain divided between those (such as La Scala when it was directed by Riccardo Muti) committed to the careful study of each opera they present, frequently with the use of integral texts, and those where performances of Italian operas in "standard versions" are hurriedly thrown together without adequate rehearsals (the situation in most smaller German theaters). The differences are often a function of whether a theater organizes its season according to the "stagione" system or the "repertory" model.

In the "stagione" system, which prevails in Italian opera houses and most American ones (such as Chicago or Houston), a company of singers is brought together for a fixed period of time. They rehearse a work and give seven to ten performances over the course of a month, after which the work is retired for the season. Rarely is the same opera produced in successive seasons. With each set of performances, it is therefore possible to study the work anew (although in practice opportunities for study may depend on how late in the rehearsal period the tenor's contract allows him to arrive—by private jet, *bien entendu*). In the "repertory" system, a larger number of operas is offered in rotation with constantly changing casts. Works are performed over a longer period of time each season and often in successive seasons. Since new singers consequently are rotated into the cast with minimal rehearsal, a "repertory" system favors the standardization of operatic texts. The "stagione" system does not guarantee great performances, nor does the "repertory" system guarantee poor ones. Yet it is important to understand how the difference between these systems affects what can appear on stage.

James Levine's Metropolitan Opera is an unusual combination of the two principles. It is a "repertory" house that aspires to offer some operas in performances normally possible only in a "stagione" system. It succeeds in doing so when Levine himself supervises the performances, when a conductor such as Carlos Kleiber demands similar working conditions, or when an opera is prepared as if it were part of a "stagione" system. Performances at the Metropolitan Opera in which the scenery overwhelms other parts of the production are often those most firmly rooted in the "repertory" concept.

Nor should we forget that union contracts have profound implications for the economic viability of artistic decisions. Some contracts provide for a standard performing time of three hours, after which fifteen-minute periods of overtime begin. Instructing a conductor that a show will *not* go into double overtime affects the decisions he makes about which version to perform. Some contracts provide more flexibility, taking into account that operas vary in length; even so, a provision that additional payments must be made after midnight affects artistic choices.

What no longer exists for nineteenth-century Italian opera, of course, is a living composer with the moral force to insist, as did Verdi, that *he* is responsible for every decision pertaining to the performance of one of his operas. But we should not exaggerate the efficacy of nineteenth-century composers in controlling the way their operas were performed. Composers rarely participated in revivals of their operas, and when they did, they often behaved just like other musicians: that is, they intervened in the text. Indeed, famous composers functioning as musical directors sometimes intervened in the text of operas by their colleagues. When Rossini's *L'assedio di Corinto* (the Italian translation of *Le Siège de Corinthe*) was performed in Genoa in 1828, Donizetti inserted a new cabaletta into a duet in the second act, replacing one of Rossini's more unusual compositions with a rather ordinary piece.[92]

What moral force a composer may have exercised in the nineteenth century lies today with conductors and stage directors, in whose hands such decisions ultimately rest. In their own self-interest and the interest of the productions for which they are responsible, these performers need to explore every area of the three-dimensional grid I have been describing before making the decisions that are within their prerogative to make. What was truly appalling about the infamous Metropolitan Opera production of *L'assedio di Corinto,* mounted for Beverly Sills in 1976, were not the many aesthetically questionable decisions made by Thomas Schippers, a most able Rossini conductor. It was rather that he did not know who wrote the music he was performing, where it came from, or the alternatives. What was truly appalling about the Houston Grand Opera production of Rossini's *La donna del lago* in 1981 was that Frank Corsaro did not understand the plot of the opera, seemed unfamiliar with Sir Walter Scott's *The Lady of the Lake,* and apparently didn't care.[93]

CHOOSING A VERSION OF BELLINI'S *I PURITANI*

There are many Italian operas for which the problem of choosing a version to perform is perplexing. It may be necessary and sufficient for a critical edition to make available the score in what we can call its authorial versions, but those versions may be neither sufficient nor even satisfactory when we seek to present the work in the theater. One opera whose many textual problems embody in a particularly thorny way many of the matters discussed in this chapter is Bellini's *I puritani,* the composer's last opera and musically one of the finest works to be written by an Italian composer during the 1830s. It is also an opera with a history that has long been considered murky, even faintly mysterious, with a version prepared for a famous prima donna but never performed. Cholera in Marseilles and subsequently the death of both the composer and the prima donna intervened. After a century and a half of uncertainty, much of the history has finally been unraveled, but the mystery and romance of the multiple versions of *I puritani* remain.[94]

Bellini had met Maria Malibran in the spring of 1833 in London, where she was singing in an English rendering of *La sonnambula*. The composer was captivated by her talent and charmed by her character ("quella diavoletta della Malibran," that little devil of a Malibran, he called her, remarking that she could learn an entire opera in a single day).[95] Engaged by the Théâtre Italien of Paris to compose what proved to be his final opera, *I puritani*, Bellini agreed simultaneously to tailor the work for a projected Neapolitan performance with Malibran. He had hoped actually to be present to stage the work in Naples, but it gradually became clear that the timing of the Parisian premiere would make that direct engagement in Naples impossible. Thus, the composer was forced to compromise: he decided instead to ship his revised version for Malibran to Naples.[96]

But first there was the original version for Paris to complete. Bellini prepared his opera for four of the greatest singers that the European theater had known during the first half of the century, singers who would become known as the "*Puritani* quartet": the soprano Giulia Grisi (Elvira), the tenor Giovanni Battista Rubini (Arturo), the baritone Antonio Tamburini (Riccardo), and the bass Luigi Lablache (Raimondo). The libretto, written by a Bolognese political exile in Paris, Count Carlo Pepoli, tells of the love between a Puritan woman, Elvira, and a cavalier, Arturo.[97] Elvira's father objects to the marriage on political grounds, but is gradually brought around by her uncle, Raimondo, even though another Puritan, Riccardo, is also in love with Elvira. An unknown prisoner at the Puritan castle turns out to be Henrietta Maria, the queen of the executed Charles I. Orders have arrived that she is to be turned over to Parliament, and it is assumed that the Puritans will execute her. Arturo arrives for his wedding with Elvira. When he realizes that the prisoner at the castle is the queen, he vows to help her escape. Aided by the wedding veil that Elvira, in her joy, has innocently draped over the head of the prisoner, Arturo escapes with Henrietta Maria, who is presumed to be the bride. Riccardo realizes what is happening, but, hoping thereby to gain Elvira's hand himself, he allows the escape. Believing that Arturo has been unfaithful to her, Elvira goes mad, as the curtain falls on the first act.

In the remainder of the work, Elvira's mind alternately clears or clouds over as she gains hope that Arturo will return to her or fears that she has lost him forever. Her state (particularly as expressed in one of the great "mad scenes" in the operatic literature) rouses pity in all, including Riccardo, but the Puritan Parliament has voted a death sentence on Arturo for having assisted in the escape of Henrietta Maria. Nonetheless, he returns to the castle in search of Elvira. After a brief moment with her, during which her reason returns, he is captured and is to be executed (while Elvira again slips into madness) when a messenger arrives from Cromwell himself: the wars are over and all political prisoners are to be freed. Elvira and Arturo are finally reunited as the opera ends, not without some discomfort for those of us brought up on Bertolt Brecht's ferocious commentary on this particular brand of deus ex machina in *The Threepenny Opera* (in the translation and adaptation by Marc Blitzstein: "But in real life the ending it is not so fine, Victoria's messenger does not come riding often").

As best we can tell, Bellini had largely completed the Parisian version of *I puritani* during the first part of December 1834, although he was still making important decisions about the second act several weeks later. In order to meet the deadline he had set for himself with the Neapolitan theater, however, he was obliged to complete and ship to Naples the revised version of the opera before the Parisian rehearsals had advanced very far. The first act and part of the second were sent before the end of 1834; the rest of the second act (at this stage the opera was divided into only two acts) followed on 5 January 1835.[98] For Naples there were to be two important shifts in vocal range among the four principal characters. Not only was the role of Elvira to be sung by Maria Malibran (a mezzo-soprano, rather than by the original soprano), but Riccardo was to be sung by a tenor, Francesco Pedrazzi, since there was no appropriate baritone on the Neapolitan roster.[99] Bellini accomplished this revision in four ways: (1) he had a copyist prepare a manuscript of the pieces for which no changes (or only the most modest changes) were necessary; (2) he had a copyist prepare a manuscript of the pieces for which the Neapolitan version was simply a transposition of the original; (3) he entered small corrections and modifications on these manuscript copies; (4) he wrote out entirely those pieces or sections of pieces for which the changes he chose to introduce were significant and extensive. As fate would have it, there was a cholera outbreak in Marseilles, as a result of which (and through no fault of the composer's) the score's arrival in Naples was delayed; in fact, the second act (which went by land) arrived several days before the first act (which went by sea from Marseilles).[100] Because of the uncertainty that had surrounded the arrival of *I puritani,* the theater decided not to wait more than a few days before proceeding with other plans. Despite an intervention in Bellini's favor from Malibran, the theater invoked its legal right to break the contract, claiming that the score had not arrived as specified in the contract. So there was no performance of *I puritani* in the "Malibran" version, and the score remained, temporarily at least, in the hands of Bellini's Neapolitan friend, Francesco Florimo.[101]

Meanwhile, rehearsals of the original version proceeded apace in Paris at the Théâtre Italien, where *I puritani* had its premiere on 24 January 1835 to enormous popular and critical acclaim. During the rehearsal period and between the first two performances, Bellini made many changes in his score, cutting sections of music, modifying his orchestration, replacing important parts, varying the order of compositions and the number of acts. Some of these changes may have been suggested by Rossini, who was serving in fact (if not in name) as musical director of the theater and as the point of reference for all Italian music in Paris, but they were adopted and executed in all details by Bellini, who was flattered by Rossini's attention and overjoyed at the success of his opera.[102] It is the version of *I puritani* Bellini himself presented at the Théâtre Italien of Paris on 24 January 1835, as further modified before the second performance, that was generally known thenceforth in the nineteenth century.[103] It was published in all printed editions of the opera and was normally performed throughout the nineteenth and twentieth centuries (often with further cuts).

Thus, leaving apart those temporary versions that appeared and disappeared from day to day during the rehearsal period (all of which came into and out of existence between the time Bellini shipped the Neapolitan version to Naples and the time of the Parisian performances), *I puritani* existed in three principal authorial versions: (1) the original version prepared for Paris; (2) the modified version of this original Parisian score, prepared for Naples; (3) the version performed in Paris. Since Bellini altered physically the autograph manuscript of the original Parisian score during the rehearsal period in Paris, adding and subtracting pages, crossing out elements of orchestration, moving sections around from one place to another, the entire original version for Paris no longer exists: only the second version (Naples) and third version (ultimately performed in Paris) can be completely reconstructed. The task of a critical edition of *I puritani* seems clear: it must produce complete texts of both the second and the third versions of the opera in a form that permits either of them to be readily used for performances. As for the first version, the edition must provide all surviving information about it. Given the fragmentary surviving materials and the evidence of Bellini's having altered the score during the rehearsal period, a critical edition is probably not the place to attempt a reconstruction of that version.

The verities of a printed edition and those of a performance, however, are not necessarily the same. What follow are the kinds of questions pertaining to the principal differences between the versions that might give us cause to reflect:

1. In some of the numbers reproduced from the original Parisian version without change for Naples or simply transposed for Naples to a new key (such as the aria for Riccardo in the first act), Bellini made important changes in the instrumentation during the Paris rehearsals. In the cabaletta of the Riccardo aria, for example, "Bel sogno beato," the melody was originally accompanied in the same rhythm by flute, two clarinets, and two horns. That orchestration was dutifully copied out for Naples, in the new key. During Parisian rehearsals, Bellini lightened the orchestration, removing the flute and horn parts (as well as other accompanimental parts for oboes and bassoons). Does it make sense to perform the Naples version with this heavier orchestration, when Bellini himself removed the extra parts during his rehearsals in Paris?[104]

2. Bellini made the Neapolitan version to favor Maria Malibran, a mezzosoprano. He had no special interest in modifying the role of Riccardo from a baritone to a tenor. In fact, the change creates a decided imbalance in the male vocal forces (two tenors and a bass instead of a tenor, a baritone, and a bass), not at all typical of Bellini's or Donizetti's operas. Even if we might wish to perform the opera with a mezzo-soprano, might it not be appropriate to keep Riccardo a baritone?

3. *I puritani* was conceived in two acts, and both the original Parisian version and the Neapolitan version have that structure. Only when Bellini manipulated the score during rehearsals, placing "Suoni la tromba" at the end of what then became the second act, did the three-act structure emerge. Does his motivation still hold valid? Or should we return the Parisian version to its original two acts?

4. Bellini announced to Florimo that he would not send a chorus to Naples because it had patriotic references that could not be performed there. This was the piece that Bellini replaced in Paris with "Suoni la tromba," which—while sent by Bellini to Florimo—was replaced in the Neapolitan version by a recitative. Since the exclusion of this highly popular number in Naples can be attributed primarily to its political content, why should we not restore "Suoni la tromba" to the score today when we perform the Malibran version?[105] If we use a baritone Riccardo, it could be added without any change; even if we use a tenor Riccardo, only minimal adjustments (of the kind that Bellini himself made on multiple occasions) would be needed.

5. During rehearsals and after the premiere, Bellini cut a number of sections from the original Parisian score because the division into three acts and the encores of two numbers demanded by the audience lengthened the evening.[106] Since most theaters today do not allow encores by audience demand,

should we not restore some of this music? If not, what justification is there to leave it in the Neapolitan version if we know that Bellini omitted it later in Paris?

6. Bellini originally ended the opera with a lyrical cabaletta for Elvira and Arturo together ("Ah senti, o mio bel angelo"). For Naples he turned it into a solo for Malibran, transposing the piece down by a third. During the course of the Parisian rehearsals, however, he substituted a choral conclusion, tearing the original ending "a 2" from his autograph manuscript of the Paris version. Fortunately, the cabaletta "a 2" is preserved in a manuscript copy of the opera at the Naples Conservatory (3.8.21–22), so it is possible to reconstruct the music as originally written for Paris. Sopranos, however, love that solo cabaletta every bit as much as mezzo-sopranos do. Joan Sutherland regularly sang this conclusion in her performances of the opera during the 1960s and 1970s, with the music transposed back up into the original register.[107] Is there any reason *not* to do this when an appropriate performer is available? Or should we insist that only a mezzo-soprano can sing the cabaletta alone, while a soprano must sing it together with her tenor?

I raise these issues as a series of questions, because establishing a performing text of an opera with a history as complex as that of *I puritani* demands that we consider the particular parameters of the performance being prepared. In the performance based on the Malibran version of *I puritani*, given by Boston Lyric Opera in autumn 1993, my colleagues and I followed the shape of the score sent by Bellini to Naples and used a tenor Riccardo, as in that score. While we did not stray from Bellini's organization, we did allow ourselves to emend the orchestration following changes introduced by Bellini during the Parisian rehearsals. It seemed absurd to insist on accompanying a passage in the first-act finale (transposed to accommodate a tenor Riccardo) with tremolo chords that interfered with the intelligibility of the text, when Bellini himself modified this accompaniment in Paris.[108] However tempted we were to introduce "Suoni la tromba" into the score, we resisted, and were happily surprised that what we lost in not performing the single most popular number from the opera was repaid by a clarity and strength in the dramaturgy that in some ways is superior to the final version. Finally, we performed essentially all the music Bellini sent to Naples, even sections later omitted in Paris, but allowed ourselves to make some cuts, adopting principles discussed in chapter 8.

Should these same decisions be taken elsewhere? Probably not. Each performance of *I puritani* will need to consider the multiple versions of the opera in terms of its own requirements. That certain procedures are appropriate for an edition does not mean that the same procedures are appropriate for a performance. The critical edition of a complex opera, though, if well prepared, provides all the musical materials a theater should need to attempt to realize that opera onstage.

Modern performers are in much the same position that prevailed in the nineteenth century, where decisions about versions were made by local musicians responsible for performances in individual theaters. These local musicians worked with the same three-dimensional grid set forth here: aesthetic criteria, historical circumstances, and the practical conditions of modern performance. That our present-day aesthetic criteria may be different, our knowledge of history both greater and lesser, and our performance conditions further from the stylistic paradigms of early nineteenth-century opera does not affect the force of these structural parallels.

In discussing the historical circumstances of nineteenth-century Italian opera, however, I have emphasized performances in which the original composer of a work participated, rather than placing all contemporary versions on the same plane. Critical editions of these works behave in much the same way. In a world that has increasingly called into question the concept of the "author," are we justified in privileging the composer? Or should contemporary musicians intervene as freely in modifying operas, making substitutions, composing new music, rearranging scores, as did some of their nineteenth-century ancestors?

At one extreme, we are under no obligation to stage these operas in a form the composer would have recognized at all. We could follow the lead of Peter Brook and invent a series of works entitled *The Comedy of Figaro, Violetta Goes to the Ball,* or *Lucy on the Stage with Daggers.* The advantage of doing so on a regular basis, however, is by no means obvious. The public does not appear to be clamoring for such adaptations, and few contemporary writers or musicians would find satisfaction in preparing them.

Any effort to gauge what constitutes acceptable or unacceptable intervention in the text of nineteenth-century Italian operas must take into account the very different social and historical position modern theaters have with respect to these works. When Rossini became director of the Théâtre Italien in 1824, he was under tremendous pressure to produce in Paris some of his legendary Neapolitan operas, word of which had been spread by travelers, critics, and other musicians. Similarly, no self-respecting theater in Italy in 1853 or 1854 could have failed to produce *Il trovatore.* It is as if a movie theater today refused to show the latest blockbuster hit. But a modern opera house is under no such obligation to perform Rossini's *La donna del lago* or Verdi's *Il trovatore* if such a performance would be possible only by having another musician heavily revise the score.

Singers in the nineteenth century, furthermore, were hired for entire operatic seasons, as we have seen. That means they were obliged to sing parts in each opera presented during the season. Although impresarios sought to avoid incompatibilities, these were inevitable. The excellent artists for whom Simone Mayr wrote *Fedra* at La Scala in 1821 were anything but ideal for Rossini's *La donna del lago*. Hence, a local musician made revisions, which the printed libretto reveals to have been numerous indeed. Modern opera houses working on the "stagione" system or producing individual operas under that system are not in the same position: they hire singers for particular roles. Unless their artistic administrators have done their job poorly, there should be no need for a modern opera house to perpetuate what were already considered abuses in the nineteenth century.

Indeed, I would press the implied question of aesthetic judgment further. Where a composer has cobbled together what we judge to be a patently inferior revised version of an opera because he lacked adequate singers to perform the original music or bowed to external pressure to permit artistically questionable changes, must a critical edition empower performers to present the inferior version (by preparing scores, parts, etc.), or does it suffice to describe the changes?

Just as a powerful prima donna can impose her will in evaluating alternative versions of a work, so too an edition of an opera can stack the deck. Placing music in the main body of a score or in an appendix might seem implicitly to favor one choice rather than another among aesthetically defensible versions, but providing only descriptions or incomplete materials places tighter constraints on performers. Rossini, for example, as we have seen, prepared two different endings to his *Tancredi* in 1813: a happy ensemble and a tragic, restrained death scene. Neither suited the desires of Giuditta Pasta, who in 1826 insisted to the composer that the opera should conclude with a showy aria for the hero *en travesti*. When Rossini equivocated, the imperious singer inserted a piece by another composer, Giuseppe Nicolini, but asked Rossini to write ornaments for her, which he obligingly did. The new critical edition prints Rossini's variants in the context of the piano reduction of the piece into which he wrote them, but does not present a full orchestral score. From information provided in the introduction, a determined prima donna could still have this version reconstructed, but as the editor I did not feel obliged to facilitate her task.[109]

If Italian opera in the twenty-first century is to remain a vital tradition, we need to recognize that part of its historical vitality lay in the process by which composers revised their operas for particular productions. The versions for which he was directly responsible offer modern performers a set of alternatives from which to make their choices. Measuring these choices against our grid of aesthetic matters, historical circumstances, and modern conditions does not ensure "correct" solutions. Indeed, the elements within this grid are so varied that no choice can ever be universally appropriate. But at least this approach recognizes that Italian opera is to be performed neither according to the idol of "tradition" nor according to the idol of "historical reconstruction." If we accept a multidimensional approach to performance decisions, we ground our theories in the actual world of opera, a world of compromise and uncertainty, a world of strong opinions and even stronger egos. We should aim to provide, not a museum for the petrification of performances of the past, but a re-creation (within the context of our own social structures) of the characteristics that made Italian opera a vital art form in the nineteenth century and can help it remain so today.

Although *Le nozze di Figaro* does not strictly fit into the subject of this book, I cannot resist adding a word about the tempest that blew over New York's Metropolitan Opera in October and November 1998, when the Susanna (Cecilia Bartoli), with the approval of the conductor (James Levine), decided to introduce at some performances two arias that were not in the original score but were inserted by Mozart himself into the opera after its first production. *Figaro* was first performed at the Burgtheater of Vienna on 10 May 1786. On the occasion of a revival at the same theater on 29 August 1789, the composer provided replacements for Susanna's original arias in the second act ("Venite, inginocchiatevi," replaced by "Un moto di gioia") and the fourth act ("Deh vieni non tardar," replaced by "Al desio di chi t'adora"). He did so, of course, because he had a new Susanna, Adriana Ferrarese, hardly an inferior artist to the original Nancy Storace: in 1790, after all, Mozart wrote for la Ferrarese the role of Fiordiligi in *Così fan tutte*.[110] But she was a different singer and must have been a very different presence onstage, if we can judge from Fiordiligi's great aria "Come scoglio!" Mozart was not altogether enamored of her, as he wrote to his wife, Constanze, on 19 August 1789: "The little aria, which I composed for Madame Ferrarese ["Un moto di gioia"], ought, I think, to be a success, provided she is able to sing it in an artless manner, which, however, I very much doubt. She herself liked it very much. I have just lunched at her house."[111] Still, he did write the two arias, and Ferrarese performed them with success. Whether or not Mozart wished them consigned to the dustbin of history we will never know, since there is no documentation whatsoever, but the arias have long been familiar to anyone with the slightest knowledge of the history of *Le nozze di Figaro*.

At the Metropolitan Opera, on the other hand, these arias gave rise to a public scandal when the stage director, Jonathan Miller, objected to their introduction. As I have tried to argue in this chapter, there is no "right" and "wrong" about such substitutions: arguments can be brought to bear from many different directions. Normally such questions are discussed backstage—whether amicably or not—and the matters are resolved before opening night. Miller chose instead to go public. *Le nozze di Figaro* is an opera regularly seen in our opera houses, season after season. Experimenting with Mozart's own added arias, even from the stage of the premiere opera house in the United States, is hardly an example of lèse-majesté. It was not Bartoli's playful substitution but Miller's almost religious fervor on the subject and his misrepresentation of the historical evidence that were unacceptable. Still smarting over the experience almost five years later, Miller gave an interview to the *Paris Review* in 2003, in which he described the arias as "concert pieces" which "should be omitted from the stage production, because the words don't match what goes on: they have nothing to do with the scene."[112] His description of the arias as "concert pieces" is historically wrong, whereas his aesthetic judgment is hardly absolute: it depends on how you conceive the scene, on how the stage director develops the action, on how the singers portray the characters. Besides, if Bartoli was "beguiling" the audience, as Miller himself affirms, something worthwhile had clearly happened in the theater.[113]

8

SERAFIN'S SCISSORS

TO CUT OR NOT TO CUT?

Should Italian operas be performed complete, or is it desirable to omit certain passages? The existence of multiple versions of Italian operas written during the first half of the nineteenth century already complicates the integrity of these operas, their status as "works." If Bellini eliminated completed passages from *I puritani* during the rehearsal period in Paris, as we saw in chapter 7, what does it mean to talk about performing the opera complete? If Rossini—before he left Paris following the first performances of *Guillaume Tell*—struck from his opera two dances, several recitatives, and an aria for Jemmy (as he joyfully waits for his father to shoot the apple from his head), what should we be performing complete? [1] If Verdi, returning to earlier works (*Macbeth, Stiffelio, Il trovatore, Simon Boccanegra*) between the late 1850s and the early 1880s, omitted entire sections of these scores and rewrote others, what search for textual purity would drive critics, scholars, and musicians to insist on integral performances?

Making cuts in nineteenth-century Italian operas has a long pedigree. [2] To pretend otherwise would falsify the historical performance record and impose a foreign aesthetic. Rarely, though, has the activity been subject to a critique that seeks to understand how that practice has been and continues to be motivated or the ways in which cuts have been effected. When a conductor omits a passage or an entire number because he honestly doesn't like it, I may disagree while respecting his motivation. When a conductor makes a cut because it is "traditional," on the other hand, he is acting without artistic integrity. [3]

Decisions about cutting, furthermore, are unrelated to what editions a performer may be using, except insofar as the critical edition may make available passages omitted from earlier published scores. Before there was any talk about critical editions of Italian opera, some performers included the "Wolf's Crag" scene in *Lucia di Lammermoor*, some did not; some tenors sang the cabalettas of their arias in *Rigoletto* and *La traviata,* some did not. While critical editions—prepared with as much knowledge as can be acquired about an opera and its textual history—tend to instill greater confidence in the credibility of the printed score, no one should need to be reminded that a performance is not an edition. Yet most objections to using critical editions in the opera house are centered not on the editions themselves but on their presumed implications for performance. There are conductors and singers who continue to believe, against all evidence, that a critical edition restricts their options, compels them to perform an opera *come scritto* (as written), abjuring cuts and performance traditions and slavishly following the dictates of the printed text. Nothing could be more remote from the position of those who prepare the editions. These fears can be understood best as a misreading of the aesthetic views of two conductors often associated with the editions, Claudio Abbado and Riccardo Muti.

Abbado was the first to use the new critical editions of Rossini's comic operas, and in his early performances he expected singers to adhere to the letter of the written text, refusing to countenance any cuts, variations, or cadenzas other than minimal ones. Given the sorry state of most Rossini performances before Abbado's work (with the exception of that most Rossinian of earlier twentieth-century conductors, Vittorio Gui), this proved a welcome sweeping away of the abuses regularly heaped upon these scores. Anyone who has heard the 1992 Abbado recordings of *Il viaggio a Reims* and *Il barbiere di Siviglia,* however, knows that he has long since abandoned such a position. Indeed, one might well argue that he has occasionally gone overboard. Placido Domingo as Figaro was hardly a choice suggested by the nature of the written score, whatever Domingo's extraordinary skills. And with Kathleen Battle as Rosina, Abbado retreated from the mezzo-soprano/contralto of Rossini's original to the vocal rescoring dear to coloratura sopranos in the first half of the twentieth century.[4] For reasons that have nothing to do with scholarly purity, I find the aesthetic results unconvincing. Also, in inserting into *Il viaggio a Reims* a citation of *La Marseillaise*—played by a trumpet, no less—Abbado served Rossini badly, an enormous irony, given the musical intelligence and spirit he lavished on other parts of the score. There are now legions of opera fans who think that Rossini bravely (or ironically) quoted the French Revolutionary anthem of 1792 in an 1825 performance of an opera at which the new King Charles X was present.[5]

Riccardo Muti, on the other hand, who has worked particularly closely with the Verdi critical edition, has remained ferocious (some think too ferocious) on the subject of singers' interpolations, refusing unwritten high notes, traditional trills and turns, and the like. There is much to be said for his position: many opera houses, as we have seen in chapter 4, continue to lament that they cannot cast the role of Manrico in *Il trovatore*, when what they really mean is that they can find no one to sing what passes today for the role of Manrico. But Muti himself is anything but rigid in his interpretation of the Verdi editions. The famous chorus of Hebrew slaves in *Nabucco*, "Va pensiero," concludes with a *pianissimo* chord in the chorus, held for one bar and cutting off at the downbeat of the next, with two further pizzicato chords in the strings to bring the piece to a close. Presenting the first performances of the new edition to open the season at La Scala in 1986, Muti had his chorus hold that sonority for so long, with such a spectacular diminuendo, that even the audience gasped for breath. And after an interminable ovation, he gave the public the unthinkable: an encore.[6]

Once any edition enters the opera house, it is subject to interpretation and emendation at every point. As in the case of choosing a version, performance decisions are dependent on the three-dimensional grid of aesthetic criteria, historical circumstances, and practical conditions, as described in chapter 7. These dimensions are not independent: our aesthetic criteria are in part determined by our historical knowledge, practical conditions tend to be closely related to our aesthetic criteria, and our view of history cannot be separated from who we are and why we are seeking information about performance decisions made at the time a work was composed. In a living art, there are no correct or definitive answers about performance decisions. Every situation is different, artists change, the same artists mature (or at least get older), instrumentalists have different characteristics from one pit orchestra to another. When a last-minute replacement tenor in *L'Italiana in Algeri* proved inadequate at the Rossini Festival of 1994, no one (administrators, conductor David Robertson, stage director Dario Fo, or scholars) had the slightest doubt that his second-act solo—a replacement piece not widely known by the public—should be snipped out of the score.[7] We were only sorry that we couldn't do the same thing with Lindoro's first-act cavatina, but "Languir per una bella" was too familiar, too integral to the score, to be omitted without incurring the wrath of a public all too willing to show its displeasure by rotund booing.

Discussions of cuts in modern performances are usually couched in aesthetic or practical terms that dehistoricize the process, or rather historicize it no further than the immediate past. It is important, instead, to measure cuts both against the social circumstances in which operas were originally prepared and against the conditions in which they are performed today. What is desirable or permissible may not be the same in San Francisco and Milan, in an American theater with supertitles and one without them, in an opera house that performs a work in the language of the audience and one that does not, in a barn that seats four thousand spectators and an intimate space that seats four hundred, at a festival in which an audience assembles from all over the world and in a regular theatrical season in which everyone has to get to work the next morning.

THE INTEGRITY OF AN OPERA AS A HISTORICAL PROBLEM

Our attitude to cuts depends on our perception of the integrity of an opera. The existence of multiple versions already problematizes that perception, as does the nature of the theatrical system for which operas were written. Equally significant is the historical position of a work within a stylistically defined continuum of nineteenth-century Italian operas. Most discussion about cuts is really about the acceptable limits within which a particular opera can be stylistically displaced along that continuum.

Every work of art belonging to a vital and living tradition is created at a specific moment in the history of that tradition. Particular solutions to political, social, compositional, and stylistic issues, often at cross purposes, inform the decisions of each creative artist. Some decisions are fully conscious, others are unconscious adaptations to the immediate environment. Nor is our understanding of a work within its historical tradition unalterably fixed. For musicians and operagoers living in the middle of the nineteenth century, each new opera by Verdi changed inexorably their vision of the immediate past as they sought to reinterpret their understanding of works by Bellini or Donizetti in the terms imposed by Verdi's accomplishment. Historical models developed by twentieth-century scholars are no less subject to reinterpretation: the widespread revival of Rossini's serious operas over the past twenty years, after a hiatus of more than a century, has had a profound effect on the way we hear the music of Bellini and Donizetti. It forces us to confront their works with operas they knew well but about which, until recently, we were ignorant. A more profound knowledge of Donizetti's operas of the early 1840s (works such as *Adelia, Maria Padilla, Caterina Cornaro,* and *Maria di Rohan*) will inevitably lead to a similar reevaluation of the operas of Verdi's first decade.

Various stylistic elements in individual works are tied to their position in this continuum. It would be as unthinkable for the protagonist of Verdi's *Luisa Miller* of 1849 to present herself in an aria with the fluid structure and dramaturgical immediacy of "Mi chiamano Mimì" from Puccini's *La Bohème* of 1896, as it would be for Cio-cio san in *Madama Butterfly* of 1904 to arrive singing a piece patterned after a great cavatina of the 1830s, such as Norma's "Casta Diva." It would be as unthinkable for the two servants, Ruiz and Ines, in Verdi's *Il trovatore* of 1852 to have a lengthy conversation about the events befalling their masters, to fall in love, and to sing *arie di sorbetto* about their feelings (as similar characters do in Rossini's *Ciro in Babilonia* of 1812), as it would be for a chorus of guards at the beginning of the last act of *Tosca* in 1900 to break into a ditty such as "Squilli, echeggi la tromba guerriera" from the third act of *Il trovatore*.

On the other hand, not every musical or dramaturgical element in a work is crucial to our perception of that work's integrity. When we make a decision about cuts in the modern performance of an opera, we are making a judgment about integrity. The more we believe in the work's integrity, the more hesitant we will be about making cuts. Yet the historical record suggests that few works for the theater lend themselves to absolutist judgments. Rather, there exists considerable evidence as to which elements seem more fragile at a given moment. Contemporary sources offer valuable insight about how operas were treated in their own time, and in some cases we can even reconstruct cuts a composer made during rehearsals.

Although many of his operas continued to pay obeisance to eighteenth-century dramaturgical models, Rossini had little interest in those conventions according to which secondary characters participate in the action; nor was he concerned with scenes of *secco* recitative that elaborately narrate past events or comment on recent ones. Donizetti's autograph manuscripts and letters, on the other hand, demonstrate his continued efforts to avoid the regular repetition of cadential formulas so characteristic of Rossini. In manuscript after manuscript Donizetti is drawn instinctively to these procedures, then crosses out the offending measures so as to streamline the musical dramaturgy.[8] For Verdi one of the most problematic elements was the cabaletta, whose formal design made sense for Rossini and Bellini, associated as it was with the practice of singer ornamentation. Increasingly it seemed useless baggage from the past to Verdi's contemporaries and to the composer himself. Revising his *Simon Boccanegra* from 1857 for performance in 1881, he tried to free it—not always successfully—from this earlier practice. Even when he did walk the path of the cabaletta in *Aida*, he constantly prodded his librettist, Antonio Ghislanzoni, with advice like, "If you could find a form somewhat more novel for the cabaletta, this duet would be perfect."[9]

Most cuts introduced by thoughtful performers in the nineteenth century and in the modern world are not arbitrary manipulations of unstable texts, but rather attempts to eliminate elements considered to be least significant or characteristic for a work's aesthetic integrity and historical position. In deciding which cuts to countenance in modern performance, we must determine how far to allow this elimination to proceed. At what point do such cuts distort the work? When does the process of cutting an opera result in such a distortion of its aesthetic premises that it would be better to abandon the effort? When should we quit trying to rescue Humpty Dumpty?

The significance of individual cuts, furthermore, will vary for different participants in an operatic performance. Too often the issues are presented as if everyone were working from a common viewpoint.[10] Aesthetic issues of musical quality rarely play a role in decisions about cutting recitative, but for a stage director the effect of recitative on the coherence of the dramatic action can be crucial. The stage director, on the other hand, needn't worry whether or not a secondary character sings an *aria di sorbetto,* but the practical capabilities of the performer (and clauses in his or her contract) may determine whether the piece is included.

In the following discussion I will consider three categories of cuts: recitative (either entire scenes or smaller sections); complete musical numbers; and portions of musical numbers.

MAKING CUTS: RECITATIVE

Early during his years in Naples, Rossini prepared an *opera buffa,* entitled *La gazzetta* (The Newspaper), for the Teatro dei Fiorentini, where it was first performed on 26 September 1816. Based on a Carlo Goldoni comedy, *Il matrimonio per concorso* (The Marriage Competition), it is a peculiar work. About 50 percent of the concerted music was derived from earlier operas still unknown in Naples, but Rossini nonetheless wrote out every note of this recycled music afresh, reorchestrating it, adapting it to new words, integrating it with new musical ideas.[11] The opera also has vast stretches of *secco* recitative (including large sections in Neapolitan dialect), not a note of which is by the composer. Some of the text is hilarious, for most situations and details of dialogue reach back to Goldoni. A stage director with a particular affinity for verbal play might luxuriate in this recitative; a stage director like Dario Fo, on the other hand, with strong roots in the *commedia dell'arte* tradition and physical comedy, was less amused. For his production at the Rossini Opera Festival in August 2001 he insisted on massive cuts.

With the performance of the new critical edition of *La gazzetta* (edited by Fabrizio Scipioni and myself) less than two months away, I traveled to Milan to discuss these cuts with Fo. His apartment was in an uproar, for his entire entourage was about to transfer its operation to Pesaro, but Fo was totally absorbed in showing off his ideas for *La gazzetta*. He is a very visually oriented man of the theater, who prepares a project by drawing countless renderings of individual scenes, arranging the entrances and exits of characters and mimes, twisting and turning scenic elements in a profusion of inventive designs. He does not work from a musical score but from a libretto. While he conceded that concerted numbers had to be sacrosanct, he treated *secco* recitative as if it were expendable, like spoken dialogue. When I tried to understand exactly which text he wanted to cut, he found the question somewhat irritating. Couldn't that be worked out in the theater? No, I tried to explain. Not only did the singers need to learn the music together with the words, but making cuts would require us to rewrite the music, so that harmonies made sense and the rhythm flowed easily. And, no, he couldn't cut two words here and three words there without taking into account what those omissions would do to the poetic structure, rhyme scheme, and the musical setting. Most of all, if he waited until the first rehearsal to inform his singers of his intended cuts (by which point they would have memorized an enormous quantity of recitative), not much of Dario Fo would remain when they had finished with him.

Italian operas from the first half of the nineteenth century are what we call "number operas": essentially closed musical forms separated by recitative, even if composers increasingly sought to override this separation. The division between recitative and numbers is not imposed by the composer. It is inherent in the structure of librettos, whose poets wrote their verses for recitative in the classical patterns of *versi sciolti* (free verses) of only occasionally rhymed *settenari* and *endecasillabi*, as opposed to *versi lirici* (lyric verses), rhymed poetry using regular poetic meters, employed for the musical numbers.

During the first two decades of the nineteenth century in Italy, recitative was almost always *secco*, accompanied by a keyboard instrument (usually the fortepiano, ancestor of the modern piano), with a violoncello and double bass doubling (and, in the case of the cello, harmonizing) the bass line.[12] Influenced in particular by French operatic practice, strongly present in Naples during the reign of Napoleon's brother-in-law Murat (1808–15), Neapolitan theaters in the 1810s began to require all recitative in serious operas to be accompanied by the orchestra. In 1813, for example, Giovanni Simone Mayr prepared *secco* recitative for his *Medea in Corinto* as he began composing the score from his home in Bergamo. When he arrived in Naples to begin rehearsals, he was compelled to rewrite all this recitative with orchestral accompaniment.[13] As of the mid-1820s, when Rossini's Neapolitan operas were being heard in theaters throughout Italy, the practice of writing only accompanied recitative in serious operas took root, although the use of *secco* recitative in comic opera persisted for several decades. Rossini's last serious opera with *secco* recitative is *Bianca e Falliero,* which had its premiere at La Scala to open the carnival season of 1819–20. Significantly, the *secco* recitative in this opera was written entirely by a collaborator, not by Rossini himself.[14] By the time he wrote *Semiramide* for the Teatro La Fenice of Venice during the carnival season of 1822–23, however, Rossini employed only accompanied recitative in this *opera seria,* and he personally prepared every note of it. While not every composer followed his lead during the 1820s, in the 1830s serious operas with *secco* recitative were practically nonexistent in Italy.

Recitative (whether accompanied or *secco*) had multiple functions in Italian opera, and recognizing them helps us develop principles for introducing cuts into modern performances. First, recitative has a narrative function: it presents developments in the plot, crucial to the dramatic structure of the opera, as they occur. Second, recitative has an expository purpose: it explains earlier events that prepared present dramatic configurations or comments on those events. Third, recitative has a formal function: it provides repose in the dramatic and emotional progress of an opera by separating closed musical numbers, which probe character, explore intense personal reactions to dramatic events, or carry emotionally charged confrontations. Fourth, recitative (and occasionally arias) can have a scenic aim, necessitated by early nineteenth-century stagecraft, in which set changes within an act were carried out in full view of the audience (or behind a drop curtain while the performance continued in front). To avoid lengthy pauses after a dramatic "long" scene (one that employs the entire depth of the stage), a bridging dramatic scene performed in front of a drop curtain (a "short" scene, often in recitative) allowed time for a new long or medium scene to be put into place.[15]

The relative weight of these functions changed during the course of the first half of the nineteenth century. Early nineteenth-century serious operas, such as Rossini's *Tancredi,* employ a full complement of handmaidens, confidants, and lieutenants, following the practices of eighteenth-century French drama (the source of many librettos) and Italian opera to librettos by Pietro Metastasio or his contemporaries. They typically receive the laments, share the joys, and execute the projects of the principal characters: Amenaide's Isaura and Tancredi's Roggiero have ample opportunity to discuss the fate of their masters. In Rossini's *Ciro in Babilonia,* as mentioned above, secondary characters actually develop sentimental attachments to one another, which must be resolved before the drama concludes.

Rossini considered the composition of *secco* recitative to be a secondary activity, and for his mature operas he usually entrusted the job to another musician. Only in some early works, written before 1815, and in the unusual *Viaggio a Reims* of 1825, did Rossini prepare *secco* recitative himself. In his first surviving autograph, *La scala di seta,* an 1812 one-act *farsa,* all the recitative is his own. But in his very next opera, *La pietra del paragone,* a two-act comedy written for La Scala later that same year, the numbing quantity of *secco* recitative invented by the librettist discouraged the composer: he prepared music for its first act, but foisted the second onto a collaborator. In fact, Rossini prepared essentially none of the *secco* recitative in his most famous comic operas, *L'Italiana in Algeri, Il Turco in Italia, Il barbiere di Siviglia,* and *La Cenerentola,* nor in semiserious or serious operas such as *La gazza ladra, Bianca e Falliero,* and *Matilde di Shabran.*

That Rossini did not prepare *secco* recitative for *Il barbiere di Siviglia* or *La Cenerentola* does not mean the job was poorly done; the musical setting is often sparkling and witty, the style fully in line with Rossini's procedures in those earlier operas for which he composed recitative (*La scala di seta,* the first act of *La pietra del paragone,* and *Tancredi*). *Il Turco in Italia* and *La gazza ladra,* both prepared for the Teatro alla Scala, offer a marked contrast. The classical rules for recitative called for notation in 4/4 meter with strong syllables falling on the first and third beats (always with the understanding that delivery would be rhythmically free and that there was no real "beat" involved). Rossini's own recitatives generally accord with this model. But his collaborators in *Il Turco in Italia* and *La gazza ladra* followed a modified convention, observing the accents on the first and third beats only when the harmony changes, while allowing strong and weak syllables to fall wherever they might during continuous recitation over a single harmony. (A still looser modified convention, adopted often by Donizetti and by Verdi in *Un giorno di regno,* his only opera with *secco* recitative, was to abandon barlines altogether, or to place them only at harmony changes, creating long run-on "bars" and abandoning all pretense of meter.) Woe to a performer who tries to sing these recitatives in a strict 4/4 meter with accents on the first and third beats. Italian singers instinctively understand this, but American singers need to be taught. Samuel Ramey and Lella Cuberli, in the first Pesaro production of *Il Turco in Italia* during the summer of 1983, painstakingly had to *un*learn the accent patterns they had assumed from the notated rhythm. Nor is it possible to fix these rhythms, as some later editions tried to do: such manipulations falsified the temporal relations between syllables, a far worse sin.

Despite the fluidity of the *Barbiere* recitatives, however, the pages devoted to this music by Serafin and Toni (to be discussed more fully below) are absurd.[16] Since these authors rather like the recitatives, they want the settings to be by Rossini, and so they invent a scenario in which the manuscripts within Rossini's autograph of the opera are the "fair copy" of a previous autograph manuscript (now lost). This fair copy "must have been" prepared by an associate from Rossini's "vocal score," because Rossini had neither the time nor the inclination to write them out a second time. How many distortions and errors can dance on the head of a pin? The recitatives in Rossini's autograph score of *Il barbiere* are composing scores, not copyists' renderings; Rossini never prepared a preliminary "vocal score" before writing out his full score; and there is no evidence that Rossini ever wrote any part of his operas, not even the most complex ensembles, "a second time." But we will return to Toni and Serafin below. The crucial issue, after all, is not who wrote these recitatives. That Rossini prepared all the *secco* recitative for *Tancredi* does not mean that every note must be played in a modern production: some dialogue, reflecting practices already old-fashioned in 1813, was always eliminated in contemporary performances and can quite properly be eliminated today.

Secco recitative can be declaimed quickly; accompanied recitative, punctuated by orchestral chords or, increasingly, enriched with sustained singing or playing, moves more slowly. Thus, the length of the verbal text decreases when recitative is accompanied, while the musical importance of these passages increases. During his Neapolitan years, Rossini invented a style for using accompanied recitative throughout an opera (and not only for the elaborate scenas that precede major arias). Much of the recitative in *Elisabetta, regina d'Inghilterra*, of 1815 is little more than *secco* recitative with interpolated string chords. (In the first performances of the new critical edition at the Rossini Opera Festival during the summer of 2004,[17] the conductor, Renato Palumbo, strove to make these recitatives highly expressive; that the music sometimes resisted his efforts reflects the limitations of Rossini's writing.) By the 1816 *Otello* the recitative is more flexible, and in the third act it reaches a consistently high level. In later works (the 1818 *Ermione*, 1820 *Maometto II*, and 1822 *Zelmira*), Rossini's accompanied recitative achieves a level of musical and dramatic intensity far different from that of his contemporaries. It comes as no surprise, then, that for operas employing accompanied recitative throughout, Rossini tended to engage collaborators only when under intense time pressure. We know, for example, that *La donna del lago*, which had its premiere at the Teatro San Carlo on 24 October 1819, was hurriedly planned by Rossini after Berlin authorities refused Gasparo Spontini permission to fulfill the contract requiring him to prepare a new opera for Naples. To help meet the unexpected deadline he was facing, Rossini assigned some accompanied recitative for *La donna del lago* (as well as the aria for Duglas, "Taci, lo voglio") to a collaborator.[18]

This reduction in the amount of recitative continued throughout the first half of the century. When Verdi first collaborated with the librettist Francesco Maria Piave on *Ernani,* he complained to Guglielmo Brenna of the excessive number of verses of recitative that Piave had written.[19] He persisted in recommending brevity to his librettist, year after year. Only a little more than a month before the premiere of *La traviata* in 1853, he commented to the president of the Teatro La Fenice, "Piave has not yet finished polishing *La traviata;* and even in the things he has finished there are some long-winded passages that will put the public to sleep, especially near the end, which must be very quick if it is to have an effect."[20] The function of recitative changed significantly as the century unfolded. With librettists and composers turning to new dramatic sources (particularly the Romantic theater), and with *secco* recitative giving way to accompanied recitative, dialogue involving secondary characters was reduced to a minimum. In works like *Rigoletto* and *La traviata,* a few brief phrases must suffice to characterize the Count of Ceprano, Merullo, the Baron Douphol, and Flora Bervoix. Only sensitive performances, both vocally and scenically, can bring such characters to life. By midcentury, the emblematic secondary role in Italian opera is the servant in Flora's party in *La traviata:* his classic and single line is "La cena è pronta" (Dinner is served).

There were also important changes in the external shape of an opera. The two-act design that dominated Italian opera during the first three decades of the century (itself a reform of eighteenth-century practice, where most operas were in three acts) grew to three or even four acts by 1850. Of Rossini's thirty-four Italian operas, only three Neapolitan works (*Otello, Armida,* and *Mosè in Egitto*) have more than two acts; of Verdi's roughly twenty-five Italian operas, only the early *Oberto* and *Un giorno di regno* have but two. Although it may seem paradoxical, this shift did not increase the amount of music in an opera: if anything, there was sometimes less music, for the intermissions obviated the need for additional scenes to bridge set changes within an act.

When Rossini wrote Italian operas in three acts, there were always unusual circumstances. Time was needed to prepare the final scene of *Mosè in Egitto,* in which the Israelites cross the Red Sea, or the beginning of the final act of *Armida,* where the action shifts from the second act's pleasure palace to an enchanted garden. Rossini and his librettists could have provided bridging scenes but preferred to introduce an intermission to enhance the dramatic and emotional resonance of the work. On scenic grounds alone, the third act of Rossini's *Otello,* which takes place in Desdemona's bedchamber (a "short" scene), could easily have followed directly the aria she sings to conclude the second act (a "long" scene). Surely the composer wished to separate this final scene of the opera not only for dramaturgical reasons but also to allow Desdemona much-needed rest. A few years earlier, however, Rossini and his librettist might have bridged the gap by introducing a short scene (both temporally and spatially), containing recitative or an *aria di sorbetto*. Indeed, in the first London performances of *Otello*, at the King's Theatre in 1822, without the participation of Rossini, a *scena e duetto* for Emilia (Desdemona's "handmaiden") and Emilio (Desdemona's father) was introduced, making it possible for the opera to be performed in two acts. (At least they don't fall in love.) When Rossini himself took responsibility for a London revival in 1824, he promptly restored *Otello* to three acts.[21]

The 1830s were a period of transition, during which the problem of bridging scenes remained. The final act of *Lucia di Lammermoor* provides a perfect example. Lucia's mad scene—after she has murdered her husband, Arturo, on their wedding night—takes place in the great hall of the castle. In the final scene of the opera, Lucia's beloved Edgardo awaits her brother Enrico, whom he has challenged to a duel, among the tombs of Ravenswood. When Edgardo learns of Lucia's death, he kills himself. Donizetti and his librettist had two problems: (1) How, after the mad scene, do they get Lucia, the chorus, and everyone else off stage? (2) How do they most effectively allow time to prepare the new setting for the final scene? They solved these problems by introducing accompanied recitative to bridge the scenes. In it, Lucia is led off by her ladies, and the remainder of the chorus exits with them. Overwhelmed by the events, Enrico too departs, while Raimondo and Normanno (Lucia's tutor and the captain of Enrico's guards) engage in dialogue about the appalling events they have witnessed. This dialogue surely took place in front of a drop curtain, behind which the final scene could be prepared. The recitative, in short, had an exquisitely practical purpose: absent these practical requirements, it could not be more superfluous. On the other hand, cutting the scene *without* solving the practical issue is an absurdity: is it really better for an audience to sit, bored, during a scene change than to hear a well-performed recitative fill in details of the plot?

With these historical issues in mind, we can offer some guidelines for making cuts in recitative (whether *secco* or accompanied) in modern performances of Italian opera:

1. Unless there is a physical change of scene or a complete break in the action between two closed musical numbers, enough recitative should be preserved to highlight the formal boundaries of these numbers. Failure to do so threatens to distort the intelligibility of an opera and create the impression

of a concert in costume. When passages of recitative between musical numbers exist primarily to bridge scenes, cover set changes, or facilitate the exit of choral masses, on the other hand, modern theatrical stagecraft can eliminate the need for such passages, thereby justifying their omission.

2. When making internal cuts in *secco* recitative, consider both the significance of the dialogue and its intelligibility (whether through direct comprehension, supertitles, or physical action). Actual dialogue must clarify significant events occurring on stage. Past events can be consigned to the synopsis that forms part of operatic programs (functioning as did the *antefatto* [background] of nineteenth-century librettos). Indeed, in these librettos, verses useful for understanding the story but omitted in performance were printed with *virgoletti* (quotation marks) to indicate that they would not be sung. In some cases, passages were cut only after the composer set them to music. In *Il Turco in Italia,* where the *secco* recitative of Rossini's collaborator is often longer than the text printed in the original libretto, the decision to abbreviate the recitative in performance apparently preceded the printing of the libretto.[22]

3. Lyrical passages in accompanied recitative, which become more prevalent as the century advances, help establish the emotional tone of an opera and should rarely be eliminated. Neither, however, should the surrounding recitative be so severely trimmed that these passages stand alone, falsifying their dramaturgical function. Recitative sustained throughout by a lyrical impulse (such as the music Verdi introduced in the prologue of the revised *Simon Boccanegra* of 1881) is a later practice in Italian opera and cannot be imposed on earlier works. Although Verdi could recast the first scene of his 1857 *Simon Boccanegra* to create a new musical dramaturgy, a pair of scissors will not allow us to achieve a similar result.

4. When cuts are made in recitative, music must be modified to guarantee an acceptable harmonic and melodic flow. The stylistic context needs to be understood: in music of the early nineteenth century a *D*-seventh chord cannot resolve to an *F-major* chord in root position. When I arranged the *secco* recitative to allow Dario Fo to make the cuts he wished to introduce into *La gazzetta,* I began by studying attentively the progressions used throughout the opera. With this point of reference against which to measure my creative instincts, I gave myself up to the pleasure of modifying the recitative in the most musically and dramatically effective way I could.

5. Finally, composers used recitative to bridge disparate tonalities between closed numbers. There are, to be sure, occasions in which these adjacencies are faulty. Particularly disturbing are cases in which a *secco* recitative points to a key, but the piece that follows the recitative turns out to be in an unrelated

tonality. This frequently happens when the recitative is by one musician and the ensuing musical number by another (there are pungent examples in *Il Turco in Italia,* as well as in *Mosè in Egitto*). While a critical edition cannot atone for breakdowns of communication between those who prepared the original score, performers disturbed by jarring adjacencies should feel free to make modifications to avoid them.[23] Modern performers, on the other hand, normally have no need to fret about places where the elimination of a recitative between numbers results in an ungracious tonal adjacency. Twentieth-century social custom, after all, encourages audiences to applaud after numbers, and such applause interrupts the succession of keys.

To those who reflect about the practical problems of operatic performance, these guidelines will come as no surprise, but there has been little reflection on such issues. Indeed, the number of occasions on which similar principles are routinely flouted is appalling. In the context of festival performances, it is not inappropriate to avoid cuts in recitative; for most theatrical circumstances, however, judicious cutting of recitative, planned for the needs of a particular performance, is justified and can be accomplished in a musically responsible fashion.

MAKING CUTS: ENTIRE NUMBERS

In 1974, Lyric Opera of Chicago sponsored a week-long international congress of Verdi studies. Lyric Opera seemed an unlikely venue for the congress, since the general manager at that time, the late Carol Fox, disliked scholars intensely: "Scholars," she said to me during the week, "I know all about scholars: my [ex-]husband was a scholar." She certainly was not pleased by the participants' criticisms of the new Lyric production of *Simon Boccanegra* by Giorgio De Lullo, whose failure to pay attention to details of the libretto turned an opera somewhat difficult to follow in the best of circumstances into a total mystery. I recall an invented procession in the first scene, in which the body of Simone's beloved Maria was carried from her house at stage right, across the front of the stage, to the church at stage left. Thus, when Simone entered the house, there was no corpse for him to find. Not only did the procession make no dramaturgical sense, it made no liturgical sense: but those were the days (before supertitles) when many Italian stage directors simply presumed an American audience wouldn't know or care.[24] In sessions of the congress where the scholars were not being actively disagreeable, Fox found the discussion arcane. But she had prepared a secret weapon to humble her academic guests. For a panel on the subject of performance practice, she produced a singer of whom everyone was in awe, Maria Callas.

As "La Divina" listened quietly, one professor after another recited the virtues of uncut performances, analyzing tonal schemes that emerged only from complete operas, demonstrating hidden melodic continuities lost when passages were omitted, and so on. When *La traviata* was discussed, every speaker deplored the practice of cutting the cabaletta "No, non udrai rimproveri" after Germont's famous baritone cantabile "Di Provenza il mar, il suol"; without this cabaletta, according to the scholars, the act lost its shape and the dramaturgy suffered considerably. By then Callas had had enough. The real problem with the end of the scene, she informed us, was that the baritone sang at all. Violetta was the principal character of the opera, and the drama's emotional center was Violetta's "Amami, Alfredo, amami quant'io t'amo... Addio!" After it, the curtain should fall and the scene come to an end. There was no baritone present to register his opinion of cutting the most famous baritone aria Verdi ever wrote, and the scholars were too cowed to take on the diva.

From the point of view of Violetta, of course, Germont may be expendable, but it is less certain that from the point of view of Verdi's opera he can be summarily dismissed. *La traviata* is not the drama of a single character, and the interaction of Germont and Alfredo, father and son, is essential for our understanding of and emotional reaction to the entire work. Nonetheless, Callas neatly raised a crucial issue: what is the justification for eliminating entire numbers from an operatic score? [25] These omissions include, in Mozart's *Le nozze di Figaro* (to extend our range slightly), the arias for Marcellina and Basilio in the fourth act; in Rossini's *Il barbiere di Siviglia,* the Count's aria just before the finale; in Donizetti's *Lucia di Lammermoor,* the "Wolf's Crag" scene, a duet for Edgardo and Enrico that precedes Lucia's mad scene; in Donizetti's *Don Pasquale,* the servants' chorus in the third act. In the less standard repertory, similar cuts are often taken: in Donizetti's *Anna Bolena,* the great tenor aria "Vivi tu" disappears; in Rossini's *Tancredi,* the aria for Argirio at the start of the second act is snipped away, as is Lucia's aria in the second act of *La gazza ladra.*

Whether aware of it or not, upholders of such traditions in the performance of Italian opera are invoking—explicitly or implicitly—the work mentioned above that appeared in 1958 (in Italian only) under the names of Tullio Serafin and Alceo Toni: *Style, Traditions, and Conventions of Italian Opera of the Eighteenth and Nineteenth Centuries.* Their book was part of a series of defensive maneuvers undertaken by Casa Ricordi to respond to the charges, spearheaded by Denis Vaughan, that their printed scores of Verdi's operas were filled with mistakes. By invoking the myth of a continuous performance tradition, Serafin and Toni sought to justify then-current (1950s) practice as both authentic and ideal. Although the volume appeared under both names, a footnote specified that these observations were "transcribed directly from the precise words of Maestro Serafin" by Toni.[26] Because they reflect much of Serafin's own performance practice, we will refer to Serafin as the author. It is not my purpose to trace the roots of Serafin's ideas or to explore their relationship to practices from earlier in the twentieth century,[27] nor do I claim that he invented the procedures he embraces. Because of his prestige, however, and because he left both written and recorded testimony, he is a convenient point of reference.

Let us hear what Serafin has to say about the tradition of omitting the Count's aria, "Cessa di più resistere" from near the end of the second act of *Il barbiere di Siviglia:*

> The omitted scena and aria are really superfluous to the action, and Rossini himself may not have written them with complete conviction: perhaps, as usual, they merely accommodated a tenor's request for a show of bravura. In any event, this piece was omitted already starting with the first performances and was never again taken up. Rossini inserted part of it wholesale into *Cenerentola.*[28]

Notice that Serafin (1) makes an aesthetic judgment (the piece is "superfluous to the action"); (2) invokes an "authorial intention" ("Rossini may not have written it with conviction"); (3) posits a singer's preference ("a tenor's request for a show of bravura"); (4) claims a historical truth (the piece "was omitted already starting with the first performances and was never again taken up"); and (5) invokes another historical circumstance (Rossini reused part of the piece in *La Cenerentola*). Let us consider further each of these statements.

Is the piece "superfluous to the action?" It depends on how we perceive that action. Certainly the absence of any solo singing by a principal character from the lesson scene through the end of the opera (absent this aria) is most unusual, and the revelation delivered in *secco* recitative, "Il Conte d'Almaviva io sono" (I am the Count of Almaviva), only to be followed by more *secco* recitative, inevitably falls flat in performance. Dramaturgically, furthermore, what should be a crucial theatrical event, the public revelation of the Count's identity (with its parallelism to the moment he reveals himself to the officers in the first-act finale) is reduced to insignificance. Stage directors flounder helplessly to identify a nonmusical device that will give this moment weight, having the Count flash a medal or remove his cloak to reveal aristocratic clothes. Then again, even if one were to grant the superfluity of the aria to the action, in the strictest sense, a great deal of solo music in Italian opera is superfluous to the action, which often takes place in recitative or ensembles. Would the action of *Il barbiere di Siviglia* be different if Figaro didn't sing "Largo al factotum" or if

Berta omitted "Il vecchiotto cerca moglie?" Would the action of *Norma* be different if the priestess omitted "Casta Diva?"

Did Rossini *not* write the piece "with conviction"? There is no evidence to that effect. Not only is the autograph score beautifully written in every detail, but a most effective alteration in the score shows that he was paying close attention to its phrase structure. The Larghetto originally concluded with a four-measure cadential phrase, repeated with a variation.[29] Rossini subsequently determined that the repetition gave the cadence too much weight, and so he decided to present the phrase only once, sensitively altering the melodic line so that it would include elements of both the unadorned and the varied versions within a single four-measure phrase (example 8.1). Consider-

EXAMPLE 8.1. GIOACHINO ROSSINI, *IL BARBIERE DI SIVIGLIA*, RECITATIVO ED ARIA CONTE (N. 17), THE CONCLUSION OF THE CANTABILE, MM. 100–103.

ing how few structural alterations there are in the autograph manuscript of *Il barbiere,* it is impossible to assert that Rossini approached the Count's aria without conviction.

Did he write the aria simply to tickle the fancy of his tenor? There is no evidence whatsoever that Rossini felt his compositional interests to be at odds with the successful utilization of the best singers of his day. It was Rossini himself, after all, who not only brought the great Spanish tenor Manuel García from Naples to Rome to take the role of the Conte d'Almaviva (the opera's original title was *Almaviva,* not *Il barbiere di Siviglia*), but also imposed this expensive choice on the management of the Teatro Argentina.[30] For Rossini, the presence of García was a guarantee of artistic quality and an extraordinary compositional opportunity, not a trial to be overcome. Were modern conductors to omit every piece an Italian composer wrote to suit the talents of a star performer, they would be better advised to make yearly pilgrimages to Bayreuth.

What about the purported historical evidence: that the piece disappeared soon after its first performance and was never taken up again in *Il barbiere di Siviglia,* while Rossini soon reused most of it for his Neapolitan wedding cantata of April 1816, *Le nozze di Teti, e di Peleo,* and some of it for *La Cenerentola* in January 1817? Although the music develops somewhat differently in the three compositions, the first phrase is essentially identical in the two operas and cantata, except for its key (example 8.2).[31] While it is false to affirm that

EXAMPLE 8.2. GIOACHINO ROSSINI, *IL BARBIERE DI SIVIGLIA,* RECITATIVO ED ARIA CONTE (N. 17), FIRST PHRASE OF THE CABALETTA, MM. 127–130; *LE NOZZE DI TETI, E DI PELEO,* ARIA DI CERERE (N. 9), MM. 125–128; AND *LA CENERENTOLA,* FINALE SECONDO: CORO, E SCENA CENERENTOLA (N. 16), MM. 154–157.

the aria was never sung again in *Il barbiere di Siviglia* (we have librettos attesting to its use well into the 1820s, and it never disappeared from Italian printed editions of the opera), there *is* an interesting historical angle to explore. After its Roman premiere in February 1816, *Il barbiere* was revived twice that same year: at the end of the summer in Bologna and in the fall in Florence. All 1816 productions featured Geltrude Righetti-Giorgi as Rosina. After the Roman premiere, Manuel García disappeared from the cast, but "Cessa di più resistere" *was* sung in Bologna, though not by the Count. Instead, Righetti-Giorgi, clearly fond of the piece, appropriated it. (Another Rosina, Catterina Lipparini, did the same for performances in Venice in 1822.) Although "Cessa di più resistere" was omitted from the Florentine revival of 1816 (as were several other pieces)—these were the performances for which Pietro Romani wrote "Manca un foglio"—it was no accident that it reappeared in a revised form as the concluding number of *La Cenerentola,* first performed in Rome on 25 January 1817, in which the title role was assumed by none other than Righetti-Giorgi. What makes the story even more piquant is that, for a performance of *Il barbiere di Siviglia* in Trieste in 1821, another prima donna, Fanny Ekerlin, inserted the *Cenerentola* aria where "Cessa di più resistere" was originally sung.[32]

An attempt to discuss these issues rationally, though, fails to take Serafin's approach into account. His book is not a thoughtful effort to come to grips with historical problems but an apologia for his own artistic instincts (themselves a part of history), as sustained by an appeal to that limited part of the performance tradition with which he was familiar. Because he considered the omission of the aria traditional, Serafin saw no reason to understand its history. Further discussion existed merely to justify the tradition. That his statements are at best debatable and often false becomes irrelevant. Yet listen to the comments of an older generation of conductors when questions of this kind arise, fine and thoughtful musicians, such as Bruno Bartoletti, or those ruled by instincts developed in the 1960s, such as Zubin Mehta: they often mimic the sentiments of Serafin. A surprisingly analogous situation is found in the monumental, three-volume Rossini biography by Giuseppe Radiciotti, written between 1927 and 1929. This superb scholar was unable to recognize that his work betrayed all the prejudices of someone who had grown up knowing the later music of Verdi and the operas of Puccini, but very little Rossini. Reading Radiciotti's diatribes against the composer's vocal style, one wonders why he bothered writing about Rossini at all.[33] Someone so evidently upset by florid vocal lines should have devoted his studies to the operas of Giordano.

There are excellent reasons for eliminating the Count's aria from *Il barbiere di Siviglia,* but they are not the ones Serafin invoked. The single most important reason for cutting "Cessa di più resistere" is that few tenors can do it justice, and even those who might succeed are often exhausted by this point.[34] The evening is getting long, and it is surely not worth prolonging for an indifferent performance of that aria. Although its disappearance creates an emotional gap in the drama, Serafin is correct that no significant element of the plot is sacrificed. With the right combination of circumstances, including a distinguished and resilient tenor, a stylish and well-paced production, and an audience not running to catch the last train home, "Cessa di più resistere" can be effective and meaningful. And a theater, in order to obtain the services of a Rockwell Blake or a Juan Diego Flórez, may find itself with contractual obligations to include the piece. Ask the audience at the Metropolitan Opera who gave Flórez a standing ovation after his debut performance as Count Almaviva on 10 January 2002 whether or not the piece should be cut. On the other hand, when the circumstances are not right for the aria's inclusion, a cut may be appropriate. The question should be decided by analyzing the circumstances of a particular performance.

Where cuts are needed in operas written during the first three decades of the nineteenth century (and occasionally in later operas)—whether to reduce performance time, to assist a challenged singer, or to meet other particular conditions—cutting entire numbers is almost always less damaging than making internal cuts in those numbers. The numbers most likely to be omitted are usually bound to earlier dramaturgical paradigms. Many operatic texts from this period embody conventional modes carried over from the eighteenth century, the *convenienze* deplored by early nineteenth-century critics. Operatic dramaturgy in the first half of the nineteenth century focused ever more attention on primary characters and their interactions. Omitting compositions sung by secondary characters or by principal characters in subsidiary circumstances nudges a work forward along an idealized historical continuum, toward a time when pieces of this kind played an ever smaller role.

We can watch the historical process at work by examining operatic librettos written and set to music early in the century, then revised for later composers. Donizetti's *Don Pasquale* of 1842, for example, is derived from a libretto by Angelo Anelli, *Ser Marcantonio,* first set by Stefano Pavesi for the Teatro alla Scala in 1810.[35] (Anelli was also the author of the text for Rossini's *L'Italiana in Algeri.*) *Don Pasquale* contains an overture and thirteen musical numbers. Dramaturgically, it presents four characters: the elder Don Pasquale, who wishes to marry; his nephew, Ernesto, who fears losing his inheritance; his nephew's beloved, Norina; and Malatesta, doctor to Don Pasquale and friend to Ernesto, with whose help Norina is disguised as Sofronia, the pretended "sister" of Malatesta, and is presented to Don Pasquale as a perfect wife. After a feigned marriage ceremony, Norina makes Don Pasquale yearn for his days of bachelorhood. In Anelli's libretto for Pavesi, there are three additional characters. Ser Marcantonio (who becomes Don Pasquale) has not only a nephew (Medoro) but also a niece (Dorina). The niece is in love with the doctor figure (Tobia), and Bettina (the Norina character), loved by Medoro, is *actually* Tobia's sister. There are also two servants with solo parts (Lisetta and Pasquino).

All these characters must be given arias and duets. If one servant laughs at Ser Marcantonio's foibles, the other must laugh; if Medoro complains of his lot, Dorina must have her chance. As a result, *Ser Marcantonio* contains nineteen numbers plus an overture, six more than *Don Pasquale.* The only numbers in *Don Pasquale* that could be considered expendable on dramaturgical grounds are two short choruses of servants (although, to my mind, the quality of the second, in particular, makes its omission a grave error).[36] A revival of *Ser Marcantonio* in which some subsidiary banter is abbreviated would not have a negative impact on the most characteristic elements of Pavesi's music or the dramaturgy of his opera.[37]

It is not just that the history of Italian dramaturgy points away from the proliferation of secondary characters: composers themselves often treated the pieces for these characters as expendable. The strongest sign is that Rossini frequently allowed the *arie di sorbetto* of secondary characters or minor arias by principal characters to be composed by associates, often the very musicians who prepared the *secco* recitative. In the second act of *L'Italiana in Algeri,* two arias (for Lindoro and Haly) are by unknown musicians, the author of the Haly aria also being responsible for all the *secco* recitative.[38] Occasionally history provides us with a name: Luca Agolini for *La Cenerentola* and Giovanni Pacini for *Matilde di Shabran* (as we have seen in previous chapters), as well as the young Michele Carafa, who in 1818 supplied Faraone's first-act aria, "A rispettarmi apprenda," for *Mosè in Egitto.*[39]

In many cases, these pieces are omissible on musical and dramatic grounds: they are not by Rossini; they play no part in the essential fabric of the musical drama; and some (but by no means all) are artistically mediocre. Although Rossini occasionally replaced pieces set to music by associates with new music of his own composition (as he did with Faraone's aria from *Mosè in Egitto* and all of Pacini's arias for *Matilde di Shabran*), the dramaturgical issue remains unchanged. Indeed, on internal grounds alone, one could make similar judgments about a number of compositions prepared originally by

Rossini: the arias for Isaura and Roggiero in *Tancredi*, the aria for Amaltea in the 1818 version of *Mosè in Egitto* (which Rossini borrowed from one of his earliest operas, *Ciro in Babilonia*, then omitted when he revived *Mosè*, still for the Teatro San Carlo of Naples, in 1819).

But opera has always been more than a fabric of essential threads. Quite apart from the inherent musical quality of some of these pieces, there are pressing reasons why they cannot all be omitted. The charming Roggiero aria in *Tancredi*, "Torni alfin ridente, e bella," for example, is dramatically expendable and tries the patience of a modern audience after a long evening.[40] But several practical factors make its omission problematic. First, the singer playing Roggiero needs to participate in major ensembles: omitting the aria considerably reduces the pool of singers prepared to take the part. Equally important, the Roggiero aria separates a major duet for Tancredi and his beloved Amenaide from Tancredi's elaborate gran scena. The Roggiero aria both allows a set change to be prepared (the concluding scene of the opera is a spectacular vista of Sicily with Mount Etna in the background) and offers the mezzo-soprano time to rest. No modern singer who has assumed the role of Tancredi, including Marilyn Horne, has *ever* countenanced cutting the Roggiero aria.[41]

On the other hand, it is hard on aesthetic grounds to justify keeping the Albazar aria (written by Rossini's collaborator) in *Il Turco in Italia*.[42] The music is poor and the situation dramaturgically feeble. The aria, however, has two practical virtues. First, as in the case of the Aria Roggiero in *Tancredi,* it allows a theater to hire a better singer for the role, which many singers will refuse if they know the aria is to be cut. Second, it provides Don Narciso time to change his costume between his big aria (N. 11)—in which he announces that he will put in an appearance at the masked ball—and his actual arrival, in Turkish garb. With goodwill, such practical problems can be overcome. For the revival of *Turco* at Cremona and Milan in the spring of 1997, the first problem was solved by arranging for the tenor taking the part of Albazar to be hired for a few performances in the more important role of Don Narciso. The second problem wasn't resolved until the dress rehearsal, when an army of personnel from the costume department lay in wait for Paul Austin Kelly, the Narciso, after his aria and poured him into his new costume.

If we can avoid simplistic responses to the question of cutting individual numbers in modern performances of Italian operas, we can approach each situation with the necessary flexibility and sensitivity to the multiple and conflicting issues involved. The historical position of different works suggests different approaches. For Rossini, there are good reasons to countenance the omission of entire numbers; by the time of Verdi, where each number tends to have a precise role in the dramaturgical structure and emotional life of the opera, the practice makes less sense. The operas of Bellini and Donizetti sit between these poles. When we consider instead the matter of cuts internal to a musical number, however, the circumstances seem to reverse themselves, and the criteria we apply to operas written after about 1830 need to be very different from those applied to earlier compositions.

MAKING CUTS: PORTIONS OF A MUSICAL NUMBER

Performers of Italian opera have been making internal cuts in musical numbers since the operas were written, and it seems unlikely they will stop in the foreseeable future. Some of their reasons are frankly venal, a category that could be defined as "vanity cuts." We have already cited an example in the closing measures of Assur's "mad scene" in *Semiramide,* where Rossini wrote a four-measure, repeated cadential phrase in the orchestra, quoted from earlier in the composition, alternating two measures on the tonic and two measures on the dominant. By removing the measures on the dominant, the singer can sit on an interpolated high *f* while the orchestra chugs helplessly away on the tonic triad (see examples 6.3 and 6.4). The cut obscures Rossini's citation of a theme from earlier in the composition and produces a dull string of measures on the tonic that Rossini would never have written, all in the service of an interpolated and prolonged high note that singers during the first half of the nineteenth century would rarely have added.

But most cuts are not "vanity cuts." They stem from a sincere belief that omitting certain passages improves an opera. There are social arguments (in the modern theater, audiences listen to works differently from the way they did in the nineteenth century); aesthetic arguments (a section is musically weak); practical arguments (by the end of a duet, singers lack the strength to repeat a cabaletta theme yet again). The results, however, tend to have the same effect, and it is similar to the effect of cutting entire numbers in Rossini or Donizetti: they push the work, sometimes gently, sometimes roughly, further along the stylistic and historical continuum. Cuts that deform Rossinian symmetries make the operas sound more like Donizetti; cuts that tighten Donizettian dramaturgy make the operas sound more like early Verdi; cuts that eliminate cabalettas or cabaletta repeats in early and middle Verdi make the operas sound more like later Verdi.

It is instructive, once again, to read Serafin, whose pronouncements regarding cuts in the Verdi operas remain those most widely invoked by self-described traditionalists. The same explanations recur time and again. Serafin recommends cuts that "do not change the equilibrium of the formal design but serve to avoid pedestrian, absolutely useless repetitions"; but he neither defines what he means by equilibrium nor provides us with a method to differentiate "pedestrian, useless repetitions" from ingenious, useful ones. He recommends trimming cadenzas, which he calls "efflorescences provoked by exhibitionistic demands of singers," but provides no evidence that Verdi wrote such cadenzas with anything but complete conviction, however much the composer may have modified elements of his style in later years. He recommends eliminating entirely or shortening concluding cabalettas of arias, which are "of little musical worth" and are "inopportune, damaging the necessary, rapid, and natural development of the action." Serafin has rarely met a cabaletta that is either musically worthy or opportune.[43] In other words, if Verdi had only known better in 1850, he would have been writing *Otello*.

This will not do. The operas forming the so-called trilogy of Verdi's middle period (*Rigoletto, Il trovatore*, and *La traviata*) were written between 1850 and 1853, just before the composer turned forty and before his second appointment with the Paris Opéra—for the composition of *Les vêpres siciliennes*—left profound traces on his style.[44] Like all works of art, those three operas show some traits that to contemporaries would have seemed conservative and others that would have seemed progressive. If Verdi sought to aim his compositional style in 1850 toward a lack of repetition, the absence of vocal virtuosity, and a rapid development of the action, he failed miserably.

That does not mean Serafin's recommendations for cuts can be disregarded. Verdi himself, less than four years after the premiere of *Il trovatore*, revised the opera for a Parisian performance, where he cut the cabaletta of Leonora's aria at the beginning of the fourth act, "Tu vedrai che amore in terra."[45] The omission is suggestive, even if it reflects a concession to practical requirements and to Parisian musical taste. Yet the disappearance of the cabaletta leaves the other sections of the aria—its cantabile, "D'amor sull'ali rosee," and its *tempo di mezzo*, the famous "Miserere"—free-floating in a formally ambiguous ether within an opera largely tied to formal conventions of the period.[46] To these contrasting considerations, one must add an aesthetic judgment about the musical quality of the cabaletta, a dramaturgical judgment about its resonance within the story, and a practical awareness that all but the studiest singers may come to grief over this difficult moment. None of the alternatives—omitting the cabaletta entirely, reducing its length, or performing the score as Verdi conceived it—provides an ideal solution to the historical and aesthetic problem, but we are obliged to pose the dilemma in all its ambiguity.

The Operas of Rossini

The cabaletta in Verdi's operas, as with so many formal gestures Verdi was to abandon or profoundly transform during his later career, prolongs a practice established firmly in the operas of Rossini and carried on (with modifications) in the works of Bellini and Donizetti during the 1830s and early 1840s. A standard aria cabaletta consists of a theme, a short transition, and what is written as an exact repetition of the theme, followed by final cadences, often in phrases of decreasing length, each of which is immediately repeated. Similar forms held sway in ensembles, whether duets, trios, or principal finales (where they were referred to as strettas). Rossini did not invent the cabaletta. Indeed, efforts to assess priority in the use of cabalettas, crescendos, and other elements of the Rossinian formal arsenal, are unlikely to produce important results. What we can say with certainty is that at the start of his theatrical career, in 1810, Rossini used a variety of related forms to conclude a piece, as did his contemporaries. By the time he wrote *Semiramide* in 1823, the tradition of bringing practically every musical number in an opera to a close with a regular cabaletta was fully established. Rossini's operas so dominated the repertory that it was with reference to them that younger composers developed their style.

In Rossini, the cabaletta was tied to a crucial element of performance practice that remained operative through the 1830s but had been greatly reduced by 1850. The repetition of the theme and of cadential fragments provided opportunities for singers to ornament the melodic line, intensifying and personalizing its dramatic meaning and musical content. As we shall see, there is ample evidence that this practice was fully embraced by Rossini. Indeed, in a group of manuscripts Rossini himself showed singers the kind of interventions he considered appropriate. Manuscripts and printed books documenting the practice and teaching of important singers from the 1830s, such as Laure Cinti-Damoreau or Adelaide Kemble, demonstrate that ornamentation remained fundamental for the operas of Bellini and Donizetti.[47] While there may occasionally be practical motives for abbreviating cabalettas and cadential repetitions in Rossini operas, doing so contravenes artistic principles that he himself developed and that are at the heart of his style. Intelligent performers must find ways to make Rossini's leisurely formal schemes effective in the modern theater, just as they are doing for the operas of Handel.[48] Indeed, singers, stage directors, and conductors who find this task unappetizing should not perform Rossini's operas: denaturing them has persistently proved a sure recipe for failure.

EXAMPLE 8.3. GIOACHINO ROSSINI, *LE SIÈGE DE CORINTHE*, INTRODUCTION (N. 1), OPENING CHORUS (MM. 23–26) AND CLOSING CHORUS (MM. 228–231).

While clarity, a balance among parallel phrases, and formal coherence were fundamental stylistic qualities for Rossini, I am not suggesting that every cut within a musical number is equally disturbing. Let me suggest an operative principle: internal cuts in a Rossini number should not create a musical form different from what the composer uses elsewhere in the same work or in works from the same stylistic period.[49] This principle would exclude many cuts that disfigured the revival of *The Siege of Corinth* at La Scala in 1969. The most notorious occurred in the opera's introduction, a closed composition beginning and ending in E♭ *major*.[50] In a slow opening chorus, the Greeks, besieged by the Turks, seek counsel from their leader. After a trio in which the Greeks debate how to respond to the Turks, the introduction concludes with another choral movement, now quick, whose theme is a melodic transformation of the one previously heard (example 8.3). In this final chorus the Greeks swear to resist the forces of Mahomet or die fighting. In the Metropolitan revival, the movement was cut, leaving the shape and sense of Rossini's music in utter shambles. It is the kind of cut no one in the nineteenth century would *ever* have made.[51]

What kinds of internal cuts might be possible in Rossini? We have already discussed those the Metropolitan Opera made in 1989 in the choruses of *Semiramide,* reducing Rossini's more leisurely

A (orchestra) A (chorus) B (choral contrast) A (repeat of chorus)
cadential phrases

to the more concentrated

A (orchestra) A (chorus) cadential phrases,

a form the composer frequently used in his mature operas. On structural grounds there can be no quarrel with such a reduction; whether it is advisable to do so in any particular case depends on other factors.

We know that the composer himself was prepared for practical reasons to emend his scores in ways he could never have approved from a musical and dramaturgical perspective. Preparing the premiere of *Guillaume Tell,* for example, Rossini found that there was insufficient time during the orchestral introduction to the chorus that opens the second act to accomplish the complex action demanded by the mise-en-scène on the enormous stage at the Opéra: mimes carrying the carcasses of deer and wild boar, the chorus and extras (some of them on horseback) executing complex stage maneuvers before preparing to sing, and the rest of the court taking up positions.[52] Rossini decided during rehearsals to repeat the orchestral introduction, a formal practice unique in his operatic production.[53] The resulting form begins:

A (orchestra) A (orchestra) opening material (chorus) A (chorus).

This musically superfluous repetition of the orchestral introduction is not present in the autograph of the opera, nor in any source other than materials deriving from the French premiere. When Elizabeth Bartlet first prepared the manuscript of her new critical edition, which in principle takes as its main text the version of the opera performed under Rossini's direction in Paris, she placed this repeat directly in the score, marking it as a suggested cut. During the first performances of the new edition at La Scala in 1988, however, Riccardo Muti accepted the repeat, leaving the stage director, Luca Ronconi, trying desperately to invent appropriate action. After that experience, we removed the superfluous music from the score, mentioning the repeat in a footnote. A conductor might still decide to repeat those bars, but the edition does not encourage him to do so.

Similar problems surround other musical forms in Rossini operas. Under what circumstances, for example, is it legitimate to abbreviate the cabaletta of a duet? Rossini employed a number of different formal designs in these circumstances. Sometimes the theme is sung partly in counterpoint, partly in harmony by both characters, who then repeat it after a brief transition.[54] Sometimes the theme is sung by one character, then by the other; after a brief transition it is again heard twice, first sung by one, then by the other, but usually with the first character providing a counterpoint to this final appearance of the melody.[55]

A1 A2 trans. A1 A2+1.

While this formal procedure can be effective, as long as the first statement of the theme in the reprise is varied, Rossini in a duet in *Mosè in Egitto* restricted the theme to only two appearances, A1 followed by A1+2, after which the music proceeded directly to cadential material.[56] More interesting still is the way Rossini abbreviated a more leisurely structured duet from *Il viaggio a Reims* (for Corinna and Cavalier Belfiore) when he adapted it to be sung by

Comte Ory and the Comtesse Adèle. Having originally written a piece in the standard design (A1 A2 trans. A1 A2+1) for *Il viaggio a Reims*, when he reused it in *Le Comte Ory* he omitted the A1 after the transition, so that the cabaletta has the structure: A1 A2 trans. A1+2.[57] Were we to make a similar abbreviation in other duets, we would not be contradicting Rossini's own practice.

A full-length Rossini duet consists of a substantial opening section (*primo tempo*) of confrontation (Allegro), a cantabile (Andante), a short *tempo di mezzo* (transitional), and the concluding cabaletta (Allegro).[58] Rossini also wrote pieces he labeled "duettinos": sometimes they are in one lyrical section ("Vivere io non potrò" for Elena and Malcom in *La donna del lago* or the remarkable duettino in *Zelmira* accompanied only by English horn and harp); sometimes they resemble full-length duets minus the internal cantabile (as in the first-act duet for Semiramide and Arsace, in which, however, Rossini integrates into the first section some elements that might be appropriate for a cantabile).[59] In one case, Rossini composed a full-length duet, then decided for dramaturgical reasons to remove its cantabile: a moment of quiet reflection during the confrontation between Desdemona and Otello in the third act of *Otello*, at the end of which the Moor kills his wife, must have seemed out of place. In the autograph manuscript one can still see where pages were removed, and the original printed libretto even provides the words, but no copy of the music is known to survive.[60] Does this kind of evidence justify introducing an analogous cut into a full-length duet, not reduced by its author? Was Richard Bonynge justified in omitting the splendid cantabile "D'un tenero amore" of the Arsace-Assur duet in his 1966 recording of *Semiramide?*[61] Whatever our answer, this further bow to the primacy of his wife and prima donna, Joan Sutherland, did not sin against Rossinian style.

Similar problems, finally, can be raised concerning the cadential formulas that pepper Rossini's scores. A series of repeated cadential phrases (sometimes with variants internally), usually of decreasing length, concludes almost every lyrical solo or ensemble section in a Rossini opera. Here is a list, for example, of the cadential phrases in the first act of *L'Italiana in Algeri*:

N. 1: Introduzione	$2\times4 + 2\times4 + 2\times2 + 3\times1$
N. 2. Cavatina Lindoro	$2\times10 + 2\times5 + 2\times2 + 3\times1$
N. 3. Duetto Lindoro—Mustafà	$2\times2 + 2\times2 + 2\times2 + 3\times1$
N. 4. Coro e Cavatina Isabella	$2\times4 + 2\times1 + 2\times2 + 3\times1$
N. 5. Duetto Isabella—Taddeo	$2\times7 + 2\times2 + 3\times1$
N. 6. Aria Mustafà	$2\times6 + 2\times2 + 3\times1$
N. 7. Finale Primo	$2\times8 + 2\times5 + 4\times1$

As phrase length decreases, possibilities for melodic or harmonic individuality, already limited, become negligible: form becomes formula. Italian critics and audiences accepted this cadential convention without hesitation, but its reception north of the Alps was more equivocal. In commenting positively on many aspects of *Le Comte Ory,* for example, Berlioz scornfully remarked on "the famous Italian final cadence, the stupid, insipid formula, reproduced thirty or forty times in the two acts."[62] Here, too, the internal repetitions— at least in arias and duets—were not meant to *sound* the way they were *written:* the singer was expected to ornament repetitions, and there is abundant contemporary evidence—to be examined in chapter 9—documenting how this was done. Simply to remove the repetitions of each phrase leaves the music limpingly asymmetrical. If a modern performer wishes to abbreviate a cadential section, it is far preferable to remove entirely one phrase (with its repetition), but there should be a good, practical reason for making such a cut (a tiring singer, for example). The few seconds saved in performance need to be measured against the resulting sacrifice in the carefully established proportions of Rossini's art.

In the musical environment of Rossini's operas, making internal cuts in individual numbers is like printing a sonnet sequence and leaving out occasional lines. It can be done, of course, but what one loses is an integral element of the formal clarity that draws us to the works in the first place. If one tries to modify Rossini's music by pushing it too far along the stylistic continuum, it will resist and ultimately lose its distinctive character. Far better to eliminate entire numbers and play the music one does choose to play as Rossini conceived it.

Donizetti and Bellini

By the 1830s, the situation had changed markedly. The concern for musical balance and formal symmetry, so essential to Rossini, became less pressing. It is not sufficient simply to listen to an opera or examine a printed edition to understand this phenomenon. What reveal it most clearly are the autograph manuscripts of operas by Bellini and Donizetti. Again and again, these composers wrote musical numbers following Rossinian patterns, then thought better of it, tightened up the dramatic motion, crossed out internal repetitions, eliminated cadential formulas, and rewrote cabalettas to vary their formal shape. Unlike the almost pristine clarity of the autograph manuscripts of Rossini and Verdi, those of Bellini's *Il pirata* and *Norma* or Donizetti's *Anna Bolena* and *Don Pasquale* show the composers in furious struggle with their material. Their music, as a result, can be decidedly out of balance, often suggesting Rossinian models while denying their proportions. Donizetti, in particular, used various techniques to sacrifice Rossinian formal balance to dramatic intensity. He would draft the final vocal cadence of a passage, following it a measure later by a new idea in the orchestra, then elide the cadence and the new idea so that the music feels more continuous. He would prepare an orchestral introduction to a solo melody, then eliminate measures of harmonic preparation or repeated repetitions of the tonic (what jazz singers refer to as "vamp until ready"). He could be ruthless with the cadential section of a solo aria, instinctively writing a cadential design à la Rossini, then crossing out a unit or eliminating internal repetitions. After devising well-behaved cabalettas, he forced them into asymmetries.[63]

Sometimes Donizetti would enter into the heart of a solo passage and excise what seemed to him its *longueurs*. In her aria in *Anna Bolena*, Giovanna Seymour, having admitted to the King that she still loves him, begs him to spare Anna's life. Donizetti originally opened this scene with a full orchestral introduction, anticipating the main theme of the cantabile "Per questa fiamma indomita." Later he eliminated the orchestral introduction, except for one measure of vamp: presumably he did not want Giovanna, who has not yet begun her plea, to indulge in a staring match with Enrico while the orchestra goes about its business. For the cantabile he originally drafted an arch design (ABCB'D), with A (the principal theme) and D (the cadential phrase) balancing one another. Having orchestrated the entire melody, however, Donizetti crossed out all of B' and half of D. The resulting cantabile is rhythmically undifferentiated (one of the sections he omitted is the only one that had provided rhythmic variety) and harmonically unbalanced, but Donizetti apparently preferred this structure to the regularity of his original idea.[64] Whether we find the result thoroughly satisfactory will depend on where we place ourselves historically with respect to *Anna Bolena;* there is no absolute answer.

Donizetti himself cut the choral movement that begins *Anna Bolena* in precisely the same way that the Metropolitan Opera cut the analogous section in *Semiramide*. Although the longer *Anna Bolena* chorus was entirely orchestrated, Donizetti abbreviated it before the opera was copied or printed. Only in the autograph does one realize that the chorus was conceived as:

A (orchestra) A (chorus) B (contrast) A' (partial reprise of chorus)
$$\text{cadential phrases.}$$

The extended form is used with great subtlety. In the first choral presentation (A), the courtiers sing in whispered fragments about Enrico's growing disaffection with Anna and his new love for another, while the principal melodic material is carried by the orchestra. The contrasting section (B) is striking for a new rhythmic figure in the accompaniment, dynamic contrasts, and a dependence on diminished-seventh chords. The partial reprise (A') continues the accompanimental rhythm in strings and timpani, while the chorus—foretelling Anna's fate—is finally assigned the principal melody. However effective this piece was as an opening to the opera and an inventive use of the typical Rossinian choral structure, Donizetti attacked its regularity by slashing and burning his way through individual phrases, thereby reducing it to:

A (orchestra) A (chorus) cadential phrases.

And so the piece has always been known. Impatient modern musicians did not have to wield their scissors: Donizetti had already done the job.

Making small internal cuts in Donizetti's operas, following the practice of the composer himself, then, is less damaging than doing the same thing with the music of Rossini. There is a wonderful letter from Donizetti to Luigia Boccabadati, preserved in the Nydahl collection (Stiftelsen Muikkulturens Främjande) in Stockholm, written on 8 September 1836. In it, the composer suggests to the singer a whole range of possible cuts in his *Lucrezia Borgia.* Referring to one of the choruses, for example, he urges, "Take out useless repetitions," sounding practically like Serafin. Nonetheless, even in the operas of Donizetti and Bellini such cuts need to be accomplished with sensitivity. When many of the major Italian operas of the 1830s first returned to the operatic stage as vehicles for the art of singers like Maria Callas, Joan Sutherland, and Beverly Sills, it seemed easy to snip out large chunks of music not associated with the divas or obeying formal conventions considered expendable. Recordings made in the 1950s and early 1960s document this practice, and one of the several recordings (some official, some pirated) made of performances of *Norma* with Maria Callas (this one with Christa Ludwig as Adalgisa and Franco Corelli as Pollione), under the baton of Tullio Serafin, gives some sense of how the cutting was accomplished.[65]

Norma is the story of a Druid priestess in love with a conquering Roman proconsul (Pollione), and mother of his two children, who is rejected for a younger initiate of the temple of Irminsul (Adalgisa). First performed at the Teatro alla Scala of Milan on 26 December 1831, *Norma* brings together many dramatic themes that dominate Italian opera: love, jealousy, friendship, conflict between nations, motherhood, and sacrifice.[66] Bellini was particularly taken with his heroine and lavished on her some of the finest music he was ever to compose. Furthermore, in writing to the singer who would be his first Norma, Giuditta Pasta, he insisted that the role was "encyclopedic," that it made a wide range of vocal and emotional demands on the heroine, surely one of the reasons why generations of prima donnas have been attracted to the opera.[67] A great Norma must be convincing not only in her prayer to the chaste goddess of the moon ("Casta Diva"), but also in the furious jealousy with which she accuses Pollione, the understanding and empathy she shows to the unfortunate Adalgisa, and the declamation with which she contemplates murdering her sleeping children. Writing about Pasta's performance in the latter scene during a summer 1832 revival of *Norma* in Bergamo, Bellini remarked, "She sings and declaims in a way that draws forth tears . . . Even I wept! . . . And I wept for all those many emotions I felt in my soul."[68] When shortly before his untimely death in 1835 Bellini contemplated a revision of his score, his plan was to prepare "a new cavatina and aria for Valini [Pollione]; a duet between him and Adalgisa in the first act, replacing the original one, which is cold; a piece for Lablache [in the role of Oroveso, Norma's father] in the second act, either a [solo] scene or a duet; and finally a new overture, as well as retouching the instrumentation here and there."[69] Did the composer realize that this list of pieces includes every number of the opera (with the exception of the brief introduction to the first act) in which Norma does not appear? But the revision was not to be, and the *Norma* we know today is, for the most part, the work Bellini composed in 1831.

Bellini prepared his opera with care. There are many melodic sketches, rejected passages in skeleton score, internal modifications in the autograph manuscript.[70] But *Norma*, too, was composed at a particular historical moment, and later musicians felt a strong urge to abbreviate its contents, particularly by eliminating "unnecessary" repetitions. Serafin's procedures are typical of the 1950s, and they continue to be imitated by conductors and singers who grew up listening to those performances, either in the theater or on recordings.

Some cuts fall into precise categories. When Bellini wrote (and left intact) a standard cabaletta in a solo aria, Serafin usually eliminates the transition after the first statement of the theme and the repetition of that theme. This happens to Pollione's cabaletta in the first scene of the opera, "Me protegge, me difende," and to the cabaletta following Norma's hymn to the moon, "Ah! bello a me ritorna." Bellini would not have expected these cuts. More likely, a singer would have ornamented the reprise, as in the operas of Rossini.[71] Likewise, in repeated cadential units of decreasing length, Serafin omits one or more phrases in Norma's cabaletta, the duet for Adalgisa and Pollione, the duet for Norma and Adalgisa in the second act, and even the duet for Norma and Pollione that opens the finale of the opera. Most of these cuts are not disruptive.

We must remember, after all, that Bellini had *already* made numerous and elaborate cuts in his autograph manuscript, adjusting the musical and dramatic proportions better to reflect his 1831 perspective. In the first-act finale, for example, a canonic movement for Norma, Adalgisa, and Pollione begins with Norma's "Oh! di qual sei tu vittima." As Bellini originally conceived this scene, it continued with Adalgisa singing the same melody (Norma providing an accompaniment), followed by Pollione doing the same (Adalgisa adopting what Norma had sung to accompany her, and Norma introducing additional material). Cadential phrases brought the section to a close. Formal procedures of this kind were common during the 1810s and 1820s.

Norma (A)	Norma (B)	Norma (C)	cadential phrases
	Adalgisa (A)	Adalgisa (B)	cadential phrases
		Pollione (A)	cadential phrases

In the course of the original season, Bellini eliminated the Adalgisa statement of the melody, so that the passage goes directly from one voice to three.[72] Rossini seems to have made a similar cut in a standard canonic movement for three voices in *Maometto II* (1820), when he revised it for *Le Siège de Corinthe* (1826).[73]

Likewise, in the duet for Norma and Adalgisa that opens the first-act finale, Bellini originally built his cabaletta with a theme for Norma ("Ah! sì, fa core e abbracciami"), followed by an exact repeat for Adalgisa ("Ripeti, o ciel, ripetimi"). A brief transition leads to a repetition sung by both together, with Norma taking the melody and Adalgisa providing an extensive accompaniment. At a later moment, probably during the opening season, Bellini himself removed the transition and the repeat, developing a part for Norma during Adalgisa's solo to make up for the resulting lack of a true passage a due.[74] If Bellini hadn't been there already, Serafin would surely have jumped in.

Still, it is important to be sensitive to more than the melodic distinction of a passage. In the cabaletta of the duet for Adalgisa and Pollione, for example, Bellini wrote a theme for Pollione ("Vieni in Roma"), begging Adalgisa to follow him; this theme is repeated immediately by Adalgisa as an aside ("Ciel! così parlar"), in which she expresses her uncertainty about what to do. The composer toyed with transitional material between the two presentations, but ultimately continued directly to Adalgisa's statement of the melody.[75] A brief "Più mosso," melodically undistinguished, provides contrast and gives Pollione a chance to plead more energetically. It leads back *not* to a repetition of the main theme, but to a passage using its tempo, with brief, strangled phrases for the lovers. Adalgisa finally agrees to join him, motivating a single reprise of the cabaletta theme, with a new text and the voices in alternation. Brief cadential phrases ("Più vivo assai"), including a reprise of the "Più mosso" for orchestra, close the duet. Serafin omitted the "Più mosso" and the reference to it in the final orchestral cadences. While the latter cut is harmless, the former leaves an unsatisfactory structure. What should have functioned as a contrast, by virtue of the change of tempo and character, disappears. Instead the music moves directly from Adalgisa's strophe to the *same* tempo for her change of heart—which is therefore musically and dramaturgically unmotivated. Everything seems woven from the same undifferentiated cloth. Even if the music Serafin cut is trivial (it certainly isn't inspired), the omission disturbs the shape of the piece. Whether what is gained in terms of the raw emotion of Adalgisa's situation justifies the omission is something each interpreter needs to face individually.

The worst detail of this recording, though, comes near the end of the first act. Bellini worked over his conclusion intensively. Not only do there exist many sketches and drafts; there were even crucial changes between the first printed edition and all later ones, changes the publisher, Ricordi, attributed explicitly to the composer. Most obvious is the introduction of an offstage chorus of druids (together with a stage band) at the end of the act,[76] but detailed modifications in the cabaletta deeply touch the structure of the music. David Kimbell has argued that Bellini's earliest published version of this passage is so much more interesting than the modified version that it should be favored in modern performances.[77] The inclusion of this earlier version in Parma during the spring of 2001 demonstrated the theatrical viability of a conclusion to the first act of *Norma* that focuses exclusively and equally on the three protagonists of the opera, with no external chorus to distract attention from their plight. Since Serafin did not have access to this version, however, I will restrict myself to the less radical but still unusual music known from modern printed editions.

Norma and Adalgisa have just learned that Adalgisa's suitor is none other than Norma's lover and father of her children, Pollione. He protests that he loves only Adalgisa; Adalgisa asserts that she can never accept the hand of a traitor; the furious Norma lashes out at both of them. Norma begins the final "Allegro agitato assai" of the act alone, in a tormented passage of short melodic fragments in *G minor* ("Vanne, sì: mi lascia, indegno"). The music arrives on the dominant, then shifts to a glorious melody in *G major* ("Te sull'onde, e te sui venti"), where she vows that her fury will pursue him everywhere, on the waves, in the wind. In its definitive version,[78] this melody consists of

EXAMPLE 8.4. VINCENZO BELLINI, *NORMA*, SCENA E TERZETTO FINALE (N. 5),
THE MAJOR MODE THEME IN THE FINAL ENSEMBLE.

a four-measure antecedent phrase (ending on the tonic), a more cadential four-measure consequent phrase (with a strong arrival at the high *g*), which shifts to the relative minor at the last moment, and an even more powerful two-measure conclusion that brings the tune to its highest point, *a,* before settling back to the tonic (example 8.4).[79]

There is no transition. The repetition of this minor/major cabaletta theme begins immediately, but the *G-minor* theme is sung now by Pollione, with Adalgisa providing counterpoint. He insists that his love for Adalgisa is stronger than himself and she asks for "mari e monti" (seas and mountains) to be placed between her and the traitor. After the arrival on the dominant, the four-measure antecedent of the *G-major* melody is sung by all three in unison. At this point Bellini strikingly modifies his earlier procedure. The four-measure consequent (closing on the tonic, *not* on the relative minor) and the two-measure conclusion is sung only by Adalgisa and Pollione. Before the theme comes to a cadence, though, Bellini assigns to Norma alone the four-measure consequent (ending on the tonic), so that there is no rest, as her furious curse on their love keeps the tension building. Then he assigns this same desperate phrase to Pollione, also overlapping Norma's statement. Only at that point do the "sacred bronzes" sound from the temple and the druids sing from inside on a diminished-seventh chord, the act rapidly proceeding to its conclusion (example 8.5). The overlapping repetitions of Norma and Pollione are marked "rinforzando sempre e stringendo" (always getting louder and faster). Introducing these unusual repetitions is how Bellini built tension in the scene and focused the conflict at the end where it belongs, on Norma and Pollione. And what does Serafin do? He cuts both overlapping repetitions (the third

EXAMPLE 8.5. VINCENZO BELLINI, *NORMA*, SCENA E TERZETTO FINALE (N. 5), THE OVERLAPPING STATEMENTS OF THE PRINCIPAL MELODY BEFORE THE FINAL CADENCES.

through the eighth measures in example 8.5), leaving what amounts to an identical repetition of the way the *G-major* conclusion to the cabaletta theme was heard the first time, when Norma sang it alone. He has reduced Bellini's carefully planned variant to banality.

Even if we accept the principle that some cuts in Bellini and Donizetti are legitimate, following the practice of the composers themselves, we must not overlook their *use* of repetition. To throw out the way in which Bellini constructed this scene to reach a powerful conclusion, thereby returning his music to the most common conventional structure, is perverse. But that is where the hunt for extraneous measures took Serafin in this recording of *Norma*. Unless we think about Bellini's music with sensitivity, we can easily follow Serafin into that artistic wasteland.

The Operas of Verdi

Verdi's career as a composer for the theater lasted some fifty-five years, a long time by any measure. When he produced his first opera at the Teatro alla Scala in 1839, Donizetti had not yet written *La favorite* or *Don Pasquale;* when he produced his final opera at the same theater in 1893, Puccini's *Manon Lescaut* had just had its premiere in Turin. From the moment *Nabucco* was performed in 1842 until the premiere of *Falstaff* more than fifty years later, every new Verdi opera was an event in the Italian and European musical spectrum, and many "made history" in the sense that they changed contemporary perspective on the nature of Italian opera. With the possible exception of a very few operas written under difficult circumstances during the 1840s, there is no evidence that Verdi wrote his music with less than complete commitment. No singer imposed his or her will on Verdi (even though the composer was mindful of their abilities and needs); no librettist escaped his insistent request for revisions.

Around him, however, other histories were being made, most particularly the Wagnerian history of music-drama and its Italian reception. And, as is the fate of every artist with a long career, Verdi saw himself hailed as an innovator, exalted as the supreme master of the art, and scorned as an old codger who stood in the way of progress in the arts. When *Aida* had its premiere in 1871, some contemporary critics shouted scandal because individual scenes have concluding sections that function as cabalettas, even if their form is treated with considerably more freedom than in Verdi's earlier operas. In private correspondence Verdi defended the continued viability of the cabaletta convention, but he was stung by the criticism.[80] How could he not have been? He had lived to see many of his early works treated as superannuated relics.

Nabucco, read as a drama of the Italian Risorgimento, escaped; a heavily cut *Ernani* continued to circulate occasionally; and the surviving canon skipped to the trilogy of the early 1850s.

As with Rossini, Serafin and Toni provided their intolerant vision of Verdi's three most beloved operas in the starkest terms. They loved these works when they seemed to adumbrate the future and loathed them when they were rooted in the past. Rather than accepting the particular moment in history to which *Rigoletto, Il trovatore,* and *La traviata* belonged, they recommended extensive cuts to create a more continuous dramaturgy, à la Puccini.[81] Rigoletto's second-act aria, "Cortigiani, vil razza dannata," was their ideal. It is constructed in three continuous and interrelated sections: a passionate "Andante mosso agitato" in *C minor,* in which the jester lashes out at the courtiers and attempts to enter the room in which the Duke and Gilda are locked; a "Meno mosso" in *F minor,* where, in tears, Rigoletto pleads with Marullo, the most responsive of the group; and finally a lyrical cantabile in *Db major,* "Miei signori, perdono, pietate," where he begs them to give him back his daughter to an accompaniment featuring arpeggios in the solo cello and a poignant English horn doubling the melody at the sixth. The order of these sections is determined not by convention (cantabile, *tempo di mezzo,* cabaletta) but by dramaturgical necessity. Verdi moves the music where he feels it must go.[82] While the phrase structure and melodic shape are quintessentially Verdian, the underlying conception shows a willingness to respond to the exigencies of the drama that marks the maturing composer. There are many equally splendid and innovative moments throughout *Rigoletto, La traviata,* and even *Il trovatore.*

Are we supposed to believe, then, that the composer fell asleep when he wrote the second-act aria for the Duke in *Rigoletto,* not to mention the major arias for Violetta, Alfredo, and Germont in *La traviata?* Each concludes with a formal cabaletta: a cabaletta theme, a short instrumental transition, a repeat of the theme, and concluding cadences. (In the Germont cabaletta, only the second half of the theme is repeated, a technique amply represented in early Rossini.) The repetition of the theme is justified dramaturgically only in the case of Violetta, who hears (or imagines) a reprise of Alfredo's "Di quell'amor" from offstage. Sure enough, "Sempre libera" is the one cabaletta in *La traviata* that usually escapes the scalpel. In the Serafin and Toni universe, however, it is not just the orchestral transition and ensuing repetition of the other cabaletta themes that must be removed: the entire sections are consigned to operatic oblivion.

No one would deny that the only one of these four cabalettas to rise to genius, musically and dramaturgically, is "Sempre libera." But each cabaletta has its musical and dramatic role, and omitting them entirely leaves gaping holes. The Duke learns from the courtiers in the *tempo di mezzo* of his aria that Gilda is in the palace. Instead of reacting with "Possente amor," he bounds offstage like a panting schoolboy. Alfredo learns from the maid, Annina, that Violetta is selling her possessions to support their country idyll. Instead of expressing his emotions in "Oh mio rimorso! oh infamia!" he hops the next stagecoach to Paris. Germont's nostalgic "Di Provenza il mar, il suol" is followed by a more direct plea from father to son in the cabaletta, "No, non udrai rimproveri." Not allowing the young man a moment to interact with his father, the cut propels Alfredo on his second headlong departure of the act (when he sees Flora's letter of invitation to her party). It is a bit comic in the best of circumstances; coming directly after the cantabile, it is intolerable.

Without their cabalettas, these scenes become a series of disconnected lyric moments, with no focus or closure. They make no structural sense and often no dramatic sense. There have been times in the history of Italian opera performances, particularly between the 1940s and 1960s, when such niceties seemed irrelevant, but I feel little nostalgia for those practices, however much I continue to love many voices associated with them. Thus, except for cases in which the repetition of the cabaletta theme is motivated musically or dramaturgically, I have long felt that the cabaletta problem in middle Verdi is best resolved by singing the cabaletta theme once and cutting to the cadential phrases. The themes themselves are worthy (especially when sung well), and by including them it is possible to maintain the basic dramatic and musical shape of the scenes, without insisting on the repetition structure of the traditional cabaletta, whose raison d'être seems slippery in the absence of the kind of ornamentation they were meant to receive.[83] I admit freely that what I advocate is pushing these works a bit forward in the historical continuum, toward a time when Verdi maintained the function of the cabaletta but not its typical structure. Push too far (by eliminating them altogether) and the remaining sections are disembodied dramaturgical and musical fragments; don't push at all (by performing them complete, without ornamentation) and the repetitions seem mechanical. Nor do I find my own solution ideal: the resulting pieces often seem short, and their proportions are not quite right. Yet each new production of an opera has its own needs, and even in the case of these cabalettas an individual response is preferable to a rigid methodology. As long as we perform Italian opera, these problems will never be definitively resolved: they will continue to demand thoughtful solutions from performers.

Cuts within cabalettas are responses to the particular historical valence of the cabaletta in the early 1850s, and they do not justify eliminating every repeated passage in a Verdi opera. The situation is quite different, for example, with two other passages frequently omitted in *La traviata,* the second strophes of Violetta's "Ah! fors'è lui," the cantabile of her first-act aria, and "Addio del passato," her aria at the beginning of the final act. These passages have a structure that is less typical, but hardly unknown, in nineteenth-century Italian opera: two parallel strophes; they belong to the *romanza* tradition.[84] Each of the *La traviata* strophes in both compositions begins in a minor key and concludes in the parallel major (the third-act *romanza* brings each strophe back to the minor at the very end). The text of the section in minor is independent in the two strophes, projecting a different dramatic quality, while that in the major is either the same (in "Addio del passato") or repeats crucial words ("Ah! fors'è lui"), thereby underlining the parallelism between the strophes. *Romanze* of this kind were particularly important among the countless songs written to be sung by amateurs in music making at home.

While Rossini used *romanze* only rarely in his operas (Mathilde's "Sombre forêt" from *Guillaume Tell* is his masterpiece in this genre), a similar strophic structure underlies one of Donizetti's most beloved compositions, "Una furtiva lagrima," Nemorino's *romanza* from *L'elisir d'amore.* Donizetti, however, allows himself considerable freedom in composing this piece. The text consists of two parallel strophes, each with five *settenari* and a concluding *quinario:*

Una furtiva lagrima	A furtive tear
Negl'occhi suoi spuntò:	Glistened in her eyes:
Quelle festose giovani	Those happy youths
Invidiar sembrò:	She seemed to envy:
Che più cercando io vo?	What more am I looking for?
M'ama, lo vedo.	She loves me, I can see.
Un solo istante i palpiti	To feel for a single instant
Del suo bel cor sentir!...	The beating of her beautiful heart!...
I miei sospir confondere	To mix my sighs
Per poco a' suoi sospir!...	For a moment with her sighs!...
Cielo, si può morir;	Heavens, I could die then,
Di più non chiedo.	I ask nothing more.

As in the classic *romanza,* the musical setting of each strophe begins with basically the same melody, in B♭ minor, but Donizetti introduced slight variants between the strophes. For example, while the accompaniment is identical for "Invidiar sembrò" in the first strophe and "Per poco a' suoi sospir" in the second, the melody in the second strophe is deliciously modified to introduce descending motion by step, a melodic detail that has been associated with the "sospir" (sigh) throughout the history of vocal music. (Later, as we shall see in chapter 9, Donizetti prepared even more elaborate ornamentation for the second strophe.)

Each strophe concludes in the major, but Donizetti gave his melodic instincts free reign even when this meant modifying the poetic structure. At the end of the first strophe, the music moves to the relative major (*D♭ major*) for "M'ama, lo vedo" (which he rendered as "M'ama, sì, m'ama, lo vedo, lo vedo" in order to obtain sufficient text for his musical needs). In the second, where Donizetti wanted an even longer passage in the *parallel* major (*B♭ major*), he continued to use all the music of the minor section but arranged it so that only the first four *settenari* were declaimed to this music (rather than all five, as in the first strophe), with many internal repetitions of words. Thus, both the last *settenario* and the *quinario* of the second stanza were available for the concluding major passage, allowing a more expansive conclusion for the second strophe, with a final cadenza to bring the number to a close. With this kind of formal manipulation defining Donizetti's art, it is impossible to reduce "Una furtiva lagrima" to a single strophe.

Verdi's treatment of the form in *La traviata* is more regular, and snipping out one of the two strophes is consequently more easily done. But why would one *want* to do it? Here are some reasons I have heard expressed:

1. *Everything significant is heard the first time: there is no reason to repeat it.* I find this a singularly unconvincing argument. Try it on Dietrich Fischer-Dieskau, who regularly colored each strophe of a song in Schubert's *Die schöne Müllerin* differently. The texts of Verdi's sections in minor are entirely different in the two strophes, and anyone sensitive to the interaction of words, music, and dramatic action can make us hear the melody in a new way. The two strophes of "Addio del passato" are particularly diverse: in the first, Violetta sings of her lost dreams of happiness and the absence of Alfredo; in the second, the mood turns even darker, as she starkly describes her fate ("no tear or flower will mark my grave, no cross with my name will cover these bones"). Furthermore, Verdi wrote quite different expressive marks in his autograph manuscript for the two strophes, providing a singer with ample suggestions for characterizing each strophe.[85]

2. *Singing both strophes tires out a singer.* An opera singer undertaking a major Verdi role should not be excessively tired by two strophes of a largely quiet and relatively short melody sitting firmly in her middle register, even if it requires great concentration and mastery to sing it well. But for many a young singer, the truth is that she has been told by her teacher (whose own teacher heard it from someone else) that she should cut as much as possible

so as to prepare for that greatest of moments in *La traviata* when she interpolates a high *e♭* as the penultimate note of "Sempre libera." Better still, why doesn't our Violetta sit out the act, and sing a few high *e♭* at the end, allowing the audience to react as if she were a contestant in the high jump in the Olympics? I am willing to admit the possible virtues of vocal athleticism and can even accept that particular *e♭* (another subject for the next chapter), but not at the price of denaturing Verdi's score.

3. *Verdi wrote two strophes because he was obeying a tired convention, and we need to save him from himself.* This argument returns us to *La traviata* as *verismo,* a false path. Verdi was indeed obeying a convention, but two-strophe arias, cantabiles, or *romanze* are relatively rare in his operas, hardly a dying breed like the full cabaletta. Who are some of the characters who sing them? Well, there is François I, the French king. While he may have become the Duke of Mantua in *Rigoletto* (when Verdi was forced to change the setting), he never lost his Gallic charm: "Questa o quella" and "La donna è mobile" are both strophic songs, popular and elegant in style. Another figure characterized by *romanze* is the page, Oscar, in the *very* French court of Gustavo III of Sweden (also known as Riccardo, Governor of Boston) in *Un ballo in maschera:* "Volta la terrea" and "Saper vorreste" both grow out of the tradition of *couplets* in opera (particularly *opéra-comique*) and *romances* in the drawing room that dominated musical life in midcentury Paris. Verdi's choices in *La traviata,* in short, were not casual.

In nineteenth-century Italian opera, in fact, the *romanza* in particular and strophic forms in general often had the character of French imports.[86] By employing this form for both of Violetta's solo cantabile moments (not to mention Germont's "Di Provenza il mar, il suol"), Verdi has added important elements to her characterization: a simple vocal style that escapes sentimentality through the composer's art, and a Parisian identity integral to the opera. The story of Marguerite Gauthier was a *French* story. Even when he was compelled for the premiere to place the story back at the end of the previous century (rather than treat it as a contemporary tale of mid-nineteenth-century vintage), Verdi never considered moving it to another location.

If we believe in Verdi's *La traviata* and not some image of it seen through a late nineteenth-century lens, Violetta needs to sing both strophes of both her *romanze.* Once they are regularly heard performed well, arguments for their omission will dissolve. That does not rule out other small cuts that can be made in *La traviata,* as well as in *Rigoletto* and *Il trovatore.* Many cadential phrases in lengthy duets, for example, are repeated in Verdi's scores. I rather like hearing them twice, but little is lost by omitting some of these repetitions.

Less acceptable is the habit of snipping away parts of the cadenzas Verdi wrote in those same duets. There is nothing superfluous in the efflorescence of the linked voices of Gilda and the Duke in the cadenza at the end of the cantabile of their duet: What authorizes Serafin to claim that Verdi surrendered to base instincts when he wrote that glorious cadenza *a due?*[87] Unless there are strong, practical reasons for trimming his scores (such as the inability of singers to keep a cadenza in tune), my general instinct is to trust Verdi.

VERDI'S *MACBETH:* THE OLD AND THE NEW

But Verdi himself occasionally fell into the very trap I have been describing, and it is fitting to conclude these two chapters on versions and cuts by examining the two versions he himself prepared of an opera he particularly loved, *Macbeth.* The operatic world of nineteenth-century Italy did not welcome, as we do, the coexistence of historically disparate styles in a repertory. As some of his mature operas fell out of fashion, Verdi sought to rescue them by bringing them up to date and removing the most blatant traces of an earlier style: *Stiffelio* of 1850 became *Aroldo* in 1857; *Macbeth* of 1847 was revisited in 1865; *Simon Boccanegra* of 1859 was heavily recast in 1881, with Boito's assistance; even the relatively late *La forza del destino* and *Don Carlos,* of 1862 and 1867, respectively, were the object of revisions in 1869 and 1884. The motivations behind each of these revisions were slightly diverse: the heavily censored *Stiffelio* could not be performed as Verdi originally planned it; *Macbeth* was revised for Parisian performance almost twenty years after its Italian premiere; *Simon Boccanegra,* despite its many strengths, had ceased to circulate, and Verdi used its revision to test a possible collaboration with Boito; the altogether bleak conclusion of the St. Petersburg *La forza del destino* never fully satisfied the composer; and the French *Don Carlos* required more than a translated text to circulate easily in Italian theaters. These revisions provide interesting examples of how the composer himself, in revising an opera, would attempt to nudge an earlier work along the historical and stylistic spectrum to rescue it from oblivion. But rarely are the revisions altogether successful, despite critical efforts—even by such superb Verdians as Julian Budden—to show that they inhabit the best of all possible worlds. However much Verdi worked over a score, the seams between the old and the new always showed.

The two versions of Verdi's *Macbeth* have already been discussed briefly in the previous chapter. When the first version, performed at the Teatro della Pergola of Florence in March 1847, was revised for performance at the Théâtre Lyrique of Paris in April 1865, Verdi carried on an elaborate correspondence about the project with his Italian and French publishers, representatives of the theater, and various friends and colleagues. Recall how the composer had described the first version of *Macbeth* in 1847 and 1848: dedicating the vocal score to his father-in-law, Antonio Barezzi, he called *Macbeth* the opera "which I love in preference to my other operas"; warning Vincenzo Flauto, impresario at the Teatro San Carlo in Naples, of the difficulties he would face in staging the opera, he wrote that "I hold this opera in greater regard than my others."[88] In short, the 1847 *Macbeth* was an opera of which Verdi was intensely (and justifiably) proud.

When the idea of a performance in French at the Théâtre Lyrique was raised in 1864 by Verdi's French publisher, Léon Escudier, first in a letter, then in a visit to the composer in Genoa during the month of June, the composer was asked simply to prepare "three *airs de ballet*," to adjust *Macbeth* to French taste.[89] Looking over his opera from the perspective of the mid-1860s, however, he "was struck by things that I would not have wished to find," and he identified several numbers "that are either weak, or lacking in character, which is worse still":

1) An aria for Lady Macbeth in act 2
2) Various passages to rewrite in the hallucination scene of act 3 [*sic;* act 2 is meant]
3) Rewrite completely Macbeth's aria in act 3
4) Retouch the opening scenes of act 4
5) Prepare from scratch the last finale, removing the death of Macbeth onstage.

What has he identified (leaving aside the small modifications in the finale of the second act)? Three solo numbers that embody pre-1850s conventions and a chorus in the Risorgimental tradition of "Va, pensiero."

While none of these pieces has ever been considered among the greatest achievements in *Macbeth* (such as the first-act duet for Macbeth and Lady, most of the second-act finale, and the sleepwalking scene), Verdi did not have a negative view of them as he prepared and rehearsed the opera. Let us consider them in the light of Verdi's own comments in his letters from 1846 and 1847.

1. *An aria for Lady Macbeth in act 2, "Trionfai!"* Hoping to counteract the prophecy of the witches that Banco's heirs will rule, Macbeth and Lady lay plans at the beginning of the second act for murdering Banco and his son. After providing Piave revised text for this recitative (he had not liked Piave's verses), Verdi concluded: "When the Lady remains alone, two quatrains are needed; but the old ones won't do, and the first one in particular must be

changed; so instead of an adagio I'll write an allegro, which will be even better." He informed the original Lady, Marianna Barbieri-Nini, that she would receive "another aria consisting, however, of a recitative and a single brilliant cabaletta." Later he decided to write this cabaletta "for you in Florence so that it will suit your voice perfectly and be sure to make an effect." [90] And so it did. According to one reviewer, "Lady Macbeth [...] sings [...] an allegro with all the vigor and energy of which Barbieri's lungs are capable. Endless calls and applause." Another described it, however, as "an aria in the worst possible style and taste, which, however, was well sung." [91]

The florid and brilliant aria, neatly described by Julian Budden as "a brash cousin of Elvira's 'Tutto sprezzo che d'Ernani,' with more than a touch of Abigaille [in *Nabucco*]," [92] is perfectly consistent with the cabaletta of Lady's first-act cavatina. Sung with conviction, it makes a strong musical effect, while dramaturgically it keeps Lady focused and forceful, rather than anticipating her psychological breakdown (as in the 1865 "La luce langue"). Would Verdi have written "Trionfai!" in 1864–65? Of course not. But "La luce langue," however accomplished, seems to have wandered into *Macbeth* from another world. Not even Verdi's perfumed reharmonizations of other sections of the score succeed in washing *Macbeth* clean of its origins.

2. *Aria Macbeth, act 3.* The return of Macbeth to consult the witches anew is the subject of the entire third act, which in its original form is an expansive gran scena for the protagonist: an introductory chorus of witches ("Tre volte miagola"), an elaborate recitative for the appearance of the apparitions, a cantabile as the heirs of Banco appear in ghostly procession ("Fuggi, regal fantasima"), a *tempo di mezzo* consisting of the descent of the aerial spirits and chorus ("Ondine, e silfidi"), and a concluding cabaletta ("Vada in fiamme"). In describing the piece to his original Macbeth, Felice Varesi, Verdi wrote: "There is a cantabile (*sui generis*) with which you have to make a big effect." As for the cabaletta, "it does not have the usual form, because, after all that has preceded it, a cabaletta in the usual mold and with the usual ritornellos would seem trivial. I'd made another one that I liked when I tried it out by itself, but when I joined it to all that went before, I found it intolerable. This one suits me fine, and I hope it will suit you too." But the third act did not excite much popular enthusiasm, and one reviewer suggested that "it might not be a bad thing to suppress all of the final cabaletta, ending with the chorus and ballet of the sylphs." [93]

The original piece had a strong internal logic, which the revision ignored. Verdi added a lengthy ballet after the initial chorus and made subtle changes in the scene of the apparitions and in the cantabile, though leaving intact the basic ideas. The cabaletta, on the other hand, he simply suppressed. Yet the appearance of Lady Macbeth in the witches' den is dramaturgically suspect, and the duet in which she and her husband goad each other toward "vengeance" is anything but inspired. While its style is unquestionably more mature than the forceful *A minor/major* cabaletta of 1847, in which Macbeth in the best baritonal fashion vowed revenge on Macduff, the revision does not improve the opera as a whole.

3. *Chorus, act 4, "Patria tradita."* Verdi knew exactly how he wanted to begin the last act in 1847, having given the following instructions to Piave: "I'd like the scene to open with a grandiose, moving chorus, which would describe Scotland's wretched state under Macbeth's rule." And he added: "Let this be a grandiose chorus. Beautiful and moving poetry, in any meter you want except *decasillabi*." Later he was even more explicit: "I've tried to set the first chorus but haven't been able to make it grandiose because, among other things, the meter is too short. So do me the favor of making four *strofette* of *ottonari*." Verdi then explained why he wanted this particular verse form: "I'd like to do a chorus as important as the one in *Nabucco*, but I wouldn't want it to have the same rhythm, and that's why I ask you for *ottonari*" ("Va, pensiero, sull'ali dorate" from *Nabucco*, "O Signore del tetto natio" from *I Lombardi*, and "Si ridesti il Leon di Castiglia" from *Ernani* all employ the poetic meter of *decasillabi*). And the composer continued, "Don't let this moment slip by, the only one in the entire opera that's affecting. So do it with passion."[94]

Verdi liked Piave's verses enough to use them without change both in 1847 and in 1865, when he completely rewrote the music of the chorus. The 1847 chorus is within a strong Risorgimento tradition.[95] For the first of Piave's four *strofette* Verdi wrote an affecting melody in the minor, sung in unison by the entire mixed chorus. In the second, in the relative major, the chorus breaks into harmony (as when the Hebrew slaves in *Nabucco* invoke their "harps of gold"). The third brings back the music of the first, still in unison, while the fourth (related to but not identical to the second) moves to the tonic major. A twinge of minor in the final cadences helps moderate what would otherwise be a questionable triumphal conclusion. The harmony is simple, the melody tuneful, though not so tuneful as "Va, pensiero": Verdi may have sought to avoid comparisons with his previous hit, yet only five years separated *Macbeth* from *Nabucco*. The 1865 chorus is very different, with its harmonic complexity, its orchestral semitone figures (both up and down), its massed harmonies and gentle counterpoints in the chorus, its avoidance of simple repetition. Then, up steps Macduff to sing a standard 1847 aria, and once again the contrast between 1865 and 1847 comes as a shock. To ask which opening chorus is *better* misses the point: Better for what? Better in which opera? Better in which context?

4. *Morte di Macbeth.* When Verdi sent a sketch of the text for this final scene to Piave, he instructed him, "Make two *strofette,* try to give them some touching quality, but don't forget Macbeth's character." To Varesi he described the concluding moments as "a very brief death scene—but it won't be one of those usual death scenes, oversweet, etc." When he sent the music, he added:

> You'll be able to make much of the death scene if, together with your singing, your acting is well thought out. You will understand very well that Macbeth mustn't die like Edgardo, Gennaro, etc. [Verdi is referring to the final cabaletta in *Lucia di Lammermoor,* with its invocation of Lucia as the "bell'alma innamorata," and to the revised finale of Donizetti's *Lucrezia Borgia,* in which Gennaro dies in the arms of his mother], therefore it has to be treated in a new way. It should be affecting, yes; but more than affecting, it should be terrible. All of it *sottovoce,* except for the last two verses, which, rather, you'll also accompany with acting, bursting out with full force on the words "Vile... crown... and only for you!..."

After the premiere, Varesi (hardly an impartial observer) referred to "my death scene" as among the most inspired parts of the opera.[96]

As in the case of the chorus opening act 4, the death scene from *Macbeth* looks back to *Nabucco,* the similar concluding passage for Abigaille, also a character whose evil deeds are finally punished. These brief, intense death scenes, with a wounded or poisoned character staggering around stage, singing a tortured solo, then collapsing, were not particularly favored by Verdi's contemporaries. Operatic deaths tended to come in duets, trios, or ensemble scenes (think of *Rigoletto, Il trovatore,* or *La traviata*), and early in the history of *Nabucco* the Abigaille scene was already cut in many performances. Still, Verdi knew that he wanted this effect in *Macbeth,* and even instructed Varesi about how to stage the ending: "You're on the ground, of course, but for this last line ['Vile... crown...'] you'll stand almost straight up and will make as great an impression as possible." When Verdi turned his back on this scene in 1865, he was criticizing not so much his specific music as a whole convention. As he told Escudier in December 1864, "I too am of the view that Macbeth's death should be changed, but the only thing that can be done is a Victory Hymn."[97] And so it was, with a marchlike phrase in a minor key, "Macbeth, Macbeth, ov'è" for the soldiers and bards, followed by the soaring major-mode phrase of thanksgiving with which the opera ends. It is a lovely chorus, and its willingness to pack all its emotion into a phrase of four measures is something that we find only in the mature Verdi. Is it a strong ending for the opera? Not so strong that many modern productions have not taken to inserting back into this final scene the "Morte di Macbeth," thereby trying to have the best of both worlds, and perhaps only succeeding in having neither.

As his work on the opera proceeded, Verdi made other significant changes, but the examples already cited provide sufficient insight. When Verdi and Boito revised *Simon Boccanegra* in the early 1880s, they faced again and again the kind of problems we have traced in *Macbeth,* and the collaborators invoked the metaphor of a wobbly table: when you fix one leg, another gets out of balance, and soon you're eating on the floor.[98] A good performance, of course, smooths out the frictions, makes the parts seem to belong together, compensates for the historically generated dissociations between elements of the opera. Even before Verdi made his revision, furthermore, performers made their own decisions about these places. To take one example, Pauline Viardot, who was to perform *Macbeth* in Dublin in 1859, informed the conductor, Luigi Arditi, of her transpositions and modifications, adding, "The cabaletta 'Trionfai' is not sung."[99] Viardot used a pair of scissors; Verdi substituted another piece. Both faced the same problem.

It would be possible to assume a stance to the problem of cutting that is absolute: the composer wrote it, the performer should follow his instructions. That is what Stravinsky told Ernest Ansermet in two letters written from Paris in 1937. In the first (14 October), he proclaimed:

> There is absolutely no reason to make cuts in *Jeu de cartes* in concert performances, any more than, for example, in *Apollo*. [...]If you propose this strange idea of asking me to make cuts, the reasoning must be that the succession of movements in *Jeu de cartes* seems a little boring to you personally. I cannot do anything about that. [...] I cannot let you make cuts in *Jeu de cartes!* I think it is better not to play it at all than to do so reluctantly.

Ansermet on 15 October persisted, although modifying his request: "I ask only one thing: permit me to cut from the second measure of 45 to the second measure of 58." The furious composer explained to him why this cut was unacceptable, and concluded, "I repeat: either you play *Jeu de cartes* as it is or you do not play it at all. You do not seem to have understood that my letter of October 14 was categorical on this point."[100] One feels a certain sympathy for

Stravinsky in all of this, but his position has never been possible in the world of Italian opera. Perhaps it has never been possible in any performance art.

It has been my purpose in this chapter to introduce some of the issues performers should be facing when they make cuts in Italian operas. Rarely are cuts neutral; rarely do all the elements suggest unmistakably that one procedure rather than another is correct. Cuts acceptable in Verdi may not be acceptable in Donizetti; cuts we can easily countenance in Bellini may be unthinkable in Rossini. Some cuts are so destructive as to be beyond reason. A performance of Rossini's *Guillaume Tell* at the Paris Opéra in the spring of 2003 was the worst example of irrational and destructive cutting that I have ever had the misfortune to witness in the theater. *Tell* is a long opera, to be sure, and for a regular theater during a normal season it probably requires trimming. But why would one choose to perform *Guillaume Tell* by sacrificing some of its most characteristic music ("Enfans de la nature" in the first act, the opening chorus of the second act, the gathering of the cantons in the second-act finale), while preserving long passages of music (such as the dramaturgically leaden trio for Mathilde, Jemmy, and Hedwige in the final act) that the composer himself chose to cut?

There may be practical reasons, as we have seen, for making decisions we know to be far from ideal. If a valued singer, beloved by the public, offers a conductor the choice between a vanity cut or no performance, the conductor may have no real choice. Such confrontations, however, are rare. Usually performers do have choices, and the care with which they exercise those choices affects the quality of their performances. Making cuts in an opera to suit the particular needs of a modern production is legitimate as long as those cuts are introduced with sensitivity to the individual nature of the work, to the stylistic characteristics of its composer, and to the relative position of each composition within the historical development of nineteenth-century Italian opera. What we must not do is abandon our own responsibilities to make such decisions in the name of standardized procedures of uncertain historical provenance and questionable aesthetic standing.

9

ORNAMENTING ROSSINI

COME SCRITTO: THE WRITTEN AND THE UNWRITTEN

In 1976, Alberto Zedda and I were installed at Zedda's home in Milan, peacefully arguing about slurs and accents in Rossini's *La gazza ladra,* the first volume to be published in the new critical edition, when we were interrupted by an urgent phone call from the Teatro alla Scala. Jean-Pierre Ponnelle was raging, Frederica Von Stade was in tears, Thomas Schippers was frantic, and the planned revival of *Il barbiere di Siviglia* threatened to dissolve before their eyes. A slow taxi ride through the appalling traffic of central Milan brought us to the theater. Von Stade had arrived for rehearsal with vocal ornamentation (variations and cadenzas) she planned to incorporate into her performance of Rosina's well-known cavatina "Una voce poco fa." Ponnelle, who had originally staged the production with Claudio Abbado on the podium in 1969, was adamant that Rossini's vocal line should be sung precisely as written, just as in the performances he prepared with Abbado.[1] They were using the critical edition of *Barbiere* and seemed to believe that interpolations by singers were therefore taboo. (The irony of a brilliant stage director's insisting to musicians on the need for textual purity was not lost on any of us.) With bruised egos on every side, Maestro Schippers found himself in the role of mediator.

In this case, thanks to Rossini, we were able to provide explicit guidance to the performers. The library of the Milan Conservatory, named "Giuseppe Verdi" after a country boy who had been refused admission in 1832, contains a manuscript in Rossini's hand of ornaments for this aria. Prepared on 12 July 1852, thirty-six years after the composition of *Il barbiere di Siviglia,* during a visit the composer made to the baths at Montecatini, the manuscript was dedicated to Matilde Juva.[2] She was a dilettante musician, sister of Emilia Branca, who was the wife of the most important Italian librettist of the first half of the nineteenth century, Felice Romani. Rossini's ornaments for Juva, we explained, were *representative* of how the composer expected singers to shape his melodic lines in performance. Although giving ground slowly, Ponnelle relented. Schippers breathed a sigh of relief, Von Stade sang her ornaments, and disaster was averted.

Only in a few cases do we possess this kind of unequivocal authorial support for modifying in performance the written notes present in an autograph manuscript (or its public face, a printed edition). Most modifications introduced into modern performances result from blind acceptance of recent practices, particularly for works widely represented in twentieth-century recordings: this is the kind of interpolation that Abbado sought to discourage. Other modifications, however, involve extrapolation from earlier historical models. Newspaper accounts often give valuable testimony concerning contemporary practice, while many specific examples of ornamentation are linked to individual composers or singers, derive from pedagogical treatises on singing, or reflect annotations in contemporary manuscripts or printed editions. Performers unaccustomed to the world of Italian opera, and wary of unexamined tradition, may or may not find extrapolation from such models convincing.

The Italian pianist Maurizio Pollini, for example, is more associated in the public mind with Bach, Beethoven, Schoenberg, and Stockhausen than with Rossini. Nonetheless, infected by the virus that prompts many instrumentalists to take up the baton, he conducted *La donna del lago* in two sets of performances from the critical edition at the 1981 and 1983 Rossini Opera Festivals. Although Pollini approached the score from a viewpoint far different from traditional attitudes toward this repertory, he brought to it musical intelligence and dramatic insight that helped even those who had worked with the repertory for years to develop a new understanding of the composer's art: the subtlety of orchestration, the richness of motivic development, the precision of harmonic pattern. That other elements of Pollini's interpretation (especially his approach to vocal style) were less successful simply reinforced a general principle: you can never get it *all* right. In this case, though, when the tempo Pollini set for Malcom's second-act cabaletta was impossibly fast, the tears flowing down the cheeks of a desperately frustrated mezzo-soprano, Martine Dupuy, night after night, were all too wet. When one tried to reason with him, Pollini would sit down at the keyboard and *play* the contested passage, saying, "You see, that's how it should go." He was right, but he was wrong. Musical works are complex organisms, and each performance can aspire only to reveal certain facets of their richness. Knowledge of a composition in the concert hall or in the opera house is a product of multiple performances; the more convincing a particular interpretation may be in certain directions, the less so it is likely to be in others.

In the Pesaro *Donna del lago,* Pollini took a purist's view toward the vocal lines, insisting that singers perform them as written. Even when cadential figures in slow movements sprouted elaborate written fioritura, he maintained a steady beat, eschewing accommodations to breath or grace. (The effect was still apparent, although somewhat tempered, when the 1983 reprise, with Katia Ricciarelli and Lucia Valentini Terrani in the roles of Elena and Malcom, was issued as a recording.)[3] Rossini scholars cited historical evidence to plead the cause of ornamentation, of rhythmic freedom, of appoggiaturas. Only in one case was Pollini moved: for the final *rondò* of the opera, Elena's "Tanti affetti in tal momento," we could show him autograph manuscripts of three different sets of ornaments prepared by Rossini later in his life for particular singers.[4] After staring at them, perplexed, for a few moments, Pollini allowed that he would permit the singer to use some of *those* ornaments if she wished, but no others.

Scholars working as consultants in the opera house often find themselves in an untenable position: they are presumed to be rigorous upholders of abstract truth, when in fact they understand full well the difference between what is written and what is unwritten. A printed edition, no matter how critical, is a point of departure for a performance, not a blueprint to be followed with architectural precision. There is no unequivocal way to agree upon the distinction in decibels between *forte* and *mezzoforte,* the difference between a horizontal accent and a vertical one, or the interpretation of melodic lines covered by slurs and those without them. But there are also conductors, ranking among the staunchest supporters of the new editions, who employ them with a rigor in some respects ahistorical. Scholars responsible for preparing those editions do not wish to quarrel publicly with distinguished proponents of their use. So we face the slings and arrows of outrageous journalists with resignation, while seeking patiently to clarify the relationship between historical knowledge and contemporary performance.

Musical performance in the western tradition is a collaboration between composers, performers, and listeners: composers provide written instructions of varying degrees of specificity, performers respond to those instructions according to changing attitudes about the function of a written score, listeners develop expectations concerning the music they will hear that cannot lightly be resisted. The balance among these collaborators has shifted over the course of the past four hundred years, and will continue to do so, even for the same works.

During the first three-quarters of the eighteenth century, composers preparing concertos, chamber music, operas, and cantatas provided only limited instructions about articulation and dynamics. They expected soloists (vocal and instrumental) to ornament lyrical lines, encouraged flexibility as to which instruments might be employed, and left much responsibility for introducing harmonic support to musicians who "realized" in performance the bass line annotated with signs indicating the harmony (the "figured bass"). Later, as composers offered ever more extensive written instructions, the necessity for performers to intervene in matters of pitch, dynamics, or instrumentation was more circumscribed. The expressive designs of the music, on the other hand, encouraged other kinds of interpretive freedom, deformations of rhythm, intensifications of dynamic levels, the inventive use of pedal effects on the keyboard.

Opera, and Italian opera in particular, while participating in this new expressivity, remained bound longer than other nineteenth-century genres to eighteenth-century traditions concerning the relationship between composer and performer. Apart from some church styles, only in Italian opera did the use of a figured bass remain prevalent well into the nineteenth century. Apart from the improvisational exploits of solo instrumental virtuosos, only in Italian opera was ornamentation integral to the performance of newly composed notated works. Nowhere else in nineteenth-century music did performers have as much freedom to choose instrumentation as in the realization of the stage band, of which composers normally provided only a sketch.

Even performers of the orchestral repertory or of German opera made modifications to suit local conditions: Wagner's autobiography and the memoirs of Berlioz demonstrate that these composer-performers did what was necessary to produce the best possible realizations of their music, often under trying circumstances. The new critical edition of *Tristan und Isolde* provides extensive details concerning changes introduced by Wagner to accommodate his singers.[5] Nonetheless, long after most European composers assumed that performers would try to respect their notation, composers of Italian opera continued to treat singers as collaborators. Indeed, to be certain that the first measures of the recitative preceding the trio in the last act of *Rigoletto* would be performed without modifications that singers might otherwise have considered self-evident, Verdi wrote in his autograph score: "This recitative must be declaimed without the usual appoggiaturas."[6]

When considering the relationship between musicians and the written text of an opera, we must bear in mind both conditions prevailing when an opera was written and those characterizing performance today. We cannot be indifferent to the intervening history, but neither must we give it undue weight, especially when that history is rooted in social and cultural practices or aesthetic preferences no longer operative. After all, the diversity of styles (both chronological and geographical) coexisting in American and European opera houses today was unknown to earlier periods. This has had a profound effect upon the way in which thoughtful modern musicians approach their task.

In the late nineteenth century, for example, the few early nineteenth-century Italian operas remaining in the repertory were routinely reorchestrated in order to render their sound more similar to operas being composed at that time: Rossini's characteristic use of the piccolo as a solo instrument was ruthlessly suppressed in favor of a flute; to operas with lighter scorings were added trombone and tuba parts, as well as elaborate percussion.[7] In a world defining the coloratura soprano by the vocal exploits of Delibes' Lakmé or Offenbach's mechanical doll Olympia in *The Tales of Hoffman,* cadenzas and ornaments introduced by such singers into earlier Italian operas tended to be stylistically akin and structurally positioned in ways reflecting this new ideal of vocal virtuosity rather than the practices of a previous era. The evidence of early recordings reflects late nineteenth-century practice, and must be evaluated accordingly.[8]

Yet we cannot pretend that knowledge of performance practice as it existed in the first half of the nineteenth century will suffice to answer the questions that invariably arise when we now perform operas in this repertory. As always, our knowledge of historical circumstances must be joined to aesthetic values and to the practical conditions of modern performance, the three-dimensional grid introduced in the discussion of multiple versions in chapter 7. This chapter examines the kinds of modifications that singers of nineteenth-century Italian opera might appropriately introduce into notated vocal lines, including ornamentation (whether improvised or learned) and *puntature* (changes made to accommodate singers unable, for whatever reason, to perform the text as written).

VOCAL ORNAMENTATION: CONTEMPORARY EVIDENCE

Rossini loved inserting notes to himself (and to posterity) in his autograph manuscripts. Some are pointed commentaries on the music he has written, transformations of the traditional "Laus Deo" (Praise God) of eighteenth-century composers. At the end of the sprightly overture to *La scala di seta,* for example, Rossini signaled his approval of the piece by commenting "Accidenti!" (probably best translated as "Awesome!"); at the conclusion of the overture to *Il signor Bruschino,* during which the second violins are instructed to beat their bows rhythmically against the metal shades of their candleholders (inauthentically replaced today by mere music stands), Rossini acknowledged his preoccupation with the reception of this unusual effect by writing, "Dio ti salvi l'anima" (God save your soul).[9]

Sometimes his comments are pointed barbs, vulgar and funny, aimed at his own musical practice or at linguistic traits of the poetry he is setting. In the closing cadences from a second-act trio in *Otello,* for example, he wrote five parallel triads, strictly forbidden according to the rules of voice-leading, annotating the passage: "Queste cinque quinte sono per li signori Coglioni" (These five fifths are for ——).[10] When I tried to quote that phrase in a Metropolitan Opera intermission feature, Gerry Souvaine came storming out of her producer's box: this is *family* radio! In *Ermione,* even the composer was unable to take seriously the florid verses with which Orestes greets Hermione after many years apart from her:

Ah mio Nume adorato! ormai la sorte	Ah my beloved Goddess! finally fate
Quel piacer mi concede,	Has granted me that pleasure I sighed for
Che sospirai ben mille volte, e mille:	A thousand times, and a thousand times more:
Vagheggio alfin le amate tue pupille!	I gaze at last into the beloved pupils of your eyes.

In his autograph score, the twenty-six-year-old Rossini put an asterisk next to the word "vagheggio" and at the bottom of the page annotated the word as "vaccheggio." Suffice it to say that the word *vacca* (cow) is a vulgar Italian term for prostitute.[11]

In two places, Rossini's commentary refers to vocal ornamentation, demonstrating unequivocally that what he wrote was not what he expected to be sung. Felice Romani's libretto of *Il Turco in Italia* is best known for the presence of a quasi-Pirandellian Poet who seeks to manipulate the action, but who instead is manipulated by it. (In fact, Romani derived much of his libretto, including the character of the Poet, from an earlier libretto by Caterino Mazzolà, best known today for reshaping Metastasio's *La clemenza di Tito* for Mozart).[12] Just before the stretta of the first-act finale (the boisterous ensemble that brings down the curtain), Fiorilla and Zaida, rivals for the affection of the opera's Turk, Selim, engage first in verbal sparring, then in physical combat. While most characters try to separate them, the Poet delights in the spectacle:

Seguitate... via... bravissime!	Go ahead... on with it... wonderful!
Qua... là... bene; in questo modo	Here... there... good; that's the way,

Azzuffatevi, stringetevi,	Go to it, get closer,
Sgraffi... morsi... me la godo...	Scratch... bite... I love it...
Che final! che finalone!	What a finale! what a great finale!
Oh! che chiasso avrà da far.	Oh! what an effect it will have

In his autograph, Rossini annotated the final verse, which leads directly into the stretta, with the following phrase: "The composer leaves it to the art of Sig.ʳ Vasoli [the singer who first played the role of the Poet] to fill out properly this..." at which point he drew an enormous fermata (example 9.1). Vasoli, in short, was expected to interpolate a cadenza.[13]

There is a similar case in *La scala di seta*. The romantic lead, Dorvil, was written for Raffaelle Monelli, the most capable tenor at the Venetian Teatro San Moisè, for which—as we have seen—Rossini prepared five one-act *farse* between 1810 and 1813. The young composer must have had a spirited relationship with Monelli. Over a notated cadenza at the end of the cantabile of Dorvil's aria, "Vedrò qual sommo incanto," the composer added: "Dolce per le cinque piaghe di Cristo" (Sweetly, by the five wounds of Christ). Just before the beginning of this cantabile, he suggested that the tenor interpolate a cadenza into the concluding phrase of his recitative by writing "a piacere del Sig.ʳ Monelli" (at the pleasure of Signor Monelli). Actually he employed yet another vulgar term, adding an "a" in a conspicuous box between "Mon-" and "-elli": "mona" is a vulgar term for vagina in Venetian dialect.[14]

Not only are Rossini's own manuscripts of complete operas filled with fermatas and instructions such as "a piacere" and "secondando il canto," invitations for singers to interpolate cadenzas, but more than thirty separate manuscripts in the composer's hand survive in which he wrote out variations and cadenzas. They are found in public and private collections in Italy, France, England, Germany, Japan, Canada, and the United States. Some provide ornamentation for a single piece; others are collections of ornaments for several pieces.[15] They pertain to recitative, arias, and duets. The earliest, written during the 1820s through the early 1840s, were prepared for singers with whom Rossini worked in the theater or whom he coached, such as Giuditta

EXAMPLE 9.1. GIOACHINO ROSSINI, *IL TURCO IN ITALIA*, FINALE PRIMO (N. 7), PREPARATION FOR THE STRETTA (MM. 510–516).

Che fi - nal! che fi - na - lo - ne! oh! che chias-so a - vrà da far.

Pasta and Giulia Grisi.[16] The latest, penned in the 1850s and 1860s, provided ornamentation either for professionals still engaged in singing Rossini's music (Adelina Patti) or for dilettantes (Matilde Juva).[17] Manuscripts prepared for dilettantes can be particularly instructive, since the composer might include details that would have seemed obvious to a professional.

According to a frequently repeated anecdote, Rossini objected to the freedom with which singers ornamented his music. Having suffered through the elaborate embellishments introduced by the last great castrato, Giambattista Velluti, at the 1813 premiere at the Teatro alla Scala of his *Aureliano in Palmira,* the anecdote continues, the composer vowed to write all vocal lines exactly as he wished them sung. However amusing this story may seem, it is totally without substance.[18] One duet from *Aureliano* involving Velluti was even printed with the ornamentation he introduced in Milan, and his interventions are quite tame.[19] Although Rossini's written melodic lines do become more florid as his career continued, at no point did he ever attempt to specify completely the kinds of variations and cadenzas that would be tailored (whether by the composer or others) to the talents of individual singers.

While we have less evidence concerning the vocal ornamentation that Bellini, Donizetti, or the young Verdi might have countenanced, there do exist some suggestive sources. A manuscript in the hand of Donizetti is an arrangement for piano and voice of Nemorino's "Una furtiva lagrima" from *L'elisir d'amore* of 1832. As we saw in chapter 8, the piece consists of two strophes: the first begins in *B♭ minor* and modulates to the relative major (*D♭ major*); the second also begins in *B♭ minor,* but concludes in the parallel major (*B♭ major*), with a cadenza underscoring the final cadence. In the original, the passages in *B♭ minor* are essentially the same in each strophe. In his arrangement, Donizetti provides some ornaments for this second strophe (as in example 9.2).[20] His manuscript also includes two alternative concluding cadenzas. The first variant is included in the principal text, the second is given

EXAMPLE 9.2. GAETANO DONIZETTI, *L'ELISIR D'AMORE,* ROMANZA NEMORINO, SECOND STANZA, WITH DONIZETTI'S OWN VARIATION.

as a footnote. It is clear, in short, that Donizetti did not consider his original cadenza to be sacrosanct.

An example from the hand of Verdi is found within his autograph manuscript of *Nabucco*. First performed at La Scala in March 1842, the work had a notable success and was revived at the same theater the next autumn, under the composer's direction. At that time, the role of Fenena, daughter of Nabucco, was assigned to a soprano, Amalia Zecchini. Since the original Fenena, Giovannina Bellinzaghi, was a mezzo-soprano, Verdi was obliged to alter the vocal line of her most important solo, Fenena's fourth-act prayer. He entitled the manuscript containing the revised melody, "Preghiera Fenena puntata per la Zecchini" (Fenena's Prayer adjusted for Zecchini). Not only did Verdi raise the tessitura of the part, he also made the vocal line more florid and provided variations for passages simply repeated in the original. Example 9.3 gives a sample of Verdi's original and "puntata" versions.[21]

Our knowledge concerning ornamentation actually applied by singers in Italian and French operas during the first half of the nineteenth century does not derive exclusively from manuscripts prepared by composers. Additional information comes from singers' notebooks, printed editions purporting to preserve the ornamentation of individual singers, anonymous annotations in printed music or manuscripts, and pedagogical treatises.

Because they can be associated with the practice of important contemporary artists, the notebooks in which Laure Cinti-Damoreau and Adelaide

EXAMPLE 9.3. GIUSEPPE VERDI, *NABUCCO*, FINALE ULTIMO (N. 13), FENENA'S PRAYER (MM. 59–63) IN ITS ORIGINAL VERSION FOR MEZZO-SOPRANO AND AS VERDI HIMSELF MODIFIED IT FOR AMALIA ZECCHINI, A SOPRANO.

Kemble jotted down ornamentation for individual arias or entire roles are of immense interest. Cinti-Damoreau was a French singer who worked closely with Rossini at the Théâtre Italien between 1824 and 1826 (she was the original Contessa di Folleville in *Il viaggio a Reims*) and then moved with him to the Opéra, where she created the soprano leads in all four of his French operas (including Mathilde in *Guillaume Tell*). Later she taught singing at the Conservatoire in Paris and published a treatise on vocal technique.[22] At Indiana University, there are seven manuscript notebooks, almost entirely in Cinti-Damoreau's hand, filled with ornamentation for works written during the 1820s and 1830s, most of which were actively in her own repertory.[23] Adelaide Kemble, on the other hand, was British. She was born in 1814, and her short career spanned the years from 1835 to 1843. In 1838 she went to Italy, where she studied with Giuditta Pasta at the older singer's home on Lake Como and performed in major Italian theaters. Kemble, too, left a notebook, with ornamentation for arias and duets (especially those written for soprano and mezzo-soprano) by Rossini, Bellini, Donizetti, and Mercadante. Among other treasures, there is extensive ornamentation for Bellini's *Norma*, surely influenced by her study with Pasta, who created the title role.[24]

Although the albums of "Cadenzas and variations composed and performed by the Marchisio sisters," prepared in 1900 by Barbara Marchisio and preserved in the Cary collection of the Pierpont Morgan Library in New York, testify to practices of a slightly later period, they are nonetheless significant.[25] Barbara and Carlotta Marchisio, contralto and soprano, respectively, were active from the mid-1850s until Carlotta's death in 1872 (Barbara lived until 1919), frequently singing together in operas by Rossini, Bellini, and Donizetti. Intimate friends of Rossini during the 1860s, they performed his *Semiramide* in a French adaptation at the Opéra in 1860 and later took part in the premiere of the *Petite Messe solennelle* in 1864.[26] Rossini deeply admired their art; hence we must treat this collection of ornamentation with particular respect.

Since the vocal exploits of individual singers fascinated the nineteenth-century operatic public, music publishers—who sought commercial gain from that public—issued many individual arias with "all the ornaments" added by famous divas. There is no reason to doubt the basic accuracy of these publications, which provide us with dated evidence pertaining to particular performers. For Rossini alone, we have sets of ornaments reflecting the practices of the castrato Velluti, Emilia Bonini (who worked with the composer at the Théâtre Italien in the 1820s), Maria Malibran, Giovanni Battista Rubini (the famed tenor with whom Rossini first collaborated in Naples in 1820, be-

fore bringing him to Paris), and many others.[27] None of these sets of ornaments is different in nature from the ones Rossini himself prepared, although
those deriving directly from the composer are often musically more inventive.

Ornamentation added by hand to printed vocal scores, manuscript copies
of an opera, or materials preserved in theater archives is more difficult to
evaluate, for only rarely can such annotations be identified with individual
singers or performances. Alongside ornaments similar to those of Rossini
or major contemporary singers, furthermore, many *puntature* (adjustments)
appear, simplifying vocal lines for performers unable to negotiate the original. While in principle *puntature* differ from ornamentation, the dividing
line is sometimes slippery. Manuscript vocal parts at the Bibliothèque de
l'Opéra in Paris, for example, reflect performance practice in the temple of
French operatic life, from which vulgar Italian custom was *supposed* to be excluded.[28] But although Rossini simplified the more florid vocal lines of his
Italian *Maometto II* and *Mosè in Egitto* when revising them for the French
stage as *Le Siège de Corinthe* and *Moïse,* performing parts at the Opéra reveal
that singers soon put back *into* the score many passages that the composer
had so carefully taken *out.*

Finally, evidence concerning ornamentation is found in theoretical treatises of the period, which provide instruction for young singers.[29] Two of the
most important are those of Cinti-Damoreau, who published her *Méthode de
chant* in 1849, and Manuel García, son of the tenor who created the role of
Count Almaviva in Rossini's *Il barbiere di Siviglia.* The first edition of the son's
Traité complet de l'art du chant was issued in Paris in 1840.[30] Didactic works
not only provide important evidence but also suggest the spirit in which ornamentation was taught by its most distinguished practitioners. These words
of advice are proffered by Joséphine Fodor-Mainvielle, a singer who worked
very closely with Rossini during the 1820s, in a passage entitled "On moder-
ation in ornaments":

> In the hope of having themselves applauded by an ignorant or unreflec-
> tive crowd, singers overload their vocal line with ornaments, with fermatas,
> with high and low notes, neither expected nor desired by the leader of the
> orchestra, who is reduced to stopping his army, which, to follow the
> caprice of the singer, is obliged to make the most awful mistakes. [...] We
> do not exclude, certainly, the possibility of adding ornaments, but they
> should not oblige us to alter the rhythm. The words should be our guide;
> conforming ourselves to them, we can be certain to give the music being
> sung the character the composer intended.[31]

Knowing the mechanisms of applying ornamentation, in short, is only a first step. As Cinti-Damoreau expressed it:

> I do not offer them [examples of ornaments and cadenzas] to you to be performed at any cost, despite your physical capabilities and your character. I propose these models of variations, rather, so that later your taste will lead you, within your individual means, to invent others that suit you properly.[32]

VOCAL ORNAMENTATION: RECITATIVE

Cinti-Damoreau's advice is exactly right: young singers, coaches, and conductors should study contemporary evidence concerning vocal ornamentation in order to develop, first, their knowledge of what a composer and his singers would have recognized as appropriate and, second, their taste in devising ornamentation that suits the needs of a modern singer. What is most encouraging about contemporary evidence is its consistency. The Rossini manuscripts, notebooks of specific singers, printed editions with variations, and added ornamentation in secondary sources offer a reasonably uniform picture. Let us review the basic techniques employed by singers during the first half of the nineteenth century, beginning with recitative and continuing with arias.

In the performance of Italian opera from this period, the tasteful use of appoggiaturas in recitative (and often in arias) is obligatory, not a matter of choice. When a composer wrote two identical notes at the end of a phrase for a word with a feminine ending ("[a]-mo-re," "[ri]-tor-no," "ba-cio"), he normally intended the first note to be differentiated in pitch from the second even though his notation did not reflect this. The first note would almost always be sung a tone or semitone above the second, but occasionally it could be approached from below.[33] This use of appoggiaturas carries over practices well established and documented in the eighteenth century.

Although the expectation that singers would apply appoggiaturas was becoming less widespread during the first half of the nineteenth century, the appoggiatura convention was by no means dying out. Rossini and Donizetti, born in 1792 and 1797, respectively, and actively involved in theatrical life by 1810 and 1818, rarely specified appoggiaturas in their notation: they were confident that singers knew what needed to be done. Bellini, on the other hand, born in 1801 and first active toward 1825, wrote out most appoggiaturas in his *Norma* of 1831, by adding grace notes. Verdi, born in 1813 and first active toward 1839, carried the process to its logical conclusion in operas such as *Nabucco* of 1842 or *Ernani* of 1844, by writing out as regular pitches in the vocal lines those appoggiaturas that would earlier have been added by singers or that Bellini would have notated as grace notes. While the need to employ appoggiaturas in early nineteenth-century Italian opera is no longer a matter of controversy, performers continue to learn the music *come scritto*. As mentioned in chapter 6, I had to beg Sam Ramey to begin Assur's "mad scene" in *Semiramide* at the Metropolitan Opera, not as written, but as Rossini unquestionably intended it to be performed, only to have to settle for a compromise. In our opera houses we face the situation in which *Norma* and *La traviata* are performed with all necessary appoggiaturas, while *Lucia di Lammermoor* and *Il barbiere di Siviglia* often are not.

Not only were nineteenth-century singers expected to add appoggiaturas to the recitative of Rossini and Donizetti, they were free to insert turns, cadential expansions, expressive leaps, and cadenzas as part of their interpretation. In a manuscript prepared by Rossini in 1858, there is fascinating evidence of variants for Tancredi's recitative and cavatina "Oh patria! dolce, e ingrata patria!" Because the recipient, Madame Grégoire, was a dilettante, the composer was especially precise in his notation, and every time it was possible to add an appoggiatura in the recitative, he did so.[34] The first phrase, as written and as realized by Rossini, is shown in example 9.4. Rossini treats the rhythm with great flexibility throughout, paying no heed to the original bar lines but encouraging instead expressive declamation of the text. He inserts ornaments to intensify emotionally charged moments, as in the concluding measures of the recitative. Notice particularly the *forte* leap and cadenza on "perire" (originally the word had a masculine ending, as "perir") and the increased pathos of the final "anima mia" (example 9.5). Similar interventions in recitative are found in manuscripts, printed editions, and pedagogical treatises associated with all those who worked in the orbit of Rossini, Bellini, and Donizetti.

EXAMPLE 9.4. GIOACHINO ROSSINI, *TANCREDI*, RECITATIVO E CAVATINA TANCREDI (N. 3), OPENING OF THE RECITATIVE (MM. 33–35) IN ITS ORIGINAL VERSION AND AS ROSSINI HIMSELF MODIFIED IT FOR MAD.[me] GRÉGOIRE.

EXAMPLE 9.5. GIOACHINO ROSSINI, *TANCREDI*, RECITATIVO E CAVATINA TANCREDI (N. 3), END OF THE RECITATIVE (MM. 63–64) IN ITS ORIGINAL VERSION AND AS ROSSINI HIMSELF MODIFIED IT FOR MAD.^{me} GRÉGOIRE.

As always, knowing the evidence and interpreting it on the modern stage are not the same. As recently as 1998, Renée Fleming ran into a wall of ignorance when she performed the title role in Donizetti's *Lucrezia Borgia* at La Scala under the direction of Gianluigi Gelmetti. Gelmetti is a fine conductor, whose *Guillaume Tell* at Pesaro in the summer of 1995 was splendid, but he is also what the Italians call *testardo*, stubborn. Somehow he had gotten it into his head that Donizetti didn't want singers to introduce appoggiaturas. There is no evidence to support this claim. Donizetti, like Rossini and the vast majority of their contemporaries, normally left appoggiaturas to the intelligence of performers. In his reluctance to add anything to a printed text, Gelmetti shares a sometimes exaggerated respect for notation with La Scala's former music director, Riccardo Muti, but Muti only occasionally performs earlier nineteenth-century operas, where singer intervention is essential, while Gelmetti often does. In *Lucrezia Borgia,* then, singers and conductor were working at cross-purposes, and the developing atmosphere was fraught with tension. On opening night, general havoc reigned, the gallery hissed and booed, and Gelmetti collapsed and was rushed to the hospital. I don't mean to suggest that appoggiaturas or ornamentation aroused all this hubbub, but they certainly played a part.

When I saw Gelmetti a few months later, recovered from his indisposition and conducting Donizetti's late opera, *Maria di Rohan* (1843), at the tent then replacing the burned-out Teatro La Fenice in Venice, he reiterated his position on Donizetti. "Finally," I replied, "you have explained to me why Verdi is a great and innovative composer. With his first well-known opera, *Nabucco*, he invented the appoggiatura." That, of course, is the logical result of the refusal to admit appoggiaturas into the operas of Rossini and Donizetti. After all, Verdi wrote out every appoggiatura he wanted in his scores, and that means essentially in all the operas he composed through the 1850s (his omissions are few in number, even if occasionally important). "If we don't admit appoggiaturas into earlier works," I concluded, "Verdi must have invented them in 1842, no?" My irony seemed lost on Gelmetti.

Knowing that the use of appoggiaturas in Italian opera is obligatory, however, is only a first step toward appropriate performance. Nineteenth-century practice is a guide for modern performers, not a recipe, and performers must never lose sight of who they are as musicians or of the audiences for whom they are performing. Appoggiaturas, after all, lend weight to phrase endings, applying stress and adding rhetorical emphasis to the poetic structure. Modern performance style, on the other hand, in the spoken drama as on the operatic stage, tends to flow more quickly, avoiding what are today perceived as excessive rhetorical devices. The emphatic Shakespearean declamation of John Gielgud, for example, reflected a powerfully different style from that of the more conversational Derek Jacobi. And while few today would imitate Marlon Brando's "method" approach in the film of *Julius Caesar*, it was widely praised during the 1950s.

Thus, in applying appoggiaturas in modern performances of Rossini or Donizetti, we must look beyond the mere opportunity to introduce an appoggiatura (two notes at the end of a phrase on the same pitch) and evaluate how the phrase or sub-phrase fits into the broader musical and dramatic discourse. A composer, for example, might set a lengthy speech as a group of shorter phrases, each of which concludes with an appoggiatura opportunity (example 9.6). If the singer were to add an appoggiatura at the end of all sub-phrases (*f; a; c*), they would emerge as weighty and separate. If the sub-phrases are declaimed more rapidly, with intervening rests practically ignored, music and drama fly across these breaks and land only at the end of

EXAMPLE 9.6. NOT EVERY APPOGGIATURA OPPORTUNITY OUGHT TO BE EMBRACED.

If you add one to ev-ery sub-phrase, there'll be too ma-ny ap-pog-gia-tu-ras.

the passage, with an obligatory appoggiatura (b♭) on the penultimate note of the passage. Modern performers and modern audiences want recitative to move along, and nineteenth-century practice can appropriately be adapted to meet these expectations.

I was responsible for preparing and coaching the ornamentation employed in the first production of Rossini's *Otello* using the critical edition of the opera, prepared by Michael Collins, at the Rossini Opera Festival during the summer of 1988. With a cast consisting of June Anderson as Desdemona, Chris Merritt as Otello, and Rockwell Blake as Iago, we had available some of the finest Rossini voices of the moment, singers who had no fear of early nineteenth-century vocal technique. My ornamentation and suggested appoggiaturas tried to recapture the style of 1816, as best I could reproduce it. While the production was a great success for all concerned, I gradually became convinced that I had exaggerated, that taking every appropriate opportunity for ornamentation slows things down too much for modern taste.

I particularly regretted introducing extra cadenzas into the recitative. I did so following the hint of Rossini's own manuscripts of ornamentation and of the practice of Manuel García, as described in his son's treatise on singing. García, after all, in addition to having been the first Almaviva in *Il barbiere di Siviglia*, was Rossini's original Otello. So on making his entrance in the opening scene, Otello sings first in recitative (no Verdian "Esultate" here), while laying before the Doge of Venice the arms and flags of the naval forces he has conquered. Example 9.7 reproduces Rossini's setting of this phrase and

EXAMPLE 9.7. GIOACHINO ROSSINI, *OTELLO*, RECITATIVO DOPO L'INTRODUZIONE (N. 1), OTELLO PHRASE (MM. 13–15) AND AN ORNAMENTED VERSION FROM THE GARCÍA TREATISE.

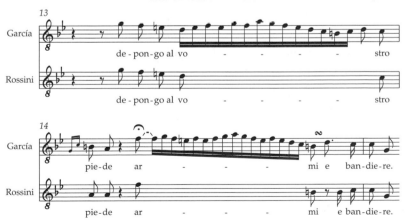

one of the three ornamented versions that the younger García prints in his treatise.[35] Not only did I adopt something akin to García's cadenza here, but I suggested similar interventions throughout the opera at points of dramatic emphasis. Each one sounded plausible individually, but the overall effect was leaden. When this stunning Pier Luigi Pizzi production was brought to the Lyric Opera of Chicago in 1992, I tried to remove most of these added recitative cadenzas, but Chris Merritt rebelled: he rather liked the vocal outbursts. Having learned that such ornamentation could be historically and stylistically justified, he only wanted more of the same!

VOCAL ORNAMENTATION:
CADENZAS AND VARIATIONS IN ROSSINI

While the tasteful use of appoggiaturas in recitative is obligatory and simple to learn, other interventions in recitative are dependent upon individual preference and taste. The music of a recitative, after all, is usually constructed to follow details of the text (in *versi sciolti*), and rarely are words or musical phrases repeated. In arias, duets, or ensembles employing *versi lirici,* on the other hand, where the musical structure is more regular, the situation changes radically. Indeed, we must bear in mind the structural precepts that underlie most fully developed arias by Rossini, Bellini, and Donizetti (and many ensembles), for these precepts were cultivated in part to permit the introduction of cadenzas and variations. One of the major problems with Verdi's early and middle operas is that he continued to use these forms while attitudes toward ornamentation were changing, hence depriving the forms of the interpretive dimension that justified their shape.

In a standard scena and aria, as we have seen, accompanied recitative prepares a slow cantabile, which may include a partial or complete repetition of the principal thematic material.[36] The cantabile is usually followed by a short *tempo di mezzo* (middle section), whose musical shape and contents depend on its dramatic purpose, on the presence or absence of other characters or chorus, on whether it motivates action or simply provides an interlude. This *tempo di mezzo* prepares the cabaletta, with its principal melodic period (the cabaletta theme), a short transition, a repetition (whole or partial) of the theme, and a series of cadential phrases of decreasing length, generally with internal repetitions.

Cadenzas

Embedded in Rossini's formal language are opportunities for singers to insert cadenzas. On some occasions they are included in the composer's autograph manuscripts (hence in vocal scores), but mostly they are left to the discretion of the singer. And nowhere is discretion more important. In these moments of soloistic abandon, the orchestra, the dramatic action, the harmonic motion come to a halt as the singer demonstrates his or her artistry. If the cadenza is poorly shaped musically, if its expressive qualities do not draw sustenance from the drama, if it seems unduly prolonged or too short, or if the singer fails to exploit successfully his or her vocal means or reaches beyond them, what should be a transcendental moment crashes to earth. Then again, how do we judge the success or failure of a cadenza? The same notes may seem magical when emerging from one throat and disappointing from another. Some members of the audience may be so outraged by not hearing a cadenza that a recorded performance has imprinted in their ear as "the text" that they are incapable of judging the artistry of a new one. And the "heavenly length" of a cadenza to one critic may seem boringly protracted to another.[37]

These are not problems exclusive to Italian opera. Cadenzas, whether written by the composer or interpolated, play a fundamental role in eighteenth-century concertos, chamber music, and solo sonatas, as well as operas. Instrumentalists, however, tend to know both what is notated in the score and the origin of cadenzas traditionally introduced into a concerto movement. Some proudly write new cadenzas; others, like Robert Levin, vaunt their ability to improvise. In Italian opera, singers too often reproduce what they have learned from teachers or heard on favorite recordings, and only strong intervention can modify their habits. Yet one of the most interesting productions with which I have worked in recent years was a *Barbiere di Siviglia* at Santa Fe Opera during the summer of 1994, conducted by Evelino Pidò and directed by Francesca Zambello. At the beginning of the rehearsal period, singers, conductor, and musicologist agreed that all cadenzas and variations would be newly devised. While this approach would hardly be viable on every occasion, its freshness communicated itself to the audience assembled in the Sangre de Cristo mountains, and the performances were an unqualified success. Dwayne Croft, debuting in the role of Figaro, was loath to give up a standard interpolated high g in "Largo al factotum," but we found compensating fireworks elsewhere: no one hearing this production could have thought for a moment that Croft didn't have high notes to burn.

Much contemporary evidence pertains to the use of cadenzas. As with appoggiaturas, though, taste has changed markedly. I have yet to find a conductor willing to permit singers to interpolate cadenzas of the length considered normal in the nineteenth century: they are more likely to shorten cadenzas already in the score. As we have seen, Verdi wrote a wonderful cadenza *a due* for Gilda and the Duke in their first-act duet in *Rigoletto,* but its heart is frequently ripped away. When Muti opened the La Scala season on 7 December 2000, anticipating the centenary of Verdi's death and using the critical edition of *Il trovatore,* his Count di Luna, Leo Nucci, boasted that he was going to sing Verdi's entire cadenza for "Il balen del suo sorriso," as if he deserved some kind of medal. Few admit that they have become unaccustomed to hearing long cadenzas. Instead they invent excuses about singers going flat, as if singing Verdi in tune were harder than singing Alban Berg, Benjamin Britten, or Luigi Nono. Only when a character is not fully lucid do we seem to countenance a long cadenza: hence our willingness to accept Lucia's interpolated fantasy with flute, an accretion to the opera dating from more than forty years after Donizetti's death.[38]

Rossini either wrote cadenzas directly in the text of a piece or provided cadenza opportunities by notating progressions such as the one given in example 9.8 from the end of Tancredi's opening period in his second-act duet with Amenaide, while adding either a fermata or the indication *a piacere.* Reproducing a cadenza opportunity in performance *come scritto* reveals ignorance of Rossini's style. One can disagree about how to fill in the cadence, not about whether or not it is meant to be filled in. Positioned at the end of musical sections or at points of musical division that prepare new sections, cadenzas usually elaborate a small number of harmonic functions. In one of the most typical functions, as in this example, the harmonic bass moves from the dominant (or fifth) degree of the scale to the tonic degree. The dominant degree supports first a tonic triad in second inversion (what musicians call a six-four chord), then a dominant sonority (V). At the end of the cadenza, voice and orchestra resolve together on the tonic (I). Depending on the length of the cadenza, the singer can muse vocally over the six-four chord or over both. Rossini himself suggested the cadenza given in Example 9.9 for Giuditta Pasta to use in the *Tancredi* duet.[39] It carefully follows the shape of the cadenza opportunity. It begins in mid-register on *bb* (supported by the six-four chord), leaps an octave higher, and then employs a repeated pattern of three notes to descend to a low *bb*, with the dominant harmony. Now the voice

EXAMPLE 9.8. GIOACHINO ROSSINI, *TANCREDI,* DUETTO (N. 14), CADENTIAL FORMULA (MM. 25–26).

EXAMPLE 9.9. GIOACHINO ROSSINI, *TANCREDI*, DUETTO (N. 14), CADENTIAL FORMULA
AS FILLED IN BY THE COMPOSER FOR GIUDITTA PASTA (MM. 25–26).

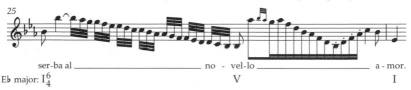

leaps to high *ab* where an arpeggio on the dominant seventh chord leads
again from high to low, then back to midregister. Finally, the voice concludes
on *eb*, the tonic, as in the original score. Pasta gets to display her leaps to registral extremes, her control of short, repeated patterns, her arpeggios, her staccato articulation, and her ability to color the entire cadenza with appropriate
dynamic levels, all to express her rage at what she believes to be Amenaide's
infidelity.

Even when Rossini wrote a cadenza in full, a singer need not feel restricted
to those pitches, although the composer's own cadenzas are usually of su-
perlative quality. In *Guillaume Tell*, for example, Rossini provided a sober
and elegant cadenza, built entirely on the dominant harmony, for Mathilde
to conclude her *romance*, "Sombre fôret." Although there is no particular
reason why a singer would not want to use this cadenza, Cinti-Damoreau,
an artist deeply knowledgeable about Rossini's style, offers five alternatives
in her treatise on singing, employing a wide range of different techniques:
simple or chromatic scales (up and down), arpeggios, complex harmonic
patterns, dissonant lower and upper neighbors, turns and trills, vocal leaps,
in a dizzying array of alternatives. While Rossini's original expresses only a
single harmony, several of Cinti-Damoreau's cadenzas complicate the harmonic progression considerably. Most performers will probably prefer the
more sober cadenza by Rossini, but experimenting with alternatives is perfectly justified.[40]

As we were preparing the critical edition of Rossini's *La gazza ladra* in the
late 1970s, I recall glancing distractedly one day at a volume of the *Strenna
marchigiana* of 1891, one of many periodicals perched casually at that time on
the shelves of the Fondazione Rossini. This one caught my fancy, because its
cover sported the picture of a pretty girl in peasant dress. Absentmindedly
I leafed through its pages, when to my astonishment I found the facsimile of
a full set of variations and cadenzas in Rossini's hand for the cavatina of
Ninetta, the heroine of *La gazza ladra*, "Di piacer mi balza il cor." The manuscript had belonged to Giuseppina Vitali, a young singer who performed this

cavatina at one of Rossini's *soirées musicales* in 1866. Although we were in final proofs, there was a blank page at the end of the first appendix, and with a little pushing and prodding we incorporated this material into the critical edition without renumbering hundreds of pages. The variations are fascinating, and the cadenza Rossini wrote in 1866 to prepare the reprise of the main theme in the cantabile is harmonically audacious with respect to his original.[41] But, of course, his taste and the taste of his singers and audience had changed considerably between 1817 and 1866. And our collective modern taste has changed between 1967 and 2006, and will certainly change again before 2037. While there are basic principles so deeply imbedded in the musical style of Rossini's operas that we ignore them at the risk of destroying the character of his music, there is great latitude about how to interpret those principles.

Ornamental Variations

Late nineteenth-century musicians (and the twentieth-century progeny that perpetuated their attitudes) approached Rossini's scores with scissors in hand. Insensitive to the stylistic context of his music, they complained about repetition, without being aware that for Rossini repetition — of short phrases, entire sections, or even cadential formulas — provided singers with an opportunity for introducing variations. Rossini and his singers inherited techniques that underscored eighteenth-century operatic tradition, where the *da capo* aria, the heart of Metastasian and post-Metastasian practice, was constructed to allow the singer to offer an ornamental variation of the first section (A) when it was repeated, *da capo* (from the top), after a brief contrasting section (B).

Da capo forms pertaining to an entire musical number almost never occur in nineteenth-century works, however, because composers and their librettists sought to incorporate greater dramatic action within each musical number, a structural approach to musical dramaturgy that remained fundamental to Italian opera well into the second half of the century. Musical numbers are therefore constructed of contrasting sections, with different tempos and employing different poetic or musical meters. Repetition, along with the ornamental variations it engenders, occurs *within* individual sections of a multipartite musical number. In order to employ variations appropriately, one must be sensitive to the structural principles underlying the art of Rossini and his followers. Contemporary sources are helpful in suggesting where to introduce variations and where to withhold them. While there may be internal repetitions *within* a lyrical period (since these periods are often constructed in four phrases, AA'BA''), for example, the *entire* melody should be heard before ornamentation is applied. That is what the overwhelming majority of contemporary models demonstrate, and these should serve as our basic frame of reference.[42] The sin of overornamenting Italian opera is just as bad as the sin of not ornamenting at all.

To treat all circumstances in which ornamental variations are appropriate in Italian opera from the first four decades of the nineteenth century would require a treatise devoted to that question alone. Some general principles can be articulated for solo arias, principles that can be applied to similar situations in ensembles. First, we need to distinguish principal lyrical sections (the cantabile and concluding cabaletta) from sections that link or introduce these lyrical sections (a *tempo di mezzo* or other subsidiary passages). Then, within the cantabile and cabaletta, we need to focus on principal melodic periods, without neglecting transitional material or cadential phrases.

While cantabile designs are so varied that attempts to embody them in a few ideal types are necessarily reductive, two structural approaches in Rossini's arias particularly favor ornamental variations. In the first, the principal melody is lyrical throughout. After it is heard in its entirety, a transition (perhaps with a cadenza) leads to a full or partial repetition. It is this repetition that requires an ornamental variation. The Ninetta cavatina from *La gazza ladra* is a perfect example. Example 9.10 gives the principal melody of the cantabile and Rossini's suggestion for ornaments from the Japanese autograph manuscript.[43] The theme is tuneful, an eight-measure period (four measures leading to the dominant at m. 45, four similar measures remaining in the tonic); it is followed by a repeated cadential figure of two measures, featuring a horn solo, and two concluding orchestral measures (these cadences are not included in the example). Rossini ornaments only the main theme, with its simple chordal accompaniment, not the cadences, where active orchestral figurations discourage intervention in the vocal line. His variation respects the basic shape of the melody but elaborates it rhythmically and melodically. The original melody sat between a low *e* and a high *f*♯, while the variation extends the range down to *b* below middle *c* and up to the high *b*, Ninetta's actual range throughout the opera. The variation, in short, does not exaggerate her tessitura; it simply exploits it more fully in the context of her cavatina. Of course, this variation should be attempted only by a singer confident of handling with precision the octave-and-a-half leap from an *e* in the upper register to a low *b* and the two-octave leap back up to the high *b*, all of it, most appropriately, to the word "balza" ("My heart *jumps* for joy!"). The singer also needs to produce both a clean arpeggio down at the end of the

EXAMPLE 9.10. GIOACHINO ROSSINI, *LA GAZZA LADRA*, CAVATINA NINETTA (N. 2), REPEAT OF MAIN THEME, WITH ORNAMENTS WRITTEN BY THE COMPOSER (MM. 42–49).

first full measure of the theme and that lovely combination of triplets and an upward scale (from *d♯* to *a*) for "ge-[nitor]." The penultimate measure, in which the original figurations on the second and third beats (an eighth note and two sixteenths) are made more florid (a sixteenth note and six thirty-seconds), looks worse than it is: in the manuscript for Vitali the composer actually wrote *col canto,* instructing the orchestra (whose part is strictly accompanimental here) to follow what should be a rhythmically free vocal rendition. Attempting to perform this ornamental variation in strict time would be profoundly antimusical. Indeed, the figuration in m. 42 is grammatically wrong: there are too many notes in the measure. And yet Rossini's notation is perfectly appropriate to the musical situation.

The second variety of Rossini cantabile that suggests variation is one that opens with a more declamatory section and only subsequently adopts a more tuneful design, where melodic repetition elicits ornamentation. The archetypical example is the cantabile of Tancredi's cavatina (known as "Di tanti palpiti" from the first words of its cabaletta), in which the mezzo-soprano hero apostrophizes his beloved Amenaide, calls for the downfall of the "empio traditore" (evil traitor) Orbazzano, and invokes glory and love to crown his fidelity. This brief, Maestoso cantabile begins with a declamatory opening (a balanced pair of two-measure phrases), followed by a two-measure lyrical theme (essentially sung twice), and concludes with a modulation to the dominant and a cadenza opportunity in that key. "Di tanti palpiti" follows in the tonic.

For this piece, too, Rossini wrote out a full set of variations later in his life, on 15 August 1858, among his suggestions for Madame Grégoire. In his ornaments for the cantabile, Rossini leaves untouched the opening figuration. While it might seem that the simple opening would welcome elaboration, the composer waits instead for the lyrical theme, intervening at the end of its first statement and more elaborately for its repetition, then provides a lovely cadenza at the end, as in example 9.11. Again, Rossini's ornaments emerge directly from the original music. The figurations concluding the lyrical phrases at the beginning of mm. 71 and 73 extend the register slightly downward and provide more rhythmic activity, while in m. 73 Rossini makes splendid use of chromatic lower neighbors (the $f\sharp$ and the $d\sharp$). The exact repetition of m. 70 in m. 72 is expertly varied, with the triplet arpeggio becoming more rhythmically active, and the final figure, which concludes with a simple triplet ($a-d-c$), becoming a sextuplet, with an extra feint downward and a graceful leap from the interpolated $e-f$ to the concluding $d-c$. It is all measured and musically compelling, the gestures capturing and extending the original musical idea, not arbitrarily imposed upon it. These examples, and the theoretical treatises supporting them, almost always require that ornamental variations consist of *diminutions* (replacing notes of longer values with shorter notes), almost never *augmentations* (replacing notes of shorter values with longer notes). Some singers and misguided coaches try to use augmentation to *simplify* repetitions, but reliance on this antihistorical device is a powerful indicator that a singer is uncomfortable performing florid music.

The Rossini cabaletta rapidly developed into a standardized form. Although he occasionally repeated only part of the principal theme, the basic form is a well-designed, tuneful melodic period (the cabaletta theme), a short transition (sometimes ending with a cadenza), and a full repetition of the theme. Often Rossini did not even write out this repetition, simply indicating that the music is to be derived "Come sopra" (as above). Later composers went further: sometimes Donizetti and Bellini did not even bother to lay out

EXAMPLE 9.11. GIOACHINO ROSSINI, *TANCREDI*, RECITATIVO E CAVATINA TANCREDI
(N. 3), THE CANTABILE IN ITS ORIGINAL VERSION (MM. 65–77) AND
AS ROSSINI HIMSELF MODIFIED IT FOR MAD.^{me} GRÉGOIRE.

empty measures, leaving instead a blank space marked "From A to B," signaling the beginning and end of the passage to be repeated with those letters. They began writing anew with the cadential phrases.

In Rossini the repetition of the cabaletta theme is *always* meant to be varied; to perform a Rossini cabaletta without ornamental variations for the repeat vitiates the meaning of the form. The music is constructed to invite variations, and the orchestral accompaniment is prepared so as not to interfere. Although every document pertaining to contemporary performance practice is in agreement, we still hear some modern performances in which cabaletta themes are repeated without change or in which a singer assumes that changing the dynamic level of the music is sufficient. On the other hand, sheer virtuosity is not the touchstone of a successful variation. What makes Rossini's own variations so delectable is that they grow out of the original musical idea, making their point by the beauty of their detail rather than by sheer glitter.

For Rosina's cavatina in *Il barbiere di Siviglia,* "Una voce poco fa," Rossini wrote out two manuscripts of ornamentation, with similar suggestions, both described earlier in this chapter. One is the 1852 manuscript for Matilde Juva; the other has neither dedicatee nor date. In this cavatina Rossini included only a partial reprise of the cabaletta theme. Example 9.12 opens with the conclusion of the transition and continues with the first eight measures (mm. 91–98) of this partial reprise; it concludes with the very last measures of the theme (mm. 104–107). The example provides both Rossini's original music and the cadenza and ornamental variations from his manuscript for Matilde Juva.[44] The "cadenza opportunity" on the tonic harmony before the reprise is filled out by what is essentially a descending arpeggiation of the tonic triad (from a high g♯ down to *e*), with each of the first four notes of that arpeggio bearing an eight-note figure, the first two with one contour, the last two with a different one. The anticipation of the decisive "Ma" at the end of the cadenza, so dear to every sweet-and-sour Rosina, stems directly from Rossini.

The partial reprise of the cabaletta theme consists of a four-measure lyrical phrase, repeated immediately with a more decisive close. While Rossini does not touch the first appearance of the lyrical phrase, he zooms in on the repetition, leaving the melodic reference points largely unchanged, while playfully bouncing the voice from register to register. At mm. 95 and 96, the figure he introduces on the first two beats is essentially an octave, but notice how differently he takes that octave in the two measures: the first pattern is a simple arpeggiation on the dominant harmony; the second begins with a piquant lower neighbor (*a*♯) before the tonic arpeggio. The scales of m. 97

EXAMPLE 9.12. GIOACHINO ROSSINI, *IL BARBIERE DI SIVIGLIA*, CAVATINA ROSINA (N. 4), THE PREPARATION FOR THE REPEAT OF THE CABALETTA AND TWO EXCERPTS FROM THAT REPEAT (MM. 89–98 AND 105–107), AS ROSSINI ORIGINALLY WROTE THEM AND AS HE HIMSELF MODIFIED THEM FOR MATILDE JUVA.

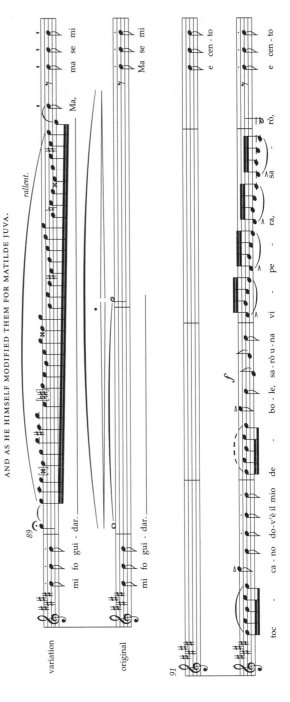

in the original (staccato, but under a slur) yield to a treacherous two-octave arpeggio. Although Rossini varies both cadential phrases, he reserves his most spectacular fireworks for mm. 104–107, where he renders the four-fold repetition of a scalar figure in the original as a breathtaking sequence of rising triplets and falling sextuplets. Developing and singing ornamental variations of this kind is just plain fun.

After the repeat of a cabaletta theme (or after the theme and variations of a *rondò* finale), Rossini normally concluded the vocal part of an aria with a series of repeated cadential phrases of decreasing length and a final one-bar cadence sung three times. Although the procedure is indeed formulaic (as French critics delighted in pointing out), Rossini's powers of invention help sustain our interest. Furthermore, each repetition of a cadential phrase was intended to be varied. The *rondò* from *La Cenerentola,* for example, concludes with a series of cadential phrases of which the first is a nine-measure, repeated phrase. Since Rossini notated all eighteen measures of the vocal line, introducing melodic changes toward the end of the repeat, one might imagine he wanted the music performed as written, but in a manuscript in the library of The University of Chicago there is a set of cadenzas and ornamental variations. While undated (physical evidence suggests the 1820s or 1830s) and without a dedicatee, the changes it introduces at the beginning of the repeat are extraordinary even by Rossini's own standards (example 9.13).[45] The transformation of the descending two-octave scales, first to an arpeggio up followed by one down, then to a series of chromatic figures, is already a difficult vocal trick, but the diminution of the four quarter notes in the original version at m. 199 into eight eighth notes, with leaps up and down, is such a tour de force that I have never succeeded in getting any singer to use it in a performance. It hasn't been for lack of trying. When Cecilia Bartoli first sang the title role in Bologna in 1992, under the direction of Riccardo Chailly, she introduced most of Rossini's own ornaments. In the process, we rehearsed those leaps again and again, but one could hardly blame her for not wanting to risk them in the theater. Ultimately we found a different solution. Nor did she change her mind when she brought her Cenerentola to the Metropolitan Opera. Sometimes I think that only a performer accomplished at scat singing will have the spirit and technique to make Rossini's notes seem both plausible and inevitable. Lovers of Italian opera glory in the past while dreaming of the future.

As the cadential phrases get shorter, the musical content grows more standardized, as do possibilities for variation, but a single note beautifully placed can do wonders. There is a repeated five-measure cadential phrase in

EXAMPLE 9.13. GIOACHINO ROSSINI, *LA CENERENTOLA*, FINALE SECONDO: CORO,
E SCENA CENERENTOLA (N. 16), THE REPETITION OF THE CADENTIAL PHRASE
(MM. 195–200) IN ITS ORIGINAL VERSION AND AS ROSSINI HIMSELF MODIFIED IT.

the cabaletta to Ninetta's cavatina in *La gazza ladra* that Rossini magically
transforms in his variations for Giuseppina Vitali by strategically inserting a
single high *b* in the repeat (example 9.14). By the time he arrives at the final
3×1 conclusion, though, even Rossini falls back on what for him was a standard formula (example 9.15). It is unwise to be overly inventive at this point:
the plane is approaching the runway and it wants to land. Neither Rossini nor
singers during at least the first four decades of the nineteenth century seem
to have thought it a good idea for the soloist to drop out for a few measures
(allowing the orchestra to chug along with its inevitable cadences), returning
in the nick of time to conclude the aria by jumping *up* from the dominant to
the tonic in a high register. We will return to concluding-high-note hijinks
below.

EXAMPLE 9.14. GIOACHINO ROSSINI, *LA GAZZA LADRA*, CAVATINA NINETTA (N. 2),
CADENTIAL REPETITION, WITH A SINGLE NOTE ADDED BY THE COMPOSER IN
THE VARIATIONS FOR GIUSEPPINA VITALI (MM. 125–127).

EXAMPLE 9.15. GIOACHINO ROSSINI, *LA GAZZA LADRA*, CAVATINA NINETTA (N. 2),
FINAL CADENCES, WITH ROSSINI'S STANDARD CONCLUDING GESTURE IN THE
VARIATIONS FOR GIUSEPPINA VITALI (MM. 132–135).

ORNAMENTATION IN BELLINI, DONIZETTI, AND VERDI

Because ornaments in the composer's own hand are extensive and fascinating, I have drawn most examples thus far from Rossini's operas. The principles advanced here, however, do not change radically for Bellini and Donizetti. Although there are fewer examples of their own vocal ornamentation
(Donizetti's varied reprise and cadenzas for the second strophe of "Una furtiva lagrime" have already been cited), there is extensive documentation from
contemporary singers known for their interpretations of the works of these
composers.

Many cadenza opportunities may be found, for example, in *Lucia di Lammermoor*. No self-respecting Edgardo could leave undecorated the final "io
moro per te" at the end of the cantabile of his final aria. And while the infamous
interpolated cadenza *a due* for flute and madwoman should never be considered obligatory, it indicates the level of intervention that seemed permissible
to Donizetti's contemporaries.[46] When Donizetti himself provided a modified
reprise for a theme, on the other hand, whether for musical or dramaturgical
reasons, modern performers should respect his notation. The dying Edgardo's
gasped reprise of his invocation to his beloved Lucia, "Tu che a Dio spiegasti

l'ali," admits no ornamental intervention, not even (despite its fermata) in the final prayer to be joined with her in heaven, "ne congiunga il Nume in ciel." Nor will any Lucia feel compelled to modify what Donizetti wrote with new text ("Del ciel clemente") as the reprise of "Alfin son tua," the cantabile of the mad scene, since the composer's ornamentation is subtle and beautiful. On the other hand, there is plenty of opportunity for fireworks in the cabaletta theme of this same scene, "Spargi d'amaro pianto," and generations of mad Lucias have let rip at this point, to excellent effect, even if their concluding high *e♭* would have made little sense to Donizetti or contemporary singers.

Bellini's messy autograph manuscripts reveal repeated efforts to get cadenzas right, documenting his concern for the vocal qualities of the particular singers with whom he was working.[47] New singers required new cadenzas, as Bellini's own revisions of his operas demonstrate. Some of the composer's cabaletta themes were born with extensive orchestral doublings, reducing the liberty with which singers could ornament a melody. On occasion, however, the composer canceled or reduced these doublings, reflecting not only his recognition (perhaps after hearing them in the theater) that the orchestration was too heavy, but also his response to the ornamenting tendencies of his singers.[48] After all, Giuditta Pasta and Giambattista Rubini cut their theatrical eyeteeth under the watchful eye of Rossini, and there is no evidence that they forgot or set aside *everything* he taught them. Many Bellinian melodies are written with simple chordal accompaniments that allow singers considerable latitude.

Rossini's attitude toward Bellini's music can be judged from two surviving examples of ornamentation he prepared for his younger colleague's operas. The first is a cadenza, written for the English soprano Clara Novello, for Amina at the end of the cantabile (which concludes *a due*) in Elvino's cavatina "Prendi: l'anel ti dono" in *La sonnambula*.[49] The second is a set of variations, surely prepared during the 1830s, for Romeo's cavatina in *I Capuleti e i Montecchi*, in which Rossini ornaments the cantabile and the cabaletta just as he would have ornamented his own music.[50] Example 9.16 offers the first eight measures of Bellini's original cabaletta theme, "La tremenda, ultrice spada," and Rossini's ornamental variation for its repetition. As always, Rossini's variations are elegant and inviting. In the first phrase (A), he keeps the strong rhythmic character of m. 126, but substitutes ascending arpeggios for the dotted rhythms, while adding a figure to ornament the bare quarter note in m. 157. He presses the arpeggios further in m. 158, but when the orchestra doubles the voice in m. 159 he leaves Bellini's melodic line unchanged. In the second phrase (A'), mm. 160–163, he continues much the same kind of treatment, with fine syncopations in m. 160.

EXAMPLE 9.16. VINCENZO BELLINI, *I CAPULETI E I MONTECCHI*, SCENA E CAVATINA DI ROMEO (N. 3), THE REPETITION OF THE CABALETTA THEME (MM. 156–163), WITH AN ORNAMENTAL VARIATION BY GIOACHINO ROSSINI.

This approach to repetitions in Bellini's vocal lines was hardly restricted to Rossini, as is clear from the contemporary singers whose notebooks are replete with variations and cadenzas for the younger composer's operas. Kemble's elaborate notations for the entire role of Norma may reflect her studies with Giuditta Pasta, who created the role, while Cinti-Damoreau's notebooks provide complete variations for aria after aria. One almost never hears in the theater, for example, the repetition of Norma's cabaletta theme "Ah, bello a me ritorno," in which she dreams that Pollione will love her again. The first four measures of Cinti-Damoreau's variation show us what we are missing (example 9.17).[51] Bellini's simple accompanimental figure cries out for vocal freedom, and while Cinti-Damoreau's virtuoso scales, arpeggios, and leaps may not be to everyone's taste, they share with Rossini's examples the ability to illuminate the original musical context rather than seeming to be imposed upon it.

More controversial is the question of Verdi's music. To what extent does the persistence of Rossinian compositional models in Verdi's operas during

EXAMPLE 9.17. VINCENZO BELLINI, *NORMA*, CORO E CAVATINA NORMA (N. 3),
REPRISE OF THE CABALETTA THEME, WITH AN ORNAMENTAL VARIATION
BY LAURE CINTI-DAMOREAU.

the 1840s bring with it earlier performance styles? That many of the same
artists sang Donizetti in the 1830s and Verdi in the 1840s suggests there should
be continuities, but there has been too little investigation of the use of variations and interpolated cadenzas in Verdi pertaining to singers who actually
worked between 1840 and 1860. A suggestive contemporary indication is
found in orchestral materials related to the first performances, under the
composer's direction, of *I masnadieri* at Covent Garden in 1847. Orchestral
lines that double the vocal part are crossed out in both the first presentation
and the repetition of the cabaletta theme in Amalia's cabaletta "Carlo vive?"
This suggests that Jenny Lind, who created the role, may well have introduced
different ornamental figures into her part, so that the orchestra could no
longer play what Verdi had originally written.[52] But when Verdi's student and
friend Emanuele Muzio commented negatively on Lind's "mania for ornamentation," he was not speaking only for himself: he claimed to be voicing
the sentiments of Verdi.[53]

Nonetheless, there is considerable later evidence, including early recordings, that nineteenth-century singers regularly made simple changes in
Verdi's melodic lines, altering and emending phrases to suit their vocal needs
and improvising cadenzas when Verdi created the occasion for one but did
not write it.[54] There are places in *I masnadieri*, for example, where the composer specifically left the task of providing a cadenza to the art of Jenny Lind.
In his music of the 1840s, Verdi had put behind him a mode of thinking
about vocal lines and the relationship between a singer and an operatic text

characteristic of Rossini, Bellini, and Donizetti; yet he continued, paradoxically, to write music whose structure reflected that earlier style.

As a practical matter, it seems to me that modest variations, an occasional diminution, a turn figure, can appropriately be applied to repeated passages in Verdi when the operas are performed complete, but ornamental variations *alla* Rossini and Bellini are to be excluded. And Verdi was absolutely clear that he wanted singers to avoid the grunts and vocal clamor that mar so many productions. A strong performance by Dolora Zajick as Azucena in Chicago Lyric Opera's *Trovatore* in 1993 was cheapened by her cackling at the end of the opera. Verdi would have been outraged. Nor is she alone in supplying superfluous sound effects. In a wonderful letter from Genoa to Léon Escudier in Paris on the occasion of the performance there of the revised *Macbeth*, Verdi wrote:

> Here we are at the *Sleepwalking* scene, which is always the high point of the opera. Anyone who has seen [Adelaide] Ristori [a famous actress who portrayed Lady Macbeth in Shakespeare's *Macbeth*] knows that very few gestures are needed, indeed everything can be limited to a single gesture, to rub away a spot of blood that she believes to have on her hand. The motions should be slow, and her footsteps should be hardly visible; her feet should drag along on the ground as if she were a statue or a ghost who walks. The eyes fixed, the body cadaverous; she is in agony and dies immediately after. Ristori made a rattling noise, a death-rattle. In music this must not and cannot be done; just as one should not cough in the last act of *Traviata* or laugh in the *È scherzo od è follia* of *Ballo in maschera*.[55]

How many sleepwalking Lady Macbeths, dying Violettas, and laughing Riccardos should have these words implanted in their memory. As Verdi continues to Escudier, the lament in the English horn supplies the effect of the death-rattle and does so "more poetically." There is room for singers to interpret Verdi's vocal lines with sensitivity and even, in certain instances, to provide small variations. There is no room for self-indulgence.

PUNTATURE AND PITFALLS

While ornamentation often bends melodic lines to the specific capabilities of a singer, it has a fundamental role to play in realizing in sound the composer's notation. *Puntature,* on the other hand, are required exclusively to assist a singer in performing passages that are awkward for his or her voice or that pose problems of breathing and syllable placement. Such *puntature* are frequently required in modern performance, and singers, conductors, scholars, and critics should not flinch before them. Few tenors, even those willing to employ a falsetto-like head voice, are likely to undertake with success the high *f* Bellini wrote for Rubini in "Credeasi, misera!" near the conclusion of *I puritani*.[56] Nor is this the only place where Rubini's legendary range has required modern singers (and most nineteenth-century singers) to modify the vocal line or even transpose entire numbers. Indeed, as we shall in the next chapter, few printed editions of Bellini's operas written for Rubini offer the solo music in its original keys.

Puntature were regularly needed in the nineteenth century, when in the course of an operatic season singers had to take multiple roles, not all of which were fully appropriate to their capabilities. Under the supervision of local music directors, the artists themselves would make necessary accommodations. As we have seen in chapter 7, when Verdi's *Ernani* was performed in Vienna in May 1844, shortly after its Venetian premiere, the composer was unable to attend rehearsals, but he sent explicit instructions. To the director of staging at the Kärntnertortheater he stressed that "the performance be accurate," adding, "Please do not allow cuts. There is nothing to take out and not even the shortest phrase could be removed without damaging the whole."[57] In a separate letter to Donizetti, music director of the theater, Verdi expressed his appreciation that the older composer had agreed to follow rehearsals, and asked him to supervise whatever *puntature* would be necessary.

Certain *puntature* tend to become traditional, passed down from teacher to student, petrified in recorded performances. One sympathizes with all the mezzo-sopranos who, faced with Rossini's written text toward the end of the cantabile of Cenerentola's final aria, take the easy way out by breaking the music at the beginning of m. 100 (the second measure in example 9.18), anticipating the final syllables of the word "rapido," breathing deep, and then singing Rossini's cadenza on the syllable "ah!" When I pointed out to Cecilia Bartoli, though, that Rossini's way of handling this passage—as a single musical gesture—was ever so much more beautiful, she steadied her extraordinary instrument, set aside the requisite air, and shot through the passage exactly as the composer conceived it. It was an object lesson that no traditional *puntatura* should be allowed to persist from one performance to another when a great singer is able to negotiate the original.

Two interesting examples of traditional *puntature* emerged during rehearsals in the spring of 2001 for Verdi's *La traviata* at the Verdi Festival of Parma, with Darina Takova in the role of Violetta and Carlo Rizzi on the podium. There are numerous places where singers over the years have

EXAMPLE 9.18. GIOACHINO ROSSINI, *LA CENERENTOLA*, FINALE SECONDO: CORO,
E SCENA CENERENTOLA (N. 16), CONCLUSION OF THE CANTABILE (MM. 99–100),
AS WRITTEN AND AS SUNG WITH A *PUNTATURA*.

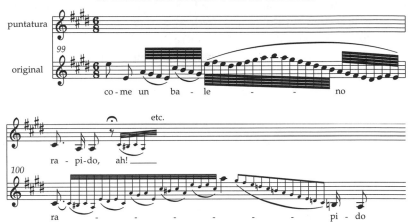

modified the music for Violetta's great aria "Ah fors'è lui," with its cabaletta
"Sempre libera," at the conclusion of the first act. One, in the middle of the cabaletta theme, just before the reprise of the opening tune, is very much like the
Rossini example cited above: the premature completion of a word, a hastily
caught breath, and an interpolated "ah!"[58] (example 9.19). The passage as written by Verdi, with its arrival at high *c* on the last syllable of "ritrovi" after a trill
on *g*, is much more beautiful than the *puntatura*, assuring a long melodic line
through the end of the phrase, but it makes difficult demands on the vocalist
in a context that is already daunting. In this case one can only be thankful for
the existence of a performance tradition to assist those singers who need help.

In the case of Violetta's cadenza at the close of the cantabile, on the other
hand, a performance tradition that simplifies the singer's task severely distorts
Verdi's musical idea. His notation suggests groupings of sixteenth notes lightly

EXAMPLE 9.19. GIUSEPPE VERDI, *LA TRAVIATA*, ARIA VIOLETTA (N. 3), WITHIN THE
CABALETTA THEME (MM. 156–158), AS WRITTEN AND AS SUNG WITH A *PUNTATURA*.

EXAMPLE 9.20. GIUSEPPE VERDI, *LA TRAVIATA*, ARIA VIOLETTA (N. 3),
THE CADENZA CONCLUDING THE CANTABILE (MM. 113–114), AS WRITTEN AND
AS SUNG WITH A *PUNTATURA*.

accented at the *beginning* of each group, so that the final "delizia al cor" can be sung as written.[59] This procedure, though, makes it difficult for a singer to catch her breath anywhere within the cadenza. In fact, the music is almost never sung this way. The notes are grouped with implied accents at the *end* of each group of four, the last accent occurring on the first of the two sixteenth notes for "delizia." All the beaming is implicitly modified, and "de-[lizia]" is postponed until the low *e*, allowing Violetta to take a good breath before finishing the phrase (example 9.20). Again, one understands the motivation for this *puntatura*, but it should represent a last resort, a change introduced to assist a singer in serious difficulty, not a tradition to be preserved. Yet faced with the imperious, unforgiving, and noisy Parma *loggionisti*, who have never actually examined Verdi's notation and know only what they hear on old recordings, Takova (perfectly capable of singing Verdi's own music) allowed their incivility to influence her decision to adopt the *puntatura*.

In today's operatic world, if a singer is capable of handling with distinction the bulk of a role, it is far preferable to remove or modify a few individual notes at the extremes of his or her register than to preserve notes that sound poor; it is far preferable to simplify a florid passage he or she finds particularly ungrateful than to allow the notes to blur; it is far preferable to make room for a breath than to have a phrase sputter to an unsatisfying conclusion. There are limits, however, beyond which the indiscriminate use of *puntature* is destructive. Beverly Sills passed that limit when she played Pamyra in Rossini's *Le Siège de Corinthe*, a part much too low for her voice. Montserrat Caballé passed that limit when she assumed the title role in *Ermione*, a part for which she no longer had the requisite vocal skills.

Other pitfalls need to be pointed out. Not one of the singers working in the first four decades of the nineteenth century would ever have introduced into a Rossini opera the kind of coloratura and variations that became standard at the end of the nineteenth century. In America, this type of vocalism is best known through an edition of "Una voce poco fa" edited by Estelle Liebling, who passed on her late nineteenth-century taste and training to several generations of American singers, including Beverly Sills.[60] I still see this execrable piece of work in the hands of young singers, and I simply cannot fathom the know-nothingism that allows such a practice to continue to flourish in American conservatories.

The problem is not that Liebling transposed the cavatina up a half step from *E major* to *F major* so that it suits a higher voice. Although I believe that Rossini's comic operas lose much when their female protagonists are sung by sopranos rather than the contraltos and mezzo-sopranos Rossini had in mind, such transpositions were already common in the early nineteenth century. Nor are there grounds for arguing against the use of variations intended to push the tessitura higher, for Rossini's own ornaments often do the same. But three elements of the Liebling variants for "Una voce poco fa" are more disturbing: all testify to historical ignorance and stylistic insensitivity. First, the voice is allowed to exhibit coloratura pyrotechnics that are totally out of style. Rossini never wrote any part resembling the Queen of the Night in Mozart's *Die Zauberflöte*, Olympia in Offenbach's *The Tales of Hoffman*, or the title role in Delibes' *Lakmé*, and a cadenza that prepares the repeat of a cabaletta theme with the kind of vocalism seen in example 9.21 is unheard of in his operas.[61] If no singer performing an Italian opera can be taken to task for failure to respect the style of that opera, as some critics apparently believe, then performers of Mozart, Mussorgsky, or Wagner should be permitted similar latitude. But that uncomfortable consequence is rarely acknowledged. I have already described the anger generated by Cecilia Bartoli's decision to interpolate Mozart's own substitute arias for *Le nozze di Figaro* into that same opera. Imagine if she had let fly a *Cenerentola* cadenza!

Second, Rossini's cadenzas and those of the singers of his age occur in well-defined structural positions. Rhythm matters, and the insertion of extraneous cadenzas in the middle of a balanced phrase, another Liebling

EXAMPLE 9.21. GIOACHINO ROSSINI, *IL BARBIERE DI SIVIGLIA*, CAVATINA ROSINA (N. 4), THE PREPARATION FOR THE REPEAT OF THE CABALETTA IN ESTELLE LIEBLING'S VERSION AND KEY (MM. 89–90).

speciality, destroys the symmetry so characteristic of the composer's art. Finally, there are many appropriate opportunities for vocal display throughout a Rossini aria. But nowhere in his operas, nowhere in the variations he explicitly wrote for singers, nowhere in the pedagogical treatises from the first half of the nineteenth century, nowhere in the notebooks of Laure Cinti-Damoreau or Adelaide Kemble, nowhere in printed editions with singers' ornaments, *nowhere* does one find a Rossini aria that concludes by simplifying Rossini's notation and then by having the singer drop out of the cadences, introduce a cadenza at a totally inopportune moment, and conclude with a high note (in this case a stratospheric *f*), as in this classic Liebling finale. Example 9.22 includes Rossini's original text and his own variation for Matilde Juva (both transposed to *F major*), as well as Liebling's version.[62]

"The audience expects it." "My public demands it." "If I don't sing it, they'll think I don't have it." "What would my mother say?" You name the

EXAMPLE 9.22. GIOACHINO ROSSINI, *IL BARBIERE DI SIVIGLIA*, CAVATINA ROSINA (N. 4), THE FINAL CADENCES OF THE CABALETTA, AS ROSSINI WROTE THEM AND VARIED THEM FOR MATILDE JUVA (TRANSPOSED TO *F MAJOR*), AND AS ESTELLE LIEBLING RENDERED THEM (MM. 111–114).

justification, I've heard it. With all the freedom to ornament, all the freedom to add cadenzas (including high notes), somehow the battle lines form over the last note of a piece, as if the audience will forget all the artistry and fireworks of an entire evening in the theater unless reminded by a final stentorian howl. In all the many cadenzas and variations in Adelaide Kemble's notebook, filled with ornamentation for *Tancredi, Il barbiere di Siviglia, Norma, Lucia di Lammermoor,* and operas by Mercadante and Pacini, there is not a single example of this practice. In the music of Rossini, it is simply an anachronism, sometimes a pleasant one, perhaps, but still an anachronism. Even in Riccardo Muti's exquisitely crafted interpretation of *Il trovatore* that opened the Scala season on 7 December 2000, a few *loggionisti* booed when the tenor, Salvatore Licitra, did not interpolate the high *c* at the end of "Di quella pira." And the late Franco Corelli, whose powerful voice was not always matched by artistic insight, was quoted as saying that *Il trovatore* was not *Il trovatore* without the high *c*. While I am not so implacably opposed to this interpolation as Muti is (so long as the singer can perform the rest of the role as Verdi wrote it), the devotion of a small part of the public to the interpolated note is absurd.[63]

Did singers improvise cadenzas and variations in the nineteenth century, or did they and their coaches (sometimes the composers themselves) work them out in advance? Contemporary sources suggest that true improvisation was rare. There are striking similarities in variations associated with different singers, and even when Rossini himself wrote out ornaments for a single piece on multiple occasions, he tended to repeat himself. The large number of surviving sources with ornamentation penciled in suggests that singers developed an interpretation and reproduced it for the most part fairly consistently.

This supposition is supported by evidence from our own century. The very queen of Rossinians, Marilyn Horne, worked from ornamentation prepared in advance (usually by her superb pianist and coach, Martin Katz). If she felt that a pattern was working poorly, of course, she was eminently capable of changing it on the spot. Of all the Rossini singers with whom I have worked over the past thirty years, however, Cecilia Gasdia is the only one whose extraordinary musicianship and mastery of *bel canto* style allowed her instinctively to spin out one complex series of variations after another. Even Gasdia, however, tended to adopt a single set of variations for a run of performances, to the immense relief of the terrorized conductors working with her.

When critics speak of improvisation in *bel canto* opera, they often invoke jazz. While there are similarities between the genres, there are also enormous differences. The presence of a large orchestra, with multiple players on each string part, means that even accomplished musicians cannot modify their pitches as they listen to the meanderings of a singer. A single solo instrument can be interactive, of course, and I will never forget the redheaded clarinettist with the Chamber Orchestra of Europe, whose name I never knew, modifying his instrumental echoes to respond to the variations used by Bernadette Manca di Nissa, in the role of Isaura, when she repeated her cabaletta theme in the first Pesaro production of *Tancredi* in 1982.[64] But an improvising singer in *bel canto* opera whose instinct leads her through a slightly different harmonic path to a cadential goal will soon find herself creating horrid dissonances with the orchestra, a situation that a fine jazz quartet could readily overcome. Nineteenth-century singers were very much like modern ones: some were superb musicians, capable of spinning out inventive variations and cadenzas; others possessed splendid instruments but had to learn everything in advance. Ultimately what matters is not whether a singer improvises cadenzas and variations, but whether he or she performs with intelligence, musicality, and stylistic acumen.

There is, to be sure, no moral obligation for singers to employ variations or cadenzas at all or, if they do, to choose those with aesthetic roots in the style of the composer. Nor should a tenor be arrested for singing the high *c* at the end of "Di quella pira." But musical art is a complex mechanism in which the separate parts have a tendency to move in tandem. The structure of Rossini's music and the character of his vocal style are beautifully adapted to the style of ornamentation Rossini favored; the structure and character of the style to which Verdi was aiming favored very different vocal techniques, even if his early works sometimes sit uncomfortably between two worlds. Singers who train their voices to accomplish certain tasks cannot move to others without a period of adjustment. That is why lovers of fine singing are horrified when promising young artists, whose voices are well suited to the *bel canto* repertory, are exploited by conductors desperate for new faces to sing such heavy parts as Verdi's Aida or Otello or Puccini's Turandot. If there is any place within the world of Italian opera where one can justifiably speak of moral obligation and high crimes, that would be a pretty good place to start.

10

HIGHER AND LOWER: TRANSPOSING BELLINI AND DONIZETTI

"ANY NOTE YOU CAN SING, I CAN SING HIGHER"

As Ethel Merman taught us in a duet/duel from Irving Berlin's *Annie Get Your Gun*, singing is both art and gymnastic competition. Fanatics in the audience treat the theater as a gladiatorial arena: they pay the price of admission to judge whether artists have cleared the high *e♭* or scored a bulls-eye on the low *f*. No Roman spectator with thumb pointed downward was ever more intolerant than a scornful *loggionista* booing a soprano who hasn't made the grade. Those fanatics know where registral extremes lie, where the tessitura sits uncomfortably high or low, where a two-and-a-half octave scale threatens the unwary. Bred on the fantasy of recorded bliss, they judge real performances by canned sound.

   Just as performers have made cuts in the written text of an opera since the dawn of the genre, so too have they transposed music up and down to suit their vocal needs. Autograph manuscripts and contemporary manuscript copies from the first half of the nineteenth century are filled with phrases like "a half tone lower," "in *G major,*" or even with two or more alternatives, some lower than the notated tonality, some higher.[1] Not only do we find the *E major* "Una voce poco fa" from *Il barbiere di Siviglia* a half tone higher, in the *F major* beloved by sopranos, but even in *G major,* where Joséphine Fodor-Mainvielle liked to sing it in Paris during the 1820s.[2] (By December 1825, however, her vocal means had so deteriorated that she was forced to withdraw after a single performance in the title role of Rossini's *Semiramide,* essentially ending her Parisian career.)[3]

   There is nothing exceptional about these transpositions. The quality of Luciano Pavarotti's performances in Donizetti's *La Fille du régiment* at the Metropolitan Opera in 1995, as his career was drawing nearer to an end, should not be judged by whether he actually sang the eight notorious high *c*s at the end of Tonio's *cavatine* "Pour mon âme quel destin," not to mention the additional high *c* usually interpolated within the final cadence, or requested that the piece be transposed down a half or a whole tone to enable him to make another stab at a demanding tenor role that he had mastered in his youth. Yes, it is thrilling to hear a fresh voice sing the *cavatine* in its original key and knock off those high notes to perfection, and Juan Diego Flórez made a sensation in a concert at Pesaro during the summer of 2000 when he sang "Pour mon âme quel destin" as an encore, but that young voice may or may not have developed the artistry of a seasoned professional in the remainder of the role.[4] Marilyn Horne's magisterial performance as Falliero in Rossini's *Bianca e Falliero* in Pesaro during the summer of 1986 was in no way compromised by her decision to lower parts of the second-act *gran scena*, "Tu non sai qual colpo atroce," by a tone, from *F minor/major* to *Eb minor/major*. Careful modifications in the *secco* recitative made the shift imperceptible to all but those few following with score in hand, and no one cried "scandal" when the several high *c*s written by Rossini, treacherous for the diva at that moment in her career, became so many high *bb*s, which she sang with conviction and passion.[5]

Pitch is not celestially ordained; it is relative. Today we usually set concert *a* between 440 and 444 vibrations per second, but some orchestras persist in pushing the pitch still higher to obtain a brighter sound. During the nineteenth century, there were enormous pitch differences from one country to another, even from one city to another. When an effort to regulate pitch throughout Europe took shape during the 1880s, Verdi was a staunch supporter of a uniform pitch level, and would have preferred that it be set at $a = 432$, despite a faction of Roman musicians who wanted it to be as high as $a = 450$. (Verdi contemptuously commented that such an *a* in Rome would be a *bb* anywhere else.)[6] Finally an international commission (with the participation of Arrigo Boito) brought a modicum of uniformity to European practice by setting standard pitch at $a = 435$.[7] Despite their formal agreements, in some countries and theaters the pitch level continued to be higher, in others lower. A soprano's high *c* today is generally higher than a similar note during the first half of the nineteenth century. Asking a prima donna to sing "Casta Diva" in *Norma* in its original key of *G major*, rather than transposing it down to *F major*, or the mad scene in *Lucia di Lammermoor* in its original key (beginning in *D minor* and concluding in *F major*), rather than transposing the whole scene down a full tone, is not the same when *a* was set at 430 vibrations per second, as it might have been heard in Milan in 1831 or Naples in 1835, rather than in the higher tunings of today.

Only rarely do we find composer-generated transposition in Rossini's operas (although that does not mean he would have disapproved of singers making transpositions), but the problem of transposition has broader importance when we consider the operas of Verdi, and it becomes fundamental for those of Bellini and Donizetti. As we gain access to more of Verdi's compositional sketches, for example, we see how often he drafted compositions in higher keys, then brought them down when he prepared his autograph manuscripts.[8] Before examining this problem from a practical viewpoint, however, it is worth considering a more general question: to what extent do choices of tonality in Italian opera depend upon a composer's vision of a coherent role for tonality in a stage work?

Over the past thirty years, the use of tonality to carry dramatic and musical meaning has been one of the more bitterly contested and politically charged terrains in the study of Italian opera. Keys and key relationships are central to German and Austrian instrumental music, after all, and scholars have demonstrated how these instrumental principles also influence the structure of operas by Mozart, Beethoven, or Wagner. Some of these demonstrations, in their insistence on the organic cohesion of entire operas, push the evidence far beyond what it seems able to bear.[9] It is true, for example, that Wagner, in *Opera and Drama,* his 1850–51 treatise setting forth some of the precepts that would inform the composition of *Der Ring der Nibelungen,* developed a theory of the "musical-dramatic period" that emphasizes the unifying role tonality could play in his evolving concept of music drama. The gulf between that important insight and the systematic theory set forth by Alfred Lorenz in his monumental *The Secret of Form in Richard Wagner,* however, is immense.[10] It is no surprise that over the past twenty years scholars and critics have tended to set aside Lorenz's massive symmetrical designs and to seek other ways of thinking about the structure of Wagner's operas. Sometimes, however, their rejection has gone too far. To ask, "What do we gain by saying that *Tristan* Act III is 'in' B major?" in order to promulgate other critical approaches is an arrogant denial of ordering principles that generations of composers and thinkers about music found of fundamental importance.[11] No one has ever claimed that the assertion of a tonal plan for all or part of an opera exhausts that opera's meaning.

Attempts to move discussion of Italian opera into the mainstream of scholarly discourse have invariably spawned efforts to show that keys and key relationships are also crucial to this repertory, as if such evidence of compositional planning might help ensure musicological respectability to the sunny South. Thus, while analysis and criticism of *oltremontani* composers were moving away from organicist tonal explanations, students of Italian opera began to embrace them.[12] Controversy still surrounds many of these efforts, but a number of highly successful studies have centered on Verdi's *Rigoletto,* an opera with a complex but convincing tonal underpinning.[13]

The prelude of *Rigoletto* begins with a phrase that recurs many times throughout the opera, referring to the curse that Monterone launches against Rigoletto and the Duke, the curse that works itself out with the seduction and death of Rigoletto's own daughter, Gilda. While centered on the pitch *c* and leading to a cadence in *C minor,* the phrase moves toward and away from a complex chord that can be heard in two ways: as a dark, dissonant sonority coloring the *c,* a momentary detail lending dramatic weight to the theme, or (respelling the *f♯* as the enharmonically equivalent *g♭* and putting the *a♭* in the bass) as a chord functioning as the dominant of *D♭ major* (or *minor*), which forces the tonality up a half tone to a resolution in a new key (example 10.1). These tonal poles recur throughout the opera: *c* seems to represent the curse or threat, *d♭* its terrible consequences. Not only does the opera begin in *C minor* and conclude in *D♭,* but this progression and related ones become implanted in our hearing. Early in his soliloquy ("Pari siamo") comparing himself to the assassin, Sparafucile, Rigoletto recalls that the old man cursed him, invoking the opening motive on *c,* then immediately moving to *d♭* for "O uomini!... o natura!..." The jester's furious attack on the courtiers, "Cortigiani, vil razza dannata," begins in *C minor,* but the aria concludes with his plea for mercy, "Miei Signori, perdono, pietate," in *D♭ major.* Composers do not begin an aria in one key and conclude a half step higher without strong motivation. When Rigoletto weeps with his daughter at the end of the second act, they

EXAMPLE 10.1. GIUSEPPE VERDI, *RIGOLETTO,* PRELUDIO (N. 1), MM. 1–3, WITH AN ALTERNATIVE INTERPRETATION OF THE HARMONY IN M. 2.

do so in *D♭*; but immediately after, when the doomed Monterone passes escorted by guards, the music is in *C minor.*

Many scholars are content to concentrate on those tonal relationships in an opera that seem central to the drama, without insisting on a scheme in which each key traversed must be thought to have profound symbolic meaning. Rossini's *Maometto II,* for example, is a tragic opera that sets the fate of four characters against a background of historical events—the wars between the Turks and the Venetians, culminating in the fall of Negroponte.[14] Paolo Erisso is in charge of the Venetian forces; Maometto II leads the assault of the Turks. It is a fourfold tragedy: of Anna, Erisso's daughter, who is in love with Maometto but cannot permit herself to surrender to feelings that betray her people; of the conqueror Maometto, who cannot have the only joy he truly desires; of Erisso, who loves his daughter above all else but feels honor-bound to supply her with the dagger she will ultimately use to take her own life; and of Calbo, the young Venetian warrior, who wishes to wed Anna but will not impose his affections on a woman who loves another.

The introduction, with which the opera begins (there is no overture), is in *E♭ major;* the entire opera will conclude in *E major* with the suicide of Anna. A casual glance at the score might suggest that Rossini was indifferent to tonal structure, since he ends the opera a semitone higher than its point of departure; but there is strong evidence that this is not the case. A central image of the opera is the tomb in which the ashes of Anna's mother lie. When Erisso asks his daughter to wed Calbo, he invokes his wife's tomb. Accompanied by tremolo strings alone, the phrase begins in *E♭ major,* then lurches upward a semitone to *E major.* The last scene of the opera takes place in the church, amid the tombs. Erisso pauses before the tomb of his wife. Within a recitative passage he breaks into a lyrical phrase, which begins not in *E♭ major* but in the closely related *A♭ major.* As Erisso invokes the heaven where his wife now resides, the music sits on the dominant (*E♭ major*) and then tortuously modulates up a semitone to the familiar *E major.* After Calbo's *E-major* aria, Anna enters. Before her mother's tomb, she vows to follow her father's wishes and accept the hand of Calbo. Her music is identical to the phrase Erisso sang earlier in the scene.

Ultimately, her vow of fidelity before the tomb of her mother and her vow to kill herself rather than be captured by the Turks are musically integrated by their similar settings and tonality. During the course of the first-act *terzettone,* Erisso hands her a dagger, her "inheritance" on this fatal day: she is to use it rather than fall captive to the Turks. It is a phrase declaimed first over a tremolando accompaniment on the pitch *e.* At the very end of the opera,

Anna turns on Maometto and tells him that, in front of her mother's tomb, she has sworn her faith to Calbo; then she stabs herself, singing:

Sul cenere materno	Over my mother's ashes
Io porsi a lui la mano;	I gave him my hand;
Il cenere materno	Let my mother's ashes
Coglie il mio sange ancor.	Now receive my blood.

In a passage that refers explicitly to the earlier phrase, the first two lines are declaimed on the pitch *e* over a tremolando accompaniment in *E major*. Hence, the *Eb major* to *E major* progression heard in Erisso's very first invocation of his wife's tomb takes on a wider musical and dramatic meaning throughout the opera and duplicates on a small scale the large-scale *Eb major* to *E major* tonality of the entire work.

Some scholars construct schemes in which every tonal choice throughout an opera is assigned deeper meaning. As their arguments become subtler, they attract dissenters, who refuse excessive claims for tonal significance and insist on the difference between more autonomous instrumental music and the complex musical and dramatic web that constitutes opera. Dissenters also point out how often composers modified keys during the composition of an opera or during later revisions, to which believers retort by insisting on the complex functioning of tonality, in which *new* relationships are brought out when keys are modified.[15] But if we cannot imagine a series of keys for which it would be impossible to find an ostensible explanation, if every tonal choice is meaningful, we are in the world of Lake Wobegon, where all the children are above average, or of *The Gondoliers:* "When every one is somebodee, then no one's anybody!" It is the principle of non-negation: if there is no way to demonstrate that a particular tonal progression is without dramaturgical meaning, then the dramaturgical significance of tonality is tautological, and why do we waste our breath?

Tonal choices for a composer of Italian opera were not without significance. Sometimes they are embedded in a web of meaning that underlies an entire work, sometimes they have local significance (ensuring a musically viable sequence of keys), sometimes they highlight particular instrumental colors. But tonal choices represent only one set of decisions: many other factors in the composition or performance of an opera can assume greater importance, leading a composer to modify the tonality of a passage or to accept the desire of a singer to do the same.[16] In practical terms, however, these modifications often create problems that are insufficiently understood and, in some cases, imperfectly resolved in the opera house.

Two of the worst transitional passages in all of Italian opera, one in Verdi's *La traviata* (the progression that links the end of the duet for Violetta and Alfredo in the last act with the "finale ultimo") and one in Bellini's *Norma* (the orchestral introduction to "Casta Diva"), are the result of transpositions gone awry, interventions made after the operas were completed and performed. Some critics have gone so far as to praise these infelicities, as if the composers had turned necessities into masterstrokes. Poppycock: no similar passages exist anywhere else in the works of Verdi or Bellini, precisely because Verdi and whoever made the modification in *Norma* (possibly Bellini) invented awkward, last-minute solutions to accommodate transpositions made to suit the needs of their singers.

VERDI TRANSPOSES VERDI: *LA TRAVIATA*

The version of *La traviata* normally performed today was prepared for a revival of the opera on 6 May 1854 at the Teatro San Benedetto of Venice, slightly more than a year after the first version of the work was launched at the Teatro La Fenice of the same city on 6 March 1853. In the revised opera, the cabaletta of the duet for Violetta and Alfredo, "Gran Dio!... morir sì giovine," concludes in *C major,* but the ensuing finale begins in *A major,* with a *c♯* in the orchestral melody. In order to move from *C major* to *A major,* Verdi jumps from a one-measure rhythmic figure on *c* to the same figure on *e.* That, in turn, functions as the dominant of *A major* (example 10.2). Julian Budden attempts to explain Verdi's modifications to the end of the duet by asserting that "in his revision Verdi tightened up the coda giving it additional urgency and harmonic strength and cutting off any possibility of applause by a purely rhythmic transition to the key of the Finale ultimo."[17] But anyone who has ever watched the behavior of an audience bent on cheering at the conclusion of such a piece—and Verdi was always attentive to his audiences—knows that the public pays little attention to niceties of the kind suggested by Budden. Even if making applause more difficult was a byproduct of Verdi's revision, it could hardly have been his motive. Why, then, did Verdi introduce this unattractive and atypical progression into his score?

Ensuring a comfortable tessitura for the singers who would most likely be engaged to perform *La traviata* had everything to do with motivating Verdi's 1854 revisions. As Fabrizio Della Seta has shown in his critical edition of the opera, which presents both the 1853 and 1854 versions, many 1854 modifications affected the part of the father, Germont, whose original tessitura was quite high. While Verdi knew Varesi's voice well (the singer had been his first

EXAMPLE 10.2. GIUSEPPE VERDI, *LA TRAVIATA*, THE TRANSITION
FROM THE DUETTO (N. 10), MM. 318–320, TO THE FINALE ULTIMO (N. 11),
M. 1, IN THE REVISION OF 1854.

Macbeth and Rigoletto), he sought to characterize the father of Alfredo in 1853 through an insistent, imperious declamation, in a register often centered above *e,* already a high note for the baritone. Before his duet with Violetta, Germont originally introduced the idea of his *two* children by declaiming "[domanda or] qui de' suoi due figli!" on high *f,* descending on the last syllable to *eb;* in the revised version the part descends and the final two notes are an octave lower (the lower *f–eb*). When Violetta at the beginning of the finale expresses her gratitude to die in the arms of those who love her, Germont responds "Che mai dite?" In the original version he leaped to high *f* for "di-[te]"; in the revision he remained more docilely on middle *c.*

In the often-eliminated cabaletta of his aria, Germont originally sang a cadential phrase that kept him in a high baritonal register, and then returned to the phrase a third still higher, insistently and aggressively repeating *f.* In the revision, down came the voice. Lowering the register of Germont was by no means the only effect of Verdi's modifications. In this same cabaletta, for example, he introduced an improved cadential phrase before the final cadenza, avoiding the more obvious symmetry of the original. Yet practical necessity certainly motivated the composer's intervention. The revised version of the cabaletta is more anodyne in comparison, one of the reasons it has proved so easy to cut: Verdi sacrificed in his revision the highly charged aggression of the original, which was in part dependent on the very high register.

Matters of register are also fundamental to Verdi's revision of the last-act duet for Violetta and Alfredo. In 1853 their cabaletta ("Gran Dio!... morir sì giovine") was in D♭ *major,* whereas in 1854 Verdi brought it down a half tone to C *major.* In the original key, the transition to the finale functioned smoothly: the duet ended on the tonic chord of D♭ *major,* while the first melodic note of the finale transformed this *d♭* to its enharmonic equivalent, *c♯.* In D♭ *major,* however, the part of Alfredo in the duet lies rather high (by comparison with the tessitura of his aria, for example), and it would have been awkward to change a melody he sings in alternation with Violetta. Yet the revision and transposition also gave Verdi the opportunity to replace a more traditional repeated cadential phrase (as he did in the Germont cabaletta), to eliminate a full stop after the cabaletta for the audience to applaud (as suggested by Budden), and to avoid insisting on the tonic D♭ (*major* or *minor*), a key that returns immediately for the final ensemble ("Prendi, quest'è l'immagine"). Ultimately he may have felt that all these apparent "goods" were sufficient to justify the poor transition that was needed to make them possible.

Verdi's autograph manuscripts and sketches are filled with examples of transpositions decided upon during the course of composition. In *Ernani,* the cantabile of Elvira's cavatina "Ernani, Ernani involami" was originally drafted in A *major* within the composer's autograph manuscript, but was transposed up (a rare occurrence) by a half tone to B♭ *major* before Verdi orchestrated the piece.[18] The final ensemble in act 2 of *Un ballo in maschera,* with its ironic laughter for the conspirators as they realize that the veiled woman Renato is escorting is his own wife, was sketched in B *major;* by the time Verdi entered the music into the skeleton score that would become his autograph manuscript, it was in B♭ *major.* The same fate befell Oscar's invitation to the masked ball, "Di che fulgor, che musiche": sketched in B *major,* it ended up in B♭ *major.* In *Stiffelio* many pieces were sketched in one key, but were placed in a different key when Verdi entered them into his autograph manuscript.[19] Thus, the cabaletta in the scena and aria for Stiffelio was sketched in B♭ *major,* but ultimately realized in A *major;* the scene and prayer for Lina was sketched in both E♭ *major* (the definitive key) and E *major;*[20] the cabaletta of Stankar's aria was sketched in A *major,* a tone higher than its definitive collocation, whereas the intensely dramatic solo for Lina in her duet with Stiffelio "Non allo sposo volgermi" is also sketched a tone higher than in the definitive version. In almost every case, the tonality for solo numbers in the completed *Stiffelio* is *lower* by a half or a whole step than the tonality in the sketch. The pattern certainly suggests that vocal range played an important, perhaps decisive, role in Verdi's decisions about keys in *Stiffelio.*

We have explicit evidence of Verdi's concern for keys and vocal range as early as 1843, thanks to a letter dated 30 May 1843 pertaining to *I Lombardi*.[21] It is from the composer to the tenor Antonio Poggi, husband of Erminia Frezzolini, the prima donna who created the role of Giselda when the opera had its premiere at La Scala on 1 February 1843. Poggi was to sing Oronte in a revival of *I Lombardi* in Senigallia during the summer of 1844 (indeed, Verdi ultimately wrote a new cabaletta for Poggi to perform in this revival). But Verdi had additional plans for it: "I intend to put in *F* [instead of *G major*] the closing stretta of the *finale secondo,* just at the point where it passes into the major mode. It seems to me that it will be less tiring and stronger, since all those high *b*s would become high *a*s, and this note is extremely effective for Signora Erminia."[22] Verdi did indeed go ahead with this transposition, which is present in many early editions of the opera. His reasons for doing so are crucial to an understanding of his developing art. While he might not have been quite so accommodating later in his career, matters of this kind were never far from his mind.

Not that the transposition, whatever its merits, is without cost. This conclusion of act 2 is a powerful moment. The act had begun in Antioch, at the court of Sultan Accian, who describes the terrible acts of the Crusaders ("Forti, crudeli, esultano di stupri e di rapine" [Strong, cruel, they exult in rape and pillage]). The Muslims, however, have taken as hostage Giselda, daughter of the Milanese leader of the crusaders, Arvino, and niece to Arvino's brother, Pagano, who is living nearby—incognito—as a hermit. Needless to say, Giselda and the Sultan's son, Oronte, have fallen in love. In the second scene, Pagano (whose identity remains unknown to his brother, from whom he is estranged) agrees to help Arvino and the crusaders rescue Giselda. The last scene of the act returns to the palace. Ladies of the harem taunt "la bella straniera" (the beautiful foreigner). Left alone, Giselda, in the cantabile of her aria, describes her own, unholy love for Oronte, and prays for assistance to her dead mother. In the *tempo di mezzo,* the Sultan's wife, Sofia (a secret convert to Christianity), describes the barbarous attack of the Crusaders, who are spreading death and destruction everywhere and have already killed her husband and her son (in fact, Oronte survives the massacre). When Arvino enters to greet his daughter, instead of welcoming him, she turns on him and ("almost as if struck by dementia") starts her cabaletta.

This unusual cabaletta is in several parts. It begins in *G minor* with an Allegro moderato, in which Giselda insists that God cannot approve of acts that shed human blood, and she concludes the section, with a modulation to the relative major (*B♭ major*), to the words "No, God does *not* wish it." Then she adopts a prophetic stance, the tempo gets faster ("Più mosso"), and she envisions a future in which "I vinti sorgono, vendetta orrenda sta nelle tenebre d'età vicina!" (The defeated will rise again and horrible revenge awaits soon in the shadows!). Her music returns to the dominant of *G minor,* but after remaining fixed there for four measures, Verdi changes the mode to major and launches, "con slancio," the vehement final section, where Giselda again insists that God rejects the "empio olocausto d'umana salma" (impious sacrifice of human corpses). In a short transition, she prophesies that Europe itself will be invaded by those who are now suffering. Again she returns to the dominant of *G minor,* in a passage essentially identical to the earlier four-measure phrase, to prepare the reprise of the *G major* theme. Its new text features her words "No, Dio nol vuole" (No, God does not wish it) and adds the image of Christ descending to spread the message of peace, not war.[23]

Verdi's transposition of the final section to *F major* creates havoc in this careful sequence of keys: *G minor, B♭ major,* dominant of *G minor, G major.* Had Verdi started the whole sequence down a tone, in *F minor,* there would have been some logic, but he was concerned only with getting maximal effect out of what he hoped would be a show-stopping moment to conclude the act.[24] While he may have been concerned that a transposition at the beginning of the cabaletta would push the part too low for Frezzolini, the result is an unfortunate compromise. It also greatly weakens the parallelism between the two four-measure phrases that prepare the section in major, since Verdi significantly modified the first of these passages in order to move down a tone. Did he not care? Yes, enough to have introduced the effect while he composed the opera. But did he care *enough* to refuse to help Frezzolini make a stronger impression? No. In this case, however, Ricordi later came to Verdi's rescue: all modern printed editions of *I Lombardi* print the music in its original key. Does that mean one should never make the transposition to assist a modern-day Frezzolini? Of course not. But it would certainly be better to sing the music as Verdi originally conceived it.

Nonetheless, for Verdi, the problems with this cabaletta from *I Lombardi* and with the end of the *La traviata* duet are rare. Most of the composer's transpositions precede the complete realization of the opera's score, and when he does introduce a transposition while revising a completed opera (as elsewhere in the 1854 *Traviata*) he is careful to make the shift seamless and to introduce necessary adjustments in the orchestral fabric. Additional transpositions should be a last resort, but—as we have seen—are not without precedent in Verdi's practice.

There is a related example in Donizetti. The role of Norina in *Don Pasquale* was originally written for Giulia Grisi, who sang the first performances at the Théâtre Italien of Paris beginning on 3 January 1843.[25] Her cavatina begins with an Andante in *G major,* in which Norina reads aloud a story about a lovesick knight, "Quel guardo il cavaliere." [26] She then laughs and throws the book away as two orchestral chords shift us from the tonic of *G major* to the dominant of *Bb major,* the key of the cabaletta ("So anch'io la virtù magica"). Despite this unusual motion from *G major* to *Bb major,* there is no evidence in the autograph manuscript of the opera that Donizetti ever considered composing any part of the cavatina in a different key.[27] It may be that he wanted to make a sharp division between the Norina who reads a sentimental love story and the sophisticated, even cynical Norina, who boasts of knowing all the fine arts of love.

When Eugenia Tadolini assumed the role in Vienna in the spring of 1843, however, and then again in the spring of 1844, Donizetti apparently transposed the cabaletta up to *C major* for her, and he seems to have liked it there. In a letter of 16 April 1844 to Ricordi's employee Giacomo Pedroni in Milan, the composer cites a melody from this cavatina in the new key.[28] But he adds, "The only thing to say is that if it seems too high, I'll lower it, but in *Bb major* it loses a lot." Apparently, then, Donizetti wrote the piece in the lower key, transposed it to the higher key for a different singer, Tadolini, and actually preferred the latter key. Ultimately, though, the piece circulated and has always been published in the original *Bb major.* While no contemporary source has been identified that shows exactly how Donizetti made the transposition, it is not difficult to make a hypothesis. If we change two notes in the vocal line and rewrite two orchestral chords, we can allow the music fluently to address *C major* for the cabaletta. On one level, of course, this resulting *G major* to *C major* progression is more "natural," more common, than Donizetti's original progression, but can we really argue that the composer didn't know what he was doing when he prepared the score for Paris? Whether Donizetti was correct when he later asserted that the cabaletta sounds better in *C major,* of course, is something each Norina needs to decide for herself, paying attention not only to her own vocality but also to the orchestral sound and the harmonic context.

If done responsibly, then, transpositions can assist a singer who has difficulty at a particular moment within the score but is able to perform the rest of a role well. What is an irresponsible transposition? Well, one could certainly argue that it is irresponsible (but not uncommon) for a tenor to insist that "Di quella pira," the cabaletta of Manrico's aria in *Il trovatore,* be transposed from *C major* to *Bb major* because, unable to sing an interpolated high *c* at the end of the piece, he wishes to transform it into a high *bb.* [29] The original key of Manrico's "Di quella pira," *C major,* is a bright, forward-sounding tonality, in part because of its extensive use of unstopped notes in the strings, with their greater resonance. When lowered a tone, the brightness of the original is sacrificed, a sacrifice all the more to be avoided in this martial context. There can be compelling reasons, of course, for making such a transposition in terms of the way a passage lies across the registral breaks in a particular singer's voice, and no abstract principle should be allowed to stand in the way of helping a singer give the best possible performance. But simply interpolating an unwritten high note at the very end of a piece may not be one of them.[30]

BELLINI (?) TRANSPOSES BELLINI: *NORMA*

While most of Verdi's modifications in tonality took place as he composed, Bellini transposed his own music constantly, during rehearsals, after an opera's premiere, or when adapting the music for different singers. He did not always ensure that the job was well done. When modifying the original Parisian score of *I puritani* for performance in Naples, with a mezzo-soprano Elvira instead of the original soprano, as well as a tenor Riccardo instead of the original baritone, Bellini often wrote only the vocal line, leaving it to a collaborator/copyist to transpose the orchestral parts. On many occasions his copyist did not produce a satisfactory result.[31] In the revised version of the Scena d'Elvira, for example, where Bellini lowered the entire scene from the original *E♭ major/A♭ major* down a third to *C major/F major*, the composer himself essentially wrote only the vocal lines and the names of the instruments at the start (see the facsimile of the autograph manuscript).[32]

While Bellini also made a few emendations in the copyist's transposition of the orchestral parts, his corrections were insufficient. Here are some musical faults in the violin parts from the orchestration in the transposition of the Scena d'Elvira:

1. When Giorgio and Riccardo enter after Elvira has first sung her melody, "O rendetemi la speme," the first violins in Paris played a series of triplets (ff. 23v–24); in the Neapolitan transposition, the first note would everywhere have been too low to be played on violins. Instead of rearranging the figuration, the copyist substituted the first available higher pitch in the chord, producing a series of unattractive octaves or fifths with the bass on successive downbeats (pp. 52–53).

2. When Elvira finally sings her theme over a triplet accompaniment, to the text "Qui la voce sua soave," Bellini changed the direction of the triplets and used a consistent pattern throughout this presentation of the theme. In the first measure, however, the second violins descended originally to *g*

(f. 25); since the parallel note for Naples would have been *e*, too low for the instrument, the copyist changed the figuration altogether, compromising the lovely effect Bellini had planned (p. 55).

3. After Elvira recalls the joyous music from the opening of the opera, she turns melancholy ("Egli piange..."), and in the original version the strings played a poignant, dissonant phrase, Largo, a memorable moment in the scene (f. 31). As originally written, all the violins and the violas are in unison, the cellos and double basses an octave below (doubled by the bassoons). When transposed down, however, a prominent pitch in the middle of the phrase is too low for the violins. Instead of rethinking the orchestration, the copyist substituted a rest for what would have been an *f♯* (p. 67). Bellini really should not have allowed this abrupt hole in the sonority to remain.

4. In the *tempo di mezzo,* as Riccardo and Giorgio are commenting on Elvira's madness, the orchestra plays a theme. The melody is played by the first violins (doubled an octave higher by the flute), with an accompanying repeated chord below the melody played in the other strings. When transposed down, the melody is fine, but the chordal notes in the second violins are too low. The copyist therefore rearranged the notes of the chord, but he did so in an awkward way, so that the notes of the accompaniment in the second violins now sit *above* the melody, where they muddy the entire sonority.

These are all serious infelicities. While those opera fans who think that their favorite art form begins and ends with the voice may not be disturbed, musicians observe Bellini's nonchalance toward the orchestra here with sadness.

As is well known, the cantabile of "Casta Diva" was written by Bellini in *G major,* the key of his autograph manuscript, not the *F major* in which it is heard today and which is preserved in most printed editions. This includes the very first reduction for voice and piano published by Ricordi in Milan on the occasion of the first performances of *Norma,* at La Scala, beginning on 26 December 1831.[33] While it is usually affirmed that the transposition was decided by Bellini himself, perhaps during rehearsals, perhaps immediately after the premiere, to suit the vocal needs of the first Priestess, Giuditta Pasta, no evidence has emerged to document Bellini's participation.[34] It is certainly relevant that in the autograph manuscript of *Norma* the first page of the orchestral introduction to the cavatina was at one point crossed out and folded in half. Still, nowhere on these pages did Bellini make any annotations pertaining to a possible transposition, nor has any other source in his hand been found with such a change.

More important, the fluent progressions Bellini used in order to arrive at this *G major* at the beginning of the cantabile and to continue, after its conclusion, with the *tempo di mezzo* leave no doubt about his original intention. The recitative preceding the cantabile concludes on an *Ab-major* chord, heard as a strong dominant, but instead of resolving to the expected *Db*, the chord is repeated by the strings alone, pizzicato, and is reinterpreted as the lowered second degree (a so-called Neapolitan sixth) in a progression that moves through *G minor* to a luminous *G major*. It is not too much to imagine that at this very moment moonlight floods the stage. After a single measure arpeggiating the tonic harmony, a solo flute intones the melody (example 10.3).[35] This is an elegant progression, unexpected, logical, and exhilarating. At the end of the cantabile, the situation is simpler: the concluding tonic note, *g*, is reinterpreted as part of an *Eb-major* harmony in the stage band (it is the third degree of the chord), and the *tempo di mezzo* begins with a reprise of the march from the choral movement preceding "Casta Diva."

Even if it was Bellini himself who decided that the cantabile should be transposed down a tone to suit Pasta's vocal requirements, we can hope that he was not responsible for the *way* in which the transposition is introduced, for the movement to the new key is both harmonically suspect and ugly. Not only do string arpeggios begin immediately (instead of awaiting the arrival on

EXAMPLE 10.3. VINCENZO BELLINI, *NORMA*, THE TRANSITION TO THE BEGINNING OF THE CANTABILE IN THE CORO E CAVATINA NORMA (N. 3) IN THE ORIGINAL KEY (*G MAJOR*).

EXAMPLE 10.4. VINCENZO BELLINI, *NORMA*, THE TRANSITION TO THE
BEGINNING OF THE CANTABILE IN THE CORO E CAVATINA NORMA (N. 3)
AS PRINTED IN THE FIRST EDITION OF THE VOCAL SCORE, WITH THE
CANTABILE TRANSPOSED TO *F MAJOR*.

Andante sostenuto assai

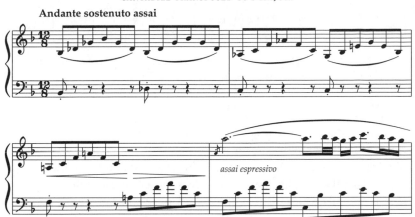

the tonic major, which justifies and exalts them), but they begin on the *first*
beat of the first measure, so that the modulation starts there instead of on the
third beat (as in Bellini's original). This causes a useless repetition of the *Gb-
major* chord, initially in first inversion (with the third degree of the chord, *bb*,
in the bass), then in second inversion (with the fifth degree, *db*, in the bass).
And that in turn leads to unfortunate parallel chords in second inversion (*Gb
major,* then *F minor*). The passage as printed in the first edition of the vocal
score is shown in example 10.4.

I am not arguing that a transposition of the cavatina to *F major* is in itself
objectionable (indeed, while we're at it, why would we want to stop a particular prima donna from singing it still lower, in *E major*,[36] or even higher, in
Ab major?), but only that the progression that introduces the *F major* in
printed editions of *Norma* is awful. What makes the situation even more
ridiculous is that a simple modification of the passage could lead fluently to
the new key. One need only use Bellini's original progression a tone lower,
employing the same pizzicato strings that he originally employed. The bass
line (*ab–bb–c–c–f*) is elegant, and the succession of chords becomes thoroughly convincing (example 10.5). At the end of the cantabile, on the other
hand, there is nothing to do. The less said about concluding a cantabile in *F
major* and beginning a *tempo di mezzo* in *Eb major,* the better. Still, given the
applause that invariably greets the conclusion of "Casta Diva," it is not a juxtaposition anyone is likely to perceive.

EXAMPLE 10.5. VINCENZO BELLINI, *NORMA*, A POSSIBLE TRANSITION TO
THE BEGINNING OF THE CANTABILE IN THE CORO E CAVATINA NORMA
(N. 3), WITH THE CANTABILE TRANSPOSED TO *F MAJOR*.

This transposition creates few problems for the orchestral instruments, which can perform the cantabile a tone lower without difficulty. Only twice did Bellini write a low *g* for the violins (their lowest note), and these can be adjusted for the *F-major* transposition by simple changes in the arpeggiated chords. When a critical edition of *Norma* is finally prepared, I hope the version of "Casta Diva" in *G major* will assume pride of place. The fear some performers express (or experience internally) when faced with the higher key may have as much to do with their expectations as with the actual difficulty of singing the music in *G major*. Had the printed editions transmitted the piece in its original key, many present-day Normas would have few qualms about performing "Casta Diva" in that tonality. Even so, I am prepared to grant that from the point of view of singing technique and the placement of the voice between registral breaks, the *F-major* tonality may be more accessible to a broad range of singers. Thus, there continues to be an important role for the transposed version, especially if the orchestral introduction is modified to remain closer to Bellini's original progression.

DONIZETTI (?) TRANSPOSES DONIZETTI:
LUCIA DI LAMMERMOOR

Just as Bellini's most famous single passage in his most enduringly successful opera was written in a different key from the one we are used to hearing, so too were three entire pieces in Donizetti's masterpiece, *Lucia di Lammermoor*, including both solo numbers sung by Lucia herself and her duet with her brother, Enrico.[37] The pieces involved are (1) the entire scena and cavatina (N. 2) for Lucia ("Regnava nel silenzio"), originally written with the scena beginning in *Eb major* and the cabaletta concluding in *Ab major*, thus, a semitone above the tonalities of the first and subsequent Ricordi editions (*D major/G major*); (2) the duetto for Lucia and Enrico that opens the second act (N. 4), which is in *A major* in Donizetti's autograph manuscript, but has normally been printed a full tone lower (*G major*); (3) the entire scena for Lucia (N. 8), from after the close of the introductory section for Raimondo and the chorus (unchanged in *E major*). The "mad scene" was written in *F major,* but has usually been printed a full tone lower (*E♭ major*).[38] There is evidence that Donizetti himself was responsible for at least some of these transpositions, but there is also evidence that, given the opportunity, he was prepared to return to his original keys.[39]

Thus far, no one has advanced an explanation for these transpositions. When were they introduced and why? Did Donizetti agree to them to accommodate the vocal needs of his original Lucia, Fanny Tacchinardi Persiani? Rather than advancing this hypothesis, those who have studied the career of the prima donna have preferred to invoke the original keys as a way of understanding the character of her voice.[40] Yet from the autograph manuscript of *Lucia di Lammermoor* it is clear that at least the transposition of "Regnava nel silenzio" was the work of Donizetti. Not that the scena and cavatina itself bears any sign of a transposition: Donizetti wrote it in *E♭ major/A♭ major* without hesitation, and at no point did he make annotations suggesting it should be sung a semitone lower. *E♭ major* is a suitable key for a scene in a park near a fountain, since this tonality has a long associative history with hunting horns and woodlands: Rossini's use of it in *La donna del lago* and *Guillaume Tell* must have been very much in Donizetti's ear. And the elaborate harp introduction in *E♭ major* would have called to mind a similar passage for harp, announcing the first appearance of another doomed heroine, Desdemona in Rossini's *Otello.* Furthermore, the passage from the *G major* of the opening scene to *E♭ major* provides a good but not excessive contrast (the tonic triads share the pitch *g*). In all these respects, the transposed *D major/G major,* with its conclusion in the same key as Enrico's preceding solo, is poorer. Yet, poorer or better, either *E♭ major* or *D major* can follow fluently Enrico's concluding *G major.*

Technical problems arise immediately *after* the Lucia cavatina, in the recitative for Alisa that precedes Edgardo's entrance. The first Ricordi edition continues the transposition down a semitone for the first part of this recitative (through Lucia's "E me nel pianto abbandoni così!"), but when the recitative picks up again with Edgardo's "Pria di lasciarti" to introduce the duet for the lovers ("Sulla tomba che rinserra"), it abruptly returns to the original tonality. The chord linking the two parts is actually printed once in the lower key, then repeated in the higher key, an absurdity Donizetti would never have sanctioned. But the modern Ricordi edition is no better. After Lucia's ca-

EXAMPLE 10.6. GAETANO DONIZETTI, *LUCIA DI LAMMERMOOR,* THE CONCLUSION OF
THE SCENA E CAVATINA LUCIA (N. 2), TRANSPOSED DOWN A HALF TONE, WITH
THREE VERSIONS OF THE OPENING OF THE ENSUING RECITATIVE.

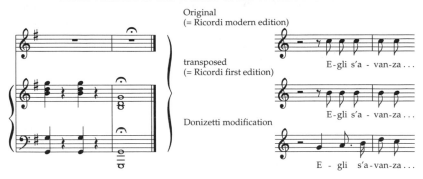

vatina closes in the transposed *G major,* it returns immediately to the original key for the recitative, so that Alisa begins with the pitch *c.* This provides
no link whatsoever between the two passages, although it was a perfect link
when the the cabaletta ("Quando rapito in estasi") concluded in its original
A♭ major (c is the third degree of the *A♭-major* chord). That Donizetti was
aware of the problem is apparent from his autograph, since at the beginning
of the recitative he revised the opening of Alisa's vocal line to link the music
more smoothly to Lucia's transposed cavatina (example 10.6).[41] Another
hand added the phrase "nel tono" (that is, in the original key). While we do
not know when Donizetti sanctioned the transposition of "Regnava nel silenzio," that he participated in no production of *Lucia* between the 1835 premiere and the French revision of 1839 certainly suggests that the change was
introduced for the first performances or soon afterwards.

In fact, Tacchinardi Persiani soon abandoned altogether "Regnava nel
silenzio," with its unusually constructed narrative cantabile, a ghost story
about an earlier unhappy love affair between an Ashton and a Ravenswood.
The very next time she sang the role of Lucia, in a revival of the opera that
opened the carnival season of 1837 (26 December 1836) at the Teatro Apollo
in Venice, she substituted a much more conventional aria, "Perché non ho
del vento," from an earlier opera written for her by Donizetti, *Rosmonda
d'Inghilterra,* which she had performed in February 1834 [42] Tacchinardi Persiani continued making this same substitution in subsequent years, and other
singers followed suit, using both the *Rosmonda* piece and others. Ultimately
Donizetti himself, when preparing his version of *Lucia di Lammermoor* in
French for the Théâtre de la Renaissance, decided to follow the lead of his

prima donna and to substitute the *Rosmonda* aria, as "Que n'avons nous des ailes," for "Regnava nel silenzio." Thus, it is the *Rosmonda* cavatina that introduces the heroine in *Lucie de Lammermoor.*

In *Lucia di Lammermoor,* however, there is no reason whatsoever not to sing "Regnava nel silenzio" in its original key. Nothing in either its recitative or its cantabile strains the voice, nor does the melody of the cabaletta. Only in the concluding cadential runs at the end of the cabaletta theme and in an exposed *db* in the final cadences of the composition is the singer's upper register highlighted. The sustained singing Lucia must accomplish in that register in the subsequent duet with Edgardo, "Verranno a te sull'aure," is considerably more arduous. Furthermore, the single most audacious moment in the melodic line of the cabaletta theme in "Regnava nel silenzio" has been misrepresented in printed editions of the opera. Not only has the theme sometimes been printed incorrectly, but Donizetti's own alternative to avoid the very highest note has been suppressed. Example 10.7 gives the original version of the passage from Donizetti's autograph manuscript (which also appears in recent editions), the version of the first Ricordi edition (transposed back up from *G major* to *Ab major*), and Donizetti's alternative in the autograph. The equivalent of the high *db* of the original version was erroneously rendered as the equivalent of *c* in the first Ricordi printed edition (with its transposed key), but the error was corrected in subsequent editions. More important, in his autograph manuscript Donizetti suggested an alternative

EXAMPLE 10.7. GAETANO DONIZETTI, *LUCIA DI LAMMERMOOR,* SEVERAL VERSIONS OF THE FINAL MEASURES IN THE CABALETTA THEME OF THE SCENA E CAVATINA LUCIA (N. 2).

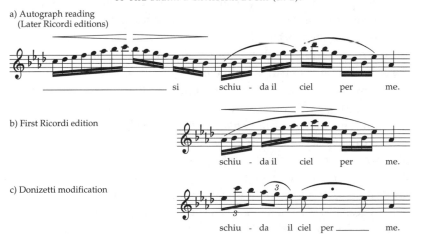

a) Autograph reading
   (Later Ricordi editions)

b) First Ricordi edition

c) Donizetti modification

for the concluding measure of the theme. The triplets at the beginning of the measure and fermata in the second half provide a perfectly appropriate way to avoid the registral extreme without transposing the entire composition.[43] Finally, given that the piece concludes either in A♭ *major* (Donizetti's original) or *G major* (the transposition), Lucia can easily interpolate a concluding high note—if she chooses—in either key.[44]

The transposition of Lucia's mad scene presents greater problems. Donizetti wrote the piece in *F major,* but it is traditionally sung a full tone lower, in *E♭ major,* and that is the key in which it is printed in the first Ricordi edition and all subsequent ones.[45] As originally written (in *F major*), there is really nothing that cannot be sung effectively by a good soprano. Even Donizetti's notated passages in which a solo flute and Lucia either play off against one another or interact in close harmony (thirds and sixths) are perfectly idiomatic for the voice.[46] As we saw in chapter 9, the interpolated cadenza for Lucia and flute at the end of the cantabile, substituting Donizetti's short notated cadenza, is based upon a late nineteenth-century interpolation for Nellie Melba, and has nothing to do with Donizetti. The composer and his original prima donna might have expected a singer to handle this "cadenza opportunity" with a certain liberty, but it is unlikely that the endless coloratura display in the very highest reaches of the voice would have made sense to a contemporary of Donizetti's, so different is it from anything else in the opera.

Why, then, was the mad scene from *Lucia di Lammermoor* transposed down? In a private communication, Will Crutchfield suggests that for many sopranos the lower key is more gracious to their voice, because those short high notes in the main theme ("Spar*gi* d'amaro pianto" and "men*tre* lassù nel cielo") are easier for them to sing with color and resonance. The same is true, he feels, about the repeated, syncopated notes at the end of the theme. He goes on to argue, though, that in the wedding scene Lucia needs to dominate the ensemble, and her part is written in a register equivalent to that of the *E♭ major* lower transposition of the mad scene, not the *F-major* original key. If you want a singer who will handle the wedding scene well, in short, you need to perform the mad scene in *E♭ major,* not in the original *F major.*

There may well be some truth to all of this, and it certainly would help explain why the transposition has such a long and enduring pedigree and why it took root even before singers habitually interpolated concluding high notes. But I cannot help suspecting that some singers, at least, who would be perfectly capable of handling the scene in *F major,* have their own reasons for accepting the transposition. They do it in order to jump around in the very highest register during the interpolated cadenza and then to conclude both the cantabile and, later, the cabaletta on a high e♭. Even the best of coloratura sopranos (and the role of Lucia was not written for a coloratura soprano) is hesitant to undertake the cadenza with the flute in the higher key or to risk a high *f* at the end of a long and difficult scene. To flub the cadenza or to crack on a concluding interpolated high note would cast into oblivion everything that preceded; to omit the cadenza or not to sing the interpolated final high note would bring down the fury of the *loggionisti* on even the finest singer. Much safer to transpose the entire piece down, even if you can sing it in the original key. That Donizetti's careful citation of earlier themes in their original keys is thereby compromised matters little. That the lovely modulation from the end of the previous chorus ("Oh! qual funesto") to Lucia's entrance is thereby sacrificed matters not at all. We come to the opera house to hear concluding high notes, don't we? Audiences should understand the cynical price they are sometimes paying for those notes.

Althought the first Ricordi edition of 1837 printed the mad scene in *E♭ major,* when Donizetti prepared *Lucie de Lammermoor* in French in 1839, he had the piece printed in its original key, *F major.* Similarly, the duet for Lucia and Enrico that opens the second act was returned from its lower transposition (*G major*) to its original *A major.*[47] This evidence need not be taken as definitive (when performing Italian opera the word "definitive" is almost always suspect), but it is certainly worth considering.[48] The important thing to remember is that no one is *obliged* to sing this music in the lower keys. Donizetti would never have sacrificed a singer's performance by insisting on a key that was awkward for a particular voice, nor should we. But in thinking about transpositions, we should be aware that the composer's own choices were rarely casual.

TRANSPOSING BELLINI: *LA SONNAMBULA* AND GIOVANNI BATTISTA RUBINI

The problem of transpositions in the operas of Bellini becomes intense whenever *La sonnambula* is mentioned, and in 1999–2000 the Metropolitan Opera of New York risked walking into this hornet's nest by preparing a new production of the opera featuring Cecilia Bartoli in the role of the sleepwalker, Amina. Although Ms. Bartoli and the Met changed their plans, the problem remains. It is not merely a matter of trying to accommodate a role written for a slightly higher soprano voice than Bartoli's to her mezzosoprano instrument (which, in any case, has gradually been ascending into a higher tessitura). No, the core of this opera has been significantly compromised by transpositions introduced into the score, and the music published in all modern editions of *La sonnambula* is not the music Bellini wrote.

Only a single source for *La sonnambula* can be associated directly with Bellini: his original manuscript, as prepared for the singers Giuditta Pasta and Giambattista Rubini when they performed the opera at its premiere at the Teatro Carcano of Milan on 6 March 1831.[49] There has been much talk of a "Malibran" version of *La sonnambula,* as if Bellini himself arranged his opera for the great mezzo-soprano, but no evidence has been produced in support of this hypothesis. In fact, Maria Malibran first sang Amina in Naples in March 1833, at the Teatro del Fondo, before she ever met Bellini.[50] When Bellini did finally come to know her in May 1833 in London, she was singing Amina in the Drury Lane Theater (and later, in June, at Covent Garden) in a version "adapted" for the English stage by Henry Bishop. Such adaptations into English were all the rage in London, one of the most famous being the 1830 Rossinian adaptation by Michael Rophino Lacy, also for Covent Garden, *Cinderella, or the Fairy-Queen and the Glass Slipper.* That was how *La Cenerentola* was generally known in England and the United States during the nineteenth century, restoring the very slipper Rossini had removed![51]

The story of Bellini's first encounter with Malibran has been told repeatedly on the basis of a supposed letter from Bellini to his friend Francesco Florimo, the director of the Library at the Naples Conservatory. After extravagantly praising Malibran's singing in *La sonnambula,* despite the English translation in which she sang ("the language of birds, or more specifically parrots"), the letter relates that the public recognized the composer sitting in the audience. Everyone sought to congratulate him:

> The first to approach me was Malibran, who, having thrown her arms about my neck, declaimed for me in the most exalted transport of joy these four notes of mine: *Ah! m'abbraccia!* adding nothing else... My emotion was at its heights: I thought I was in Paradise; I could not speak a word, and remained dumb; I do not remember anything else... The enthusiastic and repeated applause of an English public, which becomes frantic when it gets excited, called us both to the stage; we presented ourselves while holding hands: you can imagine the rest... What I can tell you is that I do not know whether in my whole life I will have a more intense emotion. From that moment I became an intimate of Malibran: she expressed to me all the admiration she felt for my music, and I all I held for her immense talent; and I promised to write for her an opera on a subject that suits her. It is a thought that already electrifies me, my dear Florimo.[52]

Florimo, unfortunately, is known to have invented or rewritten many a letter from Bellini, seeking in this way to "correct" the historical record in a way more favorable to his friend, and this scene is probably Florimo's invention.[53] Still, it seems likely that the composer did indeed present himself to Malibran for the first time after hearing her sing the role of Amina in the Bishop adaptation. That he admired Malibran is certain; but at the moment of their first meeting, Amina was already in her repertory, both in Italian and in the English adaptation. There is no evidence that Bellini sought to intervene in her interpretation of *La sonnambula,* but he did hope to collaborate with her in a future project. The Neapolitan version of *I puritani* was to be that project, his homage to Malibran. As we have seen, however, that version never reached the stage during the nineteenth century.

A trace of the English *Sonnambula* exists in the form of a reduction for piano and voice of several numbers from the opera, issued by Boosey in London later in 1833. They bear the explanatory phrase: "as sung by Mme Malibran at the Theatres Royal Drury Lane and Covent Garden." The music is often modified in this publication: "Ah! non credea mirarti" (the cantabile of her final aria) is in *F minor,* transposed down by a major third from Bellini's original key, *A minor,* while the final cabaletta, "Ah! non giunge uman pensiero," is in *F major,* a fourth below Bellini's original tonality.[54] If it is legitimate to speak of a "Malibran" version of *La sonnambula,* reflecting the vocal characteristics of a mezzo-soprano, it must be attributed to Bishop not to Bellini, although the singer could have made similar changes when she sang the role a few months earlier in Naples.

The problem of tranpositions in *La sonnambula,* however, arises not because of Amina but because of the tenor role of Elvino. Rubini had what was considered an unusual voice, even in his own day.[55] Without entering into the vexing question as to *how* he was able to sing in the extraordinarily high tessitura that characterized his art (obviously he did not maintain what is usually referred to as a "chest voice" into the upper part of his range), it is clear that composers, to favor his natural or acquired gifts, placed music written or revised for Rubini in a tessitura that the singer found grateful. For *La sonnambula,* this meant that three pieces were written in keys that seemed even in the early 1830s to be stratospheric. Indeed, one of the most amusing comments about Elvino's range is found in a midcentury edition published by Novello, Ewer and Co. in England, where the following note appears: "The principal pieces in which Elvino is concerned are here transposed in accordance with Ricordi's modern edition of this Opera. The voice for which the part was originally composed would seem to be happily extinct; even as it stands now the part is in some places beyond the ordinary tenor range."[56] By this point, of course, the "ordinary" tenor range was measured by Verdi's practice. The three pieces are (1) Elvino's cavatina "Prendi: l'anel ti dono," whose cantabile and cabaletta were both written in B♭ *major;* (2) the duettino for Amina and Elvino "Son geloso del zefiro errante," in *G major;* (3) Elvino's aria "Tutto è sciolto," which begins in *B minor,* modulating to its relative major, *D major,* and then closes with a cabaletta, "Ah! perché non posso odiarti," in *D major.* It is not merely a question of all the high, and often sustained, c♯s and *d*s. What is truly difficult is the overall tessitura of the vocal line. In its original form, for example, the cabaletta "Ah! perché non posso odiarti" moves at once to a high f♯ and then sits between that note and a still higher *b.* From the publication of the very first edition by Casa Ricordi, during the summer of 1831, a few months after the Milanese premiere of *La sonnambula,* all three pieces were transposed downward: the cavatina and the duettino by a full tone (to A♭ *major* and *F major,* respectively), the aria by a semitone (to B♭ *minor* and its relative major, D♭ *major*).

Until all contemporary sources are examined, both printed editions and manuscripts, the history of these transpositions will not be fully known. In the case of the cavatina and the duettino, however, printed editions have usually presented the pieces at this same transposition, a full tone lower than the autograph reading.[57] The manuscript tradition, however, which more often reflects actual practice in Bellini's day, is quite diverse. Of the two complete manuscripts of *La sonnambula* in the library at the "Santa Cecilia" Conservatory in Rome, for example, one (G. Mss. 714/15) transposes the cavatina even lower (down a minor third, to *G major*), while giving the duettino in its original key (*G major*). The other manuscript (G. Mss. 716/17) gives both pieces in their original keys.

Ricordi's early downward transposition by a semitone of Elvino's aria "Tutto è sciolto," on the other hand, seemed insufficient from early in the history of the opera. In the Bishop version (later reproduced in several French editions), the key was lowered everywhere by a major third: the aria therefore began in *G minor* and closed in B♭ *major.* But in Ricordi's second edition of the opera, published in 1858, the cantabile is brought only to *A minor* (down a tone), while the cabaletta is printed in B♭ *major* (a major third below the original). Thus, where Bellini provided a fluent transition between the cantabile and the *tempo di mezzo* (with the D-major harmony closing the cantabile serving as the dominant of the G-major harmony that opens the *tempo di mezzo*), in the Ricordi version regularly used in performance today (which is identical to the edition of 1858), the chords are more remote. Here, too, the readings of manuscript sources are instructive. In the two Roman manuscripts described above, one (G. Mss. 716/17) follows the original keys, while in the other (G. Mss. 714/15) the entire aria is transposed down even further, a full fourth below the original (beginning in *F♯ minor* and concluding in *A major*). In this way the entire aria is transposed in a logical and coherent manner. As in the case of *Norma,* there is no proof that any of these transpositions were Bellini's work, despite a statement in what may be an inauthentic letter to Florimo.[58]

That transposition presents an acute problem in *La sonnambula* results not simply from the tessitura of Elvino. After all, if tenors today cannot handle the original keys of the opera in an acceptable manner, practical considerations far outweigh possible objections to transposing this music.[59] While the transposition of solo numbers would not normally affect the remainder of the score, however, in this case they have a profound effect upon the part of Amina. In Elvino's "cavatina" (the title is Bellini's), in which he presents a ring to his beloved and sings of his love for her, Amina is present everywhere, a *pertichino* who reacts with joy to his words and becomes practically a protagonist. Indeed, in printed editions of *La sonnambula* the cavatina has traditionally (although incorrectly) been labeled a "duet."[60] Even in Elvino's second-act aria, which lacks a title in Bellini's autograph manuscript but is correctly called an "aria" in printed editions, Amina has an important part, especially in the cantabile but also in the *tempo di mezzo,* and her part in the printed editions is unnaturally low. Thus, in all three pieces in which Amina sings together with Elvino, the tessitura of her part is much lower in the edition used today than in Bellini's original, whereas all the music she sings alone (her cavatina and concluding aria) remains in Bellini's original keys. In short, as the role is printed in modern editions, Amina is a mezzo-soprano when she sings with Elvino, a soprano when she sings alone. No wonder singers have such a difficult time wrapping their vocal cords around the part.[61]

Only once in *La sonnambula* is there direct evidence that Bellini himself changed a key after having completed his score: the conclusion of the first-act finale was originally written in *G major,* with a transition through a common tone ("*g*"), played by the horns, between the Adagio (in *E♭ major*) and in the music leading to the stretta, "Non è questa, ingrato core." A copyist then rewrote the entire closing section a semitone *higher,* in *A♭ major* (Bellini himself seems to have indicated a cut in the cadential phrases in this copy). The copyist's manuscript was then bound into Bellini's autograph manuscript of *La sonnambula* along with the composer's original, *G-major* version. In

EXAMPLE 10.8. VINCENZO BELLINI, *LA SONNAMBULA,* FINALE PRIMO (N. 7), THE
TRANSITION BETWEEN THE END OF THE *LARGO* ("D'UN PENSIERO E D'UN
ACCENTO") AND THE TRANSPOSED VERSION OF THE *TEMPO DI MEZZO*
("NON PIÙ NOZZE") AND STRETTA.

printed editions of *La sonnambula,* on the other hand, the stretta has always
been printed in the higher key, A♭ *major,* not in Bellini's *G major.* Unlike the
situation in *Norma,* the new transition here is clever: the *g* of the horns in the
first measure of the transition is replaced by an *e♭* (the tonic of the previous
key). This note then becomes the dominant of the ensuing music, now transposed up a semitone, to A♭ *major;* example 10.8). In the same peculiar letter
Bellini is alleged to have sent Florimo in 1834, he supposedly added, "I also
lowered the largo and stretta of the finale by a semitone, since Rubini's voice
now makes its effect a semitone lower than the tessitura he required six years
ago." It is hard to believe that Bellini expressed any of these garbled ideas.
First of all, Bellini wrote the part of Elvino four years earlier, not six. Sec-
ondly, in the Largo of the first-act finale, Rubini's part in the original version
never goes higher than an insistent high *g* and *a♭,* a piece of cake for Rubini
and for any tenor specializing in *bel canto.* As for the *stretta,* in its higher version (in A♭ *major*) the voice goes up to *b♭,* but no higher. And, finally, if Rubini's voice had darkened in the way this letter suggests, how could Bellini
have written for Rubini one year later (in 1835) the role of Arturo in *I puritani*
with its legendary *f* in the final ensemble? Whatever the truth may be, if the
stretta of the first-act finale of *La sonnambula* is brought down a semitone
from the key in which it has been known in every printed edition of the opera (A♭ *major*), the resulting tonality, *G major,* is simply the key in which Bellini *originally* prepared the conclusion of the first act of his opera.

BELLINI ADJUSTS BELLINI: *LA STRANIERA*
AND GIAMBATTISTA RUBINI

Transpositions in *Norma* and *La sonnambula* occurred largely in the transmission of those operas, or were practical decisions taken by Bellini or—frequently—his publisher soon after or even before the premieres. For other

operas, however, sources in Bellini's own hand demonstrate precisely how he went about modifying a previously written part for a singer whose voice was more comfortable in a different range. It is no surprise that he undertook this work for singers he particularly admired, such as Rubini and Malibran. Since the Malibran version of *I puritani* was discussed at length in chapter 7, let us focus on revisions that Bellini made in *La straniera* to adapt its principal tenor role, Arturo, for his beloved Rubini.

When Bellini wrote *La straniera* for the Teatro alla Scala of Milan, where it was first performed on 14 February 1829, he very much wished to have Rubini as his tenor hero, Arturo. Rubini had already created the principal tenor role of Gernando for the first performances of Bellini's *Bianca e Gernando* at the Teatro San Carlo of Naples, beginning on 30 May 1826. More important, Rubini's extraordinary portrayal of the title role in the composer's *Il pirata,* at La Scala on 27 October 1827, had contributed impressively to the success of that opera. But Rubini was under contract to Naples for the carnival season of 1828–29, and even though Domenico Barbaja was serving as impresario for both theaters at the time, he was unwilling to free Rubini from those contractual obligations. Thus, Bellini had to settle for a different tenor, the young Domenico Reina. The composer wrote to him about his new opera in September 1828, and the response he received was so encouraging that he hastened to inform Florimo about it:

> I wrote to the tenor Reina in Lucca, and he answered graciously, telling me that his voice is virile, always in tune, with a chest register extending from *bb* under the staff to *a* above the staff and with falsetto notes up to high *e,* that he has agility and sings evenly, and that his style will adapt itself to my music, which he is prepared to study like a dog and perform just as I wish him to, in my own fashion, which he understands is the correct one.[62]

As it turned out, Bellini was indeed pleased with Reina's willingness to work closely with him in developing the role, and Reina's performance was well received by the Milanese public. Indeed, the vocal style of *La straniera,* much more declamatory than the still relatively florid *Il pirata,* may have been developed in part because Bellini could not count on having a singer who would be able to duplicate Rubini's style and technique.[63]

Nonetheless, when La Scala, a year later, decided to include both *Il pirata* and *La straniera* in their carnival season of 1829–30, the one significant change in the cast of *La straniera* was the replacement of Reina by Rubini, who sang in both operas. For that occasion, Bellini rewrote the principal numbers of Arturo in order to adapt them to the unusual vocal qualities of

Rubini, significantly raising the tessitura of the role. Despite Bellini's efforts, Rubini did not please the Milanese in the role of Arturo. The composer himself could not be in Milan to prepare the performances, since he was in Venice composing *I Capuleti e i Montecchi,* but he told his uncle, Vincenzo Ferlito, on 19 January 1830:

> They write me from Milan that on the 13th of this month *La straniera* was produced, that it gave the same pleasure as last year, and that Lalande and Tamburini truly distinguished themselves; but that Rubini in this opera is cold, and all wanted Reina: some claimed the revised part does not make the same effect as the original: I believe that; but it cannot be so bad as to make them desire a mediocre tenor instead of Rubini. Rather Rubini, by failing to animate a part such as this one, full of soul and fire, must have made everything languid. But enough, in general it has given pleasure, and the rest is unimportant since I did everything I could to accommodate the part for him.[64]

Although it was the original version that remained in circulation, and not the Rubini modifications, those modifications were undertaken with gusto by Bellini, and they provide a perfectly plausible alternative even today for the right singer.

Bellini entered his changes for Rubini in a copyist's manuscript of the opera, which still exists in the library of the Conservatory in Milan.[65] Not all the changes are in Bellini's hand: another hand made a few preliminary modifications, which Bellini reviewed and revised extensively. Many of the changes are in recitative. They largely maintain the rhythm and chords of the original, but significantly raise the tessitura, as shown in example 10.9, drawn from the

EXAMPLE 10.9. VINCENZO BELLINI, *LA STRANIERA,* RECITATIVE PRECEDING THE TERZETTO (N. 5), AS REVISED FOR RUBINI.

recitative that precedes the first-act trio.[66] In the quartet of the second act, Bellini apparently instructed the copyist not to reproduce the part of Arturo in the section beginning "Che far vuoi tu?" Then the composer himself wrote a higher part for Rubini into the score, always remaining close to the original rhythm and always adopting the same harmonies.

The most extreme changes occur in the duet for Arturo (tenor) and Valdeburgo (baritone) in the second act. Not only did Bellini make small changes in the vocal line, but on four occasions he extracted pages from the original manuscript and provided entirely new ones, with revised vocal lines and orchestral parts. Adjacent measures in the copy are crossed out to ensure a smooth transition from the copyist's manuscript to the new autograph pages, and back again. In some cases he transposed individual passages. In the opening section of the duet, for example, the Allegro giusto, "Sì... sulla salma del fratello" (Yes, on the corpse of her brother), Valdeburgo first sings a declamatory period in the tonic, B♭ major; Arturo responds in kind, but then the orchestra launches into a lyrical phrase in the same key, which Arturo immediately repeats with an anguished phrase describing his sorrow, "è il dolor d'un cor piagato" (it is the sorrow of a wounded heart). In the revision for Rubini, Bellini (after inserting a cadenza for his tenor) moved the lyrical phrase a minor third higher, to D♭ major. Example 10.10 shows how he inserted the new key (the oboe melody is doubled at the higher octave by piccolo and at the lower octave by clarinet).[67] The composer was to use a similar subterfuge to get back to the original key. Later in the duet Bellini transposed another lyrical phrase ("Ah! non sai d'un core ardente il delirio tormentoso" [Ah! you don't know the tormented delirium of a burning heart]) up a major second, where he felt it would sit best for Rubini's voice. Despite all these internal manipulations, however, the basic shape and overall tonality of the duet remain untouched.

Bellini's work for Rubini in *La straniera* was hardly profound. But it did not have a profound aim: he sought to allow Rubini's vocal strengths to emerge effectively by giving greater emphasis to his higher tessitura. With some modifications of the vocal line and some transpositions of entire phrases, the composer succeeded splendidly.[68] Furthermore, throughout the duet with Valdeburgo, Bellini *also* modified the baritone part, bearing in mind that the two voices needed to work together effectively. Merely raising the tessitura of the tenor was insufficient. That is a lesson that should be pondered carefully when transpositions are introduced into pieces involving more than a single singer.

If a singer today were to introduce similar manipulations to suit his or her voice, just imagine the reaction of scholars, critics, and *loggionisti*. For the last production in the Verdi Festival of 2001 in Parma, a great Lady Macbeth,

EXAMPLE 10.10. VINCENZO BELLINI, *LA STRANIERA*, DUETTO ARTURO AND VALDEBURGO (N. 8), LYRICAL PASSAGE IN ONE KEY FOR REINA, IN ANOTHER FOR RUBINI.

Tiziana Fabbricini, was having difficulty singing Verdi's final, soft, devastatingly sadistic *db* at the end of the sleepwalking scene. When I dared to suggest that she could simply take the note down an octave, I was assured that the boos would be so loud and prolonged that the woman's career would effectively be ruined. At least I hadn't suggested that she transpose the scene down from the original *Db major* to *Bb major.* Bellini (not to mention Verdi) would have been astonished at the fuss and bother. Fabbricini was replaced at the last moment by her understudy, an unexciting singer with a high *db* that was mediocre but apparently acceptable to the Parma *loggionisti.*

The puzzles we face in deciding the keys in which to perform Bellini's music (not to mention Donizetti's) are not simple to resolve, nor will the new critical edition of Bellini's complete works, launched in 2003 with the publication of *I Capuleti e i Montecchi,* be able to avoid them, whether in the case of *La straniera, La sonnambula, Norma, I puritani,* or many other operas. Unless a way is found to accommodate to responsible modern practice the music written for Rubini, the critical editions could languish unused on library shelves. Whether in the context of a critical edition, however, or simply to favor the wishes of a beloved singer, the problem of transposition will remain with us as long as Italian opera is performed. And in every case performers will need to consider the following issues. What is the best way to introduce a transposed section and, afterwards, to return to the original tonality so that the modification appears relatively seamless? Does transposing a particular passage for one singer have implications for the vocal ranges of other singers in the opera, and, if so, what can be done about it? What is the impact of a transposition on the instrumental parts, and how can anomalies in instrumental register be smoothly accommodated? Performing Italian opera well requires its practitioners to seek elegant solutions to intractable problems.

11
WORDS AND MUSIC:
TEXTS AND TRANSLATIONS

Now I know what translation means, and I have sympathy for all the awful
translations that exist, because it is impossible to make a good one.

Giuseppe Verdi to Tito Ricordi, 6 July 1855

DO WORDS MATTER? *GUGLIELMO TELL*
AT THE TEATRO ALLA SCALA

The Teatro alla Scala of Milan opened its 1988–89 season with Gioachino
Rossini's last opera, a work based on the exploits of the famous Swiss hero
William Tell, and written for the Opéra in Paris, where it was first performed
in August 1829. Riccardo Muti, then music director of La Scala and conductor for those performances, is well known for his continuing determination
to employ musical editions as close as possible to the most authentic sources
and to develop his interpretation from their readings. In this case he chose to
work from Elizabeth Bartlet's newly prepared critical edition of *Guillaume
Tell*, but Muti decided to perform not *Guillaume Tell*, using the French language in which Rossini composed the score in 1829, but *Guglielmo Tell*. This
Italian translation, with which the composer had nothing whatsoever to do,
was underlaid to Rossini's score during the 1830s in ways that grotesquely
modified his music.

As always in the world of opera, Muti's decision reflected diverse factors,
artistic, practical, commercial. Artistically, he was concerned that his largely
American and Italian cast would prove incapable of pronouncing French
idiomatically. That problem had emerged — too prominently and too recently
to be ignored — with respect to a recording in French of Verdi's *Don Carlos*,
with the orchestra of La Scala under the direction of Claudio Abbado.[1] Abbado's cast, in fact, had featured a largely Italian group of singers, including

Katia Riciarelli, Lucia Valentini-Terrani, Ruggero Raimondi, and Leo Nucci; the non-Italians—Placido Domingo as Don Carlos and Nicolai Ghiaurov as the Grand Inquisitor—did little to change the picture. Criticism of the French pronunciation was often severe.[2] Historically, after all, the language of opera performances had much to do with who was singing, and there was a strong sense that operas were more effective when performed by singers employing their own language.

Furthermore, from a practical standpoint, the entire La Scala troupe was to tour Japan during the autumn of 1988, so that the chorus needed to begin studying much earlier than normal and before materials for the new edition were available. It was therefore prudent to have the chorus relearn the Italian many were said already to know, at least in part, introducing corrections in the weeks preceding the performance. And finally, in commercial terms, opera in French by Italian composers has always perplexed the Italian public: while they are prepared to engage Bizet's *Carmen* in the original language, they remain resistant to French-language performances of Rossini's *Le Siège de Corinthe,* Donizetti's *La Favorite,* or Verdi's *Les Vêpres siciliennes.* When Muti led a fine performance of Rossini's *Moïse* in the original French to open the 2003–4 season at La Scala, he still faced criticism from the critic of the *Corriere della Sera,* Paolo Isotta, for not performing the opera in Italian.

And yet there was something inherently paradoxical in this situation: here was a conductor with a legendary reputation for his attention to dynamic markings in an edition, rhythmic details, pitch, expression, orchestral color, who was nonetheless prepared to have his singers employ a deeply problematic Italian translation. What conception of the function of text in opera would lead a Riccardo Muti to accept this compromise when he continued to find intolerable the much more limited compromise of a single high *c* at the end of "Di quella pira" in *Il trovatore,* even at the risk of infuriating the melomanes in the gallery and turning his opera house into a football stadium? After all, the high *c* is one note; in *Guglielmo Tell* tens of thousands of notes were changed from the opera Rossini actually wrote in order to underlay a metrically diverse text.

That words somehow play a subordinate role in opera is inherent, too, in a 1995 article by Will Crutchfield in *Opera News,* where he lamented the loss of "one of my favorite examples of the power of melody in Italian opera."[3] He was referring to a moment in the Adagio of this same Manrico aria at the end of act 3 of *Il trovatore,* "Ah! sì, ben mio, coll'essere." In his autograph manuscript, Verdi made a mistake in laying out the text in the varied repetition of the melody, anticipating the final line of a quatrain in place of what should have been the second line. In the original libretto, Manrico's strophe is written as follows:

Fra quegli estremi aneliti	With my last breaths
A te il pensier verrà!	My thoughts will come to you!
E solo in ciel precederti	And only to precede you into heaven
La morte a me parrà!	Death will seem to me!

But in Verdi's autograph manuscript the text is underlaid as in example 11.1. Although every copy of the score and every edition (until the appearance in 1993 of the critical edition of *Il trovatore*) followed the autograph, the text of the second phrase, "la morte a me parrà, parrà," should unquestionably be replaced (as in David Lawton's edition) by the correct words "a te il pensier verrà, verrà!"[4]

Crutchfield is too perceptive an observer of the operatic scene to suggest that singers should continue to perform the wrong words. His point is subtler: the force of Verdi's art is independent of the niceties of the text/music relationship. It is "the melody, not the word, that speaks." Indeed, he continues, after citing another gross mistake in the poetry of *Ernani*, finally corrected in Claudio Gallico's critical edition (see below), "many generations of Italian tenors, baritones, conductors and teachers have handled these arias without apparently noticing that something unintelligible was being said." Since the arias continue to speak to us despite this scrambling of their verbal messages, Crutchfield asks us to give "fresh regard for the absolute properties of voice, rhyme, melody, 'idiot sound.'"[5]

That Verdi's art transcends such errors is certain. At what point, however, do they become utterly disorienting? If the order of verses 1–4–3–4 is acceptable because blessed by a hundred and fifty years of performance, why not 1–2–3–2 or 3–2–1–4 ("E solo in ciel precederti, a te il pensier verrà,

EXAMPLE 11.1. GIUSEPPE VERDI, *IL TROVATORE*, ARIA MANRICO (N. 11), MM. 69–76, TEXTUAL ERROR IN THE CANTABILE.

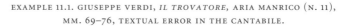

verrà, fra quegli estremi aneliti, la morte a me parrà")? Or why not a series of nonsense syllables? After all, is Verdi's art *better* because the words are wrong? Would the composer's melodic art *not* transcend the correct words as effectively as it does the wrong ones? In 2002 in Parma I sat through the presentation of a CD by a local organization interested in the history of singing, containing some twenty performances from early 78s of the Manrico aria. Whatever the positive qualities of these interpretations (and there were many), not one of the singers got the words right. That generations of tenors (tenors, so often tenors...) accepted this absurd text in Manrico's cantabile and generations of opera fans listened raptly to their interpretations is utterly irrelevant. The words are simply wrong, *punto e basta*.

WORDS AND MUSIC

Do words matter in nineteenth-century operas by Italian composers? As a theoretical question, the relative significance of text and music in opera or song has been debated by many generations of composers and critics. *Prima la musica, e poi le parole* (First the music, then the words), an eighteenth-century satire on operatic convention by Giambattista Casti, with music by Antonio Salieri, later became the inspiration for Richard Strauss's last opera, *Capriccio*. Among Casti's pointed barbs is a dialogue in which the composer misreads the libretto's words, so that the phrase "and this *costato* [literally 'rib cage'; figuratively 'windbag'] will run me through" becomes "and this *castrato* will run me through."[6] When the poet objects, the dialogue continues:

> *Composer:* *Castrato* goes extremely well and I won't change it.
> *Poet:* Are you making fun of me?
> *Composer:* What I wrote, I wrote.
> *Poet:* Have you gone crazy?
> *Composer:* I wrote *castrato,* it will remain *castrato!*
> *Poet:* And afterwards they will say, who was this poet who wrote such idiotic tripe.
> *Composer:* You won't be the first or the last.

The dialogue is so close to my dialogue with Piero Cappuccilli about *Ernani* ("your head, o traitor, there is no other choice" versus "your head *or* the traitor, there is no other choice") as to be downright frightening: "*traitor* goes extremely well and I won't change it."[7] More generally, composers have regularly been said to be indifferent to words ("Give me the telephone book, and I'll set it to music" is a modern way of putting this), and Darius Milhaud proved the case in his witty *Machines agricoles* (1919), in which he set to music descriptions of farm machinery from agricultural catalogues.

Without in any way undervaluing the terms of these debates or their significance, my own concern is a more practical one. Let us therefore rephrase our initial question. In the web of conflicting priorities that accompany every present-day operatic production, how much weight should we assign to the words? If we think about the question in those terms, it becomes apparent how many practical issues depend on our response. Should an opera be performed in its original language or in a language the local public understands? Should an opera house use supertitles? How should a singer balance the desire to produce beautiful sounds with comprehensible declamation of the text? What sorts of public spaces are most appropriate for the performance of opera? What balances should be maintained between the orchestra and the voices? Should singers' voices be amplified artificially in order to allow poorly trained voices to be heard and to ensure that the words will be better understood, as in Broadway musicals since the mid-1960s?

There are no unequivocal answers to any of these questions, for in each case the terms of the debate mean that choices need to be made. In each positive choice is embedded a negative one. If an opera house uses supertitles, members of the audience are able to follow the meaning of each phrase, but they lose visual and mental contact with the performers while their eyes and minds are focused above the stage (or, at the Metropolitan Opera, on the back of the seats in front of them). Performing in a nineteenth-century theater to 1,200 persons familiar with the language of the opera creates a different set of physical and vocal demands from performing in a twenty-first-century theater to an audience of 4,000 that for the most part does not understand the words. Yet when modern performers have to make choices—choices that may change from one theater to another, one work to another, or one performance to another—a knowledge of relevant history provides an intellectual and artistic context. Whether they embrace or reject this context, it is as much a part of the works themselves as the printed score.

A large proportion of the theater-going public continues to believe that opera composers in Italy first prepared the music (taking Casti's title literally, as a statement about compositional process), to which librettists subsequently added words. Wagner's polemical reversal of the terms, with his insistence on the priority of the words in opera, from which the composer's art would develop, became a club with which to pummel music from south of the Alps. But composers in Italy did *not* normally work this way. There is practically no evidence that Rossini ever composed music for his operas in the absence of a libretto, nor is there any reason to believe that Donizetti worked differently. When he wrote *Il barbiere di Siviglia* for the Teatro Argentina of Rome in January and February of 1816, with no time to spare, Rossini nonetheless waited until Cesare Sterbini handed him poetry, one piece at a time, before composing the music.[8]

We have, however, a fine example of the limits of any such generalization: Rossini's Neapolitan comic opera, *La gazzetta*. During the eight years in which he was involved with the Neapolitan theaters (from 1815 through 1822), Rossini wrote only one comic opera for Naples, *La gazzetta*, performed at the small, popular Teatro dei Fiorentini on 26 September 1816. As Rossini often did when facing a new audience, he recycled much earlier music in this second of his operas for Naples (as he had done in his first Neapolitan work, the serious *Elisabetta, regina d'Inghilterra*).[9] After these two works, there is very little self-borrowing in Rossini's eight subsequent Neapolitan operas.

The borrowings in *La gazzetta* include a famous quintet at a masked ball from *Il Turco in Italia*. In *Turco*, Don Geronio, in Turkish garb, is searching for his wife, Fiorilla. But she and the Turkish woman (Zaida), together with the Turk himself (Selim) and Fiorilla's admirer (Don Narciso), are also disguised in Turkish garb. The baffled Don Geronio doesn't know which way to turn. In the final ensemble they all laugh at him, while he desperately calls out "Vo' mia moglie... non capite?" (I want my wife... don't you understand?). In *La gazzetta*, the husband Don Geronio becomes the father Don Pomponio, a character who sings throughout in Neapolitan dialect. The role was created by Carlo Casaccia, a legendary figure of the Neapolitan popular stage. Pomponio, seeking an appropriately rich and upper-class husband for his daughter, Lisetta, has announced a competition for her hand in the local newspaper (hence, *La gazzetta*), but Lisetta falls in love with Filippo, an innkeeper.[10] And another couple forms during the course of the opera, Alberto and Doralice, in opposition to the wishes of Doralice's father. Toward the end of the second act they all participate in the masked ball, dressed as Turks. Don Pomponio searches in vain for his daughter, while the young couples rush off to get married.

For these two couples, the text of the quintet is essentially identical in the two operas. But a funny thing happened to Don Pomponio: in the quintet the librettist forgot to prepare a stanza for him to sing, even though there is a stanza for Don Geronio in *Il Turco in Italia*. In the libretto printed for the first performances of *La gazzetta* (and the opera was hardly ever revived during the nineteenth century), there is no text here for Don Geronio. In his autograph manuscript, Rossini includes words for the other four characters, but none at all for Don Pomponio. We have no idea what Carlo Casaccia sang at the first performances, although his powers as an improviser were legendary. Nineteenth-century manuscript copies of *La gazzetta* simply incorporate the textless part, paying no heed to the absurdity, while the only important nineteenth-century edition (prepared by Ricordi during the 1850s) imposes words from an earlier section of the quintet that have little to do with this situation.[11]

Preparing the critical edition of *La gazzetta* for performance at the Rossini Opera Festival of Pesaro during the summer of 2001, Fabrizio Scipioni and I went back to *Il Turco in Italia*, borrowed Don Geronio's stanza, but (with the help of Sergio Ragni, a Neapolitan born and bred) rendered it into Neapolitan for Don Pomponio. "Vo' mia moglie" (I want my wife) became "Vuo' mia figlia" (I want my daughter), while "Sarà questa, sarà quella" (she's this one, she's that one) became, with no change in meaning, "Sarà chessa, sarà chella." For Rossini the problem of the placement of new words under previously written music is important, as we shall see, and colors our understanding of the relationship between words and music in his operas, but there is practically no evidence that the composer exercised his art for the theater in the absence of words.

For Bellini the situation is different. The composer from Catania did indeed have a tendency to draft pages of melodic ideas, his "morning exercises," as he was wont to call them, often in the context of thinking about particular operatic plots. Some fascinating pages exist from 1834 and 1835, as he began to consider the opera he was to compose for the Théâtre Italien during the carnival of 1834–35 (*I puritani*), and then as he thought about a later project. The *Puritani* pages are filled with fragments of ideas, written down one immediately after another, sometimes a measure or two, sometimes an entire melodic period. Very little effort has been made to analyze what it is about these ideas that might have commended themselves to Bellini in the context of considering the plot of the new opera, but subconsciously, at least, there must have been something that brought them together in his mind.[12] The technique may have worked for Bellini because he tended to distribute syllables in an extremely consistent way within a phrase and was less apt than Verdi, for example, to seek a particularized relationship between words and music.

Subsequently, Bellini would develop a few of these ideas into full-fledged compositions, including the melody of Arturo's cavatina ("A te, o cara"), Giorgio's romanza ("Cinta di fiori"), and the theme of the duet for Elvira and Arturo in the last act ("Nel mirarti un solo istante"). In each case the sketched melodic fragment is significantly different from the operatic melody: the melodic cell for "A te, o cara" is notated in 4/4, rather than the characteristic 12/8 of *I puritani;* "Cinta di fiori" is represented by a two-measure fragment in B♭ *major* (the operatic melody is in A♭); and the definitive version of "Nel mirarti un solo istante" is represented by just four measures in B♭ *major* (the piece is in *C major* in *I puritani*), and is similar to the operatic melody only at its very beginning. Bellini knew that these melodies were destined for life in his operas, for when he drafted actual scenes incorporating these melodies, he crossed out the fragments, leaving untouched the themes that might still serve his needs. Turning these fragments into operatic melodies, however, was always tied to the verbal text of an opera. Even when Bellini adopted or adapted one of his exercises, it would be transformed in the process of making it into an operatic melody.

For Verdi we have vast amounts of evidence about the importance of words to his compositional process, evidence found in letters exchanged between the composer and his librettists and, increasingly, the elaborate sketches (particularly the continuity drafts) he prepared for his operas. But we also have at least one example of Verdi's having prepared preliminary melodic ideas for an opera, a page of verbal indications and musical sketches for the first act of *La traviata,* which Verdi unquestionably drafted before having received any text whatsoever from his librettist, Francesco Maria Piave.[13] On this page, the composer outlined the dramatic shape of the first act, still using the name of "Margherita" from Alexandre Dumas' *La Dame aux Camélias* and identifying her beloved simply as "Tenore." After specifying "Cena in casa di Margherita / Recc: Motivi d'orchestra. Brindisi" (Dinner in Margherita's home / Recitative: motives in the orchestra. Brindisi), he wrote a long melody that he labeled "Brindisi del tenore": it is a preliminary melodic draft of the brindisi "Libiamo ne' lieti calici" without any words. The sketch is extraordinary: not only does Verdi invent the basic theme (written out in full, very similar to the final version), but he also specifies Margherita's reprise, choral participation, the place where the soprano and the tenor alternate phrases, and even the conclusion with choral declamation beneath the melody.

The page continues with a description of Margherita's scene with the tenor, the reappearance of the guests, their departure, and Margherita alone on the stage. Then, specifying "Andante come segue," Verdi drafted the entire melody of "Ah fors'è lui," some forty measures, without any text at all. The melody differs in many respects from the final version, particularly when it turns from its minor mode opening to its major mode conclusion. What will become "A quell'amor" is here drafted in the relative major of the initial key, rather than the parallel major as in the definitive version. But the differences are matters of detail: the basic melodic material and shape are fully present, even though Verdi had received no words. Then, after some more sentences of dramaturgical explanation, he indicated "cabaletta brillante" (lively cabaletta), at which point he wrote down the first phrase of "Sempre libera," noting that the tenor will be heard from offstage singing a phrase from the duettino.[14]

This is the only such page known to exist for any Verdi opera, although similar pages might figure among the unexamined treasures in the composer's home at Sant'Agata. And for *La traviata* there is also an exceptional number of sketches without text that do not form part of longer continuity drafts, suggesting that at other points in his quite hurried work with this opera Verdi tried out melodic ideas without having poetry in hand. For the most part, however, the sketches for Verdi's operas currently available (essentially complete materials for *Stiffelio, Rigoletto, La traviata, Aroldo, Un ballo in maschera,* and *La forza del destino,* as well as smaller sections from another ten operas) show unmistakably that the composer developed his musical ideas with a particular set of words in mind. Even when sketches seem to be textless, a careful reading of Verdi's correspondence with his librettists can often explain the apparent discrepancy.

There is a fine example in the opera Verdi first conceived in 1857 as *Gustavo III,* then, prompted by censorial objections, transformed into *Una vendetta in dominò* at the end of 1857, and finally—with its premiere shifted from Naples to Rome, still because of censorship—transformed into *Un ballo in maschera.*[15] The passage comes at the end of the elaborate introduction, which comprises almost half the first act, when the Swedish king, Gustavo (later the Governor of Boston, Riccardo) and his courtiers (later citizens of Boston) decide to pay a visit to the den of the witch Ulrica, whom the "Primo giudice" (Chief Justice, a title that worked equally well in Stockholm or Boston) seeks to remove forcibly from the realm (colony).

We know exactly when Verdi was working on this final section of the introduction, because he made the following request to his librettist, Antonio Somma, on 26 November 1857:

> Excuse me: some bother on my account! It would assist me greatly in the stretta of the introduction to move this stanza to the end of the scene:
> Gustavo: *Dunque, signori, aspettovi*
> *.......................... alle tre*
> *Nell'antro dell'oracolo,*
> *Della gran maga al piè.*

Tutti: ....
          ....*alle tre*
          Nell'antro dell'oracolo,
          Della gran maga al piè.

It would serve my needs if you could find me a *parola sdrucciola* instead of "al tocco," and could include "alle tre.".... And then adjust it so that the *Tutti* can sing the entire stanza.[16]

In an undated letter, probably sent on 2 December, Somma produced the text we all know:

Gustavo:	*Dunque, signori, aspettovi,*	[*Gustavo:* So, I'll wait for you,
	Incognito, alle tre,	gentlemen, disguised, at three,
	Nell'antro dell'oracolo,	in the den of the oracle, at the
	Della gran maga al piè.	foot of the great sorceress.
Tutti:	*Teco sarem di subito,*	*Tutti:* We'll be with you right
	Incogniti, alle tre,	away, disguised, etc.],
	Nell'antro dell'oracolo,	
	Della gran maga al piè.[17]	

In the second line is Verdi's requested *sdrucciolo* ("in-*co*-gni-to," with its accent on the antepenultimate syllable) and his desired "alle tre."

In the draft of the introduction, although Verdi had entered words everywhere else, he did not put words in this passage, for he clearly was dissatisfied with Somma's original second line, "Al tocco delle tre" (when the clock strikes three). Instead, the melody he drafted, essentially identical to the final tune, left space for the *sdrucciolo* that would become "incognito," a word at the beginning of the second line that mirrors rhythmically the *sdrucciolo* at the close of the first line ("a-*spet*-to-vi"). Verdi also left room for the memorable outburst, "alle tre." In example 11.2, the text Verdi already had in hand is placed in square brackets; the text he requested of Somma is indicated in curly brackets. Ultimately the composer so much wanted to emphasize "alle tre" that he inserted extra measures to allow his singers to hold the high note longer. These changes were made only *after* he had entered the passages in his skeleton score, during work on *Un ballo in maschera.*[18]

Why is this example important? It demonstrates as clearly as possible that the lack of text in Verdi's sketch here does not mean he conceived this melody without words. He worked directly from Somma's original stanza and tried to capture its character and brio, but as he composed the music he decided that at a certain point he wanted a rhythmic effect that would have been impossible

EXAMPLE 11.2. GIUSEPPE VERDI, *UN BALLO IN MASCHERA*, INTRODUZIONE (N. 1),
MM. 470–479, THEME OF THE STRETTA AS SKETCHED FOR *GUSTAVO III*, WITH
THE IMPLICIT TEXT AND THE MODIFICATIONS REQUESTED BY VERDI.

with Somma's words. Hence the request for a modification of the original stanza. But Verdi knew exactly what he wanted the revised version to say and how he wanted the revised text to be constructed, and he drafted the melody with that ideal text in mind. Somma supplied him with an appropriate revision, and the story had a happy ending. That was not always the case. Occasionally Verdi cobbled together words of his own in order to create the text/music fusion he had in mind. But rarely did he conceive his music independently of the text to which it would give life.

SAME MUSIC, DIFFERENT TEXTS

Generations of critics have lambasted the language of Jacopo Ferretti, the Roman librettist responsible for Rossini's *La Cenerentola* and for many Donizetti texts, but their barbs are misplaced: Ferretti's poetry is hilarious (and delectably bawdy).[19] Indeed, most of the librettists working in Italy during the nineteenth century were thorough professionals, able men of the theater, who knew how to construct a text for music and had a fair ability to produce acceptable verses. And even when their inexperience showed (as in the case of Piave for Verdi's *Ernani*),[20] the composers were standing by their side to give them guidance. Much of the criticism directed at these librettists derives from ignorance. How often I have read scathing commentary on the dramaturgy of Rossini's serious operas from critics who, in their failure to know eighteenth-century neoclassical drama, center their perplexity on the sole artist through whom this drama circulates today, Rossini. In their ignorance of the poetic diction of Italian verse or verse-drama of the first half of the nineteenth century (that of Leopardi, Monti, or Manzoni), they assume that "sacri bronzi" (sacred bronzes) sound only on the operatic stage, in the melodramas of Verdi.[21] As Piero Weiss has correctly stated, "Risorgimento librettists spoke the same language as other poets of their time. It was not an 'irrational' or 'surrealist' language, nor was it 'utterly worthless.' It was Romantic, fiery, uneven; above all it was contemporary, and its message was understood." [22] Without knowledge of Romantic drama, the theater of Hugo, Dumas, Schiller, or Guttierez, or the dramatic verse of Byron, it is impossible to judge the accomplishments of the music theater of the period.

But something else is at work. The Wagnerian paradigm has accustomed us to the notion that music and text are uniquely connected and indissolubly linked. That the same music might support different texts seems, from a post-Wagnerian perspective, more than a little suspect. Yet Italian composers during the first sixty years of the nineteenth century did not share such scruples, even if their views changed over that lengthy period. Nowhere is the problem more intensely represented than in the music of Rossini, a composer who patently refused a unitary vision of the relationship between words and music.

He was not alone. The 1854 treatise by the Viennese music critic Eduard Hanslick, *On the Musically Beautiful,* set forth a program that assigned to music a role independent of any effort to bind it to words. Hanslick's famous example was the renowned aria from the *Orphée et Euridice* of Gluck, "J'ai perdu mon Euridice, / Rien n'égale à mon malheur" (I have lost my Euridice, nothing equals my sadness), whose expressivity had long been celebrated. Yet what would happen, he asked, if we simply changed the words to "J'ai trouvé mon Euridice, / Rien n'égale à mon bonheur" (I have found my Euridice, nothing equals my joy)? Music and words would form a new union, every bit as satisfying as the original. [23]

Many similar examples can be found in the operas of Rossini, but the best known is probably Elcia's aria at the conclusion of the second act of *Mosè in Egitto,* the opera first performed in Naples during the Lenten season of 1818. [24] Elcia, a Hebrew, is secretly married to the son of Faraone (the Pharaoh), Osiride. They are torn between their love for one another and their allegiance to their respective peoples. At the end of the second act, Faraone is intent on punishing the Hebrews (putting their leader, Moses, to death) and wedding his son to an Armenian princess. Elcia appears and in the cantabile of her aria begs Osiride to accept his father's will. In the *tempo di mezzo* he arrogantly refuses and, instead, moves to strike down the chained Mosè, when a lightning bolt descends and strikes Osiride dead. In the cabaletta of her aria, Elcia sings of the "tormenti" and "affanni" (torments and agitation) that tear open her heart: "Tutto di Averno, o furie, versate in me il furore" (Furies, pour into me all the fury of Hell). The music flies along, vivace, in *E major,* its vocal line replete with arpeggios and scales. The rhythmic intensity is regularly interrupted by freer passages, in which Elcia sobs "È spento il caro bene" (My beloved is dead), with the chorus and other soloists joining her laments. The whole cabaletta forms an effective tableau upon which the curtain falls at the end of the second act.

When Rossini revised *Mosè in Egitto* in 1827 to produce the second of his four French operas, *Moïse et Pharaon,* he reused this cabaletta theme but assigned it to a different character. Instead of being sung by Elcia (Anaï in Paris), the desperate lover of the son of the Egyptian ruler, Osiride (Aménophis in Paris), it is sung by Aménophis's mother, Sinaïde. In a cantabile very similar to that of Elcia, she begs her son to accept the hand of the foreign princess. During the rewritten *tempo di mezzo,* however, Aménophis yields to her pleas, at which point she launches into the cabaletta. While changed in many respects from the original composition in *Mosè in Egitto,* the principal tune is identical, but its text now reads: "Qu'entends-je, ô douce ivresse! / Il est fidèle à l'honneur" (What do I hear, oh sweet joy! He is faithful to his honor). The music flies along, vivace, in *E major,* its vocal line replete with arpeggios and scales. Example 11.3 offers the first phrase with the two texts.[25] The musical setting seems every bit as appropriate to the changed dramatic situation as it did to the earlier one. The trappings into which the main theme is inserted are, to be sure, very different; hence, Rossini did not attempt to graft an entire piece into a new dramatic situation. Nonetheless, the main melody remains intact and clearly serves both operas well. Hanslick couldn't have invented a better example.[26]

Rossini himself explained his attitude toward the relationship between text and music on several occasions.[27] In a letter from his last year, 1868, to

EXAMPLE 11.3. GIOACHINO ROSSINI, *MOSÈ IN EGITTO* AND *MOÏSE,* ARIA ELCIA (N. 10), MM. 160–163, AND ARIA SINAÏDE (N. 10), RESPECTIVELY, PRINCIPAL THEME OF THE CABALETTA.

the Italian critic Filippo Filippi, he wrote, "I will remain forever *unmovable* in my conviction that Italian musical art (especially in its vocal part) is all *ideal and expressive,* never *imitative,* as certain materialist pseudo-philosophers would want it to be."[28] But he had no need of an anti-Wagnerian stance in order to hold such convictions. Particularly revealing is a passage from a conversation with Rossini published for the first time in 1836 by Antonio Zanolini, a Bolognese friend. While it seems unlikely that Rossini himself phrased his ideas in these specific terms, they capture beautifully the nature of his art:

> Musical expression is neither so clear nor so explicit as the meaning of words, is neither so evident nor so alive as painting, with all its artifices and illusions, but it is more pleasing and more poetic than any other poetry. [...] Music produces marvelous effects when coordinated with dramatic art, when the ideal expression of music joins the true expression of poetry and the imitative expression of painting. Then, while words and deeds express the most minute and concrete particularities of the emotions, music proposes for itself a more elevated, ample, and abstract goal; music is, in a manner of speaking, the moral atmosphere that fills the place in which characters of the drama represent the action.[29]

In this conception of the coordination between words and music, the same music can easily serve to accommodate different "atmospheres" or idealize different contents. Words provide semantic suggestions, rhythmic relationships and stresses to which the composer responds. He is not immune to the particularities of the text; but his music does not "express" the emotions voiced by the poetry.

Thus Rossini felt perfectly justified in reusing music that had been composed for a particular opera in another circumstance. These reworkings rarely involve such vastly different situations as in the cabaletta from *Mosè in Egitto* and *Moïse;* in almost every case, the transported music seems fully successful in its new home. Still, one can understand Rossini's uneasiness in the world of European Romanticism, where the principle of "originality" seemed ever more important, when during the 1850s Ricordi issued the composer's complete works in reductions for piano and voice, opening the secrets of his compositional practice to any casual glance. While agreeing to assist, on 24 February 1852 he wrote to Giovanni Ricordi: "I will not fail to furnish to Sig. Stefani all that depends on me for the edition about which you spoke to me, an edition that, unfortunately, will bring all my miserable stuff back to light."[30] He returned to the matter many years later, in a letter of 14 December 1864 to Giovanni's son Tito:

> The edition you have undertaken will give rise (and with reason) to much criticism, since one will find in diverse operas the same pieces of music: the time and money given me to compose were so *homeopathic* [i.e., infinitesimal], that I barely had time to read the so-called poetry I was to set to music: the only thing that touched my heart was supporting my beloved parents and poor relatives.[31]

Leaving aside the sentimentality of the expression, the issue remains. Rossini's music was usually written to a text, but it was not indissolubly linked to that text. On the other hand, the sounds, rhythms, and character of the words provided the bases from which the music developed. When Rossini decided to reuse a theme or a piece in a later opera, it was he who gave orders to a poet to adapt new verses and a new dramaturgical situation. Words and music, in short, go together intimately but not uniquely.

In the same manner one understands Rossini's later obsession with setting again and again the same verses by Metastasio:[32]

Mi lagnerò tacendo	I will lament in silence
Della mia sorte amara;	Of my bitter fate;
Ma ch'io non t'ami, o cara,	But that I not love you, dear,
Non lo sperar da me.	Do not hope that from me.
Crudele! in che t'offesi,	Cruel one! how have I offended you,
Farmi penar così?	That you give me such pain?

Rossini set these words to music many times, a particularly poignant situation for a composer who at the age of thirty-seven had abandoned a theatrical career that had brought him to the height of European fame. He wrote hundreds of album leaves to this text, all of which can be grouped as one of some twenty-five basic settings, and then employed the Metastasian verses again toward the end of his life as the basis for much more elaborate settings in his late music, the so-called *Péchés de vieillesse.* The poetry is hardly distinguished. Indeed, a writer who gives voice to silent lamenting is standing on slippery ground. Yet Rossini responded in an impressively varied way to these verses.

In this late music, however, there is a new and fascinating phenomenon. Again and again Rossini wrote "ideal" music to these words, creating with his

EXAMPLE 11.4. GIOACHINO ROSSINI, "MI LAGNERÒ TACENDO" AND *ARIETTE POMPADOUR*, MM. 37–40, TWO TEXTS SET TO THE SAME MUSIC.

Mi la - gne - rò ta - cen - do del - la mia sor - te a - ma - ra;
La per - le des co - quet - tes ne fait que des con - quê - tes;

music many different worlds in which the Metastasian verses could come alive. Then, at a second moment, he gave those ideal worlds a new reality by arranging for original poetry to be underlaid to the music he had already written. To this end he turned most often to a Parisian friend, Émilien Pacini, whose task was to breathe in the "moral atmosphere" created by the music and give it specificity.[33] Pacini did so by seeking to capture in his text the character of Rossini's music: in one case its playfulness and eighteenth-century qualities of wit and grace, in another its barcarole-like demeanor, in another its stark drama, in another its Spanish rhythms and figurations. Thus the music, while not uniquely tied to a text, does have purely musical characteristics that suggest some kinds of verbal analogies rather than others. Example 11.4 shows the first phrase of Rossini's "Mi lagnerò tacendo" setting to which Pacini later added a text called "Ariette Pompadour," in which an eighteenth-century French beauty boasts of her ability to turn every head, as if she were a new Madame de Pompadour.[34]

Why did Rossini commission these new texts? His obsessive biographical reasons for returning to the Metastasian verses had by now become an obsessive aesthetic doctrine as well. Yet with the public performance of these compositions in Paris during the late 1850s, at the famous *samedi soirs* in Rossini's home, this obsession needed to be disguised, if only to allow the music to be performed without drawing attention to the aesthetic challenge it posed. Thus, Rossini's aesthetic stance became the basis for an elaborate game of disguises and masks. The composer who retired in silence, aware that his aesthetic roots led backwards into a more classical relationship between music and text, expressed his stance by clothing the same brief text in a myriad of different musical settings, of "moral atmospheres." Then, as if to mask the mask, he had these compositions provided in turn with a series of texts that seem to "express the most minute and concrete particularities of the emotions." And when Rossini's late music became the object of praise by modern critics, unaware of these derivations, for having achieved a close symbiosis of music and text, the irony came full circle.

SINGING OPERA IN TRANSLATION

In this context, the problem of singing translations should be relatively simple. After all, if Rossini himself was content to have a trusted friend place new French words under music written to completely unrelated Italian ones, why should we have any hesitation about singing the French operas by Rossini, Donizetti, or Verdi in Italian? On the surface it would seem that only the worst kind of pedantry would balk at that prospect. Yet the situation is considerably more complicated, and one significant problem in the performance today of operas by Italian composers active during the first six decades of the nineteenth century is the survival (and in some case the dominance) in the modern performing tradition of nineteenth-century translations into Italian of these French operas by Italian composers.

The idea that operas, for aesthetic reasons, should be sung in the languages in which they were originally written is relatively modern.[35] During the nineteenth century, certainly, the Italian public knew *L'oro del reno* or *Il profeta* and not *Das Rheingold* or *Le Prophète,* the Germans *Aschenbrödel* or *Die Macht des Schiksals* and not *La Cenerentola* or *La forza del destino,* the French *Les Noces de Figaro* and not *Le nozze di Figaro.* In countries for which the genre had strong native roots or sought to develop such roots, opera performed in a language other than the local tongue embodied distinct, albeit varied, social and cultural messages. For Jean-Jacques Rousseau, who expressed his position most strongly in his 1753 *Lettre sur la musique française,* comic opera presented in Paris in Italian by an Italian troupe was energized by a simplicity and naturalness of expression lacking in the formal *tragédie-lyrique* of the French court.[36] For Carl Maria von Weber, opera produced at the Dresden court in Italian under the direction of Francesco Morlacchi represented the loathed foreign and aristocratic influence whose presence blocked both the growth of native German forms associated with local composers and the development of an audience encompassing a broader range of social classes.[37] For composers in Russia and in the countries of Eastern Europe, opera in German or Italian hindered the development of those indigenous forms that were part of the nationalist political project.[38] And such nationalistic projects have not dimmed today. Much of the explicit and implicit criticism directed toward the performances of Verdi's *Un ballo in maschera* in Parma in January 2001, the first opera presented in that city's Verdi Festival during the centennial of the composer's death, were directed at the "Russianness" of the conductor, Valéry Gergiev, and his Slavic singers. Rather than concentrate on the accomplishments of these Russian musicians that revealed new facets of Verdi's art, some critics preferred to lament what they heard as limitations to the "Italianness" of their performance. Imagine if they had performed the opera in Russian!

Performing operas from other traditions in translation has always had both a practical and a cultural function. Practically, of course, it answered some of the objections raised in debates over the introduction of Italian opera into London during the first half of the eighteenth century: many critics perceived as absurd an entertainment performed in a language the audience did not understand.[39] But translation, and the process of adaptation that often accompanied it, also helped works conceived in other traditions be absorbed into a national sphere and, ultimately, integrated stylisically into national traditions. The effect of Rossini's style on French opera of the early nineteenth century was furthered by the performance of his operas in French adaptations, first at the Théâtre de l'Odéon,[40] then (undertaken, in this case, by the composer himself) at the Théâtre de l'Académie Royale de Musique. The effect of Wagnerism on French and Italian opera of the later nineteenth century was furthered by the performance of Wagnerian operas in the local language at the major opera houses in France and Italy.[41] Translation helped break down at least one level of public resistance to stylistic novelty.

Certain operas were more widely known during the nineteenth century in translation than in the original tongue. This was true for Eastern European operas translated into German or for French operas by Italian composers that circulated widely in Italian theaters. Because these works had many more performances outside their country of origin than within it, and because the languages in which they were written were considered either difficult to sing or not widely known, the operas were often learned and performed in German or Italian. When they were imported into countries such as England or the United States, in which native opera did not flourish, they continued to be performed in the most widely available translation. Although the situation has changed markedly, some of these nineteenth-century preferences remain operative today. The increasing rigidity and internationalization of the operatic community in the twentieth century, furthermore, provided a practical underpinning for these preferences. The same singers tended to perform the same work in different countries, often going onstage with only a few days of frenetic rehearsals, helping to foster an atmosphere that accepted French operas being sung in Italian in the United States.

Rossini's *Guillaume Tell* is such a work, and we will now take another look at the performances at La Scala in December 1988, mentioned at the beginning of this chapter.

GUGLIELMO TELL AT LA SCALA: "LIBERTÉ"

Once the decision was made to perform a critical edition of *Guillaume Tell* in Italian translation, it was necessary to determine which Italian words to sing. At first glance that seemed obvious: the standard nineteenth-century translation. In fact, performances of *Guillaume Tell* outside France were rarely given in French during the nineteenth century. Leaving aside German translations, various Italian versions are found among early editions and librettos, but the translation by Calisto Bassi, prepared for the first presentation of the opera in Italy (Lucca, 1831), is the one that has entered the modern performing tradition. A variant of it was printed in the vocal score issued by Ricordi in the middle of the nineteenth century and has been reissued with few changes until our own day.[42]

In fact, as we shall see, none of the ninteenth-century translations is adequate. One translation was even prepared with Rossini's blessing (though not his active intervention): Luigi Balocchi, librettist of the opera Rossini wrote for the coronation of Charles X, *Il viaggio a Reims,* was responsible for the translation printed in the Artaria edition, published in Vienna. But this translation was hopelessly compromised by political considerations. As Paolo Cattelan—who helped to develop the translation used at La Scala in 1988— explained, a story about Austrian tyranny could hardly be told in Vienna or Milan (ruled at the time by Austria) without significant modifications.[43] Short of attempting an entirely new translation of *Tell*, then, Calisto Bassi's work remains the best starting point for a modern Italian-language performance, and there are many advantages to this translation, including its familiarity to modern audiences (especially in Italy). Yet the translation is problematic in three ways: its failure to take into account Rossini's alterations in the text; its treatment of politics; and its use of verse forms.

Elizabeth Bartlet's study of the original performing materials of *Guillaume Tell,* which are preserved in Paris at the Bibliothèque de l'Opéra, revealed for the first time that Rossini made significant changes in the vocal lines during the rehearsal period, changes that continued to be reflected in French performances of the opera until uncertainty about the origin of these practices sent performers back to printed scores that never incorporated Rossini's alterations. A simple example is found in the chorus "Ciel qui du monde," in which the Swiss peasants and soloists bless the three couples who are to be joined in matrimony as part of the festivities that dominate the first act. Only Arnold is differentiated musically and textually from the others: just as he has set himself apart from his countrymen by his love for the Austrian princess,

Mathilde, Rossini sets him apart from the ensemble. As Professor Bartlet has demonstrated, the French text originally set by Rossini presents a quite different characterization of Arnold than the revised text found in the performing materials of the Opéra and preserved in part in the original French printed libretto.[44]

Original

Ils vont s'unir, quelle souffrance!	[They are to be united, what torment! They
Ils vont s'unir, pour moi plus d'espérance	are to be united, there is no more hope for
Quels maux j'endure! fatal amour!	me. What pains I suffer! fatal love!]

Revision

Ils vont s'unir... Qu'ils sont heureux!	[They are to be united... May they be happy!
Ils vont s'unir... Le Ciel bénit leurs vœux.	They are to be united... May Heaven bless
Ivresse pure! ô chaste amour!	their vows. Pure joy! chaste love!]

The differences between the way Arnold is pictured in these two texts is very striking. But the revised characterization, less egocentric and more sensitive to the beauty of the ceremony he is witnessing, was never adapted into the Italian translations. This problem could be solved with relative ease by developing a new translation of the French revision, following the outlines of the nineteenth-century Italian translation.

Even where the new critical edition does not provide a different reading in French, comparison of the original text and the contemporary Italian translations reveals a concerted effort to reduce the political force of the original. In Italy during the 1830s and 1840s, great caution was required when dealing with politically sensitive matters or issues having to do with religion. (Well known are the bouts Donizetti and Verdi fought, and often lost, with local censors.)[45] The original French plot of *Guillaume Tell* was considered unacceptable at various times between 1830 and 1860 in Italy, and librettos with entirely different geographical settings and transformed events were often adapted to Rossini's music. In the *Valace* that had its premiere at La Scala in 1836, Scottish followers of Robert Bruce fight against the usurper Edward I, King of England, and various MacGregors, Maxwells, and Kirkpatricks fill the stage. Pretty much the same story was performed in Bologna in 1840, but with the protagonist's name changed from Guglielmo Valace to Rodolfo di Sterlinga. (Curiously, Rossini had a hand in this revival, writing for it a new finale in Italian, a manuscript of which resurfaced only in the past decade.)[46] But even when the opera was given with its original names, as *Guglielmo Tell,* the translators had to be cautious.

Here are two characteristic examples from the Calisto Bassi translation, a translation that continued to be sung in Italy until 1988 and still circulates among the unwary today. In the second act, Guillaume and another Swiss patriot, Walter, challenge Arnold to defend his country rather than fight in the army of their oppressors. During this trio, they reveal that the Austrians have murdered Arnold's father, Melcthal, at which point all three join in a cry for revenge. The following three strophes are given in the original French, as set to music by Rossini, together with the contemporary translation, essentially that of Calisto Bassi.[47]

Tell

Quand l'Helvétie est un champ de supplices
    Où l'on moissonne ses enfants;
Que de Gesler tes armes soient complices;
    Combats et meurs pour nos tyrans!

[When Switzerland is a field of execution where its children are devoured; your weapons are Gesler's accomplices; you fight and die for our tyrants!]

    Allor che scorre—De' forti il sangue,
      Che tutto langue,—Che tutto è orror,
      La spada impugna,—Gessler diffendi,
      La vita spendi—Pel traditor.

[While the blood of heroes runs, while everything languishes, everything is horrible, you use your sword to defend Gessler, you spend your life for the traitor.]

Arnold

    Les camps rappellent mon courage;
    Aux camps règne la loyauté.
Déjà la gloire marqua mon passage;
Elle remplace aussi la liberté.

[The field of battle brings fourth my courage; loyalty reigns there. Already glory marks my path; it will thus replace liberty.]

    Al campo volo,—Onor m'attende;
      Ardir m'accende,—M'accende amor.
      Desio di gloria—M'invita all'armi,
      È di vittoria—Ardente il cor.

[I fly to the field of battle, where honor awaits me, boldness incites me, love ignites me. A desire for glory invites me to arms, and for victory my heart is yearning.]

a 3

Embrassons-nous d'un saint délire!
La liberté pour nous conspire;
Des Cieux ton père nous inspire,
Vengeons-le, ne le pleurons plus.

[Let us embrace one another in a holy delirium! Liberty conspires for us; from the heavens your father inspires us, let us revenge him and weep no more.]

    La gloria infiammi—I nostri petti,
      Il ciel propizio—Con noi cospira.
      Del padre l'ombra—Il cor c'ispira,
      Chiede vendetta—E non dolor.

[Glory inflames our breasts, propitious heaven conspires with us. The ghost of your father inspires our heart, it asks for revenge, not sorrow.]

The many strong political images of the French text are rendered pallid in the Italian: Gesler as a tyrant becomes Gessler as a traitor; the fields of the country swallowing the blood of its children disappears altogether in favor of new attention to the spilled blood of warriors; the notion that glory replaces liberty in Arnold's soul is reduced to glory inviting him to arms; and, of course, the key words of the third strophe, "La liberté pour nous conspire," disappear altogether. These are not small matters: the very essence of the concept behind Rossini's music, the ideas to which his music offers a "moral atmosphere," have lost the greater part of their power. (Notice, too, how the French *octosyllabes* and *décasyllabes,* measured in the French fashion *without* the feminine ending, are transformed without differentiation into an Italian *doppio quinario* meter. But we will return to metrical questions in the next section.)

At the very end of the opera, the grandiose conclusion celebrating the freedom of the Swiss, the French text (in *octosyllabes*) provides an ecstatic image well matched to Rossini's soaring phrase. It is derived from a popular *ranz des vaches* motif, based on a Swiss popular melody, one of the motifs that dominate much of the thematic material of the opera.[48] In the Italian translation of Calisto Bassi, however, the sentiment (here rendered in *ottonario* verse) is trivialized beyond recognition.[49]

Liberté redescends des cieux,	[Liberty, descend again from the heavens,
Et que ton règne recommence!	and may your reign begin again.]
Quel contento che in me sento	[My soul cannot explain the happiness
Non può l'anima spiegar.	I feel within me.]

Fortunately, the "moral atmosphere" of Rossini's music drives the expression well beyond the insipid words: A new translation of this text (used in the La Scala performances) has sought to imitate better the sense of the original French, reserving for the conclusion the forbidden word, "libertà":

Del tuo regno fia l'avvento	[May your reign begin on earth, o liberty.]
Sulla terra, o libertà.	

These examples are only the beginning. On page after page, the French text is compromised, and with it the verbal meaning of Rossini's opera. It is hard to imagine how these censorial interventions (whether they involved actual censorship or self-censorship) could have survived for so long. Yet the issues they raise appear simple to resolve. A modern Italian translator could modify, revise, or replace Calisto Bassi's words so that the new Italian text would correspond more closely in meaning to the original French, as in the words from the finale just quoted. Yet doing so turns out not to be quite such a simple task, after all, for there is more at work here (and in all the translations of this repertory currently in use) than just fitting new words to old music.

GUGLIELMO TELL AT LA SCALA: METRICS

More complex and far-reaching in significance is the problem of verse forms. Italian *poesia per musica* (poetry for music) had its own rules during the first half of the nineteenth century. So did French poetry. But the rules were not the same, as contemporaries were well aware.[50] In the libretto printed to accompany a performance of Rossini's *Le Siège de Corinthe* in Genoa in the spring of 1828, the following paragraph was included in the preface:

> Until now there have been three adaptations of *L'assedio di Corinto* for use in Italian theaters, but unfortunately the one destined to be employed in the theater of Genoa, having been made to agree too slavishly with the words in the French score and not with the printed libretto, cannot help but be extremely irregular and defective.[51]

This expression of caring about a national style of verse, insisting that it has its own claims, independent of the music, led Italian nineteenth-century translators to compromise without hesitation the connection between the music and the words. To come to grips with this problem, the Genoese libretto changed the printed libretto to make it more regular, less defective, but—in this case—may have allowed the words sung from the stage to continue to match the music.

For the most part, however, translations were not prepared to match musical phrases. The original text was instead transformed into a text appropriate for the other language's poetic meters, and the resulting words were made to fit, one way or another, the previously composed music.[52] Even when the composer himself was involved with the translation, as Verdi most assuredly was for *Les Vêpres siciliennes* (as we shall see), the obstacles to overcome often became insurmountable: music conceived for a set of poetic meters appropriate to one language could not be transformed to accommodate a contrasting set of poetic meters in another language without being seriously compromised.

French poetry for recitative, for example, was constructed of lines of diverse length, including classical twelve-syllable alexandrines, as well as ten-, eight-, and six-syllable lines (always measured without the feminine ending). Italian recitative, on the other hand, was constructed of *versi sciolti*, a mixture of *settenari* and *endecasillabi*. An Italian poet, translating recitative from the

French and attempting to produce recognizable verse forms in his own language, has no choice but completely to reshape the original. Here is a section from the elaborate accompanied recitative that introduces Mathilde's *Romance*, "Sombre forêt." [53]

Mathilde

Arnold! Arnold! est-ce bien toi ?	[Arnold! Arnold! Is it really you,
Simple habitant de ces campagnes,	simple inhabitant of these fields, the
L'espoir, l'orgueil de ses montagnes,	hope and pride of these mountains,
Qui charme ma pensée et cause mon effroi!	who charms my thoughts and causes
	my fear?]

Contemporary Italian (Bassi)
Arnoldo! Arnoldo! ah! sei pur tu ch'io bramo.
Semplice abitator di questi campi,
Di questi monti caro orgoglio e speme,
Sei tu solo che incanti il mio pensiero,
Che il mio timor cagioni!

Although the meaning of the translation is essentially the same as the original (with a few extra phrases added that do not affect the sense), the French text employs three *octosyllabes* and one alexandrine; to cover the same ground, the Italian text adopts four *endecasillabi* and a *settenario* (actually the final verse continues as the first part of another *endecasillabo*). The person responsible for inserting the Italian translation under the original music faced an impossible task: there were far too many syllables in the translation and all had to be accommodated. (We don't know the identity of this musician, but we do know that Rossini was not involved.) The result, musically speaking, is disastrous.

In the original it is a beautifully constructed passage, simple in outline, but with astute control of registral ascent and descent, effective use of chordal changes to underline the rhyme ("campagnes" and "montagnes"), refreshing triplets for "Qui charme ma pensée," and delicate ascending chromaticism at "et cause mon effroi." The Italian version transforms the thirty-eight syllables of the French text into fifty-one syllables, eliminates all characteristic features of the original, and substitutes a music wholly without charm, a music that nonetheless held the stage in Italy and countries where the opera was performed in Italian for a century and a half, a music that continues to be sung today by those teachers and students in conservatories and private studios who insist—mindlessly—on performing the piece in Italian, even though Rossini's own music is readily available (example 11.5). This in the most

EXAMPLE 11.5. GIOACHINO ROSSINI, *GUILLAUME TELL* [RÉCITATIF ET ROMANCE MATHILDE], (N. 9), MM. 70–76, A PASSAGE IN RECITATIVE FROM THE ORIGINAL FRENCH AND IN THE CALISTO BASSI TRANSLATION.

EXAMPLE 11.5. (*continued*)

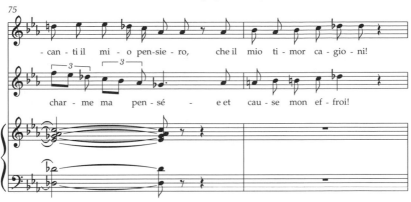

frequently sung solo composition from the opera. Yet it is typical of how Rossini's music is treated throughout.

When we turn to lyrical numbers (arias, duets, ensembles), the musical changes introduced with the Italian translation remain startling, though the musical context is more determinate and offers less opportunity for wide-ranging modification of melodic lines. French poetry for lyrical numbers allowed a certain freedom in mixing lines of differing numbers of syllables; Italian poetry required that lyrical verses normally be regular, with all lines in a stanza having the same metric structure. The first three verses of Mathilde's aria at the start of act 3 in French, for example, are *octosyllabes;* the next four are six-syllable lines (as always in French verse, not counting the feminine ending).[54] It would have been impossible for an Italian poet during the first half of the nineteenth century to render these verses in standard Italian meters, since the Italian equivalent of French octosyllabic verse would have been the shunned *novenario,* or nine-syllable verse (with feminine endings counted, as is standard in Italian poetry); changing to *settenario* for the next four, furthermore, is an internal shift that would also have been unacceptable. Instead, the seven verses in two meters of the French are changed by Calisto Bassi to six verses of *decasillabi.*

Mathilde

Pour notre amour plus d'espérance;	[There is no more hope for our love, when
Quand ma vie à peine commence,	my life has barely begun, I will never again
Pour toujours je perds le bonheur.	be happy. Yes, Melcthal, the actions of a
Oui, Melcthal, d'un barbare	barbarian separate us; my reason, which

Le forfait nous sépare;
Ma raison, qui s'égare,
A compris ta douleur.

[overwhelms me, has understood your sorrow.]

Contemporary Italian (Bassi)
Ah! se privo di speme è l'amore,
Non mi resta che pianto e terrore:
Infelice per sempre sarò.
Un delitto a me toglie il mio bene,
Fa più acerbe le immense mie pene,
Né il suo duol confortar io potrò.

[Ah! if my love has no more hope, nothing remains for me but tears and terror. I will always be unhappy. A crime deprives me of my beloved and makes my immense suffering more bitter, nor can I comfort your sorrow.]

For these Italian words to be underlaid to Rossini's music, a task accomplished by an unknown hand (certainly not Rossini), many changes in note values and text underlay were needed, so many that the original rhythm is sometimes unrecognizable.

French poetry for music made frequent use of octosyllabic verse, and the changes resulting from Italian substitutions for the *novenario* often undermine the rhythmic qualities of Rossini's music. An excellent example is the duet for Mathilde and Arnold in the second act, where the Austrian princess admits her love for the Swiss youth. In the original French, her admission takes the form of a quatrain of four *octosyllabes;* in the Italian translation this is rendered as four *ottonari.*[55]

Mathilde
Oui, vous l'arrachez à mon âme
Ce secret qu'ont trahi mes yeux;
Je ne puis étouffer ma flamme,
Dût-elle nous perdre tous deux!

[Yes, you drag from my soul this secret that my eyes betrayed; I cannot extinguish this flame, even were it to destroy us both.]

Contemporary Italian (Bassi)
Tutto apprendi, o sventurato,
Il segreto del mio cor.
Per te solo fu piagato,
Per te palpita d'amor.

[You learn, unhappy one, the secret of my heart, which bends only before you, which beats for the love of you.]

The problem is not only the change in meter but also the fixed accentuation pattern of *ottonari* verse in Italian libretto poetry, major accents falling on the third and seventh syllables. The rhythmic monotony of the opening phrases in the setting of the Italian text reflects the uniform way in which the *ottonari* are declaimed, while the French original, which differentiates the setting of

EXAMPLE 11.6. GIOACHINO ROSSINI, *GUILLAUME TELL*, DUO [MATHILDE–ARNOLD]
(N. 10), MM. 3–6, IN THE ORIGINAL FRENCH AND IN THE CALISTO BASSI TRANSLATION.

Oui, vous l'ar - ra-chez à mon â - me ce se-cret qu'ont tra-hi mes yeux,

Tut-to ap-pren - di, o sven-tu - ra - to il se - gre - to del mio cor,

the first and second verses, is rhythmically more accentuated and varied (example 11.6). But the rhythm of the Italian verse also destroys the effect Rossini has calculated at the end of Mathilde's opening section in the French original, where for several bars a single syllable is held while the voice ascends a fifth between the first and second beats (example 11.7). Only *after* this passage does Rossini use texted high notes, but on the downbeat rather than on the second beat, forcefully concluding Mathilde's stanza. In the translation, on the other hand, every single high note on the second beat is given a syllable (example 11.8). This excess of accentuation changes the way the phrase is sung and decreases the effect of the cadential phrase. The habit of singing the music in this way in Italian, furthermore, had so infiltrated the performance history of the work that Carol Vaness, performing the French original in San Francisco in 1992, for the most part beautifully, actually changed the words of the French here so as to pound out those high notes with new syllables in every measure, in utter disregard for Rossini's carefully constructed melodic line.

Metric problems can also be compounded by politics. In the second-act finale, the cantons gather around Tell. They are hesitant to revolt against their Austrian masters for fear of what may happen to their wives and children. Tell reminds them of their real plight, with two powerful *octosyllabes*, immediately repeated by the chorus.

EXAMPLE 11.7. GIOACHINO ROSSINI, *GUILLAUME TELL*, DUO [MATHILDE–ARNOLD]
(N. 10), MM. 34–38, IN THE ORIGINAL FRENCH.

Je ne puis__ é - touf-fer,__ é - touf-fer__ ma flam - me, dût-

EXAMPLE 11.8. GIOACHINO ROSSINI, *GUILLAUME TELL*, DUO [MATHILDE–ARNOLD] (N. 10), MM. 34–38, IN THE CALISTO BASSI TRANSLATION.

per te so - lo fu pia - ga - to, per te pal - pi - ta d'a - mor, sol per

> *Un esclave n'a point de femme,*   [A slave can have no wife,
> *Un esclave n'a point d'enfants.*   a slave can have no children.]

Not only are these French verses in an unloved rhythm for Italian poetry, but they also highlight the powerful word "slave." Rossini sets them as two parallel phrases, strongly underlining the political message (example 11.9). In the Calisto Bassi translation, the word "slave" is completely eliminated, while the original *octosyllabes* are rendered as two recitative verses: a *settenario* and an *endecasillabo*.

> *E cinti da' perigli*   [We see our parents, wives,
> *Vediamo i genitor, le spose, i figli...*   and children surrounded by perils.]

The sense of Rossini's music, the rhythmic power of the original, the balance of phrases, indeed the meaning of the moment is gone (example 11.10). New verses by Paolo Cattelan have tried to restore sense, rhythm, and meaning to the Italian, using a meter of nine syllables, in imitation of the French: they succeed in capturing the sense of Rossini's music and the dramaturgical significance of the passage:

> *Per noi schiavi non vi son mogli,*
> *Per noi schiavi non più de' figli...*

But these verses, or any verses like them, would not have been metrically desirable for a librettist working in Italy between 1800 and 1860. He would hardly have allowed himself to adopt the forbidden *novenario* meter.

Harold Powers, however, in an important essay, has brought forth a fascinating counterexample from 1842.[56] When the Florentine impresario Alessandro Lanari staged the Italian premiere of Fromental Halévy's opera *La Reine de Chypre* during the carnival season of 1842–43, he had its French

EXAMPLE 11.9. GIOACHINO ROSSINI, *GUILLAUME TELL*, FINAL 2e (N. 12), MM. 306–308, IN THE ORIGINAL FRENCH.

306

Un es-cla - ve n'a point de fem - me, un es-cla - ve n'a point d'en - fants.

EXAMPLE 11.10. GIOACHINO ROSSINI, *GUILLAUME TELL*, FINAL 2^e (N. 12),
MM. 306–308, IN THE CALISTO BASSI TRANSLATION.

E cin - ti da' pe - ri - gli ve-dia-mo i ge-ni-tor, le spo - se, i fi - gli . . .

text, written by Jules-Henri Vernoy de Saint-Georges, rendered into Italian by Francesco Guidi. For Guidi, Lanari established unusual parameters, as the translator explains in his preface to the printed libretto:

> I was required to make the translation of the present drama by M. de Saint-Georges not only literally, syllable by syllable and note by note, following the music already written by Maestro F. Halévy, but also preserving throughout the libretto the heterogeneous meter of the French verses, which differs greatly from our own, especially in the recitatives. The management wanted rigorously to respect the original.

What follows is an Italian libretto filled with the dread *novenario,* with shifting meters within a single stanza, and with unusual—even if acceptable—meters, such as *doppi settenari.* As a result, it was presumably possible to preserve the music of Halévy with only minimal adjustments. The history of Italian translations of French operas would have been very different indeed had Lanari and Guidi's experiment garnered further support, but it does not appear to have done so. Not until Arrigo Boito's extraordinary transformation and expansion of the metrical structure of Italian librettos from the time of his *Mefistofele* (1868) did Italian *poesia per musica* begin to allow itself this kind of poetic freedom.[57]

We are therefore left with an enigma: in the absence of a wholly separate version in each language undertaken by the composer, there is no thoroughly satisfactory way of providing an appropriate translation for an early nineteenth-century opera from Italian to French or vice versa. In order to follow the musical line, it is imperative to create verse forms that have no place in the art of libretto construction from the period; in order to follow the verbal conventions of the period, it is necessary to create verse forms that distort the vocal lines of the original score. In our world, where musical values in opera tend to be exalted over literary ones (often representing dramatic genres for which we have less sympathy), we may choose to privilege the composer's art. But if we do, it must be with the full realization that we are creating a work far removed from what would have been considered acceptable during the 1830s. To all intents and purposes, *Guglielmo Tell*, with its text by Calisto Bassi, *was* Rossini's opera for 150 years in Italy, England, the United States, even Austria. Indeed, it was to the Calisto Bassi *Guglielmo Tell* (further disguised as *Rodolfo di Sterlinga*) that, in 1840, Rossini himself added the new finale mentioned above.

TRANSLATIONS OF DONIZETTI:
SEX, RELIGION, AND "LA [FRAN]-*CIA*"

Although we often hear of performances of Italian operas with the names *La favorita* and *La figlia del reggimento*, Donizetti never wrote such operas. He did write a French score for the Paris Opéra, *La Favorite*, in 1841, and an *opéra-comique* by the name of *La Fille du régiment* in 1840, both of which were soon translated into Italian, the original works heavily recast to be rendered acceptable to Italian censors or less dependent on French conventions. After all, Donizetti had had the audacity to write a grand opera about religion and sex; worse still, he intermingled the two in ways that seemed almost sacrilegious. To tame the wild sentiments of *La Favorite*, the Italian censors rendered its plot incomprehensible, giving free rein to generations of music critics and listeners who have reacted with hostility to a plot that has very little to do with the text Donizetti set to music.[58] As for transforming a French *opéra-comique* into an Italian *opera buffa*, Donizetti and his assistants in Italy modified profoundly the original words and made many significant musical changes. In both operas, dramaturgical problems interacted with metrical problems in a way that was characteristic of mid-nineteenth-century Italy, rendering the job of producing an adequate translation even more difficult.

The changes made in *La Favorite* to overcome the objections or anticipated objections from Italian censors are quite extraordinary. The plot of Donizetti's opera is powerful. Fernand, a novice in the monastery of St. James of Compostella in 1340, admits to his prior, Balthazar, that he has fallen in love with a beautiful woman whose hand he inadvertently touched during a service. Unbeknownst to Fernand, his beloved, Léonor de Guzman, is the mistress of King Alphonse XI. Ashamed of her situation, she brushes aside Fernand's offer of marriage and instead presents him with a commission in the King's army, where Fernand distinguishes himself in battle against the Moors. But scheming courtiers have informed the Pope that the King has rejected his legitimate wife for Léonor, and Balthazar arrives, as envoy from the Pope, to inform Alphonse that he must restore his wife and banish Léonor or face excommunication.

When the King offers Fernand the opportunity to marry a noblewoman, and Fernand's choice falls on Léonor, the heartbroken King agrees and grants

Fernand a noble title. But the courtiers interpret this as the King's way to circumvent the Papal decree, and they scorn Fernand, who learns only after the marriage that Léonor has been the King's mistress. Enraged, Fernand tears off his decorations, breaks his sword, and throws its fragments at the King's feet. In the final act he returns to the monastery, where the monks are engaged in digging their own graves, an affirmation of their willingness to abandon all earthly pleasures. Fernand prepares to take final vows, while Balthazar goes to comfort a dying pilgrim. The pilgrim turns out to be Léonor, who wants only to explain herself to Fernand. His love rekindled, he still hopes to flee with her, but it is too late. As death claims her, Fernand cries out to the monks that his own death will soon follow.[59]

The Italian translation still widely used today, *La favorita*, was prepared by Francesco Jannetti for the Milanese publisher Lucca, who printed the first Italian edition of the opera. Jannetti completely obscured the nature of the drama. Baldassare is no longer the *spiritual* father of Fernando but becomes the actual father both of Fernando and of Alfonso's legitimate wife, who is therefore Fernando's sister! How is it possible, then, that Fernando does not show any sign of knowing the King? How can he refer to himself as a "soldato misero"? How can Leonora (the mistress of the King) imagine that she will raise Fernando to a high rank when he is already the brother of the Queen? One absurdity is piled upon another. And instead of a monk leaving his vocation and his spiritual father for earthly love, we have simply a young man leaving his real father to follow after his beloved, a very different level of conflict from that envisioned in *La Favorite*. The last act, in particular, becomes utterly ridiculous. Jannetti builds it around the assumption that, devastated by the cruelty of her husband, the King's wife (Baldassare's daughter and Fernando's sister) has died. Baldassare and Fernando have simply come to the monastery for her funeral (while the King apparently has stayed at home!). Since Fernando is not about to take any kind of vows (let alone final ones), why should we find his admission that he still loves Leonora to be scandalous? The story has been totally bent out of shape, and those who have complained that it makes no sense are quite correct.[60]

But metric considerations in the poetry have equally falsified the opera. While some famous compositions work effectively in Jannetti's translation or require only small changes (Léonor's aria "O mon Fernand," for example, is well served by "Oh mio Fernando"), others lose much of their character. The text of the cabaletta of the final duet for the lovers, "Viens, je cède éperdu au transport qui m'enivre," is basically in French alexandrines (in Italian the equivalent meter would be *settenari doppi*).[61] Within it, however, Donizetti

EXAMPLE 11.11. GAETANO DONIZETTI, *LA FAVORITE*, FINAL (N. 15),
MM. 285–288, IN THE ORIGINAL FRENCH.

introduces many repetitions of individual words in order to create a particular kind of melody: each measure begins with a note held for two beats and an eighth note, which serves as the first note of the two triplets that close the measure. Each of the remaining five notes has a syllable, so that the overall effect of each measure is of restraint followed by an outpouring of hammered energy (example 11.11). In Italian there is not even a hint of the original meter. Instead, the words are rendered as strophes of *ottonari*, with typically regular accents on the third and seventh syllables of each verse, and without internal repetitions of words or phrases. The result is a more poorly wrought relationship between words and music and the distinct loss of the musical and dramatic character so striking in the French original (example 11.12). There is nothing subtle about the difference between the two versions of the cabaletta. It is immediately audible to a listener who knows nothing about the technical matters that produce the change. Only a patent disregard for the musical and dramatic values inherent in Donizetti's original could have led a "translator" to this betrayal of the composer's opera. If *La Favorite* is worth our attention at all, either it must be sung in French or the translation must be modified to remain closer to the meaning of the original text and to the coordination of text and music found in the French.[62]

For *La Favorite* a new critical edition has facilitated access to Donizetti's original score and its various layers. More difficult at this point is understanding the history of *La Fille du régiment*, Donizetti's *opéra-comique*, whose first performance at the Théâtre de l'Opéra-Comique of Paris on 11 February 1840, after much equivocation on the part of the music critics, especially

EXAMPLE 11.12. GAETANO DONIZETTI, *LA FAVORITA*, FINALE 40 (N. 15),
MM. 285–288, IN THE CONTEMPORARY ITALIAN TRANSLATION.

Berlioz, was an enormous popular success. The sources of this work have not been fully studied, and we do not have reliable information about its various versions.[63] These problems are intensified because Donizetti himself took some responsibility for the Italian version of the opera, first performed at the Teatro alla Scala of Milan on 3 October 1840, transforming an *opéra-comique* with spoken dialogue into an *opera buffa* with recitative. The many significant differences among Italian sources, however, make it difficult to separate Donizetti's work from that of other arrangers.

While much of the music is basically unchanged, Donizetti introduced several significant modifications to reduce the French character of the opera and make it more Italian. Composers of *opéra-comique* peppered their scores with *couplets,* short lyrical solos in two parallel—but not necessarily identical—strophes, sometimes with a choral conclusion at the end of each strophe. Some amusing and tuneful *couplets* have a frankly popular cast; some sentimental or passionate *couplets* are composed in a more subtle fashion. The form is related to the entire French *romance* tradition, which Verdi was to transform in such an extraordinary manner in the solo music for Violetta in the first and last acts of *La traviata* (as we saw in chapter 8).

In *La Fille du régiment* Donizetti wrote four full sets of *couplets,* each with two strophes: (1) for the terror-stricken Marquise within the introduction of the opera, "Pour une femme de mon nom"; (2) for Marie, "Chacun le sait," with its refrain praising her regiment, "Il est là... Le beau Vingt-et-unième"; (3) for Marie, the *romance* "Il faut partir," within the first-act Finale, as she prepares to follow the Marquise; (4) for Tonio, a *romance* near the end of the opera, "Pour me rapprocher de Marie," in which he sings of his love for her. In the Italian version the *couplets* for the Marquise disappear altogether (in fact, they were often cut on the French stage) as do those for Tonio. Tonio gets compensated for his loss through the addition of a comic cavatina in Italian style, borrowed by Donizetti from an earlier opera, *Gianni di Calais.* Changes of this kind show a composer trying to position an opera born in one theatrical culture for a new public.

We have only sporadic evidence, however, about how much work Donizetti actually did on the Italian translation: we know neither whether he reviewed and corrected Calisto Bassi's words nor whether he himself adapted his music to the new text. One of the most popular numbers of the opera, for example, has always been Marie's air with chorus in the second act, "Par le rang et par l'opulence" (By rank and wealth) which concludes with the joyous "Salut à la France!" (Hail to France!). In the first section Marie voices the sadness she feels in her new social position as the niece (unbeknownst to her, she is actually the illegitimate daughter) of the Marquise of Berkenfield, as well as her despair at giving up her beloved Tonio for a noble marriage she feels compelled to accept. When the arrival of the French regiment that found her as a baby and has raised her (they are all her "fathers") changes her mood, she launches into the most famous melody in the opera, one that soon became an unofficial French national song. The entire text, which is in two quatrains, reads:

> *Salut à la France!*   [Hail to France! To my happy
>   *À mes beaux jours!*   days! To hope! To my loves!
>   *À l'espérance!*   Hail to glory! Here for my
>   *À mes amours!*   heart, with victory, is the
> *Salut à la gloire!*   instant of happiness!]
> *Voilà pour mon cœur,*
> *Avec la victoire,*
> *L'instant de bonheur!*

Notice that the second through the fourth verses of the first quatrain are shorter than the other verses: such metric anomalies were acceptable in French poetry for music, but frowned upon in Italy.

Donizetti set the first quatrain as shown in example 11.13.[64] The melody is conceived in two-measure units: the note on the downbeat of each unit serves as a point from which to leap to the syncopated and accented higher note on the second beat. The declamation of the text, although unusual, supports this musical structure perfectly.[65] Indeed, at the very end of the opera, when the Marquise, who now has admitted that she is Marie's mother and has blessed her marriage with Tonio, it is a reprise of "Salut à la France"—declaimed in precisely the same way—that brings down the curtain.

On 15 August 1840, from Milan, Donizetti wrote his childhood friend from Bergamo, Antonio Dolci, "I am adjusting, cutting, etc., the *Fille du régiment* for La Scala."[66] By early September, already back in Paris, he wrote to the publisher Francesco Lucca in Milan on the subject of the Italian translation

EXAMPLE 11.13. GAETANO DONIZETTI, *LA FILLE DU RÉGIMENT*, AIR ET CHŒUR MARIE (N. 9), IN THE ORIGINAL FRENCH.

of Maria's "Salut à la France!" He cited the following *senari* verses from
Marie's Aria:

Salvezza alla Francia etc.	[Salvation to France, etc.
Tornate bei giorni	Return happy days of the
Di vita guerriera	life of a soldier, let glory
La gloria ritorni	return, let love return]
Ritorni l'amor.	

He did not like this strophe because "that last *ritorni* won't do, since Maria
has always loved." Therefore he wants the translator, the same Calisto Bassi
who worked on Rossini's *Guglielmo Tell,* to find something in its place.
Donizetti himself suggested:

Chi nacque al rimbombo	[He who is born to the noise
Del bronzo guerriero	of the bronze cannon scorns the
Disprezza l'Impero	realm of vain splendor.]
D'un vano splendor.	

"They are doggerel of my own, but the idea will come across better if Bassi
converts them into good verses." Afterwards, an employee of Lucca's, one
Mandanici, was to take responsibility for underlaying the new words.[67]

What we don't know at this point is whether Bassi had written a first
quatrain beginning with the words "Salvezza alla Francia," as suggested by
Donizetti's citation, in which case the letter is specifically about the translation of the *second* quatrain. But in the Bassi translation published by Lucca,
which persists in the performing tradition today, there is no reference to
France in these quatrains at all. They become:

Di gioja bramata,	[I already feel in my breast the
Di tenero affetto	secret power of desired joy, of
Già sento nel petto	tender emotion. With the anger
L'arcano poter.	of unfriendly stars calmed, my
E l'ira calmata	thoughts return to happy days.]
Degl'astri nemici,	
A giorni felici	
Ritorna il pensier.	

Whose decision was it to remove all references to France and the French regiment in these quatrains? We don't know. It is not as if France disappears
altogether, for in the cadences of the Italian translation there are several

"evviva la Francia" and "viva la Francia." Still, the translation apparently spares the Italian audience a powerful reminder that this is an opera written to please the French.

The new words fit without difficulty under the original music, and even the regularization of the length of the verses in the Italian poetry requires only minor adjustments in the music: an added upbeat, small shifts of syllables to produce a more regular declamation in the new language, and so forth. The musical setting of the first two verses is shown in example 11.14. If one is willing to accept the decision (whether made by Donizetti or by his Italian collaborators) to decrease the dramatic emphasis on France, there is no reason not to continue using this perfectly adequate translation of Donizetti's original.

The situation is very different, however, at the end of the opera. In fact, Donizetti modified the original conclusion for the Milanese performances, removing its reprise of the opera's hit tune "Salut à la France" and substituting a concluding duet for Maria and Tonio, "In questo sen riposati." For reasons that remain obscure, however, Lucca decided *not* to print these new final pages, but instead to return to the French score. There is one important dramaturgical shift. In the French original, after Sergeant Supplice embraces the Marquise, the aristocratic guests leave the stage, so that only the soliders and soloists intone the final "Salut à la France." In the Italian translation, the guests remain on stage (a female chorus) to add a contrasting "andiam, partiam" through the end of the score.

For the first time, the translation for this final reprise of the melody returns to the French original:

Salvezza alla Francia	[Salvation to France!
A suoi lieti dì!	To her happy days! Long live the joy
Vivan le gioje	that love nourishes!]
Che amor nudrì!	

EXAMPLE 11.14. GAETANO DONIZETTI, *LA FIGLIA DEL REGGIMENTO*, SCENA ED ARIA MARIA, IN THE CONTEMPORARY ITALIAN TRANSLATION.

Di gio - ja bra - ma - ta, di te - ne - ro af - fet - to＿ già

sen - to nel pet - to l'ar - ca - no po - te - re:

EXAMPLE 11.15. GAETANO DONIZETTI, *LA FIGLIA DEL REGGIMENTO*, FINALE SECONDO,
IN THE CONTEMPORARY ITALIAN TRANSLATION, WITH A
SUGGESTION FOR FIXING THE DECLAMATION.

This is a fascinating text, because it is metrically *irregular:* the first two verses
are *senari* (with accents on the fifth syllables), the last two *quinari* (with accents on the fourth syllable). Thus, whoever made the translation actually attempted to reproduce in part the metric irregularities of the original French.
But whoever put the words under the music committed an unpardonable
sin against Donizetti "[Fran]-*cia*" (example 11.15): oh that "-cia" on the downbeat! What a horror, even if it is deemphasized by the singer! What a falsifica-
tion of the melody, with its carefully wrought two-measure units! What a denial of the symmetry and élan that gives the melody its character! And how
useless, too, for the problem could easily have been solved by following the
French, anticipating the "a'" to the downbeat and the "suoi" to the second
beat, as in the bracketed text in example 11.15, and slurring the last two notes
of the measure together. We do not know who was responsible for restoring
the original finale and arranging the translation (perhaps they were verses that
Bassi had prepared for the aria and later rejected, although the metrical irreg-
ularity makes that somewhat dubious). In any event, "-cia" is not a pretty
sound with which to bring down the curtain on one of Donizetti's most delightful operas.

"IT IS IMPOSSIBLE TO MAKE A GOOD ONE"

Verdi's experience with *Les Vêpres siciliennes* powerfully exemplifies the translation problem. Given the significant literature on the subject (including an
important study by the Italian critic Massimo Mila),[68] it is unnecessary to rehearse the issues at length. The most important difference between this example and the others we have discussed thus far is that Verdi was directly and
fully involved with the translation of this opera. Even so, the experience was
an unhappy one for the composer. However careful and conscientious he may

have been, the rules of the game in Italy before political unification (and before the loosening up of the metric rules that exercised near-tyrannical sway during the first three-quarters of the nineteenth century) made it impossible to make an adequate translation. Political and moral censorship had a devastating impact on the libretto, and the formal requirements of Italian poetry clashed with a musical style developed to suit the freer verse of the French.

The problems with the plot of *Les Vêpres siciliennes*, prepared for the Opéra of Paris, where it had its premiere on 13 June 1855, are self-evident. A rebellion in which Sicilians rise up to massacre the French rulers of their country was hardly a theme that could pass muster in Italy under the Austrians during the 1850s. The entire plot was summarily removed to the Iberian peninsula, to Portugal under the rule of the Spanish, with a new title, *Giovanna de Guzman*. Yet even when the unification of Italy made it possible to return the action to Sicily, by and large the *same* translation was employed, with modifications in the names and corrections in isolated expressions to suit the new geography. Never was the libretto carefully emended to reflect Verdi's original French text.

It could be argued, nonetheless, that these complaints are pedantic. Verdi himself, after all, was responsible for underlaying the Italian words under the original French of *Les Vêpres siciliennes*. Already on 29 April 1855, a month and a half before the premiere, he had proposed to sell rights to the opera (excluding France, Britain, Belgium, and Holland) to Ricordi, informing the publisher specifically, "I obligate myself to send you a copy of the entire orchestral score with French text and with the ballet, which constitutes a self-contained action entitled *The Four Seasons;* also an Italian translation made under my direction by an able poet, changing the subject so as to render it acceptable to Italian theaters."[69] Soon after the premiere, on 6 July, he sent a copy of the full score from Paris to Milan. The text, as *Giovanna de Guzman*, was prepared by Ettore Caimi, but Verdi himself took responsibility for placing the words under the music. As he wrote to Ricordi,

> Today I sent you the score, in six big fascicles, in one of which is the overture and the music for the ballet. Have the overture separated and placed (as is obvious) at the beginning. The words written in red are the Italian words I have entered. In the ensembles and repetitions, I avoided a chore that anyone can do; but that *anyone* needs to be a knowledgeable person who is at least as patient as I have been in this tedious work.

Now I know what translation means, and I have sympathy for all the awful translations that exist, because it is impossible to make a good one. The story chosen is a historical event; there'll still be some words that the censor may not allow; but I think the subject can be permitted.

The title we first chose was *Maria di Braganza,* but for the name of Maria I thought to substitute *Giovanna;* thus, in the score you'll find *Maria* and in the libretto *Giovanna.* It's all the same, and you can put whatever you like; just be sure to have the score adjusted according to the name you choose... I imagine you'll have a copy of the score made with all the Italian words written out in full in the repeats etc. etc.; on my way home, I will be able to review it.[70]

We don't know whether he ever did review a score of the opera, but it would not have helped very much. He could do nothing about the problem of the censors. Moreover, he could do nothing about the insistence that French poetry be transformed into Italian verse forms, with all the attendant damage.

Many verse forms translated easily, of course, and provided fluent Italian analogues, but it is remarkable how many key moments in the music drama are seriously compromised. Here are two examples from one of the most passionate moments in the score: the duet in the fourth act, in which Hélène reproaches Henri for having interrupted her act of striking down the tyrant, Monfort; this reproach compels Henri to admit that Monfort is his father. Example 11.16 gives the first part of the passage that follows, one of the most powerful in the entire opera, in which Henri laments the "horrible knot" that separates him from his beloved and leads him to perdition.[71] In French this poetry is essentially in alexandrines (the first verse opens with Hélène's previous "Ton père!"), but in Italian it has been rendered instead into *settenari.* Notice how this increases significantly the number of syllables that need to be

EXAMPLE 11.16. GIUSEPPE VERDI, *LES VÊPRES SICILIENNES*, DUO [HÉLÈNE–HENRI] (N. 12), IN THE ORIGINAL FRENCH.

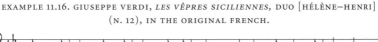

Nœud ter - ri - ble et fa - tal   que je   hais,   lien   qui nous sé - pa - re!... et

que dans sa   co - lè - re, le   ciel m'a ré - vé - lé, ____ pour me per-dre à ja - mais!

EXAMPLE 11.17. GIUSEPPE VERDI, *I VESPRI SICILIANI* OR *GIOVANNA DI GUZMAN*, GRAN DUETTO [ELENA–ARRIGO] (N. 12), IN THE CONTEMPORARY ITALIAN TRANSLATION.

No - do or-ri - bil, fa - tal_____ le-ga - me è que - sto! mor - ta - le or-ren - do vin - co-lo per sem - pre a me fu - ne - sto, che e - ter - na - men - te a per - der-mi mi ri - ve - la - va il ciel.

accommodated by the music. Thirty-four notes bear the requisite syllables in French, but in the Italian translation forty-one notes are needed (example 11.17).[72] Some of the resulting musical modifications are harmless: in the first six measures, for example, extra syllables are accommodated musically within the basic shape of the line through the addition of notes to upbeats or through declamation with two quarter notes in place of a half. The last two measures before the final note, however, are a musical disaster. In the original, Verdi sent the voice ascending to a powerful high *g* on "[révé]-lé," held for a full measure, then tied to the first note of the triplets in the next measure, reserving a final syllabic declamation for "pour me perd-re à ja-[mais]." The necessity to accommodate at this point *two* verses in *settenario* ("Che eternamente a perdermi / Mi rivelava il ciel"), the first of which is even a *sdrucciolo,* proved daunting for Verdi, even impossible. That octave leap for "perdermi" and the attack on the high *g* with "mi" are much weaker than the original French, but accommodating the extra syllables was not optional.[73] In 1855, an honest Italian poet could do nothing less.

At the end of his soliloquy, Henri compares Hélène's willingness to give her life to avenge her brother (killed by Monfort) to his own situation, and the poetry emphasizes the parallelisms: "Tu donnais tes jours pour venger ton frère" (You gave your days to avenge your brother) is set off against "J'ai donné mon honneur pour mon père" (I gave my honor for my father"). Henri's anguished final phrase is shown in example 11.18). It is elegant, with the strong "plus" repeated on two successive downbeats and an upbeat of two sixteenth notes in three successive measures. Verdi reserved the arrival at the high note for the crucial word of the passage, "[hon]-neur," while "pè-[re]" occupies the entire penultimate measure, with a fermata. Here again, the

EXAMPLE 11.18. GIUSEPPE VERDI, *LES VÊPRES SICILIENNES*,
DUO [HÉLÈNE–HENRI] (N. 12), IN THE ORIGINAL FRENCH.

J'ai fait plus... j'ai fait plus... j'ai don-né mon hon-neur pour mon pè - re!

EXAMPLE 11.19. GIUSEPPE VERDI, *I VESPRI SICILIANI* OR *GIOVANNA DI GUZMAN*, GRAN
DUETTO [ELENA–ARRIGO] (N. 12), IN THE CONTEMPORARY ITALIAN TRANSLATION.

Io più fe-ci, io più fe-ci: al cru-del pa - dre sa - gri-fi-cai l'o - nor!

Italian version, hampered by its poetry, is very poor: the two syllables of
"feci" on the downbeat make nothing like the same effect as "plus"; the
upbeat is eliminated in the phrase "al crudel padre"; and in a measure where
the French has only one syllable ("pè-[re]"), *four* must be accommodated
(example 11.19). I would differ somewhat from Verdi's opinion, for I do not
agree that it is impossible to make a good translation. But it was impossible
given the constraints within which mid-nineteenth-century translators and
musicians were working.[74]

Opera has always been an art of compromise, but rarely are the issues so per-
versely incompatible as in translation between Italian and French. I believe
that we should hear operas written by Italian composers in their original
language, whether that language be Italian or French. I do not see any justification for the belief that Italian composers did not set the French language
well. On the other hand, if performers wish to continue using Italian translations, the nineteenth-century models need to be overhauled. Sometimes they
need to be abandoned altogether; more often what is required is a strong editorial hand. The translations must be reviewed to be certain that the words
mean in Italian what they originally meant in French (rather than producing a travesty of that meaning in concession to nineteenth-century censorship). And we must abandon the impossible expectation that regular Italian
verses in the forms common during the first half of the nineteenth century
can be underlaid to music written for different metric patterns. Small shifts

in rhythm are certainly acceptable, but the musical meaning of a passage, the rhythmic matching of words and music at the heart of Italian opera, must not be compromised. Just as this chapter started with Verdi, let it end with Verdi. These are his words to Giulio Ricordi of 16 January 1883, referring to problems in the translation into Italian of the duet for King Philip and Posa at the end of the second act of *Don Carlos:* "Oh, translations are a horrendous thing! I would prefer them to be in prose (at least for the most part) in order to say everything that needs to be said and to respect more the accent and the meaning."[75] Nineteenth-century translations worked on the principle "Prima le parole, poi la musica"; those required for today's theaters must follow Verdi's advice and reverse the equation: "Prima la musica, *poi* le parole."

12

INSTRUMENTS OLD AND NEW

Among various notes I have accumulated over the past twenty years on the subject of the instrumental accompaniment of Italian nineteenth-century operas, I find the following statement in a personal communication by an evidently frustrated (and consequently nameless) Italian conductor:

> Italian conductors (real ones, not those who invent pseudo-philological groups and then cross over, with the help of record companies, to conduct modern orchestras which their talent would never have allowed them to approach) feel the need to know—before old instruments—modern ones for which they intend to prepare scores destined to be heard today, not by their ancestors. The Italian conductors to whom I allude, then, don't scorn old instruments, but they limit themselves to studying their behavior on paper or to visiting them in museums, as they do with Roman chariots or Viking ships. They follow with interest ocean crossings of the Kon-tiki [on a raft], but prefer to make the journey in jets.

Even though this statement seems to me a quintessentially blinkered vision of the problem of old and new instruments, it represents a position shared by a sizable group of musicians in Italy and elsewhere: I don't want to hear those museum specimens, since the distant past has nothing to teach me, and all this commotion about old instruments is an invention of "pseudo" philologists, sustained by record companies. Real men eat gut strings for breakfast and let natural horns rust.

There is a vast literature on instruments and instrumentation, much of it technical but some of it particularly relevant to the performance of nineteenth-century Italian opera. For the benefit of those directly involved in performances (whether as players, conductors, or scholars preparing texts), it is essential to move the conversation beyond the realm of absolute judgments.

There are excellent reasons to use period instruments, and there are excellent reasons to use modern instruments. There are even better reasons to use modern instruments with an intimate knowledge of the way earlier instruments sounded, alone and in various combinations. The treatise by Hector Berlioz, the most famous book on instrumentation of the nineteenth century, can be helpful in understanding contemporary practice, but even Berlioz's study must be understood in its chronological and geographical context: its pronouncements, as we shall see, do not automatically apply throughout Europe or throughout the first two-thirds of the nineteenth century.[1] There is also an extensive literature about individual instruments and instrumental groups, some of which will be cited in the following pages. Often, though, the most important knowledge can be grasped by studying exactly what composers wrote and by trying to understand its significance.

FABIO BIONDI AND *NORMA* AT THE VERDI FESTIVAL IN PARMA

When Fabio Biondi and his period-instrument group, Europa galante, began their performance of Bellini's *Norma* at the Verdi Festival in Parma on 7 March 2001, as part of the celebrations for the hundredth anniversary of Verdi's death and the two-hundredth anniversary of Bellini's birth, disapproval from the *loggione* was expressed almost from the first note. Although Biondi had established an extraordinary international reputation for his performances of eighteenth-century music with his hand-chosen and expertly trained orchestra of musicians playing period instruments or modern reproductions of such instruments, never had he used them for the performance of an Italian nineteenth-century work until Bruno Cagli, artistic director of the festival, invited him to make the effort. It did not take long for any of those listening to realize that traditionalists among the public wanted nothing to do with Biondi or his instruments, and they were prepared to make sure that others would be unable to enjoy the evening. Their reaction—especially in Parma—might have been expected, but all of us involved with the festival still hoped that good manners would hold sway. We were wrong.

It is not that Biondi and Europa galante, which he founded in 1989, were strangers to the opera house. They collaborated regularly with the Festival Alessandro Scarlatti in Palermo, where their performance of Scarlatti's 1718 comedy, *Il trionfo dell'onore,* just a month after the Parma *Norma,* would subsequently be awarded the most prestigious annual prize of Italy's music critics, the Premio Abbiati.[2] That award also recognized the extensive concert activity of the group and its many recordings, first with a French company, Opus 111, then with Virgin Classics. Devoted mostly to Baroque instrumental music (Vivaldi, Locatelli, Bach, and Boccherini), these recordings also explored Baroque vocal repertory, cantatas and oratorios. And "real" Italian conductors had good reason for being upset with Biondi: his recordings dominated international sales, while theirs—however accomplished—languished.

While there will always be petulant soloists who cannot imagine why anyone would want to hear the Bach flute sonatas on one of those vile old instruments, when a modern flute could do the job so much better, audiences feel no overwhelming need to hear the massed strings of the New York Philharmonic, vibrating in all their steel glory, perform Vivaldi's *Le quattro stagioni*.[3] Nor do the musicians feel a strong compulsion to set aside Brahms, Bruckner, and Mahler in order to devote themselves to the Baroque repertory, whatever they may choose to do when making music with their friends. But passions rise when later music is involved. During the 1990s there were several performances and even recordings of Rossini's early *farse*, one-act comic or "semiserious" operas, written between 1810 and 1813, using eighteenth-century instruments and performance techniques.[4] Many were beautifully realized and well received. My personal favorite is Marc Minkowski's 1997 recording of the second of these youthful gems, *L'inganno felice*, first performed at the Teatro San Moisè of Venice on 8 January 1812.[5] Using a Baroque ensemble, Le Concert des Tuileries, with many of the same musicians as in his more permanent ensemble, Les Musiciens du Louvre, Minkowski does a splendid job of bringing the opera to life. He approaches Rossini's score with imagination, energy, and sensitivity, paying particular attention to instrumental and vocal color, the declamation of the text, and vocal ornamentation. Whether one welcomes the use of older instruments or not, the singers are a delight to hear. They include the excellent Annick Massis, in one of her first Rossinian ventures; a veteran tenor (by 1997), widely acclaimed as a stylish Rossinian, Raúl Giménez; not to mention two younger Italian bass-baritones, Pietro Spagnoli and Lorenzo Regazzo. All of them sing intelligently, ornament effectively, and project the drama with conviction. They are thoroughly integrated into Minkowski's conception, without sacrificing their individuality.

But is the orchestral sound produced by Minkowski and his players similar to the sound that Rossini and his Venetian public would have heard in 1812? We have no way of accessing such information. There is much we *do* know, of course. We know that Italian string players in 1812 used instruments with gut strings. We know that natural horns were employed, not horns with valves. We know that flutes were made of wood, not metal. We know that in *secco* recitatives accompanied by the *basso continuo,* low string instruments—a violoncello and a double bass—would normally have played along with the keyboard instrument (most likely a fortepiano, although some smaller theaters may still have been using a harpsichord).[6] In all these ways Minkowski's choices approximate performance practice of Rossini's time. But, to take one controversial example, is it certain that the harpsichord (which the program booklet proudly describes as being constructed by "Émile Jobin, after a late eighteenth-century Italian harpsichord") would have intervened extensively in pieces scored for the entire orchestra, as it does in Minkowski's interpretation? There is considerable evidence for harpsichord intervention of this kind during the second half of the eighteenth century, not only in theoretical treatises but also in actual musical sources, but I don't know of any Rossinian musical source—much less in the composer's own hand—in which such participation is demonstrable.

Some evidence comes from an 1811 treatise devoted to the work of the first violinist in his role as director of the orchestra in theatrical performances: "The *Maestro al Cembalo* is nothing more than a simple player, subordinate as is everyone else to the conductor; and therefore the conductor will allow him to play only for the recitatives. In the arias and concerted numbers, he may turn the pages and nothing more."[7] The latter phrase refers to early nineteenth-century practice, in which the first cello and first double bass "al cembalo," who played the bass line during the recitatives (with the cello elaborating on the harmony), were still expected to read their parts in the musical numbers from the bass part located on the keyboard instrument. So Minkowski's decision to use the harpsichord in most tutti passages throughout the musical numbers of the opera, including the overture, is made in the absence of any evidence in contemporary musical sources. There is nothing wrong with a bit of eighteenth-century nostalgia, of course, and the sound is lovely, but we should beware of assuming that what we are hearing is what Rossini would have heard in Venice in 1812.

Some Rossinian efforts have gone beyond the early *farse,* turning to the *opera seria* repertory, even to the composer's Neapolitan operas. The most impressive modern performance of a Rossini serious opera using period instruments may have been the *Ermione* given in a concert version on 10 and 12 April 1992 by the Orchestra of the Age of Enlightenment (OAE) in London.[8] Founded in 1986 as an ensemble of players on period instruments, and still going strong today, OAE works without a fixed musical director, but the identity of its two principal guest conductors, Frans Brüggen and Sir Simon

Rattle, suggests a great deal about the ambitions of the institution. Brüggen, of course, is known for his long career as a great performer on the recorder, then as a conductor of Baroque and Classical music. Rattle has strong ties with OAE, having conducted the group in its first appearance at the Glyndebourne Festival in 1989, leading performances of *Le nozze di Figaro.* In serving as music director of the Berlin Philharmonic, he continues his relationship with the OAE, an orchestra determined to eliminate the boundaries that separate performances and performers devoted to period instruments and those who embrace modern instruments. In most of the world, save Italy, Rattle and the OAE are considered to have done so in grand style. Their American tour in the winter of 2004, with Cecilia Bartoli singing arias of Antonio Salieri, for example, was received rapturously from one end of the country to the other.

The *Ermione* performances of 1992 were under the direction of Mark Elder, hardly a period- instrument specialist. Elder served as music director of the English National Opera (which continues to perform operas in English translation) for fifteen years. Having also worked extensively with many major orchestras, he is now music director of the Hallé Orchestra. Nor was *Ermione* his only operatic project with OAE: he later pushed the period-instrument concept further with three Verdian performances, the original version of *Simon Boccanegra* (1857) in 1994, *Alzira* in 1996, and the *Messa da Requiem* in 2001, all greeted with enthusiasm by the London public and critics. The *Ermione* performances featured Anna Caterina Antonacci in the title role, Bruce Ford as Oreste, and Keith Lewis as Pirro. Reviews were splendid, and the work's London success helped convince Glyndebourne to stage the opera during the summer of 1995. As for the use of period instruments, Hilary Finch wrote, "The true confidants here are the members of the orchestra. On period instruments, the quality of Rossini's writing for clarinet and flute, for tense, stabbing trombone and tremulous strings, was pointed unmistakably. And the Rossinian crescendo will never sound the same again."[9]

Despite a spate of performances during the 1990s and into the current century, *Ermione* remains a work relatively unknown to most opera lovers. In that sense, anything goes. *Norma* is quite another matter. A century's worth of performances, seconded by numerous recordings of excerpts or of the entire opera using modern instruments, have established certain sonorities as being "correct" for Bellini's opera, or at least they are the sonorities we have in our heads. Does that mean that we *know* what Bellini's score should sound like? As we have seen time and again, "history" is taken to mean history since recordings, and usually since Serafin. Serafin, of course, was a master conductor and musician, outdated as his attitudes may seem today; but his epigones are something else. I cringe when I think of an October 2000 presentation at the Teatro dell'Opera in Rome, with three modern trombones and a tuba pumping their way, *fortissimo,* through *Norma,* as if it were written to be performed by brass band. Yet no one else seemed to object.

In that context, while I may not agree with all of Biondi's decisions, his *Norma* was a revelation, particularly in terms of sonority. If we consider the vast changes in the manufacture and diffusion of instruments during the nineteenth century, it is reasonably certain that the instruments for which Bellini composed the score of *Norma* were closer to eighteenth-century models than to those commonly used today. Furthermore, in many cases Biondi's instruments were manufactured in the nineteenth century or were copied from such instruments, so that Europa galante was hardly a Baroque group throughout. The warmth of the violins, playing with gut strings, was notable.[10] The timbre of the winds in general, and of the horns, trumpets, trombones, and cimbasso in particular, was markedly different from the sounds we usually encounter. The sounds produced by the percussion instruments belonged to another sonic world.[11] In general, the balance of instrumental groups in the Parma performances was superior to that usually attained in the theater when modern instruments are used. I say "usually" because I am not asserting that it is impossible to attain proper balances with modern instruments. With the latter, however, players must develop sensitivities to sonority that allow them to counter subsequent modifications in their instruments' structure and materials. Many fail to do so, and rare is the conductor who helps them overcome the problem.

Yet the presence of Biondi and his period-instrument orchestra helped to create a polemical atmosphere in the theater in Parma. Some of Biondi's decisions really were questionable. Continuing the practice described above in the discussion of Mark Minkowski's *L'inganno felice,* Biondi actually used a keyboard instrument (a fortepiano) in *Norma,* an opera without *secco* recitative, and allowed the instrument to play an improvised accompaniment during most ensemble passages. There is no evidence whatsoever for this usage. In an essay in the program book, Biondi invoked language in which composers are referred to as sitting "at the cembalo" during the course of the first three performances, but that does not mean they actually *played.*[12] Fortunately the instrument could barely be heard in the theater.

But what was ultimately responsible for the displeasure of even the less polemically minded members of the audience, I think, was the gulf that separated the singers from the instrumentalists. June Anderson and Daniela Barcellona, in the roles of Norma and Adalgisa, are both fine artists, but neither of them had previously worked with a period-instrument group for the *bel canto* repertory in an opera house, and neither of them had considered how to modify her singing technique to take into account the changed sonority in the pit. There was no bad will here, simply a failure to recognize that opera singers trained in the style of the twentieth century, post-Callas, and an orchestra seeking to reproduce a quite different performance style may not be able to unite effectively. One sensed throughout the opening night that Anderson, in particular, was less than confident, even though Norma was a role she had sung many times.[13] And the tenor, a young and valiant but desperately inexperienced singer, could not sustain the role of Pollione, which—unfortunately—dominates the first part of the opera. By the time Norma entered with her prayer to the moon, the audience was restive, and matters never improved.

PERIOD INSTRUMENTS: THE PROBLEM
OF TECHNICAL LIMITATIONS

Much of the rhetoric surrounding the use of older instruments in the performance of music from the first half of the nineteenth century is inflated. Many musicians, trained on modern instruments and dependent on them for their livelihood, see only the limitations of older instruments and fail to acknowledge their advantages in color and balance. Others, committed to historical instruments and riding a wave of public fascination with period orchestras, praise their tone quality and characteristic sounds while failing to acknowledge their practical inadequacies. It would be absurd to pretend that gains and losses are not present in almost equal measure.

The critical edition of an opera must respect the work in its historical context. It cannot justify rewriting instrumental parts by affirming that the composer would have prepared his score differently had modern instruments been at his disposition. Once that process begins, it is hard to know where to stop, and intervening in a published score denies performers the right to know the historical record and to make their own choices.[14] At the same time, we must avoid presuming that a composer's art is inextricably tied to specific instrumental characteristics. During the first sixty-five years of the nineteenth century, a great variety of instruments could be found in France, Italy, or Vienna. When we speak of "period" instruments, then, we need always to ask which period and in what geographical center.

Modern instrumentalists who employ historical instruments (and the conductors who lead them) cannot be indifferent to the limitations of many of these instruments. Some of these limitations are superable, whereas others must simply be accepted, just as they were accepted by composers who worked during the first half of the nineteenth century (and before). Without an awareness of these instrumental limitations, many details of contemporary musical notation are incomprehensible. Although each instrument poses its own characteristic problems, it is worth considering a few of them from different families as representative of the kinds of problems that arise when editing and performing Italian opera: double basses, oboes, timpani, and horns.

Double Basses

Italian double bass players normally employed an instrument with three strings, tuned as $A-d-g$ (all notes for the double bass, by convention, are written an octave higher than they sound). Instrumentalists in France, instead, would have been using an instrument with four strings, with the additional lowest string tuned as E (sounding E^1).[15] In those many passages in operas written for Italy in which the violoncellos and the double basses play together (either with both parts written out in full or with the cellos told to play *col basso*—"with the bass"), they normally produce sounds an octave apart. But when the cellos play in their lowest register (from C through $A\flat$), the three-stringed double bass tuned in the normal fashion cannot follow them, and hence must play the notes an octave higher, so that the sounding notes in that lowest register of the cellos are actually in unison with the notes in the double basses. No one had to be told this in the notation: everyone understood the convention, and double bass players made the adjustment automatically, using their musical sense to determine the point at which it would be best to change from one register to the other. But it would never have occurred to Rossini, when he revived for Paris operas originally written for Italian theaters, to require French double bass players to adopt an Italian three-string double bass. Rather, he must have been delighted to have the double basses at the Parisian Théâtre Italien remain in the lower register, an octave below the cello, as long as possible.[16]

Still, if one examines Rossini's 1824 *Duetto* for violoncello and double bass, written for the famous double bassist Domenico Dragonetti, at no point is the performer asked to play a note lower than written A, the lowest normal pitch on the instrument.[17] That is not quite the case with the *Sei sonate a quattro*, written by Rossini in 1804 for two violins, violoncello, and double bass; but there is still no reliable edition of either of these pieces, so we cannot be certain what the composer actually wrote.[18] In the modern edition, however, there are a few places where the double bass is asked to descend below *A,* suggesting either a *scordatura* (retuning of the lowest string) or the presence of notes Rossini wrote for musical reasons but expected to have changed by a performer using the standard three-string double bass. In the second sonata, for example, in the Andantino, there is a wayward *G♯* (sixteenth note) at m. 3, a passage in which all instruments are playing together; it was probably omitted in performance. In the third sonata, in *C major,* there are several *G*s, suggesting a possible *scordatura,* with the low *A* tuned down a tone.[19]

These practical problems of range and notation can have implications for written scores. In Verdi's *Stiffelio* (1850), for example, in the climactic duet of the opera (N. 9), Lina, having accepted the divorce Stiffelio has demanded as the consequence of her adultery, turns on him in an *E major* passage to the text "Non allo sposo volgomi, ma all'uomo del Vangelo" (I am turning not to my husband, but to a man of the Gospel). This is the passage that concludes with the infamous *parole sceniche* "Ministro, confessatemi" (Minister, hear my confession).[20] Throughout this passage (mm. 170–188), Verdi wrote the violoncellos and double basses on the same staff, since the normal cello staff is occupied by a part for a single solo cello. The cellos play in the narrow range between *A♯* and *e.* The double basses are notated below the cellos, beginning on the notated pitch *E,* but descending as low as *B*[1] before concluding on *F♯.* All of these notes are *below* the range of the standard, three-string Italian double bass of the period, and many are below the compass of the standard, four-string French double basses. In these measures it seems certain that Verdi—most unusually—has notated the pitches for the double basses as they *sound,* rather than an octave above the sounding pitches. In other words, where he wrote *E,* the double bass must actually play the pitch normally written as *e,* and so forth. Immediately after (from m. 189), Verdi's notation returns to its normal form, and the double bass part is written an octave above the sounding pitches.[21]

The problems with the "period" double bass could not only affect the notation, but could also require retuning the lowest string of the instrument to extend the downward range, what I have referred to above as *scordatura.* In *Il trovatore* (1853), Verdi expected the Italian double bass players for whom he composed the opera to be using instruments with three strings. When he wanted a sounding *A♭*[1] during the *Miserere,* he wrote in his autograph manuscript: "The double basses will lower the *A* string by half a tone," a *scordatura* that would make no sense to performers using a four-string double bass.[22] The critical edition therefore omits the indication in the score, consigning it instead to a footnote and discussing the problem in the commentary.

Oboes

Rossini was cognizant both of the expressive potential of the oboes with which he worked, and of their technical limitations: indeed, he took those limitations into account when notating his scores. The first half of the nine-teenth century was a period in which the construction of oboes was under-going many significant changes, with the proliferation of keys replacing the basic system of the late eighteenth-century oboe: finger-stopped holes, with only a small number of keys.[23] On some occasions, the composer was there-fore constrained to make musical choices that are little short of ludicrous. A perfect example occurs in the overture to *La pietra del paragone* of 1812, an overture that subsequently passed without change into the 1813 *Tancredi.* This overture already has a fully developed Rossini "crescendo," an obligatory part of all the composer's mature overtures, present in both the exposition (in the key of the dominant) and in the recapitulation (in the key of the tonic).[24] As always, a Rossini crescendo involves more than a simple increase in dy-namic level. It is a structured manipulation of dynamics, instrumentation, register, and articulation to create a powerful drive toward the final cadences of both the exposition and the recapitulation of the overture. Usually a four-measure phrase is played three times, and sometimes a shortened version of this phrase continues the effect for a few additional measures.

In *Tancredi,* the oboes enter only after the first four-measure phrase of the crescendo in the dominant key, joining other winds and the upper strings in the second statement of the phrase. For the third statement, Rossini tightens the instrumental notch one degree further and takes both the flutes and the oboes into a higher register. Were he to have done this literally, however, it would have been necessary for the first oboe to ascend to a high *e* (*e'''*), a note beyond the normal compass of Italian oboists in the 1810s.[25] Thus, Rossini modified the part, substituting a *b''* for the impractical *e'''*. In the last two measures of the crescendo, which further intensify the harmonic rhythm, he actually wrote an eighth rest where the *e'''* should fall (example 12.1). Not even the most faithful believer in period instruments could fail to appreciate that some advantage would be gained by using an oboe that can play reliably a high *e'''*.

Timpani

Describing early nineteenth-century timpani in the introduction to his recordings of the Beethoven symphonies, Roger Norrington writes, "Small and beaten with hard sticks, [they] sound as if they have come straight from

EXAMPLE 12.1. GIOACHINO ROSSINI, *TANCREDI* (*LA PIETRA DEL PARAGONE*),
SINFONIA, OBOE PARTS, MM. 108–111.

the field of Waterloo."[26] But the situation with "period" timpani is more
complicated than Norrington's enthusiasm would lead us to believe. Every
modern performer of Italian opera, for example, knows that through the first
six or seven decades of the century, Italian composers expected to find only
two kettledrums in the orchestra, usually tuned to the tonic and dominant of
the prevailing tonality.[27] They were considerably smaller than modern instruments: the drumheads of surviving examples from the first half of the
nineteenth century studied by Renato Meucci are all less than 55 centimeters
in diameter, as opposed to the dimensions specified in Grove's for a pair of
modern timpani (71 cm. and 63–65 cm.).[28] In the absence of mechanisms to
permit a rapid modification in the tension of the drumhead, it was more
difficult for the early nineteenth-century timpanist to change the pitch of his
instruments—using hand screws—than is the case with modern instruments, and therefore changes of tuning required considerable time.[29] Although three timpani were regularly available at the Paris Opéra by the 1830s,
in Italy the practice of introducing more than two timpani did not take hold
until much later in the century.[30] By contrast, the timpanist in a modern pit
orchestra regularly has available four instruments. Finally, the choice of materials for the construction of timpani remains a controversial matter: some
modern players prefer traditional calfskin for the drumhead, others a more
reliable synthetic material made of plastic. Although all agree that the resulting sound is sensibly different, some think the advantages of plastic outweigh
the disadvantages, while others do not.[31]

When Rossini wanted to employ timpani for an overture in *D major*, such
as that of *Tancredi* (*La pietra del paragone*), he had available to him only two
instruments, tuned to the tonic (*d*) and the dominant (*A*). When the music
modulates to the dominant key during the course of the exposition, however,
A major becomes the tonic. Yet the Italian timpanist had no third drum to
play the dominant pitch (*e*) of *A major*, and there was insufficient time for the
timpanist to modify the pitch of one of the two instruments he did have.
Rossini's compositional decisions reveal his sensitivity to the problems in
various ways. Realizing that the pitches available to the timpanist were insuf-

ficient to maintain a coherent part throughout passages where the sudden disappearance of the timpani might seem jarring, Rossini did not allow the timpani to play alone during ensemble passages of this overture. Instead, he added the Banda Turca (an assortment of other percussion instruments), effectively masking the sudden disappearances of the timpani.[32]

There are times, though, when he really wanted the sound of the timpani as part of the orchestral fabric, and hence was willing to compromise with respect to its pitch. At the conclusion of the exposition, for example, both at the end of the crescendo passage and in the final cadences, the music is fully settled in *A major*. The composer could call on the timpani to play *A*, the temporary tonic, but not *its* dominant, *e*. Still, it would be ugly indeed to have the timpani omit an occasional note when the chord is the dominant in the new key. Instead, Rossini asked the timpani to adopt the pitch *d*, now understood as the seventh degree of the dominant harmony ($E-G\sharp-B-D$); see example 12.2. You are unlikely ever to have heard that effect in any theater performing *Tancredi* with modern instruments, for no self-respecting timpanist would allow such a pitch to stand unchanged. Whether you believe the cautious statement in *The New Grove* that "the question of amendment is controversial" or the bolder assertion in *Grove Music Online* that "many tim-

EXAMPLE 12.2. GIOACHINO ROSSINI, *TANCREDI* (*LA PIETRA DEL PARAGONE*), SINFONIA, MM. 112–116.

panists add notes to their parts at will, ignoring earlier performing practices," performers in a normal pit orchestra simply supply the *e* at this point of the *Tancredi* sinfonia by employing a third instrument.[33]

While Rossini generally used timpani only in larger ensembles, for Verdi the timpani are commonly employed extensively throughout much of an opera, in passages that are loud and even in passages that are soft. Thus, in Verdi situations arise regularly where the timpani play notes that are not in the prevailing chords or are not desirable notes in those chords. The concluding ensemble of the third-act finale of *Ernani*, for example, the triumphant appearance of the newly elected Charles V, is in *F major*, and the two timpani are tuned to the tonic and dominant of that key. At a crucial point, the music modulates temporarily to *A♭ major*, without allowing time for the timpani to retune. As the music grows from *pianissimo* to *fortissimo*, however, Verdi is intent on including timpani in the ensemble at the climax for their percussive qualities, even if the pitches are false. He therefore continues to write the pitches *c* and *f*, although the former represents the third of the new tonic and the latter can only be understood as the ninth of an *E♭*-dominant seventh chord. It is surely true, as Fabrizio Della Seta remarks in his edition of *La traviata*, that "because of their approximate intonation, the dissonant sounds produced by the timpani were pulled into the sphere of the adjacent tones, with respect to which they produced an effect more like a dull beating than a true dissonance. The result would have been enhanced by the smaller dimensions of the instruments and their proportionately reduced sonority."[34] Modern tuning mechanisms allow a timpanist to move quickly between the tonic and dominant of *F major* and those of *A♭ major*. If one is using modern instruments, nothing would be gained in performance by forbidding such an adjustment.[35] But Norrington's Waterloo metaphor captures nicely the bracing effect older timpani can have on the sound of Verdi's more Risorgimento-tinted operas.

Horns

The horns employed by Italian composers in the first half of the nineteenth century were natural horns, without valves, instruments that could play easily only a fundamental tone (which depended on the total length of the tube) and its natural harmonic series. To move from one such series to another, the player inserted additional tubing in the instrument, called "crooks," thereby changing its length and producing a different fundamental with its corresponding harmonic series. Techniques were also developed in the late eighteenth and early nineteenth centuries to permit the natural horn to play chromatic notes lacking in its basic harmonic series. By placing a hand in the opening through which sound emerges, known as the bell, and manipulating the size of that opening (a technique called "hand stopping"), the player could produce a wider variety of pitches. But the resulting sounds were very unequal, and only virtuosos developed sufficient technique to overcome many of these problems. Some notes were simple to produce, however, and composers regularly entrusted orchestral musicians with these hand-stopped notes.

The ambiguities inherent in the choice between historical and modern horns are neatly encapsulated in Rossini's *Otello*. Rather than introduce Desdemona in a solo composition, the composer presents her together with her attendant, Emilia, in accompanied recitative, followed by a duettino for the two women. The recitative begins with a lengthy orchestral *ritornello,* which features the most elaborate horn solo in any Rossini opera.[36] But it was certainly not the first. As early as *La pietra del paragone* (1812) and *L'Italiana in Algeri* (1813), Rossini adopted the horn as his solo instrument of choice for the orchestra solos introducing the cavatinas of Clarice and of Lindoro (example 12.3).[37] Each begins with a lyrical four-measure phrase (moving har-

EXAMPLE 12.3. A) GIOACHINO ROSSINI, *LA PIETRA DEL PARAGONE*, CAVATINA CLARICE (N. 3), MM. 5–14. B) GIOACHINO ROSSINI, *L'ITALIANA IN ALGERI*, CAVATINA LINDORO (N. 2), MM. 2–9.

a) *La pietra del paragone*

b) *L'Italiana in Algeri*

monically from the tonic to the dominant), using a similar melodic gesture: an ascending sixth from the fifth degree of the scale (*g*) to the third (*e*, a sixth above). The second phrases, which duplicate the ascending melodic sixths of the first, again begin on the tonic harmony, but now close with tonic cadences. The cadential patterns of the two melodies are cut from the same cloth. Scales, with a touch of chromaticism, ascend to the high *g;* similar scales, descending, lead to arpeggiated tonic triads; until trills on the second degree of the scale (*d*), supported by dominant chords in the orchestra, resolve to the tonic. Neither in range nor in chromaticism are these melodies beyond the capabilities of a modest player of the natural horn, employing simple hand stopping.

The horn solo in *Otello* shares many of these characteristics: the lyrical opening phrase, with faint touches of chromaticism; the scales, arpeggio, and trill at the final cadence. But the expression is everywhere intensified, and with it the demands on the player.[38] Example 12.4 shows the complete horn solo as Rossini originally conceived it. The lyrical six-measure melody (with two three-measure phrases, the first leading to the dominant, the second returning to the tonic) is very much in the style of the earlier examples. It is followed, however, by four measures (14–17), whose large leaps into the lower register make notable demands for hand-stopping on the performer. As the music approaches the final cadence, Rossini lets loose. Three measures of ascending arpeggios (24–26) lead to a descending chromatic scale across a full octave from high *g* to the *g* above middle *c*, while further arpeggios bring the line down yet another octave. A two-octave leap (28) introduces a precipitous climb to the highest note in the line (high *c*), after which a gradual descent, with the expected trill on *d,* leads to a cadence on the tonic.

None of this is beyond what horn tutors of the early nineteenth century considered feasible for an experienced player,[39] but the level of virtuosity demanded—the extended range, leaps, downward arpeggios, chromaticism—all place it well beyond the level of an average orchestral musician in Italian opera houses of the time. Nowhere else in his operas does Rossini make such extraordinary demands on a horn player, and even at the Teatro San Carlo of Naples the part proved too difficult. In Rossini's autograph the penultimate and antepenultimate measures (27–28), although fully orchestrated, were heavily crossed out, presumably by the composer himself. This cut must have occurred early in the history of the opera, perhaps even before the first performance, for the measures are found in no other contemporary source.

Still later, either Rossini or another musician realized that the three measures of arpeggios (24–26) lose much of their point in the absence of the two

EXAMPLE 12.4. GIOACHINO ROSSINI, *OTELLO*, SCENA E DUETTINO
DESDEMONA–EMILIA (N. 4), MM. 7–30.

EXAMPLE 12.4. (*continued*)

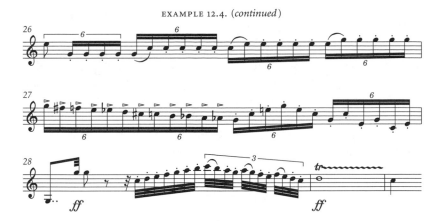

culminating measures. As a result, the first two of these three measures were marked "si passa" (cut these), and the third "si suona" (play this). This accounts for the version of the horn solo found in most contemporary printed editions of *Otello,* although in rendering the part for keyboard the editions often transformed the horn arpeggio into more pianistic scales. Contemporary manuscripts, on the other hand, normally preserve all three measures of horn arpeggios. The resulting proportions are all wrong: the labor of the arpeggios brings forth nothing more than the fabled mouse (in this case, the horn trill).

When we contemplate this music today, we are faced with a paradox: there is no doubt that Rossini canceled two measures of his horn solo, and yet the musical fabric suffers considerably from their absence. Given the problems of performing the music on a natural horn in an Italian theater during the 1810s and 1820s, Rossini's decision seems justified, but modern instruments render the passage more accessible. To which deity should we pay homage? Or, to put the matter in more practical terms, would it be better to perform this solo on a natural horn and cut the two measures or use a modern instrument and include them?

The *Otello* solo is an extreme example, to be sure, but looking carefully at the use composers made of horns and trumpets during the first half of the nineteenth century, one becomes ever more aware that they were working around quite precise technical limitations. For example, the original happy ending of *Tancredi* comes to a conclusion in *D major,* with the entire orchestra playing the tonic for five measures.[40] For four measures we hear the full *D major* triad, but in the very last measure Rossini asked all his instruments to play just the tonic note, except for the trumpets. Tuned "in A," these early nineteenth-century trumpets had no way to play that pitch in an appropriate register. Yet Rossini did not want trumpets to disappear from the orchestral sonority. Instead, he allowed them to play a written *c*, producing a sounding octave on *a*, the fifth degree of the *D major* scale. Given the overall orchestral sonority, this fifth degree is heard not as a distinct pitch but as a reinforcement of one of the overtones of the tonic.[41] Faced with an instrumentalist using a modern, valved trumpet, however, which can easily produce the tonic degree, a modern conductor may feel it appropriate to intervene.[42]

A composer writing for natural horns can overcome many technical limitations by asking his players to insert different crooks in their instruments, thereby modifying the length of the tubing and hence the fundamental notes of the instrument; but this action takes time. As a result, some nineteenth-century horn parts can seem strange, as in the second-act finale of Rossini's *L'Italiana in Algieri*. The scene in which Mustafà is inducted into the order of "Pappataci" (complaisant husbands and lovers) is in *Bb major*, and Rossini's two horns "in *Bb*" play until the very end of the scene. As the ship on which the Italians plan to escape appears, the music jumps to *D major*. Rossini wants to use horns at the beginning of this barcarolle in 6/8, but there is no time for them to change crooks. Instead, in the opening *D major* orchestral ritornello, the horns "in *Bb*" are instructed to play an octave on *e*, sounding *d*, the new tonic. Only after six measures is there sufficient time (eleven measures) for the horns to change their crooks, and at that point they are instructed to prepare "in *D*." When the opening passage returns with the chorus, the orchestral music is unchanged *except* for the horns, which are now "in *D*" (where they will remain for the rest of the finale) and therefore can play the notated octave on *c* in order to produce the same *d*. The differences between natural horns "in *Bb*" playing an octave on *e* and horns "in *D*" playing on *c* is trivial, even in nineteenth-century terms, but the example suggests how long it took a player to insert a new crook into his instrument. Rossini's frequent use of phrases such as "in Do subito" (suddenly in *C*) to announce a crook change suggests that he sometimes pressed his musicians hard.[43]

Verdi, too, frequently wrote horn parts in tutti sections that seem strange to modern players. Near the end of the trio for Elvira, Ernani, and Silva in the second act of *Ernani*, there is a cadential passage within a *fortissimo* concluding section, in which every instrument (apart from the Cassa) plays on each chord, except for the second horn.[44] In this *Bb major* section, the first pair of natural horns is "in *F*," the second pair "in *Bb*," a combination that works well most of the time, permitting all four horns to participate in most sonorities.

EXAMPLE 12.5. GIUSEPPE VERDI, *ERNANI*, RECITATIVO E TERZETTO (N. 7),
HORN PARTS, MM. 336–340.

But in the cadential phrase at mm. 336–340, Verdi introduced an unusual diminished seventh chord in the second half of 336, and no pitch in the chord is available in the lower register for a natural horn "in *F*." Hence, Verdi wrote a peculiar part for the first pair of horns (example 12.5). For a natural horn "in *F*," the written *d* above middle *c* (sounding the *g* below middle *c*) is not an easily available pitch. To produce it, the player must place his hand in the bell, significantly changing the timbre of the note. While an able soloist might in part compensate for this problem, Berlioz opines that this stopped note is "very difficult and muffled."[45] In fact, there is not a single example of this pitch for a horn in the entire score of *Ernani*. With a modern valve horn, the problem disappears.

Does that end the discussion? Should we always adopt modern instruments and add these missing pitches? Berlioz is once again a helpful witness. Since he lived in a period when the valve horn was gradually replacing the natural horn in orchestras, especially north of the Alps, his words in the *Orchestration* treatise are noteworthy. In the definitive version of his treatise he writes, "The tone of the piston horn is a little different from that of the usual horn; it would not do to substitute it on any occasion." In an earlier version of the passage, he was more strident: "I am firmly convinced that one should never consider it an improvement on the horn, from which it differs in quality of tone."[46] Indeed, if we move from the problem of technical limitations to those of sonority and balance, a largely different set of issues presents itself.

MODERN INSTRUMENTS: THE PROBLEM OF SONORITY AND BALANCE

As we saw in the discussion of the Metropolitan Opera's production of *Semiramide* (chapter 6), balancing orchestral sonorities is never simple, although the problem becomes more tractable when we take into account the significant differences in the actual instruments used by most modern musicians and those for which nineteenth-century Italian composers prepared their scores. Rossini, for example, will often join together two horns and two bassoons to form a chordal sonority in four voices: their combined sound, easier to balance with older instruments, is much more difficult with modern ones.[47] The following reflections touch on only a few of the instrumental problems that modern performers must often face, but they offer a framework within which similar questions can be addressed.

Three Trombones and a Tuba

Three modern, valved trombones and a tuba playing *fortissimo* can overpower the rest of Verdi's orchestra; the three narrow-bore trombones and cimbasso for which the composer wrote his scores do not have that effect. Even when we recognize that the problem is in part historical, it is difficult to address it successfully, given the realities of available rehearsal time in today's theaters and the stylistic diversity demanded from performers night after night. The *Semiramide* situation was hardly an isolated instance. In the winter of 2004, Eve Queler conducted a concert performance of the critical edition of Verdi's *Il corsaro* with her Opera Orchestra of New York. Working closely with her in the orchestral preparation was Italo Marchini, a sensitive conductor in his own right. After the performance, Marchini vented some of his frustrations to me in a note about dynamic levels. If you mark the three trombone parts *fortissimo* in the score, he said, the instinct of the players will be to follow the direction literally, and the resulting sound will blast you, the rest of the orchestra, and the singers out of the theater. The problem is real, even though I'm not sure I understand what a "literal" *fortissimo* would be: after all, dynamic markings are not accompanied by a scientific equivalent in decibels. Such markings are always relative: a brass *fortissimo* in a Bruckner symphony and a Verdi opera are not the same.

Those who prepare scores of this repertory constantly face the problem. Should a printed edition of a nineteenth-century opera attempt to foresee and overcome it by recommending different dynamic levels in various orchestral parts, thereby "tuning" orchestral sonorities? There are two issues to be addressed: (1) Did Italian composers themselves make those differentiations? (2) Even if they did not, should modern editors introduce them? Despite Denis Vaughan's famous polemic on the subject of dynamic levels, discussed in chapter 4,[48] there are no grounds for asserting that Verdi or other nineteenth-century Italian composers made such differentations in all but the most unusual circumstances. Before we published the critical edition of *Rigoletto* in 1983, I charted every place in the autograph manuscript of the opera where Verdi wrote a specific dynamic level, sorting them according to the instrumental parts in which these levels appeared. When there were internal discrepancies (such as *f* in some parts and *ff* in others, within a single chord played by the entire orchestra), I compared similar passages throughout the opera. I severely tried the patience of a graduate seminar, asking participants first to go over my work and then to make parallel examinations of other scores. I even delivered a boring paper on the subject to an international Verdi conference. All evidence pointed in the same direction. For Verdi an orchestral chord could be very soft (*ppp* or *pp*), soft (*p*), of moderate volume (*mp* or *mf*), loud (*f*), or very loud (*ff* or *fff*). He usually wrote these indications on every other staff and made no effort to tell the trombones to play softer and the flutes to play louder. He did not, in short, "tune" an orchestral sonority by providing different dynamic levels for different instruments, relying instead on good musicianship and stylistic acuity, as well as on the prowess of the orchestral director, whether he did his job with a violin in hand, as was typical during the first half of the century, or with a baton, the emerging practice from the 1850s onward.[49]

To assign editors the task of providing differentiated dynamic levels is unrealistic. Not only do such levels need to be different from performing space to performing space, from orchestra to orchestra, and from country to country,[50] but an invented practice of this kind would assign to notation more precision than any nineteenth-century composer or performer would have deemed reasonable. That dynamic levels in Italian opera scores refer to an overall effect, and are not instructions to particular instrumentalists, puts a special responsibility on modern performers to interpret the notation appropriately. Part of that responsibility includes a sensitivity to the way instruments have changed over the past two centuries.

In some cases the changes are largely of degree. Although early nineteenth-century practice in France still specified three differently tuned trombones (alto, tenor, and bass), in accordance with the practice of eighteenth-century composers such as Gluck, by the 1840s all three trombone parts were almost always played by tenor trombones ("incontestably the best of all the trombones"), and composers could not expect to find three different trombones in orchestras, either in France or elsewhere.[51] Modern trombones are similar to those used by Verdi and his immediate predecessors, but the use of valves changes the way in which pitches are produced, while the widening of the bore, characteristic of instruments by the beginning of the twentieth century, considerably increases the quantity of sound that emerges, a reasonable requirement for the later Wagner operas, for Bruckner, or for Mahler. Finding the proper interpretation for notated dynamic levels in earlier scores requires sensitivity to these physical modifications of the instruments.

When a fourth, lower brass instrument is called for by Italian composers, the situation becomes even more complicated. Terminological differences in composers' manuscripts, while common, may not always be meaningful: sometimes the terms simply suggest "whatever low brass the theater uses." In the few cases where Rossini requires a lower brass instrument, he refers to it as a "serpentone" (a wooden instrument) in Italy. Yet when the identical music is printed in a French score, Rossini assigns the same instrumental line to an ophicleide (a brass instrument).[52] Bellini and Donizetti do not regularly require a fourth brass instrument in Italy; when they do, they tend to use the terms "serpentone" (e.g., in Bellini's *Il pirata*) or "cimbasso" (in Bellini's *Norma*). After Donizetti moved to Paris in 1838, he wrote for the ophicleide (in *La Favorite*). Verdi, on the other hand, regularly requires a fourth instrument, which in Italy he usually refers to as a "cimbasso," at least through the 1870s. Only in a French score, such as *Jérusalem,* do we find him explicitly requesting an "ophicléide."[53]

Relating these terminological distinctions to actual instruments and performance practice remains difficult; it is highly unlikely that the terms were used with any precision. Nor must we assume that a solution appropriate for Rossini would also be appropriate for Verdi, or, for that matter, that a solution for early Verdi can be applied to *Aida.*[54] Indeed, as late as 21 December 1871, in preparing for the first performance of *Aida* at the Teatro alla Scala (20 January 1872), Verdi was trying to find an appropriate instrument to serve as the bass of the brass section:

> I still insist on the fourth trombone. That *bombardone* is impossible. Tell Faccio and, if you wish, consult the first trombonist as well to see what should be done. I would like a *trombone basso* from the same family as the others, but if it is too tiring or too difficult to play, get one of the usual *oficleidi* that go to low B. In other words, do whatever you want, but not that devil of a *bombardone* that does not blend with the others.[55]

All of this for an instrument Verdi normally referred to as a *cimbasso.*

Even for those who wish to adopt a low brass instrument consonant with documented historical practice, then, there are no simple answers. Should we use a wooden serpentone for Rossini's Neapolitan operas, but replace it with a brass ophicleide when performing the operas in their French versions? Do we accept Meucci's contention that cimbasso for Verdi did not mean a wooden "corno basso" (a successor to the serpentone), the instrument to which the word was first applied earlier in the century, but rather a brass ophicleide of the kind invented in Paris toward the beginning of the 1820s, which became the European standard by the 1840s?[56] Do we simply exclude later "improvements," making the ophicleide more sonorous and even less able to balance with the trombones? And if we accept Verdi's desire to have a bass trombone for his later operas, an instrument that blends better with the three tenor trombones, do we push this practice back to operas from the 1840s through the 1860s?

Simon Wills, a professional trombonist and composer, describes the "noisy folly" of modern brass in these terms: "The sound of brass has become denser and it projects more effectively. In many orchestras a tutti has become an assault by the brass: it is exciting for the first few sallies but ultimately exhausting and inimical to the expressiveness of the orchestra as a whole."[57] His practical solution, inherently sensible, is to follow those orchestras, such as the Chamber Orchestra of Europe, who "are adopting smaller instruments without entertaining any desire to be authentic [...] because the greater transparency of their sound allows the orchestra to play co-operatively, instead of doing battle with a monster." Even the venerable Chicago Symphony Orchestra has banished the tuba from performances of Berlioz's *Symphonie fantastique*, substituting a modern brass instrument of the kind that is being called a "cimbasso."[58] Whatever decision is taken in each particular case, Verdi expressed it best: the instrument must "blend with the others." Given the changes that took place both chronologically and geographically in the low brass during the nineteenth century, there is not likely to be much agreement about an ideal modern instrument for this repertory, although Meucci recommends the use of either a half-size tuba or a bass trombone.[59] But no matter what instrument is used, one shouldn't have to tell a brass player in a performance of *Norma* that a marked *fortissimo* in his part doesn't mean the same thing for him as it does for an oboe.

How Many Strings?

What is an "ideal" number of strings for the performance of an opera written by an Italian composer during the first six decades of the nineteenth century, and where should they be placed?[60] While these are questions I am frequently asked by theaters and conductors, I cannot pretend to offer precise guidance. The matter is of great importance, to be sure, in a repertory for which there is normally a full complement of winds (2 flutes, doubling piccolos, 2 oboes, 2 clarinets, 2 bassoons), brass (4 horns, 2 trumpets, 3 trombones, cimbasso/ophicleide), and percussion, not to mention the occasional English horn, harps, guitars, and so forth. If you search for historical evidence about the size of string sections, however, you find that opera houses in different cities had orchestras of different sizes and seating arrangements, and even within a single city the number of players and their arrangement varied over time.[61] Nor would it make sense to generalize for a Rossini comic opera intended for a small Neapolitan theater (such as the 1816 *La gazzetta* for the Teatro dei Fiorentini), a Donizetti French work aimed at the Paris Opéra (such as the 1840 *Les Martyrs*), and a Verdi opera written for Rome's Teatro Apollo (the 1853 *Il trovatore*). Even were we able to establish firm historical principles, their present applicability would remain uncertain. How, for example, should we use the knowledge that there were usually more double basses than violoncellos in an Italian opera orchestra during the 1810s and 1820s, since today's instruments are no longer the same: Rossini's three-string double bass was very different from the modern four-string double bass, the latter being an instrument of greater range and sonority.

To address such questions, we must both reconstruct accurately what composers wrote and trace the performance history of their works. Thus, while Rossini always notated his viola parts on a single staff and never specified "divise" (divided), an indication he used for first violins (as "divisi," since violins are gendered masculine in Italian and violas feminine), he regularly thought of violas as being divided into two sections. This is confirmed by contemporary performing materials, which often have separate parts for first violas and second violas. In the opening section of the first-act finale of *Tancredi,* for example, the violins, cellos, and double basses all play the same staccato figuration in their respective registers. Only violas sustain the harmony and later, along with the upper winds, double the melodic material of the four women's voices.[62] But it would have been unthinkable in the passage shown in example 12.6 for the violas to have been executed as double-stops, with each instrument playing both melodic parts. While the viola part could be played with one instrument on each line, it is unlikely that it would have balanced effectively the remainder of the ensemble. In short, Rossini's score would seem to require a minimum of four violas in the orchestra. Yet only a few Italian theaters during the 1810s could accommodate this need.[63]

Not all performance conditions are ideal, to be sure, and Rossini himself had to compromise on many occasions. As we saw in chapter 3, the absence of an appropriate cellist at the small Teatro Re in Milan seems to have com-

EXAMPLE 12.6. GIOACHINO ROSSINI, *TANCREDI,* FINALE PRIMO (N. 7), VIOLA PARTS, MM. 26–28.

pelled the composer to rewrite "Per lui che adoro" from *L'Italiana in Algeri* with a solo flute in place of a solo cello. But what happened in Italy when *Guillaume Tell* returned from the French capital to Rossini's native land? In Paris, his 1829 opera was composed for and performed by a string section of 12 first violins (in addition to the *violon principal,* who also directed the orchestra), 12 second violins, 8 violas, 10 violoncellos, and 8 double basses.[64] In the overture, furthermore, Rossini scored the initial Andante for five solo cellos, with an additional five cellos playing two accompanying parts, three cellos on the first, two on the second. Since not a single Italian theater during the 1830s or 1840s had ten resident cellos, the overture to *Guillaume Tell* was certainly not heard on the peninsula as its composer conceived it.[65] For a large opera house such as the Teatro alla Scala of Milan, there would have been enough cellos to cover the five solo parts, and it would have been relatively satisfactory to have the two accompanying parts played by some combination of cellos and double basses. Few theaters throughout Emilia-Romagna in this period, however, employed as many as five cellos, so that further compromises would have been necessary.[66] How significant might this have been? It all depends on your point of view. I wonder whether any viewers shared my discomfort with a scene in Franco Zeffirelli's 1988 film *Il giovane Toscanini* (*The Young Toscanini*).[67] As Toscanini and a traveling orchestra make their way across the Atlantic on their way to Brazil, a musician dies. When his body is committed to the waves, the other members of the orchestra gather on deck, and we witness a solemn moment of musical commemoration: the string players are all sawing away (including the violins), the flutes are fluting, and the trumpets trumpeting. From the sound track, however, come the strains of the opening of the *William Tell* overture, that is, a passage for cellos alone (give or take a double bass).

The problem was not always the presence of an insufficient number of string players. Later in his life, as orchestras grew larger, Verdi feared that in a particular theater the size of the ensemble might overwhelm the singers. In a letter of 1885, his erstwhile student Emanuele Muzio explained to Tito Ricordi that the composer felt there were too many players in the orchestra of the Teatro Apollo in Rome for a projected revival of *Don Carlo*. In Muzio's words:

> Our maestro, who wrote *Il trovatore* and *Ballo in maschera* for the Apollo in Rome, also finds that the orchestra of that theater is too numerous, and that it must certainly damage the vocal part of the operas. He is not able to write and perhaps run the risk of a refusal if he asked for a

reduction in the number, but you and Lamperti can state that the opinion of the master is such that he believes the following orchestra would be more than sufficient for the Apollo.[68]

Verdi's suggestion was for a maximum of 12 first violins, 10 second violins, 8 violas, 8 cellos, and 7 double basses, an ensemble with five fewer string players than Rossini used at the premiere of *Guillaume Tell*.[69]

There were other factors. Early in the century it was typical in Italian opera houses to divide the string players so that half of them sat on the left side, as seen by the audience, and half on the right. Sometimes this meant dividing equally first and second violinists, sometimes placing the first violinists on one side of the audience and the second violinists on the other, while dividing violas, violoncellos, and double basses.[70] The musical purpose was to produce a sound that would seem uniform throughout the theater. With his wide European experience, though, by the late 1850s Verdi had come to favor the typical northern European seating, in which most of the string families were kept together (but sometimes with the double basses arranged on both sides of the orchestra). Apparently he imposed such a seating at the Teatro San Carlo of Naples when he staged *Simon Boccanegra* during the fall of 1858, but a decade later the theater had returned to the older Italian system, as Verdi complained to Ricordi in a letter of 5 April 1869:

> Just imagine [...] that in the orchestra there are still violas and violoncellos scattered one here, another there, etc., etc. This is a vestige of olden times, when violas and violoncellos were always in unison with the basses, and it has not yet been eliminated, despite the demands of modern works, where the violas and violoncellos play independent parts like all of the other instruments. What is even stranger is that ten years ago I had these instruments united together as a group for *Simon Boccanegra*. It seems that the innovation was found to be absurd.[71]

He repeated this complaint in a letter to Francesco Florimo of 23 June 1869:

> How can you tolerate that the violas and violoncellos are still not placed together? How can there then be a downbow, dynamic shading, accent, etc.? Besides, the group of string instruments will lack fullness. This is a vestige of former times, when violas and violoncellos played in unison with the double basses. Wretched customs![72]

Surely no one is suggesting that in "historically informed" performances we must divide the string families spatially for operas from Rossini through middle Verdi, but unite them for operas beginning with *Simon Boccanegra*. In any event, Verdi's historical explanation is faulty: while there are passages where violas and cellos are *col basso* in Rossini's operas, there are also many important passages where each family of string instruments contributes in a distinctive fashion to the orchestral sonority.

More influential still on orchestral balance is the physical location of the players. While northern European opera orchestras were regularly placed in "pits" (Wagner took the process further at Bayreuth, submerging many players below the stage), Italian orchestras throughout the nineteenth century were positioned on the same level as the audience. Indeed, the Teatro alla Scala did not introduce a lowered orchestra pit until the 1907–8 season, their aim being "to obtain a more integrated sound with the singers on stage."[73] But is such a sound—perfectly reasonable for *Pelléas et Mélisande* or *Salomé*—necessarily appropriate for an opera by Donizetti or an early work by Verdi? Might other values be more important, such as the possibility of more interaction between orchestral musicians and singers? Such interaction may have been particularly significant in performances led by the principal violinist. When an effort was made in 1984 to stage *Ernani* at the Teatro Comunale of Modena in a way approximating its first Venetian performance 140 years earlier, the orchestra pit was closed and the orchestra was seated at audience level, although a modern conductor (Roberto Abbado) took responsibility for the proceedings.[74] Two of the three major performing venues at the Rossini Opera Festival, the Sala Pedrotti and the sports stadium turned Palafestival, have no orchestra pit. Only the more traditional Teatro Rossini has a standard pit. The impact on orchestral sound is considerable.

In short, there is no simple response to the question of how many strings should be used in a performance of an Italian opera written during the first two-thirds of the nineteenth century. It depends on the specific repertory, it depends on the instruments being employed, it depends on the physical space in which the modern performance is taking place. No musician should find this surprising.

ALTERNATIVES FOR MODERN PERFORMANCES: TWO DONIZETTIAN EXAMPLES

If a critical edition takes as its task not simply to produce a single performing text of an opera, but instead to explore the sources and transmission history of nineteenth-century Italian operas, it can suggest interesting and sometimes compelling alternatives for modern performers. Here are examples from two of Donizetti's most beloved operas: many others could be adduced.

Glass Harmonica or Flute?

Since at least 1941, when the autograph manuscript of *Lucia di Lammermoor* was issued in facsimile, it has been widely known that Donizetti originally wrote a part for glass harmonica in Lucia's mad scene.[75] But Donizetti crossed out this part and substituted a flute before the first performance (Naples, Teatro San Carlo, 26 September 1835), and no reference to the glass harmonica is found in nineteenth-century sources. Some critics have not considered this earlier notation particularly significant.[76] Bini and Commons, on the other hand, write:

> The quivering, supernatural sound of this instrument would have been perfect, we believe, for communicating the sense of madness, but for some reason we cannot now know—perhaps because no player of the glass harmonica was available or perhaps because the sound was too weak to be heard in the Teatro San Carlo, the part of the "armonico" in the autograph was decisively canceled and rewritten for flute.[77]

There is indeed something otherworldly about the glass harmonica, as Heather Hadlock has shown, for the instrument was quite explicitly related in the minds of the public with women, with mesmerism, with madness:

> The history of women, trance, and the armonica coalesces in the Mad Scene of *Lucia di Lammermoor*, where the instrument's sound was originally intended to conjure up anxieties about young women's vulnerability to nervous derangement, taboo eroticism, and alienation from healthy, normal society. This use of the instrument is no sign of charlatanism, however, but a genuine invocation of the uncanny.[78]

Mary Ann Smart, too, speaks of "the far more uncanny glass harmonica that Donizetti originally wanted."[79] Nor was this the first time Donizetti had employed the instrument. As Emilio Sala has pointed out, there is a glass harmonica in the composer's *Il castello di Kenilworth* (Naples, Teatro San Carlo, 6 July 1829), associated with another "female victim unjustly persecuted."[80]

Since 1970 there have been several successful attempts to restore the glass harmonica to the mad scene in *Lucia,* whether in the theater or on recordings.[81] Yet over these efforts has hung the suspicion that perhaps it is wrong to employ that instrument when Donizetti himself replaced it with a flute. Study of the autograph manuscript makes it clear, however, that Donizetti's part for glass harmonica is beautifully laid out in every detail, with extensive articulation and, twice, the characteristic indication "ondeggiante" (wavering or undulating), an indication that would make no sense for a flute and, indeed, is not copied into the flute staff. There are some lovely interactions between the glass harmonica and the flute, too, interactions that are lost when the harmonica part is rewritten for flute. The harmonica appears during the introductory recitative (to introduce "Il dolce suono"), returns extensively in the Larghetto ("Ardon gl'incensi"), where it accompanies Lucia's notated fioritura, and then is found again in the cabaletta "Spargi d'amaro pianto."

Recent research during preparation of the critical edition of *Lucia di Lammermoor* has finally clarified the historical situation.[82] Donizetti apparently wrote the part for a specific performer, Domenico Pezzi, who rehearsed the music not only with the original Lucia, Fanny Tacchinardi, but with the full orchestra. Pezzi, however, had sued the theater concerning his services for a ballet entitled *Amore e Psiche,* first performed earlier that year at the Teatro San Carlo on 30 May 1835.[83] Court papers preserved in the Neapolitan state archives make clear that there was bad blood between Pezzi and the theater, which at some point during the run of twenty-six performances of *Amore e Psiche* had substituted a flute for Pezzi's glass harmonica. Surely Donizetti was told to avoid Pezzi. With no other experienced player available, the composer fell back on a flute.

Performers today should feel free to choose between the two alternatives, and the critical edition of the opera will make both versions available. Those who wish to preserve the traditional approach to the mad scene will continue to use a flute, while those who are intrigued by the mysterious aura of the glass harmonica will want to go back to Donizetti's original inspiration. Scholars must clarify the history and make both versions available; performers must make choices for particular performances under particular circumstances.

Horn or Violoncello?

After five quick measures, in which the entire orchestra scurries from the tonic (*D major*) to an unexpected dominant of *F major,* Donizetti focuses his overture of *Don Pasquale* (first performed at the Théâtre Italien of Paris on 3 January 1843) on one of the most beautiful melodic inspirations of the opera, the serenata in the garden that Ernesto sings to Norina, "Com'è gentil," which opens the final scene. In the third act of *Don Pasquale* the melody will be presented by the tenor alone, in *A major,* accompanied by two guitars and tambourines, but in the overture the tune is played in *F major,* a pastoral interlude before the beginning of the principal movement in *D major,* derived primarily from the melody of Norina's cavatina "So anch'io la virtù magica."

EXAMPLE 12.7. GAETANO DONIZETTI, *DON PASQUALE*, SINFONIA,
ORIGINAL HORN SOLO, MM. 6–38.

Example 12.7 shows the melody in the overture as Donizetti originally conceived it, played throughout by a solo horn, tuned "in C" (that is, sounding an octave below the written pitches).[84] From the appearance of the autograph manuscript, it would seem that the melody was doubled by a solo bassoon at A2; otherwise A1 and A2 were essentially unaccompanied. At B1 and B2 pizzicato strings provided a simple chordal accompaniment, while at A3 this accompaniment continued, with bassoons now sustaining notes of the chords.[85]

This is not the orchestration as it is generally known. Donizetti himself modified his autograph manuscript, so that A1 and A2 are played by a solo violoncello (with the solo bassoon continuing to join the melody at A2). While B1 and B2 remain a horn solo, A3 is played by a solo flute and violoncello, with the horn joining only in the second half of the phrase. In its original form as a horn solo, this is not a simple melody to play, largely because of its insistence on the written melodic *f* in the middle register, already in m. 7, a "stopped note" on the natural horn, obtainable, according to Berlioz, only by "closing the bell (the lower aperture of the horn) to a lesser or greater extent with the hand." While some of these notes are of "good" or "very good" quality, according to Berlioz, this *f* "is muffled," an unfortunate quality for a note to which the melody returns again and again.[86]

And yet, thanks to the work of Bini and Commons, we now know from contemporary reviews that the entire melody was originally played in Paris by the solo horn. In *Le Corsaire* of 9 January, for example, we read, "After a charming overture in *Re* whose adagio, played by the horn, announces well the subject of the story, there is a romance for Tamburini [Doctor Malatesta]."[87] The reviewer for *La France Musicale* of 8 January says, "The clarinet and the horn begin the adagio, whose theme is the first phrase of a melody full of tenderness and originality that Mario [Ernesto] sings in the third act." While the reviewer might have confused the ensemble of wind instruments, he is unlikely to have mistaken a solo violoncello for a horn. A third review, however, suggests that Donizetti had good reason to make a change: the horn may not have accomplished his task very well. *Les Coulisses* of 5 January, in a distinctly hostile review, refers to the passage as being played by "the bassoon, and very badly by the horn of Forestier."

Donizetti apparently decided that a prominent passage for unaccompanied horn at the very beginning of his opera was simply too risky, and hence introduced the modification in his orchestration before leaving Paris on 7 January for Vienna.[88] With the knowledge that this change was made after the premiere, a modern production might certainly consider experimenting with Donizetti's original orchestration, especially with the availability of a horn with valves.

Examples of this kind allow us to glimpse the realities of the musical forces at the disposal of Italian composers during the first half of the nineteenth century. Though they can offer no sure guide to modern performers, they do reveal the extent to which the composers' problems remain our problems. Only by learning to recognize the elements of these problems and to appreciate the tentative and evolving solutions that composers undertook can we deal responsibly with instrumental problems of our own time.

Before concluding this chapter, I want to address one final question: in performing nineteenth-century Italian opera, how should one accompany *secco* recitative in the modern opera house?

SECCO RECITATIVE

While there is a considerable literature about the accompaniment of *secco* recitative in the eighteenth century, relatively little has been written about the nineteenth. That is understandable, of course, since until recently only a few nineteenth-century Italian operas using *secco* recitative were regularly performed, and those were exclusively comedies (Rossini's *L'Italiana in Algeri, Il barbiere di Siviglia,* and *La Cenerentola,* as well as Donizetti's *L'elisir d'amore*). Nineteenth-century *opera buffa* was largely thought of as a retrograde art, given the overwhelming presence of the serious, even tragic operas of Rossini (after his move to Naples in 1815), Bellini, Donizetti, and Verdi, which were generally accompanied by the orchestra throughout. Thus, it was easy to assume that eighteenth-century traditions of accompaniment lived on, unchanged, wherever composers continued to employ *secco* recitative between closed musical numbers.

That model no longer seems adequate. First of all, far more operas from the first two decades of the nineteenth century than had been realized, both serious and semiserious, employ *secco* recitative, and some of these works are being performed with increased frequency today, especially Rossini's *Tancredi* of 1813, *La gazza ladra* of 1817, and *Bianca e Falliero* of 1819. To them can be added most of the comic operas written throughout the first half of the nineteenth century, but also many serious or semiserious operas, including Meyerbeer's *Il crociato in Egitto* of 1824 and works by Donizetti (*Il furioso all'isola di San Domingo* and *Torquato Tasso,* both of 1833), by Pacini (*Il barone di Dolsheim* of 1818, *La vestale* of 1823, and *Gli Arabi nelle Gallile* of 1827), and by Mercadante (*Elisa e Claudio* of 1821). All these operas, furthermore, were first performed in major northern theaters: the Teatro alla Scala of Milan and the Teatro La Fenice of Venice, or—in the case of Donizetti—the Teatro Valle of Rome. Indeed, it was only at the Neapolitan Teatro San Carlo that *secco* recitative essentially disappeared during the 1810s: elsewhere in Italy it was widely used throughout the 1820s for serious operas and even into the 1830s for semiserious operas.

The practice of Italian theaters in the first decades of the nineteenth century, however, was considerably different from that of the eighteenth. Major eighteenth-century theaters in Italy, and elsewhere in Europe, tended to have two harpsichords in the orchestra, divided spatially, each with its attendant violoncello and double bass "al cembalo." In a musical-dramatic context in which the bulk of *secco* recitative was substantial in comparison with the length of the closed musical numbers, with most dramatic exposition and action taking place within that recitative, the interaction of this *continuo* group with the singers had to be intimate. When musical direction was provided by a "conductor" seated at one of the harpsichords, as it was during much of the eighteenth century, that instrument was likely to be placed toward the middle of the ensemble, with a second instrument positioned to one side. Toward the end of the century, when direction was generally entrusted to the principal violinist, who "conducted" with his violin in hand, the harpsichords were placed at the two extremes of the orchestra, near the stage.[89] Why *two* harpsichords? The motivation is best expressed in a letter of 1773 by Pasquale Cafaro, director of the royal chapel in Naples, reacting to the suggestion that the Teatro San Carlo give up its second harpsichord: "The second cembalo, violoncello, and double bass, in that position, are absolutely necessary to assist the singers, at those moments when they find themselves far from the first [continuo group], to ensure that the singers will not stray from the straight path of perfect intonation."[90] But neither the number nor the character of the keyboard instruments would survive into the nineteenth century.

The shifts from two keyboard instruments to one and from the harpsichord to the piano were, according to Meucci, related phenomena.[91] Despite the ambiguities that result from a single Italian word (*cembalo*) used for both the harpsichord and the piano, by the end of the eighteenth century the harpsichord was essentially a relic of an earlier age. The increased sonority of the piano, its dynamic range, its greater reliability in tuning, not to mention changing fashion, all contributed to the disappearance of the harpsichord from Italian theaters. The same factors reduced the need for a pair of keyboard instruments, and the gradual decrease in the proportion of *secco* recitative in an opera (even in an *opera buffa*), with respect to the concerted numbers, had a similar effect. Probably by the turn of the nineteenth century, but certainly by 1810, every important theater in Italy, and most smaller theaters too, had replaced their two harpsichords with a single piano (obviously of the kind manufactured early in the nineteenth century) to accompany *secco* recitative, normally joined by a violoncello and a double bass. This *continuo* ensemble maintained a role in Italian opera at least throughout the first half of the nineteenth century. There is every reason to believe that such an ensemble was still in use at La Scala when Verdi's only opera employing *secco* recitative, *Un giorno di regno*, a *melodramma giocoso*, had its premiere on 5 September 1840.[92]

Already in 1982 the Rossini Opera Festival, for its first production of *Tancredi*, began to experiment with using a *continuo* ensemble of this kind for the accompaniment of *secco* recitative. As Adriano Cavicchi explained in the program booklet for those performances, recitative accompaniment in Rossini's time was realized by the use of three players: "a 'cembalo,' actually a fortepiano, a violoncello 'al cembalo,' which played a chordal elaboration of the harmony, and a double bass 'al cembalo,' which held the bass note of the harmony."[93] There are very few indications of precisely what these players did, but there are warnings as to what they should not do. As always, such warnings need to be read with caution. Giuseppe Scaramelli in 1811, for example, primarily concerned with reining in abuses, wrote:

> Let it also be observed that there are keyboard players and cellists who, when playing recitative, love to indulge in ample preambles and florid interpolations, just about the most insufferable thing imaginable, which it would be well to prohibit, instructing them that they must play with precision only the harmonies, with the correct notes of the chords, together with the double bass, and nothing else.[94]

Similar injunctions appear in the 1876 *Trattato di Violoncello* by Giacomo Quarenghi, who is describing a practice that "is practically forgotten, but since even today there are those who want to re-hear masterpieces of the past, it is necessary to say something about accompanying *secco* recitative" (which he calls "Recitativi Parlanti"). Like Scaramelli sixty-five years earlier, Quarenghi is largely concerned with curbing abuses:

> Do not disturb the singer with ornaments of little scales or flourishes, and use them only if the singer goes flat, in order to help him return to the opportune notes. [...] Accompany sweetly and choose characteristic notes of the chord. Finally, don't try to be a master who tries to dominate the singer, but a friend who supports him.[95]

So much protesting suggests that keyboard players and cellists did indeed decorate their parts, and there is no reason why modern musicians could not do the same, as long as they stay within the constantly changing boundaries of "good taste."

Indeed, another way of accompanying *secco* recitative is documented in England, with no keyboard instrument at all; instead, the violoncello and double bass alone accompanied the recitative. This practice was associated with the cellist Robert Lindley and the double bass player Dragonetti, both of whom appeared with the Italian opera orchestra in London during the 1820s and 1830s. An example of their practice from Mozart's *Don Giovanni* was transcribed by William Smith Rockstro in the original *Grove's Dictionary*,

EXAMPLE 12.8. WOLFGANG AMADEUS MOZART, *DON GIOVANNI*, RECITATIVO
(ATTO II, SCENA XI), AS PERFORMED BY WILLIAM LINDLEY AND
DOMENICO DRAGONETTI, MM. 36–38.

reprinted in *The New Grove Dictionary* (1980), and included in *Grove Music Online*.[96] *Grove Music Online* quotes Rockstro's original comment, which is neutral, even encouraging toward the musical proclivities of these "two old friends": "The general style of their accompaniment was exceedingly simple, consisting only of plain chords, played *arpeggiando;* but occasionally the two old friends would launch out into passages as those shown in the following example [see example 12.8]; Dragonetti playing the large notes, and Lindley the small ones." Compare the snippy attitude of Nicholas Gatty in the fifth edition of *Grove's Dictionary* (1954), quoted in *The New Grove Dictionary* (1980):

> It is recorded that Lindley often embellished his share by the introduction of figures and ornamental passages; but, however ingenious this may have been, it was entirely at variance with the effect intended by the composer, which was simply to give support to the vocal line and to conjoin the modulations of the music. An example of this treatment is here shown as a curiosity.

The same example follows. By 2004, Gatty's commentary is gone and Rockstro's attitude is allowed to stand. It is a potent example of the way in which attitudes toward historical performance practice have changed over time.

Would that the matter might end there, but it does not. If theaters had given up the harpsichord in favor of the piano by the early nineteenth century, when did the harpsichord reappear as the instrument of choice for *secco* recitatives in the operas of Mozart? During the 1930s, for example, Fritz Busch, working at the Glyndebourne Festival in England, always used a piano for the Mozart operas, and apparently so did Hans Rosbaud at Aix-en-Provence as late as 1954.[97] But in a recording made at the Salzburg Festival in 1937, Bruno Walter performs Mozart with a harpsichord.[98] Perhaps of even greater importance, when Stravinsky composed his neoclassical *The Rake's Progress* (first performed at the Teatro La Fenice of Venice on 11 September 1951), with its many evocations of Mozart, the instrument he chose for his *secco* recitatives was the harpsichord (even though the printed score indicates "or piano"). By the 1960s, as the early-music movement began to establish itself strongly, the harpsichord again became the instrument of choice for theaters. Not only had the public become more used to its sound, but more instruments were being constructed. It had become perfectly obvious that using a typical eighteenth-century instrument was appropriate.

The movement that led to the performance of Mozart's music with harpsichord-accompanied *secco* recitatives, however, also led to similar performances of Rossini's music. Despite the Pesaro example, that mode of performance still prevails in most opera houses today. Thus, while the widespread acceptance of the harpsichord in the modern theater owes much to those who have worked diligently to develop a historically informed performance practice and even to employ older instruments or modern recreations of them, this particular practice was pressed upon a repertory—nineteenth-century Italian opera—where the harpsichord had no historical justification whatsoever. Yet efforts to reclaim the more modern piano (or, rather, the fortepiano) for nineteenth-century Italian opera are thought of as "musicological." It is only one of the many paradoxes we face when thinking about instruments, old and new, in history and in the opera house.

13

FROM THE SCORE TO THE STAGE

Lyric Opera of Chicago celebrated its fiftieth anniversary in 2004–5. As a prelude to the year, John von Rhein, music critic of the *Chicago Tribune* since 1977, looked back over the seasons he had witnessed and came up with lists of five "top Lyric productions" and five "top Lyric misses." His favorites consisted largely of rarely performed operas that had been beautifully and sometimes controversially staged, including Britten's *Billy Budd,* Handel's *Alcina,* Janáček's *Jenufa,* Strauss's *Capriccio,* and Wagner's *Tannhäuser.* There was not one nineteenth-century Italian opera on the list. Among the "misses" were two world premieres, Penderecki's 1978 *Paradise Lost* (on which the company almost foundered) and Anthony Davis's well-meant but poorly realized *Amistad,* as well as three operas by Verdi: *Macbeth, Rigoletto,* and *Un ballo in maschera.*[1] About David Alden's 1999 *Macbeth,* von Rhein wrote: "Campy, creepy American Eurotrash that shed more light on the director's sensibility than it did on poor Verdi's." Christopher Alden's 2000 *Rigoletto* (the Aldens are twins) fared no better: "Director Alden's screed on male-chauvinist oppression of women, set in a 19th Century Italian men's club, certainly had dramatic ideas. Too bad they weren't Verdi's." Had von Rhein been a critic in New York, he would probably have added to his least-favorite list Francesca Zambello's much-criticized 1992 *Lucia di Lammermoor* at the Metropolitan Opera.[2] As far as I can tell, von Rhein has never shown a prejudice against Italian opera; nor, I suspect, would he say that most Verdi operas (let alone those of Rossini, Bellini, and Donizetti) have been badly cast by Lyric. No, the issue is a more basic one: how should a modern theater stage a nineteenth-century Italian opera?

An important part of the audience for Italian opera in the United States and Italy tends to be exceptionally conservative when it comes to the staging of works they know and love. There are others in attendance with an appetite for more adventurous productions, to be sure, of the kind readily accepted in stagings of Wagner or Handel operas, not to mention the plays of Shakespeare or Goldoni. But a hard-core constituency wants nothing to interfere with the pleasures—musical, dramaturgical, and emotional—it associates with the works, pleasures reinforced by listening to the same recordings over and over. For this constituency, stage directors are an unfortunate necessity, and should limit their interventions to directing traffic, as they largely did in the nineteenth century. The emotion and the drama are in the music, and anything that seeks to provide another perspective on the work is a distraction. There are many music critics and scholars who agree. Writing in the *New Yorker* during the Verdi centennial, Alex Ross suggested that Verdi's operas resist radical staging:

> The greatness of Verdi is a simple thing. A solitary man, he found a way of speaking to limitless crowds, and his method was to sink himself completely into his characters. He never composed music for music's sake; every note has a precise dramatic function. The most astounding scenes in his work are those in which all the voices come together in a visceral mass—like a human wave that could carry anything before it.[3]

Pierluigi Petrobelli draws a contrast with Wagner. The operas of the German composer allow for more directorial intervention because they are "based on myth and legend" and their "dramatic rhythm allows for an overtly abstract realization of the plots." Those of Verdi do not, because "the drama is based on the complex conflicts between individuals, and even more often on conflicts within the individuals. Here the risk—in superimposing on an already complex presentation of conflicts, other meanings, other interpretations—is greater; the result is often a blurred, if not obscure picture."[4]

Yet the staging of Italian opera continues to challenge directors, and no single approach is likely to provide consistently satisfactory results. In this chapter I will explore several of its facets.

STAGING VERDI'S CENTENNIAL

In February 1816, immediately after the premiere of *Il barbiere di Siviglia*, Gioachino Rossini wrote from Rome to his mother in Bologna:

> Last night my opera went on stage, and it was solemnly booed. What madness, what extraordinary things happen in this crazy country. Despite this, I can tell you that the music is very beautiful, and already there are bets

about what will happen tonight, at the second performance, when it will be possible to hear the music, which did not happen last night, since from the beginning until the end there was nothing but an immense buzzing that accompanied the spectacle.[5]

I wish I could report that audience behavior in Italy had improved since 1816, but I fear that the celebrations in 2001 for the hundredth anniversary of Verdi's death brought out the worst tendencies of some members of the public. That Riccardo Muti had to address the *loggionisti* at La Scala during a performance of *Il trovatore*, urging them not to turn the Verdi celebrations into a circus, seems astonishing to opera lovers elsewhere.[6] It is not that members of an audience do not have the right to express their opinions at the end of an evening, by applauding, remaining silent, or even booing. But it is hard to defend the Italian custom of trying to interrupt a performance by shouting insults at the artists.

The La Scala festivities were only the most prominent in a host of events honoring Italy's most beloved composer. Many were little more than routine homages, destined to be forgotten almost before they occurred; some had more substance. Certainly we have more access to information about Verdi than could even have been imagined a decade ago. From any computer linked to the internet it was possible in 2001 to access a Web site for the Italian national committee organized to supervise and coordinate centennial celebrations. There, at your fingertips, was a vast amount of biographical information, historical data about each opera, complete librettos, images, lists of current performances and casts from around the world, bibliography, trivia, even an online store to purchase Verdi trinkets and candies (the licorice was horrid, although the little containers were charmingly decorated with scenes from the operas).

The Verdi centennial also brought with it a host of exhibitions related to the composer and his works. The Istituto Nazionale di Studi Verdiani of Parma and its stalwart director, Pierluigi Petrobelli, trotted around the globe with a show dedicated to Verdian stagecraft and set design, which brought together early stage designs for Verdi's operas, including performances he himself supervised. The exhibit had its poignant side: in some cases these beautifully executed reproductions of set designs were prepared from originals lost in the devastating fire that had destroyed the Teatro La Fenice in Venice on 29 January 1996.

Seeing these set designs side by side teaches us how the nineteenth century approached certain theatrical problems. I wish set designers for Chicago Lyric

Opera's mostly splendid *Otello* in September 2001, for example, had had a chance to see these drawings. It might have helped them appreciate the importance of performing the second act of *Otello* on a split stage, with two playing areas fully visible to the audience: one where the bulk of the action takes place, the other where Desdemona receives the homage of the people of Cyprus.[7] Lyric's setting instead presented the scene in the context of a unit-set, a front playing area and five floors of balconies and doors. In the second act, then, Desdemona (Renée Fleming) and the chorus were on the ground floor, behind a barrier of carved wood, their movements invisible from anywhere in the theater. To ensure that *something* of Verdi's effect might emerge, the director had Ms. Fleming ascend to the second floor, from whence she threw coins that clattered noisily at the feet of her assembled admirers. The libretto says "ella porge una borsa ai marinai" (she hands a purse to the sailors), a more restrained and noble gesture.

How to stage the operas of Verdi was certainly at the heart of the controversies that surrounded the Verdi Festival in Parma, a year-long centennial celebration. The festival made many important choices. It used critical editions when they were available, putting in the hands of performers the best possible texts while leaving the artists ample freedom to interpret the written signs. New editions of *Un ballo in maschera* and *Macbeth* (in its 1865 revision) were presented, essentially complete. For the first time since 1853, Italian audiences could hear *La traviata* as Verdi originally conceived it, before his 1854 revisions produced the version normally performed today. The festival brought to Parma a wonderful new orchestra and chorus. Rather than join the general lament about the lack of fine Verdi singers, it sought to develop new talent and use the best of these young voices in its productions.

Probably most controversial, however, was the festival's decision to employ important stage directors from France, Russia, and Germany, the kind of directors who believed in directorial invention, so-called *Regietheater,* precisely the kind of directors to whom Alex Ross objected. While there are many who share Ross's view, I am uncomfortable with such absolutism. During the course of the Verdi year I saw productions ranging from a highly conservative *La traviata,* to a *Macbeth* that took place in what often appeared to be an insane asylum, to the by-now-legendary *Un ballo in maschera* directed by Calixto Bieto, moved to Franco's Spain, with the conspirators in its opening scene sitting on toilets, like so many mobsters in a *Godfather* movie. Was any of these productions an "ideal" setting for an opera? No. I have stopped believing that the concept has much meaning.

My impression of *Rigoletto* is determined by all the productions I have seen, all the recordings I have heard, all the Verdi letters I have examined, all the musical sources I have studied, all the books I have read. Almost every time I see another *Rigoletto* there is something new to add to that impression. Ross would leave us no choice but to hate Jonathan Miller's infamous English National Opera *Rigoletto* set in Little Italy, with "La donna è mobile" emerging from a jukebox. And what would he have said about Bruce Beresford's Hollywood setting for Los Angeles Opera in 2000, mentioned in chapter 1, where "Duke" is a film producer and the initial party takes place around his swimming pool in southern California, after Duke (during the instrumental prologue) has screened a preview of his new film, *Vendetta.*

At the Parma Verdi Festival, Henning Brockhaus directed a *Rigoletto* that was highly sexualized in both its first and last acts. But the greatest scorn of the Parmese *loggionisti* was reserved for the scene in Rigoletto's house. It took place in Gilda's bedroom, a confined space high above stage level. Gilda's bed was a crib with adjustable sides, and she carried a teddy bear. Was this literalization of how Rigoletto had infantalized his daughter *necessary?* Did Verdi specify it? The answer is obviously no to both questions. And yet Patrizia Cioffi was eerily effective in this setting, her almost childlike singing of "Caro nome" frightening in its doomed innocence. Those images will haunt me, even when I am watching a more traditional production.

The anger of the Parma *loggionisti* reached its greatest intensity several months later, when they were faced with Dominique Pitoiset's staging of *Macbeth.* The reaction was all the more outrageous because this was Pitoiset's second production in Parma that year. The first, an inventive staging of Shakespeare's *The Tempest* at the Teatro Farnese, was received with prolonged applause. Indeed, while Pitoiset's *Macbeth* was being seen at the Verdi Festival, across town three Shakespearean plays were being presented on alternate nights in brilliant, outrageously radical productions by the Lithuanian director Eimuntas Nikrosius, while rapt theatergoers remained glued to their seats for four to five hours before exploding in standing ovations.

Pitoiset's *Macbeth* was tame in comparison. Indeed, despite his imaginative use of the stage and the strange and unsettling images that dominated much of the action, Pitoiset was deeply respectful of musical values. Never was a character asked to move unnecessarily while singing; never were members of an ensemble spread out so that they could not hear one another and watch the conductor; never did the chorus lose its compactness of sound. While I did not find Pitoiset's work everywhere convincing, I was frequently transfixed by his images. Nowhere was this more true than at the beginning of the third act, where the witches prepare for their second encounter with Macbeth. In both the 1847 and the 1865 versions of *Macbeth,* the third act opens with a chorus for the witches, the musical equivalent of the Shakespearian "Double, double, toil and trouble, / Fire burn and cauldron bubble." In 1847, Macbeth entered immediately thereafter, and the scene continued with the three apparitions. In 1865, writing for a Parisian audience (even though all of Verdi's revisions were made exclusively in Italian), the composer inserted a new ballet in three sections, just before Macbeth's entrance. During this ballet, whose music is anything but typical Parisian fare, Hecate descends among the witches. More in dramatic pantomime than in anything resembling classical ballet, she instructs the witches how they should behave during their forthcoming encounter with Macbeth.

Verdi was very much concerned about how to present "fantastic" images in his opera, and he discussed the problem at length in letters written both in 1847 and in 1865, often invoking scenic effects from the London stage. So, on the subject of the appearance of Banquo's ghost during the finale to the second act, he wrote to the Florentine impresario on 22 December 1846:

> Note that Banquo's ghost must make his entrance from underground; it must be the same actor that played Banquo in Act I. He must be wearing an ashen veil, but quite thin and fine, and just barely visible; and Banquo must have ruffled hair and various wounds visible on his neck.
>
> I've gotten all of these ideas from London, where this tragedy has been produced continually for over 200 years.[8]

Verdi also invoked practices of the Parisian *boulevard* theaters: "magic lanterns" and the "fantasmagoria" were very much on his mind.[9]

The Parma production in autumn 2001 of the 1865 *Macbeth* was anything but traditional. The witches in the third act were clothed all in black, in ankle-length dresses with ruffs on the sleeves and around the hem. Each of them carried a black purse. During the chorus in which "aerial spirits" are supposed to descend in order to bolster Macbeth's flagging courage, they moved those purses back and forth rhythmically in a gesture that was at once mesmerizing and absurd, drawing guffaws and obscene comments from the *loggione.* But those comments were nothing compared to the ruckus that accompanied the ballet, where these Mary-Poppins-like creatures gathered around what appeared to be a big soup kettle at the beginning of the scene. After their initial chorus they sat down on neat rows of chairs, and soon began to watch a powerfully disturbing movie, which employed scenes from the second World War, bombs being dropped from low-flying aircraft, flame-throwers and tanks, goose-stepping troops, desperate lines of refugees. All of this was timed with Verdi's ballet score in a way that seemed almost choreographed, rhythms of the music and rhythms of the visual images in uncanny synchronization.

The *loggione* was furious. "If we wanted a movie, we'd have gone to the movies," someone screamed. "Shame" shouted others. "And you call *this* a Verdi festival" exclaimed still another. Most significant was the cry, "What does this have to do with *Macbeth?*" Other patrons responded to these provocations: "Who's paying you?" they yelled back. "If you don't like it, go home," a man sitting in front of me boomed. Evelino Pidò and his musicians, dancers, singers, and extras continued about their business, although the noise sometimes made it impossible to hear any music.

"What does this have to do with *Macbeth?*" Well, how should one stage this scene? With nineteenth-century dancers in tutus assuming classical ballet poses? Should one summarily cut the entire ballet, as do most opera houses?[10] Parma's solution began with stylized movements, as the dancers drank some of the potion from the cauldron / soup kettle, threw off their reserve (and some of their clothes), and fell into a disturbed sleep, during which the movie was shown. From the end of the first dance and throughout the second, images of war were projected, while the dancers slept. What is *Macbeth* about? Well, it is certainly about war. It is certainly about refugees. The fourth and last act, after all, opens with one of Verdi's most distinguished choruses, added in 1865, Scottish refugees singing "Patria oppressa."[11] During this chorus and the ensuing aria for Macduff, the characters invoke the murders, executions, and casualties inflicted by Macbeth's soldiers. That the witches, who are about to predict the future, should be watching these cinematic images of war is hardly alien to the spirit of the opera.

This whole cinematic scene of death and destruction was prepared *before* the events in the United States of 11 September 2001. Seeing it in that context was chilling. Even more chilling for me and many others in the audience was the news, received just forty-five minutes before the curtain was raised on this production of *Macbeth* on 7 October, that the American bombing of Afghanistan had begun. Among the many other images from this staging that will remain with me was one from the very end, during the victory hymn. As those celebrations continued, a group of three—a father, mother, and child—gathered around the kind of large, floor-standing radio typical of the 1930s and 1940s, as if following the events of the war. And at the very end, as the victorious soldiers of Macduff and Malcolm, the Bards, and the Scottish people concluded their hymn, the child picked up a knife, walked to center stage and held it aloft, blade in the air, a new generation and a renewed cycle of violence. The gesture was in stark contrast to the victory hymn that filled the theater.

Was this an ideal *Macbeth?* Of course not. There were many aspects of the staging that I did not like and others that I did not understand. Yet it was a *Macbeth* both musically splendid and dramaturgically bracing. Whose *Macbeth* was it? It was Verdi's *Macbeth,* filtered through a modern dramaturgical sensibility, just as every note of music we hear in the theater or on recordings is filtered through a modern musical sensibility. It is basically dishonest to pretend that a performance or a staging of an opera can be anything else. Still, one needs to acknowledge that neither Verdi nor any other nineteenth-century Italian composer could have imagined the emergence during the twentieth century of interventionist stage directors and so-called "radical" stagings. Resistance to this approach has been fierce, particularly in the United States and Italy. But what should the relationship of a modern staging of an Italian opera be to historical models? Are there limits to directorial intervention that it is imprudent to cross? Is there a point at which it no longer is meaningful to refer to a performance of "Verdi's *Macbeth,*" even if the words and music of the score are being respected?

NINETEENTH-CENTURY STAGING AND SET DESIGN

At the principal scholarly conference in honor of the Verdi centennial, which took place in Parma, New York, and New Haven early in 2001, I talked about a number of the issues to which this book is dedicated, drawing examples from the new critical edition of *Un ballo in maschera,* which was about to have its first performance under the direction of Valéry Gergiev.[12] After my reflections on the way we approached modifications in the libretto due to censorship, accommodated Verdi's *banda sul palco* and offstage string orchestra in the final scene, and handled several "traditional" abuses stemming from practices of singers and choral directors that make a mockery of Verdi's score,[13] a passionate music lover spoke up: "That's all well and good, and I'm sure scholars are doing the best they can, but it hardly matters: Verdi's operas are being destroyed by ridiculous stagings." It came as no surprise that his primary example was the Bieto *Ballo,* which he had seen in Barcelona. He could barely contain his anger at the toilets in the first scene, Ulrica's den as a brothel in the second, homosexual rape and murder at the beginning of the second act, and the sadistic treatment of Oscar by Samuel and Tom in the third-act quintet (the head of the page was forcibly held underwater when he/she wasn't actually singing). And he concluded: "Why don't you scholars forbid theaters from using your work, which seeks to serve Verdi's art, when they betray him in such an outrageous manner?"

I tried to explain that even if all the scholars responsible for the critical edition of Verdi's operas agreed that it was our collective responsibility to censor the use theaters made of our editions (and it seems unlikely that any such agreement could be forged), it would be an impossible task. Not even Verdi, despite strong efforts, could stop theaters from doing as they liked with his operas. As early as 20 May 1847 the composer asked his Milanese editor, Giovanni Ricordi, to insert into rental contracts with theaters a clause forbidding them to make "any changes in the score, any mutilation, to lower or to raise the key," and the like, with punitive financial consequences for failing to live up to these obligations.[14] As far as we can tell, however, theaters signed the contracts and then proceeded to do exactly as they wished, without any serious interference from Milan.

It is reasonable to ask, however, whether critical editions of an opera might not do more to provide information about the original staging of an opera. Indeed, editions of the operas of Rossini, Donizetti, and Verdi, just like those of Mozart and Berlioz, have been criticized because they publish the *score* of an opera, its text and music in all known versions, but only those stage directions and scenic indications provided in the composer's autograph manuscript and printed or manuscript versions of the libretto, or those discussed by the composer and librettist in their letters. Rarely do they provide an account of the sometimes massive documentation that survives concerning staging, scenography, production books, and costume designs; nor do they reproduce or edit such material.[15] By doing so, these editions explicitly separate into constitutent parts something that was born as a unity of music, text, staging, and visual design. This separation of music and text from its realization onstage has often been justified on a purely practical level. Those producing critical editions of operas are largely musicians and musicologists, not experts in the history of art and theater. The practical problems of coordinating the work of scholars in diverse fields are daunting for an enterprise as poorly supported financially as the critical editing of opera. It takes years to produce the volumes dedicated only to the music and text of an opera; to add the visual and scenic dimension would multiply the problems. Scholars with specific knowledge of staging, however, are encouraged to step in: Casa Ricordi has published several volumes in a series of *Disposizioni sceniche* (production books) for Italian operas from the second half of the nineteenth century, filled with illustrations, instructions for blocking the movements of the singers and chorus, and reflections on staging and sets.[16] The Fondazione Rossini has done similar work.[17]

Despite Wagnerian rhetoric, the idea of opera as *Gesamtkunstwerk*, a coordination and integration of all the arts, was hardly invented by the German master, but the relative importance of the various elements that constitute an opera (and related musical-theatrical forms) has changed significantly over time. There are whole repertories whose meaning is inextricably tied to their original physical productions: the theatrical constructions of Inigo Jones for English masques at the turn of the seventeenth century; the stage machinery introduced into the Italian Baroque theater by masters of illusion such as Vincenzo Torelli; the scenic wonders arranged by Giovanni Niccolò Servandoni for French classical opera, including the onstage volcanic eruptions that attracted most of the public's attention when Jean-Philippe Rameau produced *Les Indes galantes* at the Paris Opéra in 1735. We cannot contemplate reviving works born under such circumstances without acknowledging the physical marvels of the original productions. That does not mean that a modern effort to stage a Ben Jonson masque, an opera by Cesti, or a French *opéra-ballet* must reproduce the stage designs and stagecraft of Jones, Torelli, or Servendoni, but neither can their work be dismissed as tangential to the fundamental aesthetic meaning of the work.

However much attention Verdi may have lavished on visual detail in his operas, no one studying or performing Italian opera has ever suggested that nineteenth-century staging and set design should dominate our view of the aesthetic character of the operas of Rossini, Bellini, Donizetti, or Verdi. Indeed, thirty years ago there was little knowledge of, or interest in, the surviving documentation. Despite occasional incursions and provocations from directors such as Luchino Visconti, Giorgio Strehler, or Luca Ronconi, most performances of the basic Italian repertory—particularly in Italy itself—were safe and predictable. They told the story (sometimes well, sometimes poorly), and they presented it in recognizable, basically naturalistic settings. Just as musicians lived under the illusion that the scores from which they were performing had roots in a continuous tradition that transmitted accurate and authentic texts, so too did audiences believe that the essential conventions of staging and set design had been passed down from generation to generation. Often they had been, and modifications were introduced within a carefully circumscribed framework, dependent on the histrionic abilities of a particular singer (like Maria Callas). This attitude toward staging remains largely pervasive today in Italy, and continues to influence performances of this repertory in other places, especially the United States. The ire of the Parma *loggione* during the 2001 Verdi Festival simply translated this conviction into boorish misbehavior.

It should come as no surprise that Tom Sutcliffe, in *Believing in Opera*, his impressive and passionate survey of contemporary operatic staging, has almost nothing to say about the repertory I'm addressing in this book. Indeed, directors widely considered to have done some of the most important work in Italy over the past thirty years—Luca Ronconi, Pier Luigi Pizzi, or the late Jean-Pierre Ponnelle—rate no more than a passing, often scornful, reference. For the staging of operas by Bellini and Donizetti in our time, whether in Italy or anywhere else, the only substantive comment made by Sutcliffe in 464 pages is: "[Robert Carsen's] approach to Bellini's *La straniera* for Wexford in 1987 was darkly stormy and romantic with fervent but vital acting and singing from its young stars."[18] Rossini does not fare much better. Of the operas of Verdi through the early 1860s, two works escape the general neglect, works that have attracted particular interest among bolder directors and designers either for their intensity (*Rigoletto*) or their unusual and ambiguous tone (*Un ballo in maschera*). For *La traviata,* however, the only things Sutcliffe finds noteworthy are that Jonathan Miller's staging for Kent Opera in the early 1980s "had a sense of Victorian photographs about it" and that Richard Eyre's *Traviata* at Covent Garden in 1994 "was conservative" and a "wasted opportunit[y]."[19]

Perhaps the gulf between those who want "traditional" stagings and those who favor "radical" ones can never be negotiated, and yet some historical knowledge and some consideration of nineteenth-century staging and stagecraft as it pertains to Italian opera can provide important points of departure. In fact, while textual scholars were discovering the musical sources for Italian opera, scholars of theater history were exploring surviving evidence for the same repertory. Thanks to their efforts we now know an enormous amount about the look and feel of the original stagings. As James Hepokoski expressed it in 1995, "Thirty years ago, the following would have been an astonishing claim: should we wish to do so, we could reconstruct the original costumes, sets, and staging of Verdi's operas from 1855 (*Les Vêpres siciliennes*) to 1887 (*Otello*)."[20] Whether such a reconstruction is also desirable, of course, is quite a different matter. Before we tackle that question, let us consider the surviving evidence, which is still unknown to most opera lovers: the *livrets de mise en scène* in France, the *disposizioni sceniche* in Italy, and stage and costume design in both countries.

Staging Manuals (*Livrets de Mise en Scène*) in France

The desire to register in written form the details of an operatic staging emerged at a particular historical moment in the nineteenth century. Not that earlier examples are altogether lacking, but descriptions and images of Renaissance entertainments in France or the spectacular stage effects of Baroque opera were intended primarily to celebrate the court or aristocratic society under whose auspices the works were produced. The pictures are meant to astonish and delight, not to serve as the basis for reproducing the effects in later productions.[21] But several new factors contributed to the emergence of written production books in the early nineteenth century: there was a sizable group of public theaters producing operas and eager for material, both new and old; the notion of a stable repertory began to emerge, operas that would be performed again and again in theaters throughout a country or even abroad; staging became more complex, so that written instructions simplified the task of those responsible for producing a work by giving them access to earlier approaches.

That staging manuals, *livrets de mise en scène,* first established themselves in France is not surprising.[22] Not only was Paris a great center of opera, featuring several major opera houses, but a host of smaller theaters with permanent or seasonal opera companies had emerged around the country during the latter part of the eighteenth century in cities such as Lyons, Bordeaux, Marseilles, Strasbourg, or Nantes, as well as Francophone centers such as Brussels. This development was given further impetus under Napoleon, who sought to regulate cultural activities throughout his dominions, and later still under the Restoration. Most new operas were produced first in the capital, and regional houses were primarily interested in reproducing (albeit in a less sumptuous fashion) recent Parisian successes. The new home of the Opéra, the Salle Le Peletier, which opened in 1821, was to be the primary opera house in Paris until its destruction by fire in 1873, two years before the inauguration of the Palais Garnier. Particularly well equipped, the Peletier permitted a wealth of scenic effects, incoporating innovative staging techniques from the popular *boulevard* theaters and employing the latest technology. The formation of a "Comité de mise en scène" at the Opéra in 1827, along with the appointment of Jacques Solomé as *directeur de la scène* and Pierre Cicéri as *peintre en chef,* resulted in a more welcoming attitude toward innovation and greater complexity in staging. Finally, with the extraordinary popularity of the music of Rossini in Paris during the 1820s and the significance of his presence at the Peletier between

1826 and 1829, which stimulated a strong desire to present Rossini's operas in other cities, the belief in a reproducible repertory gained further strength.

The manuals were also the product of new approaches to the dramaturgical construction of French operas. By the 1820s, opera librettos tended to incorporate a larger number of elaborate stage directions, indicating the increased importance of dramatic action throughout each work. The construction of these librettos was dependent upon ever more complex arrangements of the painted backdrops used for the settings and solid pieces of scenery, some purely decorative (the Italians called them *stabili*), some accommodating actors (*praticabili*). Pierre-Luc-Charles Cicéri, the principal French set painter, actually traveled to Switzerland in order to produce accurate backdrops of Swiss scenes for *Guillaume Tell,* and his sets were described in the staging manual.[23] As illumination with gas became the norm, it was possible to regulate lighting in ways unthinkable with the candles used in the eighteenth century; that too was noted. Choral masses were required to move more freely on the stage, and the manuals suggested how to avoid symmetries in the placement of the chorus and how to differentiate members of the ensemble. A highly formal style of acting among the principals gave way to one that sought more natural, although still relatively emphatic, movements, with carefully developed facial expressions and gestures.[24] As Elizabeth Bartlet points out, introducing her edition of the Solomé *mise en scène* of *Guillaume Tell* (1829),

> Soloists and chorus now needed to sing and act at the same time, and not to move only during instrumental passages. The same "modern" dynamic is apparent even more in the ensemble scenes at the end of the first and third acts, with their asymmetrical arrangements. [...] every character on stage is now asked to participate in the action with reactions and movements.[25]

Similar comments could be made about the elaborate ensemble scenes in Auber's 1828 *La Muette de Portici,* not to mention the technical skill required to stage the final catastrophe and (again) an exploding volcano. Everything is explained in detail in the printed *livret de mise en scène.*[26] If you wanted to stage the opera in Brussels in 1830 (and set off a revolution), here was a manual that described what was done in Paris.

It was long assumed that these French *livrets* were intended to guarantee a uniform staging over time (in Paris) and space (in smaller theaters throughout France and Belgium). As H. Robert Cohen contends,

> Staging in Paris and the French provinces throughout the nineteenth century and well into the twentieth was an art of preservation rather than

creation. *Régisseurs* strove to conserve, to the extent possible, the original *mise en scène* of an opera's premiere as transcribed in the production book. Staging, in a word, was *not* intended to be altered.[27]

Hence, the argument runs, the elaborate descriptions of movements, gestures, stage placement, costumes, and set designs. Hence the multiple copies existing in Parisian libraries, some printed, some in manuscript, prepared over the course of the nineteenth century and into the twentieth for operas that remained in the repertory. In the collection of the Bibliothèque de l'Association de la Régie Théâtrale alone, Cohen and Gigou found eight separate sources for *Guillaume Tell* and ten for Halévy's *La Juive.*

This theory of uniformity seemed to be supported by a well-known letter from Scribe to Louis Palianti, who was responsible for the series "Collection de mises en scènes de grands opéras et d'opéras-comiques," which began publication in 1837 and was ultimately "to encompass more than two hundred titles."[28] Scribe's letter, which Palianti used as a testimonial for his series, was written on 2 December 1849:

> I believe that your work is done with such care and intelligence, that it makes clear and apparent the thought of the author, that it stands in for him in rehearsals, that it should enormously help the fortunes of dramatic works in the provinces and abroad, and that its usefulness is indubitable. All that remains to be desired, now, is your expansion of the publication to include a much larger number of *mises en scènes;* [this publication] should be found not only in the libraries of provincial theaters, but also in our national archives. That would make it impossible to forget fine old traditions, and it is to be regretted that such a work was not started years ago.[29]

Recently, though, Arnold Jacobshagen has challenged this orthodoxy. By looking closely at various production books for Auber's *Fra Diavolo,* books prepared at various points during the course of the nineteenth century, Jacobshagen has demonstrated that the copies are quite different one from the other. While sets and costumes remained relatively constant, "the positions, movements, and dramatic actions of the performers did change over time." Thus, the *livrets de mise en scène* "functioned primarily to document the current state of a production, in order to orientate other theaters toward Paris. This does not mean that later Parisian productions were obliged to replicate earlier ones. The *livrets de mise en scène* were intended as documents for the present rather than the future."[30] The practical significance of these sources, in short, continues to be contested, and interpreting their instructions remains a challenge.

Staging Manuals (*Disposizioni Sceniche*) in Italy

It was through Giuseppe Verdi's contact with Paris that the idea of publishing staging manuals passed from France to Italy. During the first half of the nineteenth century, staging for the premiere performances of an opera in Italy was generally the responsibility of the librettist, who worked in conjunction with the composer. For later revivals, theaters turned instead to their resident poet, sometimes referred to as *direttore della scena* or *direttore degli spettacoli*.[31] It is not that staging and dramatic interpretation were considered secondary, but the public's attention focused largely on the performance by an individual singer. Giuditta Pasta, famed as Tancredi, Medea, and Norma, was praised as much for her dramatic interpretations as for her voice. This statement is taken from a review of her performances at the Théâtre Italien of Paris, beginning on 14 January 1823, in Mayr's *Medea in Corinto*:

> What words could I use to speak of the inspiration that Signora Pasta reveals with her voice and of those aspects of sublime or unusual passions she brings to life before our eyes? Sublime secrets, that surpass the limits of poetry and everything that the chisel of Canova or the brushes of Correggio can reveal of the depths of the human heart. Who, without shuddering, can think of the moment when Medea draws her children to her, while her hand already grasps the dagger, then pushes them away, as if struck by remorse? These are touches of an indescribable delicacy, that would drive even the greatest writer, I believe, to despair.[32]

In such an environment, stage directors—men like Francesco Maria Piave in Venice, Salvadore Cammarano in Naples, Calisto Bassi in Milan, most of them theatrical poets—were primarily concerned with making sure that the action moved along smoothly, entrances and exits were properly executed, and the indications of the libretto were followed.[33] Invention and innovation in staging was the furthest thing from their mind. It was also significant that in Italy there was no single center, like Paris, from which all truth flowed, but many centers, each of which believed in the validity and worth of its own theaters and its own institutions.

Rarely was the work of these stage directors documented in writing, but John Black has found a fascinating document in the library of the Naples Conservatory that gives us some insight into how they plied their craft.[34] It is the draft of a set of notes that Cammarano prepared for an unnamed colleague in another city, explaining how *Lucia di Lammermoor* (of which Cammarano himself wrote the libretto) was staged in Naples at the Teatro San

Carlo, 26 September 1835. There is relatively little detail. For the entire first scene of the opera, for example, during which we learn of the feud between the family of Enrico, brother of Lucia, and that of her beloved Edgardo, Cammarano writes only, "The huntsmen are scattered in several groups. Normanno arrives from the right (that is, the actor's right or left). The huntsmen leave from the opposite side. Enrico and Raimondo enter from the right. The huntsmen return from the left. At the end of the cavatina, everybody goes out from the right."[35] Occasionally he provides more detailed instructions for the movement of the chorus. When in the finale of the second act Edgardo arrives, interrupting the signing of the marriage contract, Cammarano indicates that the chorus must move toward the door, then draw back. "The men place their hats [which they must have been holding in their right hands] on their heads, then let their right hands grasp the hilts of their swords, but they hold back when they see Lucia fall, fainting, into a chair." He then adds something more interesting: "Make sure that the actions of the chorus are very animated. I recommend that Edgardo should not pick up his hat and cloak, it being unlikely that he would think of doing so in a moment of such desperation. For the next act, the actor will collect them from Alisa and the others." Still, none of this approaches the level of detail found in contemporaneous *livrets de mise en scène* in Paris.[36]

Presumably Verdi became aware of what a French *livret de mise en scène* was like in 1847, when he staged *Jérusalem* at the Paris Opéra.[37] Yet the composer does not appear to have commented on the practice, perhaps because he did not expect that *Jérusalem,* a revision of his popular *I Lombardi alla prima crociata,* was destined to have a significant performance history in Italy.[38] The situation was very different when Verdi wrote his first original opera for France, *Les Vêpres siciliennes,* which had its premiere at the Opéra on 13 June 1855. Now he had every interest in helping to ensure that this opera would be successful in Italy, and, as we saw in chapter 11, he personally supervised the Italian translation as *Giovanna de Guzman,* sending a score to Ricordi with the new Italian text entered in his own hand on 6 July 1855.

While no documentary evidence has been produced that Verdi also sent to his publisher a copy (whether manuscript or printed) of the *livret de mise en scène* for *Les Vêpres siciliennes* or wrote to Ricordi about the practice of publishing such volumes, an entry in the company's ledgers dated "10/1855" indicates that they were working on an Italian edition, issued in 1856 as *"Disposizione scenica* for the opera *Giovanna de Guzman* by Maestro Cav. Giuseppe Verdi, official of the Legion of Honor, compiled and regulated according to the *mise en scène* of the Imperial theater of the Opéra of Paris."[39] In a letter to Piave of 28 November 1855, however, Verdi made it clear that he believed firmly in the French practice of publishing and using such production books: "I am sending you under separate cover the description of the *mise en scène* of *Vespri*. It is beautiful, and by reading the pamphlet with care even a child could stage the opera well. If the *Vespri* are changed into *Guzman*, you only need to change the costumes. But the *mise en scène* should stay the same."[40] Nor did the composer's enthusiasm for the practice wane. Although no production books seem to have been published for either of the operas Verdi prepared in 1857 (the original version of *Simon Boccanegra* and *Aroldo*, a revision of *Stiffelio*), Ricordi issued a *disposizione scenica* for *Un ballo in maschera* on the occasion of its first performance at the Teatro Apollo of Rome on 17 February 1859, prepared by the librettist and by the *direttore di scena* associated with the theater, Giuseppe Cencetti.[41] From that moment until the end of Verdi's creative life, an Italian *disposizione scenica* was published for most of his new operas and major revisions, not to mention important operas by his contemporaries, including Luigi Ricci's *Il diavolo a quattro*, Arrigo Boito's *Mefistofele*, Amilcare Ponchielli's *I Lituani*, "Giulio" Massenet's *Il Re di Lahore* and *Erodiade*, and Giacomo Puccini's *Manon Lescaut* (the manual for which was published in 1893).[42]

The *disposizione scenica* for *Un ballo in maschera* is basically a practical document. It describes properties and costumes, mentions pieces of scenery (tables, fireplaces) that need to be moved into place, and lays out the position of the painted backdrops, specifying which scenes use the entire stage ("scene lunghe," deep scenes) and which only part of the stage ("scene a mezzo teatro," scenes on half the stage; or "scene corte," shallow scenes, or even "cortissime," very shallow). The instructions for the entrances, exits, and movements of the characters are explicit, and occasionally the *disposizione scenica* offers considerably more detail than the stage directions found either in Verdi's autograph manuscript or in the printed libretto. In the scene immediately after Renato stabs Riccardo, the chorus sings a furious "Ah! morte... infamia sul traditor" (Ah! death... infamy for the traitor), after which the small string orchestra in the wings—unaware of what has happened—continues to play as Riccardo tells the chorus to free Renato. The only stage direction is for Riccardo: "he takes out the dispatch [in which he has agreed to send Renato and Amelia away from the court], and signals Renato to approach." Riccardo then sings the Andante, "Ella è pura, in braccio a morte, te lo giuro, Iddio m'ascolta" (She is pure, in the arms of death

I swear it, with God as my witness). The *disposizione scenica* gives further information:

> Soon, their anger surpassing all other sentiments, everyone cries out: *Morte, abbominio* [Death, abomination], etc. At the last repetition of these words, two officials, members of the chorus, seize Renato to drag him to his deserved punisment, but at the words of Riccardo: *No, no... lasciatelo* [No, no... leave him alone], etc., the guilty one is set free. Then Riccardo signals Renato to approach him. Oscar immediately makes everyone else step back, while the agitated Renato draws near to the dying man; who, drawing the dispatch from his breast pocket, tells him: *Ella è pura* [She is pure], etc. The offstage music suddenly comes to an end, and other dancers and extras soon appear on stage, signaling that in the adjacent rooms, once the dreadful notice of the crime arrived, the dancing stopped.

All of this is implicit in Verdi's score, although many details throughout the *disposizione scenica* are useful in filling out the sparse stage directions.[43]

As the century went on, the *disposizioni sceniche* grew longer and more elaborate. The book for the 1858 *Un ballo in maschera* fills 38 pages; those for Boito's *Mefistofele* (published in 1877), the 1881 revision of *Simon Boccanegra*, and the 1887 *Otello*, 109, 58, and 111 pages, respectively. All three were prepared by Giulio Ricordi on the basis of stagings at Milan's Teatro alla Scala. In the *disposizione scenica* for *Otello*, the level of detail is staggering, indicating each movement during a dialogue, commenting on motivation, tone, and facial expression. So, for example, the instructions for the painful duet between Otello and Desdemona in the third act, "Dio ti giocondi, o sposo," are printed on more than four crammed pages (58–62). When the disbelieving Desdemona, trying to make light of Otello's remarks about the handkerchief, says, "Tu di me ti fai gioco, / Storni così l'inchiesta di Cassio; astuzia è questa / Del tuo pensier" (You are making fun of me in order to turn away my question about Cassio; that shows the cleverness of your thinking), there is no stage direction in either the libretto or musical score. The *disposizione scenica*, using two diagrams, provides more elaborate detail:

> To her, there is no reason for Otello's tremendous rage; it is not justified... a smile breaks on Desdemona's lips, and, almost playfully, she crosses to the left, in front of Otello, saying: *Tu di me ti fai gioco;* Otello stands still for a moment, amazed, staring at her. Desdemona turns to him and, continuing as above, says to him: *Astuzia è questa del tuo pensier.* (Here the actress has an opportunity to play a good scene of contrast: but

be careful, while bringing out this contrast between fear, first, and later, charming cunning, not to exaggerate it, thus bordering on the comic!)[44]

This is a different level of interpretation, an accumulation of details that provides a more intrusive level of instruction than we have witnessed before. Furthermore, the volume announces itself from the beginning as seeking an almost tyrannical control over future productions (recall Verdi's own "the *mise en scène* should stay the same" for *Giovanni de Guzman*). In Giulio Ricordi's words:

> It is *absolutely* necessary for the artists to study precisely the *messa in scena* and to conform to it: just as Directors and Impresarios should not permit any changes in the costumes: these were carefully studied and copied from pictures of the period and there is no reason why they should be modified according to the whim of this or that artist.[45]

The desire to consider the staging and visual appearance as integral to the opera could not be clearer. As Hepokoski has pointed out, of course, "Ricordi himself owned the commerical rights to these things: his urgings were anything but disinterested"; others have expressed similar cautions concerning the motivation behind the publication of the *disposizioni sceniche*.[46] Nonetheless, there can be little doubt that Verdi was enthusiastic about these manuals and that they provide us with a unique window into the original production of several of the most significant new operas performed in Italy between the mid-1850s and the early 1890s. The question is, what should stage directors and performers *do* with all this information?

Sets and Costumes

With the opening of the Salle Le Peletier in Paris in 1821, ever greater attention was paid to settings. Painted canvas backdrops, together with painted flats that could be brought in from the wings, dominated operatic design throughout the first two-thirds of the nineteenth century, but during the 1820s many of these scenic elements remained "generic" prison scenes, castles, country houses, or mountainous regions: the same elements could reappear with modifications from one opera to the next.[47] With the renovation of the repertory toward the end of the decade, with the four Rossini French works for the Opéra and Auber's *La Muette de Portici,* there was a much greater effort to introduce original designs. By the 1830s and 1840s, the amazing physical productions at the Paris Opéra, with their rich and elaborate settings, were frequently mentioned by travelers. Donizetti's remarks on the 1835 production of Halévy's *La Juive* are well known:

> I saw *La Juive* at the grand Opéra... and I say "saw" because there was no pleasing music [*musica popolare*]. Illusion reaches its highest point... You would swear that it was all real. Real silver and almost real cardinals. Armory of the King real, military costumes, chain mail, lances etc. real; and those that were false were copied from real ones and cost 1500 francs apiece, the chain mail of the extras. Too much reality... the last scene too horrible and more horrible for the illusion.
>
> At Constance! A Hebrew woman, for having a relationship with a Christian, is thrown together with her father into a cauldron of boiling oil. Before arriving at that point one passes through a thousand stupidities, but everything is rich and everything is magnificent, and so you let it all pass.[48]

An extensive collection of drawings, prints, and miniature models for sets, as well as costume designs, is housed at the Bibliothèque de l'Opéra, fully documenting Parisian practice. Thanks to the French illustrated press, furthermore, which followed closely the lyric theaters, reproductions of stage sets and costumes from Paris circulated all over Europe.[49] The search for historical accuracy and "local color" was particularly important. That the set designer Cicéri prepared for *Guillaume Tell* by traveling to Switzerland, as we have seen, reflects this tendency.

Italian composers from Rossini through Verdi also paid close attention to set design, and their letters reflect this involvement. The concerted effort of a group of Italian scholars, including Mercedes Viale Ferrero, Elena Povoledo, Maria Ida Biggi, and Olga Jesurum, has transformed our understanding of the surviving materials over the past twenty years. Some sources have long been known, especially the hand-colored engravings and lithographs of the painted backdrops prepared by Alessandro Sanquirico, principal scenic designer for La Scala from 1817 through his retirement in 1832. These images, classical in conception and design but gradually developing that specificity of subject matter, emotional involvement, and intense color that would characterize Romantic scene painting, circulated widely and helped suggest models for other theaters to emulate.[50] They range in style from the cool, perfectly symmetrical courtroom hall in which Ninetta, the serving girl accused of household theft, is condemned to death in Rossini's *La gazza ladra* (colored in blues and grays), first performed at La Scala on 31 May 1817, to the spectacular exploding Vesuvius (yet another volcano) in Sanquirico's set for the concluding scene of Pacini's *L'ultimo giorno di Pompei*. The premiere of this opera was in Naples at the Teatro San Carlo on 19 November 1825, but it was revived at La Scala—using Sanquirico's sets—on 16 August 1827, with red fire and smoke filling the picture and bodies scattered hither and yon.[51] Not that "generic" sets ceased to play a role in Italian opera. According to the composer himself, Verdi's *Nabucco* at La Scala in 1842 was still performed, at least in part, with recycled sets.[52] But the tendency in Italy was for the set designer to produce original drawings for each new opera.

At the Bibliothèque de l'Opéra in Paris, for example, there exist some two hundred sketches by Giuseppe Borsato, the set painter responsible for scenography at the Teatro La Fenice of Venice during Rossini's active career there (from the 1813 *Tancredi* through the 1823 *Semiramide*). Contemporary reviews refer constantly—and quite correctly—to the high quality of his work. After the premiere of *Tancredi,* the *Giornale dipartimentale dell'Adriatico* declared on 9 February 1813 that "all praise would be inadequate to the magnificence, the truth, the magic of the decorations by the famous Sig. Giuseppe Borsato [...], such is the refinement of his work, the spatial distribution, the exquisite colors with which his productions are ever more replete."[53] A reviewer of the *Semiramide* premiere a decade later reported that "the poet, composer, singers, and painter had the honor of being repeatedly called out on stage [for applause]."[54] But most of the Borsato drawings preserved in Paris are not identified with specific operas or ballets, so that it had seemed impossible to evaluate the designs in the context of the stage works for which they were prepared. Thanks to the splendid detective work of Maria Ida Biggi, most of these drawings have now been matched to specific operas, so that we have access to the original drawings for sets pertaining to several works by Rossini created or revised for the Teatro La Fenice: *Tancredi* (1813), *Sigismondo* (1815), *Maometto II* (1822), and *Semiramide* (1823).[55] Elena Povoledo describes Borsato as an artist trained in the Neoclassical tradition but open to an "imaginary exotic world" deriving from the recent Napoleonic campaigns in Africa, a "repertory of new architectonic models, an alternative to the Greek ideal."[56]

Study of iconographical sources for the Rossini operas was advanced notably in 2000 by the publication of *Rossini sulla scena dell'Ottocento,* which offers reproductions and bibliographical details for a large group of drawings, prints, and costume designs from Italian collections pertaining to the Rossini operas.[57] The images range from 1812 through 1899, although most reflect productions from the 1810s to the 1830s, when Rossini's operas dominated the theaters. They testify to a consistent approach to stage design, based on painted backdrops, until the end of the century, although many details in the realization of these images reflect changing cultural patterns. The beauty of their design demonstrates why contemporary reviewers so often pay homage to the scenic wonders accomplished by set painters such as Sanquirico and Borsato.[58]

Verdi's concern for the physical rendering of his later works has been documented extensively, but even during the 1840s there is ample evidence that he paid heed to the visual aspect of his operas. In *Attila*, for example, he was particularly preoccupied about the staging of the Prologue. The opening scene shows the city of Aquileia, destroyed by Attila and the Huns; the second scene begins in the early morning with a furious storm in a Rio Alto in the Adriatic lagoon, inhabited only by hermits, with a simple church dedicated to St. James.[59] As the storm ceases, the sun rises, and a group of refugees from Aquileia arrives by boat, vowing to construct a new city. In the final music of the Prologue, Foresto (the tenor) leads the chorus in a patently Risorgimental hymn, first lamenting the loss of Aquileia ("Cara patria, già madre e reina," Dear homeland, once mother and queen), then concluding with a strophe that announces the founding of the city of Venice: "Ma dall'alghe di questi marosi, / Qual risorta fenice novella, / Rivivrai più superba, più bella / Della terra, dell'onde stupor!" (But from the algae of these waves, as a new phoenix arising, you will live again, prouder, more beautiful, wonder of the earth and of the sea!). It is difficult to imagine a more direct reference to the audience at the Teatro La Fenice within an opera that had its premiere on 17 March 1846, just two years before the 1848 revolutionary uprisings. Verdi's efforts to ensure an appropriate staging for this scene emerges from a letter that the impresario for the season at the Teatro La Fenice, Alessandro Lanari, wrote on 29 September 1845 to the "Presidente agli Spettaccoli" of the theater (presumably Giuseppe Berti). In it Lanari quotes from a Verdi letter that has not survived: "What I really want to be sublime is the second setting (at scene 6), the birth of the city of Venice. Let the sunrise be particularly well done, since I intend to express it in the music."[60] That is precisely what Verdi does, offering a tone picture that owes much to music he had heard in Milan, *Le Désert* of Félicien David.[61]

Equally interesting is a letter Verdi wrote on 11 February 1846, during the staging of *Attila*. The composer sought to embody on the stage of the Teatro La Fenice at the end of act 1 of his opera a scene from a Raphael fresco at the Vatican. Here Leo the Great, Bishop of Rome in the fifth century, stops the advance of the Huns and their leader at the gates of the city, while apparitions of St. Peter and St. Paul with drawn swords fill the sky. Verdi specifically requested that his friend, Vincenzo Luccardi, a Roman sculptor, give him details about Attila's appearance:

> I know that in the Vatican, either in the tapestries or in the Raphael frescoes, there must be the meeting of Attila with Saint Leo. I need a description of the figure of Attila: draw me a few strokes with your pen, then explain to me with words and numbers the colors of his outfit: I particularly need information about his hairstyle. If you will do this favor for me, I will give you my saintly benediction.[62]

This effort to develop a scenic situation in tandem with a well-known painting is striking. A modern American audience might compare the effect with the first-act finale of Stephen Sondheim's *Sunday in the Park with George*, where Georges Seurat's *La Grande Jatte* takes shape before our eyes as the act comes to an end.

For *Macbeth* in Florence, Verdi went further. He took responsibility for having costume designs prepared, as he told the impresario Alessandro Lanari on 21 January 1847, a month and a half before the premiere, adding, "You can be certain that they will be well made: because I had several of them sent from London, I've had eminent scholars do research on the epoch and costumes, and then they will be looked over by [Francesco] Hayez and the other members of the commission."[63] Verdi was particularly concerned about the physical rendering of the appearance of the apparitions and the procession of kings in the third act, and he made several suggestions for the premiere and for later performances, some of them based on his experience in London. To the librettist Salvadore Cammarano, responsible for mounting the reprise of *Macbeth* at the Teatro San Carlo of Naples in 1848, he wrote:

> In the third act the apparitions of the kings (I've seen it done in London) must take place behind an opening in the scenery, with a fine, *ashen* veil in front of it. The *kings* should not be phantoms, but eight men of flesh and blood: the surface over which they pass must resemble a mound, and they must be seen clearly to ascend and descend. The scene must be completely dark, especially when the cauldron disappears, and luminous only where the kings pass.[64]

In 1865 he offered suggestions to his French publisher, Léon Escudier, about another possible solution for this scene, involving a machine in the shape of a wheel that would move the kings into and out of view without their having to walk, a solution Verdi considered "more fantastical" (più fantastico).[65]

No set designs from the original *Macbeth* have come to light, but there are sketches by Bertoja for the revival on 26 December 1847 at the Teatro La Fenice to open the following carnival season. Ricordi published five costume designs (*figurini*) by Roberto Foscosi in several issues of the *Gazzetta musicale di Milano* during November and December of that same 1847, but it is not clear whether they corresponded to costumes actually used in Florence.[66] Iconographical documents, both set and costume designs, related to the production of the revised version of *Macbeth* at the Théâtre-Lyrique in 1865 are found in Paris, and they show strong similarities to surviving Italian designs.[67]

Not only the Venetian Bertoja, but many other set and costume designers working directly with Verdi through the 1860s (or involved in contemporary productions) are coming into focus. So, for example, the career of Alessandro Prampolini is becoming better known: he contributed one splendid set for the premiere of *Il trovatore* (the scene for the gardens in the palace of Aliaferia, the second setting of act 1) and worked on sets for the revival of *Simon Boccanegra* in Reggio Emilia in 1857, directed by Verdi.[68] Since the 1985 exhibition of his set designs for the Teatro alla Scala, where he directed scenography from 1849 through 1867, Filippo Peroni has fared better.[69] According to Olga Jesurum, he "restored dignity and autonomy to scenography, through a coherent interpretation, finally in tandem with other parts of the theatrical spectacle."[70] The original sets for *La forza del destino,* first performed in St. Petersburg on 10 November 1862, were designed by Andreas Leonhard Roller, a key figure in the city's theatrical life for almost forty years, whose sketches and drawings are preserved in its Theater and Music Museum.[71] The richness of these surviving sources could hardly have been imagined thirty years ago.

STAGECRAFT AND HISTORY

If we supplement this historical documentation concerning the staging of Italian and French opera from the first two-thirds of the nineteenth century with knowledge derived from studies of theatrical gesture and movement in the prose theater, it becomes possible to present the operas of Rossini or Verdi in a way that not merely is historically informed but invokes the staging practices of the period. I am emphatically not claiming that such a presentation would be "authentic." As James Hepokoski has expressed it,

> To revive the original staging of *Otello* is not finally to see *Otello* as it was meant to be; it is first and foremost to participate in a commentary on twentieth-century staging, for we cannot escape taking the measure of the

1887 staging against a vast backdrop of later practice of which the first Italian audiences had no inkling. In order to see *Otello*—or indeed any opera— externally as it was, we are obliged to gaze at it through what it has become.[72]

I have been tangentially involved with two experimental efforts to invoke nineteenth-century stagings: a production of the St. Petersburg version of *La forza del destino* (1862) at the University of California at Irvine in 1980, and another of Verdi's *Ernani* at the Teatro Comunale of Modena in 1984. The former, directed by Clayton Garrison (with the participation of Andrew Porter), drew on actual stage designs and a published *disposizione scenica;* the latter, directed by Gianfranco De Bosio, employed contemporaneous set designs but had to fall back on standard techniques of stage movement employed in Italy during the 1840s.

Porter has recounted his experiences in 1980 at Irvine and at a 1984 production in Seattle, which he himself directed.[73] Sets in the Irvine production were based on designs prepared by Carlo Ferrario for the opera's revival at La Scala in 1869, but did not use the painted backdrops adopted at that time.[74] Instead, the Irvine team constructed three-dimensional sets, but ones that could be moved quickly about the stage.[75] The Seattle production, on the other hand, employed a facsimile of the Ferrario sets "bought from a Roman warehouse a few decades earlier, all painted in perspective canvas."[76] Not only was the result visually beautiful, it also made it possible to change settings instantaneously.

As for the *disposizioni sceniche,* Porter remarks, "the production books need not necessarily be followed in every particular nowadays, but drawing on them in certain structural aspects may well help to provide a clearer and more effective musical execution of the scores."[77] One of his examples involves Don Alvaro's leap to his death at the end of the 1862 version. Among the inaccessible cliffs surrounding the playing area, the *disposizione scenica* specifies that there are rocks and a natural arch:

> At one point the rocks rise a little higher than the practicable bridge behind it. Here one places an exact replica of Alvaro, hidden from the audience behind the raised part. Alvaro rushes across the bridge and when he gets to that point he pushes the dummy over so that it crashes down on to the stage with considerable effect; your tenor of the evening seems to have landed with a huge thud.[78]

Paying attention to the original blocking also helps achieve appropriate musical balances, as in the ensemble during the scene in the Inn that opens act 2, which involves Leonora (who must remain unseen by her brother, Don Carlo, himself disguised as a student), an offstage procession of pilgrims, and an onstage chorus with other soloists. "The stage book makes it clear how to achieve this by placing Leonora behind both the chorus and the four soloists, but well elevated so that she sings over the ensemble as an independent voice, very audible and dominant but at the same time, because she is behind them, unnoticed by them."[79] No one claims this is the *only* way to achieve the desired result, but Porter is correct in pointing out that the *disposizione scenica* helps identify and resolve such problems.

From Modena in 1984, De Bosio relates a similar set of experiences for *Ernani*. Having had the opportunity to present an *Aida* following the original *disposizione scenica,* De Bosio attempted a similar operation for the earlier *Ernani,* for which no production book existed.[80] The theater in Modena originally intended to adopt scenic designs from several different mid-nineteenth-century artists, but then discovered a complete set of drawings by a single artist from Faenza, Romolo Liverani, prepared for a performance in his native city on 30 June 1844, just a few months after the Venetian premiere (9 March). The painted backdrops in Modena were copied directly from Liverani's drawings, but instead of extending across the entire stage, as they would have done in 1844, the backdrops were inserted within a visible external frame, as if to anchor the past in the present. Costumes, too, were developed from contemporary accounts, including documents from the original Venetian performances. Working with an able young conductor, Roberto Abbado, De Bosio encouraged his singers (two of whom, the baritone Roberto Servile as Don Carlo and the bass Michele Pertusi as Silva, were to establish themselves as leading Italian artists of their generation) to adopt gestures and postures attested to in mid-nineteenth-century accounts of operatic staging, while keeping paramount the effectiveness of their performance before a modern audience.

Most unusual were the efforts to reconfigure the Teatro Comunale of Modena following structural models of nineteenth-century theaters. The proscenium was extended forward into the theater, and singers were encouraged to present their solos directly to the public. The pit was covered and the orchestra, whose numbers were adjusted to appropriate levels—although all players used modern instruments—was raised to the level of the audience. The number of choristers was significantly reduced, and the remaining chorus was brought closer to the public. This physical redistribution of singers, chorus, and orchestra compensated for adjustments in the number of performers, so that sonic balances were always maintained. The theater could not return to oil lamps and candles, but tried to reproduce electrically the distribution of lighting a nineteenth-century audience would have experienced. Critical reaction to the entire project was excellent. Mario Messinis wrote, "This exhaustive appropriation of extinct processes is not a work of arid philology, but helps to liberate us from bad habits and makes us reflect on the very genesis of the Verdian works themselves."[81]

However fascinating these productions were in bringing to the stage some sense of nineteenth-century practice, no one expected them to replace modern theatrical usage, nor did anyone seek such an outcome. It was already clear, after all, that the myth of stable productions over the course of the nineteenth century was not sustainable, even if the role of the modern stage director did not exist in nineteenth-century Italy or France. That Verdi himself changed his views between 1847 and 1865 about how the apparitions of the kings might be handled in the third act of *Macbeth* is merely one sign of the important changes in staging and set design that took place during the course of the century. Not all changes in stagecraft were improvements, of course, and the experiments from the early 1980s made abundantly clear that those involved with the performance of Italian opera needed to evaluate early practices critically.

In the area of theatrical lighting, for example, there was no turning back. Early in the nineteenth century, theaters were lit primarily by candle and oil lamps, notoriously difficult to adjust (not to mention the unpleasant smell and smoke from the oil lamps, widely mentioned in contemporary accounts).[82] More easily regulated gas illumination was gradually introduced at the Paris Opéra, first in 1822 for a fairy opera that depended upon magical effects, Isouard's *Aladin, ou La Lampe merveilleuse*. By 1833, all productions at the theater were illuminated by gas. In Italy, different theatrical centers had different traditions. At the Teatro La Fenice, gas lighting was not installed until the carnival season of 1844 – 45, so that the premiere of *Ernani* in Venice on 9 March 1844 would still have been lit with oil and candles.[83] Electric lighting at the Opéra was first introduced for a special effect in Meyerbeer's *Le Prophète* of 1849, the sunrise during the course of the third act, for which an apparatus was prepared to create a "light which is truly frightful: the sun of the Opéra threatens to eclipse the sun of the Good Lord." The *livret de mise en scène* specifies that the electric mechanism used could be purchased at the shop of a "M. Lormier, 13 Rue du Delta in Paris."[84] Not until much later in the century was electric stage lighting more generally introduced in either France or Italy, but once it became widespread, gas lighting—always a fire hazard—rapidly fell out of favor.[85] As Giulio Ricordi wrote to Verdi on 2 November

1883, while plans for the performance of *Don Carlo* at the Teatro alla Scala of Milan were being discussed: "I have had a meeting with the stage designer and another with the engineer responsible for arranging the electric lights: and I think that we have found beautiful effects that could not be achieved earlier with gas lighting." [86]

To recuperate lighting effects of the nineteenth century, then, even if fire departments were to allow it, would be an absurdity. At best, two centuries of real progress in theatrical lighting could be used to simulate the effect of candles and oil lamps, as in Modena. At a time when computer technology permits subtle lighting patterns and rapid shifts from one configuration to another that were unthinkable in the nineteenth century, not to mention effects using lasers, neon, and so forth, such a choice would make sense for the modern theater only as a curiosity.

There were also vast changes in physical staging during the late nineteenth and twentieth centuries, many in the area of set design, but here the situation with respect to today's practice is more complex. Some elements of nineteenth-century stagecraft are intimately tied to the musical rhythm of the operas for which they were devised, and some subsequent developments had a decidedly negative effect on the presentation of Italian operas. One of my first operatic experiences in Italy was a performance of *Norma* at the Teatro Comunale of Bologna during the 1966–67 season. I remember only one thing about it. In the second act there are three settings: a first scene for Norma and, later, Adalgisa that takes place "Inside Norma's dwelling"; a second scene for Norma's father, Oroveso—the chief priest of the Druids—and the male chorus, set in an "isolated place near the wood of the Druids, surrounded by ravines and caverns"; and a final scene in the "Temple of Irminsul." The entire second scene takes about nine minutes to perform. In Bologna, after the first scene, the audience sat in the darkened theater for five minutes (I couldn't help glancing at my watch) while the scenery was changed. When the curtain arose, what we saw was an enormous fallen tree in the middle of the stage, around which Oroveso and the Druids arranged themselves as best they could. After the final ensemble of this second scene ("Ah del Tebro al giogo indegno"), the curtain fell. And—as the restive audience sat once again in darkness—it took another five minutes (by my watch) to lug the tree off the stage and to set in place the Temple of Irminsul.

Such a theatrical abomination could never have happened in Italy during the first two-thirds of the nineteenth century. No composer would have accepted it. The stage, after all, was arranged with a series of positions at which painted backdrops could be lowered or raised instantaneously, or where decorated side panels or pieces of scenery could be brought in from the wings. When, for large ensemble scenes, a few larger pieces of scenery were needed, on which one or more characters could walk (the *praticabili*), these were put into place either between acts or when a scene was performed using only part of the stage. We have many drawings that show how Italian stages were constructed to accommodate this kind of setting, but more important is the physical example of the Drottningholm Court theater in Stockholm, the best-preserved late eighteenth-century theater in Europe. It owes its exemplary condition to having been abandoned after the assassination of King Gustaf III (of *Ballo in maschera* fame) in 1792. Only in the 1920s did its exemplary character begin to be understood, thanks to its well-preserved mechanisms for changing painted backdrops and side flats, for wind and thunder effects, for descending gods *ex machina* in cloud machines, and all the rest. Diagrams in books could now be compared to an operational theater.

Since operas written in Italy through the middle of the 1830s were normally in two acts, it was necessary to establish a sequence of set changes within each act that guaranteed continuity. The assumption was that only insignificant amounts of time would be needed to pass from one scene to another and that changes would be made in full view of the audience (*a vista*). This was accomplished by alternating deeper scenes, which filled most of the stage, with shallower ones, filling only the front part of the stage. At the beginning of an act, for example, most of the stage might be used. Then a new painted backdrop could be lowered into position nearer the front of the stage, and while a scene was played in that smaller space, a new deep scene could be prepared behind it. Something of this kind is what Romani and Bellini had planned for the second act of *Norma*.

Because Verdi communicated extensively with his librettists by letter, we have written evidence that he was directly concerned about the rhythm of scene change. He wrote to Piave on 3 December 1846, for example, discussing the structure of the second act of *Macbeth*. Its first scene begins with a dialogue between Macbeth and Lady, and then has Lady remain alone to sing a solo number (for which he asked Piave to supply "two quatrains"). "Next," Verdi continued, "comes the Chorus of the Assassins, and the scene should go on a bit, so that the Banquet can be prepared."[87] As the composer explained to Antonio Somma on 29 June 1853, at the beginning of their first effort to prepare *Re Lear:*

> [I am concerned that] there are too many set changes. The only thing that has always held me back from treating Shakespearian subjects more

often is precisely this necessity to change the set at every moment.[88] When I used to frequent the theater it was something that made me immensely unhappy, and it seemed to me I was attending a magic lantern show. In this the French are right: they plan their dramas so that only one setting is needed in each act. In that way the action moves along expeditiously, without obstacle, and nothing distracts the public's attention.[89]

Verdi's description of French practice is not quite correct, but there are fewer set changes within an act than in Italian opera, rarely more than one per act, with a simpler setting always giving way to a more complex one. Thus, the third act of *Guillaume Tell* begins with a duet for Mathilde and Arnold alone, a "shallow" set, followed by the "deep" set in the central square of Altorf—the place where Gesler forces the Swiss to bow down before his hat, where the *divertissement* is sung and danced, and where the rebellious Tell, renowned as an archer, is compelled by Gesler to shoot an apple off the head of his son, Jemmy. As French stagecraft grew ever more elaborate—often adopting techniques from the popular, *boulevard* theaters that sought to astonish audiences with scenic effects—and as large pieces of furniture, functional monumental staircases, or architectural elements proliferated, changing scenery within an act became more difficult. It also became more central to the success of the total spectacle. In a work such as *Le Prophète* of 1849, the effectiveness of the fourth act is partially dependent on a fabulous set change *à vue:* while the audience watches, a public square in Münster is transformed into a set representing the inside of the cathedral for the Coronation Scene. Even in Verdi's own *Vêpres siciliennes* of 1854 there is an impressive change of set within the third act, when the first "shallow" setting, in Montfort's study, "changes and represents a sumptuous ballroom [a "deep" set] prepared for festivities."

In this regard, it is instructive to think about the three serious operas Rossini wrote for Naples—*Otello, Armida,* and *Mosè in Egitto*—in which the composer and his librettists divided the action into three acts instead of the standard two. In each case there are good psychological and dramaturgical reasons for this unusual organization. To pass from Desdemona's despair at her father's curse directly to the bedroom scene would be psychologically disastrous; to move from the pleasure palace and *divertissement* that dominates most of act 2 of *Armida* into act 3, where the illusion is destroyed, would seriously compromise the sense of the opera; and to shift without pause from Elcia's horror at the death of her beloved Osiride to the scene of the passage of the Red Sea would allow no time for the Hebrews to regroup for the departure from Egypt. But alongside these dramaturgical considerations are some eminently practical ones. In *Otello,* no Desdemona could sing the Ave Maria, willow song, and final duet immediately after the major aria that concludes act 2. In both *Armida* and *Mosè in Egitto,* not only does the second act conclude with a "deep" set (a magnificent palace in *Armida,* Pharaoh's throne room in *Mosè in Egitto*), but the third act must begin with one (an "enchanted garden" in *Armida,* the shore of the Red Sea in *Mosè in Egitto*).

The gradual movement away from painted backdrops to three-dimensional scenery, growing ever more massive, continued during the first half of the twentieth century and—in some circles—into the twenty-first, establishing itself for a long period as the dominant approach to stage design. The Franco Zeffirelli productions that continue to hold the boards at the Metropolitan Opera are simply the decadent remnant of this tradition. Countertendencies grew during the course of the twentieth century: after World War II, the spare Wieland Wagner productions at the Bayreuth Festival were among the most important. But the tendency toward heavy, often awkward scenic display continued in many productions of Italian opera throughout the century and in all countries. While some of these productions were attractive to look at, their negative aspect was well described almost thirty years ago by Luciano Alberti: "This three-dimensional, volumetric, 'constructed' complication [which Alberti calls "a violent reaction to the old pictorial tradition of scenography"] in the last analysis risks being a betrayal, to the extent that it involves the systematic dissolution of that fluid continuity in changes between scenes that the music explicitly requires."[90]

The fashion for complicated scenery had other unfortunate consequences. As settings became more elaborate, a strange phenomenon occurred: operas written in two or three acts began to be played in three or four, primarily to allow for set changes. It became "traditional," for example, to perform the first act of Rossini's *Il barbiere di Siviglia* in two separate parts, with an intermission, because the first scene (in which the Count serenades Rosina outside her window and then encounters Figaro) would be given such an elaborate setting that the second scene (inside Don Bartolo's house) could not be prepared behind it. The same problem affected the second act of *La traviata,* where the first scene, in the country home of Violetta and Alfredo, became ever more picturesque in its setting, a regular villa with full garden in the background, occupying more and more of the stage. The party at Flora's, therefore, which actually forms the finale of the act, had to be treated as a separate unit in order to allow time for the set of the first scene to be removed and the new set to be put in place. In both cases, but particularly in *La traviata,* the effect is destructive. A curtain after the Germont aria is hardly how Verdi would ever have imagined closing an act, and, indeed, the theatrical effect is always very poor.[91] It is absurd that these divisions persisted throughout most of the twentieth century, long after improved stage machinery and new approaches to set design had rendered them unnecessary. Yet it does not improve matters simply to play these acts as units, as the composers wrote them, if this means the public must sit in a darkened theater for several minutes while the sets are being changed. It is essential that the dramatic rhythm be continuous.

Some directors and director/designers consider the necessity for continuity within an act so obvious that they wonder why it is even worth mentioning.[92] Yet at the opening of the centennial Verdi Festival in Parma, that very problem had surfaced. In the third act of *Un ballo in maschera,* there are three separate settings. The *disposizione scenica* for the opera is precise about how they must be handled.[93] The first scene, "a study in the home of Renato," is intended to occupy half the stage. At its conclusion the front curtain should fall just long enough to allow for the lowering of the second painted backdrop, closer to the front of the stage.[94] The new setting, in Riccardo's chamber, thus uses a very shallow set. While Riccardo signs the paper that will send Renato and Amelia back to England, the first backdrop of the act is raised invisibly, revealing a painted backdrop for this last scene, which has been in place at the very rear of the stage since the beginning of the act. Additional columns and chandeliers are brought in toward the rear of the stage, behind the second backdrop, thus completing the setting for the ballroom scene. As Riccardo exits, then, the second backdrop "is raised in plain view of the audience, and the ballroom is discovered behind it." Between the second and the third scenes Verdi's music is continuous, so we can tell *exactly* how much time is available for the scene change: fifteen seconds. With no choice but to move continuously, Andrej Konchalovskij's staging, supported by the sets of Ezio Frigerio, did the latter change beautifully, but between the first two scenes we waited in darkness for *four* minutes as heavy constructions were pushed and prodded into place.

The situation was worse in act 1, whose two settings reproduce the same configuration as the last two settings in act 3: a shallow setting for a hall in the governor's residence and a deep setting for the dwelling of the sorceress, which should already be largely set up toward the rear of the stage, behind the first backdrop. Again the *disposizione scenica* is explicit: the first setting "va via a vista, e scopre l'abituro" (is removed in full view of the audience, and behind it is found the dwelling). How long should the change take? Recall that the same procedure in act 3, which is accompanied by Verdi's music, takes fifteen seconds. In Parma the change of set took *five minutes.* Five minutes in the dark, five minutes of restive quasi silence. Frigerio's sets were beautiful, but Verdi's stunning juxtaposition of the "can-can" that concludes the first scene and the three hammerlike dissonant chords for the entire orchestra that open the second scene was utterly lost. No one imagines that theaters should return to painted backdrops, should give up massive scenery where such scenery seems desirable, or should reject other, more original approaches to set design; but to require an audience to sit patiently for a long scene change within an act is a failure both of historical knowledge and of artistic imagination.

There can be moments in which a modern production plays brilliantly with our sense of time in a way that could not have been contemplated by those who brought the opera to life at its premiere. I recall Graham Vick's *Moïse* at the Rossini Opera Festival during the summer of 1997. The production was staged in the Palafestival, the basketball stadium intelligently transformed into a theater. Normally the stage was constructed at one of the longer sides of the rectangular space, and the public sat on bleachers on three sides of the room and on chairs placed where the basketball court used to be. In this case, though, Vick and his designer, Stefanos Lazaridis, constructed an enormous thrust stage starting from one of the shorter sides of the rectangle. The public was seated on the other three sides of the stage, which could be adjusted hydraulically so that at one moment it would be flat, at another raked. Probably the most remarkable moment in the production was the famous Prayer in act 4, "Des cieux où tu résides" (From the heavens where you reside), where Vick avoided all direct reference to the Red Sea. Instead, he had the Hebrews, many dressed as East European Jews at the time of the Holocaust and carrying makeshift valises, appear at the back of the raked stage and then gradually descend the long distance toward the front. As the music turned from the minor key in which it begins to a major key for the final section, the now-assembled chorus sang directly to the audience, confronting them with the enormity of the biblical story and the twentieth-century disaster. It was a profoundly disturbing, yet beautiful moment.

It was in the third act, though, that Vick played with time. The act, which takes place in the portal before the Temple of Isis, begins with a choral march, "Reine des cieux" (Queen of the heavens). For this act Vick flattened the stage, around the whole of which was a channel filled with water. When the lights came up, standing in the channel, barefoot, were the priestesses who later in the act would participate as dancers in the *divertissement.* They were dressed in flowing, diaphanous white robes, and they proceeded slowly and with beautiful gestures to walk in measured fashion around the entire channel. No music played: the entire theater was silent. I do not know how long the procession took, for time seemed to stand still. When I first heard what Vick had been planning, I worried that members of the audience might grow impatient, but the fear was groundless: the sheer beauty of the movements and the hypnotic quality of the action testified to the director's genius.

"DISPLACED" AND "RADICAL" STAGINGS

What freedom should a stage director have to modify an opera in a modern production? As we saw at the beginning of this chapter, many lovers of Italian opera become incensed when faced with directorial interventions, whether a simple transposition of period or a more radical reinvention of the action. Perhaps it would console them to know that similar controversies swirl around the staging of plays, although in the United States, Britain, and Italy, at least, the theater has in general been more open than the operatic world to radical staging. For many years I have kept a file of interesting cases. One is a 1994 debate that intrigued me because of the respect I have for both the author and the performers: Deborah Warner directed Fiona Shaw in a revival of Samuel Beckett's *Footfalls* at the Garrick Theater in London.[95] According to Edward Beckett, his uncle's executor, the production "destroyed the play's timing, atmosphere, the ghostly aspect." Warner replied that the text was unchanged, but that it was time to move away from what she referred to as "a Beckett cliché": "someone standing in a white light in a black box set." What may have seemed innovative in the theater thirty years ago, in short, needed to be studied anew. "Beckett," Warner concluded, "will withstand productions that will delight some and offend others. The estate is reluctant to allow him to take on sure wings of his own." The Beckett estate, furious, withdrew permission for a European tour.

There are times, though, in which the artists themselves rebel. Such a rebellion preceded the performances planned for the Teatro alla Scala on 6 and 8 November 2001 of Verdi's *Luisa Miller* in a production by Götz Friedrich. The head of the Deutsche Oper in Berlin from 1981 until his death in December 2000, Friedrich was one of Europe's most distinguished, if controversial, stage directors. His last opera production, which had its premiere in Berlin on 22 November 2000, shortly before his death, was a *Luisa Miller* conducted by Lorin Maazel. That production, still under the direction of Maazel, was scheduled for revival in Munich in October 2001 with a new cast, Barbara

Frittoli and Vincenzo La Scola in the roles of Luisa and Rodolfo, to be followed by the performances in Milan with the same team. In both Munich and Milan, however, the staged production became a concert performance. Paola Zonca, writing in the pages of *La repubblica*, explained that "the first to protest was Frittoli, who narrated what, according to her, were the exaggerations and incongruencies of the staging: her Luisa was supposed to take a bath dressed in underwear, have a lesbian relationship with Federica (the contralto), be raped by Wurm (the bass), improvise a striptease, and remain on stage always with scanty clothes and suggestive makeup."[96] La Scola commented that "the staging betrayed the spirit of the opera." Whether Friedrich might or might not have been willing to adapt his ideas to Frittoli and La Scola is something we will never know.

When speaking about directorial intervention today, we need to differentiate two approaches, "displaced stagings" and "radical stagings," without pretending that the division is absolute. Indeed, within each tendency there is a range of differing attitudes. In what I have called displaced stagings, a story is moved either temporally or spatially, but the subject, characters, situations, and action are basically unchanged. In radical stagings, in the words of Roger Savage, the operatic text is treated as "a sheer, unprescriptive stimulus to the free play of theatrical imagination." He adds, "It is the text itself, unshackled by time or authorship, which is alive; and its untrammelled life triggers new responses in the imagination of directors and designers."[97]

About displaced stagings it is possible to lay out a coherent historical argument. There are Italian operas, such as Verdi's *Aida*, with strong roots in a particular historical moment or geographical location. Others float more freely from one venue to another, although composers were never indifferent to where they landed. Subject to the intervention of theatrical censors, Verdi himself was compelled on multiple occasions to shift an opera in time and/or space. As we have seen, *Rigoletto* was originally conceived as occurring at the court of the French Renaissance king, François I, who reigned from 1515 to 1547. Verdi was willing to displace the story either temporally (he suggested moving it to an earlier period, before the reign of Louis XI, which began in 1461, when France was not a unified kingdom) or geographically (to an independent duchy of Burgundy or to an Italian principality), as long as there was "an absolute ruler." Ultimately the King of France became the Duke of Mantua, while the period remained the sixteenth century.[98] The early nineteenth-century German narrative of the 1850 *Stiffelio*, along with much of its music, flowed seven years later into a Scottish story set in 1200 for the revised *Aroldo* (whose last act, entirely new, takes place on the banks of Loch

Lomond). As we saw in chapter 11, in order to make *Les Vêpres siciliennes,* which takes place in Palermo, Sicily, in 1282, acceptable to the Italians, Verdi himself displaced it to Lisbon, Portugal, in 1640, as *Giovanna de Guzman.*[99]

The tormented travels of *Un ballo in maschera* are well known, but some of Verdi's letters on the subject are particularly apposite at defining the composer's attitude toward displacements. Although he regretted that the censors would not permit him to maintain the drama at the royal court of Gustaf III of Sweden in 1792, he was hardly surprised. The problem was to find an acceptable alternative. Among Somma's first notions was to move the story back to medieval times ("It wouldn't be bad to place it in Pomerania—a part of Prussia—and an independent Duchy in the twelfth century, when the Teutonic knights fought to eliminate the idolatry that persisted in many parts of the Duchy").[100] Verdi's response was unequivocal:

> The twelfth century seems to me too remote for our *Gustavo.* It was such a coarse and brutal period, especially in those lands, that it seems to me a grave contradiction to insert characters cut in the French manner, like Gustavo and Oscar, and a lively drama, fashioned according to our modern customs. It would be better to find a little prince, a duke, a devil, even one from the North, who had seen something of the world and smelled the odor of the court of Louis XIV.

Displacement was fine, so long as it was accomplished with sensitivity to the characters and situations. Verdi did finally agree to move the drama to Stettin, capital of Pomerania, but set it in the second half of the seventeenth century.

When the Neapolitan censors sought to displace his opera yet again, under the name *Adelia degli Adimari,* to Florence in 1385, Verdi returned to the same theme in his letter of 14 February 1858 to Vincenzo Torelli, impresario of the Teatro San Carlo: "Shift the action back by five or six centuries?! What an anachronism! Cut the scene where the name of the assassin is chosen by lot?!... but that is the most powerful and novel situation in the drama, and you want me to give it up?!"[101] After failing to reach a satisfactory compromise in Naples, Verdi began negotiations with Rome, but similar problems surfaced. Finally, exhausted by the squabbles and concerned that his completed opera would languish unperformed, he wrote to Somma on 8 July 1858: "The censors might permit the subject and situations, etc., etc., but they would want the setting removed from Europe. What do you think about North America at the time of the English domination? If not America another place. The Caucasus perhaps?"[102] A whiff of the court of Louis XIV in the Caucasus?[103] What was he thinking?

For Verdi, there was no compromising on the situations and the characters, but he was prepared to discuss and effect displacements—even improb-
able ones—in both time and space. Given these histories (and their number
can be multiplied to include other operas by Verdi and many works by
Donizetti), arguments against modern displaced stagings ring hollow. A New
York Mafia don "Duke" from the 1920s in the manner of Jonathan Miller, or
a Holywood mogul "Duke" with a swimming pool in the manner of Bruce
Beresford, would never have crossed Verdi's mind, for obvious reasons, but
the composer's own displacements were just as significant. In a 2003 interview
in *The Paris Review*, referring to his *Rigoletto*, Miller offered a way to think
about what he called "isomorphic" displacements in operatic staging:

> Ah, but now we are talking about plays or operas which are written in
> one period, apparently *about* another, but the world to which these "his-
> toric" works nominally refer is nonexistent. For example, none of the ac-
> tions that are represented in Verdi's *Rigoletto* could possibly have happened
> in the Gonzaga world to which it refers. It is a *virtual* historic world. It is
> *generically* historic. You have to find a world with some sort of common
> structure, one in which a man has absolute power of life and death over his
> followers, and who can behave as badly as he wishes because he is the boss.
> And that happens in the Mafia. [...] Underneath the surface differences
> there are common structures which allow some plays and operas to be
> transposed without distortion.[104]

Of course, Verdi and his librettists were prepared to adjust the language of
the libretto and even the music to make sure that their displacements were
coherent.

While extensive adjustments are rarely made in operatic scores today, minor changes can help a particular displaced production cohere. An American
wild-west version of Rossini's *Il viaggio a Reims* in Brian Dickie's Chicago
Opera Theater in the spring of 2004, for example, substituted Abraham Lincoln's second inauguration for the coronation of Charles X, an amusing and
engaging displacement that did not require changing the plot. Similarly,
manipulations in the simultaneous translations projected over the stage have
become quite common. In general, though, audiences are not disturbed by
hearing an occasional "King" or "Duke" addressed to a character without
dynastic pretensions. Of course, we smile inwardly at those cases in which
an apparent inconsistency is cleverly removed. The best example I know
is not operatic but cinematic, the first scene of Baz Luhrman's displaced
Shakespeare's R & J, which begins with a fight between two feuding Latino

gangs, equipped with submachine guns, at a gas station in Verona Beach, California. When Benvolio calls out, "Fools, put up your swords," the camera zooms in on the barrel of the guns, where the manufacturer's name is engraved: "Sword."

In modern productions of Italian opera, then, displaced stagings seem entirely appropriate, although it must be acknowledged that modern displacements tend to bring the events of an opera into the present, a different kind of displacement from the ones Verdi undertook. Nonetheless, the practice is historically defensible as long as the works preserve, in Verdi's words, "the subject and situations." Even the occasional and inevitable incoherence is admissible. What matters is whether the displacement functions effectively in the theater, and whether it illuminates those elements of the drama that are independent of time and place. Those are judgments each member of the audience must make.

"Radical" stagings by their very nature ask different kinds of questions, questions for which the history of a work, the thinking of the composer and the librettist, and the niceties of character, action, and stage directions provide little guidance. Roger Savage summarizes the problem neatly when he speaks of the "untrammelled life" of an opera that "triggers new responses in the imagination of directors and designers" (quoted above). In David Alden's 1999 *Macbeth* at Chicago, defined by von Rhein as "campy, creepy American Eurotrash," the witches were conceived—in Alden's words—as "Strong, power-suited executives." [105] At the end of the opening scene, after their first encounter with Macbeth and Banco, they reached into their purses, pulled out bright red lipsticks, and applied them with aggressive menace toward any men in their vicinity, including the audience. Most of us may not believe in witches today, but are the sentiments and insecurities that caused our ancestors to burn at the stake women considered dangerous altogether absent from modern society? And how do we react to characters like Macbeth and Lady, who continue to embody the problem of the power relationship between a man and a woman? While Alden's staging of *Macbeth* was filled with provocations emerging from the text of Verdi's opera, it was certainly not a presentation of the opera as conceived by its authors. Yet I often found the production powerful and effective, and it has stayed with me where many more conventional treatments have rapidly faded.

When critics speak of *Regietheater* or of productions with a *Konzept,* this is the kind of production they intend to invoke. That the words are German is not coincidental, for the dominance of the stage director in opera was strongly felt in Berlin already by the 1920s, as exemplified in operatic productions of the Kroll Theater (in particular the abstract, antinaturalistic staging by Jürgen Fehling of Wagner's *Der fliegende Holländer* in 1929) and closely related ideas of epic theater being developed by Bertolt Brecht.[106] There is an enormous literature about the increasing significance of the stage director in the opera house during the twentieth century, a good deal of it associated with the staging of Wagner. Among the key individuals were Walter Felsenstein at the Komische Oper of East Berlin, later succeeded by Harry Kupfer; Götz Friedrich at the Deutsche Oper in Berlin; Hans Neuenfels and Ruth Berghaus, both of whom worked at the Frankfurt opera house under Michael Gielen; and the French director Patrick Chéreau (known principally for his *Ring* at Bayreuth in 1976).

Nineteenth-century Italian opera, especially as produced in Italy, the United States, and Britain, largely held aloof from these tendencies. Writing in 2001, Mike Ashman commented:

> A cursory glance at Verdian performance history will focus first on singers and impresarios, then conductors, but rarely on the directors' work, where, in terms of "progressive" (read "committed" or "theatrical") stagings, Verdi seems to lag behind. Critical and public outrage at novel Verdi productions both outweighs that at like-minded Wagner (or other German-composer) productions—where it is currently regarded as *de rigueur*—and remains less willing to tolerate attempts to move beyond historically informed fourth-wall naturalism.[107]

If this is true of Verdi productions, how much more so is it of Rossini, Bellini, and Donizetti. Even when innovative directors from the cinema and theater, like Luchino Visconti, Giorgio Strehler, Luca Ronconi, and Lina Wertmüller, began to enter the opera house in Italy after 1950, their productions only rarely tried to endow a work with "untrammelled life." At most they stressed the blatant theatricality of the Italian operatic repertory, as when Visconti in his 1955 *Sonnambula* at La Scala turned the houselights on for the final cabaletta, "which focused the attention of the audience and the other singers on the performance of the protagonist."[108] This technique is similar to the one Pier Luigi Pizzi would employ almost thirty years later when he directed the tragic ending of Rossini's *Tancredi* at the Rossini Opera Festival in 1982 as a hallucination of the sorrowing Amenaide. When her vision subsided, the victorious Tancredi made his return from the battle with Solamir, the house lights came up, and the evening concluded with a spirited rendition of the *vaudeville* that originally brought the opera to a happy conclusion.

Ronconi developed other innovative methods. Sometimes he sought to emphasize the relationship of a work to the culture that gave it birth (treating *Nabucco* as a Risorgimental myth at the Maggio Musicale of Florence in 1977) or in which it was being performed (celebrating the discovery of *Il viaggio a Reims* at the Rossini Opera Festival in 1984). Sometimes he luxuriated in a work's inherent theatricality: his *Guglielmo Tell* at La Scala in 1988 used filmed Swiss travalogues and semicircular rows of graded benches from which the chorus could observe the proceedings during the first act, while in his *Moïse* at the same theater in 2003, a massive Baroque organ emerged from the sands in the middle of the desert. Yet, however theatrically compelling, Ronconi's productions are not "radical stagings" in the sense described by Savage or by Guccini in his survey of Italian practice:

> the type of direction that addresses the show in complete liberty, precisely as though [...] the musical text did *not* in its own right describe settings, situations, and characters. When directors apply their creativity to opera without accepting any degree of compromise, they produce shows with a double identity: on the one hand, the staged interpretation and, on the other, the musical text.[109]

Searching for an Italian example of such a staging, Guccini falls back on a production of *Tristan und Isolde* by Jurij Ljubimov at the Teatro Comunale of Bologna.[110]

For many years it was largely left to German theaters to explore radical stagings of Italian opera, and the techniques were applied for the most part to a number of operas by Verdi. The legendary staging by Hans Neuenfels of *Aida* at the Frankfurt opera in 1981 was "booed and maligned to an unprecedented extent," but later "advanced to cult status, playing to sold-out crowds for years."[111] Neuenfels began by staging the prelude, that is, introducing stage action as soon as the music began to play. Many directors have done this even in highly traditional productions. After all, by opening *La traviata* with a prelude that will be reheard at the start of act 3 as Violetta lies dying of tuberculosis, Verdi himself "stages" the opera as a flashback. Introducing Violetta in her sickbed during the prelude, then, as in countless modern productions, simply confirms what is already in the score, although one could argue that it does it in a way significantly more banal than the composer's. But Neuenfels had other aims. This is Samuel Weber's description:

> Radames, captain of the Egyptian palace guard, appears dressed in the civilian clothes of a nineteenth-century European businessman. At a certain

moment in what seems to be a dream, he seizes a shovel (implausibly located in what appears to be an office) and begins to dig in the earth, or, rather, to tear up the floorboards of the stage, bringing to light first sand, then a sword, and finally the sculpted head of Aida.[112]

Weber attempts to define the meaning of this gesture in the context of Freud's theory of the dream. The following sentences give the flavor of his discussion:

> For when Radames takes the shovel—which, with oneiric incongruity, just happens to be ready at hand—and begins to dig, what comes to light is not merely a number of obviously symbolic objects—swords and sculpted head—but also, and perhaps more important, *the materiality of the scene itself* in all of its equivocal overdetermination. The gesture of Radames forces the spectators to direct their glance at the physical foundation of theatrical representation, the flooring of the stage, the "basis" of the scene.

And Neunfels's concern with the position of the spectators with respect to an operatic representation carries over into the opening scene of the second act:

> In this scene, the curtain rises to reveal a surprising, indeed even breath-taking tableau: the chorus assembled as the elegant audience gathered for the opening night of *Aida* at La Scala in 1872. What quite literally takes one's breath away in this image is not merely the unexpectedness of its content but its location. The chorus, ranged horizontally and vertically in a grid representing the Scala loges and covering most of the visible area, is placed at the very front of the stage, just behind the curtain... One audience looks at another. And the other stares back.

In describing this production and other radical stagings of *Aida,* Clemens Risi—thinking about recent critical controversies surrounding the opera—insists: "Seeking out new and provocative images proves to be necessary in order to visualize *Aida*'s implicit statement about colonialist and imperialist tendencies."[113]

As I hope I made abundantly clear in my discussion of Dominique Pitoiset's staging of *Macbeth* earlier in this chapter, I am not prepared to condemn radical stagings of this kind in principle, even if they simply create a parallel universe to experience and to reflect upon alongside the music and libretto of a Verdi opera. I can only nod in agreement with Graham Vick, who—in the wake of his controversial staging of *Il trovatore* at the Metropolitan Opera in December 2000—contended that "a production should offer a surprising dialogue with the stage, which an audience is prepared to engage in. The notion of going to see a familiar opera is at its worst when it is like putting on a familiar pair of old carpet slippers. That has nothing to do with the spirit of why Verdi created his operas."[114]

Whether it is *necessary* to visualize *Aida's* Orientalist tendencies in the theater, in Risi's sense, is quite another matter. There are many ways to stage Italian opera, and it is every bit as dangerous to insist on radical stagings as it would be to insist on displaced or traditional ones. That is why I am saddened when a director for whom I have great respect, Francesca Zambello, is quoted as saying, "If I have to think of a work of Verdi that moved me on stage, that's going to be pretty hard." I rather agree with David Levin that there are convincing and original traditional stagings and convincing and original radical stagings, just as there are failures across the spectrum.[115] Verdi's reaction to any such controversy would have been to look at the box-office receipts. We could do worse.

Whereas many works by Verdi have at least been the object of controversy, relatively little thought has gone into the staging of serious or semiserious operas by Rossini, Bellini, and Donizetti. Widespread acceptance of the Rossini serious operas, in particular, has been hindered by the failure of stage directors to realize these works effectively in the theater. That an unusual number of operas such as *La donna del lago* are regularly presented in concert form, rather than being staged, attests to this failure. Since 1981, I have seen four productions of the opera, by Frank Corsaro, Gae Aulenti, Werner Herzog, and Luca Ronconi, all highly respected names in the theater, but none has succeeded in giving the opera a convincing profile on stage. The most successful stagings of Rossini serious operas over this period have probably been those of Pier Luigi Pizzi, many for the Rossini Opera Festival. Pizzi has such a splendid eye for theatrical space that his productions of *Tancredi, Maometto II, Bianca e Falliero,* and *Otello* have been extraordinarily beautiful. Only in the case of *Maometto II,* however, did he produce what I considered to be a convincing dramatic action. Others have followed in Pizzi's footsteps, without his genius, and have given us Rossini productions that involve little more than shifting singers around the stage to form beautiful but static images.

Is it Rossini's fault? That is hard to tell. Certainly his operas emerge from a theatrical tradition quite different from the more rapid dramaturgy that often characterizes the operas of Verdi. In Rossini, events come more slowly: arias, duets, ensembles expound the drama in a more formal way. In a slow ensemble, each character will sing the same melodic line and from those separate melodic lines, with added counterpoints, an overall emotional state emerges. The music can be stunningly beautiful, but it suspends time, rather than moving it along. Arias set forward one dramatic position in a broad opening section; a brief transition establishes a new dramatic position; and the latter gives rise to a lengthy concluding section. Within duets there are long melodic periods, first sung by one character, then repeated by the other. Conflicts are often stereotyped: love versus duty is the most common, often embodied in a daughter who refuses to wed the man chosen by her father for political reasons, but insists on following her own romantic instincts. Extended choral movements establish a mood against which the drama will develop. Given this more deliberate dramatic and musical pacing, traditional stagings of Rossini's serious operas often seem like concerts in costume.

Yet much the same thing could have been said until recently about the operas of George Frideric Handel, which are even further from familiar theatrical traditions. Productions of Handel operas in major opera houses in England and the United States used to be as rare as they still are in Italy. The "da capo" aria tradition, with its almost obligatory ABA structure, the castratos that roamed the eighteenth-century stage, the formal poetic language, all seemed to place a barrier between a modern audience and the successful revival of Handel. Yet the situation has turned itself completely around in the past decade. Instead of trying to prod Handel's operas into mid-nineteenth-century conventions, musicians have accepted the structure of the works and discovered their beauties. Stage directors have invented new ways of bringing them to life, not by deconstructing them in the German manner, but by treating their general plots with ironic distance—placing them in fanciful settings or laughing gently at the complications of their plots—while continuing to take seriously the emotions of their characters. They have discovered that it is possible to stage *through* a "da capo" aria, to make an aria tell a story that begins at the beginning of the first "A" and concludes only at the end of the repeated "A." The music and art of the singer can therefore be enjoyed on one level, while the staging keeps the action going across the entire aria. One cannot argue with the extraordinary success these operas have been having: Who would have imagined that in the past few years delighted audiences in major American opera houses from Chicago to Houston to New York would vigorously applaud essentially complete performances of *Partenope, Giulio Cesare, Agrippina, Xerxes,* and *Alcina?*

We need directors who attempt to think through the Italian repertory anew, not directors who impose extreme settings in order to stir life into works in which they do not believe. I infuriated the head of the Rossini Opera Festival by referring to Pesaro's *Semiramide* from the summer of 2003, directed by Dieter Kaegi, as "just silly." And so it was: not terrible, not disgusting, not outlandish, just silly. The basic set, an enormous table with television monitors, evoked the control room of the Enterprise from *Star Trek*. At the very beginning of the opera, the ambassadors to Babylonia seemed to come not from all over the ancient world but from all over the universe. So far so good. And then the *Konzept* disintegrated, leaving the awkward table, around which characters struggled to sing their duets (*Semiramide* is largely an opera of duets). Arsace arrived with a shopping bag containing little cut-out hearts to present to his beloved Azema. (He abandoned the bag after his aria, and it had to be picked up by an extra.) The control table was then transformed into a gaming table—filled with characters tossing in chips—for the duet between Arsace and Assur, who could hardly get near to one another in the pandemonium. It was worse when Arsace and Semiramide were served dinner on opposite sides of the table during one of their duets. Assur sported a Dr. Strangelove prosthesis instead of an arm, and when it came time for him to descend into the tomb of Assur, he writhed around the middle of the table from which smoke emerged. If there was a point, even a *Konzept,* no one seemed to have understood what it was, and I have yet to see it explained.

Because they emerge from Neoclassicism, but also initiate the glorious tradition of Italian Romantic opera, the Rossini serious operas pose special opportunities and challenges to contemporary directors. As debates about staging continue, the operas themselves demand our attention for their musical beauty, their dramatic truth, and the complex and continually changing ways in which they interact with the artistic visions of performers. What theaters can do is make available to stage directors and set designers the best possible texts of the operas and all relevant secondary materials (including staging manuals and contemporary set designs), and then turn them loose to do their work as they conceive it. Whether designers and directors choose traditional, displaced, or radical stagings, such as those discussed in this chapter, or seek other innovative approaches, it is only through their artistry that these operas can come to life in the theater.

CODA

14

TWO KINGS HEAD NORTH: TRANSFORMING ITALIAN OPERA IN SCANDINAVIA

While divas and scholars alike may spend most of their time learning the score—in one or more of its surviving versions—and developing the stylistic sensitivity and skills needed to perform an opera, there are occasions when contemporary theatrical life allows them, even encourages them, to take a role that goes significantly beyond the kinds of interventions discussed thus far. In the spoken theater, performers are assumed to have ample liberty to modify and invent, even when faced with the works of the very greatest playwrights. To what location *hasn't* one stage director or another moved "To be or not to be" in order to give "his" or "her" *Hamlet* a particular aura? When the film director Baz Luhrman, known for his Latino *Shakespeare's R & J*, mounted Puccini's *La Bohème* on Broadway on 8 December 2002, he boasted about maintaining the musical and verbal integrity of the opera, while allowing his invention full reign within the realm of contemporary stagecraft and updating the action to 1957. But in many countries (including the United States), operatic performers, critics, scholars, and audiences tend to be impatient with inventions that transform the musical and verbal substance of a familiar work, which is why there have been relatively few efforts to renew the repertory of Italian opera by manipulating it from within.

In the world of theater, after all, there is no expectation that the version of an important play produced by a great director—such as Deborah Warner's *Medea* with Fiona Shaw, which opened in New York at the Brooklyn Academy of Music on 2 October 2002—will be around five years later. Such a version will be performed many times in succession within a single season (sometimes night after night), toured from one venue to the next, or revived in subsequent seasons, until the audience begins to lose interest, and then will be retired, often encased in an electronic form for home viewing. The economic and artistic realities of operatic production, on the other hand, do not encourage similar freedom. Textual uniformity is economically advantageous. While a play script is a relatively simple document to manipulate, modifying operatic performing materials (parts, scores) is more time-consuming and costly. There are also practical considerations. With operas from the standard repertory, it is difficult enough for singers to learn new stagings and remember a new set of musical cuts; asking them to change text or rearrange sections of music often proves impossible, especially when they will perform the work in that version no more than eight to twelve times before moving on with the same work to a different country, a different opera house, a different stage director, and a different conductor.

And yet there are occasions when unusual interventions seem justified. By studying carefully the history of a work, scholars and performers may be able to produce or resurrect a version sufficiently interesting to a particular opera house that it justifies the unusual effort required to bring it before the public. A singer such as Natalie Dessay can be so entranced with a particular version of an operatic warhorse (the French *Lucie de Lammermoor,* for example), that multiple opera houses may decide to mount the work for her.[1] Or a world-famous stage director may come up with an idea for producing an opera that requires significant creative interventions in the version or versions with which the composer was involved—interventions that involve not only staging but even text and music.

Is there a limit to the extent of such interventions? Since no one can assert moral rights in the theater, certainly not for nineteenth-century works long out of copyright, the rule of the marketplace holds sway. As Verdi would have said, what matters is whether the public buys tickets. The only moral imperative, it seems to me, is absolute honesty in describing what a theater is doing. When the Martina Franca opera festival in Italy's Puglia region put on several important Rossini productions during the summers of 2000, 2001, and 2002, I criticized them not for their initiative in producing the shows (a most appropriate effort) or for the quality of their realizations (I didn't see them), but for pretending that the 1831 "revision" of *Otello* with Maria Malibran in the title role, *Ivanhoé* at the Odéon Theater in Paris in 1826, or *Robert Bruce* at the Opéra in 1846 were composer-sanctioned texts.[2] One understands a theater's desire to sell tickets, but to do so by falsifying the historical record is unconscionable.

During the 2002–3 season, I had the opportunity to work with two fascinating productions in Scandinavia, in which major new "versions" of operas by Verdi and Rossini were successfully performed. While Gothenburg's

Gustavo III was the "hypothetical reconstruction" of an opera that Verdi had "completed" (the composer's word) in 1858, and Helsinki's *Il viaggio a Reims* involved considerable rewriting of the libretto by Dario Fo, each production demonstrated that the cooperative efforts of performers and scholars need not stop at the establishing of composer-sanctioned scores and their theatrical realization. In the best of senses, the theater is a site for play: so let's play.

RESTORING VERDI'S *GUSTAVO III*
Sweden's National Opera

The new opera house is one of the most characteristic buildings on the waterfront in Gothenburg, Sweden's major southwestern port and its second largest city. Founded in the seventeenth century to give the country a military foothold near the North Sea, where battles with adjacent Denmark and Norway were common, the town soon became a significant trading center. It attracted merchants from England and the Netherlands, who helped establish its East India Company and provided some of the economic strength needed to develop a major industrial and commercial area. As the town grew, a series of semicircular canals and ring roads provided a frame through which urban life could sprawl. The Gothenburg Opera, which opened in October 1994, is perched at the very center of this design. While many of the older buildings within the innermost canal are constructed of the yellow bricks that dominate the appearance of old Gothenburg, the side of the opera house facing the city is largely concrete. Its wondrous seaside facade, however, opening into the lobby where patrons enter the theater and congregate during intermissions, is made of glass, and its shape calls to mind the great ships that used to ply the port. The city's shipbuilding days are largely over, although some large freighters and even passenger ships continue to use the port, but maritime museums, floating restaurants and hotels, and architectural landmarks (a parking garage in the shape of a tanker, an office building that resembles a smokestack constructed from Lego building blocks) nostalgically invoke past glories.

Opera had been produced in Gothenburg with regularity since the nineteenth century, often by visiting companies, but the art form became an ever more central part of cultural life during the twentieth. Performances were held in the Grand Theater, built during the 1850s, but its small seating capacity and inadequate stage prompted efforts to provide Gothenburg with a modern opera house. After almost fifty years of discussion, in which some of Sweden's most prominent performers, including Birgit Nilsson and Jussi

Björling, were involved, the new theater was finally erected. During 2002 the city continued beautification efforts around its imposing presence, constructing a tunnel for the city's principal roadway so that the space in front of the theater could become a park. Culture continues to matter in Sweden, and in Gothenburg the opera house is arguably the most important cultural site.

Ever since the Gothenburg Opera opened its doors, there had been talk of producing Verdi's *Un ballo in maschera*. The work had been tentatively scheduled for 1998, but the theater learned that the rival Royal Opera in Stockholm also intended to offer *Ballo* that season. Rather than mount a competing production, the theater asked the stage director already hired, Anthony Pilavachi, to substitute *La traviata*. As it turned out, Stockholm changed its plans, so that neither house produced Verdi's *Ballo* that year. Bear in mind that *Un ballo in maschera* is not just any opera in Sweden. Despite a native tradition of operatic composition, *Ballo* is as close as the Swedes come to having a "national opera," since everyone knows that Verdi's work was based on a historical event: the assassination of that most European and cultivated of Swedish monarchs, Gustaf III. Indeed, one of the treasures in the fabled collection of musical manuscripts assembled by Rudolf Nydahl, housed today in Stockholm, is the autograph manuscript of the 1833 French opera by Daniel François-Esprit Auber, to a text by Eugène Scribe, *Gustave III;*[3] this libretto, in turn, was the direct source for the libretto of Verdi's *Un ballo in maschera.*

There are star-crossed works of art, born under circumstances that challenge their very integrity. Donizetti's *Maria Stuarda* and *Poliuto,* ravaged by Neapolitan censorship, could be rescued simply by locating and editing the original, complete manuscripts (that of *Maria Stuarda,* in fact, is in the same Nydahl collection in Stockholm): and so Maria once again refers to Elisabetta as "vile bastard" and Saint Polyeuctus goes to his martyrdom on the operatic stage. Undoing the censor's last-minute effort to improve the moral tone of *Rigoletto* by pretending that the Duke has not shown up at Sparafucile's inn looking for the assassin's "sister" required no more than looking with care at Verdi's original manuscript and realizing that his text had been altered by another hand. Even after Verdi decided that *Stiffelio,* with its explosive mixture of sex, hypocrisy, and religion, would never be permitted to remain in the repertory without extensive revisions, he carefully preserved almost all the pages he had removed from his manuscript, allowing scholars some 150 years later to reconstruct the work in its written form precisely as he had envisioned it.

But *Un ballo in maschera* has quite a different history, and some of that history has been known for a long time.[4] During the autumn of 1857 Verdi and his librettist, Antonio Somma, began to prepare an opera on the theme of

Gustavo III for performance during the carnival season of 1858 at the Teatro San Carlo of Naples. That the assassination of a Swedish king in 1792 during a masked ball might raise censorial hackles did not surprise the composer, and by the end of November Verdi and his librettist had agreed to shift the action away from the Swedish royal court at Stockholm to a smaller ducal court in the Pomeranian province of Stettin, with the title of the opera becoming *Una vendetta in dominò.* For Verdi this change was not unlike what he had accepted during the composition of *Rigoletto,* moving his story from the Renaissance French court of François I to a ducal court in Mantua.[5] What neither Verdi nor the Neapolitans expected was that on 14 January 1858, just as the composer was ending his sea voyage from Genoa to Naples, Felice Orsini and three accomplices would attempt to assassinate Napoleon III and his empress in Paris. The reverberations from the Italian anarchists' bombs, which killed eight people and wounded another one hundred and fifty, were felt all over Europe. Thus, although Verdi was prepared to begin rehearsals for *Una vendetta in dominò* immediately, he soon understood that even this revised story had become impossible. The Neapolitans suggested a libretto set in medieval Florence, *Adelia degli Adimari,* the masked ball becoming an unmasked banquet. Verdi was outraged. A legal battle with the theater ensued, and as part of his evidence the composer had a copyist write the two librettos (*Vendetta* and *Adelia*) in parallel columns. Then, in a series of pungent footnotes, Verdi explained why he would not be party to this substitution, concluding, "A composer who respects both his own art and himself could not nor would not dishonor himself by accepting as the subject for his music, written to quite a different text, these absurdities, which manhandle the most obvious dramatic principles and insult the conscience of an artist."[6] Ultimately Verdi and the theater came to an agreement: the contract was dissolved and the composer agreed to return during the autumn of 1858 to mount an opera that had not yet been produced in Naples, *Simon Boccanegra.*

But what was to become of *Una vendetta in dominò?* By coincidence, a play on the subject of the life and death of the Swedish monarch was staged in Rome during that same winter, apparently without significant censorship. Upon learning of it, Verdi sought to interest the Roman impresario Vincenzo Jacovacci in mounting the opera he had originally conceived. Toward the beginning of March 1858 he therefore sent Jacovacci a copy of the libretto for what he claimed was *Gustavo III.* In fact, it was *Una vendetta in dominò,* but with the setting returned from Stettin to Stockholm, thus, from a ducal court to the royal one. The enthusiastic Jacovacci forwarded it immediately to the Papal censors, only to find them as inflexible as their Neapolitan brethren: their suggested substitute libretto, *Il Conte di Gothemburg,* heavily modified both the structure of the drama and the individual verses.[7] Verdi was again outraged, but this time he did not suspend negotiations with the theater. Gradually a compromise was reached: if Verdi wanted to keep the essential characters and plot, he would be compelled to move the story out of Europe; if he insisted on keeping it in Europe, he would have to introduce most of the modifications demanded by the censors.[8] Ultimately he and Somma shifted the setting to colonial Boston, and the composer acknowledged receipt of the new libretto, *Un ballo in maschera,* on 11 September 1858. During the remainder of the year, first in Sant'Agata, then in Naples, Verdi elaborated the new version, although not without constant harrassment from the censors, who continued to demand modifications in phrases they found immoral or politically daring. Having now decided, come what may, that he was going to stage his new opera in Rome, the composer accepted changes he might otherwise have resisted. And so, complaining all the while, Verdi arrived in Rome in early January 1859 with a completely orchestrated opera, whose first performance took place on 17 February.

Un ballo in maschera has not ceased to be a problem ever since. There are, of course, those who claim that there really is no problem: if Verdi had wanted to change the opera, they say, he had ample opportunity to do so once Italy became united in 1860 and regional censorship disappeared.[9] That argument, of course, fails to recognize that Rome, where *Ballo* was first performed, did not become part of a united Italy until 1870, by which time Verdi had no motivation whatsoever to alter an opera that was more than a decade old and continued to circulate successfully. It is easy, on the other hand, to understand why the Swedes would want to return Verdi's opera to its original historical setting: the court of Gustaf III, one of the most important of Sweden's monarchs, was often compared with that of the French king Louis XIV.[10] The prospect of experiencing on the operatic stage the magnificence of Gustaf's court and the unhappy history of his demise, especially when accompanied by Verdi's music, seemed irresistible. The best-known adaptation was made by a Swedish poet, Erik Lindegren, who rewrote the text in Swedish, introducing characters and situations he claimed to be truer to the historical record, and adopting actual words attributed to the King.[11] Lindegren did not simply "adapt" Somma's verses: he rewrote the text, introducing references that did not figure in the original libretto. After being shot by Count Holberg (the "Renato" figure), for example, Gustaf addresses him with the classical and Shakespearean "Ej du, min Brutus!" This version, performed at the Royal Opera of Stockholm in 1958, makes no secret of Gustaf's purported homosexuality, and the King seems every bit as interested in his page Oscar (a woman in the role of a young man) as in Amelia.

But dissatisfaction with the Boston setting of *Ballo* has hardly been restricted to Sweden. Edward Dent had already made a version set in Sweden for Covent Garden in 1952, in which he restored the names from the Scribe libretto. At London's Sadler's Wells, which produced the work in 1965, a new English version was provided by Leonard Hancock, with a Swedish setting; this text was published in 1989, side by side with the Italian text as *A Masked Ball, Un ballo in maschera,* an absurd mixture.[12] Many American productions simply transport the story from Boston to Stockholm, with as few interventions as possible, modifying explicit references to "America" and to the "New World." The Metropolitan Opera's production from the 1980s and 1990s, revived again in 2005, had the King of Sweden continue to send Amelia and Ankastrom across "l'immenso Oceàn."[13] For anyone who knows American history, of course, colonial Boston was hardly associated with masked balls, and conspirators named Sam and Tom evoke an unmistakably comic tone. Verdi knew that Gustavo and particularly Oscar were characters "cut in the French mode" and could exist only in a European court that had "breathed the atmosphere of the court of Louis XIV."[14] And his use of a can-can *alla Offenbach* ("Dunque, signori, aspettovi," So, comrades, I'll await you) to celebrate a visit in disguise to the den of Ulrica hardly captures the spirit of a culture known for the Salem witch trials. Boston, in short, far from being an example of "local color," has been an embarassment to *Ballo;* most contemporary stagings—whether in Milan, Paris, or Chicago—have done their best to ignore or override it.[15]

How should the change in venue be accomplished? That is the question. Do we really want the dying ruler to sing "Addio, diletta Amelia" (Farewell, beloved Amelia) instead of the "Addio, diletto America" of *Ballo,* thereby undoing all his efforts to avoid compromising the name of his beloved?[16] And who wants to hear Renato referred to as "Ankastrom" (the Italianized form of the name of the actual assassin, Johann Jacob Anckarström)? Although both names have three syllables, their accents fall differently (on the second syllable for Renato, on the first for Ankastrom). Do we assume that a European Ulrica continues to be of the "immondo sangue dei negri" (even in those countries where political correctness does not automatically require "foul blood of the negroes" to be changed)? Is "immondo sangue dei gitani," substituting one oppressed minority for another ("gypsies" for "negroes") and awkwardly adding a syllable to the text, really any better? And to what "natio tuo cielo" (your native sky) does the ruler intend to send Amelia and her husband if they are not English colonists in Boston: surely not "in Inghilterra!" (to England!). These problems have attached themselves to *Ballo* for generations, like so many barnacles: we can pretend that it doesn't matter, but it does. A Swedish setting for this opera is as relevant as a French one for *La traviata*. To place *Ballo* in Boston is like setting *La traviata* in Munich: one can do it, of course; indeed, one can make an appropriate postmodern statement in the process. But we shouldn't delude ourselves into thinking that the physical setting and the opera Verdi wrote have much to do with one another.

The early history of *Ballo* has always been told (just as I have told it) on the basis of its libretto alone. Yet during work on the critical edition of the opera, which opened the Verdi Festival in Parma in February 2001, celebrating the hundredth anniversary of the composer's death, it became clear both to Ilaria Narici, editor of that edition, and to me that there was much more to be said. When Verdi wrote to his Neapolitan friends that he had "completed" *Una vendetta in dominò* as his opera for Naples, he meant it. Tracing the musical history of *Un ballo in maschera* and its earlier versions allows us to think about performing it in new ways.

Una Vendetta in Dominò (Gustavo III)

By October 1857 Verdi had proposed for the following carnival season at the Teatro San Carlo of Naples an opera to be entitled *Gustavo III,* based on the libretto Scribe had prepared for Auber at the Paris Opéra in 1833. Verdi himself wrote a prose outline, which he sent to Somma for versification some time before 24 October.[17] Somma sent his original verses scene by scene to the composer, who commented on them and requested revisions (*CVS* 50–77, pp. 185–260). As Verdi's musical sketches preserved at the Villa Verdi at Sant'Agata reveal, the composer seems not to have written down any music before the arrival of Somma's textual revisions.[18]

Throughout his career Verdi made clear that sketching was the most important creative task in preparing an opera. As we have seen, the heart of the sketching process consists of a "continuity draft," in which Verdi traces in detail the shape and melodic content of the score. In some cases, such as *La traviata,* these drafts are primarily at the level of the individual piece or section. In other cases, such as *Rigoletto* and *Ballo,* drafts start at the beginning of an opera and essentially continue until the end. For *Ballo* there is a continuity draft for all of act 1, followed immediately by the scena before Amelia's aria in act 2. Then there is a gap: no full continuity draft exists for the aria or for the following duet and trio, although there are isolated sketches. The continuity draft resumes with the finale of act 2 and follows without hesitation through all of act 3.

Verdi spent much of November and early December 1857 sketching act 1 of *Gustavo III* in its original Swedish setting. In his continuity draft, all references are to Sweden, to King Gustavo, and to Carlo, Duke of Ankastrom. In the first measures of the introduction, the chorus invokes the "King," whom every Swedish heart adores; when Ankastrom enters, he addresses Gustavo as "Sire"; at the end of his solo he sings, "With you lost, what would remain of Sweden?" When the people stream in at the end of the Ulrica scene, they sing "Viva Gustavo" and "Glory to our King." Verdi would not have continued in this way once he and Somma had agreed about the Pomeranian setting as *Una vendetta in dominò*. Thus, the continuity draft of act 1 and the ensuing scena must have been completed by early December.

We can establish even more precise dates. Since Verdi did not like the poetry Somma originally sent for Ulrica's invocation, the librettist forwarded new text on 17 November (*CVS* 63, p. 236), with which Verdi expressed satisfaction on the 26th (*CVS* 67, p. 242). Only the revised text is in the composer's sketch: hence, he could not have drafted music for the scene until he had the new words. At that very moment, in fact, he was completing the introduction, for in a second letter on 26 November Verdi added this request: "In the stretta of the introduction it would [...] be wonderful if you could find me a dactyl [a *sdrucciolo* in Italian metrics] instead of "al tocco," and allow me to say "alle tre" (*CVS* 69, p. 244). Meanwhile, though, as we saw in chapter 11, Verdi drafted the introduction using Somma's words, *except* for this final passage, which he wrote without text. Thus, between mid-November and approximately 26 November, Verdi sketched the introduction of *Gustavo III*; from 26 November to early December, he sketched the scene in Ulrica's den and the scena that opens act 2. Then he abruptly broke off work on the continuity draft.

By mid-November, Verdi reluctantly informed Somma that the Neapolitan censors would not accept *Gustavo III*: there could be no Swedish court, no King, no firearms, no political conspiracy. Instead, he and Somma moved the action from Sweden to the Swedish province of Pomerania, from Stockholm to Stettin. the King of Sweden became the Duke of Pomerania, the Duke of Ankastrom became Count Renato, and so on. Composer and versifier worked together during Somma's visit to Verdi's home over Christmas; by Somma's departure, around 27 December, the libretto of the now-retitled *Una vendetta in dominò* was finished.

What about the music? Behind schedule, the composer decided to remain at Sant'Agata until he had completed "everything that requires imagination." [19] On 9 January he wrote to Naples, "The opera is done and even here I am working on the full score; I hope to depart on board the *Sicilian Courier*, and as soon as I land in Naples I will be able to deliver music to the copyist." [20]

It is uncertain when Verdi began sketching again, since only fragmentary sketches survive for Amelia's aria at the beginning of the second act and the following duet and trio, but once the continuity draft resumes with the finale of act 2, Verdi is setting *Una vendetta in dominò*. He makes no mistakes. There is no hint of a "King" or a Swedish royal court. Gustavo is always "Duke" and Renato "Count." Verdi's work could not have begun before Somma arrived at Sant'Agata a few days before Christmas and was surely completed by the time the composer left Busseto on 5 January.[21]

A composer's continuity drafts are private documents. From them no one, not even singers, could rehearse or perform. That is the significance of Verdi's words, "even here I am working on the full score [...] and as soon as I land in Naples I will be able to deliver music to the copyist." As we saw in chapter 2, Verdi prepared a full score in two stages. First, working from the continuity draft, he prepared a skeleton score, entering all the vocal lines, with important instrumental solos and the instrumental bass. In a second stage, he completed the orchestration.

Preparation of a skeleton score was urgent: only from this document could copyists derive the vocal parts. While rehearsals with singers proceeded, Verdi would then complete the orchestration. It is unlikely that he waited until the entire continuity draft was finished before beginning his skeleton score. We know from other operas that these stages overlapped. Creative artists divide their time between moments that depend on inspiration, when a work takes shape, and the arduous task of taming that inspiration into a practical document. However, Verdi did not begin preparing the skeleton score for *Una vendetta in dominò* before composer and versifier decided on the Pomeranian setting, and the work must have been far advanced when Verdi left for Naples.

Although the complete autograph manuscript of what we know as *Un ballo in maschera* has been in the Ricordi archives since 1859 and has been consulted by many, no one until the beginning of the twenty-first century had fully appreciated that 75 percent of that manuscript is, in fact, the skeleton score of *Una vendetta in dominò*, with modifications and orchestration for *Ballo* introduced directly on the same pages. When he began work on *Ballo* in September 1858, nine months after having "completed" the earlier opera, Verdi modified the names, scraped away some words and music, crossed out superseded passages, manipulated tonalities he had decided to change, and completed the orchestration. By reading beneath these superimposed alterations, one can discover what was there in January 1858. Here are two examples from the second scene of the first act, all but two folios of which were prepared for *Una vendetta in dominò* and transformed on the same pages into *Un ballo in maschera*.

1. Ulrica originally sang the words "le chiavi del futuro" (the keys to the future), as in all sources for *Gustavo III* and *Una vendetta in dominò;* for *Ballo*, Verdi replaced "the keys" with "la face" (the torch). As Somma later wrote, "And they don't want Satan to have in hand the keys to the future, but the books of the future and who knows what" (*CVS* 90, p. 278). In Rome, only St. Peter is permitted to have keys.

2. The final choral hymn, for which there is no text in the continuity draft, was originally entered into the skeleton score with the text of *Una vendetta in dominò:* "Gloria a te, grande e pio, / Che come volle Iddio / Le nostre sorte moderi: / Gloria e salute a te." (Glory to you, great and pious one, who guides our fortune, as God wills: glory and long life to you). For *Ballo*, Verdi subsequently crossed out this text celebrating the divine right of kings, substituting "American" verses, which address the tenor: "O figlio d'Inghilterra / Amor di questa terra" (O son of England, beloved of this land).

Almost 80 percent of the manuscript pages of the concluding *festa da ballo*, which fills forty-six folios of the composer's manuscript, show the same kind of modifications as in in these two examples from the second scene of act 1. Verdi, in short, completed a skeleton score of *Una vendetta in dominò* in preparation for what he expected to be its Neapolitan premiere.

Although Orsini's bombs failed to assassinate Napoleon III, the explosions resonated in Naples. As a result, instead of rehearsing *Una vendetta in dominò* and orchestrating the score, Verdi engaged in complex negotiations about the text of the opera, about his legal responsibilities, about compromises that would salvage honor and purses. With his "completed" (but not fully orchestrated) opera intact, the composer sent a libretto of *Gustavo III* to the Roman impresario at the beginning of March 1858. This libretto was essentially identical to the one he had set to music, that is *Una vendetta in dominò*, but with the original setting and names restored. There could be no clearer indication that he considered this text to be the proper one for his opera. When the Roman censors, too, insisted on elaborate modifications, Verdi set aside *Gustavo III*, returning to it only after he acknowledged receipt from Somma of the libretto for *Un ballo in maschera*, on 11 September 1858.

And what had the composer been doing while negotiations with the Roman theaters and with Somma proceeded? As far as we can tell, nothing. It made no sense to return to the score until matters pertaining to its libretto were resolved. As Giuseppina Strepponi said in a letter of 12 July 1858, written from the baths at Tabiano, to their Neapolitan friend, Cesarino De Sanctis,

"Verdi is very busy... doing nothing. His most demanding activity at present is to get dressed and undressed, to eat and sleep, so that his stomach is beginning to get round, to his great satisfaction."[22] That idleness would soon be coming to an end.

From the time he received the libretto of *Un ballo in maschera* in Busseto until his arrival in Rome on 10 January 1859, Verdi was completing and orchestrating the opera. There is relatively little information about the chronology of his work. Most was accomplished in Naples, where he remained after mounting *Simon Boccanegra* on 30 November. With the skeleton score of *Una vendetta in dominò* before him, Verdi had several tasks to accomplish:

> He had to transform the setting and character names, substituting "Riccardo," "Silvano," "Samuel," and "Tom" for "Gustavo," "Cristiano," "Ermanno," and "Manuel." He had to emend titles: Riccardo is a "Count," not a "Duke"; Renato loses his title of "Count."
>
> He had to modify text throughout the score to agree with the libretto of *Ballo*, not that of *Una vendetta in dominò*. This meant eliminating Somma's earlier text, normally by scraping away or crossing out earlier words and inserting new ones. In some cases Verdi also made changes in the melodic lines.
>
> He had to complete the orchestration. It is impossible to tell how much of the orchestration was written down when Verdi worked out the skeleton score of *Una vendetta in dominò* during the winter of 1857–58, but it is unlikely to have been extensive.
>
> He took the opportunity, having thought further about the opera, to make aesthetically motivated musical changes.

For several important parts of the opera Verdi did away with the earlier skeleton score of *Una vendetta in dominò* and started anew. This is particularly evident when he entered names and vocal text that did not exist before September 1858. Here are two examples:

> After receiving the libretto of *Ballo* in September 1858, Verdi removed the first part of the original introduction, which includes the instrumental prelude and introductory choral scene, and completely rewrote it on new paper. Riccardo's name is entered directly (rather than replacing "Gustavo"), as are the new words. But Verdi would not have rewritten the gathering just to fix the text. A comparison of the continuity draft and the autograph manuscript of *Ballo* shows that he made significant musical changes in the melodic lines and in the structure of the prelude.

The very last gathering of the opera was written anew for *Ballo*. The names and American verses are entered without a previous layer. But there were other differences between the continuity draft and this manuscript. Most striking, the entire passage after the choral outburst "Ah! morte... infamia" (Ah! death... infamy) and the beginning of Riccardo's final Andante, "Ella è pura" (She is pure), was originally drafted as a continuation of the 2/4 meter of the choral music. The idea of a final reprise of the offstage dance music, after the assassination, came to Verdi only as he worked on *Un ballo in maschera,* that is, after 11 September 1858.

It is easiest to identify the new pages when they involve American verses or modified names, but there are other possibilities. Verdi originally wrote a continuity draft for what would become Renato's scena ed aria in act 3, for example, using a largely different melody (its first words are "E sei tu," And it is you). From that draft he must have prepared a skeleton score by January 1858, one that no longer survives. Later, after 11 September 1858, Verdi made a second, independent sketch for this scena ed aria, corresponding to the famous "Eri tu" (It was you) from *Ballo*. We know this because two phrases from "E sei tu" associated with the Swedish court had become problematic by the fall of 1858. In the scena, Renato wants revenge against "altro e più nobil sangue" (other, more noble blood), while in the aria he refers to himself as "vassallo tuo primo" (your principal vassal). For the New World setting of *Ballo,* both phrases were modified: the first became "altro, ben altro sangue" (other, very different blood) and the second "l'amico tuo primo" (your closest friend). The revised continuity draft has the revised text, as do the new pages in the autograph manuscript. Thus, "Eri tu" must have been composed between September 1858 and January 1859.

While working on *Un ballo in maschera,* then, Verdi introduced such extensive changes that he felt obliged to replace 25 percent of the original skeleton score pages of *Una vendetta in dominò* (some 80 to 85 folios of a manuscript of 329 folios). On these added pages, Riccardo, Renato, Sam, and Tom are the only names found; no original Swedish verses are peeking out from under the "American" ones; and references to the political situation in Europe are gone. As far as we know, the rejected 25 percent of the skeleton score of *Una vendetta in dominò* no longer exists.[23]

Reconstructing *Gustavo III* for Gothenburg

Anders Wiklund, a genial Swedish musicologist and conductor, has collaborated closely in both the critical editions of the works of Rossini (for which he edited *La scala di seta* and, in collaboration with Patricia Brauner, *La pietra del paragone*) and those of Donizetti (*Maria Stuarda* and, in collaboration with Roger Parker, *Le convenienze ed inconvenienze teatrali*). After a trip I made to Copenhagen for the Verdi Festival in that city at the end of May 2001—where I admired the Calixto Bieto staging of *Un ballo in maschera* in Fascist Spain[24]—I visited Wiklund at his home in nearby Gothenburg and saw a fascinating new opera by Jan Sandström, *Macbeth²* (*Macbeth* squared), at the Gothenburg opera, where Wiklund works as an adviser. The production showed off beautifully the remarkable scenic capabilities of the new theater and its first-rate orchestra.

While taking a long walk through one of the parks on the outskirts of the city, we began to talk about *Ballo*. I related the history to Wiklund and shared my thought that it might be possible to reconstruct *Gustavo III*. "And we can perform it in Gothenburg," he immediately added. From a hypothetical "might" to a performance less than sixteen months later was hardly what I had in mind, but he was absolutely serious. In September, Wiklund and the director of the theater, Kjell Ingebretsen, himself a conductor, flew from Sweden to Parma to see the production of Verdi's revised *Macbeth* (1865) that concluded the 2001 Verdi Festival, and was the first to use the new critical edition prepared by David Lawton. Before the evening was over, Ilaria Narici, editor of *Ballo*, and I had agreed to undertake the reconstruction of *Gustavo III* for the September opening of the 2002–3 season of the Gothenburg Opera.

Three-quarters of an opera is not an opera, but we had available to us not only three-quarters of Verdi's skeleton score for *Una vendetta in dominò*, but also the continuity draft from which he had prepared that skeleton score. For the 75 percent of the skeleton score of *Vendetta* that still exists, embedded in the autograph of *Un ballo in maschera*, the versions of the continuity draft and the skeleton score are amazingly similar: the differences are in details or in the addition of brief orchestral conclusions to closed numbers (Verdi often stopped sketching a piece with the last notes of the vocal line). For the 25 percent of the skeleton score that no longer exists, the problem often involved a transposition, so that there were only minimal musical changes. One can differentiate two situations:

> *Passages where neither an original continuity draft nor an original skeleton score exists.* This involves primarily the duet for Amelia and Gustavo/Riccardo in the second act.[25] All 20 folios of this duet in the autograph manuscript were added after 11 September 1858. While it is possible to modify the words of *Ballo* in accordance with the libretto of *Gustavo III*,

we have no certain knowledge about the original music.[26] Still, the changes that can be introduced in the text are dramaturgically significant. Whereas Riccardo promises Amelia the universe, "La mia vita... l'universo, l'universo per un detto..." (My life... the universe, the universe for a word...), Gustavo offers her something more tangible, "Il mio nome e la corona, la corona per un detto..." (My name and the crown, the crown for a word...).

Passages where only a continuity draft exists, but where the music underwent minimal changes for "Un ballo in maschera." The canzone for Oscar in the first scene began with the words "Pallida, pallida, / Volta alle stelle" (Pallid, pallid, turned toward the stars) in *Gustavo III*, but with "Volta la terrea / Fronte alle stelle" (Her earth-colored face turned toward the stars) in *Un ballo in maschera.*[27] This piece was originally entered into the skeleton score of *Una vendetta in dominò / Gustavo III* in B major; for *Un ballo in maschera* Verdi transposed it down to B♭ major. Musical differences between the two versions are minimal. Thus, there is every reason to believe that the original skeleton score (nine missing folios) was essentially the same as the music we know from *Ballo,* but written a half tone lower.

For a good half of the missing 25 percent of the original skeleton score, then, the music of *Gustavo III* was probably the same as *Un ballo in maschera,* but in a different key.

In several places, though, the versions of the continuity draft for *Una vendetta in dominò / Gustavo III,* on the one hand, and *Ballo,* on the other, are strikingly different. There are important changes in significant melodies (such as the opening chorus), structural differences (the entire scena for Amelia that opens the second act, through the beginning of her aria), heavily modified passages (the end of Gustavo/Riccardo's romanza in the last act), or even largely new pieces (Ankastrom/Renato's aria in the last act). But wherever there is a hint remaining in the autograph manuscript of *Ballo* of what was once there for *Vendetta,* that hint is very close to the continuity draft. Here are three examples:

I. THE SCENA PRECEDING AMELIA'S ARIA AT THE BEGINNING OF ACT II. The last measures of the original version of Amelia's scena are still visible in the autograph manuscript of *Ballo:* never orchestrated, Verdi crossed them out as he worked on *Ballo.*[28] These surviving measures, however, are basically the same as those in the continuity draft. All preceding pages for *Vendetta* were removed by Verdi as he prepared *Ballo.* Given the way Verdi constructed his manuscripts physically, however, we know that the passage he removed was about half as long as the music he added. Indeed, the version found in Verdi's continuity draft is half as long as the music he introduced for *Ballo*.[29] The text of this draft is basically what Somma sent to Verdi on 5 November 1857 (*CVS* 56, p. 211), and this same text occurs in the libretto of *Una vendetta in dominò* that Verdi prepared in February 1858 to press his case in the legal proceedings, as well as in the libretto of *Gustavo III* he sent to Rome in March 1858. There is every reason to assume that the music of the scena currently found in the autograph manuscript of *Un ballo in maschera,* with its partially different text, was prepared for *Ballo,* after 11 September 1858.

The original passage is fascinating, because the music explicitly refers back to the orchestral introduction to the second scene of the opera, in Ulrica's den. The opening sonority and the ensuing orchestral figuration that play such an important part in that scene also dominate Amelia's scena. But the continuity draft of Amelia's scena (and presumably its transformation into a skeleton score) lacks what is the most striking melodic reference here in *Ballo.* the return of the lyrical theme that Amelia sang during her trio with Ulrica and Gustavo, to the text "Concedimi, o Signore, virtù ch'io lavi il core" (Grant me, Lord, virtue to cleanse my heart). This is the passage which, in his autograph manuscript of *Ballo,* Verdi associates with the stage directions "Appare Amelia dalle eminenze" (Amelia appears from the hills) and "A questa ripresa Amelia s'inginocchia e prega" (At this reprise Amelia kneels and prays). There is no such respite for Amelia in *Una vendetta in dominò* until her aria: the scena itself is stark and terrifying from the first note to the last.

This change in Verdi's conception of the scene between *Una vendetta in dominò* and *Un ballo in maschera* has an effect similar to the removal of specific references to the gallows on the "orrido campo" (horrible field), a change mandated by the Roman censors. There is something faintly sentimental, even pietistic, about Verdi's modification. The pure-hearted maiden appears to the heavenly sound of the flute, accompanied by high string tremolos (shades of *La traviata*), then kneels to pray as the first violins, second violins, and cellos take the tune over a three-octave range, with the flute and first clarinet playing celestial arpeggios (shades of Gilda's "Lassù in ciel").

Stage directors today, of course, are not much given to sentimentality and pietism, and most audiences would snicker at an Amelia kneeling in prayer. Nonetheless, Verdi's music for *Ballo* speaks clearly. In one of the productions I saw recently, the problem was resolved by keeping Amelia out of sight until the embarrassing moment had passed and the music again became agitated. Calixto Bieto simply ignored the music (to put it bluntly), or (to put it generously) used it as an ironic counterpoint for the action introduced by the director: act 2 began with a homosexual rape and murder on the "orrido campo." Even the grandest of grand musical gestures, in short, cannot be treated as an absolute guide to staging Verdi's operas today. Once we understand the composer's own ambivalence about this scene, that knowledge plays inevitably into our thinking about it.

2. A CADENZA IN THE SECOND-ACT FINALE. The continuity draft of the laughing-chorus finale of the second act was originally notated in *B major*, but Verdi lowered the tonality to *B♭ major* before preparing his skeleton score. The original text reads "l'innamorato Conte riposa!" (the Count in love [Ankastrom in *Gustavo III*, Renato in *Una vendetta in dominò*] takes his ease), as it did in the skeleton score; after 11 September 1858 the composer changed it to "l'innamorato campion" (the champion in love) for *Ballo*, since the creole Renato is no longer a Count. Explicit references to cuckoldry, such as "Tal marchio fitto mi volle in fronte" (he wanted that deep mark [i.e., horns] on my forehead), which Verdi had copied into the skeleton score, he modified for the Roman censors to "per lui non posso levar la fronte" (because of him I cannot raise my head). The continuity draft, skeleton score, and final version remain structurally identical until near the end, when in the continuity draft there appears a two-measure repeated phrase, the first measure of which is the concluding one on folio 213v in the autograph manuscript, crossed out, but fully orchestrated. After that single measure, Verdi removed an entire leaf from this finale (the original folio 214) when preparing *Un ballo in maschera,* adding a new leaf with new music pertaining to the revised score. When the *Una vendetta in dominò* layer begins again, at folio 215, it picks up with Ankastrom's invitation to the conspirators to come to his home the next day, as in the final version.[30]

The music in the continuity draft, from the two-measure repeated phrase through Ankastrom's invitation, includes a cadenza for Amelia and Ankastrom. Here they could seem to be warbling in the mode of Gilda and the Duke, yet most of their singing in the cadenza is actually done separately, suggesting their alienation (example 14.1). Verdi stepped back from this solution, but—given that the first measure of the phrase was orchestrated in Verdi's autograph—it seems likely that the entire passage we know from the continuity draft, including the cadenza, had been orchestrated before Verdi modified his score.

For performers, the principal interpretive challenge in this final scene, in *Gustavo III* as in *Un ballo in maschera,* is the interaction between Ankastrom/ Renato and Amelia. Scholars tend to focus on details, of which performers are

EXAMPLE 14.1. GIUSEPPE VERDI, *GUSTAVO III*, CADENZA
FOR AMELIA AND ANKASTROM IN FINALE II.

often heedless or even contemptuous. How much ink has been spilled on the subject of the veiled moon and the veiled lady, the inadvertent dropping of the veil as Amelia seeks to stop the conspirators from attacking her husband, while the moon's rays illuminate her face. A nice idea, but just try to get a veil to fall inadvertently while a singer rushes forward and simultaneously strives to produce an effective melodic line. In Gothenburg, Amelia wore a mask, and the conspirators could not remove it without harming her, so she removed it herself. In Parma a more standard veil was employed, and I struggled mightily to have the performers obey Verdi's instructions. The conductor, Valéry Gergiev, and the stage director, Andrej Konchalovskij, were supportive, yet the effort was ultimately abandoned as Amelia ostentatiously ripped off her veil and threw it as far from herself as she could so as not to trip over it. To my eye, the gesture made her seem more like an exhibitionistic Salomè than a hesitant Amelia, but no one in the audience seems to have minded.

What audiences cannot help but notice, on the other hand, is the interaction between Amelia and Ankastrom / Renato. Here Somma's verses are quite explicit. At the beginning of the finale, their dialogue, while strained, is direct. After the revelation they inhabit different spheres—both speak aside, he of the dishonor his "friend" has brought on him, she of her isolation and shame. Only after summoning the conspirators to his home the next morning does Ankastrom / Renato address Amelia directly, asserting his resolve to fulfill his promise, while she—still unable to speak to him—begs pity from heaven. Verdi's modification in the final scene addresses the problem of situating

Amelia and Ankastrom/Renato and intensifies the alienation of the characters. The omission of the cadenza avoids a musical gesture that threatens to bring the characters together in musical terms, contradicting their dramaturgical separation. The Bieto production, with its visual immediacy in his Fascist setting, translated alienation into more violent confrontation between husband and wife, with much physical interaction. Despite my intellectual conviction that the Parma production's effort to keep the characters apart— so that they neither touched nor addressed their words to one another—was more "correct," the effect was less theatrically compelling. In Gothenburg, on the other hand, a production about which I will speak more fully below, the characters came together poignantly to sing their anti-cadenza, and then Ankastrom broke away to address the conspirators.

3. THE ORIGINAL VERSION OF "ERI TU." We have already seen that the famous Renato aria "Eri tu" was written specifically for *Un ballo in maschera*, not for *Una vendetta in dominò*. After 11 September 1858 the skeleton score of the aria Verdi had composed for *Una vendetta in dominò* at the end of 1857, "E sei tu," was removed from the manuscript of that opera. Verdi made a continuity draft of the new piece, using Somma's revised text, and then wrote out an entirely new autograph manuscript of the new aria. Changes in the text involved not only elements pertaining to the revised plot mentioned above (with "dell'amico tuo," for example, replacing "del vassallo tuo"), but also images considered objectionable by the Papal censors. They would not allow Amelia to be referred to as "Paradiso dell'anima mia" (Paradise of my soul) or as "simile ad un angel" (like an angel), preferring the less exalted "la delizia dell'anima mia" (delight of my soul) and "sì bella, sì candida" (so beautiful, so chaste). The continuity draft of the original "E sei tu" is complete, however, so that the original aria can be fully reconstructed.

The dark, introverted atmosphere with which "E sei tu" begins is profoundly different from the simmering rage that pervades the first part of "Eri tu," with its well-known punctuating rhythmic figure for trumpets and trombones. In "Eri tu" Verdi moves from this intense *D minor* to the relative major (*F major*) after eighteen measures, about two-fifths of the way into the aria, as Renato invokes his love for Amelia ("O dolcezze perdute!" Oh lost sweetness!). The composer accompanies the shift of key and mode with the first appearance of a celestial, arpeggiating harp and flutes. Only after this sixteen-measure lyrical outpouring is there a brief return to the parallel minor (*F minor*, at "È finita! non siede che l'odio, / E la morte nel vedovo cor!" (It is over! only hate and death remain in this widowed heart!), after which Verdi concludes the aria with an eight-measure cadence in *F major*, taking up again the words "O dolcezze perdute! O speranze d'amor!" (Oh lost sweetness! Oh hopes of love!).

In "E sei tu" the brooding opening in *F minor* continues and builds through "Traditor! che in tal guisa rimunerei del vassallo tuo primo la fé" (Traitor! that is how you would repay the faith of your principal vassal"). At that point the music shifts to *A flat major* for the more lyrical setting of "O dolcezze perdute!" (example 14.2). Although there is only a faint hint of an accompaniment in the continuity draft, the harp and flutes of "Eri tu" work perfectly well, and that is how we orchestrated the phrase in our reconstruction. In one of the most striking moments in the piece, the voice sits on middle *c* to conclude the phrase "brillava d'amor!" (shone with love!), while the opening tune returns in the accompaniment back in *F minor* for a more extended reprise and cadence at "È finita! non siede che l'odio, / E la morte nel vedovo cor!" Thus, the initial mood—less aggressive, more inward, than in "Eri tu"—plays a much more consistent role in "E sei tu." Only at the very end does the original version anticipate the revision, returning to *F major* for the brief concluding phrase ("O dolcezze! o memorie d'amor!"), using a tune essentially the same as the one Verdi would employ in the same place in "Eri tu." The vocal climax, with the baritone sustaining a high *f,* attacked softly, followed by a crescendo, is shared by both versions.

This is not the place to suggest possible reasons for Verdi's rewriting the Ankastrom aria for *Un ballo in maschera.* Without claiming for a moment that "E sei tu" is superior to "Eri tu"—one of the most popular arias Verdi ever wrote for baritone—one can justifiably say that had Verdi not revised the piece for *Un ballo in maschera,* the original aria would have continued to be performed over the decades to the delight of singers and audiences alike. Certainly the nightly ovations that would greet Gothenburg's Ankastrom, Krister St. Hill, testify to the aria's ability to give pleasure, even to a public that knows and loves "Eri tu."

EXAMPLE 14.2. GIUSEPPE VERDI, *GUSTAVO III,* ARIA ANKASTROM ("E SEI TU"), OPENING PHRASE AND LYRICAL PHRASE.

Performing *Gustavo III*

If scholars can indeed reconstruct with conviction the skeleton score of *Una vendetta in dominò,* as Verdi carried it with him to Naples in January 1858, where does that leave us? A skeleton score, after all, is not an opera that can be performed. Here we exit the realm of scholarship and enter the hypothetical. Given the widespread dissatisfaction with the compromised fate of *Un ballo in maschera,* the temptation to intervene is great. Two operations seem both possible and sensible: (1) reconstruct the opera Verdi brought with him in skeleton score to Naples in January 1858, but by using the revised libretto Verdi offered the Roman impresario in March 1858, *Gustavo III;* (2) transform *Un ballo in maschera* into a version with no historical precedent, *Un ballo in maschera (Gustavo III),* by underlaying Verdi's libretto of March 1858 to the definitive opera, making only those few musical changes required by specific changes in the text that cannot be accommodated to the music for *Ballo.* So, for example, the vocal line must be changed in order to replace "S'appella Ulrica, dall'immondo sangue dei negri" (She's called Ulrica, of the foul blood of the negroes) by the original text, "S'appella Ulrica, la sibilla" (She's called Ulrica, the sybil).

The first, "maximalist," intervention is what was performed at the Gothenburg Opera in September 2002. The second, "minimalist," intervention—which is possible, thanks to the reconstruction of *Gustavo III*—was used in a concert performance of the opera at New York's Carnegie Hall on 31 March 2004, with the Collegiate Chorale under the baton of Robert Bass. The following passage from the trio of conspirators in the third act gives the flavor of what we have been missing. Although the music is unchanged between *Una vendetta in dominò* and *Un ballo in maschera,* the quality of the text Verdi actually set to music (in the right-hand column) is profoundly better than the compromised verses for Rome:

Una vendetta in dominò/Gustavo III	Un ballo in maschera
Tutti stretti alla fede d'un patto,	*Dunque l'onta di tutti sol una,*
Tutti ardenti d'un solo desio,	*Uno il cor, la vendetta sarà,*
Noi giuriamo per l'anima a Dio	*Che tremenda, repente, digiuna*
Questo rege esecrato immolar.	*Su quel capo esecrato cadrà.*
[All joined by the faith of a pact,	[Thus, the shame of all is one shame,
all burning with a single desire,	our hearts are one, revenge will be
we swear to God on our souls to	one, terrible, sudden, hungry it will
murder this execrated King.]	fall on that execrated head.]

One cannot help wondering how any opera company could perform anything else.

Operas are also historical documents, and the original text of *Gustavo III* included a phrase that would return to Italian history in a striking fashion two years later. At the end of the first scene, Gustavo explains his plan to visit Ulrica's den to the assembled courtiers. The first stanza of his poetry originally went as follows:

Ogni cura si doni al diletto,	[Let us give ourselves over entirely to pleasure,
E s'accorra al fatidico tetto.	and let us hurry under the prophetic roof.
Per un dì si folleggi, si scherzi,	For one day let us frolic and play, let the
S'affratelli al suo popolo il Re.	King be a brother to his people.]

With the King demoted to a Governor General and the "prophetic" roof softened to a "magical" one, the strophe in *Un ballo in maschera* becomes:

Ogni cura si doni al diletto,	[Let us give ourselves over entirely to pleasure,
E s'accorra nel magico tetto.	and let us hurry under the magical roof. Among
Tra la folla de' creduli ognuno¸	the crowd of the credulous, let each of you
S'abbandoni e folleggi con me.	abandon himself and frolic with me.]

Two years later, on 20 September 1859, the Italian patriot Giuseppe Mazzini wrote an open letter to the would-be King of Italy, Victor Emanuel II, in which he rebuked him in these words: "Voi non v'affratellaste al Popolo d'Italia" (You have not made yourself a brother to the people of Italy).[31] There is a precise correspondence between Mazzini's letter and a phrase from a version of Verdi's *Un ballo in maschera* that he could not have known. Even if it should prove that the phrase was a common idiom of the period, its pointed use in *Gustavo III* is significant for those who care about the history and culture of the Italian Risorgimento; in comparison, the bland revised text in *Ballo* is without interest.

Neither of these operations can be anything more than a "hypothetical reconstruction": even assuming that our interpretation of the skeleton score is basically correct, we have no way of knowing what Verdi himself would have done had he had a free hand. For *Gustavo III,* in particular, we do not know what alterations the composer might have made as he orchestrated his score, nor what modifications might have emerged during rehearsals, nor whether he might have made still other changes when he decided to return the opera to its original setting in Stockholm. In some cases, indeed, there are hints that the score he brought to Naples might have been different from *Ballo,* but the evidence is insufficient to allow us to reconstruct a hypothetical original.

EXAMPLE 14.3. GIUSEPPE VERDI, *GUSTAVO III*, ARIA ANKASTROM
("E SEI TU"), ADDED ORCHESTRAL FIGURE.

Even more important, we do not know how the composer's orchestration for Naples in January 1858 might have differed from the orchestration of *Un ballo in maschera* for Rome. When the music is basically the same, Ilaria Narici and I followed his later orchestration. When the music is similar, we followed his later orchestration wherever possible, making only required emendations. When the music is largely different, as in Ankastrom's "E sei tu," we orchestrated the passage anew, remaining always within the orbit of Verdi's own procedures. But we could not resist allowing trumpets and trombones to add the rhythmic counterpoint in the Ankastrom aria shown in example 14.3. Anyone who knows "Eri tu" will understand why.

The Gothenburg production, by Anthony Pilavachi, was one of the most convincing stage treatments of the opera I have ever seen, not only for the coherence of its libretto but also for the inventive manner in which the opera was realized both visually and dramaturgically. The story was updated to a timeless present, and an effort was made to portray Gustavo as a ruler more interested in his private life than in matters of state. His indifference to the political realities surrounding him was established from the beginning. In receiving petitions in the first scene, for example, the King pronounced his words ironically, and the documents were soon strewn across the stage. The Chief Judge, seeking Ulrica's banishment, was a nerdish figure, bowing and scraping before the King. He was physically abused by Oscar, who tore up the documents, tripped him, and rode him like a horse, all to the King's evident amusement. The reactions of the conspirators, dressed in dark three-piece suits with red ties, some already sporting hidden weapons at this point, made clear their disgust with the lack of dignity surrounding the court, however "popular" Gustavo might be. One could argue that these antics are hardly inherent in Verdi's score, but I found wholly convincing Pilavachi's effort to reverse visually the earliest objections of the Neapolitan censors, by suggesting the existence of a well-justified "political conspiracy."

Without insisting on Gustavo's active homosexuality, the production gave Oscar a central role, establishing him as a rival to Amelia for Gustavo's affections, at least in the mind of the page. His erotic presence was felt by everyone on stage, male and female alike. Even in the quintet of the last act, Oscar shamelessly rubbed up against the conspirators (Ribbing and Dehorn), who did not seem displeased in the least by the resulting sexual charge. The two scenes of the first act were joined by Oscar, who moved directly from the end of the scene in the royal palace into Ulrica's den, where he struck the ground with his staff three times on the opening chords, as if a stage manager in a French classical drama. Ulrica herself seemed like the leader of a carefully organized séance, surrounded by excited well-to-do ladies from the court, carrying shopping bags, out for an afternoon's *frisson*. And when Amelia's fright increases at the end of her aria opening the second act ("Mezzanotte!.. ah! che veggio? Una testa / Di sotterra si leva... e sospira... "; Midnight!.. ah! what do I see? A head rises from underground... and sighs...), it was the appearance of a masked, shadowy Oscar that terrified her, an Oscar who was accompanying the King to the "orrido campo." At the end of the opera the grieving Amelia was upstaged by a distraught Oscar, who dragged the final curtain across the stage, as he collapsed in front of her.

Masks were everywhere on the stark set of Piero Vinciguerra. Throughout the entire opera the stage was bounded on both sides by enormous flats, on the upper half of which were assembled rows of red masks against a black surface, electromagnetically fixed in place. When Ankastrom shot Gustavo in the final scene, the current was switched off and the masks crashed to the stage. (One always worries about accidents in such cases—even one mask falling too early would have ruined the effect—but during the two weeks of rehearsals and performances I witnessed, there was never a problem.) The remainder of the stage consisted of platforms and a back cyclorama, with a rotating platform on which was placed a large, three-dimensional mask. Its front faced the audience during the first scene,[32] but at the start of the second scene the mask and its platform turned, so that its back faced the audience, revealing Ulrica on the platform. A similar shift occurred between the two scenes of the third act, so that at the end of the opera the platform supported not only a ghostly Ulrica observing the fulfillment of her prophecy, but also the string instruments playing at the ball. And masks dominated Markus Pysall's costumes: the absurdly comic, grotesque masks that the courtiers donned for their visit to Ulrica; the white, ghostlike mask that Oscar wore in the second act, which was then passed to Amelia (instead of a veil); and the many masks that dominated the third act.

There were those who objected to this visual and dramaturgical modernization in support of a musical edition which, after all, prided itself on having tried to reestablish the original historical setting and text of *Gustavo III*. Wouldn't it therefore have been more appropriate to set the opera in the Swedish court in 1792? I don't think so. The updating worked for me because it found appropriate ways to stage the most characteristic elements of Verdi's drama. Even when the production toyed with the original (in its treatment of the Chief Judge, for example), it never falsified: Verdi's orchestral figure for the Judge's entrance is readily heard as pompous and ironic. At the emotional heart of the opera, however, the interactions of Gustavo, Amelia, and Ankastrom were never treated with less than complete dramaturgical integrity, and Verdi's magnificent score was given every opportunity to dominate the proceedings.

What emerged clearly from the production of *Gustavo III* in Gothenburg was that Verdi had composed a superb opera for Naples. Had it not been for the assassination attempt on the life of Napoleon III in January 1858, which made compromise with the Neapolitan censors impossible, the opera by Verdi that we would know and perform today would be *Una vendetta in dominò.* And then, had it not been for the fears of the Roman censors, it would instead be *Gustavo III,* that is, not the work Verdi and Somma had begun preparing (in October and November 1857), but *Una vendetta in dominò* with a somewhat revised text, as sent by Verdi to Rome in March 1858.

DARIO FO AND *IL VIAGGIO A REIMS*
Rossini's Coronation Opera and its Stagings

Luca Ronconi's brilliant 1984 staging in Pesaro of Rossini's *Il viaggio a Reims* was directly tied to the notion of "rediscovery," ironically reflecting the media event that had been created around these performances: the production was replete with multiple television screens, reporters, microphones on booms, and postmodern efforts encouraging the audience to be inside and outside the theater (and the text) at the same time.[33] Similar effects have been seen in the theater for many decades. How often has Claudius given his first speech in *Hamlet* ("Though yet of Hamlet our dear brother's death") as if he were engaged in a news conference, microphones and all. Yet this image has continuing strength, for it helps illuminate Claudius's words by invoking the widespread belief that on such formal occasions truth is bent for political purposes. The Pesaro staging of *Viaggio* was more explicitly tied to a single historical moment, and nothing ages so badly in the theater as a *Konzept* that celebrates the particularities of a production's birth.

Ronconi's *Il viaggio a Reims* lost credibility when it continued to proclaim the opera's rediscovery fifteen years after the premiere. In 1992, when the production returned to Pesaro and Ferrara to help celebrate the Rossini bicentennial, it still remained amusing and effective, especially under the baton of

Claudio Abbado. But by the time the Rossini Opera Festival brought it back yet again during the summer of 1999, with a largely new generation of fine singers (among them Elizabeth Norberg-Schulz, Eva Mei, Valeria Esposito, Antonino Siragusa, Juan Diego Flórez, Michele Pertusi, Bruno Praticò, and Roberto Frontali) and with Daniele Gatti in the pit, the Ronconi production was interesting only for helping a knowledgeable audience to recall the intensity of a past theatrical experience: its too familiar devices had little significance for operagoers who had not seen the productions of 1984 or 1992. Many details of brilliant acting tied to the original singers lost their effectiveness with the new cast. It was pointless, for example, to have Norberg-Schulz and Esposito mimic the hilarious interplay between two singers who were known to have personal animosities, the Corinna of Cecilia Gasdia (with her hair in the shape of a lyre) and the Cortese of Katia Ricciarelli (who maliciously "strummed" Corinna's coiffed lyre during the "Gran Pezzo Concertato"—Rossini's piece for fourteen solo voices). Different singers, different personalities: not only could no one reproduce Gasdia's waspish glances, no one should have been asked to try. Fine vocal fireworks were insufficient to rescue this return to the Ronconi staging.[34]

But this 1984 staging is not the only one to have circulated in recent years, and several other productions focus on political themes in *Il viaggio a Reims*. Balocchi's tale, after all, features representatives from all over Europe, who meet at a spa in Plombières (named after the symbol of the Bourbon family—the "giglio d'or" or golden lily), on their way to attend the coronation of Charles X at Rheims. Although at the beginning of the opera Ronconi wrapped the travelers in bath towels decorated with the flags of their respective countries, his political references stopped there. He made no effort to communicate the historical meaning of the sextet, in which the jealous Russian Count Libenskof and the proud Spanish admiral Don Alvaro almost come to blows in their jealousy over the Polish Marquise Melibea, until they are reconciled by the voice of the poetess Corinna, who enjoins all the people of Europe to unite in peace under the sign of the Cross so as to fight more effectively the threat from the "falcata luna" (Turkish crescent). As Janet Johnson has pointed out, this situation duplicates almost precisely the historical conflict over Poland, one of the key issues for Tsar Alexander I of Russia (represented in the opera by Count Libenskof) at the congresses of Vienna (1814–15) and Verona (1822).[35] Nor did Ronconi become involved with the politics of the opera's finale, in which the guests address the new king in their various national hymns and styles, followed by Corinna's improvisation in praise of Charles X and by concluding ensembles (with Rossini's variations on the venerable French tune, "Vive Henri IV"). In Ronconi's 1984 staging the scene provided the opportunity for a parade of fine singing, leveraged by the amusing entrance of the King and his train into the theater (after a mad dash up the stairs—projected inside the theater by video cameras).

Two stagings of *Viaggio* during the 1990s were more interventionist with regard to the opera's politics. Despite the Caballé shenanigans that exasperated the public (see chapter 1), John Cox's Covent Garden production of 1992 had a number of distinctive moments that reflected England's effort at that time to keep its distance from the European Community. There were amusing dances near the beginning of the finale, where figures representing England, Denmark, and Sweden twirled apart from the common core of France, Germany, Italy, and Spain. At New York City Opera in 1999, James Robinson took a different tack, looking not to replicate today's political situation but rather to explore the political realities of 1825. He prepared a set of notes for the company in which he sketched the historical background of the Bourbon restoration, from the downfall of Napoleon in 1814–15 to the 1830 revolution.

In 1793, according to Robinson's accurate reconstruction, the French Revolutionaries had chopped off the heads of King Louis XVI and his Queen, Marie Antoinette. Their son (who would have been Louis XVII) died in prison two years later. After the fall of Napoleon, then, it was to Louis XVI's younger brother that the European allies looked to grace the throne of France. Louis XVIII reigned as a constitutional monarch until his death in 1824, but found himself under constant pressure both from those who favored a return to an "ultra"-royalist society and from those who believed in a constitutional monarchy informed by "liberal" ideals inherited from the French Revolution. The situation became more explosive when Louis XVIII, who died in 1824, was replaced by *his* younger brother, the Count d'Artois. Ruling as Charles X, he led a government that sought to stamp out as many traces of liberalism as possible. New taxes were instituted that weighed most heavily on the bourgeoisie; the French government paid indemnities to the returning nobility; severe restrictions were placed on the press; the church was given new power, and the educational system was largely turned over to the clergy; crimes defined as "sacrilegious" were punishable by death. Since the King reigned as the representative of God on earth, political debate was stifled. The situation became so oppressive that Charles ultimately lost the support of a vast majority of Frenchmen, even among the upper classes. After the so-called "July Revolution" of 1830, Charles went into exile, and Louis-Philippe, who traced his lineage back to Louis XIII through another branch of the Bourbon dynasty (the "Orléans" side), became King.

On only a few occasions did Robinson point his production of *Il viaggio a Reims* in a markedly political direction. After the Gran Pezzo Concertante for fourteen solo voices, the travelers reconcile themselves to missing the coronation. In the libretto they decide instead to leave the next day for Paris, where they will greet the King on his arrival in the capital, after having "un bel convito" (a lovely banquet) that very night at the spa. They can pay for the entertainment by using the sums already collected from all the travelers for the voyage, now *manqué*, to Rheims. And what should we do with the money that will be left over, asks the Baron, to which Libenskof replies: "For the poor." "Do you all agree?" the Baron asks the company, who respond in unison, "Sì." There is nothing about this interchange, musically or poetically, that would lead us to interpret it as anything but sincere. Seeking to expose the mendacity and greed of the nobility under Charles X, however, Robinson had the company laugh long and hard at the suggestion of sharing their wealth with the poor, and their "Sì" provided the opportunity for more uncontrollable laughter and cynicism.

This cynicism returned in an even more striking fashion at the end of the opera, when Charles X, bewigged, powdered, and dressed in formal seventeenth-century garb à la Louis XIV, appeared onstage during the final ensemble, scattering paper money, while the nobles madly dashed around picking up the bills: "Viva la Francia ed il prode regnator" (Long live France and its proud ruler) indeed! While one could appreciate the reasoning behind Robinson's decision not to play these final moments straight, the grotesque movements of the nobles seemed unsupported by Rossini's celebratory music, and it wasn't easy for them to sing their vocal lines while scrambling to accumulate cash. Perhaps Robinson would have liked to provide an even more politically inflected reading of the opera, but had not quite figured out how to do it. As a result, the final moments seemed curiously out of place in the context of the remainder of his staging.

Dario Fo was prepared to go much further toward politicizing *Il viaggio a Reims*. One of Italy's foremost actors, playwrights, and stage directors, as well as the Nobel Prize laureate for Literature in 1997, Fo has been a controversial artistic and political figure from the beginning of his long theatrical career in the 1950s.[36] He is one of the few artists in the West who has succeeded in antagonizing both the left and the right. His ferocious belief in combating through his art what he views as political, economic, or social injustice, wherever he perceives it, has earned him vociferous acclaim and intense opposition. Although his plays continue to be extensively performed in the United States, he and his wife, Franca Rame, were on several occasions in the early

1980s denied visas to enter the United States because of their political associations, leading to demonstrations, articles, denunciations. On 18 September 1984 the American Civil Liberties Union and other organizations (including the American Academy of Arts and Sciences) held a conference in Washington, D.C., on "Free Trade in Ideas," from which not only Fo and Rame were among the excluded, but also literary figures such as Gabriel García Marquez. When asked whether he was truly anti-American, Fo responded, "Our highest recognition goes to the U.S. State Department. It is, in fact, the only institution in the whole world to be so sensitive and aware of the thought and creative imagination of artists, it is convinced that those ideas advertised on the stage are even more explosive than the nuclear bomb."

As a man of the theater, Fo's allegiances have long been to the theatrical traditions of the middle ages and early modern periods. His Nobel address in 1997 was entitled "Contra Jogulatores Obloquentes," the Latin title of a law promulgated in 1221 by Frederick II (at that point the Holy Roman Emperor) that allowed the public to attack *jongleurs* (minstrels or entertainers) without fear of legal sanctions.[37] In it he thanked the Swedish Academy "in the name of the strolling players, *jongleurs*, clowns, acrobats, and bards, particularly those of my own region on Lago Maggiore, where I was born and grew up." And he cited as his two most important influences Molière and especially Angelo Beolco, known as Il Ruzzante, to whom he offered half of his medal, with these words in the local dialect he and Ruzzante shared:

Beolco Ruzzante,	[Beolco Ruzzante, beastly
bestia animal de palco,	stage-animal, take this piece
cata 'sto tòco del méo medajón,	of my medal, it's also yours!
l'è anca tòo! Salùt!	I salute you!]

A playwright from the first half of the sixteenth century, Ruzzante was known particularly for his transgressive art, which sought to break down the more literary traditions of contemporary theater with a strong dose of popular, peasant culture. Identifying his own theatricality with that of Ruzzante, Fo described the playwright as "the greatest author for the theater that Europe had in the Renaissance, even before the advent of Shakespeare" and called him

> my greatest teacher, together with Molière: both actor-authors, both ridiculed by the highfalutin literati of their time, scorned most of all because they brought to the stage daily life, the joy and desperation of the common people, the hypocrisy and arrogance of the powerful, the injustice and horrendous massacre of the innocent.

Ruzzante, father of the *commedia dell'arte,* constructed a language for himself, a lexicon entirely theatrical, composed of diverse idioms: dialects from the Po region, Latin, Spanish, even German expressions, mixed with entirely invented onomatopoeic sounds. From him, from Beolco Ruzzante, I learned to free myself from a conventional literary language and to express myself with unusual words, with strange sounds, with different rhythms and pauses, arriving even at the mad orations in *grammelot.*[38]

It is in this spirit that Fo mounted Rossini's *Il viaggio a Reims* for Finnish National Opera in January 2003.

The Voyage to Finland

The occasion was auspicious. As a country, Finland has made a concerted effort since the 1960s to strengthen musical education for all its citizens. The prestige and cultural significance of the Finnish composer Jean Sibelius helped justify this agenda, and much of its success reflects the intensive, enlightened training young musicians receive at the Sibelius Academy in Helsinki. As a result, Finnish conductors (Esa-Pekka Salonen, Jukka-Pekka Saraste, Mikko Franck), singers (the late Martti Talvela, Matti Salminen, Karita Mattila), and composers (Aulis Sallinen, Kaija Saariaho) are represented in the international arena in numbers far greater than the size of their country might suggest.[39] Musical organizations have cultivated an attitude both sympathetic and adventurous toward the traditional repertory and a solid commitment to new and experimental art. With a musically well-educated citizenry, these efforts continue to bring outstanding artistic results and large audiences, even in times of financial stress.

The new opera house in Helsinki, which opened in 1993, is a beautifully designed building on the Töölö bay near the center of the city, and a short distance from the equally impressive Finlandia Hall, home of the Helsinki Philharmonic. With excellent acoustics and state-of-the-art stage facilities, the opera house quickly developed an enviable reputation for the quality of its productions (which have included a complete staging of the *Ring*), even as some lamented its massive concrete facade. Most roles are sung by native singers in productions that stress ensemble work, and the theater does not normally attempt to compete for the more expensive international stars. Even so, Finnish National Opera regularly sells out its productions, and draws overflow crowds to its educational programs. Governmental presence is not restricted to monetary support: the President of the Republic and the Prime Minister both attended the opening night of *Il viaggio a Reims.*

When Erkki Korhonen, a pianist, conductor, and opera administrator, became general director of the Finnish National Opera during the summer of 2001, one of his earliest projects was to develop a Rossini Festival week for early 2003. His idea, formulated in conjunction with his artistic administrator, Aviel Kahn, was to revive two current productions of Rossini operas, *Il barbiere di Siviglia* and *La Cenerentola,* adding to them a new staging by Dario Fo of *Il viaggio a Reims.* The choice of Fo as his stage director was not wayward. Fo and his wife are well known in Scandinavia, not only for Fo's Nobel Prize, but also for the visits of their theatrical troupe. While opera has not played a significant part in Fo's theatrical life, he had made several forays into the art, always with comic operas by Rossini. After a staging of *Il barbiere di Siviglia* at the Amsterdam Opera in 1987, later revived in many other opera houses, he was responsible for two new productions at the Rossini Opera Festival in Pesaro: *L'Italiana in Algeri* in 1994 and *La gazzetta* in 2001.

I supervised vocal ornamentation for the *Italiana* performances, so I followed the rehearsals carefully. It was a brilliant staging, inventive to a fault: at every point there was something to engage the eye. Some argued that the staging overwhelmed the music, but it is hard to submerge Rossini's spirit, and in any event Fo—while not a musician—is eminently sensitive to music, especially its rhythmic side. During the overture, for example, he adopted the standard stage trick of imitating the sea by means of a set of tautly stretched colored silks that could be manipulated to give the appearance of moving water. When the Allegro began, and Rossini lets loose his main theme, with its explosive syncopated chords (example 14.4), those chords were visually punctuated with flying fish. With all the twirling and twisting the cooperative Jennifer Larmore had to endure as Isabella, I had to be rather parsimonious with ornamentation, since it was hard enough for her to get through the part without becoming seasick. She also had to resign herself to audience hilarity during her gorgeously seductive aria "Per lui che adoro" in the second act, which entranced not only her three hidden would-be lovers

EXAMPLE 14.4. GIOACHINO ROSSINI, *L'ITALIANA IN ALGERI,* SINFONIA, MM. 33–34.

but also the very plants, which, standing straight up, reacted to each lascivious strain by growing a little more erect.

Fo, the playwright, did not intervene in the vocal text of *L'Italiana in Algeri,* but with *La gazzetta* he failed to show similar restraint. There was some justification. The 1816 printed libretto of the first act includes several scenes adapted from Goldoni's *Il matrimonio per concorso* (the primary source of the libretto) that Rossini does not seem to have set to music. These scenes, which appear in no musical sources—not even in the composer's autograph manuscript—contain events significant to the drama, establishing relationships and providing information to be drawn upon later. They include not only verses of recitative but also the text for a major quintet. Unless something is done to include their gist, the plot descends into incoherence.[40] Scholars tend to adopt a minimalist approach to interventions. Thus, for the purposes of the critical edition of *La gazzetta,* I had set to music one scene of recitative, without which the second pair of lovers is never introduced, and had suggested a group of smaller changes to cover the remainder of the missing action: removing references to the action of the quintet and introducing stage business (such as one character's overhearing others in conversation) to account for knowledge that pertains only to the scenes Rossini did not set to music. My coeditor and I were not prepared to take responsibility for composing from scratch a quintet in Rossinian style. All of this worked well in the first production of the new edition of *La gazzetta,* which had its premiere on 12 June 2001 at the Garsington Festival outside of Oxford (before Fo's Pesaro première), and will, I trust, continue to work well in future productions.

But *bestia animal de palco* that he is, Fo disdained "overhearing" as a technique: "old stuff," he said, and never very effective (I resisted citing Polonius). No, he felt there was a dramaturgical hole in the middle of act 1, where the quintet ought to have gone, and he was determined to fill it. Fill it he did, with a newly devised rhymed and metrical text, developed in part from the verses in the printed libretto not set to music. The whole *tamurriata,* as he called it, a dialectic derivative of the word *tamburo* or small drum, was inflected with a Neapolitan accent and recited while the continuo group in the orchestra played Rossini's tarantella, *La danza,* in the background. As Fo wrote in the program notes: "The first to enjoy themselves, declaiming it in a rhythmic manner, were the singers themselves, protagonists of the opera. All of us on the stage, from stagehands to musicians, were enormously amused."[41] And so was the audience, as they watched the entire cast engaged in the most frenetic gyrations. Fo had taken what was a significant textual problem and turned it into a scenic opportunity.

Having seen and been entranced by the *Gazzetta* production in Pesaro, Korhonen and Kahn invited Fo to direct *Viaggio* in Helsinki. Fo accepted the challenge. His extraordinary theatrical imagination, of course, readily found a way to create a visually entrancing spectacle, full of movement and scenic wonders. Whereas some directors prepare a stage book that charts blocking and positions—a document used both to record ideas pertaining to the first production and to guide subsequent revivals (very much like the *disposizioni sceniche* discussed in chapter 13)—Fo works differently.[42] Trained originally as an artist, he typically executes hundreds of pages of drawings, with costume designs, characters in motion, grotesques, montages of historical events or characters and *commedia dell'arte* figures, tracing in this form the progress of the entire spectacle from beginning to end. These exuberant designs provide him with a starting point for his actual work in the theater: costume designs, the elaborately flexible stage design, the blocking of the principal characters, the dancers, acrobats, and clowns that populate every part of the stage, on the ground and in the air.

As he began to study *Il viaggio a Reims* more closely, however, Fo realized that he had a serious problem. What was the sense of all this elaborate scenic paraphernalia in the service of an opera glorifying the coronation and the regime of a corrupt king, whose politics could not have been more foreign to the political and social views of Fo? He could, of course, have presented a staging that treated the text in an ironical manner (as Robinson did at New York City Opera), but he soon developed a different perspective: why not *change* the text?

Dario Fo was, of course, not the first to discover that Rossini had written a musical masterpiece to problematic words. The composer himself was keenly aware of the dilemma, although he tended to see it not as political but as generic. *Il viaggio a Reims* was born as an occasional piece, a celebratory cantata. What could one do subsequently with long "improvisations" by Corinna praising Charles X and the restored Bourbon monarchy or celebrating the victories of the "cross" against the Turkish crescent? How could one make sense of a succession of European travelers singing patriotic songs in honor of Charles X? *We* may live in a world where the intersection of history and opera can delight, but Rossini's audience wanted well-oiled dramas. As we have seen, the composer withdrew the opera/cantata and reused parts of it in 1828 for his comic opera *Le Comte Ory*, abandoning the rest. Among the abandoned sections were those most directly tied to the historical circumstances of the coronation: the sextet and the entire finale.

Yet, despite Rossini's best efforts to suppress them, some sources circulated and led to two nineteenth-century revivals, as discussed in chapter 5. In both cases the text was heavily modified. Rossini's music had become a chameleon, changing its identity for these new occasions. The 1848 *Andremo a Parigi?* (Shall we go to Paris?) recast characters and situations. Don Profondo, described in *Viaggio* as "learned, friend of Corinna's, member of various academies, and a fanatic for antiquities," became Don Pandolfo. This "symbol of *petite bourgeoise* society" (in the words of Janet Johnson)[43] is interested only "a salvar la pelle" (in saving my skin), as Don Pandolfo says in recitative preceding his aria. Representative is the first strophe of the Profondo/Pandolfo aria in the two versions. Don Profondo lists the personal items that he plans to take on the trip to Rheims; Don Pandolfo worries about his future:

Il viaggio a Reims	Andremo a Parigi?
Medaglie incomparabili,	*Consiglio nel mio cerebro*
Camei rari, impagabili,	*Politico economico*
Figli di tenebrosa	*Io debbo qui tenere*
Sublime antichità.	*Per la mia sicurtà.*
In aurea cartapecora	*Allontanar gli ostacoli,*
Dell'accademie i titoli,	*Non affrontar pericoli,*
Onde son membro nobile	*Prudenza usare cauto*
Di prima qualità.	*Schivar la società.*

| [Incomparable medals, rare, priceless cameos, children of dark, sublime antiquity. In golden parchment the titles of the academies of which I am a noble member of the first order.] | [I need to think through the political and eonomic situation so as to guarantee my safety. Put aside obstacles, don't confront dangers, use cautious prudence, avoid society.] |

In the Viennese adaptation of 26 April 1854 as *Un viaggio a Vienna*, Corinna's concluding "Improvisation" becomes an encomium for Franz Joseph, recalling his lineage and proclaiming his virtues:

Il viaggio a Reims	Un viaggio a Vienna
All'ombra amena	*Del Gran Rodolfo*
Del Giglio d'Or,	*O Germe Augusto*
Aura serena	*Di gloria onusto*
Inebbria il cor.	*Qual brilli Tu!*
Di lieti giorni	*Sul Tron degli Avi*
Più dolce aurora	*Da un lustro appena,*
Sorger la Francia	*Già l'Austria hai piena*
Non vide ancor.	*Di Tue Virtù.*

[In the lovely shade of the Golden Lily, a serene breeze intoxicates the heart. France has never seen a more lovely dawn of happy days.]

[Oh majestic seed of the great Rudolph, you shine with the weight of glory! Though you have been on the throne of your ancestors for barely five years, Austria is already filled with your virtues.]

The opera concludes with a "New Popular Hymn on Haydn's melody, here expressly translated into Italian," with a text beginning: "Dio Conservi, Dio Protegga / Sempre il Nostro Imperator" (God conserve, God protect our Emperor forever).

New Words in the Service of Theatrical Invention

The notion of performing Rossini's coronation opera with a modified text, in short, has illustrious historical precedent, and Fo seized upon it. His realization was both simple and audacious: locate those moments in the score where the original libretto extravagantly praises the new King and the social, political, or economic policies he represented, and substitute verses that "tell the truth" about Charles X and his world, verses that would resonate for a public in the first years of the twenty-first century. Despite certain reports in both the Italian and the Finnish press, my role in all of this was not to give scholarly "approval" to the operation: Dario Fo needs no external approval to do whatever he wants to do. I was simply there to help him make certain that his new verses worked fluently with Rossini's music. When needed, I introduced small changes in declamation and rewrote short sections of *secco* recitative (for some parts of which I had already helped to compose the music in the critical edition). When Fo's verses in concerted numbers seemed awkward musically, I told him so directly, and he modified them with alacrity. Not a single change had to be made in the orchestral parts. Implicit in the entire operation was Fo's conviction that *Il viaggio a Reims* is not an opera we treasure because of its dramaturgical brilliance or plot construction: it is frankly an entertainment, rendered notable by Rossini's magnificent score. Yet however piquant Fo's verses may be, not all of them had the same resonance in the theater, and that is a story worth telling.

Operatic time is largely determined by the music, and only in the rarest cases can a stage director successfully modify the temporality that music imposes. While two stanzas of poetry may be equal in length on the page, in their musical realization they can occupy vastly different theatrical space. In some cases, Fo's textual changes freed his directorial imagination and allowed him to introduce action and images that would have been unthinkable with the original poetry. In other cases, however, his changes involved text declaimed so quickly that the differences could hardly be perceived in the theater. There was insufficient time for the staging to reflect the new words, which were more apparent to an audience reading translated supertitles (in Finnish) than hearing Fo's words in Italian.

That Fo might choose to intervene massively in the text of the Don Profondo aria, one of the jewels of the score, came as no surprise. In Luigi Balocchi's original libretto, after having Don Profondo list his own personal items for the trip to Rheims, Balocchi provides several eight-line stanzas, each naming the nationality of one of the travelers and describing—in a brief vignette of national character—what he or she is transporting to the coronation. Rossini set all of this as the first half of his aria, with Don Profondo declaiming the words rhythmically, often on a single pitch. An orchestral melody recurs in each strophe, shifting from one key to another as the poetry focuses on each character in turn. Once all their possessions have been described, Balocchi changes the meter of the verses (to *quinari*) for a brief cabaletta, in which Don Profondo announces with delight that everything is ready for the trip. The entire aria flies by. In the 1984 recording of the Pesaro production, where Don Profondo was sung by Ruggero Raimondi, the 309 measures of this aria took exactly 5 minutes and 20 seconds to sing. Yet it is scarcely an exaggeration to say that Raimondi received a nightly ovation in the small Sala Pedrotti that lasted longer than the piece itself. Some of that public enthusiasm acknowledged a brilliant interpretive maneuver: while Rossini did little to differentiate the musical presentation of the seven national travelers, Raimondi declaimed each stanza using a different accent (his German, English, French, and Russian-accented Italian were particularly hilarious). Although almost every successive Don Profondo has imitated this "invented tradition," none has matched Raimondi's grace.

In Balocchi's libretto, the Spaniard declaims the following stanza, which gently satirizes the Spanish taste for family genealogy and decorations, referring, too, to Spain's colonial history in South America:

Gran Piante genealogiche	Great genealogical charts
Degl'avoli e Bisavoli,	Of grandfathers and great-grandfathers,
Colle notizie storiche	With historical information
Di quel che ognuno fu.	About each one.
Diplomi, Stemmi e Croci,	Diplomas, coats of arms, and crosses,

Nastri, Collane ed Ordini,	Decorations, medals, and orders,
E, grosse come noci,	And, large as walnuts,
Sei perle del Perù.	Six pearls from Peru.

Dario Fo took Balocchi's invocation of colonialism and made it the heart of this rewritten stanza:

E qui i bottini storici,	And here the historical spoils,
Raccolti dagli Iberici,	Collected by the Iberians,
Saccheggio inimitabile	Inimitable sacking
Su Aztechi del Perù.	Of the Peruvian Aztecs.
Selvaggi privi d'animo	Savages without souls
Che in cambio del massacro,	Who, instead of being massacred,
Furono battezzati,	Were baptized
A colpi di cannon.	To blasts of the cannon.

Fo's text is essentially identical in its rhythm to that of Balocchi, with only small differences, easily reconciled with the music. Alas, it does give up the rhymes so characteristic of the original...

On stage, however, this textual change, and the many others throughout the aria, had no impact whatsoever. There is only so much a Don Profondo can be asked to do in the midst of an aria that resembles a fifty-yard dash: if he demonstrates sufficient endurance and keeps enough breath to arrive intact at the end, he has accomplished much. And even in the frenetic theatrical universe of Dario Fo, with acrobats, dancers, crocodiles, and balloons, the eleven seconds it took Raimondi to declaim the Spaniard's stanza (I did not clock Damon Nestor Ploumis's performance in Helsinki) provides insufficient time to recount visually the history of the Spanish conquest of the New World.

The improvisation of Corinna near the end of the opera created quite a different opportunity for Fo. Balocchi had modeled her after the heroine of Madame de Staël's 1807 novel *Corinne, ou l'Italie,* where Corinne is a poet, an "improviser," recognized by the Arcadian Academy of Rome and crowned on the Campidoglio. In the famous painting by François Gérard of 1819, "Corinne au Cap Misène," Madame de Staël herself is portrayed as Corinne, lyre in hand and dressed in the Greek robes of the Cumaean Sybil, with the bay of Naples and an erupting Vesuvius in the background.[44] In one form of improvisation, the poet/singer was expected to receive suggestions for a theme from the assembled listeners and would choose one at random, declaiming her improvised verses over an accompaniment of her own devising. In Balocchi's libretto, each assembled voyager writes a subject on a piece of paper and hands it to Don Profondo, who reads the theme to the company and places the paper in an urn. (In most modern productions, the voyagers themselves read out their own subjects—a theatrical solution that provides more variety.) The themes are all from French history, including Joan of Arc, St. Louis, the three royal lineages of France, and so on. It is the French Cavalier Belfiore who suggests "Carlo Decimo, Re di Francia" (Charles X, King of France), and when Melibea draws one subject from the urn, the topic chosen is indeed the new King. Corinna, lyre in hand, then improvises five stanzas, in extravagant praise of Charles X. Rossini set these stanzas with a harp accompaniment alone, alternating two principal sections (ABABA, followed by final cadences). The form is repetitive, as befits "improvised" music and poetry, but it also allows ample opportunity for a fine singer to ornament the melodic line.

Nonetheless, this "improvisation" seems long and the poetry provides little opportunity for scenic expansion. In the opening stanza (whose first eight verses, beginning "All'ombra amena," were quoted above) Corinna sings of the happy days that France can now anticipate. The second stanza refers to Charles as bestowing new splendor and nobility on the crown of France. He has been on the throne only a short time, the third stanza relates, but already the country is happy and hymns of love are sung everywhere. In the fourth stanza the coronation itself is described. By setting the ceremony for Sunday, 29 May—Trinity Sunday in 1825—Charles had tapped into a long medieval tradition and symbolically emphasized the divine right of kings:[45]

Appiè dell'are,	At the foot of the altars,
Ei chiese al cielo,	He asked heaven
Che secondare	That it deign to lend support
Degni il suo zel;	To his zeal.
Non fia deluso	Let his fine wish
Il bel desio,	Not be disappointed,
Figlio dell'almo	Divine progeny
Suo nobil cor.	Of his noble heart.
Sacro il diadema	God has already
Già rese Iddio,	Made sacred his crown,
Né più del fato	Nor need it fear any longer
Teme il furor.	The fury of fate.

The final stanza augurs long life and divine favor on "Carlo, de' Franchi / Delizia e amor" (Charles, the delight and love of the French). Already in the 1984 production, Abbado had cut the third and fourth stanzas, and almost every subsequent revival has done the same, reducing the ABABA of the original to ABA. When I have advised productions of the opera, I too have recommended that cut.

The greatest triumph for Fo's rewriting of Balocchi at Helsinki came precisely in this scene. What makes the triumph ironic is that this production—with its altered words—is the only one I know in which the music of Corinna's "improvisation" was presented successfully without cuts. Fo drew his inspiration from the original text, specifically its fourth stanza, with its image of Carlo X kneeling before the altars at Rheims, as God blesses his future reign. Fo had already let loose a savage critique earlier in the scene. After the travelers had announced what they had written on their slips of paper (many modified for the Finnish context), Don Profondo read the subject chosen for the improvisation, "Carlo X, Re di Francia." At that point, however, a servant holding the urn stumbled, and all the other proposals fell out. Characters scurried to pick them up, and on every one had been written: "Carlo X, Re di Francia." Commenting on an election in which only one result was possible, Count Libenskof opines, "La votazione è legale" (The vote is legal). Electorates worldwide would have had no trouble understanding Fo's gibe.

Now Corinna steps forward, and Fo's verses relate actual events from the coronation. She tells of Carlo stretched out on the cold marble, anointed with holy oil. The King, who is supposed to have the divinely granted power to cure the sick, is surrounded by the "scrufolosi" and "rognosi" (those with tumors and scabs), but, miserable with the damp and cold, he pays them no heed. His sneezes are greeted by shouts of "Santé!" from the crowd. When he tries to rise, a cardinal steps on him to hold him still. Here is Fo's description of the consequences in the fourth stanza, corresponding to "Appiè dell'are" cited above:

Sente un prurito,	He feels an itching
Pel corpo intero,	Over his entire body,
Il foco addosso	A fire all over him
E un gran febbron.	And a high fever.
Non ha guarito	He didn't cure
Manco un fetente,	Even a single stinking wound,
Però in compenso	But in recompense
Ha il morbo blù.	He has syphillis.
Perde i capelli,	He loses his hair,
È tutto a chiazze,	He is covered with blotches,
E il coro canta	And the chorus sings
"Salute al Re."	"Health to the King."

In the final stanza Corinna describes other elements of Charles's reign: how he turned over control of public education to the clergy, closed newspapers, banned satire and bordellos; and she concludes, "Senza più fiato / Muore il pensier" (With no room to breathe, thought itself dies).

In his staging, Fo transformed Corinna into a medieval *cantastoria*, the kind of entertainer who participated in popular festivals during the Middle Ages, relating a story—religious or secular—as it was simultaneously acted out by his or her colleagues in mime. A simply painted ecclesiastical backdrop was carried onstage. Dressed in white, the actors seemed like statues descended from the portico of a cathedral—the King, a cardinal, and a group of *scrufolosi* and *rognosi*. Thus, in the long-standing tradition of comic theater, Fo transmuted one kind of poetry, the extravagant encomium, into another, the mock epic, thereby overcoming the scene's dramaturgical stasis.

From there until the end, his invention never flagged. As the assembled company broke out to the strains of "Vive Henri IV," the celebratory verses of Balocchi became a commentary on *Plus ça change, plus c'est la même chose:*

Balocchi	Fo
Viva il diletto	*Gran vita a Carlo.*
Augusto regnator,	*L'oracol vede il Re...*
Ond'è l'aspetto	*Fuggir cacciato,*
Forier di gioia e amor	*Un altro Re verrà*
Che desta in petto	*D'altro casato,*
Rispetto, e vivo ardor.	*Evviva sempre il Re.*
[Long live our beloved, august ruler, whose appearance, harbinger of joy and love, evokes in our hearts respect and keen ardor.]	[Long life to Carlo. The oracle sees the King... driven away in flight, another King will come from another lineage, but still, Long live the King.]

As for the ordinary people, the "chorus," so dear to Fo's heart, sang in Fo's words,

Per noi del Coro	[For us of the Chorus, that's the way
La musica è cotal.	the music goes. Yes, what matters is
Sì, quel che importa è	that everything stays the same. The
Che tutto resti ugual.	government is everything, The grand
Il regno è tutto,	finale doesn't change.]
Non cambia il gran final.	

But Fo had a final trick up his sleeve. As these verses were sung, a small air-borne vehicle crossed the stage at a distance, then reappeared, full size and closer up. It was a helicopter-like contraption, with a bicyclist in full view pedaling through the skies what seemed to be a glistening *Fabergé* egg. When the device landed in the center of the stage, out popped a sabled and ermined Charles X, who acknowledged the people, sat for a moment on an improvised throne, then returned to his egg, which soon lifted off, with flags of all the European nations jubilantly waved and juggled. As the last strains of the opera sounded, the smaller version of the vehicle again crossed high over the back of the stage, but now attacked by antiaircraft missiles, one of which blew it out of the sky as the curtain descended. Putting words to Fo's anarchical images would be utterly superfluous.

Adjustments in the text, nonetheless, were not made exclusively for political purposes. Since Fo is a director who often allows images to inspire his staging, in at least two scenes the visual was determinate. He conceived the jealousy duet between the Polish Marquise Melibea and the Russian Count Libenskof as being dominated by a tempest, with dark colors, protective coverings buffeted by the wind, torrents of rain, and flying umbrellas everywhere (sometimes with mimes attached to them), "una tempesta in cielo, in terra un omicidio" (a storm in the heavens, on earth a murder), as Rigoletto would have commented. While the effect may have had little to do with Rossini and Balocchi's duet—which, after all, is mostly about reconciliation, not conflict—Fo's darker reading of jealousy had its own rationale. No words were changed in the duet, but a small modification in the preceding recitative introduced the idea that the skies were threatening ("il ciel non promette nulla di buono").

In the aria of the Countess Folleville too, some of the text changes went hand-in-hand with the staging. The piece itself is a parody of Italian operatic arias of Rossini's generation, an ironic commentary on their structure and dramatic shape. As we have seen, the standard form of a Rossini aria (not to mention a Bellini, Donizetti, or early Verdi aria) involves two principal sections: the first is a slow cantabile, often both lyrical and florid, in which the singer reacts to a specific dramatic situation or expresses a particular emotion; then a change of tone, set up either by an external event or by an internal change of mood, leads to a quicker second section, normally called a cabaletta, in which a lyrical period is sung once, repeated (providing an opportunity for singers to vary the melodic line) after a transition, and brought to a conclusion with elaborate cadential phrases.

What makes the aria in *Il viaggio a Reims* a parody is the emotional gulf between the events that call it forth and the extraordinary music Rossini uses to give it dramatic depth. The tragic tones of the first section are a reaction to the "calamity" that the coach containing the Countess's clothes has over-turned, so that she has nothing appropriate to wear on the trip to Rheims: she sings, "Donne, voi sol comprendere / Potete il mio dolore" (Women, only you can comprehend my sorrow"). What changes her mood is the appear-ance of the one item rescued from the debacle, a hat: she thanks God for hav-ing heard her prayer, and continues, in some of the most exuberant col-oratura Rossini ever wrote, "A tal favor quest'anima / Grata ognor sarà" (For such a favor, this soul will always be grateful). When the composer reused the music of the aria (practically unchanged) three years later in *Le Comte Ory,* the subject of the text touched a deeper emotion: Should Adèle, the Count-ess of Formoutiers, keep her vow to seclude herself from the society of men until her brother returns from a crusade, or should she allow herself to ex-press the love she feels for her cousin and Count Ory's page, Isolier? In a stun-ning reversal, Rossini had first written the parody, and only later transformed it into what was being parodied.

Staging this aria from *Il viaggio a Reims,* Fo envisioned not one hat but a sequence of hats, beginning with one of normal size, then growing larger and larger, out of all proportion. They multiplied like rabbits and began to fly through the air with abandon. Certainly it was that image of flying hats that led Fo to modify the words of the cabaletta to read: "È vivo il mio capell, ha l'ali, è vivo il mio capell" (My hat is alive, it has wings, my hat is alive). The final hat—unveiled as the Countess began the ornamented reprise of the ca-baletta theme—was large enough for Folleville to stand on and be lifted into the air by her attendants, as she continued to sing her coloratura.

On opening night, the not normally hyperexpressive Finns granted *Il vi-aggio a Reims,* as seen through the eyes of Dario Fo, a fifteen-minute stand-ing ovation. *Viaggio* is a work that delights in its original version but also wel-comes the kind of creative intervention that he brought to Finnish National Opera. Certainly a modern audience can react only with amused distance to the original libretto's extravagant praise of a Restoration monarch whose so-cial and political actions were despised not only by liberal thinkers but even by those who sought to build a peaceful post-Napoleonic Europe. By taking the politics of Charles X seriously and by describing and commenting on them in his modified text, Fo offered a modern audience a way to experience Rossini's opera from a very different perspective. Instead of retaining in full a libretto that can be heard only across a vast historical gap, he introduced new words in crucial places, forcing us to come to grips with elements of the history of Charles X that resonate with our own time. When asked by various journalists about ways in which his *Viaggio* adaptation seemed to reflect elements in the politics of Italy's Silvio Berlusconi or America's George W. Bush, Fo—in his patented brand of wide-eyed innocence—demurred: no such connection had occurred to him. He could hardly be blamed for the perception that, unwittingly, those national leaders have taken Charles X as their model. Through Dario Fo's work, *Il viaggio a Reims* became a voyage of political discovery for today.

Some opera lovers reacted to Fo's production both with genuine appreciation and sincere fear. Yes, it was enormously appealing, they said, but suppose we started to change the words of all operas? What would happen to the art form? I do not share their concern. Just as Peter Brook's *La Tragédie de Carmen* did not result in a host of epigones, neither will Dario Fo's *Il viaggio a Reims.* And each of these highly personal efforts was made with great respect for the music, whether it was a question of arranging the original for a new context à la Brook or of showing sensitivity to the way words and music interact à la Fo. Far better an inventive operation under the guidance of one of the great theatrical geniuses of our time than the kind of plodding, ordinary performances, unstylistic and sometimes musically decimated, that we hear too often in the theater.

One more story needs to be told in conclusion. *Opera News,* the magazine published by the Metropolitan Opera Guild, instead of covering the Gothenburg *Gustavo III* in its print edition, decided to send readers to its online pages for a review. Although George Loomis's notice was both accurate concerning the nature of the project and laudatory about the performance, I found unacceptable the phrase the magazine printed as a way to draw attention to Loomis's online review: "Göteborg's 'authentic' *Un ballo in maschera.*" [46] Of course, "authenticity" had nothing to do with our Gothenburg project, and I explained as much to the then editor, Rudolph Rauch. He responded, "Your letter demonstrates that opera scholars are as passionate as opera fans about the art form."

Yes, opera scholars are as passionate as opera fans about the art form. Indeed, opera scholars *are* opera fans. But in a world where there is such a paucity of serious thought about performing Italian opera, the task of bringing divas and scholars together seems positively quixotic. Nonetheless, those of us who love this art form in all its complexity, who are negotiating the past with the present, the practical with the theoretical, the needs of staging with the vocal health of singers, the written score with performances based on it, will continue to work diligently to raise the level of discourse. It is to that end that my book has been dedicated.

NOTES

(Authors' and editors' first names, subtitles of works, and publication details are omitted in the notes. After first mention, long titles are shortened. Full details are to be found in the bibliography.)

PREFACE

1. See Miggiani, "Il teatro di San Moisè (1793–1818)."

2. At the Teatro alla Scala in Milan, for example, of the 242 opera performances in 1823, at the height of Rossinimania, 162 were of operas by Rossini; comparable figures for 1824 are 191 performances out of 232. See Gatti, *Il teatro alla Scala nella storia e nell'arte (1778–1963)*, 2:30–32.

3. Pacini, *Le mie memorie artistiche,* 54. All translations from foreign languages, unless otherwise noted, are my own.

4. There are, to be sure, important continuities to be observed in Verdi's two next operas, *Don Carlos* (1867) and *Aida* (1871), but the repertory and social context I am describing largely come to an end with *Un ballo in maschera* (1859) and *La forza del destino* (1862).

5. Contract of 26 December 1815 between Rossini and Francesco Sforza Cesarini, published in Rossini, *Lettere e documenti,* 1:124–25.

6. One area I have touched upon only tangentially is early recordings. As Crutchfield has shown in an important study, "Vocal Ornamentation in Verdi," there is much we can learn about performance traditions from a careful consideration of this evidence. Because I have a relatively limited knowledge of these recordings, however, I prefer to leave this analysis to those, like Crutchfield, who know better how to negotiate its many pitfalls. These recordings have documentary value for singers such as Victor Maurel or Francesco Tamagno, who participated in the first performances of Verdi's late works, *Otello* and *Falstaff;* what they teach us about *La traviata* or *Rigoletto,* not to mention *Il barbiere di Siviglia,* is more ambiguous.

7. See, in particular, Rosselli's *The Opera Industry in Italy from Cimarosa to Verdi: The Role of the Impresario; Music and Musicians in Nineteenth-Century Italy;* and *Singers of Italian Opera.* Two fine recent studies are Banti, *La nazione del risorgimento,* and Sorba, *Teatri: L'Italia del melodramma nell'età del Risorgimento.*

8. Marvin, "Aspects of Tempo in Verdi's Early and Middle-Period Italian Operas"; see also Mauceri, "Verdi for the Twenty-first Century."

9. Brown, *Classical and Romantic Performing Practice 1750–1900.*

10. Hansell, "Il ballo teatrale e l'opera italiana"; Jürgensen, *The Verdi Ballets.*

11. Gossett, "Scandal and Scholarship."

12. Gossett, "Trasporre Bellini."

13. Gossett, "Staging Italian Opera: Dario Fo and *Il viaggio a Reims.*"

CHAPTER ONE

1. For the early history of the Santa Fe Opera, see Scott, *The First Twenty Years of the Santa Fe Opera.* There is a similar treatment of the Rossini Opera Festival by Lorenzo Arruga, *Medaglie incomparabili.*

2. For a chronology of performances at the Teatro San Carlo, see *Il Teatro di San Carlo 1737–1987,* vol. 2, *La cronologia,* ed. Roscioni, esp. 161. See also the critical edition of the opera, Rossini, *Ermione,* ed. Brauner and Gossett.

3. Escudier and Escudier, *Rossini,* 122–23.

4. Ibid.

5. Hiller, *Plaudereien mit Rossini,* in particular 94.

6. For both *The Works of Giuseppe Verdi* and the *Edizione critica delle opere di Gioachino Rossini,* my colleagues and I consider a critical edition to be "provisional" until it is published, by which time the experience of working through actual performances usually allows the editors to present a text tempered by theatrical fire.

7. I recall that the score on his podium had never before been physically opened. He might, of course, have studied the opera from another source, but *Ermione* was not a work in circulation.

8. *Puntature* and ornamentation in Rossini and throughout the repertory of Italian opera are discussed in chapter 9, where bibliographical references are provided.

9. Allan Kozinn, "Greek Legend No Match for Bel Canto Heroics," *New York Times,* 7 August 2000, E1. Why does our paper of record ask critics whose likes and dislikes are so clearly scripted in advance to review such events?

10. The problem of stagings, radical and conventional, is discussed more fully in chapter 13.

11. Verdi, *Rigoletto,* ed. Chusid.

12. Kalmus reprinted and sold as *Il Turco in Italia* a French edition from the 1820s, reflecting a set of performances organized by Ferdinando Paër at the Théâtre Italien of Paris in 1820, in which Rossini's opera was intentionally mutilated. See the preface to Rossini, *Il Turco in Italia,* ed. Bent. This Parisian revival of *Turco* is discussed further in chapter 7.

13. Although elsewhere in the opera both Rigoletto and Monterone ascend from this *c* to *e♭*, the passages usually return to the *c* and never produce a dominant/tonic relationship between the *e♭* and a subsequent *A♭ major.*

14. Among studies touching on this moment of transition are Fulcher, *The Nation's Image;* Gerhard, *Die Verstädterung der Oper,* trans. Whittall as *The Urbanization of Opera;* and Lacombe, *Les Voies de l'opéra français au XIXe siècle,* trans. Schneider as *The Keys to French Opera in the Nineteenth Century.* Gasparo Spontini anticipated Rossini's revolution, with his *La Vestale* (1807) and other works.

15. Rossini, *Guillaume Tell,* ed. Bartlet.

16. Will Crutchfield informs me that opera professionals frequently speak about rehearsing the "duettone" from *La traviata,* meaning the long "duetto" (Verdi's term) for Violetta and Germont.

17. For the Troupenas orchestral score of the cavatina, see Rossini, *Le Siège de Corinthe,* ed. Gossett. The phrase quoted above occurs in the edition (with the plate number 12817) by the Milanese publisher, Francesco Lucca, issued in approximately 1860. For this date, see Antolini, *Dizionario degli editori musicali italiani 1750–1930,* 213.

18. Rossini, *La scala di seta*, ed. Wiklund.

19. Information of this kind was accumulated by Rossini's major biographer, Giuseppe Radiciotti: see his *Gioacchino Rossini*, 3:193–94. Work on the critical edition of Rossini's works over the past decades has increased our knowledge greatly.

20. I saw this performance at the Teatro Olimpico of Rome in November 1976. In the program, Handt attempted to justify his belief that this overture is by Rossini. For further information, see the preface to Wiklund's critical edition, Rossini, *La scala di seta*, xxvi, as well as Gossett, "Le sinfonie di Rossini," esp. 95–99.

21. *Rossini Arias/Alle voci della gloria*, Teldec 9031-73242-2, with Gabriele Ferro conducting the orchestra of Welsh National Opera.

22. There has been some excellent work recently on the problem of substitute arias in the nineteenth century. See Poriss, "Making Their Way through the World" and "A Madwoman's Choice."

23. Rossini, *La Cenerentola*, ed. Gossett.

24. Rossini, *La Cenerentola*, ed. Zedda.

25. The critical edition of Rossini's operas includes music by other composers as long as Rossini himself was directly involved in the performances where they were inserted. We know about Agolini's compositions through their presence in various early nineteenth-century sources. For further details, see chapter 3.

CHAPTER TWO

1. There is an extensive literature about the social milieu in which Italian opera flourished. Apart from the contributions by Rosselli, Banti, and Sorba mentioned in the preface, see the essays, with extensive bibliography, in *Storia dell'opera italiana*, ed. Bianconi and Pestelli, particularly vol. 4, *Il sistema produttivo e le sue competenze*, trans. Cochrane as *Opera Production and Its Resources*. Della Seta provides an important overview in his *Italia e Francia nell'Ottocento*. Also useful is de Angelis, *Le carte dell'impresario*.

2. *Il Teatro di San Carlo 1737–1987*.

3. Cametti's *Il teatro di Tordinona poi di Apollo* continues to serve as a model for histories of a single theater.

4. Girardi and Rossi, *Il Teatro La Fenice*.

5. For precise timetables, see my introductions to the facsimile editions of the autograph manuscripts of *Il barbiere di Siviglia* (English, 12–26; Italian, 63–79) and *Don Pasquale* (English, 86–90; Italian, 15–20).

6. Verdi used the phrase "anni di galera" in a letter to his friend Clara Maffei of 12 May 1858, published in *I copialettere di Giuseppe Verdi*, ed. Cesari and Luzio, 572.

7. For the finest short biography of Bellini, see Rosselli, *The Life of Bellini*. The most significant overall study continues to be Pastura, *Bellini secondo la storia*. Although a number of new letters and documents have appeared since its publication, Cambi's *Bellini: Epistolario* remains the most important and best-annotated collection. For Donizetti, see Ashbrook, *Donizetti and His Operas*. Of great importance is Bini and Commons, *Le prime rappresentazioni delle opere di Donizetti nella stampa coeva*. As in the case of Bellini, the most important collection of letters and documents remains one printed in the 1940s, Zavadini, *Donizetti*, supplemented by more recent articles and monographs.

8. See Piperno, "Il *Mosè in Egitto* e la tradizione napoletana di opere bibliche," as well as his "'Stellati sogli' e 'immagini portentose.'"

9. See, for example, Verdi's contract with La Fenice for *La traviata*, as reproduced in Verdi, *La traviata*, ed. Della Seta.

10. The best overall treatment of the Neapolitan operas of Rossini remains Cagli, "All'ombra dei gigli d'oro." See also the excellent chapter by Kimbell, "Rossini in Naples," in his *Italian Opera*, 448–66.

11. For historical information about these operas, see the prefaces to *L'Italiana in Algeri*, ed. Corghi, and *Semiramide*, ed. Gossett and Zedda.

12. For studies of the most important librettists of this later tradition, see Black, *The Italian Romantic Libretto*, and Roccatagliati, *Felice Romani librettista*. There is no comparable work for librettists of the earlier tradition, but an important article is Castelvecchi, "Walter Scott, Rossini e la *couleur ossianique*."

13. See his letter to Simone Mayr of 15 June 1826, published in Zavadini, *Donizetti*, 246–47.

14. See Rossini's letter to Romani of 31 August 1819 approving the choice of a subject, in Rossini, *Lettere e documenti*, 1:393.

15. The page is reproduced in facsimile in *I copialettere*, between 422 and 423.

16. Verdi's language for various elements associated with his compositional process has been studied by Folena, "Lessico melodrammatico verdiano."

17. The manuscript is found among the composer's papers at the Villa Verdi in Sant'Agata. I was able to examine it in a microfilm copy at the American Institute of Verdi Studies. Although only the *selva* for the second act seems to survive, Verdi's correspondence with Piave, his librettist, suggests that the composer prepared a similar manuscript for each act.

18. Piave would follow Verdi's instructions precisely, employing a *senario* meter (basically with six syllables to each line, as explained later in this chapter).

19. The most elaborate studies of the genesis of a Verdi libretto concern the original version (1847) of *Macbeth*. See [Folena], "Il *Macbeth* verdiano"; and Degrada, "Observations on the Genesis of Verdi's *Macbeth*" and "The 'Scala' *Macbeth* Libretto."

20. The compositional history of Donizetti's *Le convenienze ed inconvenienze teatrali* has been sorted out in exemplary fashion in the 2002 critical edition, ed. Parker and Wiklund.

21. Here, too, the terminological pitfalls are legion. See Beghelli, "Tre slittamenti semantici."

22. Letter to Piave of 2 October 1843, published in Conati, *La bottega della musica*, 91–92. The compositional history of the opera is discussed in the preface to *Ernani*, ed. Gallico.

23. As far as we know, Solera's original manuscript librettos have not survived.

24. Letter to Brenna of 15 November 1843, published in Conati, *La bottega*, 102–3.

25. An intriguing sheet, with several melodies subsequently used in *I puritani*, is reproduced in Pastura, *Bellini*, facing 385.

26. In some unusual cases comic dialogue was written in prose: this is the case particularly in operas with characters singing in Neapolitan dialect, such as Don Pomponio in Rossini's *La gazzetta* of 1816.

27. Among basic studies on musical forms in Italian nineteenth-century opera are Gossett, "Verdi, Ghislanzoni, and *Aida*"; Powers, "'La solita forma' and the Uses of Convention"; Balthazar, "Rossini and the Development of the Mid-Century Lyric Form."

28. In fact, Rossini introduces the new lyrical section in *senari* with a transitional passage, already in common time, that continues to employ the *settenari* of the Andantino.

29. This example cites the text as printed in the original publication of Cammarano's libretto, not as set to music by Verdi; the composer made a number of small modifications.

30. Although ostensibly each verse pattern has "ten" syllables, *doppi quinari* are distinct from *decasillabi*, with their characteristic accents on the third, sixth, and ninth syllables. The quintessential example of *decasillabi* in Italian opera is Somma's text for Verdi's most famous

chorus (accented syllables are printed in boldface): "Va pen**sie**ro sull'**ale** do**ra**te, / Va ti **po**sa sui **cli**vi, sui **col**li / Ove o**lez**zano **te**pide e **mol**li / L'aure **dol**ci del **suo**lo na**tal!**" The text is quoted, as Verdi set it to music, from the critical edition of *Nabucodonosor*, ed. Parker.

31. Letter to Cammarano of 4 April 1851, published in *Carteggio Verdi–Cammarano (1843–1852)*, ed. Mossa, 188–89.

32. The effect of the structure of verses on a composer's activity has been studied extensively by Friedrich Lippmann. See, in particular, his *Versificazione italiana e ritmo musicale*, trans. Bianconi, the revision of an earlier study in German.

33. For the *Barbiere* documents, see my preface to the facsimile edition, 12–19 (English) and 63–70 (Italian); for the composition of *Beatrice di Tenda*, see Rosselli, *Bellini*, 105–15; for *Parisina*, my introduction to Donizetti, *Parisina*.

34. Verdi kept up a formidable correspondence all his life, and it is the primary source of our knowledge of his activities and opinions. The Istituto Nazionale di Studi Verdiani, which has assiduously collected photocopies of these letters for decades, has begun to publish parts of this correspondence, reserving a volume or volumes to the letters exchanged with significant figures in Verdi's life: Boito, Cammarano, the Ricordi firm, and Somma. Apart from the *Copialettere* and Conati's *La bottega*, other significant collections of letters are found in Abbiati, *Giuseppe Verdi;* Alberti, *Verdi intimo;* and Luzio, *Carteggi verdiani*. The most significant series of books about Verdi's operas remains Budden's three-volume *The Operas of Verdi*.

35. For an overview of these materials, see Gossett, "Compositional Methods." The *Semiramide* sketches are transcribed fully as appendix 1 to the critical edition of the opera, 1421–41. The *Moïse* sketch is published in facsimile and discussed in Gossett, "Gioachino Rossini's *Moïse.*"

36. Gatti, *L'abbozzo del Rigoletto di Giuseppe Verdi*. On Verdi's preliminary sketches, see Gossett, "Der kompositorische Prozeß." See also Petrobelli, "Remarks on Verdi's Composing Process" and "Thoughts for *Alzira*," and Gossett, "Verdi the Craftsman."

37. Gatti, *Verdi nelle immagini*. There is good reason to believe that Verdi also sketched earlier operas, at least in part, and important manuscripts have been identified for *I due Foscari*, *Alzira*, and *Jérusalem*.

38. For a lovely example, pertaining to the cabaletta of the Duke's aria at the beginning of act 3 of *Rigoletto*, see the introduction by Martin Chusid to his critical edition of the opera, xviii (English) and xlii (Italian).

39. The sketches have been studied by Gossett in "New Sources for *Stiffelio,*" and Hansell in "Compositional Techniques in *Stiffelio.*"

40. The most important single publication to come out of the celebrations in honor of the hundredth anniversary of Verdi's death in 1901 was Verdi, *La traviata: Schizzi e abbozzi autografi*, ed. Della Seta, a facsimile of the sketches for *La traviata* with an ample introduction, transcription, and analysis. The explanatory "Commento critico" was published in 2002.

41. For a consideration of the music as it existed in January 1858, see chapter 14.

42. On the basis of manuscripts in St. Petersburg, Holmes discussed some of these changes in "The Earliest Revisions of *La forza del destino*." At the time he wrote this essay, the sketches were not available.

43. See the preface to Rossini, *La donna del lago*, ed. Slim, as well as my introductions to Rossini, *Elisabetta, regina d'Inghilterra*, and to Rossini, *Mosè in Egitto: A Facsimile Edition of Rossini's Original Autograph Manuscript*.

44. Similar problems arise in *Mosè in Egitto*, in whose autograph manuscript there are, in the second act, five recitative passages whose textual history remains elusive and whose author is uncertain. These issues are discussed in the preface and critical notes to Rossini, *Mosè in Egitto*, ed. Brauner.

45. See Bellini, *Il pirata,* ed. Gossett. The vocal parts of this final section are on folios 162–65, the orchestral parts on 173–78.

46. These performances of *Semiramide* are the subject of chapter 6.

47. For further details, see the critical commentary to Verdi, *Alzira,* ed. Castelvecchi with Cheskin.

48. See the critical commentaries to Rossini, *Otello,* ed. Collins, and *Guillaume Tell,* ed. Bartlet.

49. See the critical commentary to Rossini, *Tancredi,* ed. Gossett.

50. See the critical notes to the Cavatina Elvira (N. 3) in the critical edition of Verdi, *Ernani,* 35–40.

51. As if that were not bad enough, twentieth-century orchestras have had to cope with the disappearance of the cimbasso from today's orchestras, so that modern judgments on such matters have usually been made with the sound of the tuba in mind, a *very* different sound from the one intended by Verdi (see chapter 12).

52. I first advanced this hypothesis, which by now has been generally accepted, in my article "The Composition of *Ernani*" (see particularly 33–35).

53. See my introductory essay to the facsimile edition of Donizetti, *Don Pasquale,* pp. 37–45 (Italian) and 108–15 (English).

54. I discuss the problems associated with the structure of this chorus in my introduction to Bellini, *Norma.*

55. The standard chorus at the San Carlo in 1816—men and women—was thirty (see the description of expenses from February 1816 in Rossini, *Lettere e documenti,* 1:142). For the witches in *Macbeth* in Florence, Verdi asked for eighteen women, divided into three groups, but he treated this as an unusual request: see his letter to Alessandro Lanari of 21 January 1847, in Rosen and Porter, *Verdi's "Macbeth,"* 33.

56. Gossett, *Le sinfonie di Rossini,* particularly 56–68. Rossini may well have known the overture to Gluck's *Iphigénie en Tauride* (1781), in which what seems at first to be a strictly instrumental composition soon becomes a formidable vocal ensemble.

57. See the introduction to the critical edition of Verdi, *Alzira,* xvi (English) and xxxiv (Italian).

58. The best discussion of this incomplete opera is Pastura, *Bellini,* 245–76. Two autograph pages, from the collection in the Museo Belliniano of Catania, are reproduced in *Bellini,* ed. Andò, De Meo, and Failla, 212.

59. The libretto was edited by Lo Presti as "*Le Duc d'Albe:* The Livret of Scribe and Duveyrier." See also Ashbrook, *Donizetti and His Operas,* 434–36.

60. There are two articles about *L'Ange de Nisida,* together with an edition of Alphonse Royer and Gustave Vaëz's libretto, in the *Donizetti Society Journal* 7 (2002): Lo Presti, "Sylvia prima di Léonor (con interferenze di un duca)," and Desniou, "Donizetti et *L'Ange de Nisida*"; the transcription of the libretto, by Lo Presti and Desniou, follows. See also Donizetti, *La Favorite,* ed. Harris-Warrick. For a serious corrective to earlier accounts of Stolz and her art, see Smart, "The Lost Voice of Rosine Stolz."

61. These documents are all cited in the preface to Rossini, *Edipo Coloneo,* ed. Tozzi and Weiss.

62. Letter to Piave of 5 February 1851, published in Conati, *La bottega,* 250–51.

63. See the discussion of the chorus that opens the final act in its 1847 version, "Patria oppressa" (N. 12a), in the introduction and commentary to Verdi, *Macbeth,* ed. Lawton.

64. In the cavatina "Fragolette fortunate" for the heroine of *Adina,* an opera he prepared on commission for a Portuguese nobleman, Rossini wrote the first nineteen measures in full. For

the remainder of the piece (mm. 20–118), he notated only a skeleton score, leaving the orchestration to another musician. See Rossini, *Adina,* ed. Della Seta.

65. The contemporary banda realization for *Semiramide* is printed as vol. 4 of this critical edition.

66. See the facsimile edition of the autograph manuscript of *Mosè in Egitto,* vol. 2, ff. 289–291, as well as the critical edition, 786–96.

67. For further information, see the preface to vol. 3 of the critical edition of *La donna del lago.* What no one in the nineteenth century could have imagined, however, is a scoring in which horns inappropriately took the place of the martial trumpets, precisely what audiences at the Rossini Opera Festival heard in a particularly unfortunate production of *La donna del lago* during the summer of 2001.

68. Rossini, *La gazza ladra,* ed. Zedda; the problem occurs at m. 172 (p. 741).

69. The critical edition of *Rigoletto,* ed. Chusid, places the chord on the second beat (see p. 81).

70. For a typical example, see the facsimile of the autograph manuscript of *Mosè in Egitto,* ff. 34v–37v, in the Quintetto, where Rossini originally indicated "Come Sopra" for the repetition of the theme of the cabaletta ("Voce di giubilo"), writing only a single measure in the vocal part and two measures in the bass. This 47-measure passage was meant to be identical to an earlier passage on ff. 28–31v. A copyist later erased the "Come Sopra" and added the vocal and orchestral parts, but his readings are not philologically significant: a critical edition must independently fulfill Rossini's original instruction.

71. Recall Berlioz's description of rehearsals on his travels in his *Memoirs of Hector Berlioz,* trans. Holmes and Holmes: "The first clarinet is ill, the wife of the oboe has just been confined, the child of the first violin has the croup, the trombones are on parade—they forgot to ask for an exemption from their military duty for today; the kettle-drum has sprained his wrist, the harp will not come to the rehearsal because he needs time to study his part" (267).

CHAPTER THREE

1. See Verdi's letter to Barbieri-Nini of 2 January 1847 and to Varesi from the last week of January, both printed in Rosen and Porter, *Verdi's "Macbeth,"* 28–30 and 36–37. On 4 February he sent Varesi the vocal part of the "Scena Aria e Morte di Macbet," which survives at the Accademia Chigiana in Siena.

2. Letter to Barezzi of 16 June 1847, published in Garibaldi, *Giuseppe Verdi nelle lettere di Emanuele Muzio ad Antonio Barezzi,* 329.

3. See the introduction to Verdi, *I masnadieri,* ed. Marvin, xxx–xxxi (English) and lx (Italian). Characteristic is Verdi's addition of ascending staccato arpeggios at mm. 61 and 65 of the Scena e Cavatina Amalia (N. 4): compare the final version of the cavatina (on pp. 102–3 of the edition) and the early version (in appendix 1B, p. 492, mm. 58a and 62a).

4. The correct note is printed in the critical edition of *Rigoletto,* ed. Chusid (see the commentary to the Aria Gilda [N. 6], Note 65, 69, on p. 51).

5. Both versions are printed in the critical edition of *Guillaume Tell,* ed. Bartlet. The original version, without the reprise of the chorus, is given in appendix 2, pp. 1513–1607 (see, in particular, mm. 427–442); the revised version, with the reprise, discovered by Bartlet in performing parts at the Bibliothèque de l'Opéra, is in the main score, on pp. 992–1068 (see, in particular, mm. 358–375).

6. The revised duet is discussed in Gossett, *"Anna Bolena" and the Artistic Maturity of Gaetano Donizetti,* 151–76. In the most recent Ricordi vocal score (the 1986 reprinting, with modifications, of a nineteenth-century score), this Duetto is included on 105–27.

7. I discuss Donizetti's modifications in the Duetto for the Dottore and Don Pasquale (N. 11) in the introduction to the facsimile edition of *Don Pasquale*, 48–61 (Italian) and 119–31 (English).

8. See Geltrude Righetti-Giorgi, *Cenni di una donna già cantante* (Bologna, 1823), 35. Thanks to the recent recovery of a highly significant group of letters from Rossini to his family from the 1810s and 1820s, published as vol. 3a of *Lettere e documenti,* we now have access to the letters Rossini himself wrote to his mother after opening night of *Il barbiere di Siviglia* and after the next performance, and his statements support the anecdotal evidence (see 3a:119–23). The letters were sold as lot 175 at the Sotheby's auction of 7 December 2001.

9. The contract is reproduced in Conati, *La bottega,* 290–92.

10. Letter to Tito Ricordi of 4 February 1859, published in *I copialettere,* 556–57. There has been important recent work on the history of this opera. See Izzo, "Verdi's *Un giorno di regno.*"

11. See Harwood, "Verdi's Reform of the Italian Opera Orchestra."

12. See Jensen, "The Emergence of the Modern Conductor in 19th-Century Italian Opera."

13. In her description of the manuscript sources of *Guillaume Tell* in the commentary to the critical edition (23–33), Bartlet analyzes the history in considerable detail.

14. Verdi's most famous letter on the subject was to Camille Du Locle, dated from Genoa on 7 December 1869. See *I copialettere,* 219–22.

15. Rossini, *Lettere e documenti,* 2:154–56.

16. For further information, see *L'occasione fa il ladro,* ed. Carli-Ballola, Brauner, and Gossett, xxix; and *Il signor Bruschino,* ed. Gazzaniga, xxvii.

17. The sources are described in Selk, "*Matilde di Shabran,*" 69–79. See also Gossett, "Le fonti autografe delle opere teatrali di Rossini."

18. The history is told in my introductory essay to the facsimile of the autograph manuscript of *Il barbiere di Siviglia,* 29–32 (English) and 82–86 (Italian).

19. Rossini, *Lettere e documenti,* 1:150. See my introduction to the facsimile of the autograph manuscript of *La Cenerentola,* as well as the introduction to the critical edition of the opera, xxii.

20. Fortunately, a unique copy of this chorus, "Ah! Della bella incognita," survives in a copyist's manuscript in Rome.

21. Since autograph manuscripts were rarely pristine documents, however, this was no guarantee of a satisfactory edition, as Bartlet has demonstrated throughout her critical edition of *Guillaume Tell.*

22. For further information, see Devries and Lesure, *Dictionnaire des éditeurs de musique française: Des origines à environ 1820,* and *Dictionnaire des éditeurs de musique française II: De 1820 à 1914.*

23. The standard reference source for Italian publishers is Antolini, *Dizionario degli editori musicali italiani 1750–1930.*

24. An excellent study of Roman publishers in this period is Antolini and Bini, *Editori e librai musicali a Roma nella prima metà dell'Ottocento;* see pp. 146–90 for a complete list of the publications of Ratti and Cencetti, organized by plate number.

25. For detailed observations on a particular case, the distribution of Rossini's *Semiramide,* which contractually was owned by the Teatro La Fenice of Venice, see Gossett, "Piracy in Venice."

26. These extracts, published by the Litografia Annibale Patrelli of Naples, are described in the commentary to the critical edition of *Ermione,* 22. For further information about Patrelli, see the entry by Rosa Cafiero in Antolini, *Dizionario degli editori musicali italiani,* 258–59, as well as Cafiero and Seller, "Editoria musicale a Napoli attraverso la stampa periodica," in particular items 18 and 19 on p. 66.

27. Verdi's *Ernani,* for example, had its premiere in March 1844, and the complete vocal score was advertised by Ricordi in August; see the commentary to the critical edition, 8–10.

28. All pieces are printed in the critical edition of *Tancredi:* the original first-act aria (N. 4) on 131– 47, the Milanese substitution (N. 4a) on 718–39.

29. The manuscript is Florence, Biblioteca del Conservatorio "L. Cherubini," D-III-176. The reorchestration is discussed in the commentary to the critical edition, 248.

30. The letter is printed in Barblan and Walker "Contributo all'epistolario di Gaetano Donizetti," 27–28 (letter 32, identified also as Z. 151ᵃ).

31. Cambi, *Bellini: Epistolario,* 287.

32. Ibid., 335.

33. The 173-page score, published in 1832 in oblong format, has the plate numbers 5900–5911. The original passage is printed on 85–100.

34. In his Cambridge Opera Handbook, *Vincenzo Bellini: " Norma,"* 83–86, for example, David Kimbell concludes, "It would be opportune to reinstate the evidently superior original readings."

35. For an account of the controversy and many of the relevant documents, see Seller, "Il *Marin Faliero* da Napoli a Parigi," "Il libretto," and "La pirateria musicale e *Marin Faliero:* nuovi documenti." See also Girardi, *Gaetano Donizetti,* which is filled with important studies and documents.

36. Zavadini, *Donizetti,* 387.

37. Ibid., 420–21.

38. For further details, see both the preface and the commentary to the critical edition of *L'Italiana in Algeri.* The Neapolitan manuscripts of the opera, which will be discussed in the following paragraphs, are described in the critical commentary, 20–21.

39. Reviewing the first Milanese performance of *Tancredi,* which had inaugurated the Teatro Re several months earlier, on 18 December 1813, the critic of the *Corriere Milanese* commented that "not all the instruments foreseen in the score were actually present in the orchestra." See the preface to the critical edition of *Tancredi,* xxx.

40. According to Will Crutchfield, in a private communication, the recording was made for Moscow Radio in about 1950.

41. The history of the libretto is discussed in greater detail in Fabbri and Bertieri, *L'Italiana in Algeri.* Anelli's 1808 libretto is reproduced on 51–102.

42. In a private communication, Will Crutchfield informs me that these symbols are found in some engraved Italian vocal pieces published in the British Isles as early as 1781.

43. See Beghelli and Piana, "The New Critical Edition." The essay describes and compares the sources for *L'equivoco stravagante:* see 37– 44 (Italian) and 45–53 (English).

44. A copy of the libretto prepared on that occasion is found in the library of the Civico Museo Bibliografico Musicale of Bologna (4663).

45. On the Martorelli *copisteria,* see Antolini and Bini, *Editori e librai musicali,* 13–19.

46. A copy of this libretto, published for performances at the Teatro Valle during the autumn of 1819, is found in the Biblioteca di Santa Cecilia in Rome, XXII 147.

47. Roman censorship remained strong as long as the Papacy retained political control of the region. For a fascinating study of a later period, see Giger, "Social Control and the Censorship of Giuseppe Verdi's Operas in Rome (1844–1859)."

48. The events are summarized in the historical introduction to Donizetti, *Poliuto,* ed. Ashbrook and Parker, xiii–xiv, as well as in Black, "The Contract for Paris." For the historical context of this disaster-laden season, see Maione and Seller, "L'ultima stagione napoletana di Domenico Barbaja (1836–1840)."

49. Bellini told Florimo in a letter of 21–22 December 1834 that he would not send the duet to Naples because the singers engaged there could not do it justice and because "both love of country and Liberty are invoked" (Cambi, *Bellini: Epistolario,* 492).

50. I discussed this example in "The Tragic Finale of *Tancredi*"; see, in particular, 71–77 (English) and 156–62 (Italian).

51. The manuscripts are Venice, Biblioteca del Conservatorio "B. Marcello," Busta 89; and Vicenza, Biblioteca Civica Bertoliana, FF.2.6.5–6.

52. Among the many studies of the effects of censorship in *Rigoletto*, the most important is Lavagetto, *Un caso di censura*.

53. This letter was published for the first time in Evan Baker, "Lettere di Giuseppe Verdi a Francesco Maria Piave 1843–1865," 156–57; Verdi discusses the problem in another letter, written a few days later, on 29 November (see Conati, *La bottega*, 227). Many of Verdi's letters to Piave are now in the Koch collection at the Beinecke Rare Book Library of Yale University.

54. *I copialettere*, 497.

55. For an even worse situation, see the discussion of Donizetti's *La Favorite* in chapter 11. This opera continues to be performed today in an execrable Italian translation of the French original. Bowing to religious proprieties as they existed in Italy during the 1840s, the relationships among the protagonists and their very identity were altered in this translation, rendering the story incomprehensible. This is *not* a matter of whether the opera should be sung in French or Italian, a question to which serious responses can be advanced from both sides. Even if *La Favorite* is to be performed in Italian, it is impossible to understand how a travesty of the opera can continue to be foisted on a confused public to the discredit of the composer. The vocal score (Milan, 1999), derived from Rebecca Harris-Warrick's critical edition of 1997, has both the original French words and a partially new translation by Fausto Broussard, which finally makes it possible to perform the opera responsibly in Italian. There can be no excuse for continuing to use the deeply flawed nineteenth-century translation.

56. All the substitute arias by Rossini mentioned here are printed as appendixes to the critical edition.

57. See chapter 7.

58. For a fuller discussion of these issues, see chapter 12.

59. Meucci, "Il cimbasso e gli strumenti affini nell'Ottocento italiano."

60. The manuscript prepared for the Teatro La Fenice at the time of the first performance on 7 March 1824 is reproduced in Meyerbeer, *Il crociato in Egitto*.

61. For an overview of the Ricordi firm in the nineteenth century, see Antolini, *Dizionario degli editori musicali italiani*, 286–313. The publishing house itself has issued two important surveys of its production: Sartori, *Casa Ricordi 1808–1958;* and *Musica Musicisti Editoria: 175 anni di Casa Ricordi 1808–1983*.

62. There has been little work on copyright issues for Italian opera composers. For one interesting contribution, see Kallberg, "Marketing Rossini." Kallberg's most important contributions to the history of musical copyright, however, are associated with the music of Chopin: see, in particular, "Chopin in the Marketplace."

63. White, *Stravinsky*, 99; for White's comments on the *Petrushka* revision, see 165.

64. Many of the documents from which the following paragraphs are derived are found in Sartori, *Casa Ricordi*, 11–46.

65. Let me thank that inveterate Rossini collector and friend, Colwyn Philipps (Lord St. Davids), who first pointed out this relationship to me.

66. These negotiations are described more fully in the introduction to the critical edition of *Rigoletto*, xi–xii (English) and xxxv–xxxvi (Italian).

67. In his *Giuseppe Verdi and Giovanni Ricordi*, Luke Jensen provides an overview of the business dealings between Verdi and Giovanni Ricordi, who died in 1853, together with a listing of all Ricordi publications pertaining to the operas through *La traviata*.

68. Letters from Muzio to Barezzi of 14 April 1847 and 22 April 1847, in Garibaldi, *Giuseppe Verdi,* 315 and 316, respectively.

69. For full details, see the introduction and commentary to the critical edition of *Alzira,* ed. Castelvecchi with Cheskin. Verdi's reduction of the overture for piano solo is printed as appendix 2 of the edition, 415–20.

70. Letter from Verdi to Tito Ricordi of 24 October 1855, published in *I copialettere,* 168.

71. As we saw in chapter 2, the remark is found in a letter of 12 May 1858 to his friend Clarina Maffei: "From *Nabucco* on I have not had, you might say, one hour of calm. Sixteen years on the galleys" (ibid., 572).

72. These proof sheets, pertaining to the "Lux æterna" movements, are described in Verdi, *Messa da Requiem,* ed. Rosen, critical commentary, 20–21.

73. Letter from Donizetti to Giovanni Ricordi of 13 June 1833, published in Zavadini, *Donizetti,* 313.

74. Letter from Donizetti to Giovanni Ricordi of 1 August 1833, ibid., 325.

75. Letter from Donizetti to Giovanni Ricordi of 5 July 1839, ibid., 497.

76. Letter from Donizetti to Francesco Lucca of 7 March 1841, ibid., 533.

77. The pages pertaining to *Rigoletto* are reproduced in *I copialettere,* the first as table III (between 114 and 115), the second as table IV (facing 116). Unfortunately, the editors of *I copialettere* did not transcribe this material; nor did they include any other information of this kind in their publication.

78. The remark is from a letter to Tito Ricordi in the Ricordi archives in Milan of 17 January 1863, a letter in which he particularly takes the publisher to task for the sloppy way in which articulation and dynamics are handled in the "Rataplan" in the act 3 *Accampamento* scene.

79. Gui relates the story in his 1971 text "Storia avventurosa di alcuni capolavori del passato."

80. In a more extreme vein, it is also quite possible to concern oneself with the historical problem of how successive generations have modified a musical text, and the reasons that prompted them to do so. For an excellent example, see Senici, "'Adapted to the Modern Stage.'" But few, if any, would urge us to allow the perceived necessities of London performers in 1821 to guide our behavior in mounting Mozart's opera today.

CHAPTER FOUR

1. Vaughan, "Discordanze fra gli autografi verdiani e la loro stampa." In other articles he turned his attention to several Puccini operas.

2. In his *"Arpa d'or dei fatidici vati,"* Roger Parker finds little evidence that the *Nabucco* chorus was singled out during the early years of the opera. While I disagree with some of his conclusions, I think he is correct in his assessment that the immense prestige of this chorus is largely a product of mythmaking in postunification Italy. For recent studies of twentieth-century Verdian mythmaking, see Polo, *Immaginari verdiani,* and Basini, "Cults of Sacred Memory."

3. Let me thank the Dutch critic, J. R. Evenhuis, who kindly sent me a copy of the printed invitation to the public "debate between Maestro Denis Vaughan and Maestro Giulio Confalonieri about the vexed question of errors and differences between the autograph manuscripts of Verdi and Puccini and the current editions of their works."

4. In the first issue of *Verdi* (1960), the president of the Istituto Nazionale di Studi Verdiani, Mario Medici, wrote that one of the institute's goals was "the publication of a critical edition of Verdi's complete works" (x, Italian; xviii, English).

5. Gavazzeni, "Problemi di tradizione dinamico-fraseologica e critica testuale, in Verdi e in Puccini." I am quoting from the English translation included in the Ricordi reprint.

6. See the famous letter from Puccini to Toscanini of 23 June 1910, inviting him to review and correct the dynamic levels, slurs, etc., so that he can finally have "a definitive *Manon*." The letter is printed in Gara, *Carteggi pucciniani*, 377. For *La fanciulla del West,* consult Dotto, "Opera, Four Hands."

7. On the occasion of the performances at the Teatro Comunale of Bologna in the fall of 1993, Riccardo Chailly reintroduced the "canzone" most effectively. See Mandelli, "I 'fiori' ritrovati, che Puccini non voleva eliminare."

8. At least one scholar has made a case for the primacy of the printed score of *Falstaff:* see Hepokoski, "Overriding the Autograph Score." My own position would tend to favor a mixed approach to the editing of *Falstaff:* choosing the autograph as a copy text, but accepting later modifications that can reasonably be attributed to Verdi. It will be up to the editor of the critical edition, however, to make a final determination.

9. Vaughan, "Discordanze."

10. Vaughan, "Discordanze"; Gavazzeni, "Problemi," 68.

11. To the extent that it is possible to distinguish Verdi's *f* from his *ff,* not always an easy task, the markings are as follows: *ff* in piccolo, clarinets, trumpets, timpani, violins, and cello; *f* in the second pair of horns, violas, and double basses; nothing in the other parts. Vaughn failed to realize that Verdi habitually (but *not* exclusively) places his dynamic markings beneath an instrumental staff.

12. See Verdi, *Messa da Requiem,* ed. Rosen, 119.

13. The passage discussed by Vaughan and Gavazzeni occurs several pages later, when the theme is embedded in a complex ensemble (mm. 645–49, printed in the critical edition on 122–23). See Vaughan, "Discordanze"; Gavazzeni, "Problemi," 67.

14. Vaughan, "The Inner Language of Verdi's Manuscripts," 80.

15. Verdi's autograph manuscript was issued in facsimile, *La Messa da Requiem di Giuseppe Verdi,* in three hundred copies, in 1941, on the fortieth anniversary of the composer's death. There is no better way to understand these problems than to consult this passage directly, as it appears in the composer's hand.

16. The recording was issued by the Decca Record Company, London (425-520-2). Patané's statement "A traditional recording of *Barbiere*" is archetypal of the inability of some artists to differentiate the contents of a printed score from performance decisions quite properly made by interpreters.

17. There had been important publications of documents pertaining to the librettos and their genesis, however, including those in Abbiati, *Giuseppe Verdi;* Luzio, *Carteggi verdiani;* and a host of individual studies, such as Pascolato, *"Re Lear" e "Ballo in Maschera."*

18. For those who aspired to work in this field, the appearance of Ashbrook's first book on the composer, *Donizetti* (1965), and of Weinstock's *Donizetti and the World of Opera in Italy, Paris and Vienna in the First Half of the Nineteenth Century* (1963) was a revelation.

19. The fruits of Lawton and Rosen's research was published in their fundamental study, "Verdi's Non-definitive Revisions."

20. See Gui, "Storia avventurosa."

21. These problems will be addressed in the critical edition of *Il barbiere di Siviglia* that I am preparing.

22. New York Public Library, *MSI, Special Collections. A manuscript in the collection of the Bibliothèque Nationale (Fonds du Conservatoire) in Paris was once thought—without any justification—to be Rossini's original manuscript (Mss. 8330–8331). A page of that manuscript was even published as representing Rossini's handwriting, in Hürlimann, *Musikerhandschriften von Schubert bis Strawinsky,* facsimile 14.

23. Rossini, *Il barbiere di Siviglia,* ed. Zedda.

24. Ibid., Commento Critico, 15.

25. For a good introduction to the problem of critical editions of music, see Grier, *The Critical Editing of Music.* Grier's book, however, is primarily devoted to the editing of music written before 1800.

26. The comment is found in his letter to Camille Bellaigue of 2 May 1898, published in Luzio, *Carteggi verdiani,* 2:312.

27. See, for example, the cabaletta melody "Sventurata, anch'io deliro" in Imogene's cavatina in *Il pirata,* where Bellini experimented with two entirely different accompaniments in the upper strings, first writing out the entire section with a continuous arpeggiation, then crossing out these string parts and substituting a series of chords off the beat. See the facsimile edition of *Il pirata,* ff. 74r–77r.

28. For a balanced approach to Schumann's orchestration, see the article by Brian Schlotel, "The Orchestral Music," especially 313–23. While most orchestras today use Schumann's own orchestrations, the problem continues to exercise musicians, critics, and scholars.

29. Performances with "early" instruments, while fascinating, do *not* make all such problems disappear; see chapter 12.

30. D'Amico, "C'è modo e modo (*I Capuleti e i Montecchi* di Bellini nella revisione di Claudio Abbado)."

31. Some sense of Abbado's approach can be gleaned from the studio recording he made shortly after with Deutsche Grammophon, 2561 214-216. It includes several members of the La Scala cast (Teresa Berganza as Rosina, Luigi Alva as the Conte d'Almaviva, Hermann Prey as Figaro, Paolo Montarsolo as Basilio, and Stefania Malagú as Berta), with the London Symphony Orchestra.

32. Patané's recording was cited in n. 16 above.

33. For complete details of the operation, see my review of the recording of *L'assedio di Corinto* on Angel Records, which preceded by several months the Metropolitan Opera performances and featured all the same principal singers (Gossett, Review of Gioachino Rossini, *L'assedio di Corinto*).

34. The section in question is a cabaletta near the end of the third act, "Parmi vederlo ahi misero," added anonymously for Giuditta Grisi when she performed the role of Pamyra at the Teatro La Fenice of Venice during the carnival season of 1829, beginning on 17 January 1829. The next year, on 11 March 1830, Grisi created the role of Romeo in Bellini's *I Capuleti e i Montecchi* at the same theater. Although propaganda for the performance and the edition hinted that Rossini was responsible for this addition, there is not a shred of evidence that this is the case. See my review (cited in n. 33 above), 637.

35. There have been several recent studies of the Rossini Neapolitan operas, with particular attention to *Maometto II.* An early and significant contribution was Isotta, "I diamanti della corona" (1974). Later studies include Grondona, *La perfetta illusione* (1996) and Tortora, *Drammaturgia del Rossini serio* (1996). See also my "History and Works That Have No History."

36. See the fine treatment of the relationship between the two operas in Osborne, *Rossini,* 237–42.

37. The Greek revolt against their Turkish rulers in the 1820s had caught the imagination of much of Europe. Byron's sojourn in Greece and his death at Missolonghi in 1824 are well known. While the poet's 1816 verse tale *The Siege of Corinth* gave its name to Rossini's opera, the poem has only a rhetorical resemblance to *Le Siège de Corinthe;* witness Byron's first invocation of the city (stanza 1, lines 46–49): "Many a vanish'd year and age, / And tempest's breath, and battle's rage, / Have swept o'er Corinth; yet she stands, / A fortress form'd to Freedom's hands."

38. Rossini may have overcompensated in his effort to suit what he believed to be French taste. As Damien Colas has shown, in his study of singers' parts at the Bibliothèque de l'Opéra, individual performers at the Opéra often returned to the original florid lines or interpolated other, equally florid passagework. See Colas, *Les Annotations de chanteurs dans les matériels d'exécution des opéras de Rossini à Paris (1820–1860)*, particularly the musical examples related to *Le Siège de Corinthe* in 4:103–19.

39. It should come as no surprise that during the revolutionary movements in 1848, this music was arranged (not by Rossini) as a "National Hymn by Francesco Ilari, dedicated to the mobilized civic legions of Rome." The text begins, "Italiani! È finito il servaggio! Dio ci chiama la patria a salvar!" (Italians! Our servitude is over! God calls us to save the homeland!). A copy of the publication is in the Library of the Conservatory "G. Verdi" of Milan (A-55-222-40).

40. To be honest, Rossini himself had inserted this piece into *Mosè in Egitto* in its first Neapolitan performances during 1818, but when he returned to the opera in 1819, he wisely removed it. The situation with this inserted cabaletta for Sills was even worse, however, since the copy of the aria used as the basis for what she performed lacked the horn and trumpet parts certainly written by Rossini, making the orchestral fabric even sparser; the question is treated fully by Charles Brauner in the preface and notes to the critical edition of *Mosè in Egitto*.

41. Some of this talk was subsequently published in my review (see n. 33 above) of the recording cited in the same note.

42. Wills, "Gorgeous Sills." It is not altogether certain whether I was the direct or indirect object of Sills's scorn, since a number of New York critics quoted my words.

43. Interview published in the *Corriere della Sera* (Milan), 28 November 1982, 28. Presumably it is under this rubric that he can justify to himself a relatively liberal approach to matters of tempo and dynamics.

44. I will return to the question of French opera in Italian translation in chapter 11.

45. The *loggione,* the uppermost tier of seats in a traditional Italian theater, is known in Italy as the home of the "true" opera lovers, and winning their approval is considered fundamental to the success of a singer in Italy. It needs to be said, though, that denizens of the *loggione,* the so-called *loggionisti,* tend to be among the most conservative members of the operagoing public, and they often object vociferously to any stylistic or textual modification from the music they know and love (usually from mid-twentieth-century recordings). I cite Bentivoglio's article after Beghelli, "Per fedeltà a una nota," 296.

46. Verdi, *Il trovatore,* ed. Lawton.

47. For a full discussion of the problem, see Beghelli, "Per fedeltà a una nota."

48. The situation is not quite so simple, since there is a significant problem in Verdi's autograph at this point. For further details, see ibid., 306–10. Although I do not think Beghelli's solution is correct (see his example 3 on 309), he does point out an inconsistency in the critical edition.

49. Baucardé himself is said to have introduced the high *c* in a reprise of *Il trovatore* in Florence at the Teatro della Pergola in October 1853, just a few months after the premiere of the opera (see Rescigno, *Dizionario verdiano,* 85–86). A few years later, when seeking to arrange a cast for the premiere of *Aroldo* (Rimini, Teatro Nuovo, 16 August 1857), Verdi refused to consider Augusta Albertini, the wife of Baucardé. As he said in a letter to Piave of 31 October 1856, "I had more than enough with her husband, and I want nothing more to do with lunatics." We don't know if his feelings had anything to do with high *c!* The letter is printed in Morazzoni, *Verdi: Lettere inedite,* 42.

50. The anecdote is related in Budden, *The Operas of Verdi,* 2:98–99, who says that he heard it in a public lecture given by Giovanni Martinelli. Clearly Verdi did not disdain Tamberlick's

high *c,* since he constructed the end of the third act of the original version of *La forza del destino* in order to highlight it.

51. The anecdote—which refers specifically to Tamberlick's *c♯*—is related by Giuseppe Radiciotti, in his charming *Aneddoti rossiniani autentici* (Rome, 1929), 67.

52. Interview published in the *Corriere della Sera* (Milan), 28 November 1982, 28.

53. Indeed, when he first projected this finale, Verdi did not plan to include even the canta-bile ("Infelice! e tu credevi") for Silva. For more complete details, see the introduction, xix (En-glish) and xliii (Italian), as well as the commentary, 48–49, in the critical edition of *Ernani.* Verdi's earliest version, without a cantabile, is reconstructed in skeleton score in appendix 1B. of the edition, 420. The cantabile was added before the Venetian premiere.

54. For Budden's commentary, see *The Operas of Verdi,* 1:167–69.

55. Parker announced his discovery in his article "'Infin che un brando vindice.'" See also the introduction to the critical edition of *Ernani,* xxi–xxii (English) and xlv–xlvi (Italian), as well as appendix 2, where the added cabaletta is printed, together with the revised measures leading up to it. Verdi's letter to Marini, written on 15 November 1841, was sold at the Sotheby's auction in London of 9–10 May 1985 (lot 218). The letter was then deposited at the Pierpont Morgan Library of New York. Today it forms part of the Koch collection at the Beinecke Library of Yale University.

CHAPTER FIVE

1. It would be both presumptuous and inappropriate to attempt to provide a list of works devoted to the history of textual criticism in literature. Those interested in pursuing the ques-tions raised here should consult Greetham, *Textual Scholarship,* for both an introduction to the most important issues and an extensive bibliography. In the following notes I will cite only the sources most relevant to my concerns.

2. The standard theory of traditional textual criticism is laid out in Greg, "The Rationale of Copy-Text." See also Bowers, "Greg's Rationale of 'Copy-Text' Revisited."

3. The introduction of computer-based editions using hypertext, allowing the reader to move freely between one version of a text and another, has given impetus to this approach. Mc-Gann and his colleagues at the University of Virginia have done remarkable work on the poetry of Dante Gabriel Rossetti. For a theoretical statement concerning his aims, see McGann's *Radi-ant Textuality.*

4. McGann, *A Critique of Modern Textual Criticism.*

5. Among statements about the aims of the new editions, see Martin Chusid, Claudio Gal-lico, Philip Gossett, and David Lawton in *Nuove prospettive nella ricerca verdiana.* See also Parker, "A Donizetti Critical Edition in the Postmodern World."

6. In addition to the critical edition itself, see Chusid's "Editing *Rigoletto,*" in *Nuove prospet-tive nella ricerca verdiana,* 49–56. For the documentary evidence pertaining to the following paragraphs, see the introduction to the critical edition, as well as Conati, *La bottega* and Budden, *The Operas of Verdi,* 1:477–87.

7. The history of *Stiffelio* is considered in full in the introduction to Verdi, *Stiffelio,* ed. Hansell.

8. Letter to Carlo Marzari of 14 December 1850, printed in Conati, *La bottega,* 232–33.

9. The relevant passage from this letter is printed in Conati, *La bottega,* 251.

10. Letter of 18 December 1886, printed in *Carteggio Verdi–Boito,* ed. Medici and Conati, 1:118.

11. Among important writings are Ingarden, *The Work of Music and the Problem of Its Iden-tity;* Goodman, *Languages of Art;* and Goehr, *The Imaginary Museum of Musical Works.* For a re-cent collection of essays, see Talbot, *The Musical Work.*

12. This is decidedly not the case with every work by Verdi: often there are multiple sources providing information, not simply the basic autograph manuscript. But I have chosen *Rigoletto* as an example here precisely because it represents the problem in an extreme form.

13. Letter of 14 January 1851, printed in Conati, *La bottega*, 243–44.

14. The passage is found in the critical edition in the Introduzione (N. 2), at mm. 389–393, on pp. 34–35.

15. In some cases Verdi uses a shorthand, indicating that one part should be derived from another.

16. The passage is found in the critical edition in the Scena ed Aria Duca (N. 8), at mm. 89–93, on p. 168.

17. I have reflected on some of these matters in "Editorial Theory, Musical Editions, Performance."

18. The manuscript is discussed in the preface to Rossini, *La gazzetta*, ed. Gossett and Scipioni, xl. On Noseda and his collection, see Moreni, *Vita musicale a Milano 1837–1866*.

19. The Bologna manuscript (UU 5) also bore what should have been an authoritative attestation, "Full score, partly autograph, of the *Stabat Mater*, entrusted in deposit to the city [of Bologna] by the family of the *Marchesi* Bevilacqua." The Bevilacquas were an important Bolognese family, and Gherardo Bevilacqua Aldobrandini was a close friend of Rossini's who worked with the composer on librettos for *Adina* and *Eduardo e Cristina*, and even provided some verses for *Semiramide*. See the prefaces to the critical editions of *Adina* (xxvii–xxxi) and *Semiramide* (xxx–xxxi).

20. I reported my findings in 1968 in "Rossini in Naples."

21. To Rossini scholars, Michotte is primarily known for his two books of memoirs, *Souvenirs personnels: La Visite de R. Wagner à Rossini (Paris 1860)*, and *Souvenirs: Une Soirée chez Rossini à Beau-Séjour (Passy)*. For translations, see Weinstock, *Richard Wagner's Visit to Rossini (Paris 1860) and An Evening at Rossini's in Beau-Séjour (Passy) 1858 by Edmond Michotte*. For bibliographical information about the Rossini literature, see the invaluable work of Gallo, *Gioachino Rossini*.

22. The verso of this page, with the dedication to Vaëz, is reproduced in Gossett, "Rossini in Naples," facing 331.

23. Budden, *The Operas of Verdi*, 1:262–63.

24. See Lawton and Rosen, "Verdi's Non-definitive Revisions," 206–7 (English) and 236–37 (Italian). For a fuller discussion of the *Attila* romanza, consult Gossett, "A New Romanza for *Attila*."

25. See Seebass, *Musikhandschriften in Basel aus verschiedenen Sammlungen*, item no. 61. At the time, the aria was in the collection of the widow of A. Wilhelm. Its present whereabouts are unknown.

26. Azevedo, *G. Rossini*, 259. On the other hand, we recently learned that the composer's autograph manuscript of the third-act finale of *Moïse* is found in the collection of the Deutsche Staatsbibliothek in Berlin.

27. See Gossett, "Der kompositorische Prozeß," 175–76. Verdi apparently gave this seven-page sketch for the "Grande scène de la dégradation" to Gilbert-Louis Duprez, the tenor for whom the scene was written.

28. Fortunately the existence of the microfilm made it possible for Rebecca Harris-Warrick to prepare the critical edition of *La Favorite*, but many matters will remain unclear until the autograph itself resurfaces.

29. See the Christie's catalogue for its sale of 4 April 1979, under lot no. 136.

30. See Rossini, *Quelques Riens pour album*, ed. Tartak.

31. For further details and references, consult Gossett, "Rossini e i suoi *Péchés de Vieillesse*," and Bruson, "Olympe, Pacini, Michotte ed altri."

32. There is a description of this colorful character by his great-nephew, Michael Grant, in *My First Eighty Years* (Henley-on-Thames, 1994), 191–93. Let me thank Ronald Mellor for bringing this memoir to my attention.

33. A copy of the catalogue, with annotations concerning the disposition of each lot and a list of those who acquired the manuscripts, is in the British Library.

34. Vitoux, *Fin de saison au Palazzo Pedrotti*, 77.

35. The recording, with Richard Bonynge conducting the London Symphony Orchestra, was issued by Decca (London A-4383). Sutherland and Horne had previously sung the opera together in concert performances in Los Angeles and New York (in 1964) and in a staged performed in Boston (1965).

36. The notice was published in Venice on 27 March in the *Giornale dipartimentale dell'Adriatico*.

37. The relevant documents are published in Gossett, "The Tragic Finale of Rossini's *Tancredi*," and in the critical edition of the opera.

38. The page is reproduced in "The Tragic Finale of Rossini's *Tancredi*" as plate V.

39. The letter is published in Foscolo, *Edizione nazionale delle opere di Ugo Foscolo*, vol. 16, Epistolario, bk. 3, 58.

40. Ibid., 317.

41. See the critical edition of *Tancredi*, 704–5 and 710–11. The edition, of course, contains both the original ending (in the bulk of the score as part of the original version of the opera) and the tragic ending (in an appendix featuring all the music Rossini prepared for Ferrara).

42. In a most interesting study, Benjamin Walton has recently argued that Charles's coronation itself was "operatic": see his " 'Quelque peu théâtral.' "

43. For full details, see the preface to *Il viaggio a Reims*, ed. Johnson.

44. Gossett, *The Operas of Rossini*, 506–21.

45. Most, but not all. I had hypothesized (see *The Operas of Rossini*, 517–19), on the basis of the structure of the poetry, that the duet for the Marchese Melibea and the Conte di Libenskof (N. 8) in *Il viaggio a Reims* was derived from a duet from Rossini's *Armida*, the famous "Amor! (Possente nome!)"; see N. 5 in *Armida*, ed. Brauner and Brauner. In fact, although the poetry was indeed identical in shape, form, and meter, and had clearly been modeled on the *Armida* text, the duet from *Il viaggio a Reims* was a brand-new composition.

46. The page is reproduced as Tavola 3 in the critical edition.

47. I have only recently been informed, by Annalisa Bini, librarian of the Accademia Nazionale di Santa Cecilia, that the manuscript had belonged to Queen Margherita of Savoy (the widow of Umberto I) and was donated to the conservatory, along with an important group of other manuscripts, during the 1920s.

48. See the section of the article "Römische Handschriften" written by Emilia Zanetti, in Blume, *Die Musik in Geschichte und Gegenwart*, 11:765–66.

49. See, in particular, Johnson, "A Lost Rossini Opera Recovered."

50. The Italian critics gave it their Abbiati prize for the best operatic production of the year. For Andrew Porter's withering attack, see his "Un viaggio a Pesaro."

51. Herbert Weinstock, who died in 1971, was the author of the important *Rossini: A Biography*.

52. It is printed in the critical edition of *Il viaggio a Reims*, 762–825.

53. See the Recitativo Dopo l'Aria Don Profondo, mm. 39–55 (on pp. 569–70).

54. Donizetti, *Maria Stuarda*, ed. Wiklund. In fact, the autograph incorporates changes made by Donizetti when the opera was given in Milan at the end of 1835, so that a complete

reconstruction of the Neapolitan version may never be possible. The remarkable collection of musical manuscripts in Stockholm is described in Lomnäs and Lomnäs, *Stiftelsen Muikkulturens främjande (Nydahl Collection)*.

55. The reconstruction of *Gustavo III* will be discussed in chapter 14.

56. For complete information, see Hansell's introduction to the critical edition of *Stiffelio*. For a discussion of the early Ricordi vocal score, see her commentary to the edition, 22–26; the surviving manuscript copies are discussed on 14–18.

57. There are those, such as Julian Budden (see his discussion of *La traviata* in *The Operas of Verdi*, 2:165–66), who utterly reject the notion that Verdi's art and his personal life might have interacted. My sympathies are much more with Luzio's interpretation in "La 'Traviata' e il dramma intimo personale di Verdi," in *Carteggi verdiani*, 4:250–76, which I do not find "sentimental" at all (the word is Budden's), but wise and sensitive to the complex ways in which art and life intermingle.

58. See the chorus near the beginning of the Scena, Coro, e Finale Primo (N. 5) at mm. 75–77, etc. (pp. 185–86). The changes begin as soon as the curtain goes up, where Verdi's autograph manuscript indicates that Jorg "sta leggendo la Bibbia" (is reading the Bible), whereas other contemporary sources have him simply "leggendo" (reading).

59. No written evidence has been produced to that effect, but so the story has been passed down from one generation to the next. See Abbiati, *Giuseppe Verdi*, 4:666, as well as Phillips-Matz, *Verdi*, 760, who reports it using much the same terms as Abbiati: "One of his main concerns was to provide for the destruction of the two wooden crates that contained his early compositions, which he had gathered in over many years. At the end of 1900 he asked Maria [Carrara] to take care of this for him." For a fuller consideration of these questions, see Martin, "Two Unpublished Early Works: 'La madre e la patria' and 'Marcia funebre,'" in his *Aspects of Verdi*, 139–56. See also the important contributions by Marvin, "A Verdi Autograph and the Problem of Authenticity," in which she discusses a youthful *Sinfonia* in D major, and by Rizzo, "'Con eletta musica del Sig. Verdi da Busseto, fu celebrata la Messa solenne,'" in which he announces the recovery of a *Messa di gloria*, part of which he convincingly attributes to the early Verdi. See also the publication of the facsimiles of Verdi's autographs for three early works whose manuscripts are in the Museo teatrale alla Scala, with descriptions and critical editions of the music, in *Giuseppe Verdi*: the *Sinfonia in D major*, ed. Roberta Montemorra Marvin; the *Tantum ergo* for tenor and orchestra (1836), ed. Dino Rizzo; and the *Notturno a tre voci* with flute and piano (1839), ed. Marco Marica.

60. From the unpaginated preface to Gatti, *L'abbozzo del Rigoletto di Giuseppe Verdi*.

61. See Girardi and Petrobelli, *Messa per Rossini*.

62. Verdi, *Libera me domine (Messa per Rossini)*.

63. The missing pages included the Preghiera e Finale Ultimo (N. 10), which needed to be reconstructed (see 397–412 in the critical edition) from a contemporary manuscript and—for the censored sections—from Verdi's quite complete continuity draft.

64. See, in particular, the studies by Gossett ("New Sources for *Stiffelio*") and Hansell ("Compositional Techniques in *Stiffelio*").

65. See the Scena, Coro, e Finale Primo (N. 5), at mm. 284–288 (pp. 212–13), where Verdi's "Del perfido Giuda il vil tradimento" was changed to "Antico. Dell'empio il vil tradimento" or "Antico. Dell'empio sarà il tradimento," as well as the Duetto, Quartetto, Finale Secondo (N. 7), at mm. 323–324 (p. 336) and mm. 335–338 (p. 338), where Verdi's "Ah! Sacerdote sono!" and "Da questa Croce agli uomini ha Cristo perdonato" were changed to "Assasveriano io sono!" or "Ah! sì, Stifellio io son!" and "Da questa Croce agli uomini ha il Giusto perdonato" or "Da questa Croce agli uomini il Giusto ha perdonato."

66. This Scena e Duetto (N. 9) is printed on 362–96 of the critical edition; see also the commentary, 136–51, for a discussion of the censored passages.

67. For thoughtful, if somewhat contradictory, analyses of this term, see Della Seta, "'Parola scenica' in Verdi e nella critica verdiana"; and Folena, "Lessico melodrammatico verdiano."

68. Verdi also used the form "Dunque perdere volete."

69. I first presented this example in "New Sources for *Stiffelio*." For an imaginative effort to interpret its possible meaning, see Parker, "Lina Kneels; Gilda Sings," chap. 7 in his *Leonora's Last Act*.

70. Della Seta's critical edition of *La traviata* and edition of the sketches are both in print; work on the other two operas is proceeding.

71. See Gossett, "Rossini's *Petite Messe Solennelle* and Its Several Versions." A first performance in the United States, sponsored by the Juilliard School of Music and under the direction of Judith Clurman, took place at Alice Tully Hall in New York's Lincoln Center on 19 March 2004.

72. See Marvin's introduction and commentary to *I masnadieri*.

CHAPTER SIX

1. A bibliography pertaining to general issues of performance practice goes beyond the framework of this book. Readers interested in exploring some of the most recent work in this field should consult the pages of *Early Music*, a journal devoted to these matters, or the late and lamented *Performance Practice Review*, which ceased publication after ten years in 1997. Many of the historical issues mentioned in this section are highly controversial and have engendered acrimonious debate. For the most part, I will limit myself here to documenting matters that have general theoretical significance or pertain specifically to the performance of Italian opera.

2. See Herz, "Johann Sebastian Bach in the Early Romantic Period" (esp. 100–109) and "The Performance History of Bach's *B Minor Mass*." A more recent discussion of these issues is Stauffer, *Bach—the "Mass in B Minor,"* esp. chapters 6 ("The B-Minor Mass after Bach's Death: Survival, Revival, and Reinterpretation") and 7 ("Issues of Performance Practice"), 175–249.

3. Publication began in 1851. Rossini's name appears as a subscriber during most of the years he lived in Paris (1855–68), from vol. 7 (1857) through vol. 16 (1868), with the sole exception of vol. 8. Traces of Bach's style are to be found in many pieces from Rossini's *Péchés de vieillesse*.

4. Later it would become de rigueur, for example, to accompany *secco* recitative with a harpsichord—rather than a piano—in operas by Mozart and Rossini, a practice widely accepted even among musicians who scorned other features of the growing interest in early instruments. For further observations on the accompaniment of *secco* recitative, see chapter 12.

5. The new edition, which began publication in 1954, revolutionized our knowledge of much of Bach's output—especially of his vocal music—thanks in part to the brilliant work of Alfred Dürr and Georg von Dadelsen.

6. The debate was provoked by Rifkin's recording on Nonesuch 79036 (New York, 1982), which was accompanied by Rifkin's explanatory article "Bach's 'Chorus.'" A critical response by Robert Marshall, "Bach's 'Choruses' Reconstituted," was followed by a Rifkin rebuttal, "Bach's 'Choruses': The Record Cleared."

7. For a suggestive discussion of the problem of early pianos, see Winter, "The Emperor's New Clothes." Malcolm Bilson himself has written extensively in the pages of *Early Music*. See also the remarks by Charles Rosen in his essay "The Benefits of Authenticity," originally published in the *New York Review of Books* (19 July 1990) as "The Shock of the Old," reprinted in *Critical Entertainments*, 201–21, esp. 208–10.

8. I am thinking of a performance of the Bach *Brandenburg Concerto* No. 3 for strings and continuo that I heard a few seasons back at Chicago's Symphony Center, in which Barenboim placed the soloists in a semicircle around him, and signaled to them for more and more expression: the vibrato regularly grew so intense that it was impossible to make out the intricate contrapuntal lines.

9. See Brendel, "Schubert's Last Sonatas," esp. 79–84. See, too, the responses in the *New York Review of Books* by Walter Frisch (16 March 1989), 42–43, with a reasoned rebuttal by Brendel, and by Neal Zaslaw (23 April 1989), with a Brendel wisecrack substituting for a rebuttal.

10. See, for example, the beginning of his chapter "Chopin: Counterpoint and the Narrative Forms," in *The Romantic Generation*, 279–82.

11. Taruskin, *Text and Act*. Those interested in pursuing the debate should begin their exploration with Kenyon, *Authenticity and Early Music*. I recommend particularly the contributions of Philip Brett and Howard Mayer Brown as correctives to Taruskin's polemic in the same volume. For remarks aimed at performers, see le Hurray, *Authenticity in Performance*. Two philosophical treatises on the subject are Kivy, *Authenticities*, and Scruton, *The Aesthetic of Music*, esp. chapter 14, "Performance," 438–56. As always, Charles Rosen, in "The Benefits of Authenticity," brings to the discussion strong beliefs, elegant prose, and the ability to separate good arguments from bad. The most important recent contribution, and one that attempts for the first time to deal seriously with historical, critical, and philosophical arguments, while developing a genuinely new approach to the issues, is Butt, *Playing with History*.

12. For Stravinsky's most prominent compositional interaction with Baroque music, see Brook, "Stravinsky's *Pulcinella*." In most cases Stravinsky accessed the Baroque repertory from printed sources edited by twentieth-century musicians or scholars working from manuscripts and printed editions in the British Library or the library of the "S. Pietro a Majella" Conservatory in Naples. Edmund van der Straeten, who worked with the sources in the British Library, is best known as a cellist concerned with early instruments—the viol and viol playing, in particular—and unknown Baroque and Classical works. His most important book is *History of the Violoncello, the Viol da Gamba, their Precursors and Collateral Instruments with Biographies of All the Most Eminent Players of Every Country*. That only some of the music adopted by Stravinsky is by Pergolesi, as we now know, is of relatively minor interest for understanding *Pulcinella*. The questions that do matter are (1) What music did the scholars choose and why? (2) How did the manuscripts submitted by Diaghilev to Stravinsky reflect editorial decisions made by early twentieth-century musicians and scholars? That Stravinsky did with the music what he needed to do as an artist is, of course, unaffected by these questions, nor is there any presumption that Stravinsky's music, in turn, did not have an effect upon modern attitudes toward music of the Baroque era. As ever, though, the relation between scholarship and composition or performance cannot be reduced to slogans.

13. In fact, Kivy seeks to rehabilitate the term by referring to what he calls the "personally authentic performer" (*Authenticities*, 286).

14. Furie, "An 'Authentic' Cavpag!" reviewing Angel SZCX 3895.

15. Righetti-Giorgi, *Cenni di una donna già cantante*, 29–37. As we saw at the beginning of chapter 3, Rossini's own reactions were expressed in recently recovered letters to his mother: they were written after opening night and again after the much more successful second performance: see Rossini, *Lettere e documenti*, 3a:119–23.

16. Stendhal's *Vie de Rossini* is filled with piquant observations about the social life of Italian theaters. See, for example, chapter 6, "L'Impresario et son théâtre," 136–48 (translated in Coe, *Life of Rossini by Stendhal*, 110–19). Balzac's finest description of life in an Italian theater is found

in his short novel *Massimilla Doni* (1839), which includes the imaginary reconstruction of a performance of Rossini's *Mosè in Egitto* at the Teatro La Fenice of Venice.

17. These matters are discussed in chapters 9, 12, and 13, respectively.

18. Perhaps the most fascinating effort to achieve a modern performance using nineteenth-century techniques of staging, lighting, singing, and orchestral placement was in the production of Verdi's early opera *Ernani* at the Teatro Comunale of Modena, in December 1984, the first Italian performances of the critical edition. Papers delivered at a conference held during the same period are gathered in *Ernani ieri e oggi*.

19. Rosen, "The Benefits of Authenticity," 204.

20. Some of them, of course, may have known the Voltaire tale, *Candide,* thanks to Leonard Bernstein's musical.

21. Donal Henahan, "Met Season: Better Than It Looked," *New York Times,* 21 April 1991, 25.

22. All matters pertaining to the critical edition of *Semiramide* are fully documented in that edition, and I have not repeated in footnotes what can be found through a perusal of the edition.

23. Ricordi had moved its most precious autograph manuscripts to safer quarters, but not the bulk of its musical archive.

24. We now know, however, that many nineteenth-century editions are derived from the first Italian edition, published in 1825 by Ricordi of Milan, an edition that partially depends on imperfect oral transmission (see Gossett, "Piracy in Venice").

25. Available vocal scores, either reprintings or reproductions of the Ricordi "edizione economica" or the Boosey vocal score, were fairly complete, so that it was immediately apparent where the full score was deficient.

26. A small number of changes are needed to use these materials today. Because of the poor quality of the trumpets available in typical bands of the period, for example, arrangers often used trumpets tuned in different keys and parceled out a melody among these various trumpets, one note here, one note there, depending on which trumpets could play a particular note more easily. In today's theaters it is wiser to trust the artistry of a trumpet player, whether he or she is employing a historical or a modern instrument, and—where possible—to assign the entire melody to a single instrument.

27. Indeed, when it came time to print the critical edition of *Semiramide* in 2001, we abandoned that earlier score altogether and had the entire opera processed anew: it was more work, to be sure, but we felt decidedly more confident in the likely accuracy of the resulting score.

28. The surviving sets and costumes from early productions in Italy are reproduced in Biggi and Ferraro, *Rossini sulla scena dell'Ottocento*.

29. An ample selection of surviving ornamentation from the nineteenth century is reproduced in the commentary to the critical edition. Rossini's own ornamentation is given in an appendix to the main score.

30. Usually orchestral rehearsals begin after those with the singers, but in the case of *Semiramide* the Metropolitan Opera schedule required that the first orchestral readings actually preceded work with the singers.

31. Butt's chapter "Negotiating between Work, Composer and Performer: Rewriting the Story of Notational Progress," in his *Playing with History,* 96–122, should be reread with this modern example in mind: the theoretical models Butt so carefully sets forth, however interesting, need to be evaluated in terms of actual performance situations, which often suggest quite a different reality. As for contemporary evidence, I wonder whether Butt has ever seen a set of parts—either printed or manuscript—actually used in the performance of a nineteenth-century French or Italian opera. Citations of a theoretical manifesto by Parker ("A Donizetti

Critical Edition in the Postmodern World") and an article by Hepokoski, applicable—if at all—only to Verdi's last two operas ("Overriding the Autograph Score"), provide insufficient evidence to draw any conclusions (see Butt, 99–100). But, like most writers on performance practice, Butt has little interest in Italian nineteenth-century opera or the vast literature surrounding its performance. (To be fair, he does mention two important articles to demonstrate the interaction of a composer and his singers: Armstrong, "Gilbert-Louis Duprez and Gustave Roger in the Composition of Meyerbeer's *Le Prophète*," and Smart, "The Lost Voice of Rosine Stolz.")

32. That it covers those situations, of course, does not necessarily mean that orchestral players will follow the instructions.

33. The *banda sul palco,* a military band not consisting of professional musicians, should not be confused with the orchestral ensembles playing on the stage or the wings that Mozart uses, for example, in *Don Giovanni.*

34. For *Guillaume Tell,* see the preface to the critical edition, xxxii–xxxviii; for *Don Carlos* the problems are outlined briefly in Budden, *The Operas of Verdi,* 3:24–25.

35. See my introduction to the facsimile edition of *Il barbiere di Siviglia,* 20–21 (English) and 73–74 (Italian).

36. Among the many discussions of appoggiaturas by modern scholars, see Crutchfield, "The Prosodic Appoggiatura in the Music of Mozart and his Contemporaries." Beghelli focuses his attention primarily on Italian nineteenth-century opera in his *I trattati di canto italiani dell'Ottocento,* 423–47. Both Crutchfield and Beghelli give a host of contemporary references. I will discuss this matter at greater length in chapter 9.

CHAPTER SEVEN

1. There are, of course, more subtle ways of thinking about continuity, ways that recognize that there have been changes over time, some of which remain valid, some of which ought properly to be reconsidered.

2. For a thoughtful position paper on these problems by one of our most distinguished scholars of medieval and Renaissance music, Margaret Bent, see her "Impossible Authenticities."

3. Serafin and Toni, *Stile, tradizioni e convenzioni del melodramma italiana del Settecento e dell'Ottocento.*

4. The recording was reissued by EMI Classics in 1997, as D 220703.

5. See Charles Rosen, "The Benefits of Authenticity," in *Critical Entertainments,* 214–21. For amusing and instructive instances of some of these conditions, see Kelly, *First Nights.*

6. A superb introduction to these problems from a literary perspective is Gaskell, *From Writer to Reader.* I recommend, in particular, the discussion of Tom Stoppard's *Travesties* in Gaskell's final chapter, 245–62. The complex issues surrounding *King Lear* are summarized effectively in the edition by R. A. Foakes, 110–46. The relationship between Dreiser's manuscript of *Sister Carrie* and the printed edition is discussed in Pizer, "Self-Censorship and Textual Editing."

7. I exclude the unique case of *La traviata,* which Tito Ricordi had engraved in full score no later than 1 November 1855, as demonstrated by Della Seta in the commentary to his critical edition of the opera (12–16). Ricordi's purpose, though, was to counteract piracy by providing a printed score, which he hoped theaters would consider superior to manuscript copies. Ricordi described his score in the following terms in a circular to theaters he shared with Verdi on 2 August 1854: "Whoever wishes to consider how much advantage a copy of the score prepared in this way offers for its precision of engraving, its distinctness in legibility, the exactness of proofreading, the certainty of conformity with the original score of the maestro, and the economic advantage with respect to the usual manuscript copies, will rush to ensure a copy of it for the repertory of his own theater." But it is clear from the letter of Tito to Verdi of 1 November 1855 that the com-

poser had never even seen this score, let alone assisted with its preparation. The effort must have been unsuccessful, since Ricordi did not print another operatic full score until *Otello* in the late 1880s. Verdi certainly took more interest in the editions of *Otello* and *Falstaff,* and surely helped to determine what music was included and what was left out, as well as providing corrections to individual passages. Despite the view of Hepokoski, "Overriding the Autograph Score," however, there is no evidence that Verdi concerned himself with Ricordi's realization of details, such as articulation or dynamic levels, and—in the absence of serious compositional emendations—there is therefore no reason to grant greater authority to the early printed score than to the composer's autograph manuscript. This is especially the case since the printed edition is filled with discrepancies no thoughtful musician seriously examining the score—either in 1895 or today—could sanction. It may be the product of the "socialization" of the text, but it is an excellent example of how badly the process worked when it was done under intense pressure of time.

8. The Venetian revision of *Maometto II* is considered in Emanuele, *L'ultima stagione italiana,* 161–218.

9. There has been little recent work on this early Bellini opera, but see the discussion by Pastura, *Bellini,* 125–38, as well as details on the source situation in Adamo and Lippmann, *Vincenzo Bellini,* 530–33.

10. The forthcoming critical edition of *Maria di Rohan,* edited by Luca Zoppelli, will clarify this history. For the moment, see his "I burattini del Cardinale," in the program for the first performance of the new edition at the PalaFenice al Tronchetto (Venice, 1999). See also Bini and Commons, *Le prime rappresentazioni,* 1146–75.

11. The best treatment remains Budden, *The Operas of Giuseppe Verdi,* 2:425–521. For a different viewpoint, compare Parker, "Leonora's Last Act: *La forza del destino,*" in *Leonora's Last Act,* 61–99.

12. This is the way the matter is formulated in the guidelines to the critical edition, and it is valid for every opera through *Aida.* That does not deny that there exist isolated cases in which Verdi's later modifications fail to be reflected in his autograph manuscript. His revisions for *Macbeth* in 1865 were done in a separate manuscript altogether, sent by the composer to Paris. Several important examples of modifications from *Aida* are not reflected in the autograph manuscript: they are mentioned by Lawton in "The Autograph of *Aida* and the New Verdi Edition." The Verdi edition has adopted similar modifications in its edition of the *Messa da Requiem,* and it will do the same in Ilaria Narici's forthcoming edition of *Un ballo in maschera.* But again and again, as late as his revision of *Simon Boccanegra* in 1880–81, Verdi made modifications to an opera by having Ricordi send him his original autograph manuscript and by sending the revised form back to Ricordi for the Milan archives. The passages he no longer considered definitive he placed in his personal collection at Sant'Agata.

13. For a sophisticated treatment of this problem, with reference to the finales of the two operas, see Fabio Vittorini, *"Quelque chose pour le ténor."* I will discuss further the two versions of *Macbeth* at the end of chapter 8.

14. Dahlhaus's position is most easily available in his *Nineteenth-Century Music,* 9–10.

15. This quotation is from his letter of 20 May 1847, in *I copialettere,* 39.

16. In a paper delivered to the American Musicological Society's national meeting in Houston in November 2003, Hilary Poriss has demonstrated a similar history for Donizetti's *Marin Faliero,* to which the soprano Carolina Ungher, perhaps with Donizetti's approval, regularly added a cavatina for herself.

17. The Roman revival of *Otello* is discussed fully by Michael Collins in the preface (xxxvi–xxxvii) and commentary (155–60) to his critical edition of the opera. Because no musical sources whatsoever are preserved for the revised finale, and because the conclusion neither

had any significant diffusion in the nineteenth century nor seemed aesthetically justified to the editors of the *Edizione critica delle opere di Gioachino Rossini*, it was decided not to attempt a hypothetical reconstruction of the new finale in the critical edition. The edition did, however, through careful analysis of the libretto, provide a road map for how such a reconstruction could be carried out. That road map was subsequently followed by the English company *Opera Rara*, which issued in 2000 a CD (ORC 18) with both the original finale and a reconstruction of the happy ending.

18. Many have marveled at Pasta's ability to sing roles as diverse as Rossini's Tancredi and Bellini's Norma, but in many cases she manipulated the vocal lines to suit her own talents. The question whether she should sing the soprano title role in Rossini's *Semiramide* or the contralto role of Arsace was at the heart of a serious feud in Paris in 1825: for details, see my preface to the critical edition of *Semiramide*, lii–lviii.

19. For details, see the prefaces to the critical editions of *La donna del lago* (xxvii–xxx) and *Semiramide* (lv).

20. Rossini, *Lettere e documenti*, 3:304.

21. For a modern reprint of the first edition of the Vaccai opera, see Vaccai, *Giulietta e Romeo and Excerpts from Zadig ed Astartea*. On Romani and Bellini, see Roccatagliati, *Felice Romani librettista*, esp. 110–11, and Lippmann, "Romani e Bellini," esp. 90–92.

22. These borrowings are analyzed by Brauner, "Parody and Melodic Style in Bellini's *I Capuleti e i Montecchi*."

23. For an excellent summary of the history and reception of *I Capuleti e i Montecchi*, see Bellini, *I Capuleti e i Montecchi*, ed. Toscani, xi–xxix.

24. According to Giazotto, *Maria Malibran*, 228, Rossini himself may have advised Malibran to make the substitution. As Toscani has shown in his introduction to the critical edition (xxii–xxiii), the substitution had been made earlier, in the carnival season of 1831 at the Teatro della Pergola in Florence, but not during the regular run of performances: it was an innovation introduced to help draw crowds to a benefit evening on behalf of the prima donna Santina Ferlotti. In his "Bellini and the *Pasticcio alla Malibran*" (134), Collins claims that Malibran did not actually make this substitution until her performances at La Scala in the autumn of 1834, but the evidence he presents is not altogether clear.

25. The article appeared in the *Gazzetta Ufficiale Piemontese* of 18 January 1836. I consulted the complete text in the ample program, edited by Maria Rosaria Adamo, accompanying performances of the opera at the Teatro Bellini of Catania during the fall of 1994; selections are printed in Basso, *Il teatro della città dal 1788 al 1936*, 216–17. Mesenzio is the cruel Etruscan king, protagonist of the latter part of the tenth canto in Vergil's *Aeneid*.

26. The currently available vocal score from Ricordi (pl. no. 42043) continues to include Vaccai's music, with the note: "To be substituted, if desired, as is generally done, for the last piece of Bellini's opera."

27. I quote this letter in the translation of Weinstock, *Vincenzo Bellini*, 249. His source is an 1885 publication in Italian by Scherillo, *Belliniana: Nuove note*, 35, but Scherillo was in turn quoting from Florimo, *La scuola musicale di Napoli e i suoi conservatorii* (1880–83), 3:192–93. Toscani (xxiii; see n. 23 above) cites the same source. One would not like to think it inauthentic, but Florimo was sometimes a less than reliable witness: see Rosselli, *The Life of Bellini*, 6–11.

28. See the critical edition of *Armida*, where Brauner and Brauner, in their preface (xxxv–xxxvi) mention the reuse by Rossini himself of entire numbers and melodies from *Armida* in the Roman revival of *Otello* in 1820, in the Alidoro aria added to *La Cenerentola* in 1821, in *Il viaggio a Reims*, in *Moïse et Pharaon*, and in the *Cantata in onore del Sommo Pontefice Pio Nono* (1847). Famous pieces, such as the duet for Armida and Rinaldo "Amor! (Possente

nome!)," however, were introduced—without Rossini's blessing—into revivals of many other operas, those by Rossini and those by other composers.

29. There are copies of this libretto in many different libraries. I consulted a copy at the Bibliothèque de l'Opéra in Paris (Lib. 1189).

30. Goodman, *Languages of Art*, 116–18.

31. There are several excellent treatments of the social situation of theaters, performers, administrators, and the public during the first half of the nineteenth-century. See especially the books by Rosselli already cited, as well as his summation, "Il sistema produttivo, 1780–1880." Also important are Kimbell, *Italian Opera*, 417–29, and Sorba, *Teatri*. My concern here is not to duplicate their work but to understand the impact of this social organization on problems that affect today's performers.

32. See Rossini, *Bianca e Falliero*, ed. Dotto. Information about the original libretto is given in the commentary, 39–41. A detailed description of *Cimene* can be found in Ritorni, *Commentarii della vita e delle opere coredrammatiche di Salvatore Viganò e della coregrafia e de' corepei*, 298–301. The entire genre is described by Hansell in her "Il ballo teatrale e l'opera italiana." The term "atto" in ballet would seem to be the equivalent of "scene" in opera, with only some of the "atti" involving actual changes of scenery.

33. Stendhal's classic description of an evening at La Scala in February 1818, although inaccurate—as always—about details (see Hansell, "Il ballo teatrale," 258n, and "Theatrical Ballet," 258n), captures the spirit of theatrical life at the time. See his *Vie de Rossini*, 2:577–80 (447–48 in the Coe translation).

34. See Hansell, "Il ballo teatrale," 288–90, and "Theatrical Ballet," 288–90.

35. Descriptions of the structure and social practices at individual theaters throughout the peninsula should be consulted for a more detailed picture. An excellent summary remains Rosselli's "An Industry in a Hierarchical Society," chapter 3 of his *The Opera Industry*, esp. 39–49.

36. For a full description of the physical structure of the first Teatro San Carlo and of the theater which replaced it after the earlier structure was burned down in 1816, see vol. 1 of *Il teatro di San Carlo 1737–1987*, "la storia, la struttura" by Franco Mancini.

37. A good introduction to the problem of theatrical lighting is provided by Capra, "L'illuminazione sulla scena verdiana ovvero L'arco voltaico non acceca la luna?"

38. See Brombert, *Cristina*.

39. Stendhal, *Vie de Rossini*, 2:575 (444 in the Coe translation).

40. See Rosselli, *The Opera Industry*, 47–48.

41. For details, see Gatti, *Il teatro alla Scala*, 2:29.

42. See Gossett, "Rossini's Operas and Their Printed Librettos."

43. Some of those problems will be discussed in chapter 10.

44. The eight operas are *Un giorno di regno, Alzira, I masnadieri, Il corsaro, La battaglia di Legnano, Luisa Miller, Rigoletto,* and *Un ballo in maschera*. Of these works, of course, the first four had only a limited performance history. Verdi himself wished mightily to revise *La battaglia di Legnano,* but the right opportunity never came, while *Un ballo in maschera* is itself the end product of a complex process of revision.

45. On the complicated history of this opera and its libretto, see Scarton and Tosti-Croce, "*Aureliano in Palmira*."

46. Romani (1791–1877) was still a mainstay of the Florentine staff more than thirty years later, when Verdi presented his *Macbeth* there. Verdi refers to him several times in his 1846–47 letters (see Rosen and Porter, *Verdi's "Macbeth,"* 17 and 33–35).

47. Rossini had written two earlier roles specifically for Rosich, Buralicchio in *L'equivoco stravagante* (1811) and Taddeo in *L'Italiana in Algeri* (1813), but neither role has any music

approaching the difficulty of "A un Dottor della mia sorte." The original Bartolo, Bartolomeo Botticelli, was not a singer of great reputation, and neither Alberto Cametti nor Annalisa Bini mentions any contemporary reports citing either Botticelli or the aria: see Cametti, "La musica teatrale a Roma cento anni fa," and Bini, "Echi delle prime rossiniane nella stampa romana dell'epoca," esp. 173–76.

48. Among manuscripts of the opera which include Romani and omit Rossini are copies in F-Pn (D. 13.546), I-PAc (SL b 47, 48), and I-MOe (F.995). While Rossini's aria was generally sung in Paris and London, according to contemporary printed librettos, it was almost always replaced in Italy by Romani's. Among librettos attesting to this substitution are those printed in Florence (1816, 1831), Livorno (1821), Lucca (1818, 1821), Milan (1819, 1820, 1835), Prato (1822), Ravenna (1831), Trieste (1821), Turin (1818, 1833), and Venice (1822). None of the Italian librettos I have examined has the text of Rossini's original aria, nor do they have other substitutions. Some, however, deprive Bartolo of an aria altogether.

49. All three editions published by Ricordi's Milanese rival, Lucca, the first c. 1838, the last c. 1856, substituted Romani for Rossini without acknowledging the author. The note cited in the text, which does recognize Romani's contribution, is found in the full score published by Guidi of Florence in 1864 (pl. No. 2342).

50. These include editions published by G. M. Meyer and Henry Litolff's Verlag in Braunschweig; Breitkopf und Härtel, Philipp Reclam, and Peters in Leipzig; and Pietro Mechetti in Vienna.

51. On the other hand, if an accomplished singer were to decide, with full knowledge of this history, to adopt "Manca un foglio" for a particular occasion or even in alternation with "A un dottor della mia sorte," I would find no cause for alarm. I say this independently of the assertion of Righetti-Giorgi (*Cenni di una donna già cantante*, 37), whose accuracy we cannot test, that "the aria for Don Bartolo, substituted for the original piece in Florence, is a composition by Sig. Pietro Romani. It is a lovely aria, and Rossini does not object to it being introduced into his opera."

52. In the review, which appeared in the *Gazzetta privilegiata di Venezia* on 17 March 1830, Tommaso Locatelli wrote, "A happier and more complete triumph theatergoers of a certain age do not remember after that of *L'Italiana in Algeri*." It is quoted in its entirety in Pastura, *Bellini*, 238–39.

53. See Corghi's preface to his critical edition of *L'Italiana in Algeri* (xxvii–xxx), as well as appendix 3 and the relevant commentary (176–84).

54. For further information, see Bent's preface to her critical edition of *Il Turco in Italia* (xxi–xxvii). The history of the libretto has since been examined more fully by Nicolodi, *Il Turco in Italia*; see, in particular, her essay "Da *Mazzolà* a *Romani* (e *Rossini*)," ix–lix.

55. No moral code can be invoked to stop a singer from falsifying the sense of an opera. But why would one want to do it? In this case, the joke quickly wore thin. What Sills gained in immediate adoration from her public, she lost by having made *Turco* seem silly and unworthy of subsequent revival in New York. This for an opera that continues to play in major theaters all over the world.

56. Several contemporary reviews are cited in the preface to the critical edition, xxiv–xxvi.

57. The Roman revival is discussed in the preface to the critical edition, xxvii–xxx, and the music is printed as appendix 2 (928–1040); see also the related commentary, 207–48.

58. For Paër's version of *Turco*, see the preface to the critical edition, xxx–xxxiii and the commentary, 252–59. The entire Parisian libretto is reproduced in Nicolodi, *Turco*, 427–501. See also her introductory essay, cxvii–cxix.

59. See the anonymous pamphlet *De MM. Paër et Rossini* (Paris, 1820), attributed to the poet Émile Deschamps and a certain Massé, who has not been better identified. See also Stendhal, *Vie de Rossini*, 1:27–28 (27–28 in the Coe translation).

60. Contemporaries were perfectly aware of this problem. Indeed, the administrators of the Opéra, officially responsible for the Théâtre Italien, in a letter to Paër of 27 October 1820 formally forbade him to insert music from other operas by Rossini into the composer's works he was planning to stage, "with the exception of those which might still be taken from *La Cenerentola*, the only opera from which it is permitted for now to draw, since it has already been used to that end" (i.e., in Paër's version of *Il Turco in Italia*). See Rossini, *Lettere e documenti*, 1:435.

61. A manuscript of the Zandonai *Gazza* is to be found in the library of the Pesaro Conservatory.

62. The critical edition of *Macbeth*, ed. Lawton, includes both arias. See the end of chapter 8, where the two versions of *Macbeth* are considered further.

63. The music of the alternative cavatina is printed in the critical edition, 681–712. See also Corghi's preface, xxvi–xxvii, where he traces the history of the two compositions.

64. See chapter 3, n. 6.

65. The new composition was published for the first time in appendix 3 of the critical edition, 447–76; Gallico describes its historical context in his preface, xxii (English) and xlvi (Italian). For a rather negative evaluation of the substitution, see Budden, *The Operas of Verdi*, 1:169–70.

66. See Bini and Commons, *Le prime rappresentazioni*, 375–76. The complicated history will be clarified, I trust, in Roger Parker's forthcoming critical edition of *Lucrezia Borgia*.

67. No modern edition of this cabaletta is currently available, although the revised finale to the opera is printed in the modern Ricordi score (pl. no. 41690). The cabaletta was published by Ricordi, however, in an appendix to its comprehensive edition (pl. nos. 32731–32754), issued in the early 1860s. For a thoughtful discussion of Frezzolini and her art, see Smart, "Verdi Sings Erminia Frezzolini."

68. The same unidentified collaborator was also responsible for Don Geronio's cavatina in the first act, Albazar's aria in the second, and all the *secco* recitative. While Rossini often called on collaborators to prepare short solos or recitative, *Turco* is the only work in which a collaborator wrote a finale.

69. A preliminary critical edition of *Matilde di Shabran*, in the Neapolitan version, edited by Jürgen Selk, was performed at the Rossini Opera Festival of Pesaro during August 1996 and reproduced in 2004. The opera, in all versions associated with the composer, will eventually be published. For further information see the essay by Selk ("*Matilde di Shabran*") in the program accompanying those performances.

70. This summary is the result of recent work on the opera—much of it based on newly available manuscript sources—by Ilaria Narici, who is editing *Un ballo in maschera* for *The Works of Giuseppe Verdi*; by Simonetta Ricciardi, editor of the *Carteggio Verdi–Somma*; and by me. Among earlier publications that have proven useful are: Pascolato, "*Re Lear*" *e* "*Ballo in Maschera*"; Alessandro Luzio, "Le lettere del Somma sul libretto del *Ballo in maschera*" and "Il libretto del *Ballo in maschera* massacrato dalla Censura borbonica," in *Carteggi verdiani*, 1:219–40 and 1:241–75, respectively; and Rosen and Pigozzi, "*Un ballo in maschera*" *di Giuseppe Verdi*.

71. There is a wonderful document in which Verdi sets the libretto of *Una vendetta in dominò* alongside that of *Adelia degli Adimari*, adding a series of piquant footnotes. It is described and transcribed in *Carteggio Verdi–Somma*, 342–405.

72. Ilaria Narici and I were responsible for just such a reconstruction, performed for the first time at the Gothenburg Opera in Sweden during the fall of 2002. The project is described in chapter 14.

73. Although there is no documentary evidence concerning this substitution, we have already seen in chapter 3 that the original *rondò* with its introductory chorus was looked on with

suspicion in both Venice and Rome. The composition was published for the first time in Corghi's critical edition; see appendix 4, 751–81.

74. The manuscript, Fondo Noseda I.86 of the Milan Conservatory, belonged to the Milanese collector Gustavo Adolfo Noseda. See Moreni, *Vita musicale a Milano.*

75. The letter of 31 January 1847, is published (with a translation) in Rosen and Porter, *Verdi's "Macbeth,"* 39–41.

76. The original version has been reconstructed by David Lawton in the critical edition of *Macbeth.*

77. The letter, written during the last week of January 1847, is also in Rosen and Porter, *Verdi's "Macbeth,"* 36–37.

78. The letter is cited in Abbiati, *Giuseppe Verdi,* 1:507–8; see also Claudio Gallico's preface to the critical edition of *Ernani,* xxi (English) and xlv (Italian).

79. The original version of the opera is printed in facsimile in Giacomo Meyerbeer, *Il crociato in Egitto.* For information about the various versions, see Mongrédien, "Les débuts de Meyerbeer à Paris," and Pinamonti, "*Il crociato in Egitto* da Venezia a Parigi."

80. H. Colin Slim amply documents the Parisian revival in his critical edition of *La donna del lago* (see, in particular, the preface, xxvii–xxx, and the commentary volume, 178–94). Because he did not want to encourage performers to employ this version, which he judged distinctly inferior to the original, Slim decided to include in appendix 3 only newly composed music: those who might wish to use the pieces from *Bianca e Falliero* (or *Semiramide* or *Armida,* both of which were also sources for music introduced into the opera in Paris) need to consult the editions of those operas—all of which are in print—together with the commentary to *La donna del lago.*

81. A number of Stendhal's reviews are gathered in *Notes d'un dilettante,* 227–32.

82. See Mauceri, "Rossini a Roma nel 1821." The crucial letter for *La donna del lago,* however, is not found in Mauceri but is printed in Rossini, *Lettere e documenti,* 1:472–73.

83. For complete details, see the introduction to Toscani's critical edition of *I Capuleti e i Montecchi* (xx–xxii), as well as the music printed in appendix 1 (509–624) and its accompanying commentary (103–13).

84. The strangest transposition, though, occurs in the second-act finale (N. 9), where Bellini transposed down by a full tone *Romeo's* beautiful solo "Deh! tu, bell'anima," even though the same singer, Giuditta Grisi, performed the part in both Venice and Milan. It suggests that Grisi found the rather high tessitura of this passage a strain.

85. The passage is found in the critical edition, 591–94.

86. Alessandro Rolla was usually identified as the "Primo violino, Capo d'orchestra" at La Scala, and as such was responsible for leading the orchestra. On Rolla, see Inzaghi and Bianchi, *Alesandro Rolla.*

87. Cambi, *Bellini: Epistolario,* 264–65.

88. On the other hand, I cannot subscribe to the apparent decision of the Donizetti editors to publish *Maria Stuarda* but to ignore *Buondelmonte:* if scholars are to bring out critical editions of this repertory, they should offer to opera lovers and to performers the widest possible set of alternatives that can be traced to each composer. Extensive sources are extant for *Buondelmonte,* including a full score, partly autograph, in the Naples Conservatory Library and some 31 pages of autograph music in the Pierpont Morgan Library, New York. See Turner, *Four Centuries of Opera,* 54–56.

89. See the discussion in Budden, *The Operas of Verdi,* 1:198–99. Verdi's letter to Mario of 1 January 1847, requesting the return of the composer's original manuscript, was first published in Simone, "Lettere al tenore Mario de Candia sulla cabaletta de *I Due Foscari.*"

90. A much more appropriate venue for the Vaccai finale was found when Roberto Abbado recorded *I Capuleti e i Montecchi*, with a cast featuring Vesselina Kasarova and Eva Mei, and included the Vaccai finale on a supplementary CD. The recording was issued in 1998 by RCA Victor Red Seal, as 09026-68899-2.

91. See Giazotto, *Maria Malibran*, 142–43. Her friend the Countess de Merlin, in *Memoirs of Madame Malibran*, 1:144–45 (I quote from the English version), wrote, "The result was a decided failure. The small and feminine form of Madame Malibran was in no respect adapted to the manly and heroic character of Otello. The dusky colour, too, with which she tinged her countenance, not only deformed the beauty of her features, but concealed all that flexibility of expression which was their peculiar charm."

92. "Pietoso all'amor mio" was frequently performed during the nineteenth century, in part because Ricordi published it in its first edition of the complete score of the Italian translation of *Le Siège de Corinthe* (*L'assedio di Corinto*). Ricordi issued the Scena e Duetto with Donizetti's cabaletta late in 1828, with the plate number 3650, identifying it as having been "written in Genoa by Donizetti." When it came to printing a complete edition of the score in 1829, however, Ricordi included the Donizetti cabaletta but no longer named its composer. The title at the beginning of the number reads simply: "Scene and Duet / Che veggo oh Ciel / in L'Assedio di Corinto / by Maestro Rossini. / Sung by Sig.ª A. Tosi and Sig. A. Tamburini / in the opening of the Theater in Genoa."

93. In the opening scene, for example, Corsaro was simply unaware that the mixed chorus (Scottish peasants) at the beginning of the introduzione constituted a *different* group of people from the male chorus at its close (hunters in the service of King Giacomo). No wonder the audience seemed totally confused by what was happening onstage.

94. A full accounting of the opera's history and problems must await Fabrizio Della Seta's critical edition, to be published in the *Edizione critica delle opere di Vincenzo Bellini*. For the moment, it is possible to consult a facsimile of the autograph manuscript (the latter housed in the Biblioteca Comunale in Palermo) of what was essentially the version performed in Paris at the end of January 1835, together with the pages in which Bellini himself made modifications for Naples (these pages were inserted by Bellini into a copy of the opera preserved today in the Museo Belliniano of Catania): see Bellini, *I puritani*, ed. Gossett. For a brief, largely accurate introduction to the sources, see the description by Lippmann in Adamo and Lippmann, *Vincenzo Bellini*, 544–48. As always, Pastura, *Bellini*, 396–468, provides a highly useful treatment of the history. Two publications of the 1980s, on the other hand, are unfortunately confused: Monterosso, "Le due redazioni dei *Puritani*"; and Pugliese and Vlad, *I puritani ritrovati*.

95. See Bellini's letter to Florimo of 5 January 1835 in Cambi, *Bellini: Epistolario*, 497. This meeting in London and the problem of the so-called "Malibran" version of *Sonnambula* will be discussed in chapter 10.

96. One can follow the chronology through a series of letters, printed in Cambi, *Bellini: Epistolario*. Bellini had originally expected to finish the Parisian opera and have it performed in November 1834, then to travel to Naples to present an entirely new opera for Malibran in February 1835. By 24 July 1834 he is beginning to have doubts about the feasibility of this project, and he mentions for the first time the possibility of revising *Puritani* for Malibran (ibid., 418), although he rejects the idea. By 13 October he realizes that there will be no time to compose a new opera, and suggests instead coming to Naples to adapt *Puritani* "for Malibran and the rest of the company, perhaps composing some new pieces when I think it necessary, in agreement with Malibran, who will be consulted by me throughout, and in this way I will make it practically a new opera" (ibid., 454). In letters of 18 and 21 November he finally admits that he can't come to

Naples: instead, he will make the necessary changes and send the score to Naples: "So, tomorrow [22 November] I begin to make all the necessary modifications that the opera requires"; and he expects "to consign the score at the latest by 1 January [1835]" (ibid., 476–77).

97. Bellini tried to speak well of Pepoli most of the time, but he knew his limitations, as he said in a letter to his friend Alessandro Lamperi of 7 October 1834, "the book isn't bad, but it isn't Romani" (ibid., 446). Pepoli wrote the poetry for eight of the twelve songs that Rossini set to music in *Les Soirées musicales,* published in 1835 (the other four use older texts by Metastasio).

98. The most significant letters for determining this chronology are those from Bellini to Florimo of 21–22 December and 5 January (ibid., 488–93 and 494–98).

99. In some seasons, at least, the theater continued the practice, prevalent in Rossini's time, of engaging two contrasting tenors.

100. Bellini reports this outcome in a letter to Alessandro Lamperi of 27 February 1835 (ibid., 524).

101. After Bellini's death, Florimo sent this score to Bellini's family in Catania, whence it made its way to the Museo Belliniano of that city. See Lippmann in Adamo and Lippmann, *Vincenzo Bellini,* 546.

102. For astute comments on the relationship between Rossini and Bellini, see Rosselli, *The Life of Bellini,* 130–34. See also Pourvoyeur, "Rossini et les Puritains."

103. Bellini writes about post-premiere cuts in a letter to his uncle, Vincenzo Ferlito, of 26 January (Cambi, *Bellini: Epistolario,* 504).

104. Both versions are reproduced in Bellini, *I puritani:* see the revised Parisian version on ff. 39v and 41–42v of the Palermo manuscript and the Neapolitan version on pp. 78–82 of the Catania manuscript.

105. Bellini told Florimo in a letter dated 5 January 1835 that this duet was "d'un *liberale* che fa paura" (so *radical* as to be terrifying; Cambi, *Bellini: Epistolario,* 498).

106. The cuts include two beautiful movements: a slow trio within the first-act finale, Larghetto affettuoso, "Se il destino a te m'invola," actually removed from the Palermo autograph (the cut is evident in the final Parisian version on f. 114v) but present in the Neapolitan version on pp. 235–47 of the Catania manuscript; and a cantabile, Andante sostenuto, in the duet for Elvira and Arturo, "Di qual dì che ti mirai," present in the Palermo autograph (ff. 121v-127v in the second volume) but marked to be cut.

107. This is the ending found in the recording issued by Decca in 1975, under the direction of Richard Bonynge, OSA-13111.

108. The passage begins on f. 112r in the Palermo manuscript, where Bellini entered the change in the accompaniment only for a few measures, but presumably intended it to continue for the entire passage (through f. 114r). The equivalent passage in the Neapolitan version is found on pp. 231–35 of the Catania manuscript, where no trace of the revised version can be seen.

109. See my preface to the critical edition of *Tancredi,* xxxiv–xxxv. The music is printed on pp. 802–18, and the relevant Notes are on pp. 284–90 of the commentary.

110. The history is recounted in many sources. Easily available titles in English include Carter, *W. A. Mozart,* 125–26, and Daniel Heartz, *Mozart's Operas,* 151–54. All the relevant music is available in the critical edition of Mozart, *Le nozze di Figaro,* ed. Finscher. Ferrarese was apparently romantically involved with the librettist, Lorenzo Da Ponte.

111. I quote from Marshall, *Mozart Speaks,* 371.

112. I read the interview, with Shusha Guppy—published in the *Paris Review 165* (spring, 2003)—online at http://www.parisreview.com/tpr165/miller1.html.

113. See Miller's interview with Martin Bernheimer, in Bernheimer, "Operating Theater."

CHAPTER EIGHT

1. In her critical edition of *Guillaume Tell*, while making available all the music Rossini prepared for the opera, Bartlet tries to address these questions in her preface and by the way she organizes the volume into a main text and appendixes.

2. The critical editions of the Rossini operas, in particular, regularly indicate in their commentary volumes all the cuts either made (by omitting measures) or indicated (by annotations) in contemporary sources, whether printed editions or manuscripts. When the cuts can be traced back to the composer himself, the measures are included in the score but are marked in the standard Italian fashion with the indication "Vi-" "-de."

3. I am aware that this is a recurring theme in *Divas and Scholars,* and it may be that in the United States it is a theme that does not require quite as much repetition as it may have needed a decade ago. Half of my professional activity, though, is in Italy, where—I fear—there are still many conductors, old and young, who continue to invoke "tradition" as an excuse for perpetuating questionable practices. There is much that is good in the performing tradition, but a blind acceptance of cuts reflecting another generation's sensibility is not one of them.

4. The recording was issued by Polygram in 1993, as no. 435763. The one advantage of a soprano Rosina is that she can sing the soprano aria "Ah! se è ver che in tal momento" that Rossini added to the second act for Joséphine Mainvielle-Fodor, who sang the role at the Teatro San Samuele of Venice during the spring of 1819, while Rossini was in the city preparing *Eduardo e Cristina* for the same theater. It should be added that even during periods when Rosina was primarily sung by sopranos, there were always important mezzo-sopranos who performed the role, singers such as Conchita Supervia, Jennie Tourel, and Giulietta Simionato.

5. The reference was added—as a rather awkward counterpoint—within the "Canzone Francese" during the finale, "Madre del nuovo Enrico de' Franchi," a duet sung by the two French travelers, Contessa di Folleville and Cavalier Belfiore (see Rossini, *Il viaggio a Reims,* 866–71). That piece, in fact, is one of the "national hymns" based on a popular tune, the old French folksong "Charmante Gabrielle," as Janet Johnson recounts in her preface, xxx. The Abbado insertion can be heard on his recording, issued by Polygram in 1985 as Deutsche Gramophon 415 499-501. For an example of a scholar who assumed that the insertion was authentic, see Kern, "Verfassungsgeschichtliche Aspekte der Oper *Il viaggio a Reims* von Rossini." He writes: ". . . spielt das Orchester in den gemeinsamen Gesang beider Franzosen zur Huldigung an die Schwiegertochter Karls X. im Schlußbild der Oper die Anfangstakte der Marseillaise" (247).

6. See Beghelli, "Per fedeltà a una nota," in which he points out (and not in a negative spirit) how far Muti's readings stray from those indicated in the printed score.

7. Rossini originally had an assistant compose this second-act solo for Lindoro, "Oh come il cor di giubilo" (see the critical edition of *L'Italiana in Algeri,* 320–26); for a later performance, at the Teatro Re of Milan in early April 1814, he replaced it by a beautiful piece of his own composition, "Concedi, amor pietoso" (see ibid., appendix 3, 724–49). The festival had expected to include Rossini's replacement aria, and Fo had designed an imaginative staging, which had to be sacrificed at the last moment.

8. See my essay accompanying the facsimile edition of *Don Pasquale* and my *"Anna Bolena" and the Artistic Maturity of Gaetano Donizetti.* Similar evidence is visible throughout the autograph manuscript of Donizetti, *Lucia di Lammermoor.*

9. See his letter of 5 November 1870 to Ghislanzoni in *I copialettere,* 662. For the dating and a discussion of the problem of cabalettas in *Aida,* see Gossett, "Verdi, Ghislanzoni, and *Aida,*" 298 and 316–21. The problem of the Verdi cabaletta will be considered at the end of this chapter.

10. That, of course, is the lesson of the dispute over *Le nozze di Figaro* between Cecilia Bartoli and Jonathan Miller, discussed at the conclusion of chapter 7.

11. For complete information, see the preface and commentary to the critical edition of *La gazzetta*. The derivations were described earlier by Mauceri, "*La gazzetta* di Gioachino Rossini."

12. For further details about the accompaniment of *secco* recitative, see the concluding section of chapter 12.

13. See my introduction to Mayr, *Medea in Corinto*, where I accept the hypothesis of Schiedermair, *Beiträge zur Geschichte der Oper*, 2:121–54. The basic point remains unchanged, however, even if it turns out that Mayr wrote first the accompanied recitative for Naples, then transformed it into *secco* for a performance in Bergamo, as suggested by Roccatagliati, "Il giovane Romani alla scuola di Mayr," 313n. See also Russo, "*Medea in Corinto*."

14. See the preface by Gabriele Dotto to his critical edition of *Bianca e Falliero*, xxvii.

15. These elements of stagecraft will be discussed in chapter 13.

16. Serafin and Toni, *Stile, tradizioni e convenzioni*, 1:71–72.

17. This edition was prepared by Vincenzo Borghetti.

18. H. Colin Slim discusses the history in the preface to his critical edition of *La donna del lago*, xxi–xxiv. It is less clear why Rossini appears to have assigned a good deal of accompanied recitative to a collaborator in *Mosè in Egitto* (Naples, Teatro San Carlo, 5 March 1818).

19. Verdi's letter of 15 November 1843, published in Conati, *La bottega*, 102–3, was cited in chapter 2 at the end of the section "Orchestrating the opera."

20. Letter from Verdi to Carlo Marzari, postmarked 30 January 1853, published in Conati, *La bottega*, 312–13.

21. The two London versions are compared by Michal Collins in his critical edition of *Otello*: see the commentary volume, 165–69.

22. For an example, see mm. 72–103 in the Recitativo Dopo il Quartetto of *Il Turco in Italia*, which precedes the duet for Fiorilla and Don Geronio, "Per piacere alla signora" (N. 6). The measures are included in the critical edition, pp. 360–62, but the cut is clearly indicated, and the modifications necessary to make the cut are shown. In fact, with two accomplished actors in the roles, the scene is hilarious.

23. To take a particularly egregious example, in *Il Turco in Italia* the Recitativo Dopo la Cavatina Geronio concludes in E♭ *major;* the following Cavatina Fiorilla begins in A *major:* see the critical edition, 171–72. In this case the solution is very simple: starting at m. 61, Zaida could continue declaiming on a d♭, and everything else (vocal lines and continuo) needs to be taken up a semitone from 61 through the end of the recitative. The recitative thus concludes in E *major,* dominant of the key of the following cavatina.

24. Verdi was particularly concerned about this scene, and laid out details of Simone's motions in a letter to Piave written toward the end of 1856 (letter LXI in Morazzoni, *Verdi: Lettere inedite*, 38, reprinted in Abbiati, *Giuseppe Verdi*, 2:375).

25. To be fair to "La Divina," Will Crutchfield reminds me that in an interview she once opined that in the second act of *Tosca*, "Vissi d'arte," her own showstopper, held up the action and ought to be cut. Of course, an opera is not a play, and holding up the action is not always a bad thing. One wonders whether remarks of this kind might not have reflected her interactions with Visconti.

26. See Serafin and Toni, *Stile, tradizioni e convenzioni*, 1:11n. My criticism of the pretences and influence (acknowledged or unacknowledged) of this book should not be taken as criticism of Serafin as a conductor, as a trainer of voices, as a significant participant in the *bel canto* revival during the 1950s and 1960s. But the list of operas he conducted at La Scala during the 1910s included hardly any Italian operas written before 1855: his specialties seem to have been Wagner

and Strauss (between 1911 and 1914 he conducted *Siegfried, Die Meistersinger, Lohengrin, Parsifal,* and *Tristan,* as well as *Der Rosenkavelier, Feuersnot,* and *Salome*) and the young Italian school (composers such as Mascagni, Laparra, Wolf-Ferrari, Montemezzi, Smareglia, and Alfano). See the useful repertory and cast lists in Gatti, *Il teatro alla Scala,* 2:71–73. Hence, to imagine that Serafin formed a significant link to nineteenth-century performance practice (and particularly to practice reflecting atittudes from the first half of the nineteenth century) seems little more than wishful thinking, even if the dues he paid in the opera house as a young conductor and coach included preparation of some of the earlier Italian repertory.

27. This would be a complicated task at best, since one must not be misled by the recorded evidence, whose shape was often determined by the physical limitations of early technology.

28. Serafin and Toni, *Stile, tradizioni e convenzioni,* 1:88.

29. Example 8.1 is transcribed directly from Rossini's autograph manuscript: the rhythmic imprecisions in the two measures marked "[sic]" give a better indication of how the phrase should be performed than an artificially "corrected" text could offer.

30. For all the relevant documents, see my introduction to the facsimile edition of the autograph manuscript of *Il barbiere di Siviglia,* 6–8 (English), 58–60 (Italian).

31. The examples are drawn from the critical editions of *La Cenerentola,* and of *Le nozze di Teti, e di Peleo.* The example from *Il barbiere di Siviglia* is transcribed directly from the autograph manuscript.

32. Printed librettos document the entire history. This argument will be developed further in the preface to the critical edition of *Il barbiere di Siviglia,* which I am preparing.

33. This, for example, is what he says about the solo arias for Giacomo and Elena that bookend the second act of *La donna del lago:* "Lacking for inspiration, he [Rossini] had recourse to rhetoric and to the ostentation of vocal ornaments. Thus arose the cavatina for Uberto, "Oh fiamma vorace"; and likewise the rondo finale ["Tanti affetti"]: both are bravura arias and nothing more." See Radiciotti, *Gioacchino Rossini,* 1:387.

34. So, when the fine tenor Paul Austin Kelly interpreted the role of the Count at the Rossini Opera Festival of Pesaro in the summer of 1997, he sang the aria some nights and not others, depending on how he felt physically. In principle, the festival wanted to include it, but never to the detriment of the singer's performance.

35. For useful analyses of the relationship between the operas of Pavesi and Donizetti, see Anselmo, *"Don Pasquale" di Gaetano Donizetti,* 51–92, as well as Cronin, "Stefano Pavesi's *Ser Marcantonio* and Donizetti's *Don Pasquale.*" Compare also my introduction to the facsimile edition of the autograph manuscript of *Don Pasquale,* 20–22 (Italian), 91–94 (English).

36. Sometimes the pieces are cut for economic reasons: by removing these choruses, the choral accompaniment to the Serenata, and the brief choral interventions in the Rondò Finale, it is possible to eliminate the need for a chorus in *Don Pasquale* altogether.

37. A modern edition of *Ser Marcantonio,* prepared by Paolo Fabbri and Maria Chiara Bertini, was performed at the Teatro Rossini of Lugo in April 2000, but I don't know whether the opera was given complete or with cuts.

38. See the critical edition of *L'Italiana in Algeri,* 320–26 and 448–55, and the relative commentary. The editor of this volume, the composer Azio Corghi, tells of a performance from his edition, conducted and staged by colleagues who constructed the entire spectacle around "Le femmine d'Italia," blissfully unaware that it isn't by Rossini (they had read neither the preface nor the commentary to the edition). The evening began with the conductor walking down the aisle of the theater humming the tune. I am not saying that this was a bad or inappropriate choice, only that a little knowledge could have spared them the embarassment of commenting on their innovative use of *Rossini's* great tune in their production.

39. In Charles Brauner's critical edition of the opera, which had its premiere at the Teatro San Carlo of Naples on 5 March 1818, "A rispettarmi apprenda" appears as an appendix. The principal text includes instead the new aria with which Rossini replaced the Carafa piece, "Cade dal ciglio il velo," added for a revival of the opera at the same theater in February and March 1820. See Rossini, *Lettere e documenti,* 1:310. Rossini placed the new aria within his autograph manuscript of *Mosè in Egitto,* where it occupies ff. 69–80.

40. It is worth pointing out that the Roggiero aria, printed in the critical edition of *Tancredi,* pp. 500–504, uses an orchestral melody (mm. 5–9) that Rossini borrowed from what was widely considered to be his first completed composition, a song, "Se il vuol la mulinara." An autograph manuscript of the song is in the Pierpont Morgan Library in New York; see *The Mary Flagler Cary Music Collection,* 41. As the annotators of this catalogue point out, although the piece bears the autograph date of "li 20 marzo 1801," the manuscript is likely to have been written a few years later, as a presentation copy for Vincenza Viganò Mombelli, who prepared the libretto of his first opera, *Demetrio e Polibio.*

41. I made a similar argument in chapter 1 about the duettino for Pilade and Fenicio in the second act of *Ermione,* a piece that allows the singer portraying Ermione a moment of respite between her gran scena and the duet finale with which the opera concludes.

42. The Aria Albazar (N. 12) is found in the critical edition of *Il Turco in Italia,* 698–710. In order to make this cut, it is necessary to perform the dialogue between Albazar and the Poet (Recitativo Dopo l'Aria Narciso, mm. 1–29), which concludes on the dominant of C *major,* then to continue directly with the Coro, N. 13, in C *major.*

43. Serafin and Toni, *Stile, tradizioni e convenzioni,* 2:62, 2:167–68, 2:177.

44. For an assessment, see Budden, *The Operas of Verdi,* 2:167–242, and Mila, *Giuseppe Verdi.*

45. See Lawton, "*Le Trouvère,*" where he comments, "Since Verdi himself cut Leonora's *cabaletta* in Act IV for Paris, this traditional practice is well justified" (102). As I am suggesting in this chapter, however, the composer's decision to cut this cabaletta in a later performance, for different performers, in a different language, and for a different audience should constitute only one factor in our thinking. Lawton's critical edition of *Le Trouvère* is forthcoming in *The Works of Giuseppe Verdi.*

46. Verdi himself, however, was ever more prepared to take this path, as is apparent with the first-act finale of *Luisa Miller,* where Cammarano originally provided him text for a final quick movement, which he rejected. See Verdi's letter to Cammarano of 17 May 1848, cited in the introduction to Verdi, *Luisa Miller,* xvii (English) and xli (Italian).

47. Ornamentation is the subject of chapter 9, where full bibliographical references and descriptions of Rossini's own manuscripts and of those of his contemporaries are provided.

48. Performances of Handel's operas over the past decade have demonstrated as clearly as possible that these works seem much shorter when given in their entirety. What was needed to make them live in the modern theater was a way to stage effectively the "da capo" aria. Notable recent successes, such as two I have seen at Lyric Opera of Chicago (the 1999 *Alcina* of Robert Carsen, first performed at the Opéra National of Paris, and the 2003 *Partenope* of Francisco Negrin, first performed at Glimmerglass Opera) have tended to present each of these arias as miniature dramas, so that the formal musical repetitions are balanced by a dynamic, constantly evolving stage action. I do not in any way consider such directorial interventions to be "compromises": they are thoroughly appropriate. This topic will be developed at greater length in chapter 13.

49. It might be objected, of course, that composers themselves occasionally introduced modifications in their music that had precisely this effect (Verdi's revision of *Simon Boccanegra* after more than two decades is the classic example). Still the ways in which a great composer

might have modified his own music must not be confused with the ways in which present-day interpreters should feel free to intervene.

50. Tonal closure in a musical number in several sections was as crucial for Rossini as it was for Mozart in his multimovement symphonies. This introduction is taken over without significant structural change from *Maometto II*. But Verdi, for example, was prepared to abandon such a formal principle.

51. A few years later, in December 1982, I was engaged by the Teatro Comunale of Florence to lecture about the opera before the opening of their new production. As soon as I realized that they were introducing the same cut, I discussed it with the conductor, Eliahu Inbal. Unaware that the cut was first introduced for the Milanese performances of 1969, he assured me that it was "traditional." When I pointed out the structural consequences and the thematic transformation, he seemed genuinely crestfallen, but the two days remaining before the performance offered insufficient time to make amends.

52. The maneuvers are described as follows in the stage director Solomé's mise-en scène: "Rodolphe, three hunters, and two women in riding habits arrive on horseback, with falcons on their fists. They cross the scene at a gallop, from the left to the right of the Public. As soon as they have disappeared, six soldiers carrying braziers place them on the slopes of the mountains and rocks so as to illuminate the hunting party, which is reposing at the *rendez-vous*. Then the pages of the hunt and valets bring in the dogs and stop in the middle of the stage. The horses likewise place themselves in the middle; the riders step down. Six pages of the hunters, with falcons on their fists, cross the stage and exit to the left of the Public. Then peasants carrying deer and wild boar follow the same path. The horsemen mount the horses again and leave to the left, with the pages and valets. As the horsemen, pages, and valets depart, the hunters and the *piqueurs* on foot enter from the right. They have javelins, gourds, etc. They too come to a halt and sing the Chorus, 'Quelle sauvage harmonie.'" See the volume *Commento Critico: Testi* in the critical edition of *Guillaume Tell*, 132–33.

53. The repeated measures are 1–41 of the Chœur (N. 8): see pp. 531–39 of vol. 2 in the critical edition of *Guillaume Tell*.

54. Two particularly beautiful examples are the cabaletta, "Perché soave calma," from the duet for Ermione and Pirro in *Ermione* (N. 3, mm. 240–326, on pp. 237–58 of the critical edition) and "Ah! dopo cotanto penar per trovarsi" from *Bianca e Falliero* (N. 5, mm. 178–275, on pp. 483–507 of the critical edition).

55. Some characteristic examples are the cabaletta "Cielo! in qual'estasi," from the duet for Elena and Uberto in *La donna del lago* (N. 2, mm. 280–404, on pp. 213–47 of the critical edition) or the cabaletta "Va, superbo: in quella Reggia," from the duet for Arsace and Assur in *Semiramide* (N. 3, mm. 161–276, on pp. 401–33 of the critical edition).

56. See the cabaletta "Dov'è mai quel core amante," from the duet for Elcia and Osiride in *Mosè in Egitto* (N. 3, mm. 180–220).

57. For the *Viaggio a Reims* cabaletta "Oh! quanto ingannasi," see N. 5, mm. 114–324, on pp. 492–513 of the critical edition. All musical sources for *Le Comte Ory* omit the equivalent of mm. 215–256 of *Il viaggio a Reims* for the cabaletta "Ce téméraire," in the duet for Comte Ory and the Comtesse Adèle (N. 7); see, for example, Rossini, *Le Comte Ory*, 340–52.

58. Since Harold Powers' important article "'La solita forma' and the Uses of Convention" was published in 1987, many musicologists have referred to the first section in this model as a "tempo d'attacco." I stubbornly resist the name. In the entire nineteenth century it is used only by Abramo Basevi in his famous *Studio sulle opere di Giuseppe Verdi*, 191, where it immediately precedes the description of a very particular kind of *primo tempo* (the standard term in the

period), that is, a short introductory section which *prepares* the cantabile, much as a *tempo di mezzo* prepares the cabaletta. The example is the duet for Rigoletto and Gilda in the first act of *Rigoletto;* a similar piece is the duet for Alfredo and Violetta in the last act of *La traviata.* It seems to me inappropriate to use it for the typical Rossinian duet, where the *primo tempo* is a fully developed section, both musically and dramatically.

59. For the *Donna del lago* duettino (N. 5), see the critical edition, 345–52; the *Zelmira* duettino (N. 7) is published in the critical edition of Rossini, *Zelmira,* 475–83; the *Semiramide* duettino (N. 6), so named to differentiate it from the duetto for the same characters in act 2 (N. 11), is in the critical edition of *Semiramide,* 561–615.

60. For a discussion of this problem in *Otello,* see the commentary by Michael Collins (141) to his critical edition of the opera (note 478–479). The page in Rossini's original autograph manuscript, with the revised version visibly replacing an earlier one, can be seen in the facsimile edition of *Otello,* ed. Gossett, vol. 2, f. 133v. (102).

61. See the Andantino of N. 3 (mm. 83–132) in the critical edition of *Semiramide,* pp. 380–92. For bibliographical information about the recording, see chapter 5, n. 35.

62. Berlioz's article was published in the *Journal des Débats* of 28 May 1839. I am citing the phrase after the Italian translation in Radiciotti, *Gioacchino Rossini,* 2:92.

63. For fuller information about these modifications, see my *"Anna Bolena" and the Artistic Maturity of Gaetano Donizetti.* Similar examples are described in the introduction to my facsimile edition of the autograph manuscript of *Don Pasquale.* The autograph manuscripts of Bellini's *Il pirata* and *Norma* are also available in facsimile editions.

64. For further details about Giovanna's aria, with musical examples, see my *"Anna Bolena,"* 68–72. The introductory chorus for the opera (mentioned in the next paragraph of this chapter) is discussed in *"Anna Bolena,"* 77–90.

65. The recording analyzed here was made as a studio recording at La Scala in September 1960 and was issued by Angel Stereo with the number 3615 C/L (35919-21). Of all the operas in the serious *bel canto* repertory, it should be said, *Norma* remained a favorite challenge for sopranos and is practically the only such work (along with *Lucia di Lammermoor*) regularly performed throughout the nineteenth century and into the twentieth, so at least some of these cuts may have a longer pedigree. But no one has analyzed the history of cuts made to *Norma.*

66. For an important treatment of the relationship between these operatic themes and the Italian Risorgimento, see Banti, *La nazione del Risorgimento.*

67. See Bellini's letter of 1 September 1831 to Pasta, published in Cambi, *Bellini: Epistolario,* 278–79.

68. See Bellini's letter of 24 August 1832 to Felice Romani, ibid., 319–21.

69. See the fragmentary letter from Bellini to Francesco Florimo, written in March 1835, ibid., 533.

70. My 1983 facsimile edition of the autograph manuscript of *Norma* contains reproductions of all the sketches and canceled skeleton scores known to survive at that time. Several additional sources have been identified subsequently.

71. An elaborate set of variations by Laure Cinti-Damoreau for the repeat of "Ah! bello a me ritorna" will be discussed in chapter 9. Variants by the tenor Mario for the repeat of Pollione's cabaletta theme are found in the Biblioteca di Santa Cecilia in Rome.

72. This complete version of the music is present in the first edition of the vocal score, 85–90, cited in chapter 3, n. 33. In the autograph manuscript, the ensemble occupies ff. 133–138. When Bellini made the cut, he crossed out the last measure of f. 134r and all of f. 134v. Between ff. 134 and 135 there was originally one additional folio, which Bellini physically removed from his autograph manuscript. It survives in a collection of canceled material from the opera preserved in the

Museo Belliniano of Catania. Since it no longer figured in the manuscript, Bellini did not need to cross it out. The folio was paginated as 117–118 in the Catania collection, but the correct order should be 118–117 (i.e., p. 118 is the recto of what was originally f. 134bis, and p. 117 is the verso of the folio). It is reproduced in my facsimile edition of the opera among the sketches for the Scena e Terzetto Finale (N. 5).

73. The terzettino before the final scene of *Maometto II*, "In questi estremi istanti," originally consisted of a canon in A♭ minor/major, with the principal melody sung, in turn, by Calbo, Anna, and Erisso. The same piece figures in *Le Siège de Corinthe*, with the words "Céleste providence," transposed up a half tone to A minor/major. According to the printed orchestral score of *Le Siège*, issued soon after the premiere in 1826 by Rossini's French publisher Troupenas (see chapter 1, n. 17), the composer eliminated the solo statement by Calbo altogether and began instead with Pamira (= Anna) singing the tune and Néocles (= Calbo) accompanying her (see *Le Siège de Corinthe*, ed. Gossett, 469–77). In the original vocal score with piano accompaniment issued at the same time by Troupenas (pl. no. 180, pp. 304–13), however, all three entries are present, as in *Maometto II*. To make the matter even more confusing, in the first complete Italian edition of *Le Siège de Corinthe* (translated as *L'assedio di Corinto*), issued after the performance of the opera at La Scala in Milan on 26 December 1828 and probably reflecting the way the opera was performed there, the melody is presented only a single time, with all three voices in harmony: nothing whatsoever remains of the canon. There is no reason to believe that Rossini would have sanctioned this radical treatment of his score, but only a critical edition of the opera will make it possible to unravel the complicated history of this terzettino.

74. The original version of the cabaletta is found in the first edition of the vocal score of *Norma*, 76–80. In the autograph manuscript the entire passage is included in the correct order (see vol. 1, ff. 120–126), but Bellini marked the cut of the transition and repeat (see his signs before the last measure on f. 123v and after the second measure on f. 125r), and he added a part for Norma during Adalgisa's solo statement of the theme (see ff. 122v-123v). This part for Norma is a later addition to the score and was never intended to be sung when the cabaletta is performed in its entirety.

75. In the facsimile of the autograph, part of a rejected transition is found between ff. 94v and 95r. Some rejected pages, present in the Museo Belliniano collection, are included in the appendix. They are not absolutely continuous (some are replacements for others, but their correct order is pp. 71/72, 69/70, 75/76, 74/73, and 77/78.

76. There is no choral entry in the rejected skeleton score of the final cadential phrases for Norma, Adalgisa, and Pollione preserved in the Museo Belliniano (pp. 59–61, reproduced in the appendix to the facsimile edition), nor in the first edition of the vocal score (see 99–100). In the autograph manuscript it seems clear that ff. 145–147 (the concluding part of the act and the pages on which the chorus and banda are present) were a later addition to the manuscript. At this point the paper type changes (from 20-stave paper to 24-stave paper), the vocal staves are relabeled, and so forth.

77. Kimbell, *Vincenzo Bellini*, 83–84.

78. The autograph manuscript and rejected drafts provide considerable information about earlier versions of this melody (some of them a half tone higher than the final version, in A♭ major instead of G major), but by the time Ricordi printed the first edition of the vocal score, the melody existed in the form we know today.

79. I have transcribed examples 8.4 and 8.5 directly from Bellini's autograph manuscript, which does not always agree with the printed editions. The shift to the relative minor (rather than the tonic) in the eighth complete measure, which does not affect the vocal line, is not shown

in the autograph, even though it is present in all printed editions subsequent to the first, and presumably stems from Bellini.

80. See, in particular, his letter to Giulio Ricordi of 20 November 1880, discussing the revision of *Simon Boccanegra,* in which he wrote: "Musically it would be possible to conserve the cavatina of the soprano, the duet with the tenor, and the other duet between father and daughter, even if there are cabalettas!! *Rend thyself asunder, o earth!* I do not have such an aversion to cabalettas, however, and if a young man were born tomorrow who knew how to make one for me of the worth of "Meco tu vieni o misera" [from Bellini's *La straniera*] or "Ah perché non posso odiarti" [from Bellini's *La sonnambula*], I would listen to it with all my heart, and I would renounce all the harmonic trifles, all the affectations of our learned orchestrators." The letter is published in *Carteggio Verdi—Ricordi 1880–1881,* 69–71 (citation p. 70). After that spirited defense, however, the composer did either omit or change the structure of the cabalettas in the revised *Simon Boccanegra.*

81. See, for example, Serafin and Toni's suggestion for rewriting the beginning of act 2 of *Rigoletto,* in *Stile, tradizioni e convenzioni,* 2:177–79 (in which the Duke is given a big dominant seventh chord for "Ah, tutto il ciel non mi rapì," whose resolution is provided by Rigoletto's entrance, a procedure Serafin actually followed—with disastrous results—in his recording with Callas) or their remarks on the Leonora cabaletta from act 4 of *Il trovatore* (2:251–52) and the Germont aria from *La traviata* (2:295–98).

82. A very strong case has been made, however, that the progression from *C* minor to *D♭* major is already embedded in the "Maledizione" motive itself and informs the tonal activity of the opera as a whole. See, in particular, Conati, *"Rigoletto" di Giuseppe Verdi,* 124–37.

83. For a discussion of ornamenting the repetitions in Verdi, see chapter 9.

84. James Hepokoski has had the most interesting things to say about Verdi's use of this tradition in *La traviata* and *Il trovatore.* See his essays "Genre and Content in Mid-Century Verdi" and "*Ottocento* Opera as Cultural Drama."

85. See the critical edition of *La traviata,* ed. Della Seta, 333–39, and compare especially the articulation markings at mm. 138–145 and 175–183. Even where the edition has chosen to extend markings from one strophe to the other, it differentiates Verdi's own markings from editorial integrations, so that the singer can always be aware as to precisely what the composer wrote.

86. Often, but not always; as Hepokoski has shown in his "*Ottocento* Opera as Cultural Drama," there is little French about Azucena's "Stride la vampa."

87. Perhaps the following will give some flavor of Serafin and Toni's prose (see 2:167–68): "The unaccompanied cadenza, *a 2,* [...] is a gross concession of Verdi's, perhaps the most tawdry we know, stuck on like a *coda di gala* [the train of a wedding dress or a set of tails], exclusively decorative, to meet the public's taste for bravura vocal pyrotechnics." These authors compare it to "extraneous" cadenzas in classical violin or piano concertos, "a sort of efflorescence provoked by exhibitionistic needs deriving from the inevitable, invasive virtuosity of concertos."

88. See Verdi's letters of 25 March 1847 to Barezzi and of 23 November 1848 to Flauto, both in Rosen and Porter, *Verdi's "Macbeth,"* 57 and 66. Translations are either cited directly from those in this volume or lightly modified. My understanding of the opera has been greatly enhanced by my work with David Lawton on his critical edition of the opera.

89. See the letters from Escudier to Verdi of 27 September 1864 and of Verdi to Escudier of 22 October 1864, both in Rosen and Porter, *Verdi's "Macbeth,"* 70–71.

90. See the letters from Verdi to Piave of 3 December 1846 and to Barbieri-Nini of 2 January and 31 January 1847, in ibid., 18–20, 28–30, and 39–41.

91. These reviews (Vincenzo Meini of 15 March in *La moda* and Alessandro Gagliardi in the *Revue et Gazette Musicale* of 28 March) are published in translation in ibid., 373 and 378.

92. Budden, *The Operas of Verdi,* 1:294.

93. See Verdi's letter to Varesi of 23–30 January 1847 and the review (in translation) by L. F. Casamorata from the *Gazzetta musicale di Milano,* both in Rosen and Porter, *Verdi's "Macbeth,"* 36–37 and 390.

94. See the letters from Verdi to Piave of 10 and 22 December 1846, in ibid., 20–24 and 26–27.

95. The critical edition of *Macbeth* includes the music of both versions; for a vocal score of the 1847 chorus, see Rosen and Porter, *Verdi's "Macbeth,"* 511–16.

96. See the letters from Verdi to Piave of 10 December 1846 and to Varesi of 23–30 January and 4 February 1847, as well as from Varesi to Ranzanici of 17 March 1847, in Rosen and Porter, *Verdi's "Macbeth,"* 20–24, 36–37, 41, and 54–56.

97. See Verdi's letters to Varesi of 4 February 1847, and to Escudier of 2 December 1864, in ibid., 41 and 75.

98. See *Carteggio Verdi–Boito,* 1:7–12 (Boito to Verdi, 8 December 1880), 1:12–13 (Verdi to Boito, 11 December 1880), 1:40 (Boito to Verdi, 5 February 1881), and 1:40–41 (Verdi to Boito, 6 February 1881).

99. See Viardot's letter to Arditi of 15 March 1859, in Rosen and Porter, *Verdi's "Macbeth,"* 364–65.

100. I first came across these letters in Milan Kundera's lovely article, "You're Not in Your Own House Here, My Dear Fellow." For a fuller treatment of them, see Craft, *Stravinsky,* 225–28, from which my citations are derived.

CHAPTER NINE

1. These 1969 performances were discussed in chapter 4, in the section "Claudio Abbado and a tenor Romeo."

2. It is one of the peculiarities of the Zedda critical edition of *Il barbiere di Siviglia* that Zedda provides many ornaments in his critical notes to Rosina's cavatina, most introduced as "Rosina can vary as follows" (see pp. 68–70 of the commentary), but not one of his examples corresponds to Rossini's own variations, neither those in Milan nor a similar set published a few years later by Edition Eulenberg (General Music Series 108), based on an autograph manuscript owned at that time by the editor, Franz Beyer; see Rossini, *Varianten zur Cavatine der Rosina "Una voce poco fa."*

3. This recording has been available as Sony S2K 39311.

4. The first appendix to the critical edition of *La donna del lago* includes the original version of the vocal line of the Rondò Finale (N. 13), with the three sets of variants superposed: see 896–904. These autograph variants are found in manuscripts currently preserved, respectively, in Paris, Bibliothèque de l'Opéra, Rés. 525; Forli, Biblioteca Comunale, Fondo Piancastelli, MS 406 CR 306; and Milan, Biblioteca Nazionale Braidense, MS AC XIII 48/9. For full details, consult the commentary to the edition, 159–63.

5. Wagner, *Tristan und Isolde,* ed. Vetter.

6. See the critical edition of *Rigoletto,* 289–90 (N. 13, mm. 1–28). Notice, by the way, that immediately after these first measures (the dialogue between Rigoletto and Sparafucile, where Rigoletto pays Sparafucile half the money in advance for killing the Duke), Verdi began once again to write out explicitly almost every possible appoggiatura in the recitative. As we shall see, already by the early 1840s Verdi had begun to provide more explicit written instructions to his singers concerning the use of appoggiaturas.

7. Problems concerning the reorchestration of early nineteenth-century operas toward the end of the century are discussed in chapter 3, under the rubric "Transforming *L'Italiana:* The orchestration."

8. Although there has been relatively little published work concerning recorded evidence pertaining to ornamentation in Rossini, see the significant essay by Crutchfield, "Vocal Ornamentation in Verdi: the Phonographic Evidence." Another important contribution is that of Shawe-Taylor, "Verdi and His Singers."

9. The autograph of *La scala di seta* is found in Stockholm, Sweden, in the Nydahl collection of the Stiftelsen Musikkulturens främjande; that of *Il signor Bruschino* is in Paris, Bibliothèque Nationale (fonds du Conservatoire, Ms. 1337). These manuscripts are discussed fully in the critical editions of *La scala di seta,* ed. Wiklund, and of *Il signor Bruschino,* ed. Gazzaniga.

10. How should one translate "coglioni" in this phrase? My Italian-English dictionary says "blockheads"; I rendered it as "stupid pedants." The word is actually an Italian vulgarism for testicles. The passage is found in the critical edition of *Otello* (N. 8, mm. 331–333, on pp. 664–65); in my edition of the facsimile of the original manuscript, see the second volume, f. 66v.

11. See the critical edition of *Ermione* (Recitativo Dopo l'Aria Pirro [N. 6], mm. 66–74 , on pp. 400–401).

12. The relationship of Romani's text to previous incarnations of the libretto is discussed in detail by Nicolodi, *Il Turco in Italia.*

13. The entire passage is given in the critical edition of *Il Turco in Italia,* 494–96 (mm. 493–516).

14. For the conclusion of the cantabile, see the critical edition of *La scala di seta,* N. 3, m. 49 of the aria (p. 174); for the reference to Monelli at the end of the accompanied recitative, see N. 3, m. 11 of the accompanied recitative (p. 159).

15. The most important of these is a collection in Paris at the Bibliothèque de l'Opéra, prepared by Rossini for "Mlle E. Rouget." This was the French singer Eugénie Rouget, who became Mme de Chambure before 1839; hence it is most likely that the manuscript predates her marriage (see Slim, in his commentary to the critical edition of *La donna del lago,* 159–60). This manuscript is the basis for all the variations published in the second appendix to Ricci's *Variazioni—Cadenze—Tradizioni per canto,* vol. 4, "Variazioni e cadenze di G. Rossini."

16. For several sets of variations prepared for Giuditta Pasta, often with cadenzas, see the critical edition of *Tancredi,* 606–7 (for the Duet, N. 14, "Lasciami: non t'ascolto") and 802–18 (for the composition by Giuseppe Nicolini, "Il braccio mio conquise," which Pasta sometimes introduced as a final aria). For Giulia Grisi, Rossini prepared variants for the scene for Desdemona opening act 3 of *Otello* (see the critical edition, 955–61). According to the commentary of Michael Collins, 148–49, it seems likely that the composer wrote this manuscript when Grisi performed the role at the Théâtre Italien of Paris during the 1833–34 season.

17. Rossini wrote a variation for the second-act finale (N. 16) of *La gazza ladra* and a cadenza for the opening section of the duet between Ninetta and Pippo (N. 12) when Patti sang the role of Ninetta at the Théâtre Italien of Paris in 1867. See the critical edition of the opera, 1076–78. The variants for Matilde Juva for "Una voce poco fa" have been discussed earlier in this chapter.

18. As Rodolfo Celletti demonstrated in his article "Origine e sviluppi della coloratura rossiniana."

19. I have seen two separate editions of these ornaments for the section "Mille sospiri e lagrime" (sung by Zenobia and Arsace) from the trio (N. 11), which later includes Aureliano. One edition was published by T. Boosey in London, with the indication, "Expressly published with the modifications of Sig. G. B. Velluti to serve for teaching at his Academy in London"; the other, issued in Vienna by Pietro Mechetti in the series Aurora d'Italia e Germania, has the indication, "with the ornaments of Sig.ʳ G. Battista Velluti."

20. In the autograph manuscript from which example 9.2 is taken (Paris, Bibliothèque Nationale, Département de la Musique, Ms. 4062 [2]), the *romanza* is written in *G minor* and is

reduced by the composer for voice and piano. Donizetti wrote both the original version and the variation. I print this example in the original tonality. Unfortunately there is a tear in the upper left-hand corner, so that the first few notes of the variant in the first measure are missing.

21. The original version of Fenena's prayer, which is part of the Finale Ultimo (N. 13), is printed in the critical edition of *Nabucco,* 453–56; the version "puntata per la Zecchini" is given as appendix 4 (519). The music of the latter, in the composer's own hand, is present in his original autograph manuscript (conserved in the archive of BMG Ricordi), on ff. 145–146.

22. The soprano in Balzac's *Massimilla Doni* is named la "Tinti" in homage to Cinti-Damoreau. See her *Méthode de chant composée pour ses classes du Conservatoire.*

23. These notebooks, which are in the Everett Helm collection of the Lilly Library, have been studied by Austin Caswell. See his "Mme Cinti-Damoreau and the Embellishment of Italian Opera in Paris: 1820–1845."

24. Photocopies of the Kemble manuscript have been in circulation for more than twenty years. I do not know where the original currently resides. Kemble performed the title role in *Norma* for the first time in a special performance of the opera at the Teatro La Fenice of Venice on 2 December 1838: see Girardi and Rossi, *Il Teatro La Fenice,* 1:140.

25. The manuscript is described in *The Mary Flagler Cary Music Collection,* 33 (item 142); see also Turner, *Four Centuries of Opera,* 122. All the examples attributed to the "Sorelle Marchisio" in Ricci, *Variazioni,* vol. 1 ("Voci femminili"), are derived from this source.

26. Their ornamentation for *Semiramide* is included as alternative readings in the vocal score of the French adaptation, issued by Heugel in 1860. Most of these have been printed in the commentary to the critical edition of the opera.

27. A Velluti example has been cited above. Bonini was the first Cenerentola in Paris (1822), and the Parisian publisher Pacini dedicated his edition of the opera to her. In it, the final aria (pl. no. 2114) is printed with variations that surely reflect her performance at the Théâtre Italien. They are reproduced in the commentary to the critical edition, 190–91. In 1870 the Parisian publisher Heugel issued a new edition of the "Romance du Saule et Prière de Desdémone" in Rossini's *Otello,* "with the ornaments and variants of Mme Malibran" (pl. no. 3667, "as sung by Gabrielle Krauss at the Théâtre Italien"). These can be studied in the commentary, 151–53, to appendix 1 of the critical edition of *Otello.* In the second edition of his vocal score of *La donna del lago,* Pacini included a piece from *Ermione* that Rubini inserted into the opera for performances at the Théâtre Italien in November 1825, printing it "with all the ornaments that Mr Rubini adds to it" (pl. no. 1097). The composition and ornaments are reproduced in appendix 2 of the critical edition of *La donna del lago,* 907–41, and the commentary, 173–76. The singer had earlier made this insertion for performances in Naples in 1820. We must not assume, of course, that these variation sets include *every* modification introduced by a singer: the addition of single ornamental notes or turn figures was so much part of the stylistic vocabulary, that it would not normally have been necessary to write them in.

28. These manuscripts have been collected and analyzed by Colas in his doctoral dissertation, *Les Annotations de chanteurs.*

29. See Beghelli, *I trattati di canto italiani.*

30. A modern edition, while not complete, is most helpful: Ginevra, *Manuel García.*

31. Mainvielle Fodor, *Réflexions et conseils sur l'art du chant,* 13–14. I am grateful to Marilyn Horne for bringing this lovely little pamphlet to my attention.

32. Cinti-Damoreau, *Méthode de chant,* 2. For further information about Cinti-Damoreau and other singers of the period, see Caswell, *Embellished Opera Arias.*

33. Less frequently, it is possible to embellish these two identical notes by inserting a small ornament before the second: thus, before the second of two *g*s one could sing quickly *b–a.* There has been no full study of appoggiatura techniques for nineteenth-century Italian opera. Most

scholarly work has focused on the eighteenth century, and there is considerable controversy about a number of important issues. See, for example, Crutchfield, "The Prosodic Appoggiatura," as well as two articles by Frederick Neumann, "The Appoggiatura in Mozart's Recitative," and "Improper Appoggiaturas in the *Neue Mozart Ausgabe*," in which he attacks some of the practices in the Mozart edition, focusing especially on the edition of *Così fan tutte*, ed. Ferguson and Rehm.

34. The manuscript, prepared "for the use of Mad.^me Grégoire by her friend G. Rossini," is dated 15 August 1858. It is part of the collection of the Pierpont Morgan Library in New York: see item 177 in *The Mary Flagler Cary Music Collection*, 42. Nothing is known about Madame Grégoire except that there was a family of Belgian musicians and critics by the name of Grégoir, to which she probably belonged. The variants are transcribed in the critical edition of *Tancredi*, 602–5; see also the commentary, 197–99.

35. See García, *Traité complet de l'art du chant en deux parties*, 65. The modern edition by Stefano Ginevra reproduces the text of the 1872 version of García's treatise, which is considerably abbreviated and does not have this example.

36. Despite modern usage, it is historically and structurally wrong to use the word "cavatina" to describe this cantabile: in nineteenth-century usage the term "cavatina" always refers to an entire composition, usually an independent aria sung by a character entering for the first time (such as Figaro's cavatina or Rosina's cavatina in *Il barbiere di Siviglia*). In some of Rossini's early operas, such as *Tancredi*, the composer also used the word "cavatina" to refer to pieces in a single section for a major soloist in the second act (of a two-act opera), a usage that carries over from eighteenth-century conventions. The latter are explored by Osthoff in "Mozarts Cavatinen und ihre Tradition." The terminological issues for nineteenth-century Italian opera are explored by Beghelli in "Tre slittamenti semantici."

37. The phrase "heavenly length," of course, is usually applied to lengthy movements in Schubert's instrumental music.

38. Thanks to the work of Pugliese, *"Un idillio a fili d'argento,"* we now know for certain that the basic cadenza was written for Nellie Melba by Mathilde Marchesi in 1889. See also her article "The origins of *Lucia di Lammermoor's* cadenza." According to Pugliese, there is no evidence of an important cadenza with flute in the mad scene in nineteenth-century musical sources or journalistic accounts before 1889.

39. This cadenza is part of a longer variant, an ornamented version of the entire passage that Tancredi sings at the beginning of the duet. Based on an autograph manuscript prepared by Rossini for Giuditta Pasta and now preserved at the Pierpont Morgan Library in New York (item 170 in *The Mary Flager Cary Music Collection*, p. 40), the complete variant is transcribed in appendix 1 of the critical edition of *Tancredi*, 606.

40. The cadenzas of Cinti-Damoreau are all reproduced in Bartlet's commentary to her critical edition of *Guillaume Tell*, 147–49. For three cadenzas by Carlotta Marchisio, who sang the part of Mathilde during the 1860s, see 153.

41. See the critical edition of *La gazza ladra*, 1080. What we did not know at the time was that another set of variations for this same cavatina would be auctioned by Sotheby's in London in their sale of 3–4 December 1992 (item 599 in the catalogue, on p. 280). It, too, was certainly penned during Rossini's final years in Paris, since the manuscript also has variants for one of his *Péchés de vieillesse*. The manuscript was purchased by a Japanese collector, who very kindly supplied me with a photocopy. For an excerpt from this manuscript, see example 9.10.

42. This pertains specifically to *lyrical* sections: contemporary evidence suggests that passages more declamatory in character may present ornamentation earlier.

43. The version for Giuseppina Vitali is transcribed in the critical edition, 1080; there is a photocopy of the relevant portion of the manuscript auctioned at Sotheby's in their catalogue cited in n. 41 above, 280.

44. The original melodic line has been edited directly from Rossini's autograph manuscript of *Il barbiere di Siviglia*, the variation from the autograph manuscript at the Milan Conservatory.

45. For a complete transcription, see appendix 1 to the critical edition, 1067–69.

46. As we have seen, the cadenza in its original form was almost certainly written in 1889 for Nellie Melba. Interpolated cadenzas of a similar length and difficulty, however, are found in many earlier sources for Italian *bel canto* operas, including a source for *Lucia di Lammermoor*, as Pugliese demonstrates in her *"Un idillio a fili d'argento."*

47. See, for example, Bellini's rewriting of the cadenza at the end of the cabaletta "Ah! non fia sempre odiata!" within Gualtiero's second-act aria in the facsimile of the autograph manuscript of *Il pirata* (vol., 2, f. 125r) or his recasting for Giambattista Rubini of a cadenza in *La straniera* originally written for Domenico Reina: see Bellini, *La straniera*, ed. Gossett, 2:121. In the first case Bellini makes the cadenza more elaborate; in the second he simplifies it.

48. For Bellini's various efforts to reduce the number of doubling orchestral parts in the cabaletta of Pollione's first-act cavatina in *Norma*, "Mi protegge, mi difende," see the facsimile of the autograph manuscript, vol. 1, ff. 40r-41v. An even more extensive reduction of doublings occurs in the cabaletta of the Riccardo aria in *I puritani*, "Bel sogno beato," as we saw in chapter 7.

49. This cadenza is reproduced in Mackenzie-Grieve, *Clara Novello 1818–1908*, facing 214.

50. For information about this manuscript, see n. 15 above. The original vocal line is reproduced from Claudio Toscani's critical edition; Rossini's variation is transcribed from his autograph manuscript.

51. The original text is transcribed from the facsimile of the *Norma* autograph; the variant is derived from the Cinti-Damoreau notebooks at the Lilly Library, Indiana University.

52. Roberta Marvin discusses this passage in her commentary to the Scena ed Aria Amelia (N. 6) of *I masnadieri;* see the critical commentary, 76 (note 253–254, 285–286).

53. Muzio's letter is quoted in the third paragraph of chapter 3.

54. See, in particular, Crutchfield, "Vocal Ornamentation in Verdi."

55. Letter of 11 March 1865, published in Rosen and Porter, *Verdi's "Macbeth,"* 110–13.

56. Those who would like to see this fabled pitch for themselves should consult Bellini, *I puritani*, ed. Gossett, vol. 2, f. 157r, last measure and f. 157v, first measure. The part of Arturo is, of course, written in tenor clef.

57. The letter is cited and translated in the preface to Claudio Gallico's critical edition of *Ernani*, xxi (English) and xlv (Italian). For Verdi's letter to Donizetti, see chapter 7, in the section "Historical circumstances."

58. The passage is found in the critical edition of the Aria Violetta in *La traviata*, ed. Della Seta (N. 3, mm. 155–158), 93.

59. The passage is found in ibid., (N. 3, mm. 113–114), 89.

60. The Liebling variations are available in various formats; see, for example, Liebling, *Arrangements and Editings for Coloratura Voice with Piano*, the source from which I am quoting.

61. For the original notation of this passage and Rossini's own added cadenza, see example 9.12.

62. The music is transcribed from Rossini's own manuscript of *Il barbiere di Siviglia* and from the manuscript for Matilde Juva at the Conservatory of Milan, cited in the second paragraph of this chapter.

63. For a well-balanced and interesting treatment of this interpolation, see Beghelli, "Per fedeltà a una nota."

64. The passage for clarinet in question is found in the Aria Isaura (N. 9) in the critical edition of *Tancredi*, 335–36. Isaura should appropriately sing a varied form of the melody at mm. 50–54, giving the clarinet the opportunity to echo the vocal ornamentation at mm. 54–56.

CHAPTER TEN

1. In the autograph manuscript of Rossini's *L'Italiana in Algeri*, preserved at the Ricordi Archives in Milan, for example, the *F-major* cavatina for Isabella, "Cruda sorte," is marked twice "in Sol" (in *G*) by another hand. In other sources for this cavatina (which exists in two versions), there are actual transpositions or indications of transpositions to *G♭ major, A major,* and even *B♭ major.* See the commentary to Corghi's critical edition, 64–65 and 151–52. Will Crutchfield tells me that librarians of Her Majesty's Theatre in London in the midnineteenth century actually printed up gummed labels reading "one note higher," "one note lower," "one half-note higher," and "one half-note lower." Apparently at that time orchestral musicians were prepared to transpose at sight; today's players are unlikely to be entrusted with such a responsibility.

2. Transpositions to *F major* were common already in the decade after the opera's premiere, but an extract issued by Carli, a Parisian publisher, presents the cavatina in *G major*. On this edition, a copy of which is to be found in the Bibliothèque Nationale of Paris, Fonds du Conservatoire, D. 11808(5), Carli specifies "Cavatina sung by M.ᵉ Fodor in the *Barbier de Seville,* music by Rossini, with all the ornaments that M.ᵉ Fodor adopts, written by herself." On the other hand, an extract published by a British company, Falkner's Opera Music Warehouse, also invoking "Mad.ᵐᵉ Fodor," prints the piece in *E♭ major,* a tonality *lower* than the original key.

3. For the history of these Parisian performances, see the introduction to the critical edition of *Semiramide,* lii–lviii.

4. A performance of the Tonio *cavatine* is found on Flórez's 2003 CD, *Una furtiva lagrima* (Universal B00008CLJK). During the 2003–4 season he sang the entire opera at the Bologna Teatro Comunale, to wide public and critical acclaim.

5. One cannot be entirely indifferent, however, to how much more difficult it is to make the string parts sound as bright and forceful in *E♭ minor* as they do in *F minor.* In addition, several exposed notes in the strings in the original key fall below the instruments' range when the piece is transposed down by a whole tone.

6. See Verdi's letter to Antonio Bazzini of 10 February 1884, printed in *Carteggio Verdi–Ricordi 1882–1885,* 417. The history is discussed in full by Renato Meucci in "Verdi, Bazzini e l'unificazione del diapason in Italia." For many of the relevant documents, see *Carteggio Verdi–Ricordi 1880–1881,* appendix 27 (308–9) and *Carteggio Verdi–Ricordi 1882–1885,* appendix 26 (409–25).

7. See Verdi's letter to Boito of 8 November 1885 (no. 65 in the *Carteggio Verdi–Boito,* 93); commentary to the letter is on 334–35.

8. Verdi more rarely transposed a piece upward, but there are several examples, such as Preziosilla's "Al suon del tamburo" from act 2 of *La forza del destino.* This music not only was originally sketched in *B♭ major* in 1861 but was sung in that key in the version of the opera performed in St. Petersburg in 1862. Only when Verdi revised the opera for Milan in 1869 did he transpose the music up a semitone, to *B major.* Much more typical is the first set of *couplets* for Oscar in the introduction of *Un ballo in maschera,* "Volta la terrea," known today in *B♭ major* but originally planned for *Una vendetta in dominò / Gustavo III* as "Pallida, pallida" in *B major.*

9. The classic study of the concept of "organicism" in nineteenth-century music is Solie's "The Living Work."

10. See Lorenz, *Das Geheimnis der Form bei Richard Wagner,* 4 vols. The first volume is devoted to the *Ring,* the others to *Tristan, Die Meistersinger,* and *Parsifal,* respectively.

11. See Abbate, "Wagner, 'On Modulation,' and *Tristan*," 37. In citing Abbate at her most intolerant, I nonetheless invoke one of today's most able thinkers about opera.

12. My own first exposure to these problems came in a seminar at Columbia University in 1962 led by a distinguished theorist and composer, Peter Westergaard, who also happened to love opera. I remember very well how strange it seemed to all of us when he suggested that one could think in analytically and dramaturgically interesting ways about the tonal structure of *Il trovatore*. Verdi and tonality? At the time it seemed like an odd pairing indeed. It was not until a decade later that Petrobelli delivered a paper in which he began to develop these ideas further: "Per un'esegesi della struttura drammatica del *Trovatore*," translated as "Toward an Explanation of the Dramatic Structure of *Il trovatore*."

13. The best discussion of these issues is by Conati in *"Rigoletto" di Giuseppe Verdi*, 124–37. For a related argument, in English, see Chusid, "The Tonality of *Rigoletto*."

14. The following paragraphs are derived from Gossett, "History and Works that Have No History," 110–12.

15. The literature is quite extensive. For two recent examples, with many other references, see Powers, "One Halfstep at a Time," and Greenwald, "Puccini, *Il tabarro*, and the Dilemma of Operatic Transposition." For another interesting contribution see Parker's discussion of "tonal 'plot'" in the two versions of *La forza del destino* in his essay, "Leonora's Last Act: *La forza del destino*," in *Leonora's Last Act*, 61–99.

16. This point has been made effectively by Webster in "Mozart's Operas and the Myth of Musical Unity."

17. Budden, *The Operas of Verdi*, 2:161.

18. This transposition is discussed in Gossett, "The Composition of *Ernani*," 38–41. All relevant materials are published in Claudio Gallico's critical edition of the opera.

19. For a brief treatment of the transpositions in *Stiffelio*, see Gossett, "New Sources for *Stiffelio*," 32–36.

20. The compositional history of the Scena e Preghiera Lina is analyzed fully in Hansell, "Compositional Techniques in *Stiffelio*, 52–59. For further information, see Hansell's critical edition of the opera.

21. According to Lawton and Rosen, in "Verdi's Non-definitive Revisions," 197–98 and 230–31, this letter was first cited by Radiciotti, "Giuseppe Verdi a Senigallia." See also Chusid, *A Catalog of Verdi's Operas*, 101.

22. As Smart writes: "it seems likely that the problem was not simply a higher tessitura, but the fact that the *Lombardi* cabaletta requires the soprano to sing in this high range loudly and with considerable force over a sustained period, while what Frezzolini excelled in was delicate, pianissimo high notes" ("Verdi Sings Erminia Frezzolini," 22, note 17). It remains noteworthy, however, that in his letter Verdi refers exclusively to the top of her register.

23. This discussion of keys and transpositions should not blind us to the realization that no one in Europe or the United States can read the text of this scene today with indifference.

24. Thus, I cannot agree with Powers that in a case like this one Verdi has decided "for one or another reason to allow the passage in question to participate in the web of tonalities in a different manner, but not one that is random or without tonally expressive implications" ("One Halfstep at a Time," 164). However clever the music analyst might be in inventing an explanation, Occam's razor tells us that the composer simply set aside tonal matters here in favor of considerations that—at a particular moment—seemed to him more important.

25. For an introduction to Grisi's life and career, see Forbes, *Mario and Grisi. Don Pasquale* is discussed on pp. 59ff. Grisi was the soprano of the legendary "*Puritani* Quartet" at the Théâtre Italien (Grisi, soprano; Giambattista Rubini, tenor; Antonio Tamburini, baritone; Luigi Lablache,

bass), the same quartet (with the substitution of Giovanni Mario, Cavaliere de Candia, for Rubini) for which Donizetti composed *Don Pasquale*. See also the very helpful article by Kaufman, "Giulia Grisi," with a chronology of her career and a summary of her repertory.

26. The parallelism with the composer's earlier *L'elisir d'amore* (1832), in which the heroine begins her solo within the opera's introduction by reading aloud, in that case from the story of Tristan and Isolde ("Della crudele Isotta"), has been noted many times.

27. See my facsimile edition of the autograph manuscript of *Don Pasquale;* the manuscript is preserved in the Ricordi Archives in Milan.

28. The letter is mentioned in Johnstone, "Treasure Trove in Gloucester," esp. 55–56). Let me thank H. Diack Johnstone for bringing his article to my attention.

29. The practice of interpolating a high note at the end of this cabaletta is discussed in chapter 8.

30. And I must insist that thirty years of experience in the theater has made clear to me that singers do make demands of this kind frequently, not because of particular characteristics in their vocal production, but specifically to allow them to interpolate a high note.

31. The four examples listed below can be verified in Bellini's original autograph manuscript and the pages on which he made his Neapolitan revision in my facsimile edition of *Norma.*

32. Bellini, *I puritani,* ed. Gossett, ff. 23–47 in acts 2–3, and pp. 51–94 in the appendix (the scene starts on p. 51).

33. See the first volume in the facsimile edition of the autograph manuscript, where the cantabile occupies ff. 57v–64. In a very early issue of the first Ricordi edition of *Norma,* where the cavatina has the plate number 5904 and occupies pp. 35–50, the cantabile is indeed in the transposed *F major.*

34. The evidence is reviewed in Kimbell, *Vincenzo Bellini,* 10 and 76.

35. Example 10.3 is derived from Bellini's notation in his autograph manuscript. See the facsimile edition.

36. Will Crutchfield informs me that in the materials rented by Kalmus, the parts include the piece in both *F major* and *E major,* and he believes that Zinka Milanov sang it in the latter key in at least some of her performances as Norma at the Metropolitan Opera.

37. It is strange that Bini and Commons, in their excellent treatment of the initial performances of *Lucia* in *Le prime rappresentazioni delle opere di Donizetti nella stampa coeva,* 513–32, make no reference to these transpositions; nor do they treat Donizetti's own 1839 revision of the opera for Paris as *Lucie de Lammermoor.* The transpositions are mentioned by Ashbrook, *Donizetti and His Operas,* 376. While he does not assess their significance, Ashbrook prints an example from "Regnava nel silenzio" in the original key (377). Smart, in "The Silencing of Lucia," cites the two solo scenes for Lucia in their original keys, but nowhere calls attention to the fact that those keys neither appear in modern editions nor are used on most recordings of the opera. In her critical argument, Smart invokes moments where Donizetti makes precise tonal references in her original keys, but she does not mention that in most performances these tonal references are disguised by the transpositions. Indeed she goes so far to silence the problem that she "corrects" her quotations from McClary's *Feminine Endings,* 90–99, making it appear—quite mistakenly—that McClary cites the music in its original keys. Jésus Lopez-Cobos was responsible for editing a version of the opera based on the readings of the autograph manuscript and using the original keys, which he has now conducted for several decades. I am grateful to Maestro Lopez-Cobos for several illuminating conversations about his work.

38. Gabriele Dotto, who together with Roger Parker is preparing a new critical edition of *Lucia di Lammermoor,* informs me that in the earliest Neapolitan edition of the opera, published in 1835 by the firm of Girard, the duet for Lucia and Edgardo "Sulla tomba che rinserra" is also

transposed down a half step, but this transposition never made its way into later editions of the opera or into the modern performing tradition. Dotto and Parker's edition was performed for the first time at London's Covent Garden on 29 November 2003.

39. The facsimile of the autograph is widely available in major libraries; the manuscript itself today resides in the collection of the Fondazione Donizetti in Bergamo. A copy of the first complete Ricordi edition (plate numbers 10076–10094) is in my collection. Although Ricordi had published excerpts from *Lucia* by October 1835, the firm did not issue the complete opera until the summer of 1837, confirming Ashbrook's point that *Lucia* was not immediately popular after its premiere. See his "Popular Success, the Critics and Fame."

40. See Ciarlantini, *Giuseppe Persiani e Fanny Tacchinardi,* 108–13, as well as the same author's "Fanny Tacchinardi Persiani." See also Kaufman, "Giuseppe and Fanny Persiani."

41. Although Donizetti's modification never made it into the Ricordi edition, it does appear in some other sources, and modern performance practice tends to adopt it.

42. See Ciarlatini, *Giuseppe Persiani,* 75–76, and "Fanny Tacchinardi Persiani," 139–41, as well as the list of Fanny's operatic appearances in Kaufman, "Giuseppe and Fanny Persiani," 140–41. On the broader problem of aria substitution in *Lucia,* see Poriss, "A Madwoman's Choice"; on "Regnava nel silenzio," see 2–3. What is most remarkable in Poriss's study is her demonstration that the mad scene itself was often replaced in early performances of *Lucia,* usually with a composition taken from Donizetti's *Fausta,* first performed at the Teatro San Carlo of Naples on 12 January 1832.

43. Donizetti may have provided yet another variant, substituting a *g* for the high *d♭,* but he may also have made other changes in the following two sixteenth notes, changes not altogether clear from the facsimile of the autograph manuscript. I trust that the forthcoming critical edition will help clarify the matter.

44. Although Natalie Dessay used the lower transposition of the mad scene in her debut in the role at Lyric Opera of Chicago in January 2004 (she had earlier sung only Donizetti's French revision of the opera), she sang "Regnava nel silenzio" in its original key with no apparent difficulty.

45. The transposition, which—as Gabriele Dotto informs me—is found in the early Girard Neapolitan print, is independent of Donizetti's original instrumentation of the mad scene with a solo for "armonico" or glass harmonica, which he changed in his autograph manuscript to a flute, already for the original performances. This problem in the instrumentation of the mad scene will be discussed in chapter 12.

46. There is no hint of the transposition in Donizetti's autograph. Nonetheless, even taking into account the transposition, there are very few errors in the vocal line in printed editions, except for the measure immediately preceding Donizetti's written-out cadenza to the cantabile. For that measure, modern editions distrust Donizetti's notation, in which Lucia begins a third below the flute, then crosses over the flute line to conclude a third above. In its place, these editions substitute a more banal melodic line that keeps the vocal line strictly a third below the flute. Two measures earlier, where the flute and voice begin to come together in thirds and sixths, Donizetti actually wrote in his autograph, "If [the singer] does not want to be united with the flute, it is possible to stop the flute and continue *a piacere.*" Needless to say, this phrase has never made its way into printed editions of the opera!

47. Rather than being an adjustment for the soprano, this transposition may have reflected the particularly high tessitura for the baritone in the original key. Even in comparison with Enrico's solo in the introduction, the duet in *A major* lies in the baritonal stratosphere. And, of course, should Enrico wish to conclude the duet by ascending with Lucia to a high note at the end of the cabaletta, high *g,* in the transposed version, is one thing, high *a* quite another!

48. Dotto, in a private communication, has suggested that the transpositions may have been intended only for salon usage, not for the theater. Yet ornamentation for Lucia's solos is present in the album of the English singer Adelaide Kemble, and all of it is in the lower keys.

49. The autograph manuscript is housed in the Archivio Ricordi of Milan, now deposited at the Biblioteca Nazionale Braidense. According to Lippmann, in Adamo and Lippmann, *Vincenzo Bellini,* 540, the manuscript was issued in facsimile by the Reale Accademia d'Italia in Rome in 1934, but copies are difficult to find.

50. See Giazotto, *Maria Malibran,* 198.

51. See Graziano, *Cinderella (1831) adapted by M. Rophino Lacy from Gioacchino Rossini's "La Cenerentola."* See also Rogers, *"Cenerentola a Londra."*

52. Fragments from three letters supposedly written to Florimo by Bellini from London were published by Florimo. They are reprinted in Cambi, *Bellini: Epistolario,* 363–66. Cambi refers to them as being "of doubtful authenticity." The letter quoted here is in Florimo, *Bellini: Memorie e lettere,* 137–39, where it is specifically referred to as an "anecdote derived from a Bellini letter" and is *not* included in the section of the book devoted to actual letters. The words "Ah! m'abbraccia!" are part of Amina's final cabaletta, "Ah! non giunge uman pensiero."

53. The most judicious and yet devastating presentation of the evidence is by the distinguished historian John Rosselli, in *The Life of Bellini.* On Florimo's forgeries, see 6–13; on the Malibran incident, 9–10.

54. Let me thank Emanuele Senici, who, on the occasion of a conference concerning Bellini held at the Accademia Chigiana of Siena in May 2000, where we both presented papers, kindly shared with me some of his research into the transpositions for *La sonnambula,* including information about this early Boosey print. His essay is now available as "Per una biografia musicale di Amina," in Della Seta and Ricciardi, *Vincenzo Bellini,* 297–314.

55. There is a considerable literature about Rubini. A good point of departure is Brewer, "Il cigno di Romano—Giovan Battista Rubini," which includes a summary of his repertory and extensive information about his performing career, as well as Gara, *Giovan Battista Rubini nel centenario della morte.* See also Huber, "Giovanni Battista Rubini als Donizetti-Interpret," and Johnson, "Donizetti's First 'Affare di Parigi,'" esp. 340–42.

56. I examined a copy of this vocal score in the library at the "Santa Cecilia" Conservatory in Rome.

57. Senici ("Per una biografia musicale di Amina," 305) identified only one vocal score that diverged from this publishing tradition; Boosey, in 1849, printed both pieces in their original tonalities.

58. See the composer's letter to Florimo of 24 October 1834 (Cambi, *Bellini: Epistolario,* 462), another document that must be treated with great caution: "To give him [Rubini] greater mastery of his part, I lowered his cavatina from B♭ major to A major." Even if Rubini's voice had changed since Bellini had written the part of Elvino specifically for the tenor, the Ricordi edition had *already* lowered the piece to A♭ major, so that bringing it to A major was neither novel nor significant. There is no indication in the letter, furthermore, whether Bellini personally made revisions or merely handed the aria to a copyist with instructions to bring the piece down.

59. Of course, it depends on which kind of tenor and using what kind of vocal technique. Excluding the highest of the high Rubini notes, like the infamous high *f* in *I puritani,* a singer such as Juan Diego Flórez could sing with relative ease most of this music at its original pitch level. The tessitura, after all, is rarely higher than most of the music Rossini wrote for Giovanni David during the 1810s and early 1820s in Naples, a repertory that Flórez has mastered.

60. On f. 32v of his autograph manuscript, Bellini wrote, "Rec. e Cav. Elvino"; and on f. 48r, at the beginning of the next composition (which Bellini referred to in a letter as "la sortita di Rodolfo"), he wrote, "Dopo la Cavatina d'Elvino." The indication "Duetto" is found already in the first Ricordi vocal score, prepared during the summer of 1831 (see p. 38, pl. no. 5275, "Rec. e Duetto"), and that title continues to appear in all later Ricordi vocal scores until the present. Too many critics have been fooled, including Rosselli, *The Life of Bellini*, 85–86.

61. In the cantabile of "Prendi: l'anel ti dono," the voices come together in sixths at "Caro/a! dal dì che univa," the melody sung by Elvino, with Amina a sixth above. Senici ("Per una biografia musicale di Amina," 37–38) has documented how singers, including Maria Callas, frequently changed the design by moving Elvino down a third (hence, an octave below the part originally written for Amina), while Amina sang Elvino's part an octave higher. The result was a series of tenths, with a considerable distance between the two voices and Amina definitely "on top" in Elvino's cavatina, an unsatisfactory solution both musically and dramaturgically.

62. See Cambi, *Bellini: Epistolario*, 161–65; the reference is to 161. This is an authentic letter, and Cambi verified its contents with Bellini's autograph manuscript in the Library of the Conservatorio di Musica "S. Pietro a Majella."

63. For an astute analysis of the opera, its sources, and its singers, see Lippmann, "Su 'La Straniera' di Bellini."

64. The original text of the letter is found in Cambi, "Bellini: Un pacchetto di autografi."

65. Milan, Biblioteca del Conservatorio di Musica "G. Verdi," Ms. 20: this is the manuscript of *La straniera* reproduced in the Garland series Early Romantic Opera, ed. Gossett.

66. Example 10.9 is transcribed from vol. 1, p. 315, of the Milanese manuscript, in *La straniera*, ed. Gossett.

67. The original version is taken from the modern Ricordi vocal score of *La straniera*; the Rubini version is transcribed from the manuscript, vol. 2, p. 113, of *La straniera*, ed. Gossett.

68. In a concert performance of *La straniera* on 7 February 1993, with the Opera Orchestra of New York under the baton of Eve Queler, Gregory Kunde performed the role of Arturo in the Rubini version. Although most attention was focused on the Straniera herself, a young Renée Fleming, Kunde managed his role in what Bernard Holland, reviewing the performance for the *New York Times*, described as "a calm control and a musical forthrightness in a part that weightier modern tenors might have approached with some terror."

CHAPTER ELEVEN

1. The recording was issued in 1985 by Deutsche Grammophon, 415316-1.

2. Thus, Alan Blyth in the pages of *Gramophon* (December 1985), consulted online at http://www.tenorissimo.com/domingo/Articles/cdreviews2.htm: "All the singers here have made a valiant attempt to sing idiomatic French but none, I feel, Domingo possibly excepted, actually makes much of the language." There is similar criticism by William Huck in the pages of the *Opera Quarterly*, 5, nos. 2–3 (1987), 234: "It must be noted that the 'Frenchness' of this recording is severely impaired because Abbado's singers, uniformly more accustomed to singing in Italian, rarely use the French text dramatically."

3. Crutchfield, "Crutchfield at Large." The following paragraphs are adapted from my study "Critical Editions and Performance."

4. The passage is in the Aria Manrico (N. 11) at 294; see also the critical commentary, 93 (note 70–72).

5. Crutchfield was responding to an article by John Rockwell that had recently attacked the stereotypical opera fan for glorifying "idiot sound."

6. I quote this interchange in the translation from Smith's *The Tenth Muse,* 162–63. Salieri's *divertimento teatrale* had its premiere at Vienna, in the Orangerie of Schönbrunn Palace, on 7 February 1786 on the same occasion as Mozart's *Der Schauspieldirektor.* For a full discussion of the opera, see Rice, *Antonio Salieri and Viennese Opera,* 376–84.

7. This incident is related in chapter 7 in the subsection "Practical conditions of modern performance."

8. For a precise timetable, see my introductory essay to the facsimile of Rossini's autograph manuscript, 16–19 (English), 68–72 (Italian).

9. For complete information about Rossini's self-borrowings in *La gazzetta,* see the introduction to the critical edition of the opera, xxix–xxxi. See also Marco Mauceri, "*La gazzetta* di Gioachino Rossini."

10. The story is derived from a 1763 play by Carlo Goldoni, written first as a bilingual comedy, *Les Deux Italiennes,* then rendered entirely into Italian as *Il matrimonio per concorso.* The work is most readily available in the 1999 edition by Fabiano (Goldoni, *Il matrimonio per concorso*).

11. For further information, see the commentary to the critical edition, 172–73 (note 190–268).

12. See, in particular, two pages in Bellini's hand reproduced in Pastura, *Bellini secondo la storia,* facing 385 and 400. I have discussed several sketches related to the duet for Elvira and Arturo in the last act of *I puritani* in "Verdi the Craftsman," 91–93.

13. See Della Seta's edition of Verdi, *La traviata: Schizzi e abbozzi autografi.*

14. Roger Parker first pointed out to me in private conversation that isolated textless sketches for some of these melodies are likely to precede the page that lays out the entire first act.

15. For a preliminary discussion, see Gossett, "La composizione di *Un ballo in maschera.*" The history will be discussed more fully in chapter 14.

16. The letter was first printed in Pascolato, "*Re Lear*" e "*Ballo in Maschera,*" 87–88. For a new, complete edition of the correspondence between Verdi and Somma, see *Carteggio Verdi–Somma,* where the letter is printed on 243–45. The second verse of the first stanza was originally "Al tocco delle tre."

17. See *Carteggio Verdi–Somma,* 246–48.

18. This is perfectly clear in the autograph manuscript, preserved in the Archives of Casa Ricordi, where the following pairs of measures were each originally a single measure: 469–470, 479–480, 499–500, and 555–556. See ff. 47v, 49, 50v, and 55.

19. Here, for example, is Giuseppe Radiciotti, Rossini's most important biographer, on the libretto of *La Cenerentola*: "*Cenerentola* is a realistic comedy, in which the laments of the poor, persecuted girl and the affections of the two lovers are suffocated in the midst of more or less insipid and vulgar buffoonery. Only the extraordinary genius of Rossini could make it possible to tolerate for so many years on the stages of the world such a miserable action, covering with vivacity and his exquisite spirit the triviality of those gags, filling with his inexhaustible melodic vein the emptiness in that unhappy drama" (*Gioacchino Rossini,* 1:277). For a quite different perspective, see the essays in Bini and Onorati, *Jacopo Ferretti e la cultura del suo tempo.* Compare also the extraordinary document containing Ferretti's response to his critics in Bini, "'Altro è l'Arcadia.'"

20. For the famous letter from Verdi to Brenna of 15 November 1843 about Piave's lack of experience as a librettist, see chapter 2, end of section "The librettist and *Le convenienze teatrali,*" and n. 24 of that chapter.

21. The example is featured in a famous essay by Luigi Dallapiccola, most easily available in English as "Words and Music in Italian Nineteenth-Century Opera," 195–96.

22. Weiss, "Sacred 'Bronzes,'" 49.

23. Hanslick, *On the Musically Beautiful,* 17. According to Hanslick, this observation was first made by a French contemporary of Gluck's, Pascal Boyé.

24. For further information, see Brauner's introduction to his critical edition of *Mosè in Egitto.* Two other studies comparing the Italian and French versions of this opera are Isotta, "Da Mosè a Moïse," and Conati, "Between Past and Future."

25. The example from *Mosè in Egitto* is taken from the critical edition; that from *Moïse* is derived from the original full score published in Paris by Troupenas.

26. After having taken a position strongly in favor of the *Mosè in Egitto* setting in his article "Da Mosè a Moïse," Isotta acknowledged in his "I diamanti della corona," 339–40, that both versions function well.

27. For a helpful introduction to Rossini's aesthetic views, consult Fabbri, "Rossini the Aesthetician."

28. *Lettere di G. Rossini,* ed. Mazzatinti, Manis, and Manis, 332.

29. I cite this essay after Zanolini, *Biografia del Maestro G. Rossini e Passeggiata del medesimo col Signor A. Zanolini di Bologna,* 21. See also Lippmann, "Sull'estetica di Rossini."

30. *Lettere di G. Rossini,* 202.

31. Ibid., 284–85.

32. The Metastasian verses are taken from his *Siroe, re di Persia,* first set to music in January 1726 by Leonardo Vinci. For further information, see the preface to Rossini, *Musique anodine, Album italiano,* ed. Tartak, xvii–xviii.

33. Émilien Pacini (1810–98) was the son of Antonio Pacini, one of Rossini's principal publishers in Paris. For information about Émilien, see Rossini, *Album français, Morceaux réservés,* ed. Dalmone, xxi–xxii. Several autograph manuscripts of poetic texts by Pacini, texts intended to be underlaid under music previously written by Rossini to other words, usually the Metastasian verses, are found in the collection of the Fondazione Rossini in Pesaro. They are discussed in ibid., 319–20.

34. Both versions of the piece are published in ibid., 27–37 and 145–55.

35. This phenomenon should not, however, be exaggerated. Many cities during the first half of the nineteenth century (including London, Paris, and Vienna) had specific theaters in which Italian operas were normally performed in Italian, with Italian singers, Italian composers in residence, and Italian or Italian-trained musical staffs.

36. Rousseau, *Lettre sur la musique française.* For a general treatment of the intellectual role of music in France during this period, see Verba, *Music and the French Enlightenment.* Rousseau's explicit criticism of French operatic style is discussed by Dill, in *Monstrous Opera,* 60–66.

37. The standard biography in English remains Warrack, *Carl Maria von Weber.* For Italian and German opera in Dresden, see his chapter 10. Italian perspectives are provided in Brumana and Ciliberti, *Francesco Morlacchi e la musica del suo tempo (1784–1841).*

38. See, for example, Taruskin, *Defining Russia Musically.*

39. See Dean and Knapp, *Handel's Operas,* esp. chapter 9, which treats the state of Italian opera in England before Handel's arrival in London late in 1710.

40. The nature and significance of the activity at the Odéon is thoroughly investigated in Everist, *Music Drama at the Paris Odéon 1824–1828.*

41. For an important set of essays on Wagnerism in Italy, see Rostirolla, *Wagner in Italia.* For Verdi's reactions to the first Italian performances of *Lohengrin* at the Teatro Comunale of Bologna in November 1870, see Phillips-Matz, *Verdi,* 583–86.

42. See Bartlet's introduction and commentary to her critical edition of *Guillaume Tell,* in which many of these issues are discussed. On the subject of early Italian performances of the opera, see Cametti, "Il *Guglielmo Tell* e le sue prime rappresentazioni in Italia."

43. Cattelan, "I libretti italiani." On the other hand, Bartlet is correct when she says that the Balocchi translation always bears in mind Rossini's music, whereas Bassi's seems to have been prepared without any thought for the original musical setting. Her discussion, with a complete edition of the Balocchi translation, is found as part of the critical edition, in the volume *Commento Critico: Testi*, 155–253. Some of the following discussion of the translation of *Guillaume Tell* is derived from Gossett, "Translations and Adaptations of Operatic texts."

44. The passage is from the Marche, Récitatif et Chœur (N. 3), mm. 118–133; see Rossini, *Guillaume Tell*, 276–79 in the critical edition and note 119–133 through note 133 (pp. 109–10) in the commentary.

45. I have discussed several examples throughout this book, including Donizetti's *Maria Stuarda*, Verdi's *Ernani*, *Stiffelio*, and *Rigoletto*. One of the most severe cases, Verdi's *Un ballo in maschera*, is treated in detail in chapter 14.

46. See the introduction to *Guillaume Tell*, xlvi–xlix. The music is edited as appendix 6 of the edition, 2025–50; see also the critical commentary to appendix 6, 320–24.

47. In the critical edition, see the Trio [Arnold—Guillaume—Walter] (N. 11). The passages are found on 672–77, 678–85, and 722–27.

48. Rossini's use throughout the opera of melodic lines deriving from Swiss popular traditions has long been noted. The most extensive analysis of this aspect of the score is by Straeten, *La mélodie populaire dans l'opéra "Guillaume Tell" de Rossini*.

49. In the critical edition, see the [Final 4ᵉ] (N. 19). The passage is found on 1473–83.

50. There is a considerable literature on the metrics of Italian and French libretto poetry from the nineteenth century, and in recent years a number of scholars have become interested in the problem. An excellent introduction is Fabbri, "Istituti metrici e formali." See also Lippmann, *Versificazione italiana e ritmo musicale*, and Giger, "The Triumph of Diversity."

51. A copy of the libretto of *L'assedio di Corinto* is found in the British Library, 11715.cc.10.

52. For some fascinating examples of contemporary efforts to introduce non-Italian metrical patterns so as to match the words more closely to previously composed music, see Della Seta, "Un aspetto della ricezione di Meyerbeer in Italia."

53. In the critical edition, see the [Récitatif et Romance Mathilde] (N. 9). The passage is found on 573–74.

54. In the critical edition, see the [Scène et Air Mathilde] (N. 13). The passage is found on 869–74.

55. In the critical edition, see the Duo [Mathilde–Arnold] (N. 10). The passage is found on 592–602.

56. Powers, "'. . .il vario metro dei versi francesi. . .'"; I want to thank Harold Powers for sharing with me a typescript of his essay, which was presented at a conference in Paris in 2000.

57. Unusual characteristics of the *Mefistofele* libretto are the subject of Ashbrook, "The *Mefistofele* Libretto as a Reform Text."

58. *La Favorite*, ed. Harris-Warrick. The standard Ricordi edition used until the publication of Harris-Warrick's edition in both full score and vocal score was a reprint of their late nineteenth-century standard edition, issued originally in 1879, with the plate number 46268 (357 pp.). Several music critics (especially Andrew Porter) have written often and with great clarity about these problems, but their observations have largely gone unheeded.

59. In his review of the first performance, Berlioz expressed great admiration for the libretto, which was devised by Alphonse Royer, Gustave Vaëz, and Eugène Scribe, although it comes as no surprise to learn that his admiration did not also extend to Donizetti's musical setting. See Glasow, "Berlioz on the Premiere of *La Favorite*": "I believe I have said, and I repeat (although my approval counts for naught) that I love this libretto very much, as much for the pathos that it offers as for the clarity and naturalness of the action" (37–38).

60. In conjunction with its publication of the new critical edition of *La Favorite* in French, Casa Ricordi also issued a vocal score (Milan, 1999) with an Italian translation prepared by Fausto Broussard, based on nineteenth-century translations, that of Jannetti and another that Calisto Bassi prepared for the Teatro alla Scala in 1843. Broussard intervenes in order to rectify most of these faults. See his discussion (lvii) of both the dramaturgical problems discussed thus far and the metric problems to be discussed below.

61. In the critical edition, see the [Final] (N. 15). The cabaletta is found on 735–45 in the full score and 355–58 in the vocal score.

62. If the opera is to be presented in Italian, Broussard's translation should certainly become the standard. Nonetheless there remain weaknesses even here, including the very phrase cited above, "Viens! je cède éperdu," for which he simply replicates the inadequate nineteenth-century Italian setting of the text.

63. The most useful summary remains that of Bini and Commons, *Le prime rappresentazioni delle opere di Donizetti nella stampa coeva,* 750–56. They also provide an extensive collection of early reviews (756–93). See also Ashbrook, *Donizetti and His Operas,* 436–40.

64. In the absence of either a reliable edition or an autograph (the location of Donizetti's own manuscript remains unknown), this transcription is derived from a vocal score published by Henry Lemoine (pl. no. 7969, 218 pp.). The Italian version is from the standard Ricordi vocal score (pl. no. 46263, 216 pp.).

65. One might find awkward the use of "à" on the downbeat of the second through fourth phrases and the downbeat position for "beaux" and "a-[mours]," but these details do not strike me as errors: surely Donizetti was fully aware that the second syllable of "amours" is accented. Rather, his decision to set the text in this way gives the melody its particular character and charm.

66. Zavadini, *Donizetti,* 518; the letter to Lucca is on 520–21.

67. This was almost certainly the composer Placido Mandanici, a friend of Donizetti's from at least the mid-1830s. His name figures frequently in the Donizetti correspondence (for a list of the letters in which he is mentioned, see Zavadini, *Donizetti,* 1003), especially in the composer's correspondence with Lucca. In a letter to his brother-in-law, Antonio Vasselli, of 16 February 1842, Donizetti describes Mandanici as a "man of very great learning" (Zavadini, *Donizetti,* 578).

68. Mila, *Giuseppe Verdi.* See also Budden, *The Operas of Verdi,* 2:167–242, as well as Giger, "The Triumph of Diversity." Although Giger is critical of Langford's "Poetic Prosody and Melodic Rhythm in *Les Vêpres siciliennes,*" the latter remains an essay well worth consulting. See also Toscani, "Verso francese e prosodia italiana."

69. *I copialettere,* 160–61.

70. Abbiati, *Giuseppe Verdi,* 2:297–98. (The epigraph at the beginning of chapter 11 is drawn from Abbiati 2:297.)

71. In the absence of a critical edition of *Les Vêpres siciliennes,* the examples from the French score are derived from the first edition of the vocal score, published in Paris by Léon Escudier in 1855 (pl. no. L.E. 1500 [L.E. 1501 for the ballet], 415 pp.). See Hopkinson, *A Bibliography of the Works of Giuseppe Verdi, 1813–1901,* 2:112–13, edition 56A (a).

72. In the following examples, the passages (including the words) are identical in the vocal score with Caimi's Italian text published in Paris by Léon Escudier, presumably in 1855, as *I vespri siciliani* (pl. no. L.E. 1583, 400 pp.), an edition not mentioned in Hopkinson (see 2:111–16), and the vocal score issued by Ricordi in 1856 as *Giovanna de Guzman* (pl. nos. 28116–28150, 482 pp.), Hopkinson 56B (a).

73. Nor is the sequence of syllables "[perder]-mi mi" particularly attractive. When working with his librettists during the original composition of an opera, this is precisely the kind of fault the composer rejected on countless occasions.

74. For a fascinating essay on Verdi's efforts to revise the words and music of an opera written in Italian for performances in French, see Lawton, "The Revision of Recitatives from *Il trovatore* to *Le Trouvère.*"

75. *Carteggio Verdi–Ricordi 1882–1885,* 72–73.

CHAPTER TWELVE

1. The Berlioz treatise can be consulted in a fine English translation: Macdonald, *Berlioz's Orchestration Treatise.* Macdonald lays out the history of the book in his preface (xiii–xxxii).

2. Franco Abbiati, author of a four-volume biography of Giuseppe Verdi in 1959 (frequently cited in this book), was for many years the principal music critic of the *Corriere della sera* in Milan.

3. The materials used in string construction changed significantly over the twentieth century. In particular, what had normally been an *a* or an *e* string on the violin made exclusively from gut was almost universally replaced with a steel string or a string with metal over a gut (or sometimes a nylon) core. The consequences for reliability and flexibility were positive, but there were also consequences for the nature of the sound.

4. These *farse,* whose premieres fall between 3 November 1810 and 27 January 1813, include *La cambiale di matrimonio, L'inganno felice, La scala di seta, L'occasione fa il ladro,* and *Il signor Bruschino.* For a discussion of stagings of *La scala di seta,* see the section "Rummaging in a trunk for *La scala di seta,*" in chapter 1.

5. The opera was issued by Disques Erato in Paris (0630-7579-2).

6. At the end of this chapter, I will consider the vexed question of which keyboard instrument is most appropriate to use for Rossini's operas.

7. Scaramelli, *Saggio sopra i doveri di un primo violino direttore d'orchestra.* I quote the passage after Meucci, "La trasformazione dell'orchestra in Italia al tempo di Rossini," 448.

8. Would that I had been there! I know the performance from a tape kindly sent me by the orchestra.

9. I have consulted clippings of those by Max Loppert in the *Financial Times* and Hilary Finch in the *London Times* (both published on 14 April 2001). Loppert wrote, "On Friday it burst over a packed QEH with the force of a thunder-clap; noisy cheering greeted several of the numbers and ovations the finale."

10. On the other hand, for practical reasons Biondi adopted four-string double basses, instead of the standard three-string instruments in use at La Scala in 1831. He told me that he had been unable to identify in Italy a sufficient number of adequate players of the three-string double bass (see the section "Double basses" later in this chapter).

11. Timpani from the first half of the nineteenth century, however, made available to composers and performers a more limited number of pitches than we are used to hearing with modern drums (see the section "Timpani" later in this chapter).

12. See Biondi, "Riflessioni interpretative su *Norma.*" Composers were expected to direct the first three performances from the cembalo (after which the job of coordinating orchestra and stage was left to the "violino principale," who played the violin and conducted simultaneously, just as Biondi did in Parma. There was no conductor in the modern sense in Italian theaters until after 1850, and even then the practice spread slowly. Composers may have accompanied the *secco* recitative when appropriate, but nowhere does anyone refer to them as playing during concerted music. If the performance got out of kilter, of course, they could have used the keyboard instrument to get back into gear, but that is merely speculation. As late as in the autograph manuscript of *Il bravo* (1840), Mercadante signals a cello solo by writing "violoncello al cembalo." He does not mean that there is a cembalo playing in an opera whose elaborate orchestral scoring would make such an addition absurd: he is merely using a conventional term to refer to the principal cellist in the orchestra. In personnel lists at major theaters, the term persisted even longer.

13. I have been assured that her nerves settled down in subsequent performances.

14. A critical edition, however, should offer alternatives in particularly problematic musical situations, as we shall see.

15. Berlioz describes both the three-string and four-string double bass, asserting that: "The three string bass is tuned in fifths, written *G—d—a*" (see Macdonald, *Berlioz's Orchestration Treatise,* p. 54). Later, however, he speaks of "English double basses" tuned to *A—d—g.* According to Macdonald (p. 55), Berlioz added "the sentence about English double basses [...] to the 1855 edition after visiting England several times." It seems as if Berlioz either did not know that the English were following Italian practice or chose to ignore it. The evidence from Verdi's *Il trovatore,* cited later in this chapter, leaves no doubt about the lowest string a composer expected to find on an Italian double bass at midcentury.

16. I am positing a uniform practice on the part of players within a single country, a single city, or a single opera house, but the reality is likely to have been much messier, with some players having different kinds of instruments within the same orchestra and some players employing nonstandard tunings. To the extent that there was a normative behavior, however, it is the one described here. There are occasional notes in double bass parts, where they are not doubling the violoncello, that extend below the normal compass: players took these in stride and modified their parts according to the practical limitations of their instruments.

17. See Rossini, *Duetto per Violoncello e Contrabasso,* ed. Slatford, an edition based on Rossini's autograph manuscript and instrumental parts in Dragonetti's hand.

18. See Rossini, *Sei sonate a quattro,* based on manuscript parts, authenticated by Rossini, conserved in Washington, at the Library of Congress. The history of the pieces is complex, however, and no one has sorted out the extensive evidence found in manuscript and printed materials of the period, both pertaining to the original scoring and to adaptations of that scoring for regular string quartet, wind ensemble, and so forth.

19. Such a *scordatura* among Italian sources, with the *A* tuned down to *G,* is mentioned in Rodney Slatford, "Double bass," in *Grove Music Online* (accessed 4 May 2004). A single *F* at m. 26 of the Andante, however, may well have been played an octave higher.

20. Contemporary sources, under censorial constraints, changed the first phrase to "Ma all'uom di santo zelo" (to the man of saintly zeal) and the second to "Rodolfo, ascoltatemi" (Rodolfo, listen to me). Both phrases were restored to their original form in Hansell's critical edition of the score (see Verdi, *Stiffelio,* 377–79, as well as notes 171–173 and 186–189 on pp. 145 and 146 of the commentary). The reconstruction of the score of *Stiffelio* has been described in chapter 5.

21. When the critical edition of *Stiffelio* was first rehearsed at the Metropolitan Opera in 1993, this passage created considerable consternation in the double bass section, since many of these very low notes can be played on the modern double bass, whose lowest normal string is tuned as *E* but which frequently has an extension string that extends the range as low as *C* or even B^1. Still, there is no reason to think that Verdi wanted these sonorities. Hansell's published critical edition therefore clarifies the matter by annotating the notes at mm. 170–188 "note effettivi" (sounding notes), returning to "note normali" (normal notes) at m. 189 (see pp. 377–79). As Hansell remarks, "It seems clear that he [Verdi] was notating the part at *sounding* pitch so as not to produce a notation in which the written notes for Vc are below those for Cb on a single staff" (commentary, 145).

22. See the Scena ed Aria Leonora (N. 12) in the critical edition of the opera, at m. 71 (p. 328 in the score); see also note 71 on p. 101 in the commentary. It cannot be excluded, of course, that some players had a four-string bass, even in Rome, in which case they would simply have played the part as written.

23. For some nice photographs of late eighteenth-century oboes, see the article "Oboe" by Philip Bate in Sadie, *The New Grove Dictionary of Music and Musicians,* 13:466–67. See also the

revised portion of the article "Oboe" by Geoffrey Burgess, concerning the nineteenth-century oboe, in *Grove Music Online* (accessed 4 May 2004). Burgess's assertion, however, that "the virtuoso solos in Rossini's operas—notably *La scala di seta* (1812) and *La gazza ladra* (1817)—were written for Baldassare Centroni (1784–1860), who for most of his career played a two-key oboe," cannot be sustained. Centroni lived and worked in Bologna, teaching ultimately at the Liceo Musicale, and there is no evidence that he was involved in performances either at the Teatro San Moisè of Venice (where *La scala di seta* had its premiere) or at the Teatro alla Scala of Milan (where *La gazza ladra* had its premiere). Nonetheless, Rossini was a close friend of Centroni's, and he wrote for the kind of instrument Centroni employed. Indeed, Centroni participated in the first Italian performance of the *Stabat Mater* in Bologna in 1842 (see *Lettere e documenti*, 3a:722n). The most recent study of the early oboe is Haynes, *The Eloquent Oboe*. The best general history remains Bate, *The Oboe*.

24. See Gossett, "Le sinfonie di Rossini," 13–30. The overture is printed in the critical edition of *Tancredi:* for the crescendo in the dominant, see pp. 14–18 (mm. 96–112); for that in the tonic, see pp. 21–23 (mm. 142–158).

25. Even Berlioz, writing several decades later and after significant improvements in the mechanisms introduced by nineteenth-century instrument makers, remarks that "the two highest notes, *e* and *f,* must be used with great caution" (Macdonald, *Berlioz's Orchestration Treatise,* 102). In later operas, Rossini does occasionally write *e‴* for oboe, but never when the pitch is exposed. For another excellent Rossinian example of an omitted *e‴*, see the Sinfonia of *Ermione,* at m. 204. For a similar example, in the same Sinfonia, where the flute avoids the high *b‴* in a musically unconvincing fashion, see mm. 130 and 138.

26. I quote from Norrington's essay, copyright 1988, in the booklet accompanying Symphonies 1 and 6 (EMI, CDC 7 49746 2), 4. I

27. Frequently the pitches were notated as *c* and *G,* i.e., "tonic" and "dominant," with the tuning specified in the margin, "in Fa," "in Re," etc. Donizetti used this system extensively, although Rossini mostly preferred to write sounding pitches in his scores, as did Verdi. In some early operas, however, such as *Ernani* (but not *Nabucco*), Verdi continued to use the older *c/G* notation.

28. For an extensive treatment of changes in the physical construction of the timpani during the nineteenth century in Italy, as well as the ways in which composers used them, see Meucci, "I timpani e gli strumenti a percussione nell'Ottocento italiano." A general discussion of the history of the timpani by James Blades and Edmund A. Bowles is found in their article "Timpani," in *Grove Music Online* (accessed 8 May 2004). Differences in size and material, of course, had a profound influence on pitch and resonance.

29. As Meucci demonstrates in "I timpani" (see p. 187), only after 1860 did timpanists in Italian orchestras adopt one of the various "machine" mechanisms for retuning the timpani, even though many timpanists were familiar with and had even experimented with innovations in this area.

30. See the discussion in Macdonald, *Berlioz's Orchestration Treatise,* 265–70.

31. In the article "Timpani" in *Grove Music Online,* some of the differences are described in the following terms: "Animal skin is particularly susceptible to humidity, a moisture-laden atmosphere causing the membrane to expand and consequently to produce flatter notes. Indeed, on a damp night high notes may be unobtainable, for the tension required to reach them may cause the skin to split. Conversely, a cold, dry atmosphere may cause the skin to shrink so much that high notes are sharp and low notes cannot be reached because there is no slack. Because of these problems many players using natural skins install heating or moisture-carrying units, fitted inside at the bottom of the kettles. Plastic heads have a different tone quality, with less resonance

and elasticity; notes produced on them have a faster decay and more sound, or noise, at low frequencies, thus producing uneven dynamics."

32. See, for example, m. 61, where after eleven measures of the transition in the exposition (50–60), during all of which there has been a tonic pedal on *d*, the chord changes momentarily to the dominant of *B minor*, *F♯* dominant seventh, a chord that has no room for either a *d* or an *A*. As a result, Rossini drops the timpani out for that one measure, having it return in m. 62, where it plays the third degree (*d*) of a *B minor* chord, hardly an ideal choice, but at least within the chord. This passage is on pp. 9–11 of the critical edition.

33. For the first statement, see the article "Timpani" by James Blades in Sadie, *The New Grove Dictionary*, 18:835; the revised opinion is found in the Bowles revision of the article in *Grove Music Online*. I want to acknowledge a number of very helpful conversations about modern practice with Richard Horowitz, who served for many years as principal timpanist at the Metropolitan Opera. Meucci, "I timpani" (249) reproduces a page from a marked timpani part for Verdi's *Otello* as adapted and performed by the timpanist at La Scala, David Searcy. For a Web page devoted to questions of this kind, consult *http://members.cox.net/datimp/*. I am grateful to Renato Meucci for bringing my attention to this page, which includes an analysis of some problematic moments in the Verdi *Messa da Requiem*.

34. See his introduction to the critical edition of *La traviata*, xl (English) and lxxiv (Italian).

35. For other Verdian examples, some in louder passages, some in softer ones, see Meucci, "I timpani," 200–202.

36. I have treated this example previously in "Rossini's *Ritornelli*."

37. See the provisional edition of Rossini, *La pietra del paragone*, ed. Brauner and Wiklund, Cavatina Clarice (N. 3), mm. 4–14; and the critical edition of *L'Italiana in Algeri*, ed. Corghi, Cavatina Lindoro (N. 2), mm. 1–9 (pp. 73–74). In example 12.3 I am printing these horn parts as Rossini wrote them, so that they seem to be in *C major*, and I refer to the pitches in that key; since the horn has an *E♭* crook, however, the notes sound a major sixth lower, in *E♭ major*.

38. See the critical edition of *Otello*, Scena e Duettino Desdemona–Emilia (N. 4), mm. 7–30 (pp. 248–52).

39. For an overview of this literature, see Morley-Pegge, *The French Horn*, and Fitzpatrick, *The Horn and Horn-playing and the Austro-Bohemian Tradition 1680–1830*. For a more general treatment of brass instruments, see Herbert and Wallace, *The Cambridge Companion to Brass Instruments*, especially chapters 8 ("The horn in the Baroque and Classical periods," by Thomas Hiebert) and 9 ("Design, technology and manufacture since 1800," by Thomas Myers).

40. See the Secondo Finale (N. 17) in the critical edition of *Tancredi*, mm. 101–105 (p. 598).

41. All pitches produced by acoustic instruments are complex sounds, containing not only the basic pitch, but to varying degrees other pitches in the overtone series. That is what gives these sounds their characteristic timbre.

42. Whether a conductor today should intervene simply to avoid overbalance of one pitch or another because of instrumental limitations in the nineteenth century is more controversial, but I am certainly not prepared to exclude it, so long as it is done with due caution.

43. The phrase is found in the critical edition of *L'occasione fa il ladro* (p. 123). There are similar phrases in many other Rossini operas, including *La scala di seta*, *Otello*, and *La Cenerentola*.

44. See the Recitativo e Terzetto (N. 7) in the critical edition of *Ernani*, mm. 336–340 and 344–348 (on pp. 241–2). There are similar passages in the Cavatina Elvira (N. 3), at mm. 122–128, 138–140, 157–159, 173–175, and 183–185 (pp. 75–84); in the Scena e Duetto, indi Terzetto (N. 4) at mm. 209, 217, 284, and 288 (pp. 116–17 and 126–27); in the Finale Primo (N. 5) at mm. 26, 34, 41, 151, 196–197, and 200–201 (pp. 132–34, 154, and 161–63); in the Recitativo e Terzetto (N. 7) at mm. 84–85, 88–89, 120–122, and 212–215 (pp. 206–7, 213, and 227); in the Scena ed Aria Carlo

(N. 8) at mm. 231, 234, 279, and 283 (pp. 272–73 and 279–80); and in the Scena e Terzetto Finale (N. 14) at mm. 26 and 271 (pp. 379 and 414).

45. See Macdonald, *Berlioz's Orchestration Treatise*, 167. Berlioz goes on to say that this pitch (and several others) "should never be used for filling in but only for the special effect of their harsh, muffled, savage sound" (170).

46. Ibid., 181, 182.

47. For a characteristic example, see the Introduzione (N. 1) to *Semiramide*, mm. 333–362 in the critical edition (pp. 171–85). In the accompaniment to Assur's solo "A que' detti, a quell'aspetto," Rossini wrote for pizzicato strings (violins, violoncellos, and double basses on the beat, violas off the beat). The off-beat violas are joined by chords in four-part harmony for two bassoons and two horns.

48. Recall Gianandrea Gavazzeni's response: "Nothing and nobody will ever convince me that Verdi intended in the first bar [of *Falstaff*] to differentiate, *f* from *ff*, instrumental sections and instruments belonging to the same section."

49. According to Meucci, "La trasformazione dell'orchestra," 451–57, the first musician to assume the role of "maestro concertatore e direttore dell'opera" was Alberto Mazzucato at the Teatro alla Scala in 1854, even before Angelo Mariani, whose influence was so great throughout the 1860s. For further information about the introduction of modern, baton-wielding conductors into Italian opera house, see Jensen, "The Emergence of the Modern Conductor in 19th-Century Italian Opera," and Chusid, "A Letter by the Composer about *Giovanna d'Arco* and Some Remarks on the Division of Musical Direction in Verdi's Day." For the earlier history of the practice in Paris, see Holoman, "The Emergence of the Orchestral Conductor in Paris in the 1830s."

50. Even today there are different instrumental preferences and performing styles between French orchestras, for example, and Viennese ones.

51. See Macdonald, *Berlioz's Orchestration Treatise*, p. 210. According to Berlioz (p. 212), even when composers used terms such as "alto trombone" or "bass trombone" in their scores, the parts were not only played by "tenor trombones," but were intended for those instruments, which were more agile than the old "bass trombones." According to Clifford Bevan, "The Low Brass," in Herbert and Wallace, *The Cambridge Companion to Brass Instruments* (p. 151), during Verdi's lifetime "it was Italian practice to use a section of three tenor trombones."

52. This is the case with the two Neapolitan operas, *Mosè in Egitto* and *Maometto II*, that Rossini adapted for Paris as *Moïse* and *Le Siège de Corinthe*. He did not include a fourth brass instrument in either of his other French operas, *Le Comte Ory* and *Guillaume Tell*, but he did require a serpentone in two further Neapolitan scores, *Armida* and *Ricciardo e Zoraide*. Helen Greenwald points out to me that in *Zelmira*, Rossini indicates "Tromboni e Serpan[tone]" in the list of instruments for one number, the Aria Antenore (N. 6), but writes no separate part for the instrument.

53. Meucci, in "Il cimbasso e gli strumenti affini nell'Ottocento italiano," refers to a place in *Il corsaro* where the term "bombardone" appears on an added leaf (f. 87), rather than "cimbasso." He neglects to point out, however, that this leaf is in a copyist's hand. See Verdi, *Il corsaro*, ed. Hudson, Note 58–66 to the Cavatina Gulnara (N. 6), pp. 46–48.

54. Thanks to Renato Meucci, real progress has been made. See his "Il cimbasso."

55. The letter to Ricordi is cited in part in Abbiati, *Giuseppe Verdi*, 3:525–26. This translation is taken from Busch, *Verdi's "Aida,"* 266–67.

56. Meucci, "Il cimbasso," 110–16.

57. See Simon Wills, "Brass in the Modern Orchestra" in Herbert and Wallace, *The Cambridge Companion to Brass Instruments*, 157–76 (esp. 175–76).

58. Bevan, in "The Low Brass," identifies the modern instrument with the Verdian bass trombone ("*trombone Verdi,* or late nineteenth-century *cimbasso*"), which "assumed a distinctive 'T'-shape, its mechanism and associated tubing positioned vertically and the bell facing forwards over the player's shoulder" (152).

59. Meucci, "Il cimbasso," 130–31.

60. Precisely the same question could be asked about the chorus.

61. The standard work on the subject remains Koury, *Orchestral Performance Practices in the Nineteenth Century.* Koury's scope, however, extends to all performance venues and all countries, so that he provides rather scanty information about the situation in Italian opera houses.

62. See the Finale Primo (N. 7) in the critical edition to *Tancredi,* mm. 10–30 (pp. 209–17).

63. Harwood, "Verdi's Reform of the Italian Opera Orchestra," cites considerable evidence that "Italian orchestras seemed to lack a sufficient number of strings, especially violas and cellos, but often had relatively large double bass sections" (109).

64. See the preface to the critical edition of *Guillaume Tell,* lix, as well as Note 1–48 in the commentary to the overture (p. 70). According to Harwood, "Verdi's Reform," 114, this was the size of the Parisian string section also in 1837 (Table 5); see also Koury, *Orchestral Performance Practices,* 157.

65. For some representative data, see Harwood, "Verdi's Reform," 109–12, Meucci, "La trasformazione dell'orchestra," 438–39; and Conati and Pavarani, *Orchestre in Emilia-Romagna nell'Ottocento e Novecento,* 33–35. More recent research into a number of Italian orchestras (including those of Parma, Trieste, Milan, Florence, and Naples) is reported in Piperno, "Le orchestre dei teatri d'opera italiani nell'Ottocento."

66. According to Bartlet (see *Guillaume Tell,* commentary to the overture, p. 70), Troupenas, Rossini's Parisian publisher, prepared a set of performance materials for a smaller ensemble than that of the Opéra, assigning the third and fourth solo violoncello parts to two solo violas.

67. There were probably not many viewers at all, since the film—which I caught in a Roman theater together with six other hardy souls—was never released in the United States. A pity: so many lovers of camp lost the opportunity to watch Elizabeth Taylor mouth the words of "Ritorna vincitor" from *Aida* as if she were speaking, while the lush sounds of Aprile Millo poured from the sound track.

68. Cametti, *Il teatro di Tordinona,* 2:588–96. In the last sentence, Muzio is presumably referring to Francesco Lamperti, an important musician and singing teacher in Milan, whose sons Giuseppe and Giovanni Battista were the impresarios for the 1886 and 1887 seasons at the Teatro Apollo. As Muzio says, Verdi would have been more hesitant about approaching the impresarios directly. There were indeed eight performances of *Don Carlo* at the Teatro Apollo, beginning on 26 April 1887.

69. Harwood, "Verdi's Reform," 129.

70. See the seating arrangement for the Teatro San Carlo of Naples in 1818, as printed in the *Allgemeine musikalische Zeitung,* reproduced in Harwood, "Verdi's Reform," 121, or the similar charts for the Teatro alla Scala from 1825, in Harwood, 122. These same charts are reproduced in Koury, *Orchestral Performance Practices,* 251 and 253.

71. The letter is given in Abbiati, *Giuseppe Verdi,* 3:262. I cite it after the translation in Harwood, "Verdi's Reform," 124.

72. Quoted in a slightly modified translation from Harwood, "Verdi's Reform," 124.

73. Gatti, *Il teatro alla Scala nella storia e nell'arte,* 1:237.

74. The production is described by the stage director, Gianfranco De Bosio, in his "Un'ipotesi di regia dell' 'Ernani,'" esp. 326. This production is described at greater length in chapter 13.

75. See *Lucia di Lammermoor,* ff. 151–177. The instrument is a more practical version, as first developed by Benjamin Franklin in the early 1760s, of traditional musical glasses.

76. Ashbrook, for example, does not mention it in his discussion of the opera in *Donizetti and His Operas,* 94–98 and 375–82; nor does Catherine Clément refer to it in her rapturous description of "The song of lunatic women" in her book *Opera, or The Undoing of Women,* 87–90.

77. Bini and Commons, *Le prime rappresentazioni delle opere di Donizetti nella stampa coeva,* 520–21.

78. Hadlock, "Sonorous Bodies," esp. 534.

79. Smart, "The Silencing of Lucia," 129n.

80. Sala, "Women Crazed by Love," 40 (n. 39).

81. They include a 1970 recording with Beverly Sills on ABC (ATS 200006-3) and the 1992–93 Metropolitan Opera production of *Lucia di Lammermoor,* as well as the recent staging at Covent Garden during the fall of 2003, under the direction of Evelino Pidò, with Andrea Rost in the title role.

82. The edition, being edited by Gabriele Dotto and Roger Parker, was first used for performances at Covent Garden in 2003. I wish to thank Mr. Dotto for sharing with me the fruits of the work on this edition, on which I have drawn for much of the following paragraph.

83. See *Il Teatro di San Carlo,* 2:245.

84. Occasionally one reads that Donizetti originally wrote this melody for a basset horn. See, for example, Zedda, "La strumentazione nell'opera teatrale di Donizetti," esp. 491. There is no such indication in the autograph manuscript of *Don Pasquale:* it is one of those urban legends that continue to weave themselves around Italian opera. Zedda also refers to the percussion instrument used in the act 3 serenata as "Tamburo basso," misreading Donizetti's "Tambours Basques" (see f. 192r), i.e., tambourines.

85. The passage appears on ff. 1–3 of the autograph manuscript of *Don Pasquale:* see the facsimile edition. I briefly discussed this example in the introductory essay to that facsimile, 48 (Italian) and 118–19 (English).

86. Problems associated with the natural horn have been discussed earlier in this chapter. See Macdonald, *Berlioz's Orchestration Treatise,* 164–68.

87. Bini and Commons, *Le prime rappresentazioni,* 1121; these quotations are found on 1099.

88. He did not bring his autograph manuscript with him to Vienna, but had it forwarded from Paris to Ricordi in Milan so that a vocal score could be prepared. As far as we know, he never came into contact with the manuscript again.

89. For a discussion of late eighteenth-century practice, with historical seating charts, see Koury, *Orchestral Performance Practices,* 31–35. An excellent diagram from the Teatro Regio of Turin is found in Galeazzi's *Elementi teorico-pratici di musica con un saggio sopra l'arte di suonare il violino.* Galeazzi's diagram has been widely reproduced, most conveniently in Sadie, *The New Grove Dictionary,* 13:686.

90. Prota-Giurleo, *La grande orchestra del R. Teatro San Carlo nel Settecento (da documenti inediti),* 27.

91. Meucci, "La trasformazione dell'orchestra," 443–51. The following paragraph draws on Meucci's research.

92. Although the list of orchestral personnel for the Teatro alla Scala for the carnival season 1845–46 (see Meucci, "La trasformazione dell'orchestra," 461–62), does not explicitly mention a keyboard player, there was indeed a very well-known "maestro al cembalo," composer, and teacher, Giacomo Panizza, who was a regular member of the theater orchestra during the early 1840s (see the commentary to *Nabucco,* 13). The indications in both the *Nabucco* libretto of 1842 and the 1845–46 personnel, identifying Vincenzo Merighi as "Primo Violoncello al Cembalo"

and Luigi Rossi as "Primo Contrabbasso al Cembalo," therefore, were not merely remnants of an earlier practice.

93. Cavicchi, "Per una nuova drammaturgia rossiniana," esp. 88.

94. Quoted in ibid., 90.

95. Quoted in ibid., 88.

96. See Grove, *A Dictionary of Music and Musicians.* In Sadie, *The New Grove Dictionary,* the example is found in the article on Robert Lindley by Lynda Lloyd Rees, 11:4; in *Grove Music Online,* see Lynda MacGregor and Christina Bashford: "Robert Lindley" (accessed 26 September 2004).

97. Let me thank Michael Steinberg, who was there, for that information.

98. Richard Burke kindly brought that recording to my attention.

CHAPTER THIRTEEN

1. Von Rhein's article was published in the *Chicago Tribune Magazine* of 5 September 2004. As he informed me privately, he had actually made "top 10" and "top 10 misses" lists, but only half of his choices made their way into the magazine. Still, the overall picture was unchanged. The only Italian opera among the original "top 10" was a *Lucia di Lammermoor* of 2004, notable—as von Rhein himself remarked—for the performance by Natalie Dessay in her first American Lucia. The totally conventional production by John Copley was—to my mind—otherwise dreary. Among von Rhein's original 10 misses there is a fourth Verdi opera (*La traviata*) and one by Puccini (*Tosca*).

2. Seven years later, when the opera had recovered enough finally to return to the Met, now in a conservative production by Nicolas Joël with sets by Ezio Frigerio, Peter G. Davis commented in *New York Magazine* on 4 January 1999: "I realize that the Met is probably still reeling from its last *Lucia* production, an experimental feminist interpretation by Francesca Zambello that went haywire somewhere along the line, but at least that misguided effort was not completely brainless." (I consulted Davis's review at http://www.newyorkmetro.com.)

3. Ross, "Verdi's Grip."

4. Petrobelli, "Response to David J. Levin," 486.

5. Rossini, *Lettere e documenti,* 3a:119. This letter is part of the recently recovered group of 250 autograph letters, almost all by Rossini and for the most part addressed to his mother, written between 1812 and 1829.

6. For an amusing report, see the notice by Jay McInerney in the *New Yorker* of 25 December 2000 / 1 January 2001, 60.

7. That Boito and Verdi conceived the scene in this way is clear both from Boito's letter of 17 June 1881 (see *Carteggio Verdi–Boito,* 1:51–57), together with which he sent the words of the scene to Verdi, and from the production book in which the actual staging of the 1887 premiere is recorded. The latter is reproduced in Hepokoski and Ferrero, *"Otello" di Giuseppe Verdi:* see 35 and 41–46 in the reproduction of the *Disposizione scenica.* For further observations about the significance of these published production books, see the sections "Staging manuals (*livrets de mise en scène*) in France" and "Staging manuals (*disposizione sceniche*) in Italy" later in this chapter.

8. Rosen and Porter, *Verdi's "Macbeth,"* 27.

9. For an evaluation of Verdi's indebtedness to the *boulevard* theater, see Sala, "Verdi e il teatro di boulevard parigino degli anni 1847–1849."

10. For information about the composition and original staging of the *Macbeth* ballet, see Jürgensen, *The Verdi Ballets,* 77–92 and the accompanying illustrations.

11. The poetry was the same in 1847, but Verdi's music for the earlier version was more in the style of his Risorgimental choruses from the 1840s.

12. The history and staging of *Un ballo in maschera* will be discussed further in chapter 14.

13. I was particularly disturbed by the practice of having women's voices join what Verdi intended to be a male chorus at the conclusion of the first scene. My remarks are printed as "Verdi's Ideas on Interpreting His Operas" in *Verdi 2001*.

14. A draft of the letter is included in *I copialettere*, 39.

15. The issue is raised by Parker, in his "Reading the 'Livrets' or the Chimera of 'Authentic' Staging," 345–47; see also Rosen, "On Staging that Matters." There have been important individual exceptions to this practice. The critical edition of *Guillaume Tell*, edited by Bartlet for the Fondazione Rossini, for example, includes in a separate volume an edition of the *mise en scène* prepared by Jacques Solomé, the *directeur de la scène* for the original 1829 production (see *Commento Critico: Testi*, 107–51). Four years later the Fondazione Rossini also published an iconographical volume, which provides ample documentation concerning the original staging of *Guillaume Tell* and its significance for the history of nineteenth-century French operatic practice: Bartlet, with Bucarelli, *Guillaume Tell di Gioachino Rossini*.

16. Volumes devoted to Boito's *Mefistofele* and Verdi's *Simon Boccanegra, Un ballo in maschera*, and *Otello* are in print.

17. In addition to the iconographical volume devoted to *Guillaume Tell*, cited in note 15, a full study of the iconographical sources for Rossini's *Otello* may be found in Scarton and Tosti-Croce, *Otello*.

18. Sutcliffe, *Believing in Opera*, 169.

19. Ibid., 330 and 353.

20. Hepokoski, "Staging Verdi's Operas." Hepokoski, who is no proponent of historical stagings, provides a strong statement of what he calls the "paradox" of stagings that seek to reproduce Verdi's own practice: "in restoring an original staging we do not so much 'see' the original work as experience a modern, historicized commentary on what has continued to extend into our own time" (19).

21. The classic treatment of the French *ballet de cour* is McGowan, *L'Art du ballet de cour en France*. The most important early example of the genre, the *Balet Comique de la Reine*, was presented on 15 October 1581 to commemorate the wedding of the sister of the Queen, Mademoiselle de Vaudemont, and the Duc de Joyeuse, a favorite of King Henri III (see McGowan, 42–43). The "livret" published in 1582 to commemorate this event has many illustrations, as well as the text and music of the spectacle. Clearly the publication was meant to celebrate the power and splendor of the court: there was no thought of reproducing the *Balet Comique* elsewhere. Likewise, no one would have considered reproducing the staging of Antonio Cesti's lavish *Il pomo d'oro*, commissioned by the Viennese imperial court, and first performed in 1668 to celebrate the Empress's birthday, with extravagant sets by Ludovico Burnacini, many of which were engraved by Matthäus Küsel and figure in early printed librettos. For further information, see Schmidt, "Antonio Cesti's *Il pomo d'oro*." The engravings are reproduced in Guido Adler's edition of those sections of the work known to survive at the end of the nineteenth century in *Denkmäler der Tonkunst in Österreich*, Jg. III/2 (vol. 6) and IV/2 (vol. 9) (Vienna, 1896–97). Schmidt subsequently discovered additional music. For a description of early librettos, see Schmidt, 401–2.

22. Although similar documents were earlier studied by theater historians such as Marie-Antoinette Allévy, in her *La mise en scène en France dans la première moitié du dix-neuvième siècle*, the first person to bring these sources to the attention of musicologists was H. Robert Cohen. See, in particular, his volume with Marie-Odile Gigou, *One Hundred Years of Operatic Staging in France*, as well as Cohen's *The Original Staging Manuals for Twelve Parisian Operatic Premières*, which includes the staging manuals for Verdi's *Les Vêpres siciliennes* and *Le Trouvère*. Also of importance is the article by Pendle and Wilkins, "Paradise Found."

23. See Bartlet, *Guillaume Tell di Gioachino Rossini*, 74–81, for information about Cicéri's Swiss travels in search of "vérité locale" (local truth) and several reproductions of the sketches he made.

24. In "Staging Verdi's Operas" (15–16), Hepokoski has pointed out that views of what constitutes *naturalezza* in stage action varied over the course of the nineteenth century, so that the term is by no means self-explanatory.

25. See *Commento Critico: Testi*, 110, in Bartlet's critical edition of *Guillaume Tell*; the *mise en scène* of Solomé follows on 117–51. The latter is also reproduced as appendix 2 of Bartlet, *Guillaume Tell di Gioachino Rossini*, 177–89.

26. *Indications Générales et observations pour la mise en scène de "La Muette de Portici"* (Paris, [1829]), which Cohen has described as "the first independently published operatic *livret scènique*": see his "A Survey of French Sources for the Staging of Verdi's Operas," 14n. For further commentary, consult Pendle and Wilkins, "Paradise Found," 184–90.

27. Cohen, *The Original Staging Manuals for Twelve Parisian Operatic Premières*, xxiii.

28. Cohen and Gigou, *One Hundred Years of Operatic Staging in France*, xliii.

29. I cite the translation, slightly edited, as in Jacobshagen "Staging at the Opéra-Comique in Nineteenth-Century Paris," 242. The matter is considered at length, but primarily with respect to German sources and stagings, in Langer, *Der Regisseur und die Aufzeichnungspraxis der Opernregie im 19. Jahrhundert*. See, however, his discussion of "Veröffentliche 'mises en scène' in Frankreich" (198–226) and "Gedruckte Inszenierungsanweisungen in Italien und Rußland" (274–90).

30. Jacobshagen, "Staging at the Opéra-Comique in Nineteenth-Century Paris," 259.

31. The history of stage direction in Italy is traced by Guccini in his essay "Direzione scenica e regia," revised and translated as "Directing Opera." I will cite the English version.

32. This review, from the Parisian *Moniteur*, is cited after Ferranti-Giulini, *Giuditta Pasta e i suoi tempi*, 54–55. Another reviewer comments, "When has Paris ever seen a lyric tragedy not only sung but acted with such profound sensibility, with such rapturous ardor?" (49).

33. See Guccini, "Directing Opera," 146.

34. Black, "Cammarano's Notes for the Staging of *Lucia di Lammermoor*"; see also his "Cammarano's Duties as Producer," chapter 15 of *The Italian Romantic Libretto*, 272–90.

35. Black, "Cammarano's Notes for the Staging of *Lucia di Lammermoor*," 36. The following quotations are from Black's translation, 36–38, slightly edited (the actual document is reproduced at 32–35).

36. Donizetti had an opportunity to work in the French system at the Opéra three times in the early 1840s, and *livrets de mise en scène* were published for *Les Martyrs*, *La Favorite*, and *Dom Sébastien*, not to mention the French *Lucie de Lammermoor* and the opéra-comique, *La Fille du régiment*. But the composer does not seem to have attempted to introduce the practice into Italy. In her critical edition of *La Favorite*, Harris-Warwick draws extensively on the *mise en scène* for her critical notes. See also Smith, "The *Livrets de Mise en Scène* for Donizetti's Parisian Operas," which concentrates particularly on *Les Martyrs*.

37. Although no printed *livret* for *Jérusalem* has been located, several manuscript versions exist: see Cohen, "A Survey of French Sources for the Staging of Verdi's Operas," 16, 26, and 32.

38. Kaufman, in his *Verdi and His Major Contemporaries*, points out that the opera was extremely popular in France and French-language theaters "but was a great rarity in its Italian translation, being unable to supplant the earlier *I Lombardi*" (361n).

39. According to Hopkinson, *A Bibliography of the Works of Giuseppe Verdi, 1813–1901*, 2:113–14, Ricordi first announced publication of the vocal score of *Giovanna de Guzman*, whose plate numbers extend from 28116 through 28150, on 20 January 1856. The plate number of the *disposizione scenica* (28556) therefore suggests a publication date several months later. See Peterseil,

"Die 'Disposizioni sceniche' des Verlags Ricordi," 150–55, where she provides a list of all the *disposizioni sceniche* published by Ricordi, with bibliographical information and the location of a surviving copy. It is surprising how many of the *disposizioni sceniche* announced in various Ricordi catalogues have not been located, among them—most surprisingly—the *disposizione scenica* for *Falstaff,* registered in the Ricordi ledgers on 25 July 1893 with the plate number 96585 (155). Some fifteen years ago I saw a catalogue card for this *Falstaff* volume in a Roman anti-quarian book dealer's shop off the Via della Scrofa, but the dealer was unable to produce the book or to give me further information about the source of his annotation. When I returned a few years later, still intrigued, he was gone, and the premises were occupied by a gadget store.

40. Abbiati, *Giuseppe Verdi,* 2:316.

41. For information about Cencetti, son of the publisher Giovanni Battista Cencetti, see Rosen and Pigozzi, *"Un ballo in maschera" di Giuseppe Verdi,* 21–23. According to Rosen (22–23), there is no evidence that Verdi actively participated in the preparation and publication of this *di-sposizione scenica,* although he certainly played a central role in the Roman staging of his opera.

42. No *disposizione scenica* seems to have been printed for the *Macbeth* revision for Paris of 1865 (and no Parisian *mise en scène* for this opera is listed in Cohen, "A Survey of French Sources for the Staging of Verdi's Operas"); nor—as we have seen—has a copy been located of the *Fal-staff* volume, supposedly published in 1893. For further details, see Peterseil, "Die 'Disposizioni sceniche' des Verlags Ricordi." The *disposizione scenica* for *Manon Lescaut* (1893) is the last of the Ricordi volumes in Italian known to survive. It is not clear why Ricordi decided to abandon these efforts.

43. The description is somewhat confused: the music for the dancers concludes *before* Riccardo sings "Ella è pura."

44. I cite the text after the facsimile of the *disposizione scenica* (59), published in Hepokoski and Viale Ferrero, *"Otello" di Giuseppe Verdi.* For the translation, I have adopted, with slight modifications, the text given by Hans Busch in his *Verdi's "Otello" and "Simon Boccanegra" (re-vised version) in Letters and Documents,* 2:560.

45. Ricordi makes this pronouncement on p. 7 of the *disposizione scenica* (see the facsimile edition cited above).

46. Hepokoski, "Staging Verdi's Operas," 13.; see also Parker, "Reading the 'Livrets,'" and Peterseil, "Die 'Disposizioni sceniche' des Verlags Ricordi."

47. See Pendle and Wilkins, "Paradise Found," 175–82.

48. See his letter to Antonio Dolci of 16 March 1835, in Zavadini, *Donizetti,* 369.

49. For the surviving iconographical evidence pertaining to operas written in 1828 and 1829, see Schneider and Wild, *"La Muette de Portici,"* and Bartlet, *Guillaume Tell di Gioachino Rossini.* There is a vast literature concerning sets and costumes for operas performed in Paris during the nineteenth century. Of great importance has been the work of Nicole Wild, in particular her *Dé-cors et costumes du XIXe siècle.* For reproductions of sets and costumes from the popular press, see Cohen, Lacroix, and Léveillé, *Les Gravures musicales dans l'Illustration, 1843–1899.* On Pari-sian opera in this period more generally, with important comments on the physical productions, see Gerhard, *The Urbanization of Opera.*

50. For information about nineteenth-century publications pertaining to Milanese theaters through the retirement of Sanquirico in 1832, see the chapter on "Scenografie nell'editoria teatrale" in Viale Ferrero, *La scenografia della Scala nell'età neoclassica,* 91–95. The most impor-tant publications to include reproductions of sets by Sanquirico are the engravings in *Raccolta di Scene Teatrali eseguite e disegnate dai più celebri Pittori Scenici in Milano* (Milan, c. 1824–29), ed. Santislao Stucchi; the engravings in *Raccolta di varie Decorazioni Sceniche inventate, ed eseguite da Alessandro Sanquirico Architetto* (Milan, c. 1824–32); and the lithographs in *Nuova raccolta di*

scene teatrali inventate dal celebre Sanquirico (Milan, 1827–32), ed. Giovanni Ricordi. All these sources are described in Viale Ferrero, "Per Rossini."

51. For information about how this effect was achieved in the Neapolitan performances, see Black, "The Eruption of Vesuvius in Pacini's *L'ultimo giorno di Pompei*."

52. Verdi claims this in his "Racconto autobiografico," in Pougin, *Giuseppe Verdi*, 40–47 (in particular 45), based on a text Verdi is supposed to have dictated to Giulio Ricordi on 19 October 1879. In it the composer puts the following words in the mouth of the Scala impresario, Bartolomeo Merelli: "I cannot have costumes or sets specially made for *Nabucco!*. . .and I'll have to patch up as best I can the most suitable material I find in the storeroom." See also Parker's introduction to his critical edition, xvii (English) and xxxvii (Italian).

53. The entire review is cited in the preface to the critical edition of *Tancredi*, xxiv–xxv.

54. The article from the *Gazzetta privilegiata di Venezia* of 6 February 1823 is cited in the preface to the critical edition, xlii.

55. Biggi, "Scenografie rossiniane di Giuseppe Borsato."

56. Povoledo, "Le prime esecuzioni delle opere di Rossini e la tradizione scenografica italiana del suo tempo," 293.

57. Biggi and Ferraro, *Rossini sulla scena dell'Ottocento.*.

58. There has been little work on stage design or scenography for either Bellini or Donizetti, but see Francesco Bellotto, "L'immaginario scenico di *Marino Faliero*." Bellotto also speaks about Donizetti's attitude toward staging in his "'Fa' le cose da pazza': Una lettera inedita di Gaetano Donizetti su *Lucrezia Borgia*," unpublished. Let me thank Dr. Bellotto for sharing this study with me.

59. Budden points out that "Rio Alto" is a "piece of pseudo-antiquarianism on Solera's part suggesting the origin of the Rialto" (*The Operas of Verdi*, 1:252n).

60. See Conati, *La bottega*, 159. Verdi's work with Bertoja is discussed by Baker in his article "Verdi's Operas and Giuseppe Bertoja's Designs at the Gran Teatro la Fenice, Venice," 225–28. The original stage designs of Bertoja for both these scenes from the Prologue, and related drawings and lithographs, are found in "*Sorgete! Ombre serene!*" 33–37. See also Muraro, "Nuovi significati delle scene dei Bertoja alla Fenice di Venezia."

61. See the letter from Emanuele Muzio to Antonio Barezzi of 17 July 1845 in Garibaldi, *Giuseppe Verdi nelle lettere di Emanuele Muzio*, 208–10. At that point Verdi had thought to include a similar sunrise in the opera preceding *Attila*, that is, *Alzira*.

62. *I copialettere*, 441.

63. The letter is cited in both Italian and English in Rosen and Porter, *Verdi's "Macbeth,"* 33; this translation is a slightly emended version. The great artist Francesco Hayez was a member of the supervisory committee to oversee set and costume design at the Teatro alla Scala. For further information about this committee, see Agosti and Ciapparelli, "La Commissione Artistica dell'Accademia di Brera e gli allestimenti verdiani alla Scala alla metà dell'Ottocento."

64. Rosen and Porter, *Verdi's "Macbeth,"* 67.

65. Letter of 11 March 1865, in ibid., 112.

66. For color reproductions of the Bertoja drawings, several later scenic designs, and two costume designs from the *Gazzetta musicale di Milano*, which published the designs in the issues of 3 November and 8 and 22 December, see "*Sorgete! Ombre serene!*" 40–49 and 153–54. For a consideration of the five *figurini*, and reduced reproductions of them all in black and white, see Rosen and Porter, *Verdi's " Macbeth,"* 413–20.

67. See Cohen, "*Macbeth* in Paris."

68. See Pigozzi, "Prampolini scenografo verdiano." His *Trovatore* set is beautifully reproduced in "*Sorgete! Ombre serene!*" 131. The revival of *Simon Boccanegra*, on which Prampolini

worked together with Girolamo Magnani (who was also responsible for sets for the revised version of the opera in 1881 at the Teatro alla Scala), is the subject of Conati, *Il "Simon Boccanegra" di Verdi a Reggio Emilia (1857)*. See also Conati and Grilli, *"Simon Boccanegra" di Giuseppe Verdi*.

69. See Grilli, *Filippo Peroni scenografo alla Scala (1849–1867)*. Important new information is provided by Jesurum, "Lo spazio del dramma."

70. Jesurum, "Lo spazio del dramma," 214. Peroni was known both for his *figurini* and his stage designs. Indeed, Verdi specifically asked that Peroni design the *figurini* for *Simon Boccanegra* in Reggio Emilia in 1857. Although he was not yet the head of the service, Peroni designed a set for the premiere of *Giovanna d'Arco* (see Jesurum, 219), at La Scala on 15 February 1845. Many of his set and costume designs are reproduced in Degrada, *Giuseppe Verdi*, passim.

71. See Metelitsa and Fedosova, "A.L. Roller, the First Scenographer of 'La forza del destino.'" Set designs of Roller's from *La forza del destino* (sometimes variant versions of the same scena) are reproduced in ibid., 107–8; additional designs are found in "*Sorgete! Ombre serene!*" 57–62.

72. Hepokoski, "Staging Verdi's Operas," 19. For a beautiful essay on this theme, with examples from both opera and theater, see Fenton, "The Cherry Orchard Has to Come Down."

73. Porter, "In Praise of the Pragmatic"; see also his *"La forza della ricerca."*

74. Carlo Ferrario worked as an assistant at the Teatro alla Scala in 1859, taking the place of Filippo Peroni as director of scenography in 1867 (see Jesurum, "Lo spazio del dramma," 215). In that capacity he designed the 1869 revival of *La forza del destino*. By 1871 his relations with La Scala had disintegrated. In a letter to Verdi of 23 May 1871, Ricordi informs the composer that "the management (which wants to stage *Aida* in the best possible way) has determined to change the scenic designer, replacing Ferrario with some better artist": see Busch, *Verdi's "Aida,"* 161. But Ferrario was again on the scene in 1886–88, preparing the sets for Verdi's *Otello*. His designs are printed in Bignami, *Cinquecento bozzetti di scenografia di Carlo Ferrario*. Several drawings for the 1869 *Forza* can be found in "*Sorgete! Ombre serene!*" 63–65. Verdi must have liked the *Forza* sets greatly, for he apparently wrote congratulating Ferrario, a letter the designer wanted to produce, but could not find, in 1886 when he was competing for an academic position (see Giulio Ricordi's letter to Verdi of 23 October 1886, in Busch, *Verdi's "Otello" and "Simon Boccanegra,"* 247). In the early 1980s the Verdi community did not know the original Roller sets for the St. Petersburg production.

75. I will have more to say on this point later in this chapter.

76. Porter, "In Praise of the Pragmatic," 24.

77. Ibid., 23.

78. Ibid., 24.

79. Ibid., 25.

80. De Bosio, "Un'ipotesi di regia dell' 'Ernani.'" In 1982 De Bosio had reconstructed for the Arena of Verona the production of *Aida* that opened the Arena's operatic programming in 1913, "constructing the entire production by rigorously following the *disposizione scenica* of Verdi and Ricordi" (324).

81. Messinis's article appeared in *Il gazzettino* of Venice on 14 December 1984.

82. Several accounts of nineteenth-century staging and set design in Italy discuss theatrical lighting. The most exhaustive treatment is Capra, "L'illuminazione sulla scena verdiana, ovvero L'arco voltaico non acceca la luna?"

83. See Baker, "Verdi's Operas and Giuseppe Bertoja's Designs at the Gran Teatro la Fenice, Venice," 219.

84. See Pendle and Wilkins, "Paradise Found," 199. (The first quotation is from an article of 25 March 1849 in *Le Ménestrel*.) For further information about the use of electricity for the sunrise in *Le Prophète*, see Gerhard, *The Urbanization of Opera*, 298–303.

85. According to Capra, "L'illuminazione sulla scena verdiana" (232), the Teatro alla Scala of Milan was the first theater to introduce electric lighting for an entire production, on 26 December 1883, when Meyerbeer's *La stella del nord* (*L'Étoile du Nord*) was produced.

86. *Carteggio Verdi–Ricordi 1882–1885,* 157. For some considerations as to how advantages in theatrical lighting affected the music of Puccini, see Greenwald, "Realism on the Opera Stage."

87. See Rosen and Porter, *Verdi's "Macbeth,"* 18–19. The phrase in Italian reads: "Dopo viene il Coro dei Sicarj, e qui va la scena assai avanti per prepare il Banchetto." The phrase "qui va la scena assai avanti" is slightly ambiguous: Does it refer to the temporal length of the scene or to the structure of the stage? In any event, if the banquet was to be prepared while the scene of the assassination was taking place, the latter had to be played on only the front part of the stage, using a "scena corta."

88. In Elizabethan theaters, of course, there was no "scenery" to change. Here, too, the nineteenth and early twentieth centuries imposed a system of formal sets that seriously misrepresented the rhythm of the original plays. That the original rhythm must be preserved, even in modern stagings, is now universally recognized.

89. *Carteggio Verdi–Somma,* 47–48.

90. Luciano Alberti, "'I progressi attuali [1872] del dramma musicale,'" 137. Andrew Porter makes a similar point in "In Praise of the Pragmatic," 25.

91. Another example is the first act of *Rigoletto,* so often played during the middle of the twentieth century as two acts, separating the "Introduzione" in the palace of the Duke of Mantua from the scene incorporating a street and the houses of Rigoletto on one side and Ceprano on the other. But the stage direction is clear: "the curtain is lowered for a moment [*un istante*] in order to change the set."

92. That was the reaction of the director/designer Pier Luigi Pizzi when I raised this issue in a symposium devoted to the staging of the Verdi operas, "Didascalie e immaginario, fedeltà e libertà," organized by Lorenzo Arruga in Prato on 31 March 2001, as part of the Verdi centennial celebrations. And it is certainly true that the many Pizzi productions I have enjoyed over the past twenty years at the Rossini Opera Festival, where he has been—in fact if not in name—a resident director/designer, have always been sensitive to this problem.

93. See Rosen and Pigozzi, *"Un ballo in maschera" di Giuseppe Verdi,* especially the "description of the scenes," 159–64.

94. Meanwhile, various small pieces of constructed scenery, all of which are behind the second backdrop, can also be removed: a fireplace, a portrait of Riccardo, a flat with a painted bookcase, and flats with door frames.

95. I report this incident after Mel Gussow, "Modify a Beckett Play? Enter, Loud Outrage," *New York Times,* 26 March 1994; the quotations are all derived from Gussow's article.

96. Zonca's article, entitled *"Luisa Miller* da scandalo," from which I quote, was published in *La repubblica* on 5 November 2001.

97. See the excellent essay by Savage, "The Staging of Opera," esp. 282.

98. For details and the relevant letters, see Chusid's introduction to his critical edition of *Rigoletto,* xvi–xvii (English) and xl–xlii (Italian).

99. For the composer's own work with this Italian translation of *Les Vêpres siciliennes* see chapter 11.

100. Letter from Somma to Verdi of 19 November 1857, *Carteggio Verdi–Somma,* 238–39; for Verdi's reply of 26 November 1857, see 243.

101. Abbiati, *Giuseppe Verdi,* 2:472.

102. *Carteggio Verdi–Somma,* 280.

103. The history of *Gustavo III* and *Un ballo in maschera* will be considered more fully in chapter 14.

104. I consulted this interview, "A Talk with Jonathan Miller," conducted by Shusha Guppy, in the online version of the *Paris Review* (no. 165, Spring 2003) at: http://www.parisreview.com/tpr165/miller1.html (accessed 13 October 2003).

105. I quote from Alden's article in the Lyric Opera program. This *Macbeth* was a coproduction with Houston Grand Opera.

106. For an overview and critique of the history I am summarizing here, see Savage, "The Staging of Opera"; Levin, "Reading a Staging/Staging a Reading"; and Guccini, "Directing Opera." Modern thinking about operatic staging is also influenced by late nineteenth-century and early twentieth-century innovators such as the Swiss Adolphe Appia, the German Max Reinhard, the British Gordon Craig, and the Russian Constantin Stanislavski.

107. Ashman, "Misinterpreting Verdian Dramaturgy."

108. Guccini, "Directing Opera," 160.

109. Ibid., 167.

110. Ibid. Guccini's essay was originally published in 1988, but the translation did not appear until 2002. Today he would have been able to choose from a much broader range of examples in Italian theaters, some of which have already been cited in this book.

111. Risi, "The Performativity of Operatic Performances as Academic Provocation," 489.

112. Weber, "Taking Place," 107; the subsequent quotations are found at 121–22 and 123–24.

113. Risi, "Shedding Light on the Audience," 208. He refers to the controversy between Said, "The Empire at Work: Verdi's *Aida*," and Robinson, "Is *Aida* an Orientalist Opera?"

114. I have taken this quotation, as well as the following one attributed to Francesca Zambello, from the article by Matthew Gurewitsch, "Poking Holes in Verdi to Let Audiences In" in the *New York Times*, 4 March 2001.

115. Levin, "Reading a Staging / Staging a Reading," 51–52.

CHAPTER FOURTEEN

1. The first performances, in January 2002 in Lyon (Dessay's native city), conducted by Evelino Pidò and featuring also Roberto Alagna, are preserved on a Virgin Classics recording, 45528. Donizetti himself prepared this French version of *Lucia di Lammermoor* for performances at the Théâtre de la Renaissance in Paris on 6 August 1839. It is different in many important respects from the Italian original.

2. I mentioned the Martina Franca *Otello* in chapter 7. For a careful assessment of the extent of Rossini's likely participation in *Ivanhoé*, see Everist, *Music Drama at the Paris Odéon 1824–1828*, 100–101 and 177–88. The composer *did* participate in part of the preparations, for he wrote a brief recitative intended for insertion into the opera (the autograph manuscript is in London, at the British Library, Add. Ms. 30,246, ff. 23–27), but the rest of the score was arranged and prepared by Antonio Pacini. Rossini certainly conversed with the librettist Gustave Vaëz and the composer Abraham-Louis Niedermeyer about transforming *La donna del lago* into *Robert Bruce*, a French opera for the Académie Royale de Musique, where it was first performed on 30 December 1846. The two Frenchmen visited Rossini in Bologna in July 1846, and he seems to have advised them about which pieces to incorporate, including pieces not only from *La donna del lago* but also from other operas. But he had absolutely nothing to do with the realization, which involves extensive rewriting of his original music.

3. See Lomnäs and Lomnäs, *Stiftelsen Musikkulturens främjande*, i and 18. They describe Nydahl as "the Swedish music lover, wine merchant, and officer."

4. See, among others, Budden, *The Operas of Verdi*, 2:361–76; Abbiati, *Verdi*, 2:447–529; Luzio, *Carteggi verdiani*, 1:219–75; Pascolato, *"Re Lear" e "Ballo in Maschera."* The most important source, however, is Ricciardi's 2004 edition of the correspondence between Verdi and his

librettist, *Carteggio Verdi–Somma*. I first formulated some of these ideas in "La composizione di *Un ballo in maschera.*"

5. As we saw in chapter 5, before the change in *Rigoletto* was introduced, Verdi had written out his continuity draft of the entire first act, and the new location required essentially no changes to the music. The names in the sketch were simply modified when the composer laid out his skeleton score: "Triboletto" became "Rigoletto," "Bianca" became "Gilda," and "Il Re si diverte" became "Il Duca si diverte."

6. For a complete transcription of this wonderful document (preserved in Rome, Biblioteca Corsiniana dell'Accademia nazionale dei Lincei, Arch. Linceo 90), see appendix 6 in *Carteggio Verdi–Somma*, 340–402 (the passage appears on 401). The manuscript is also analyzed, with several facsimiles, in Luzio, "Il libretto del *Ballo in maschera* massacrato dalla censura borbonica," *Carteggi verdiani*, 1:241–75.

7. This manuscript, which has never been transcribed for publication or reproduced in full, is preserved in the Archivio di Stato of Rome.

8. The compromise was explained to Verdi by his Roman friend Antonio Vasselli in a letter of 10 June, cited by Luzio, *Carteggi verdiani*, 4:141n.

9. See, for example, Roncaglia, "Riccardo o Gustavo III."

10. For a fine series of essays on the performing arts during and after Gustaf's reign, see Mattsson, *Gustavian Opera*.

11. Lindegren, *Maskeradbalen (Gustaf III)*.

12. See John, *A Masked Ball, Un ballo in maschera*. For the reference to Edward Dent, see p. 8.

13. I verified this in the recently issued DVD of a performance from 1991, conducted by James Levine, with Luciano Pavarotti, Leo Nucci, and Aprile Millo, ASIN: B00006CXFD.

14. See his letter to Somma of 26 November 1857, *Carteggio Verdi–Somma*, no. 69 (p. 243).

15. David Rosen, in the third chapter of his essay on the *Disposizione scenica* of *Ballo* (in Rosen and Pigozzi, *"Un ballo in maschera" di Giuseppe Verdi*, 46–53), makes a valiant effort to justify the Boston setting historically, but I do not find the argument convincing.

16. In some performances I have heard this as "Addio, diletto mia patria." For the Swedish setting, Verdi actually wrote, "Mia dolce patria, addio," and words and music fit beautifully together.

17. *Carteggio Verdi–Somma*, no. 49 (p. 184); future references will be in the text, as *CVS*.

18. I wish to thank Pierluigi Petrobelli, the director of the Istituto Nazionale di Studi Verdiani, and the Carrara-Verdi family for having made the sketches for *Un ballo in maschera* available to those of us working on the critical edition of the opera. The principal continuity draft includes text throughout, except in those places where the composer and the librettist had still not agreed on a final version; where isolated sketches are without text, they involve later revisions (in order to work out contrapuntal details, for example), rather than preliminary ideas.

19. Letter to Vincenzo Torelli in Naples of 26 December, printed in *I copialettere*, 564.

20. See Walker, "Lettere inedite," 285–86.

21. On 30 December, after Somma returned to Venice, Verdi asks for another stanza in the second-act finale (*CVS* 80, pp. 263–64): "I have already done the music, and preserve as much as you can that somewhat comic character." This is the first letter to Somma after the latter's departure. The continuity draft, in fact, has text everywhere *except* for this choral passage. Thus, Verdi's draft must have been prepared between 27 and 30 December. In that same letter of the 30th, Verdi tells Somma, "If you are not opposed, I would omit the allegro of that [Renato's] aria, 'Son dessi che debito.' The piece becomes long; the action is cold, and all those strophes are useless." Somma had conceived the aria in two principal parts, with a concluding cabaletta, but Verdi tells him for the first time on 30 December that he is omitting the cabaletta, a decision he

must have made *after* Somma's departure from Busseto. This act 3 aria, then, which exists in the continuity draft in a version very different from the "Eri tu" of *Ballo,* must have been sketched after 27 December. Since none of Verdi's observations in his letter of 30 December touch on the following *romanza* for Gustavo and the concluding *festa da ballo* (ball scene), he probably did not complete their continuity drafts until early January 1858.

22. Luzio, *Carteggi verdiani,* 1:49.

23. At least one fragmentary rejected page, however, survives from the skeleton score: it was auctioned at Sotheby's in London on 6 December 2002, as item 197. It is part of a passage from the trio, quartet, and quintet in act 3 that Verdi removed during his work on *Ballo* (the original ff. 260–261). This surviving page contains the reprise of the conspiracy tune with the addition of Amelia, a passage in which she originally sang "tre pugnali scintillano già" (three daggers are already gleaming), which in *Ballo* became "i lor ferri scintillano già" (their steels are already gleaming"). Apparently "ferri" were acceptable, but "pugnali" were not. As expected, the version of this skeleton-score fragment is essentially identical to what is in the continuity draft of *Una vendetta in dominò.*

24. This staging is mentioned in chapter 13.

25. Recall that there is a gap in the continuity draft within act 2: Verdi was working on this section of the opera during December 1857, before Somma came to Sant'Agata over Christmas to finalize the libretto as *Una vendetta in dominò.* Because the composer presumably felt that he needed to move cautiously during this period, the continuity draft includes neither the aria of Amelia, nor the duet for Amelia and Gustavo, nor the trio for Amelia, Gustavo, and Ankastrom.

26. There is good evidence within several surviving fragmentary sketches for this duet — as it was conceived for *Una vendetta in dominò* and within the definitive form of the piece from *Un ballo in maschera* — that its music was first written in skeleton score in different keys than in the final version. Verdi's decision to change these keys was probably the main reason why he substituted all the pages of the original skeleton score.

27. Notice that the sybil Ulrica in *Gustavo III* becomes "pallid" as she looks at the stars, whereas the black Ulrica in *Ballo* turns her "earth-colored face" to the stars.

28. Harold Powers described these measures in his article "*La dama velata.*" Because of disruptions in the structure of its autograph manuscript, Powers knew that the passage must have been revised by Verdi. Yet he could not determine the nature of the revisions because the continuity draft was not available and because he did not try to imagine the original structure of the autograph.

29. The entire scena and aria originally filled a fascicle of seven nested bifolios. When preparing *Un ballo in maschera,* Verdi snipped away the first five folios, leaving two nested bifolios and five single folios (ff. 152–160). He subsequently replaced the five canceled folios with five new nested bifolios (ff. 141–150) and a single folio (f. 151). The canceled measures appear at the beginning of f. 152.

30. This section is notated quite differently in the continuity draft and the autograph manuscript, although the sense is similar. But the change was made as Verdi prepared the skeleton score of *Una vendetta in domino,* and he did not alter it significantly for *Un ballo in maschera.*

31. See Salvatorelli, *Pensiero e azione del Risorgimento,* 151.

32. While the prelude was being played, workmen painted the mask an intense red against the largely blackened stage.

33. For an account of the rediscovery of this, Rossini's last Italian opera, written in 1825 and considered lost for 150 years, see chapter 5.

34. During the summer of 2004, Ronconi himself said to me in a private conversation that stagings have their natural life cycles, and that the effort to preserve them over an extended period of time is usually misguided.

35. See Johnson's preface to the critical edition of *Il viaggio a Reims,* xxviii–xxix. She first developed these ideas in her 1983 article, "A Lost Rossini Opera Recovered."

36. His wife and collaborator, Franca Rame, has set up an Internet "Archivio Franca Rame Dario Fo" (http://www.archivio.francarame.it), which presents an impressive number of documents pertaining to their life and work, artfully arranged and beautifully reproduced. The documents quoted in the following paragraphs are all taken from this Archivio.

37. I am translating from both the talk Fo actually delivered and from his original, longer statement: both are available in the Archivio Franca Rame Dario Fo.

38. *Grammelot* is Fo's "invented" language, with words that sound real and are spoken as if they were meaningful, but are actually nonsense syllables. Part of their "meaning," of course, is a function of the elaborate gestural vocabulary that Fo uses in his theater presentations.

39. On 9 January 2003, just a few weeks before the premiere of *Il viaggio a Reims* in Helsinki, Warren Hoge published an article in the *New York Times,* "Finland's Multitude of Maestros," that brought the country's efforts to the attention of American readers.

40. For full details, see the introduction to the critical edition of *La gazzetta,* xxxii–xxxiv and xliii–xlv.

41. See Fo, "Il teatro comico e la situazione."

42. See also chapter 8, in the section "Making cuts: Recitative."

43. See Johnson's preface to the critical edition of *Viaggio,* xlviii–xlix.

44. The painting is reproduced at the end of Janet Johnson's preface to the critical edition of *Viaggio,* lxv.

45. Let me thank my colleague Anne Walters Robertson for pointing this out; see her *Guillaume de Machaut and Rheims,* 246.

46. See *Opera News* 67, no. 8 (February 2003): 96.

GLOSSARY

ACCOMPANIED RECITATIVE   **Recitative** accompanied by the orchestra, without a keyboard player. In 1815 for Naples, following French practice, Rossini began to accompany his recitative in serious operas with a full complement of strings. Earlier he had used accompanied recitative only in **scenas**, more elaborate recitatives introducing arias or ensembles, often with wind instruments as well as strings. By the 1820s and 1830s, recitative in all but comic operas was accompanied by the orchestra. Among Verdi's works, only his youthful comic opera, *Un giorno di regno* (1840), uses *secco* recitative.

ACCOMPANIMENT   Music with a strong lyrical impulse is often thought of as being divided between a "melody" and an "accompaniment." The latter frequently uses standard devices, such as the **arpeggiation** of chords in the upper strings or favorite rhythmic patterns (Verdi favored a Polonaise rhythm). Italian opera composers were criticized for devoting too much attention to the melody, and insufficient attention to the accompaniment.

ALEXANDRINE   In French verse drama (Racine, Corneille), the alexandrine is the basic unit of verse, a twelve-syllable line with a caesura in the middle; there can be mute endings in both halves of each line. In Italian verse this would be the equivalent of *doppio settenario* (for a similar meter, see *quinari doppi*), a verse form found only rarely in opera librettos of this period.

ANTEFATTO   The action that has taken place before the beginning of an opera and must be understood if the dramaturgy of the opera as laid out in the libretto is to make sense. In published librettos, the *antefatto* is often printed at the opening of the volume.

APPOGGIATURA   When Italian composers in the first decade of the nineteenth century (extending a technique widespread in the eighteenth) set the last two syllables of a *verso piano* with two identical pitches, it was understood that the part would not actually be sung that way. Normally the first note, on the accented penultimate syllable, would be sung a step higher or—more rarely—a step lower; the second note, on the accented final syllable, would be sung as written.

ARIA   The generic name for a composition featuring a solo voice. Subcategories are **cavatina** or **rondò.** Although arias always feature a solo voice, many also employ the chorus or one or more **pertichini,** other characters who play a subsidiary role in the music of the aria.

ARIA DI BAULE   Literally a "trunk aria." Famous singers would have a group of favorite arias ready at hand to insert into operas when they felt their parts did not give sufficient scope to their art or that they lacked a sufficient number of solo compositions.

ARIA DI SORBETTO   A short solo composition sung by a secondary character (a *comprimario*). The name reflects the custom of selling and consuming ices in Italian theaters when the principal characters were offstage. Rossini often asked collaborators to take responsibility for composing *arie di sorbetto.*

ARPEGGIATION   The notes of a chord can be played together as a single sonority or they can be played successively, one at a time. Arpeggiation is the technique of developing an accompaniment from a series of chords whose notes are played successively.

ARTICULATION   Composers provide not only pitches and rhythms but also accents, slurs, and staccati, indicating to performers *how* they should interpret the pitches. The totality of such performance indications within a musical passage is known as the articulation of the passage.

AUTOGRAPH MANUSCRIPT   The manuscript of an opera primarily or entirely in the hand of its composer. Sometimes—within an autograph manuscript— passages of **recitative** (*secco* or accompanied) or entire individual pieces (often *arie di sorbetto*) by other musicians are preserved as composing scores. At other times, one or more pieces we believe to be the work of the primary composer are nonetheless preserved only in the hand of a copyist. We nonetheless continue to refer to the entire manuscript as representing the composer's autograph manuscript of the opera.

A VISTA   When a change of stage setting between one scene and another was meant to be done in full view of the audience, it was said to be a change *a vista.* The nineteenth-century system of painted backdrops and a limited number of three-dimensional elements made such rapid changes eminently feasible.

BALLATA   A simple, usually strophic song with a distinctly popular flavor. In the operas of Verdi, *ballate* are often embedded within larger scene complexes (such as Oscar's "Volta la terrea" in the introduction of *Un ballo in maschera*).

BANDA SUL PALCO "Stage band." Beginning in 1818, during Rossini's Neapolitan years, the composer developed the practice of bringing a fully costumed brass band on stage at certain points within an opera, generally to play music (marches, processions) actually heard by the protagonists. The band musicians were usually supplied by local military garrisons. As late as *Rigoletto* (1851), Verdi too employed a *banda sul palco*. Nowadays these bands are usually placed offstage, in the wings.

BEL CANTO "Beautiful singing." The term has many uses in modern parlance. It can refer, generically, to the style of operas written in the first decades of the nineteenth century by Rossini, Bellini, Donizetti, and their contemporaries. It can also refer to a style of singing that stresses vocal flexibility and beautiful sound, rather than dramatic declamation. It should be obvious, though, that the music of the *primo Ottocento* often has strong declamatory passages, whereas the music of Verdi is filled with *bel canto* passages.

BIFOLIO A single sheet of paper, folded in half, with a separate series of musical staves drawn on each of its four sides. Rossini, who did not prepare **continuity drafts,** normally constructed his autograph manuscripts as a series of bifolios; Verdi, who did prepare continuity drafts and hence knew the precise length of each piece before preparing his autograph manuscript, organized his manuscripts as a series of nested bifolios, one inside the other, known also as "fascicles" or **gatherings.**

BRINDISI Literally a toast, and that is how the term is used for the *brindisi* of Violetta (then Alfredo) in Verdi's *La traviata* and Lady in Verdi's *Macbeth*. Often the term simply signifies a drinking song.

CABALETTA The final, usually quicker section of a multipartite **aria** or ensemble. Through the first half of the nineteenth century, cabalettas were normally constructed with a theme, a brief transition, a repetition of the theme, and cadences. Rossini (and to a lesser extent Bellini and Donizetti) expected that the repetition would be ornamented by the singer.

CANTABILE A lyrical, slow section of a multipartite number. In an **aria,** the opening section is usually a cantabile; in a **duetto,** it is the second section that can be described as a cantabile, often with the two voices singing together in close harmony (thirds or sixths). More generally the term is used for any lyrical melodic line.

CARNIVAL SEASON The theatrical calendar in nineteenth-century Italy was divided into several seasons, dependent on the liturgical year. The most important was the season of carnival, which began on 26 December and continued through the beginning of Lent or even the beginning of Holy Week, depending on the city. Carnival 1818 is the season that began on 26 December 1817.

CAVATINA   In the nineteenth century, a cavatina is normally an entrance **aria** for a character who has not previously appeared on stage. The term does not refer to a specific musical form and is never used in the nineteenth century to stand for the first, lyrical section of a multipartite aria (the correct term is **cantabile**). Occasionally in the music of Rossini one finds remnants of an eighteenth-century usage, in which cavatina meant a short aria, in one section, normally found toward the end of an opera.

CAVATINE   A French term for the Italian **cavatina;** its meaning is the same.

CHOREGUS   The leader of the chorus, a term derived from ancient Greek drama.

COL BASSO   "With the bass." When orchestrating their scores, opera composers often used this phrase to instruct instruments such as the bassoons, cimbasso, violas, and violoncellos to play together with the double basses, thereby reinforcing the bass line.

COME SCRITTO   "As written." Some performers believe that they should follow strictly the indications of a written or printed score. In doing so, they fail to understand that implicit within a composer's notation are a series of conventions for interpreting that notation.

COME SOPRA   "As above." Composers in their **autograph manuscripts** (and, subsequently, scribes preparing copies) used this phrase to avoid writing out passages that were to be repeated without modifications. Instead, they specified that the music from point A to point B was to be repeated in full. In some cases the composer would write out the vocal lines and orchestral bass part, using *come sopra* to refer to the remainder of the orchestration.

CONCERTATORE   In the era before the introduction of formal conductors (during the 1850s), the *concertatore* was the musician principally responsible for the performance of an opera, almost always the first violinist of the orchestra. In the absence of the composer, he would direct rehearsals. At the performances themselves, he would give cues to other instrumentalists and singers and would lead by playing his violin from a specially marked part known as ***violino principale.***

CONTINUITY DRAFT   A compositional sketch that provides a continuous draft (usually the principal vocal lines, with their words and music, and hints of the **accompaniment**) for a single composition within an opera or for an entire opera. Verdi regularly used such drafts; earlier composers less so.

CONVENIENZE   The set of practices that determined the basic layout of an Italian opera early in the nineteenth century: the mix of musical numbers and **recitative,** the quantity of **arias** or **duets** and their ordering, the vocal ranges of the principal and secondary characters, and so on. These practices were satirized in operas such as Donizetti's *Le convenienze ed inconvenienze teatrali.*

COPISTERIA   Copyists of Italian operas preparing complete manuscripts and manuscript parts (for individual instruments and singers) worked in *copisterie,* sometimes independent businesses, sometimes associated directly with a theater. The Ricordi firm in Milan, founded by Giovanni Ricordi in 1808, was originally a *copisteria.*

CRESCENDO   A gradual increase in volume, indicated either by a musical sign or by the abbreviation *cresc.* The "Rossini crescendo" is a particular kind of crescendo, with a regular, repetitive phrase structure, the gradual addition of new instruments, an expansion of the register both upward and downward, and so on. Rossini regularly adopted his trademark crescendo within overtures.

CROOK   Natural horns were of a fixed length and hence could play only certain notes within a particular key. By inserting metal tubes of varying lengths (crooks) into the mechanism, it was possible to change the notes produced by the horns and adapt them for various keys. By instructing the players to change crooks, the composer ensured that the horns could play throughout a composition. As the nineteenth century unfolded, the addition of a series of valves allowed horns to play a much broader range of notes, rendering superfluous the system of crooks.

DA CAPO ARIA   An eighteenth-century **aria** form, in which the composer wrote a principal section (A) and a brief middle section to new poetry (B), then signaled a repeat of the entire principal section (A) *da capo* (from the top). In the eighteenth century, singers knew that in the reprise of a *da capo* aria they were expected to vary the notes of the melodic line.

DECASILLABO   A line of Italian verse with ten syllables as a ***verso piano,*** with accents usually on the third, sixth, and ninth syllables. It was frequently used by Verdi in his Risorgimento choruses (such as "Va pensiero sull'ale dorate") during the 1840s.

DÉCASYLLABE   A line of French verse with eleven syllables. French verse is parsed without counting the final syllable if it is mute.

DIMINUENDO   A gradual decrease in volume, indicated either by a musical sign or by the abbreviation *dim.*

DISPOSIZIONE SCENICA   A printed book providing information about how an opera was staged at its premiere, including sets and properties, the movements on stage of the principal characters and the chorus, and so on. It was intended to guide other performances of the work. Introduced into Italy by Verdi after his experience in Paris with *Les Vêpres siciliennes* (1855), *disposizioni sceniche* became more and more complex as the century progressed. By 1893 Ricordi stopped publishing them.

DIVERTISSEMENT French operas were constructed so that once or twice during the course of an evening the action would stop and an entertainment would be presented, including several contrasting dance movements, together with choruses. In some cases the *divertissement* is cleverly integrated into the plot (in the third act of *Guillaume Tell,* for example, Austrian soldiers compel Swiss maidens to dance with them); in others the dances are wholly decorative. When Verdi revised his *Macbeth* (1847) for Paris (1865), he was compelled to introduce a *divertissement* (the descent of Hecate in the third act).

DOMINANT A technical term in music theory meaning the fifth degree of the major or minor scale; the major chord constructed on that degree (or sometimes the seventh chord, when an additional note is added); or a tonality built on that degree, now serving as a new, temporary **tonic.**

DUETTINO A short duet, usually in a single section and entirely lyrical. Often duettinos have a special accompaniment. In *Zelmira* (1822), for example, Rossini wrote a duettino accompanied only by English horn and harp.

DUETTO A multipartite musical number featuring two singers. Already with Rossini, duets were usually constructed in four sections: an initial confrontation (known to contemporaries as the ***primo tempo***), a lyrical second section (**cantabile**), a transitional passage (***tempo di mezzo***), and a final quicker section (**cabaletta**). Verdi tended to abbreviate the opening section. His contemporary Abramo Basevi in 1859 referred to this abbreviated first section of a duet as a *tempo d'attacco,* probably a neologism.

ENDECASILLABO Line of Italian verse consisting of eleven syllables as a ***verso piano,*** with an accent on the tenth syllable. Librettists used *endecasillabi* largely in **versi sciolti;** the meter was not commonly employed for **versi lirici.**

EN TRAVESTI It was typical in Italian opera during the first decades of the nineteenth century for a female singer—usually a mezzo-soprano or a contralto—to sustain the role of a young, masculine hero, hence *en travesti,* or cross-dresssed. Parts such as Rossini's Tancredi or Arsace (in *Semiramide*) would have been sung by castratos during the eighteenth century. While widespread in Italy, the use of a hero *en travesti* was rejected in France.

FARSA, PL. FARSE For several small or regional opera houses (the Teatro San Moisè in Venice, the Teatro Nuovo in Naples), composers were frequently asked to write shorter, one-act operas, known as *farse.* Rossini wrote five *farse* for the San Moisè between 1810 and 1813; Donizetti prepared numerous *farse* for the Teatro Nuovo or Teatro del Fondo of Naples during the 1820s and 1830s. Unless recast as two-act operas, these *farse* rarely circulated in nineteenth-century Italy.

FIGURED BASS In a *secco* **recitative,** the bass line was marked with a series of numbers or symbols indicating the chords that were to be played. The keyboard player and the cellist were expected to improvise an **accompaniment** using those chords.

GATHERINGS   Verdi regularly constructed his **autograph manuscripts** as a series of nested **bifolios,** one inside the other, known also as "fascicles" or gatherings. Because Verdi frequently revisited his previously written operas, disturbances in the structure of the gatherings help us to understand where the composer made changes.

GRAN SCENA   A gran scena is an elaborate **aria** with many different, and contrasting, lyrical sections (as many as four or five), together with connecting passages. There is almost never more than one such piece in an opera. It generally falls within the second act and is given to the most important member of the cast. (Tancredi, Ermione, and Anna in *Maometto II* are all graced with pieces that can be described as gran scenas.)

GREEN ROOM   A backstage room in a theater, where performers can relax when they are neither on stage nor in their dressing rooms, where they can warm up, or where they can encounter guests.

HORNS, NATURAL AND MODERN   Natural horns are constructed of a single tube; in order to change the available pitches it is necessary to introduce **crooks** to change the length of the tube. Modern horns use valves to effect the same kinds of modifications in a much simpler way. Nonetheless the sound of a natural horn is quite different from the sound of a modern horn, so that gains on the one hand are compromised on the other.

IMPRESARIO   A key figure in the social system of Italian theaters during the first half of the nineteenth century, the impresario was expected to run the theater (managing its financial affairs, often with a subsidy from the government or the box holders), and choose the repertory and singers. The finest impresarios, Domenico Barbaja in Naples, Vienna, and Milan, and Alessandro Lanari in Florence, maintained their theaters both financially and artistically. In many cases, however, unsuccessful impresarios jumped ship, leaving the government or box holders with unpaid bills.

KEY   In tonal music, compositions are said to be "in a key," whether a major key (like *C major*) or a minor key (like *A minor*). The principal note of that scale or chord is known as the **tonic.** Composers use motion from one key to another as a way to underpin musically dramatic happenings. While in most circumstances the individual musical number is the unit within which composers control the sequence of keys, there are many examples in which composers employ keys to give musical shape to a sequence of numbers or even to an entire opera.

LARGO (OF A FINALE)   Most major ensembles, and particularly full-scale finales of the first act (for a two-act opera) or one of the internal acts (for operas in more than two acts), include a slow, lyric ensemble, often called generically a *largo*. Famous examples include "Freddo, ed immobile" from *Il barbiere di Siviglia* and the so-called Sextet from *Lucia di Lamermoor* ("Chi mi frena in tal momento"). Although Verdi often concluded finales without a final quicker movement (or **stretta**), he continued the practice of including a largo movement even in an opera as late as *Otello* (in the third of four acts).

LIBRETTO   The dramatic text of an opera, normally in verse. The word is also used to specify the printed text distributed for nineteenth-century performances and generally reflecting the words of the opera as they were sung in a particular group of performances.

LOGGIONE   Above the **palchi** in a theater was a section reserved for those of the most limited means, who would take seats in the upper reaches of the theater, where they could barely see what happened on stage. Most Italian opera companies continue to use theaters built in the nineteenth century (or rebuilt in the same mode), so that *loggioni* continue to exist.

LOGGIONISTI   The regular denizens of a **loggione** are known as *loggionisti*. They believe themselves to be the most knowledgeable part of the theatrical audience, and they have no compunction about making their opinions known vociferously during the course of a performance.

MAESTRO AL CEMBALO   In operas with **secco recitative**, the keyboard player who accompanies the **recitative** and realizes the **figured bass.** The composer himself was required to fulfill this function for three evenings when an opera had its premiere.

MANUSCRIPT COPY   Operas normally circulated not in printed editions of the orchestral score, but in manuscript copies prepared in local **copisterie.** Many serious problems associated with operatic scores made available by modern publishers reflect the derivation of these scores from indifferent manuscript copies of the period, rather than from the composer's own **autograph manuscripts.**

MESSA IN SCENA   The Italian translation of *mise-en-scène,* referring to the staging of an opera, including its physical production.

MISE-EN-SCÈNE   The French term refers to the broad range of issues involved in the staging of an opera: the sets, costumes, lighting, as well as the movements of the characters (the blocking) and of the chorus. The French began to publish this information already in the 1820s, in the *livrets de mise-en-scène,* with the aim of providing information about staging to provincial theaters and for future revivals.

MODULATE   When a composer actually moves from one **key** to another during a section of music, he is said to modulate from the first key to the second. The term is not used when one piece or section of a piece concludes in one key and the next one begins in a new key.

NOVENARIO A line of Italian verse with nine syllables as a *verso piano,* with an accent on the eighth syllable. It was not considered a grateful poetic meter and was rarely used by librettists during the period covered by this book.

NUMBER OPERA Most Italian operas in the first two-thirds of the nineteenth century were composed as a series of musical units, referred to as "numbers," often separated by **recitative.** The poetry of the musical numbers would be in *versi lirici;* the poetry of the recitative in *versi sciolti.* In their more adventurous moments, composers sought to create a more continuous dramaturgy, resulting in some of their most unusual forms (the *terzettone* in Rossini's *Maometto II* of 1820 or the two scenes in act 1 of Verdi's *Un ballo in maschera* of 1858).

OBLONG FORMAT Paper that is wider than it is tall is said to be in oblong format. (Paper taller than it is wide is said to be in **vertical format.**) Rossini, Bellini, and Donizetti generally used paper in oblong format. Although more measures could fit on each page, fewer staves were available.

OCTOSYLLABE A line of French verse with nine syllables. French verse is parsed without counting the final syllable if it is mute. This verse form, common in French opera, was the equivalent of the Italian *novenario.*

OLTREMONTANE A term used by Italians to refer to a person from the other side of the mountains (the Alps or Dolomites), hence a foreigner. Artists from abroad, such as Wagner, whose music introduced new tendencies into Italian opera, were frequently referred to as *oltremontani.*

OPERA BUFFA Comic opera. The term is carried over from eighteenth-century practice. Rossini and Donizetti still composed a considerable number of comic operas, but this kind of opera was losing its hold on the public. After *Un giorno di regno* (1840), Verdi did not compose another entirely comic opera until *Falstaff* (1893), although many of his operas have individual comic scenes.

OPERA SEMISERIA A sentimental opera, which seems to be moving toward a tragic ending but which, often at the last moment, ends happily. Many signals, including the frequent presence of one or more *buffo* characters (such as the poet Isidoro in Rossini's *Matilde di Shabran*), suggest that these works are not to be read as tragic.

OPERA SERIA The eighteenth-century term *opera seria,* which normally refers to a certain kind of dramatic action associated with the **librettos** of Pietro Metastasio, is not altogether appropriate for the Romantic melodrama that dominated Italian theaters after the 1820s. Still, it was widely used at the time, and this book does not refrain from adopting it.

ORCHESTRAL SCORE   A printed edition of an opera that contains not just the vocal lines, but all the orchestral parts in full. Conductors today direct operas from orchestral scores, and musicians study them in that format when such scores are available. Critical editions are always printed as orchestral scores, from which can be derived reductions for piano and voices (**vocal scores**).

ORNAMENTATION   Composers throughout the first three decades of the nineteenth century—and, in some cases, beyond—expected singers to add ornamentation, variations, **appoggiaturas,** cadenzas, to the music the composers had written down. In that sense, the performance of an Italian opera became a collaboration between a composer and his performers. Providing tasteful and appropriate ornamentation, however, requires a thorough understanding of contemporary practice.

OTTONARIO   A line of Italian verse with eight syllables as a ***verso piano,*** with an accent on the seventh syllable.

PALCHI   In a standard nineteenth-century Italian theater, several rows of boxes, or *palchi,* in a horseshoe shape, surrounded the ***platea.*** The *palchi* were often owned by the nobility or by wealthy families. In many theaters box holders were financially responsible for theatrical activities. Some used their *palchi* not only to follow operatic performances, but also as a site for social interaction. In many cities, curtains could be drawn to ensure privacy.

PARLANTE   Sections of the vocal line, particularly in comic opera, were often performed by declaiming on a single pitch, giving the effect of speaking in rhythm, hence the term *parlante* from *parlare* (to speak).

PARTICELLA   In order to begin rehearsing a new opera, composers allowed vocal parts or *particelle* to be copied from their **skeleton scores,** even before they orchestrated an opera. These manuscripts, which were given to singers as soon as possible, included the complete vocal lines for that singer, indications of what other singers might be performing, and the instrumental bass line.

PERTICHINO   Within an **aria** for one character or a **duet** between two characters, the dramatic situation sometimes required the presence of one or more additional singers, known as *pertichini.* They were not necessarily secondary characters. In *La sonnambula,* Elvino's **cavatina,** or entrance **aria,** features a lengthy part for the prima donna, Amina, as a *pertichino.*

PLATEA   In an Italian theater of the Ottocento, the *platea* is the area in front of the stage, on the same level as the orchestral players. Merchant classes, military personnel, and students would take their places in the *platea,* sometimes in individual seats, sometimes on benches, sometimes on foot: practices changed over time and from city to city.

PRATICABILI   Functional three-dimensional pieces of scenery (such as a staircase), on which actors could walk. They are to be distinguished from **stabili** (such as the representation of a massive piece of furniture), which were not intended to be walked upon by the actors.

PRIMO OTTOCENTO   The period from about 1800 to 1840 in Italy, that is, before the advent of Verdi. When **bel canto** is used to describe a historical period, it tends to be equivalent to *primo Ottocento.*

PRIMO TEMPO   The first section of a standard four-part **duetto.** In Rossini, Bellini, and Donizetti the *primo tempo* consisted almost always of an elaborate confrontation between the two characters. Verdi often used a similar design, but there are also examples where he abbreviated this section to lead more directly to the second movement, the lyrical **cantabile.**

PSEUDO-CANON   In constructing the **cantabile** movement of an ensemble, Rossini often employed a canonic structure. In a trio, for example, one character would sing a melody, which would pass to a second character and then to a third, while counterpoints would be developed for the other characters. Thus:

A   B   C

A   B

A

Cadences involving all three singers would bring the cantabile to a close.

PUNTATURE   Small adjustments made to a melodic line. They accommodate places where a specific voice is unable momentarily to cope with the requirements of the music, because the music is especially high, low, or florid, because it demands great breath control, and so on. Singers should avoid parts that they cannot perform without a large number of *puntature.*

QUINARIO   A line of Italian verse with five syllables as a **verso piano,** with an accent on the fourth syllable.

QUINARIO DOPPIO   A line of Italian verse consisting of two consecutive **quinari.** In each half of the verse there are accents on the fourth syllable. Since each half is parsed independently, a verse in *quinari doppi* can have as many as twelve syllables (two *quinari sdruccioli*) or as few as eight (two *quinari tronchi*).

RADICAL STAGING   A staging in which the director does not seek to tell the story as set forth in the **libretto,** but rather uses elements of the opera to inspire a parallel action on stage, one that can be said to comment critically on the original libretto.

RANZ DES VACHES   Traditional Swiss melodies, associated with the care of animals, in particular cows. Rossini quoted and developed many such melodies in his *Guillaume Tell.*

RECITATIVE   Italian opera was divided into musical numbers and intervening recitative, the latter almost always constructed of *versi sciolti* ("heroic verse"), a free mixture of *settenari* and *endecasillabi.* When accompanied by a keyboard instrument, violoncello, and double bass, the recitative was called *secco;* when joined by the orchestra (whether strings alone or a fuller orchestra), without a keyboard instrument, the recitative was called **accompanied.**

ROMANZA   The Italian *romanza* is derived from the French *romance.* It is normally a strophic, sentimental song in a serious style (not the more lighthearted style of the *ballata*). Famous examples are the two *romanze* for Violetta in *La traviata* ("Ah! fors'è lui" and "Addio al passato") and the *romanza* for Nemorino in *L'elisir d'amore* ("Una furtiva lagrime"). Sometimes the *romanza* is used to refer to a Parisian setting or ambience.

RONDÒ   The concluding **aria** of an opera from the *primo Ottocento* was frequently referred to as a *rondò.* The term could refer to the specific structure of the final section (a kind of **cabaletta,** but whose theme recurs three times, with elaborate variations written out in full by the composer). Often, though, the final section is a normal cabaletta, so that the term does not have specific structural implications.

SCENA   When an elaborate **accompanied recitative,** often with an extended orchestral introduction, precedes an **aria,** it is referred to as a scena. Many of Rossini's most famous **cavatinas** include scenas (Tancredi's cavatina is preceded by the scena "Oh patria!"; Malcom's cavatina in *La donna del lago* is preceded by the scena "Mura felici"; Arsace's cavatina in *Semiramide* is preceded by the scena "Eccomi alfine in Babilonia"). The term was also used simply to mean accompanied recitative.

SCORDATURA   String instruments were sometimes tuned in unconventional ways to accommodate notes that would not otherwise have been possible. In the *Miserere* movement, the *tempo di mezzo* of the **aria** for Leonora in act 4 of *Il trovatore,* for example, the double basses are instructed to tune their lower string (*A*) down a half tone to A♭. Unconventional tunings of this kind are referred to as *scordatura.*

SECCO RECITATIVE   **Recitative** sung with the **accompaniment** of a keyboard instrument improvising chords over a written bass line (**figured bass**). A violoncello and double bass also play the bass line. The violoncello was free to arpeggiate chords or to join the musical and dramaturgical discourse; the double bass was expected to sustain the bass notes. In *opera seria* during the 1820s, in *opera semiseria* and *opera buffa* during the 1830s, *secco* recitative was everywhere replaced by **accompanied recitative.**

SELVA   In the nineteenth century, the rough draft of a **libretto,** sometimes prepared by a librettist, sometimes by the composer himself (especially in the case of Verdi). It laid out the division into **recitative** and musical numbers, provided prose renderings of the text to be versified, and specified the meters to be used for *versi lirici* in the musical numbers.

SENARIO   A line of Italian verse with six syllables as a *verso piano,* with an accent on the fifth syllable.

SETTENARIO   A line of Italian verse with seven syllables as a *verso piano,* with an accent on the sixth syllable. Librettists used *settenari* in both *versi lirici* and *versi sciolti.*

SINFONIA   The Italian word for overture. During the first part of his career Rossini wrote standard overture forms, with a slow introduction and a sonata-form allegro (usually without a development section); later he experimented with other models or eliminated the sinfonia altogether. Later composers followed his lead, but also developed potpourri overtures (as in Bellini's *Norma*). While Verdi wrote relatively few overtures, preferring brief orchestral preludes, there are some first-rate examples of more elaborate overtures, such as the 1869 sinfonia to *La forza del destino.*

SKELETON SCORE   Composers would begin laying out their **autograph manuscripts** by writing the vocal lines and the bass, entering also an occasional instrumental solo. In this form the skeleton score could be given to copyists to prepare vocal parts. Afterwards the **autograph manuscript** was returned to the composer, who would fill in the flesh around the skeleton he had earlier notated.

SOTTOVOCE   A performance instruction telling the singers or instrumentalists to play a passage as if whispering it, very softly.

SPARTITINO   When composers were unable to fit all the instrumental parts needed for a large ensemble into the main section of an **autograph manuscript,** they would add a *spartitino* to accommodate the parts that did not fit into the main section. With autograph manuscripts written on **oblong paper,** *spartitini* were more prevalent; with those written on **vertical paper,** fewer were necessary.

STABILI   Decorative three-dimensional pieces of scenery (such as the representation of a massive piece of furniture), which were not intended to be walked upon by the actors. They are to be distinguished from *praticabili* (such as a staircase), upon which actors could walk.

STRETTA   The concluding section of a multipartite ensemble or finale was often known as a stretta. Structurally the section normally had the same design as a **cabaletta.**

STROPHIC   When the same music is used for a series of different poetic stanzas, the piece is called strophic. Strophic compositions are more frequent in German *Lieder* or French *romances* than in operas, but the compositional types known as *ballate* and *romanze* are basically strophic forms.

TEMPO DI MEZZO   The section in nineteenth-century operatic forms that follows the **cantabile** and prepares the **cabaletta,** either in multipartite **arias** or ensembles, was known as a *tempo di mezzo* (middle section). It was normally constructed quite freely, even though the poetry generally continued to be built out of ***versi lirici.*** During the *tempo di mezzo* some event usually occurs that justifies the change of mood represented by the cabaletta.

TERZETTONE   A very long, complicated trio. Rossini used the term to refer to a particularly extended trio in his 1820 opera *Maometto II.*

TESSITURA   The effective range of a singer is known as that singer's tessitura; similarly, in describing the kind of voice needed to sing a particular operatic role, one frequently refers to the role's tessitura. This is not merely a matter of the highest and lowest notes, but rather reflects where the voice sits, how it moves from one register to another, and so on.

TONIC   The principal note of a scale or chord. See also **key.**

VERSO PIANO   In Italian poetry, a *verso piano* is one that concludes with a feminine ending, so that the accent is on the penultimate syllable. Verse in Italian is measured on the basis of *versi piani.* Hence, a *verso piano* in **settenario** has seven syllables, with the accent on the sixth syllable.

VERSO SDRUCCIOLO   In Italian poetry, a *verso sdrucciolo* is one that concludes with an accent on the antepenultimate syllable (like "Pé-sa-ro," "rá-pi-do," or even "sdrúc-cio-lo"). Verse in Italian is measured on the basis of ***versi piani.*** Hence, a *verso sdrucciolo* in **settenario** has eight syllables with the accent on the sixth syllable.

VERSO TRONCO   In Italian poetry, a *verso tronco* is one that concludes with a masculine ending, so that the accent is on the final syllable. Verse in Italian is measured on the basis of ***versi piani.*** Hence, a *verso tronco* in **settenario** has six syllables with the accent on the sixth syllable.

VERSI LIRICI   The words for sections within a musical number are generally written in a single poetic meter, with several lines of poetry (one or two quatrains, for example) and a regular rhyme scheme. This poetry is referred to as *versi lirici.* For a multipartite composition the librettist and composer could achieve variety by changing the poetic meter from section to section.

VERSI SCIOLTI   A combination of ***settenari*** and ***endecasillabi*** with occasional rhymes. Italian librettists used it for verses of **recitative.** This type of verse alternated with ***versi lirici*** for musical numbers.

VERTICAL FORMAT   Paper that is taller than it is wide is said to be in vertical format. (Paper wider than it is tall is said to be in **oblong format.**) Verdi generally used paper in vertical format. Although fewer measures could fit on each page, more staves were available.

VIOLINO PRINCIPALE When the first violinist of the orchestra directed the performance, he normally played from a part (manuscript or printed) identified as the *violino principale*. This part contains the entire first violin line, as well as important instrumental cues for other instruments and the text, together with indications of the vocal line. From this material, the director could set tempos, cue important solos, and follow closely the interaction between the orchestra and the singers.

VIRGOLETTI Quotation marks (or *virgoletti*) in printed **librettos** signal lines of poetry not set to music by the composer or cut in a particular production. Thus, even if an opera were abbreviated in performance, audiences could follow the drama by reading the entire libretto.

VOCAL SCORE When operas were printed, they generally included all vocal lines and a reduction for piano of the orchestral fabric. Even today, singers learn their parts and music students study operas largely from vocal scores. Often full **orchestral scores** have never been printed.

NOTE RANGES

Throughout this book, I have largely avoided referring to exact pitch levels for "high *c*" or similar notes. When, in the chapters on transposition and instrumentation, I have needed to be more precise, the following equivalents are used:

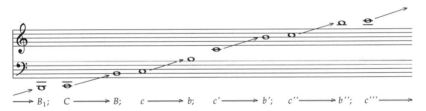

BIBLIOGRAPHY

Abbate, Carolyn. "Wagner, 'On Modulation,' and *Tristan*." *Cambridge Opera Journal* 1 (1989): 33–58.

Abbate, Carolyn, and Roger Parker, eds. *Analyzing Opera: Verdi and Wagner*. Berkeley, 1989.

Abbiati, Franco. *Giuseppe Verdi*. 4 vols. Milan, 1959.

Adamo, Maria Rosaria, and Friedrich Lippmann. *Vincenzo Bellini*. Turin, 1981.

Agosti, Giacomo, and Pierluigi Ciapparelli. "La Commissione Artistica dell'Accademia di Brera e gli allestimenti verdiani alla Scala alla metà dell'Ottocento." In Petrobelli and Della Seta, *La realizzazione scenica dello spettacolo verdiano*, 215–29.

Alberti, Annibale. *Verdi intimo: Carteggio di Giuseppe Verdi con il Conte Opprandino Arrivabene [1861–1886]*. Verona, 1941.

Alberti, Luciano. "'I progressi attuali [1872] del dramma musicale': Note sulla *Disposizione scenica per l'opera 'Aida' compilata e regolata secondo la messa in scena del Teatro alla Scala da Giulio Ricordi*." In *Il melodramma italiano dell'Ottocento*, 125–55.

Allévy, Marie-Antoinette. *La mise en scène en France dans la première moitié du dix-neuvième siècle*. Paris, 1938.

Anselmo, Francesco Attardi. "*Don Pasquale*" di Gaetano Donizetti. Invito all'opera, 6. Milan, 1998.

Antolini, Bianca Maria, ed. *Dizionario degli editori musicali italiani 1750–1930*. Pisa, 2000.

Antolini, Bianca Maria, and Annalisa Bini. *Editori e librai musicali a Roma nella prima metà dell'Ottocento*. Rome, 1988.

Antolini, Bianca Maria, Teresa M. Gialdroni, and Annunziato Pugliese, eds. *Et facciam dolci canti: Studi in onore di Agostino Ziino in occasione del suo 65° compleanno*. Lucca, 2003.

Antolini, Bianca Maria, and Wolfgang Witzenmann, eds. *Napoli e il teatro musicale in Europa tra Sette e Ottocento: Studi in onore di Friedrich Lippman*. Florence, 1993.

Armstrong, Alan. "Gilbert-Louis Duprez and Gustave Roger in the Composition of Meyerbeer's *Le Prophète*." *Cambridge Opera Journal* 8 (1996): 147–65.

Arruga, Lorenzo. *Medaglie incomparabili: Vent'anni di storia del Rossini Opera Festival*. Milan, 2001.

Ashbrook, William. *Donizetti*. London, 1965.

———. *Donizetti and His Operas*. Cambridge, 1982.

———. "The *Mefistofele* Libretto as a Reform Text." In Groos and Parker, *Reading Opera*, 268–87.

———. "Popular Success, the Critics and Fame: The Early Careers of *Lucia di Lammermoor* and *Belisario*." *Cambridge Opera Journal* 2 (1990): 65–81.

Ashman, Mike. "Misinterpreting Verdian Dramaturgy: History and Grand Opera." In Latham and Parker, *Verdi in Performance*, 42–46.

Atti del 1° Convegno internazionale di studi donizettiani, 22–28 Settembre 1975. 2 vols. Bergamo, 1983.

Atti del III° Congresso internazionale di studi verdiani: Milano, Piccola Scala, 12–17 giugno 1972. Parma, 1974.

Azevedo, Aléxis. *G. Rossini: Sa vie et ses œuvres.* Paris, 1864.

Baker, Evan. "Lettere di Giuseppe Verdi a Francesco Maria Piave 1843–1865." *Studi verdiani* 4 (1986–87): 136–66.

———. "Verdi's Operas and Giuseppe Bertoja's Designs at the Gran Teatro la Fenice, Venice." In Radice, *Opera in Context*, 209–40.

Balthazar, Scott L. "Rossini and the Development of the Mid-Century Lyric Form." *Journal of the American Musicological Society* 41 (1988): 102–25.

Banti, Alfredo. *La nazione del risorgimento: Parentela, santità e onore alle origini dell'Italia unita.* Turin, 2000.

Barblan, Guglielmo, and Frank Walker. "Contributo all'epistolario di Gaetano Donizetti: Lettere inedite o sparse." *Studi donizettiani* 1 (1962).

Bartlet, M. Elizabeth C., with the collaboration of Mauro Bucarelli. *Guillaume Tell di Gioachino Rossini: Fonti iconografiche.* Iconografia rossiniana 1. Pesaro, 1996.

Basevi, Abramo. *Studio sulle opere di Giuseppe Verdi.* Florence, 1859.

Basini, Laura. "Cults of Sacred Memory: Parma and the Verdi Centennial Celebrations of 1913." *Cambridge Opera Journal* 13 (2001): 141–61.

Basso, Alberto. *Il teatro della città dal 1788 al 1936.* Vol. 2 of *Storia del Teatro Regio di Torino.* Turin, 1976.

Bate, Philip. *The Oboe: An Outline of Its History, Development and Construction.* 3rd ed. London and New York, 1975.

Beghelli, Marco. "Per fedeltà a una nota." *Il saggiatore musicale* 8 (2001): 295–316.

———. *I trattati di canto italiani dell'Ottocento.* Doctoral diss., Università degli Studi di Bologna, 1995.

———. "Tre slittamenti semantici: cavatina, romanza, rondò." In Nicolodi and Trovato, *Le parole della musica, III*, 185–217.

Beghelli, Marco, and Stefano Piana. "The New Critical Edition." In the program for *L'equivoco stravagante* at the Rossini Opera Festival (Pesaro, 2002), 45–53.

Bellini: mostra di oggetti e documenti provenienti da collezioni pubbliche e private italiane. Edited by Caterina Andò, Domenico De Meo, and Salvatore Enrico Failla. Catania, 1988.

Bellini, Vincenzo. *I Capuleti e i Montecchi.* Edited by Claudio Toscani. In *Edizione critica delle opere di Vincenzo Bellini*, vol. 6. Milan, 2003.

———. *Norma: A Facsimile Edition of the Original Autograph Manuscript and the Surviving Sketches.* Edited by Philip Gossett. New York, 1983.

———. *Il pirata: A Facsimile Edition of the Original Autograph Manuscript.* Edited by Philip Gossett. New York, 1983.

———. *I puritani: A Facsimile Edition of Bellini's Original Autograph Manuscript together with the Naples Revision.* Edited by Philip Gossett. New York, 1983.

———. *La straniera: A Facsimile Edition of a Contemporary Manuscript with Bellini's Autograph Annotations.* Edited by Philip Gossett. New York, 1982.

Bellotto, Francesco. "'Fa' le cose da pazza': Una lettera inedita di Gaetano Donizetti su *Lucrezia Borgia*." Unpublished.

———, ed. *Giovanni Simone Mayr: L'Opera teatrale e la musica sacra. Atti del Convegno internazionale di studio 1995.* Bergamo, 1997.

————. "L'immaginario scenico di *Marino Faliero*." In Girardi, *Gaetano Donizetti: Marino Faliero*, 89–102.

————, ed. *L'opera teatrale di Gaetano Donizetti: Atti del Convegno internazionale di studio, Bergamo, 17–20 settembre 1992*. Bergamo, 1993.

Bellotto, Francesco, and Paolo Fabbri, eds. *La vocalità e i cantanti: Bergamo 25–27 settembre 1997* (*Il teatro di Donizetti: Atti dei Convegni delle celebrazioni 1797/1997–1848/1998*). Bergamo, 2001.

Bent, Margaret. "Impossible Authenticities." *Il saggiatore musicale* 8 (2001): 39–50.

Bergeron, Katherine, and Philip V. Bohlman, eds. *Disciplining Music: Musicology and Its Canons*. Chicago, 1992.

Berlioz, Hector. *Memoirs of Hector Berlioz*. Translated by Rachel Holmes and Eleanor Holmes; annotated and translation revised by Ernest Newman. New York, 1932.

Bernheimer, Martin. "Operating Theater." *Opera News* 66, no. 12 (June 2002): 20–25.

Biggi, Maria Ida. "Scenografie rossiniane di Giuseppe Borsato." *Bollettino del centro rossiniano di studi* 35 (1995): 61–83, followed by 31 full-page plates.

Biggi, Maria Ida, and Carla Ferraro. *Rossini sulla scena dell'Ottocento: Bozzetti e figurini dalle collezioni italiane*. Iconografia rossiniana 2. Pesaro, 2000.

Bignami, Vespasiano, ed. *Cinquecento bozzetti di scenografia di Carlo Ferrario*. Milan, 1919.

Bini, Annalisa. "'Altro è l'Arcadia, altro è poi Valle': *Jacopo*, un *divertissement* letterario di Jacopo Ferretti a proposito di *Cenerentola*." *Bollettino del centro rossiniano di studi* 36 (1996): 5–43.

————. "Echi delle prime rossiniane nella stampa romana dell'epoca." In *Rossini a Roma— Rossini e Roma*, 165–98.

Bini, Annalisa, and Jeremy Commons, eds. *Le prime rappresentazioni delle opere di Donizetti nella stampa coeva*. Rome, 1997.

Bini, Annalisa, and Franco Onorati, eds. *Jacopo Ferretti e la cultura del suo tempo: Atti del Convegno di studi, Roma, 28–29 novembre 1996*. Rome, 1999.

Biondi, Fabio. "Riflessioni interpretative su *Norma*." In the program for *Norma* at the Verdi Festival (Parma, 2001), 91–94.

Black, John N. "Cammarano's Notes for the Staging of *Lucia di Lammermoor*." *Donizetti Society Journal* 4 (1980): 29–45.

————. "The Contract for Paris." *Donizetti Society Journal* 7 (2002): 11–21.

————. "The Eruption of Vesuvius in Pacini's *L'ultimo giorno di Pompei*." *Donizetti Society Journal* 6 (1988): 95–105.

————. *The Italian Romantic Libretto: A Study of Salvadore Cammarano*. Edinburgh, 1984.

Bloom, Peter, ed. *Music in Paris in the Eighteen-Thirties*. Stuyvesant, NY, 1987.

Blume, Friedrich, ed. *Die Musik in Geschichte und Gegenwart*. 16 vols. Kassel, 1949–79.

Bornstein, George, and Ralph Williams, eds. *Palimpsest: Editorial Theory in the Humanities*. Ann Arbor, 1993.

Bowers, Fredson. "Greg's Rationale of 'Copy-Text' Revisited." *Studies in Bibliography* 31 (1978): 90–161.

Brauner, Charles S. "Parody and Melodic Style in Bellini's *I Capuleti e i Montecchi*." In *Studies in Music History, II: Music and Drama*, 124–51. New York, 1988.

Brendel, Alfred. "Schubert's Last Sonatas." *New York Review of Books* 36 (2 February 1989): 32–36. Reprinted and expanded in *Music Sounded Out*, 77–141. London, 1990.

Brewer, Bruce. "Il cigno di Romano—Giovan Battista Rubini: A Performance Study." *Donizetti Society Journal* 4 (1980): 115–65.

Brombert, Beth Archer. *Cristina: Portraits of a Princess*. Chicago, 1977.

Brook, Barry S. "Stravinsky's *Pulcinella*: The 'Pergolesi' Sources." In Fauquet, *Musiques–Signes– Images*, 41–66.

Brown, Clive. *Classical and Romantic Performing Practice 1750–1900*. Oxford, 1999.

Brumana, Biancamaria, and Galliano Ciliberti, eds. *Francesco Morlacchi e la musica del suo tempo (1784–1841): Atti del Convegno internazionale di studi, Perugia, 26–28 ottobre 1984*. Florence, 1986.

Bruson, Jean-Marie. "Olympe, Pacini, Michotte ed altri: La vendita dei *Péchés de vieillesse* e le sue vicende." *Bollettino del centro rossiniano di studi* 34 (1994): 5–68.

Bucarelli, Mauro, ed. *Rossini 1792–1992: Mostra storico-documentaria*. Perugia, 1992.

Budden, Julian. *The Operas of Verdi*. 3 vols. London, 1973–1981. Revised edition, Oxford, 1992.

Busch, Hans. *Verdi's "Aida": The History of an Opera in Letters and Documents*. Minneapolis, 1978.

———. *Verdi's "Otello" and "Simon Boccanegra" (revised version) in Letters and Documents*. 2 vols. Oxford, 1988,

Butt, John. *Playing with History*. Cambridge, 2002.

Cafiero, Rosa, and Francesca Seller. "Editoria musicale a Napoli attraverso la stampa periodica: Il *Giornale del Regno delle Due Sicilie* (1817–1860)." *Le fonti musicali in Italia* 3 (1989): 57–90; and 4 (1990): 133–70.

Cagli, Bruno. "All'ombra dei gigli d'oro." In Bucarelli, *Rossini 1792–1992*, 161–96.

Cambi, Luisa, ed. *Bellini: Epistolario*. Verona, 1943.

———. "Bellini: Un pacchetto di autografi." In *Scritti in onore di Luigi Ronga*, 53–90.

Cametti, Alberto. "Il *Guglielmo Tell* e le sue prime rappresentazioni in Italia." *Rivista musicale italiana* 6 (1899): 580–92.

———. "La musica teatrale a Roma cento anni fa." *Annuario* of the Regia Accademia di Santa Cecilia 330–32 (Rome, 1916): 44–69.

———. *Il teatro di Tordinona poi di Apollo*. 2 vols. Rome, 1938.

Capra, Marco. "L'illuminazione sulla scena verdiana ovvero L'arco voltaico non acceca la luna?" In Petrobelli and Della Seta, *La realizzazione scenica dello spettacolo verdiano*, 230–64.

Carteggio Verdi–Boito. Edited by Mario Medici and Marcello Conati, with the collaboration of Marisa Casati. 2 vols. Parma, 1978. Translated and edited by William Weaver as *The Verdi–Boito Correspondence*. Chicago, 1994.

Carteggio Verdi–Cammarano (1843–1852). Edited by Carlo Matteo Mossa. Parma, 2001.

Carteggio Verdi–Ricordi 1880–1881. Edited by Pierluigi Petrobelli, Marisa Di Gregorio Casati, and Carlo Matteo Mossa. Parma, 1988.

Carteggio Verdi–Ricordi 1882–1885. Edited by Franca Cella, Madina Ricordi, and Marisa Di Gregorio Casati. Parma, 1994.

Carteggio Verdi–Somma. Edited by Simonetta Ricciardi. Parma, 2004.

Carter, Tim. *W. A. Mozart: Le nozze di Figaro*. Cambridge, 1987.

Castelvecchi, Stefano. "Walter Scott, Rossini e la *couleur ossianique*: Il contesto culturale della *Donna del lago*." *Bollettino del centro rossiniano di studi* 33 (1993): 57–71.

Caswell, Austin. *Embellished Opera Arias*. Vols. 7–8 of *Recent Research in the Music of the Nineteenth and Early Twentieth Centuries*. Madison, WI, 1989.

———. "Mme Cinti-Damoreau and the Embellishment of Italian Opera in Paris: 1820–1845." *Journal of the American Musicological Society* 28 (1975): 459–92.

Cattelan, Paolo. "I libretti italiani." In the program for *Guglielmo Tell* at the Teatro alla Scala (Milan, 1988), 24–25.

Cavicchi, Adriano. "Per una nuova drammaturgia rossiniana." In the program for *Tancredi* at the Rossini Opera Festival (Pesaro, 1982), 86–90.

Celletti, Rodolfo. "Origine e sviluppi della coloratura rossiniana." *Nuova rivista musicale italiana* 2 (1968): 872–919.

Cesti, Antonio. *Il pomo d'oro*. Edited by Guido Adler. In *Denkmäler der Tonkunst in Österreich*, Jg. III/2 (vol. 6) and IV/2 (vol. 9). Vienna, 1896–1897.

Chusid, Martin. *A Catalog of Verdi's Operas.* Hackensack, NJ, 1974.

———. "Editing *Rigoletto*." In *Nuove prospettive nella ricerca verdiana,* 49–56.

———. "A Letter by the Composer about *Giovanna d'Arco* and Some Remarks on the Division of Musical Direction in Verdi's Day." *Performance Practice Review* 3 (1990): 7–57.

———. "The Tonality of *Rigoletto*." In Abbate and Parker, *Analyzing Opera,* 241–61.

———, ed. *Verdi's Middle Period, 1849–1859: Source Studies, Analysis, and Performance Practice.* Chicago, 1997.

Ciarlantini, Paola. "Fanny Tacchinardi Persiani: Ritratto biografico ed artistico della prima Lucia." In Bellotto and Fabbri, *La vocalità e i cantanti,* 125–52.

———. *Giuseppe Persiani e Fanny Tacchinardi: Due protagonisti del melodramma romantico.* Ancona/Bologna, 1988.

Cinti-Damoreau, Laure. *Méthode de chant composée pour ses classes du Conservatoire.* Paris, 1849.

Clément, Catherine. *Opera, or The Undoing of Women.* Translated by Betsy Wing. Minneapolis, 1988.

Cohen, H. Robert. "*Macbeth* in Paris: New Iconographical Documents." In Rosen and Porter, *Verdi's "Macbeth,"* 182–98.

———. *The Original Staging Manuals for Twelve Parisian Operatic Premières.* Stuyvesant, NY, 1990.

———. "A Survey of French Sources for the Staging of Verdi's Operas: 'Livrets de mise en scène,' Annotated Scores, and Annotated Libretti in Two Parisian Collections." *Studi verdiani* 3 (1985): 11–44.

Cohen, H. Robert, and Marie-Odile Gigou. *One Hundred Years of Operatic Staging in France.* New York, 1986.

Cohen, H. Robert, Silvia L'Ecuyer Lacroix, and Jacques Léveillé. *Les Gravures musicales dans l'Illustration, 1843–1899.* 3 vols. Québec, 1982–1983.

Colas, Damien. *Les Annotations de chanteurs dans les matériels d'exécution des opéras de Rossini à Paris (1820–1860): Contribution à l'étude de la grammaire mélodique rossinienne.* 4 vols. Doctoral diss., University of Tours, 1997.

Collins, Michael. "Bellini and the *Pasticcio alla Malibran:* A Performance History of *I Capuleti e i Montecchi*." *Note su note* 9–10 (2002): 109–52.

Conati, Marcello. "Between Past and Future: The Dramatic World of Rossini in *Mosè in Egitto* and *Moïse et Pharaon*." *19th Century Music* 4 (1980): 32–47.

———. *La bottega della musica: Verdi e La Fenice.* Milan, 1983.

———. "*Rigoletto*" *di Giuseppe Verdi: Guida all'opera.* Milan, 1983.

———. *Il "Simon Boccanegra" di Verdi a Reggio Emilia (1857): Storia documentata; Alcune varianti alla prima edizione dell'opera.* Reggio Emilia, 1984.

Conati, Marcello, and Natalia Grilli. "*Simon Bocannegra*" *di Giuseppe Verdi.* Musica e spettacolo: Collana di Disposizioni sceniche. Milan, 1993.

Conati, Marcello, and Marcello Pavarani, eds. *Orchestre in Emilia-Romagna nell'Ottocento e Novecento.* Parma, 1982.

I copialettere di Giuseppe Verdi. Edited by Gaetano Cesari and Alessandro Luzio. Milan, 1913.

Craft, Robert, ed. *Stravinsky: Selected Correspondence.* Vol. 1. New York, 1982.

Cronin, Charles Patrick Desmond. "Stefano Pavesi's *Ser Marcantonio* and Donizetti's *Don Pasquale*." *Opera Quarterly* 11, no. 2 (1995): 39–53.

Crutchfield, Will. "Crutchfield at Large." *Opera News* 59, no. 13 (18 March 1995): 50.

———. "The Prosodic Appoggiatura in the Music of Mozart and His Contemporaries." *Journal of the American Musicological Society* 42 (1989): 229–71.

————. "Vocal Ornamentation in Verdi: the Phonographic Evidence." *19th Century Music 7* (1983): 3–54.

Dahlhaus, Carl. *Nineteenth-Century Music.* Translated by J. Bradford Robinson. Berkeley, 1989.

Dallapicola, Luigi. "Words and Music in Italian Nineteenth-Century Opera." In Weaver and Chusid, *The Verdi Companion,* 193–215.

D'Amico, Fedele. "C'è modo e modo (*I Capuleti e i Montecchi* di Bellini nella revisione di Claudio Abbado)." *Nuova rivista musicale italiana* 1 (1967): 136–42.

Dean, Winton, and John Merrill Knapp. *Handel's Operas: 1704–1726.* Oxford, 1987.

de Angelis, Marcello. *Le carte dell'impresario: Melodramma e costume teatrale nell'Ottocento.* Florence, 1982.

De Bosio, Gianfranco. "Un'ipotesi di regia dell' 'Ernani.'" In *Ernani ieri e oggi,* 324–27.

Degrada, Francesco, ed. *Giuseppe Verdi: L'uomo, l'opera, il mito.* Milan, 2000.

————. "Observations on the Genesis of Verdi's *Macbeth*" and "The 'Scala' *Macbeth* Libretto: A Genetic Edition." In Rosen and Porter, *Verdi's "Macbeth,"* 156–73 and 306–38.

Della Seta, Fabrizio. "Un aspetto della ricezione di Meyerbeer in Italia: Le traduzioni dei Grands opéras." In Döhring and Jacobshagen, *Meyerbeer und das europäische Musiktheater,* 309–51.

————. *Italia e Francia nell'Ottocento.* Turin, 1993.

————. "'Parola scenica' in Verdi e nella critica verdiana." In Nicolodi and Trovato, *Le parole della musica I,* 259–86.

Della Seta, Fabrizio, Roberta Montemorra Marvin, and Marco Marica, eds. *Verdi 2001: Atti del Convegno internazionale, Parma–New York–New Haven, 24 gennaio–10 febbraio 2001.* 2 vols. Florence, 2003.

Della Seta, Fabrizio, and Simonetta Ricciardi, eds. *Vincenzo Bellini: verso l'edizione critica (Atti del Convegno internazionale, Siena, 1–3 giugno 2000).* Città di Castello, 2004.

[Deschamps, Émile, and Massé (first name unknown)]. *De MM. Paër et Rossini.* Paris, 1820.

Desniou, William. "Donizetti et *L'Ange de Nisida.*" *Donizetti Society Journal* 7 (2002): 177–218.

Devries, Anik, and François Lesure. *Dictionnaire des éditeurs de musique française: Des origines à environ 1820.* 2 vols. Geneva, 1979.

————. *Dictionnaire des éditeurs de musique française II: De 1820 à 1914.* Geneva, 1988.

Dill, Charles. *Monstrous Opera: Rameau and the Tragic Tradition.* Princeton, 1998.

Döhring, Sieghart, and Arnold Jacobshagen, eds. *Meyerbeer und das europäische Musiktheater.* Laaber, 1998.

Donizetti, Gaetano. *Le convenienze ed inconvenienze teatrali.* Edited by Roger Parker and Anders Wiklund. In *Edizione nazionale delle opere di Gaetano Donizetti.* Milan, 2002.

————. *Don Pasquale.* Facsimile edition of the autograph manuscript; edited by Philip Gossett. Rome, 1999.

————. *La Favorite.* Edited by Rebecca Harris-Warrick. In *Edizione critica delle opere di Gaetano Donizetti.* Milan, 1997; vocal score, Milan, 1999.

————. *Lucia di Lammermoor: Dramma tragico,* riprodotta integralmente per mandato di Giovanni Treccani degli Alfieri. Milan, 1941.

————. *Maria Stuarda.* Edited by Anders Wiklund. In *Edizione critica delle opere di Gaetano Donizetti.* Milan, 1991.

————. *Parisina: A Facsimile Edition of Donizetti's Original Autograph Manuscript.* Edited by Philip Gossett. New York, 1981.

————. *Poliuto.* Edited by William Ashbrook and Roger Parker. In *Edizione nazionale delle opere di Gaetano Donizetti.* Milan, 2000.

Dotto, Gabriele. "Opera, Four Hands: Collaborative Alterations in Puccini's *Fanciulla.*" *Journal of the American Musicological Society* 42 (1989): 604–24.

Emanuele, Marco. *L'ultima stagione italiana: Le forme dell'opera seria di Rossini da Napoli a Venezia.* Turin, 1997.

Engelhardt, Markus, ed. *Giuseppe Verdi und seine Zeit.* Laaber, 2001.

Ernani ieri e oggi: Atti del Convegno internazionale di studi (Modena, Teatro San Carlo, 9–10 dicembre 1984. Published by the Istituto Nazionale di Studi Verdiani in Parma as *Verdi* 10 (1987).

Escudier, Léon, and Marie Escudier. *Rossini: Sa vie et ses œuvres.* Paris, 1854.

Everist, Mark. *Music Drama at the Paris Odéon 1824–1828.* Berkeley, 2002.

Fabbri, Paolo, ed. *Gioachino Rossini 1792–1992: Il testo e la scena.* Pesaro, 1994.

———. "Istituti metrici e formali." In *Teorie e techniche, imaggini e fantasmi,* vol. 6 of *Storia dell'opera italiana,* 163–233. Revised and translated as "Metrical and Formal Organization." In *Opera in Theory and Practice* (see *Storia dell'opera italiana*), 151–219.

———. "Rossini the Aesthetician." *Cambridge Opera Journal* 6 (1994): 19–29.

Fabbri, Paolo, and Maria Chiara Bertieri, eds. *L'Italiana in Algeri.* I libretti di Rossini, published by the Fondazione Rossini, vol. 4. Pesaro, 1997.

Fauquet, Joël-Marique, ed. *Musiques-Signes-Images: Liber amicorum François Lesure.* Geneva, 1988.

Fenton, James. "The Cherry Orchard Has to Come Down." *New York Review of Books* 43 (4 April 1996): 16–17.

Ferranti-Giulini, Maria. *Giuditta Pasta e i suoi tempi.* Milan, 1935.

Fitzpatrick, Horace. *The Horn and Horn-playing and the Austro-Bohemian Tradition 1680–1830.* Oxford, 1971.

Florimo, Francesco. *Bellini: Memorie e lettere.* Florence, 1882.

———. *La scuola musicale di Napoli e i suoi conservatorii.* 4 vols. Naples, 1880–83.

Fo, Dario. "Il teatro comico e la situazione." In the program for *La gazzetta* at the Rossini Opera Festival (Pesaro, 2001), 56–57.

Folena, Daniela Goldin. "Lessico melodrammatico verdiano." In Muraro, *Le parole della musica, II,* 227–53.

[Folena], Daniela Goldin. "Il *Macbeth* verdiano: Genesi e caratteri di un libretto." In *La vera fenice: Librettisti e libretti tra Sette e Ottocento,* 230–82. Turin, 1985.

Forbes, Elizabeth. *Mario and Grisi: A Biography.* London, 1985.

Foscolo, Ugo. *Edizione nazionale delle opere di Ugo Foscolo.* Vol. 16, *Epistolario,* bk. 3 (1809–1811). Edited by Plinio Carli. Florence, 1953.

Fulcher, Jane. *The Nation's Image: French Grand Opera as Politics and Politicized Art.* Cambridge, 1987.

Furie, Kenneth. "An 'Authentic' Cavpag!" *High Fidelity* 30, no. 9 (1980): 79–81.

Galeazzi, Francesco. *Elementi teorico-pratici di musica con un saggio sopra l'arte di suonare il violino.* 2 vols. Rome, 1791, 1796.

Gallo, Denise. *Gioachino Rossini: A Guide to Research.* New York and London, 2002.

Gara, Eugenio, ed. *Carteggi pucciniani.* Milan, 1958.

———. *Giovan Battista Rubini nel centenario della morte.* Bergamo, 1954.

García, Manuel. *Traité complet de l'art du chant en deux parties.* Paris, 1847. Reprinted by Minkoff, Geneva, 1985.

Garibaldi, Luigi Agostino, ed. *Giuseppe Verdi nelle lettere di Emanuele Muzio ad Antonio Barezzi.* Milan, 1931.

Gaskell, Philip. *From Writer to Reader: Studies in Editorial Method.* Oxford, 1978.

Gatti, Carlo. *L'abbozzo del Rigoletto di Giuseppe Verdi.* Milan, 1941.

———. *Il teatro alla Scala nella storia e nell'arte (1778–1963).* 2 vols. Milan, 1964.

———. *Verdi nelle immagini*. Milan, 1941.

Gavazzeni, Gianandrea. "Problemi di tradizione dinamico-fraseologica e critica testuale, in Verdi e in Puccini." *Rassegna musicale* 29 (1959): 27–41, 106–22. Reprinted by Ricordi, with additional commentary and translations into English and German. Turin, 1961.

Gerhard, Anselm. *Die Verstädterung der Oper: Paris und das Musiktheater des 19. Jahrhunderts.* Weimar, 1992. Translated by Mary Whittall as *The Urbanization of Opera: Music Theater in Paris in the Nineteenth Century.* Chicago, 1998.

Giazotto, Remo. *Maria Malibran.* Turin, 1986.

Giger, Andreas. "Social Control and the Censorship of Giuseppe Verdi's Operas in Rome (1844–1859)." *Cambridge Opera Journal* 11 (1999): 233–65.

———. "The Triumph of Diversity: Theories of French Accentuation and their Influence on Verdi's French Operas." *Music & Letters* 84 (2003): 55–83.

Giger, Andreas, and Thomas J. Mathiesen, eds. *Music in the Mirror: Reflections on the History of Music Theory and Literature for the 21st Century.* Lincoln, NE, and London, 2002.

Ginevra, Stefano, ed. *Manuel García: Traité complet de l'art du chant en deux parties: Trattato completo dell'arte del canto in due parti.* Turin, 2001.

Girardi, Michele, ed. *Gaetano Donizetti: "Marino Faliero."* Program for *Marino Faliero* at the Teatro Malibran (Venice, 2003).

Girardi, Michele, and Pierluigi Petrobelli, eds. *Messa per Rossini: La storia, il testo, la musica.* Quaderni dell'Istituto di Studi Verdiani, vol. 5. Parma, 1988.

Girardi, Michele, and Franco Rossi. *Il Teatro La Fenice: Cronologia degli spettacoli 1792–1936.* 2 vols. Venice, 1989, 1992.

Giuseppe Verdi: Gli autografi del Museo teatrale alla Scala. Milan, 2000.

Glasow, E. Thomas. "Berlioz on the Premiere of *La Favorite*." *Opera Quarterly* 14, no. 3 (1998), 33–43.

Goehr, Lydia. *The Imaginary Museum of Musical Works: An Essay in the Philosophy of Music.* Oxford, 1992.

Goldoni, Carlo. *Il matrimonio per concorso.* Edited by Andrea Fabiano. In the series Carlo Goldoni, Le opere, Edizione nazionale. Venice, 1999.

Goodman, Nelson. *Languages of Art: An Approach to a Theory of Symbols.* Indianapolis and New York, 1968.

Gossett, Philip. *"Anna Bolena" and the Artistic Maturity of Gaetano Donizetti.* Oxford, 1985.

———. "Compositional Methods." In Senici, *The Cambridge Companion to Rossini*, 68–84.

———. "The Composition of *Ernani*." In Abbate and Parker, *Analyzing Opera*, 27–55.

———. "La composizione di *Un ballo in maschera*." In the program for *Un ballo in maschera* at the Verdi Festival (Parma, 2001), 31–58.

———. "Critical Editions and Performance." In Latham and Parker, *Verdi in Performance*, 133–44.

———. "Editorial Theory, Musical Editions, Performance: 19th-Century Faultlines from a 21st-Century Perspective." In Giger and Mathiesen, *Music in the Mirror*, 217–31.

———. "Le fonti autografe delle opere teatrali di Rossini." *Nuova rivista musicale italiana* 2 (1968): 936–60.

———. "Gioachino Rossini's *Moïse*." In Newsom and Mann, *Music History from Primary Sources*, 369–74.

———. "History and Works That Have No History: Reviving Rossini's Neapolitan Operas." In Bergeron and Bohlman, *Disciplining Music*, 95–115.

———. "Der kompositorische Prozeß: Verdis Opernskizzen." In Engelhardt, *Giuseppe Verdi und seine Zeit*, 169–90.

———. "A New Romanza for *Attila*." *Studi verdiani* 9 (1993): 13–35. Published in shortened form as "Giuseppe Verdi's *Attila*" in Newsom and Mann, *Music History from Primary Sources*, 436–43.

———. "New Sources for *Stiffelio:* A Preliminary Report." *Cambridge Opera Journal* 5 (1993): 199–222. Reprinted in Chusid, *Verdi's Middle Period*, 19–43 (to which citations refer).

———. *The Operas of Rossini: Problems of Textual Criticism in Nineteenth-Century Opera*. Doctoral diss., Princeton University, 1970.

———. "Piracy in Venice: The Selling of *Semiramide*." In Rosen and Brook, *Words on Music*, 120–37.

———. Review of Gioachino Rossini, *L'assedio di Corinto*, recording on Angel Records SCLX-3819. *Musical Quarterly* 61 (1975): 626–38.

———. "Rossini e i suoi *Péchés de Vieillesse*." *Nuova rivista musicale italiana* 14 (1980): 7–26.

———. "Rossini in Naples: Some Major Works Recovered." *Musical Quarterly* 54 (1968): 316–40.

———. "Rossini's Operas and their Printed Librettos." In *Report of the Tenth Congress of the IMS, Ljubljana 1967*, 194–202.

———. "Rossini's *Petite Messe Solennelle* and Its Several Versions." In Reardon and Parisi, *Music Observed*, 139–46.

———. "Rossini's *Ritornelli:* A Composer and his Orchestral Soloists." In Fauquet, *Musiques-Signes-Images*, 133–41.

———. "Scandal and Scholarship." *New Republic* 225, no. 1 (2 July 2001): 23–32.

———. "Le sinfonie di Rossini." *Bollettino del centro rossiniano di studi* [19] (1979).

———. "Staging Italian Opera: Dario Fo and *Il viaggio a Reims*." In Antolini, Gialdroni, and Pugliese, *Et facciam dolci canti*, 1447–65.

———. "The Tragic Finale of Rossini's *Tancredi*." *Bollettino del centro rossiniano di studi* [16] (1976): 5–79 (English) and 89–164 (Italian).

———. "Translations and Adaptations of Operatic Texts." In Bornstein and Williams, *Palimpsest* 285–304.

———. "Trasporre Bellini." In Della Seta and Ricciardi, *Vincenzo Bellini*, 163–85.

———. "Verdi, Ghislanzoni, and *Aida:* The Uses of Convention." *Critical Inquiry* 1 (1974): 291–334.

———. "Verdi's Ideas on Interpreting His Operas." In Della Seta, Marvin, and Marica, *Verdi 2001*, 399–407.

———. "Verdi the Craftsman." *Revista Portuguesa de Musicologia* 11 (2001): 81–111.

Grant, Michael. *My First Eighty Years*. Henley-on-Thames, 1994.

Graziano, John, ed. *Cinderella (1831) Adapted by M. Rophino Lacy from Gioacchino Rossini's "La Cenerentola."* Italian Opera in English, vol. 3. New York and London, 1994.

Greenwald, Helen M. "Puccini, *Il tabarro*, and the Dilemma of Operatic Transposition." *Journal of the American Musicological Society* 51 (1998): 521–58.

———. "Realism on the Opera Stage: Belasco, Puccini, and the California Sunset." In Radice, *Opera in Context*, 279–96.

Greetham, D. C. *Textual Scholarship: An Introduction*. New York and London, 1994.

Greg, Sir Walter. "The Rationale of Copy-Text." *Studies in Bibliography* 3 (1950–51): 19–36.

Grier, James. *The Critical Editing of Music: History, Method, and Practice*. Cambridge, 1996.

Grilli, Natalia, ed. *Filippo Peroni scenografo alla Scala (1849–1867)*. Catalogue of the exhibition at the Museo Teatrale alla Scala, 12 January–9 February 1985. Milan, 1985.

Grondona, Marco. *La perfetta illusione: "Ermione" e l'opera seria rossiniana*. Lucca, 1996.

Groos, Arthur, and Roger Parker, eds. *Reading Opera*. Princeton, 1988.

Grove, Sir George, ed. *A Dictionary of Music and Musicians.* 4 vols. 1878–1890. For a revised edition, see Sadie, *The New Grove Dictionary of Music and Musicians.* See also *Grove Music Online.*

Grove Music Online. Edited by L. Macy. http://www.grovemusic.com.

Guccini, Gerardo. "Direzione scenica e regia." In *La spettacolarità,* vol. 5 of *Storia dell'opera italiana,* 123–74. Revised and translated as "Directing Opera." In *Opera on Stage* (see *Storia dell'opera italiana*), 125–76.

Gui, Vittorio. "Storia avventurosa di alcuni capolavori del passato." *Bollettino del centro rossiniano di studi* [25] (1985): 56–60.

Hadlock, Heather. "Sonorous Bodies: Women and the Glass Harmonica." *Journal of the American Musicological Society* 53 (2000): 507–42.

Hansell, Kathleen Kuzmick. "Il ballo teatrale e l'opera italiana." In *La spettacolarità,* vol. 5 of *Storia dell'opera italiana,* 175–306. Revised and translated as "Theatrical Ballet and Italian Opera." In *Opera on Stage* (see *Storia dell'opera italiana*), 177–308.

———. "Compositional Techniques in *Stiffelio:* Reading the Autograph Sources." In Chusid, *Verdi's Middle Period,* 45–97.

Hanslick, Eduard. *On the Musically Beautiful: A Contribution towards the Revision of the Aesthetics of Music.* Translated and edited by Geoffrey Payzant. Indianapolis, 1986.

Harwood, Gregory W. "Verdi's Reform of the Italian Opera Orchestra." *19th Century Music* 10 (1986–87), 108–34.

Haynes, Bruce. *The Eloquent Oboe: A History of the Hautboy, 1640–1760.* Oxford, 2001.

Heartz, Daniel. *Mozart's Operas.* Edited, with contributing essays, by Thomas Bauman. Berkeley, 1990.

Hepokoski, James. "Genre and Content in Mid-Century Verdi: 'Addio del passato' (*La traviata,* Act III)." *Cambridge Opera Journal* 1 (1989): 249–76.

———. "*Ottocento* Opera as Cultural Drama: Generic Mixtures in *Il trovatore.*" In Chusid, *Verdi's Middle Period,* 147–96.

———. "Overriding the Autograph Score: The Problem of Textual Authority in Verdi's *Falstaff.*" *Studi verdiani* 8 (1992).

———. "Staging Verdi's Operas: The Single 'Correct' Performance." In Latham and Parker, *Verdi in Performance,* 11–20.

Hepokoski, James, and Mercedes Viale Ferrero. "*Otello*" *di Giuseppe Verdi.* Musica e spettacolo: Collana di Disposizioni sceniche. Milan, 1990.

Herbert, Trevor, and John Wallace, eds. *The Cambridge Companion to Brass Instruments.* Cambridge, 1997.

Herz, Gerhard. "Johann Sebastian Bach in the Early Romantic Period" and "The Performance History of Bach's *B Minor Mass.*" In *Essays on J. S. Bach,* 67–109 and 187–202. Ann Arbor, 1985.

Hiller, Ferdinand. *Plaudereien mit Rossini.* As edited in Guido Johannes Joerg, "Gli scritti rossiniani di Ferdinand Hiller." *Bollettino del centro rossiniano di studi* 32 (1992): 63–155.

Holmes, William C. "The Earliest Revisions of *La forza del destino.*" *Studi verdiani* 6 (1990): 55–98.

Holoman, D. Kern. "The Emergence of the Orchestral Conductor in Paris in the 1830s." In Bloom, *Music in Paris in the Eighteen-Thirties,* 387–430.

Hopkinson, Cecil. *A Bibliography of the Works of Giuseppe Verdi, 1813–1901.* 2 vols. New York, 1973, 1978.

Huber, Konrad. "Giovanni Battista Rubini als Donizetti-Interpret." In Kantner, *Donizetti in Wien,* 114–21.

Hürlimann, Martin, ed. *Musikerhandschriften von Schubert bis Strawinsky.* Zürich, 1961.

Ingarden, Roman. *The Work of Music and the Problem of Its Identity.* Originally published in 1966. Translated by Adam Czerniawski and edited by Jean G. Harrell. Berkeley and Los Angeles, 1986.

Inzaghi, Luigi, and Luigi Alberto Bianchi. *Alesandro Rolla: Catalogo tematico delle opere.* Milan, 1981.

Isotta, Paolo. "I diamanti della corona: Grammatica del Rossini napoletano." In *Gioacchino Rossini: "Mosè in Egitto," "Moïse et Pharaon," "Mosè,"* edited by Paolo Isotta. In *Opera: Collana di guide musicali,* 145–346. Turin, 1974.

———. "Da Mosè a Moïse." *Bollettino del centro rossiniano di studi* [11] (1971): 87–117.

Izzo, Francesco. "Verdi's *Un giorno di regno:* Two Newly Discovered Movements and Some Questions of Genre." *Acta Musicologica* 73 (2001): 165–88.

Izzo, Francesco, and Johannes Streicher, eds. *Ottocento e oltre: Scritti in onore di Raoul Meloncelli.* Rome, 1993.

Jacobshagen, Arnold. "Staging at the Opéra-Comique in Nineteenth-Century Paris: Auber's *Fra Diavolo* and the *livrets de mise en scène.*" *Cambridge Opera Journal* 13 (2001): 239–60.

Jensen, Luke. "The Emergence of the Modern Conductor in 19th-Century Italian Opera." *Performance Practice Review* 4 (1991): 34–63.

———. *Giuseppe Verdi and Giovanni Ricordi, with Notes on Francesco Lucca: From "Oberto" to "La Traviata."* New York and London, 1989.

Jesurum, Olga. "Lo spazio del dramma: Le scenografie di Filippo Peroni." In La Via and Parker, *Pensieri per un maestro,* 211–26.

John, Nicholas, ed. *A Masked Ball, Un ballo in maschera.* English National Opera Guide 40. London, 1989.

———, ed. *Simon Boccanegra.* English National Opera Guide 32. London, 1985.

Johnson, Janet. "Donizetti's First 'Affare di Parigi': An Unknown Rondò-Finale for *Gianni da Calais.*" In Bellotto, *L'opera teatrale di Gaetano Donizetti,* 329–51.

———. "A Lost Rossini Opera Recovered: *Il viaggio a Reims.*" *Bollettino del centro rossiniano di studi* [23] (1983): 5–112.

Johnstone, H. Diack. "Treasure Trove in Gloucester: A Grangerized Copy of the 1895 Edition of Daniel Lysons' History of the Three Choirs Festival." *RMA Research Chronicle* 31 (1998): 1–90.

Jürgensen, Knud Arne. *The Verdi Ballets.* Parma, 1995.

Kallberg, Jeffrey. "Chopin in the Marketplace." In *Chopin at the Boundaries: Sex, History, and Musical Genre,* 161–214. Cambridge, MA, 1996.

———. "Marketing Rossini: Sei lettere di Troupenas ad Artaria." *Bollettino del centro rossiniano di studi* [20] (1980): 41–63.

Kantner, Leopold M., ed. *Donizetti in Wien (Musikwissenschaftliches Symposion, 17.–18. Oktober 1997).* Vienna, 1998.

Kaufman, Thomas G. "Giulia Grisi: A Re-evaluation." *Donizetti Society Journal* 4 (1980): 180–226.

———. "Giuseppe and Fanny Persiani." *Donizetti Society Journal* 6 (1988): 122–51.

———. *Verdi and His Major Contemporaries: A Selected Chronology of Performances with Casts.* New York and London, 1990.

Kelly, Thomas Forrest. *First Nights: Five Musical Premieres.* New Haven, 2000.

Kenyon, Nicholas, ed. *Authenticity and Early Music.* Oxford, 1988.

Kern, Bernd-Rüdiger. "Verfassungsgeschichtliche Aspekte der Oper *Il viaggio a Reims* von Rossini." In Kilian, *Dichter, Denker und der Staat,* 233–59.

Kilian, Michael, ed. *Dichter, Denker und der Staat: Essays zu einer Beziehung ganz eigener Art.* Tübingen, 1993.

Kimbell, David. *Italian Opera.* Cambridge, 1991.

———. *Vincenzo Bellini: "Norma."* Cambridge, 1998.

Kivy, Peter. *Authenticities: Philosophical Reflections on Musical Performance.* Ithaca, 1995.

Koury, Daniel J. *Orchestral Performance Practices in the Nineteenth Century: Size, Proportions, and Seating.* Ann Arbor, MI, 1986.

Kundera, Milan. "You're Not in Your Own House Here, My Dear Fellow." *New York Review of Books* 42 (21 September 1995): 21–24.

Lacombe, Hervé. *Les Voies de l'opéra français au XIXe siècle.* [Paris], 1997. Translated by Edward Schneider as *The Keys to French Opera in the Nineteenth Century.* Berkeley, 2001.

Langer, Arne. *Der Regisseur und die Aufzeichnungspraxis der Opernregie im 19. Jahrhundert.* Frankfurt, 1997.

Langford, Jeffrey. "Poetic Prosody and Melodic Rhythm in *Les Vêpres siciliennes.*" *Verdi Newsletter* 23 (1996): 8–18.

Latham, Alison, and Roger Parker, eds. *Verdi in Performance.* Oxford, 2001.

Lavagetto, Mario. *Un caso di censura: Il "Rigoletto."* Milan, 1979.

La Via, Stefano, and Roger Parker. *Pensieri per un maestro: Studi in onore di Pierluigi Petrobelli.* Turin, 2002.

Lawton, David. "The Autograph of *Aida* and the New Verdi Edition." *Verdi Newsletter* 14 (1986): 4–14.

———. "The Revision of Recitatives from *Il trovatore* to *Le Trouvère.*" *Verdi Forum* 26–27 (1999–2000): 17–32.

———. "*Le Trouvère:* Verdi's revision of *Il trovatore* for Paris." *Studi verdiani* 3 (1985): 79–119.

Lawton, David, and David Rosen. "Verdi's Non-definitive Revisions: The Early Operas." In *Atti del III° Congresso internazionale di studi verdiani,* 189–237.

le Hurray, Peter. *Authenticity in Performance: Eighteenth-Century Case Studies.* Cambridge, 1990.

Letterature comparate, problemi e metodo: Studi in onore di Ettore Paratore. Bologna, 1981.

Lettere di G. Rossini. Edited by Giuseppe Mazzatinti, Fanny Manis, and G. Manis. Florence, 1902.

Levin, David J., ed. *Opera through Other Eyes.* Stanford, 1994.

———. "Reading a Staging / Staging a Reading." *Cambridge Opera Journal* 9 (1997): 47–71.

Liebling, Estelle, ed. Gioachino Rossini's "Cavatina from the opera *Il barbiere di Siviglia.*" In *Arrangements and Editings for Coloratura Voice with Piano.* New York, 1938.

Lindegren, Erik. *Maskeradbalen (Gustaf III): Opera i tre akter av Verdi.* Stockholm, 1958.

Lippmann, Friedrich. "Romani e Bellini: I fatti e i principi della collaborazione." In Sommariva, *Felice Romani,* 83–113.

———. "Su 'La Straniera' di Bellini." *Nuova rivista musicale italiana* 5 (1971): 565–605.

———. "Sull'estetica di Rossini." *Bollettino del centro rossiniano di studi* [8] (1968): 62–69.

———. *Versificazione italiana e ritmo musicale: I rapporti tra verso e musica nell'opera italiana dell'Ottocento.* Translated by Lorenzo Bianconi. Naples, 1986.

Lomnäs, Bonnie, and Erling Lomnäs. *Stiftelsen Muikkulturens främjande (Nydahl Collection): Catalogue of Music Manuscripts.* Stockholm, 1995.

Lo Presti, Fulvio Stefano. "*Le Duc d'Albe:* The Livret of Scribe and Duveyrier." *Donizetti Society Journal* 5 (1984): 243–316.

———. "Sylvia prima di Léonor (con interferenze di un duca)." *Donizetti Society Journal* 7 (2002): 145–75.

Lorenz, Alfred. *Das Geheimnis der Form bei Richard Wagner.* 4 vols. Berlin, 1924–33.

Luzio, Alessandro. *Carteggi verdiani.* 4 vols. Rome, 1935–47.

Macdonald, Hugh. *Berlioz's Orchestration Treatise: A Translation and Commentary*. Cambridge, 2002.

Mackenzie-Grieve, Averil. *Clara Novello 1818–1908*. London, 1955.

Mainvielle Fodor, Joséphine. *Réflexions et conseils sur l'art du chant*. Paris, 1857.

Maione, Paologiovanni, and Francesca Seller. "L'ultima stagione napoletana di Domenico Barbaja (1836–1840): Organizzazione e spettacolo." *Rivista italiana di musicologia* 27 (1992): 257–325.

Mandelli, Alfredo. "I 'fiori' ritrovati, che Puccini non voleva eliminare." In the program for *Il trittico* (Bologna, 1993), 43–65.

Marshall, Robert. "Bach's 'Choruses' Reconstituted." *High Fidelity* 32, no. 10 (1982): 64–66 and 94.

———. *Mozart Speaks: Views on Music, Musicians and the World*. New York, 1991.

Martin, George. *Aspects of Verdi*. New York, 1988.

Marvin, Robert Montemorra. "Aspects of Tempo in Verdi's Early and Middle-Period Italian Operas." In Chusid, *Verdi's Middle Period*, 393–412.

———. "A Verdi Autograph and the Problem of Authenticity." *Studi verdiani* 9 (1993): 36–61.

The Mary Flagler Cary Music Collection. The Pierpont Morgan Library. New York, 1970.

Mattsson, Inger, ed. *Gustavian Opera: An Interdisciplinary Reader in Swedish Opera, Dance, and Theatre 1771–1809*. Royal Swedish Academy of Music, publication no. 66. Uppsala, 1991.

Mauceri, John. "Verdi for the Twenty-first Century." In Della Seta, Marvin, and Marica, *Verdi 2001*, 2:749–57.

Mauceri, Marco. "*La gazzetta* di Gioachino Rossini: Fonti del libretto e autoimprestito musicale." In Izzo and Streicher, *Ottocento e oltre*, 115–49.

———. "Rossini a Roma nel 1821: Nuovi documenti su un'opera mai scritta." *Bollettino del centro rossiniano di studi* 28 (1988): 27–46.

Mayr, Giovanni Simone. *Medea in Corinto: A facsimile edition of the printed piano-vocal score*. Edited by Philip Gossett. New York, 1986.

McClary, Susan. *Feminine Endings: Music, Gender, and Sexuality*. Minnesota, 1991.

McGann, Jerome J. *A Critique of Modern Textual Criticism*. Chicago, 1983.

———. *Radiant Textuality: Literature after the World Wide Web*. New York, 2001.

———, ed. *Textual Criticism and Literary Interpretation*. Chicago, 1985.

McGowan, Margaret M. *L'Art du ballet de cour en France*. Paris, 1963.

Il melodramma italiano dell'Ottocento: Studi e ricerche per Massimo Mila. Turin, 1977.

Merlin, Countess de. *Memoirs of Madame Malibran*. 2 vols. London, 1840.

Metelitsa, Natalia, and Helene Fedosova. "A.L. Roller, the First Scenographer of 'La forza del destino.'" In Petrobelli and Della Seta, *La realizzazione scenica dello spettacolo verdiano*, 72–82.

Meucci, Renato. "Il cimbasso e gli strumenti affini nell'Ottocento italiano." *Studi verdiani* 5 (1989): 109–62. For an abbreviated English version, see "The *Cimbasso* and Related Instruments in 19th-Century Italy." Translated by William Waterhouse. *Galpin Society Journal* 49 (1996): 143–79.

———. "I timpani e gli strumenti a percussione nell'Ottocento italiano." *Studi verdiani* 13 (1998): 183–254.

———. "La trasformazione dell'orchestra in Italia al tempo di Rossini." In Fabbri, *Gioachino Rossini 1792–1992*, 431–64.

———. "Verdi, Bazzini e l'unificazione del diapason in Italia." In *Milano musicale 1861–1897*, Quaderni del Corso di Musicologia del Conservatorio Giuseppe Verdi di Milano, no. 5, 393–403. Lucca, 1999.

Meyerbeer, Giacomo. *Il crociato in Egitto: A Facsimile Edition of the Original Version.* Edited by Philip Gossett. New York, 1979.

Michotte, Edmond. *Souvenirs personnels: La visite de R. Wagner à Rossini (Paris 1860)—détails inédits et commentaires.* Paris, 1906. See also Weinstock, *Richard Wagner's Visit to Rossini (Paris 1860).*

———. *Souvenirs: Une soirée chez Rossini à Beau-Séjour (Passy).* Privately printed, after 1893.

Miggiani, Maria Giovanna. "Il teatro di San Moisè (1793–1818)." *Bollettino del centro rossiniano di studi* 30 (1990): 5–213.

Mila, Massimo, ed. *Giuseppe Verdi: "Les Vêpres siciliennes," "I Vespri siciliani."* In *Opera: Collana di guide musicali.* Turin, 1973.

Mongrédien, Jean-Robert. "Les débuts de Meyerbeer à Paris: *Il crociato in Egitto* au Théâtre Royale Italien." In Döhring and Jacobshagen, *Meyerbeer und das europäische Musiktheater,* 64–72.

Monterosso, Raffaelle. "Le due redazioni dei *Puritani.*" In *Letterature comparate, problemi e metodo,* 1589–1609.

Morazzoni, Giuseppe, ed. *Verdi: Lettere inedite.* Milan, 1929.

Moreni, Carla. *Vita musicale a Milano 1837–1866: Gustavo Adolfo Noseda collezionista e compositore.* In *Musica e Teatro. Quaderni degli Amici della Scala* 1 (1985).

Morley-Pegge, Reginald. *The French Horn.* 2nd ed. London, 1973.

Mozart, Wolfgang Amadeus. *Così fan tutte.* Edited by Faye Ferguson and Wolgang Rehm. In *Wolfgang Amadeus Mozart: Neue Ausgabe sämtlicher Werke,* series 2:5, vol. 18. Kassel, 1991.

———. *Le nozze di Figaro.* Edited by Ludwig Finscher. In *Wolfgang Amadeus Mozart: Neue Ausgabe sämtlicher Werke,* series 2:5, vol. 16. Kassel, 1973.

Muraro, Maria Teresa. "Nuovi significati delle scene dei Bertoja alla Fenice di Venezia." In Petrobelli and Della Seta, *La realizzazione scenica dello spettacolo verdiano,* 83–108.

———, ed. *Le parole della musica, II: Studi sul lessico della letteratura critica del teatro musicale in onore di Gianfranco Folena.* Florence, 1995.

Musica Musicisti Editoria: 175 anni di Casa Ricordi 1808–1983. Milan, 1983.

Neumann, Frederick. "The Appoggiatura in Mozart's Recitative." *Journal of the American Musicological Society* 35 (1982): 115–37.

———. "Improper Appoggiaturas in the *Neue Mozart Ausgabe.*" *Journal of Musicology* 10 (1992): 505–21.

Newsom, Jon, and Alfred Mann, eds. *Music History from Primary Sources: A Guide to the Moldenhauer Archives.* Washington, 2000.

Nicolodi, Fiamma, ed. *Il Turco in Italia.* I libretti di Rossini, published by the Fondazione Rossini, vol. 9. Pesaro, 2002.

Nicolodi, Fiamma and Paolo Trovato, eds. *Le parole della musica, I: Studi sulla lingua della letteratura musicale in onore di Gianfranco Folena.* Florence, 1994.

———, eds. *Le parole della musica, III: Studi di lessicologia musicale.* Florence, 2000.

Nuove prospetive nella ricerca verdiana: Atti del Convegno internazionale in occasione della prima del "Rigoletto" in edizione critica. Vienna, 12/13 marzo 1983. Parma/Milan, 1987.

Osborne, Richard. *Rossini.* London, 1986.

Osthoff, Wolfgang. "Mozarts Cavatinen und ihre Tradition." In Stander, Aarburg, and Cahn, *Helmuth Osthoff,* 139–77.

Pacini, Giovanni. *Le mie memorie artistiche.* Edited by Ferdinando Magnani. Florence, 1875.

Parker, Roger. *"Arpa d'or dei fatidici vati."* Parma, 1997.

———. "A Donizetti Critical Edition in the Postmodern World." In Bellotto, *L'opera teatrale di Gaetano Donizetti,* 57–66.

————. "'Infin che un brando vindice': From *Ernani* to *Oberto*." *Verdi Newsletter* 12 (1984): 5–7. Revised as "'Infin che un brando vindice' e le cavatine del primo atto di *Ernani*." In *Ernani ieri e oggi*, 142–60.

————. *Leonora's Last Act: Essays in Verdian Discourse*. Princeton, 1997.

————, ed. *The Oxford History of Opera*. Oxford, 1996.

————. "Reading the 'Livrets' or the Chimera of 'Authentic' Staging." In Petrobelli and Della Seta, *La realizzazione scenica dello spettacolo verdiano*, 345–66. Reprinted in Parker, *Leonora's Last Act*, 126–48.

Pascolato, Alessandro. *"Re Lear" e "Ballo in Maschera": Lettere di Giuseppe Verdi ad Antonio Somma*. Città di Castello, 1913.

Pastura, Francesco. *Bellini secondo la storia*. Parma, 1959.

Pendle, Karin, and Stephen Wilkins. "Paradise Found: The Salle le Peletier and French Grand Opera." In Radice, *Opera in Context*, 171–207.

Peterseil, Michaela. "Die 'Disposizioni sceniche' des Verlags Ricordi: Ihre Publikation und Ihr Zielpublikum." *Studi verdiani* 12 (1997): 133–55.

Petrobelli, Pierluigi. *Music in the Theater: Essays on Verdi and Other Composers*. Translated by Roger Parker. Princeton, 1994.

————. "Per un'esegesi della struttura drammatica del *Trovatore*." In *Atti del III° Congresso internazionale di studi verdiani*, 387–400. Translated as "Toward an Explanation of the Dramatic Structure of *Il trovatore*." In Petrobelli, *Music in the Theater*, 100–112.

————. "Remarks on Verdi's Composing Process" and "Thoughts for *Alzira*." In Petrobelli, *Music in the Theater*, 48–74 and 75–99.

————. "Response to David J. Levin." In Della Seta, Marvin, and Marica, *Verdi 2001*, 2: 485–87.

Petrobelli, Pierluigi and Fabrizio Della Seta, eds. *La realizzazione scenica dello spettacolo verdiano: Atti del Congresso internazionle di studi, Parma, Teatro Regio—Conservatorio di musica "A. Boito," 28–30 settembre 1994*. Parma, 1996.

Phillips-Matz, Mary Jane. *Verdi: A Biography*. Oxford, 1993.

Pigozzi, Marinella. "Prampolini scenografo verdiano." In Petrobelli and Della Seta, *La realizzazione scenica dello spettacolo verdiano*, 109–26.

Pinamonti, Paolo. "*Il crociato in Egitto* da Venezia a Parigi." *Rassegna veneta di studi musicali* 7–8 (1991): 219–40.

Piperno, Franco. "Il *Mosè in Egitto* e la tradizione napoletana di opere bibliche." In Fabbri, *Gioachino Rossini 1792–1992*, 255–71.

————, ed. "Le orchestre dei teatri d'opera italiani nell'Ottocento. Bilancio provvisorio di una ricerca." *Studi verdiani* 11 (1996): 119–221.

————. "'Stellati sogli' e 'immagini portentose': Opere bibliche e stagioni quaresimali a Napoli prima del *Mosè*." In Antolini and Witzenmann, *Napoli e il teatro musicale*, 267–98.

Pizer, Donald. "Self-Censorship and Textual Editing." In McGann, *Textual Criticism and Literary Interpretation*, 144–61.

Polo, Claudia. *Immaginari verdiani: opera, media e industria culturale nell'Italia del XX secolo*. Milan, 2004.

Poriss, Hilary. "A Madwoman's Choice: Aria Substitution in *Lucia di Lammermoor*." *Cambridge Opera Journal* 13 (2001): 1–28.

————. "Making Their Way through the World: Italian One-Hit Wonders." *19th Century Music* 24 (2001): 197–224.

Porter, Andrew. "*La forza della ricerca*: Bringing a Verdi Opera to the Stage." In Rearson and Parisi, *Music Observed*, 393–99.

————. "In Praise of the Pragmatic." In Latham and Parker, *Verdi in Performance*, 23–27.

———. "Un viaggio a Pesaro." *New Yorker,* 1 October 1984, 129–32.

Pougin, Arturo. *Giuseppe Verdi: Vita aneddotica, con note ed aggiunte di Folchetto* [Jacopo Caponi]. Milan, 1881.

Pourvoyeur, Robert. "Rossini et les Puritains." In *Bellini, Les Puritains,* published as *L'Avant scène Opéra* 96 (March 1987): 23–25.

Povoledo, Elena. "Le prime esecuzioni delle opere di Rossini e la tradizione scenografica italiana del suo tempo." In Bucarelli, *Rossini 1792–1992,* 285–313.

Powers, Harold. "'La dama velata': Act II of *Un ballo in maschera.*" In Chusid, *Verdi's Middle Period,* 273–336.

———. "One Halfstep at a Time: Tonal Transposition and 'Split Association' in Italian Opera." *Cambridge Opera Journal* 7 (1995): 135–64.

———. "'La solita forma' and the Uses of Convention." *Acta Musicologica* 59 (1987): 65–90.

———. "'...il vario metro dei versi francesi...'" In *La traduction des livrets,* edited by Gottfried R. Marschall, 83–106. Paris, 2004.

Prota-Giurleo, Ulisse. *La grande orchestra del R. Teatro San Carlo nel Settecento (da documenti inediti).* Naples, 1927.

Pugliese, Giuseppe, and Roman Vlad. *I puritani ritrovati: La versione inedita dedicata a Maria Malibran.* Bari, 1986.

Pugliese, Romana Margherita. *"Un idillio a fili d'argento": La cadenza della Lucia di Lammermoor e la rappresentazione musicale della follia.* Laureate thesis, University of Milan, 2000/2001.

———. "The origins of *Lucia di Lammermoor's* cadenza." *Cambridge Opera Journal* 16 (2004): 23–42.

Radice, Mark A. *Opera in Context: Essays on Historical Staging from the Late Renaissance to the Time of Puccini.* Portland, OR, 1998.

Radiciotti, Giuseppe. *Aneddoti rossiniani autentici.* Rome, 1929.

———. *Gioacchino Rossini: Vita documentata, opere ed influenza su l'arte.* 3 vols. Tivoli, 1927–29.

———. "Giuseppe Verdi a Senigallia." *Rassegna marchigiana* 1, no. 4 (1923): 137–40.

Reardon, Colleen, and Susan Parisi. *Music Observed: Studies in Memory of William C. Holmes.* Warren, MI, 2004.

Report of the Tenth Congress of the IMS, Ljubljana 1967. Ljubljana, 1970.

Rescigno, Eduardo. *Dizionario verdiano.* Milan, 2001.

Ricci, Luigi. *Variazioni—Cadenze—Tradizioni per canto.* 4 vols. Milan, 1937–41.

Rice, John A. *Antonio Salieri and Viennese Opera.* Chicago and London, 1998.

Rifkin, Joshua. "Bach's 'Chorus': Less Than They Seem?" *High Fidelity* 32, no. 9 (1982): 42–44. Published in revised form as "Bach's Chorus: A Preliminary Report." *Musical Times* 123 (1982): 747–53.

———. "Bach's 'Choruses': The Record Cleared." *High Fidelity* 32, no. 12 (1982): 58–59.

Righetti-Giorgi, Geltrude. *Cenni di una donna già cantante.* Bologna, 1823.

Risi, Clemens. "The Performativity of Operatic Performances as Academic Provocation." In Della Seta, Marvin, and Marica, *Verdi 2001,* 489–96.

———. "Shedding Light on the Audience: Hans Neuenfels and Peter Konwitschny Stage Verdi (and Verdians)." *Cambridge Opera Journal* 14 (2002): 201–10.

Ritorni, Carlo. *Commentarii della vita e delle opere coredrammatiche di Salvatore Viganò e della coregrafia e de' corepei.* Milan, 1838.

Rizzo, Dino. "'Con eletta musica del Sig. Verdi da Busseto, fu celebrata la Messa solenne.'" *Studi verdiani* 9 (1993): 62–96.

Robertson, Anne Walters. *Guillaume de Machaut and Rheims: Context and Meaning in His Musical Works.* Cambridge, 2002.

Robinson, Paul. "Is *Aida* an Orientalist Opera?" *Cambridge Opera Journal* 5 (1933): 133–40.

Roccatagliati, Alessandro. *Felice Romani librettista.* Lucca, 1996.

———. "Il giovane Romani alla scuola di Mayr: Intese drammaturgiche di primo Ottocento." In Bellotto, *Giovanni Simone Mayr,* 309–24.

Rogers, Stuart W. "*Cenerentola* a Londra." *Bollettino del centro rossiniano di studi* 37 (1997): 51–67.

Roncaglia, Gino. "Riccardo o Gustavo III." *Verdi: Bollettino quadrimestrale dell'Istituto di studi verdiani* 1, no. 2 (1960): liii–lv.

Rosen, Charles. *Critical Entertainments: Music Old and New.* Cambridge, MA, 2000.

———. *The Romantic Generation.* Cambridge, MA, 1995.

Rosen, David. "On Staging That Matters." In Latham and Parker, *Verdi in Performance,* 28–33.

Rosen, David, and Claire Brook, eds. *Words on Music: Essays in Honor of Andrew Porter on the Occasion of his 75th Birthday.* Hillsdale, NY, 2003.

Rosen, David, and Marinella Pigozzi. "*Un ballo in maschera*" *di Giuseppe Verdi.* Musica e spettacolo: Collana di Disposizioni sceniche. Milan, 2002.

Rosen, David, and Andrew Porter, eds. *Verdi's "Macbeth": A Sourcebook.* New York, 1984.

Ross, Alex. "Verdi's Grip." *New Yorker,* 21 September 2001, 82–87.

Rosselli, John. *The Life of Bellini.* Cambridge, 1996.

———. *Music and Musicians in Nineteenth-Century Italy.* Portland, OR, 1991.

———. *The Opera Industry in Italy from Cimarosa to Verdi: The Role of the Impresario.* Cambridge, 1984.

———. *Singers of Italian Opera: The History of a Profession.* Cambridge, 1992.

———. "Il sistema produttivo, 1780–1880." In *Il sistema produttivo e le sue competenze,* vol. 4 of *Storia dell'opera italiana,* 77–165. Translated as "Opera Production, 1780–1880," in *Opera Production and Its Resources* (see *Storia dell'opera italiana*), 81–164.

Rossini, Gioachino. *Adina.* Edited by Fabrizio Della Seta. In *Edizione critica delle opere di Gioachino Rossini,* series 1, vol. 25. Pesaro, 2000.

———. *Album français, Morceaux réservés.* Edited by Rossana Dalmonte. In *Edizione critica delle opere di Gioachino Rossini,* series 7, vol. 2. Pesaro, 1989.

———. *Armida.* Edited by Charles S. Brauner and Patricia B. Brauner. In *Edizione critica delle opere di Gioachino Rossini,* series 1, vol. 22. Pesaro, 1997.

———. *Il barbiere di Siviglia.* Edited by Alberto Zedda. Milan, 1969.

———. *Il barbiere di Siviglia.* Facsimile of the autograph manuscript. Edited by Philip Gossett. Rome, 1992.

———. *Bianca e Falliero.* Edited by Gabriele Dotto. In *Edizione critica delle opere di Gioachino Rossini,* series 1 vol. 30. Pesaro, 1996.

———. *La Cenerentola.* Edited by Alberto Zedda. In *Edizione critica delle opere di Gioachino Rossini,* series 1, vol. 20. Pesaro, 1998.

———. *La Cenerentola.* Facsimile of the autograph manuscript. Edited by Philip Gossett. Bibliotheca Musica Bononiensis, Sezione IV, N. 92. Bologna, 1969.

———. *Le Comte Ory: A Facsimile Edition of the Printed Orchestral Score.* Edited by Philip Gossett. New York, 1978.

———. *La donna del lago.* Edited by H. Colin Slim. In *Edizione critica delle opere di Gioachino Rossini,* series 1, vol. 29. Pesaro, 1990.

———. *Duetto per Violoncello e Contrabasso.* Edited by Rodney Slatford. London, 1969.

———. *Edipo Coloneo.* Edited by Lorenzo Tozzi and Piero Weiss. In *Edizione critica delle opere di Gioachino Rossini,* series 2, vol. 1. Pesaro, 1985.

———. *Elisabetta, regina d'Inghilterra: A Facsimile Edition of Rossini's Original Autograph Manuscript.* Edited by Philip Gossett. New York, 1979.

———. *Ermione.* Edited by Patricia B. Brauner and Philip Gossett. In *Edizione critica delle opere di Gioachino Rossini,* series 1, vol. 27. Pesaro, 1995.

———. *La gazza ladra.* Edited by Alberto Zedda. In *Edizione critica delle opere di Gioachino Rossini,* series 1, vol. 21. Pesaro, 1979.

———. *La gazzetta.* Edited by Philip Gossett and Fabrizio Scipioni. In *Edizione critica delle opere di Gioachino Rossini,* series 1, vol. 18. Pesaro, 2002.

———. *Guillaume Tell.* Edited by M. Elizabeth C. Bartlet. In *Edizione critica delle opere di Gioachino Rossini,* series 1, vol. 39. Pesaro, 1992.

———. *L'Italiana in Algeri.* Edited by Azio Corghi. In *Edizione critica delle opere di Gioachino Rossini,* series 1, vol. 11. Pesaro, 1981.

———. *Lettere e documenti.* Edited by Bruno Cagli and Sergio Ragni. Vols. 1–3 and 3a. Pesaro, 1992, 1996, 2000, 2004.

———. *Mosè in Egitto.* Edited by Charles Brauner. In *Edizione critica delle opere di Gioachino Rossini,* series 1, vol. 24. Pesaro, 2004.

———. *Mosè in Egitto: A Facsimile Edition of Rossini's Original Autograph Manuscript.* Edited by Philip Gossett. New York, 1979.

———. *Musique anodine, Album italiano.* Edited by Marvin Tartak. In *Edizione critica delle opere di Gioachino Rossini,* series 7, vol. 1. Pesaro, 1995.

———. *Le nozze di Teti, e di Peleo.* Edited by Guido Johannes Joerg. In *Edizione critica delle opere di Gioachino Rossini,* series 2, vol. 3. Pesaro, 1993.

———. *L'occasione fa il ladro.* Edited by Giovanni Carli-Ballola, Patricia Brauner, and Philip Gossett. In *Edizione critica delle opere di Gioachino Rossini,* series 1, vol. 8. Pesaro, 1994.

———. *Otello.* Edited by Michael Collins. In *Edizione critica delle opere di Gioachino Rossini,* series 1, vol. 19. Pesaro, 1994.

———. *Otello: A Facsimile Edition of Rossini's Original Autograph Manuscript.* Edited by Philip Gossett. New York, 1979.

———. *La pietra del paragone.* Edited by Patricia Brauner and Anders Wiklund. Provisional edition, to be published in *Edizione critica delle opere di Gioachino Rossini,* series 1, vol. 7.

———. *Quelques Riens pour album.* Edited by Marvin Tartak. In *Edizione critica delle opere di Gioachino Rossini,* series 7, vol. 7. Pesaro, 1982.

———. *La scala di seta.* Edited by Anders Wiklund. In *Edizione critica delle opere di Gioachino Rossini,* series 1, vol. 6. Pesaro, 1991.

———. *Sei sonate a quattro.* Vol. 1 of *Quaderni rossiniani.* Pesaro, 1954.

———. *Semiramide.* Edited by Philip Gossett and Alberto Zedda. In *Edizione critica delle opere di Gioachino Rossini,* series 1, vol. 34. Pesaro, 2001.

———. *Le Siège de Corinthe: A Facsimile Edition of the Printed Orchestral Score.* Edited by Philip Gossett. New York, 1980.

———. *Il signor Bruschino.* Edited by Arrigo Gazzaniga. In *Edizione critica delle opere di Gioachino Rossini,* series 1, vol. 9. Pesaro, 1986.

———. *Tancredi.* Edited by Philip Gossett. In *Edizione critica delle opere di Gioachino Rossini,* series 1, vol. 10. Pesaro, 1984.

———. *Il Turco in Italia.* Edited by Margaret Bent. In *Edizione critica delle opere di Gioachino Rossini,* series 1, vol. 13. Pesaro, 1988.

———. *Varianten zur Cavatine der Rosina "Una voce poco fa."* Edited by Franz Beyer. Adliswil-Zürich, 1973.

————. *Il viaggio a Reims.* Edited by Janet L. Johnson. In *Edizione critica delle opere di Gioachino Rossini,* series 1, vol. 35. Pesaro, 1999.

————. *Zelmira.* Edited by Helen Greenwald and Kathleen Kuzmick Hansell. In *Edizione critica delle opere di Gioachino Rossini,* series 1, vol. 33. Pesaro, 2005.

Rossini a Roma—Rossini e Roma: Convegno di studi, 25 marzo 1992. Rome, 1992.

Rostirolla, Giancarlo, ed. *Wagner in Italia.* Turin, 1982.

Rousseau, Jean-Jacques. *Lettre sur la musique française.* 2nd ed. Paris, 1753. For an abridged English translation, see Strunk, *Source Readings in Music History,* 636–54.

Royer, Alphonse, and Gustave Vaëz. *L'Ange de Nisida.* Transcribed from the original manuscripts by Fulvio Stefano Lo Presti and William Desniou. *Donizetti Society Journal 7* (2002): 219–290.

Russo, Paolo. *"Medea in Corinto" di Felice Romani: Storia, fonti e tradizioni.* Florence, 2004.

Sadie, Stanley, ed. *The New Grove Dictionary of Music and Musicians.* 20 vols. London, 1980. See also Grove, *A Dictionary of Music and Musicians.*

Said, Edward. "The Empire at Work: Verdi's *Aida.*" In *Culture and Imperialism,* 111–32. New York, 1993.

Sala, Emilio. "Verdi e il teatro di boulevard parigino degli anni 1847–1849." In Petrobelli and Della Seta, *La realizzazione scenica dello spettacolo verdiano,* 187–214.

————. "Women Crazed by Love: An Aspect of Romantic Opera." Translated by William Ashbrook. *Opera Quarterly* 10, no. 3 (1994): 19–41.

Salvatorelli, Luigi. *Pensiero e azione del Risorgimento.* Turin, 1963.

Sartori, Claudio. *Casa Ricordi 1808–1958.* Milan, 1958.

Savage, Roger. "The Staging of Opera." In Parker, *The Oxford History of Opera,* 235–85.

Scaramelli, Giuseppe. *Saggio sopra i doveri di un primo violino direttore d'orchestra.* Trieste, 1811.

Scarton, Cesare, and Mauro Tosti-Croce. *"Aureliano in Palmira:* Un percorso storico-drammaturgico da François Hédelin d'Aubignac a Felice Romani." *Bollettino del centro rossiniano di studi* 41 (2001): 83–165.

————. *Otello: Un percorso iconografico da Shakespeare a Rossini.* Iconografia rossiniana 3. Pesaro, 2003.

Scherillo, Michele. *Belliniana: Nuove note.* Milan, 1885.

Schiedermair, Ludwig. *Beiträge zur Geschichte der Oper um die Wende des 18. und 19. Jahrhunderts: Simon Mayr.* 2 vols. Leipzig, 1907, 1910.

Schlotel, Brian. "The Orchestral Music." In Walker, *Robert Schumann,* 277–323.

Schmidt, Carl B. "Antonio Cesti's *Il pomo d'oro:* A Reexamination of a Famous Hapsburg Court Spectacle." *Journal of the American Musicological Society* 29 (1976): 381–412.

Schneider, Herbert, and Nicole Wild. *"La Muette de Portici": Kritische Ausgabe des Librettos und Dokumentation der ersten Inszenierung.* Tübingen, 1993.

Scott, Eleanor. *The First Twenty Years of the Santa Fe Opera.* Santa Fe, 1976.

Scritti in onore di Luigi Ronga. Milan and Naples, 1973.

Scruton, Roger. *The Aesthetic of Music.* Oxford, 1997.

Seebass, Tilman, ed. *Musikhandschriften in Basel aus verschiedenen Sammlungen.* Basel, 1975.

Selk, Jürgen. *"Matilde di Shabran:* Rossini's last *opera semiseria."* In the program for *Matilde di Shabran* at the Rossini Opera Festival (Pesaro, 1996).

Seller, Francesca. "Il *Marin Faliero* da Napoli a Parigi: Raffronti testuali," "Il libretto," and "La pirateria musicale e *Marin Faliero:* nuovi documenti." *Donizetti Society Journal 7* (2002): 31–134.

Senici, Emanuele. "'Adapted to the Modern Stage': *La clemenza di Tito* in London." *Cambridge Opera Journal* 7 (1995): 1–22.

———, ed. *The Cambridge Companion to Rossini*. Cambridge, 2004.

———. "Per una biografia musicale di Amina." In Della Seta and Ricciardi, *Vincenzo Bellini*, 297–314.

Serafin, Tullio and Alceo Toni. *Stile, tradizioni e convenzioni del melodramma italiana del Settecento e dell'Ottocento*. Milan, 1958.

Shakespeare, Willliam. *King Lear*. Edited by R.A. Foakes. In *The Arden Shakespeare*. 3rd series. Walton-on-Thames, 1997.

Shawe-Taylor, Desmond. "Verdi and His Singers." In John, *Simon Boccanegra*, 27–35.

Simone, Cesare. "Lettere al tenore Mario de Candia sulla cabaletta de *I Due Foscari*." *Nuova Antologia* 69 (1 October 1934): 327–34.

Smart, Mary Ann. "The Lost Voice of Rosine Stolz." *Cambridge Opera Journal* 6 (1994): 31–50.

———. "The Silencing of Lucia." *Cambridge Opera Journal* 4 (1992): 119–41.

———. "Verdi Sings Erminia Frezzolini." *Verdi Newsletter* 24 (1997): 13–22.

Smith, Marian. "The *Livrets de Mise en Scène* for Donizetti's Parisian Operas." In Bellotto, *L'opera teatrale di Gaetano Donizetti*, 371–93.

Smith, Patrick J. *The Tenth Muse: A Historical Study of the Opera Libretto*. New York, 1970.

Solie, Ruth. "The Living Work: Organicism and Musical Analysis." *19th Century Music* 4 (1980): 147–56.

Sommariva, Andrea, ed. *Felice Romani: Melodrammi, poesie, documenti*. Florence, 1996.

Sorba, Carlotta. *Teatri: L'Italia del melodramma nell'età del Risorgimento*. Bologna, 2001.

"*Sorgete! Ombre serene!*": *L'aspetto visivo dello spettacolo verdiano*. Parma, 1994.

Stander, Wilhelm, Ursula Aarburg, and Peter Cahn, eds. *Helmuth Osthoff zu seinem siebzigsten Geburtstag*. Tutzing, 1969.

Stauffer, George B. *Bach—the "Mass in B Minor" (the Great Catholic Mass)*. New York, 1997.

Stendhal. *Notes d'un dilettante*. In *Mélanges d'Art*. Edited by Henri Martineau, 223–398. Paris, 1932.

———. *Vie de Rossini*. 2 vols. Paris, 1824. Translated and edited by Richard N. Coe as *Life of Rossini by Stendhal*. London, 1956; revised edition 1970.

Storia dell'opera italiana. Edited by Lorenzo Bianconi and Giorgio Pestelli. The series is planned in six volumes, of which three have been published: vol. 4, *Il sistema produttivo e le sue competenze* (Turin, 1987), translated by Lydia Cochrane as *Opera Production and Its Resources* (Chicago, 1998); vol. 5, *La spettacolarità* (Turin, 1988), translated by Kate Singleton as *Opera on Stage* (Chicago, 2002); vol. 6, *Teorie e techniche, imaggini e fantasmi* (Turin, 1988), translated by Kenneth Chalmers and Mary Whitall as *Opera in Theory and Practice, Image and Myth* (Chicago, 2003).

Straeten, Edmund van der. *History of the Violoncello, the Viol da Gamba, their Precursors and Collateral Instruments, with Biographies of All the Most Eminent Players of Every Country*. London, 1915.

Straeten, Edmond vander. *La mélodie populaire dans l'opéra "Guillaume Tell" de Rossini*. Paris, 1879.

Strunk, Oliver, ed. *Source Readings in Music History*. New York, 1950.

Sutcliffe, Tom. *Believing in Opera*. Princeton, 1996.

Talbot, Michael. *The Musical Work: Reality or Invention?* Liverpool, 2000.

Taruskin, Richard. *Defining Russia Musically: Historical and Hermeneutical Essays*. Princeton, 1997.

———. *Text and Act: Essays on Music and Performance*. New York and Oxford, 1995.

Il Teatro di San Carlo. 2 vols. Naples, 1987. See particularly vol. 2, *La cronologia 1737–1987,* edited by Carlo Marinelli Roscioni.

Il Teatro di San Carlo 1737–1987. 3 vols. (vols. 1 and 3 edited by Franco Mancini, vol. 2 edited by Bruno Cagli and Agostino Ziino). Naples, 1987.

Tortora, Daniela. *Drammaturgia del Rossini serio: Le opere della maturità da "Tancredi" a "Semiramide."* Rome, 1996.

Toscani, Claudio. "Verso francese e prosodia italiana: Ossservazioni sulla traduzione delle *Vêpres siciliennes.*" In Della Seta, Marvin, and Marica, *Verdi 2001,* 499–517.

Turner, J. Rigbie. *Four Centuries of Opera: Manuscripts and Printed Editions in the Pierpont Morgan Library.* New York, 1983.

Vaccai, Nicola. *Giulietta e Romeo and Excerpts from Zadig ed Astartea: A Facsimile Edition of the Printed Piano-Vocal Scores.* Edited by Philip Gossett. New York, 1989.

Vaughan, Denis. "Discordanze fra gli autografi verdiani e la loro stampa." *La Scala,* no. 104 (1958): 11–15, 71–72.

———. "The Inner Language of Verdi's Manuscripts." *Musicology* 5 (1979).

Verba, Cynthia. *Music and the French Enlightenment.* Oxford, 1993.

Verdi, Giuseppe. *Alzira.* Edited by Stefano Castelvecchi with the collaboration of Jonathan Cheskin. In *The Works of Giuseppe Verdi,* series 1, vol. 8. Chicago and Milan, 1994.

———. *Gli autografi del Museo teatrale alla Scala.* Milan, 2000.

———. *Il corsaro.* Edited by Elizabeth Hudson. In *The Works of Giuseppe Verdi,* series 1, vol. 13. Chicago and Milan, 1998.

———. *Ernani.* Edited by Claudio Gallico. In *The Works of Giuseppe Verdi,* series 1, vol. 5. Chicago and Milan, 1985.

———. *Libera me domine (Messa per Rossini): Facsimile dell'autografo.* Edited by Pierluigi Petrobelli. Parma, 1988.

———. *Luisa Miller.* Edited by Jeffrey Kallberg. In *The Works of Giuseppe Verdi,* series 1, vol. 15. Chicago and Milan, 1991.

———. *Macbeth.* Edited by David Lawton. In *The Works of Giuseppe Verdi,* series 1, vol. 10. Chicago and Milan, 2005.

———. *I masnadieri.* Edited by Roberta Montemorra Marvin. In *The Works of Giuseppe Verdi,* series 1, vol. 11. Chicago and Milan, 2000.

———. *Messa da Requiem.* Edited by David Rosen. In *The Works of Giuseppe Verdi,* series 3, vol. 1. Chicago and Milan, 1990.

———. *La Messa da Requiem di Giuseppe Verdi.* Milan, 1941.

———. *Nabucodonosor.* Edited by Roger Parker. In *The Works of Giuseppe Verdi,* series 1, vol. 3. Chicago and Milan, 1987.

———. *Rigoletto.* Edited by Martin Chusid. In *The Works of Giuseppe Verdi,* series 1, vol. 17. Chicago and Milan, 1983.

———. *Stiffelio.* Edited by Kathleen Kuzmick Hansell. In *The Works of Giuseppe Verdi,* series 1, vol. 16. Chicago and Milan, 2003.

———. *La traviata.* Edited by Fabrizio Della Seta. In *The Works of Giuseppe Verdi.* series 1, vol. 19. Chicago and Milan, 1997.

———. *La traviata: Schizzi e abbozzi autografi.* Edited by Fabrizio Della Seta. Parma, 2000; Commento critico, Parma, 2002.

———. *Il trovatore.* Edited by David Lawton. In *The Works of Giuseppe Verdi* series 1, vol. 18A. Chicago and Milan, 1993.

Viale Ferrero, Mercedes. "Per Rossini: Un primo tentativo di iconografia scenografica." *Bollettino del centro rossiniano di studi* [22] (1982): 5–28.

———. *La scenografia della Scala nell'età neoclassica.* Milan, 1983.

Vitoux, Frédéric. *Fin de saison au Palazzo Pedrotti.* Paris, 1983.

Vittorini, Fabio. "*Quelque chose pour le ténor:* I finali del *Macbeth* verdiano." *Rivista Italiana di Musicologia* 31 (1996): 327–62.

Wagner, Richard. *Tristan und Isolde.* Edited by Isolde Vetter. In *Richard Wagner: Sämtliche Werke,* vol. 8. Mainz, 1990.

Walker, Alan, ed. *Robert Schumann: The Man and His Music.* London, 1972.

Walker, Frank. "Lettere inedite: Contributo alla storia di *Un ballo in maschera.*" *Verdi: Bollettino quadrimestrale dell'Istituto di studi verdiani* 1, no. 1 (1960): 279–304.

Walton, Benjamin. "'Quelque peu théâtral': The Operatic Coronation of Charles X." *19th Century Music* 26 (2002): 3–22.

Warrack, John. *Carl Maria von Weber.* London, 1968; 2nd ed., 1976.

Weaver, William and Martin Chusid. *The Verdi Companion.* New York, 1979.

Weber, Samuel. "Taking Place: Toward a Theater of Dislocation." In Levin, *Opera through Other Eyes,* 107–46.

Webster, James. "Mozart's Operas and the Myth of Musical Unity." *Cambridge Opera Journal* 2 (1990): 197–218.

Weinstock, Herbert. *Donizetti and the World of Opera in Italy, Paris and Vienna in the First Half of the Nineteenth Century.* New York, 1963.

———, tr. and ed. *Richard Wagner's Visit to Rossini (Paris 1860) and An Evening at Rossini's in Beau-Séjour (Passy) 1858, by Edmond Michotte.* Chicago, 1968. See also Michotte, *La visite de R. Wagner à Rossini (Paris 1860)—détails inédits et commentaires.*

———. *Rossini: A Biography.* New York, 1968.

———. *Vincenzo Bellini: His Life and His Operas.* New York, 1971.

Weiss, Piero. "Sacred 'Bronzes': Paralipomena to an Essay by Dallapiccola." *19th Century Music* 9 (1985): 42–49.

White, Eric Walter. *Stravinsky: The Composer and His Works.* Berkeley, 1969.

Wild, Nicole. *Décors et costumes du XIXe siècle.* 2 vols. Paris, 1987, 1994.

Wills, Gary. "Gorgeous Sills." *New York Review of Books* 22 (1 May 1975): 37.

Winter, Robert. "The Emperor's New Clothes: Nineteenth-Century Instruments Revisited." *19th Century Music* 7 (1984): 251–65.

Zanetti, Emilia. "Römische Handschriften." In Blume, *Die Musik in Geschichte und Gegenwart,* 11:765–66.

Zanolini, Antonio. *Biografia del Maestro G. Rossini e Passeggiata del medesimo col Signor A. Zanolini di Bologna.* Milan, 1837.

Zavadini, Guido. *Donizetti: Vita–Musiche–Epistolario.* Bergamo, 1948.

Zedda, Alberto. "La strumentazione nell'opera teatrale di Donizetti." In *Atti del 1° Convegno internazionale di studi donizettiani,* 1:453–542.

Zoppelli, Luca. "I burattini del Cardinale: *Maria di Rohan:* Spazio privato e drammaturgia dell'angoscia." In the program for *Maria di Rohan* (Venice, 1999), 57–71.

INDEX OF PRINCIPAL OPERAS DISCUSSED

Bellini, Donizetti, Rossini, and Verdi

VINCENZO BELLINI

GIOACHINO ROSSINI

GIUSEPPE VERDI

GENERAL INDEX

Note: For operas of Bellini, Donizetti, Rossini, and Verdi, please consult the *Index of Principal Operas Discussed.*